Office 97

fast & easy

How to Order:

For information on quantity discounts contact the publisher: Prima Publishing, P.O. Box 1260BK, Rocklin, CA 95677-1260; (916) 632-4400. On your letterhead include information concerning the intended use of the books and the number of books you wish to purchase. For individual orders, turn to the back of this book for more information.

Office 97

fast & easy

Elaine Marmel

PRIMA PUBLISHING

Publisher: Matthew H. Carleson
Acquisitions Manager: Alan Harris
Managing Editor: Tad Ringo
Product Marketing Specialist: Julie Barton

Acquisitions Editor: Jenny L. Watson
Assistant Acquisitions Editor: Christy Clinton
Development and Project Editor: Kelli Crump
Copy Editor: Theresa Mathias
Editorial Coordinator: Stacie Drudge
Technical Reviewers: Diane Koers, Ray Link
Interior Design and Layout: Marian Hartsough
Cover Design: Vanessa Perez
Indexer: Emily Glossbrenner

Microsoft is a registered trademark of Microsoft Corporation.

IMPORTANT: If you have problems installing or running Microsoft Office 97, notify Microsoft Corporation at (206) 635-7056. Prima Publishing cannot provide software support.

Prima Publishing and the author have attempted throughout this book to distinguish proprietary trademarks from descriptive terms by following the capitalization style used by the manufacturer.

Information contained in this book has been obtained by Prima Publishing from sources believed to be reliable. However, because of the possibility of human or mechanical error by our sources, Prima Publishing, or others, the Publisher does not guarantee the accuracy, adequacy, or completeness of any information and is not responsible for any errors or omissions or the results obtained from use of such information. Readers should be particularly aware of the fact that the Internet is an ever-changing entity. Some facts may have changed since this book went to press.

ISBN: 0-7615-1162-8
Library of Congress Catalog Card Number: 97-66154
Printed in the United States of America

97 98 99 DD 10 9 8 7 6 5 4 3 2

Acknowledgments

Special thanks to Theresa Mathias, Diane Koers, Ray Link, Marian Hartsough, and Emily Glossbrenner.

—Prima Publishing

Contents at a Glance

PART IV
POWERPOINT 157

PART V
OUTLOOK. 209

PART VI
USING OFFICE 97 TOOLS 281

PART VII
OFFICE 97 AND THE WEB 327

PART VII
APPENDIXES 357

Contents

PART III
EXCEL. 101

PART IV
POWERPOINT 157

PART V
OUTLOOK 209

PART VII
OFFICE 97 AND THE WEB 327

PART VIII
APPENDIXES 357

Introduction

This new Visual Learning Guide from Prima Publishing will help you master Microsoft Office 97, whether you are computer-challenged or a sophisticated power-user. This book uses a step-by-step approach with color illustrations of what you will see on your screen, linked with instructions for the mouse movements or keyboard operations to complete a task.

Office 97 is a powerful and popular suite of programs that will support all aspects of your everyday work style. Whether you want to write a letter, create a spreadsheet, produce a professional-quality presentation, or manage your schedule and electronic mail, you will find the information that you need to get the job done quickly and easily in the *Office 97 Visual Learning Guide*.

Office 97 is a suite of products where each of the individual programs interact with the other programs in the suite. For example, you may need to prepare a business report in Word that contains graphs and charts based on data you enter in an Excel spreadsheet. Perhaps later, after you have delivered your report (possibly using Outlook's e-mail), you'll find you need to prepare and schedule a PowerPoint presentation. The *Office 97 Visual Learning Guide* will show you how to use the tools that makes Office a suite of programs. In addition, you'll learn how to use Office 97 products to interact with the Internet.

WHO SHOULD READ THIS BOOK?

At first glance, the easy-to-follow, highly visual nature of this book makes it seem like the perfect learning tool for a beginning computer user. Computer terms and phrases are clearly explained in non-technical language, and expert tips and shortcuts help you achieve quality results. However, it is also ideal for those who are new to this version of Office, or those who feel comfortable with computers and software, but have never used the Office programs before.

In addition, anyone using a software application needs an occasional reminder about the steps required to perform a particular task. Visual Learning Guides are a quick and easy way for any user of Office to look up steps for a task without having to plow through pages of description or advanced topics to find them.

In short, this book can be used by a beginning to intermediate user as a learning tool or as a step-by-step task reference.

ADDED ADVICE TO MAKE YOU A PRO

You'll notice that this book uses steps and keeps explanations to a minimum to help you learn faster. Included in the book are a few elements that provide some additional comments to help you master the programs, without encumbering your progress through the steps:

✦ **Tips** often offer a shortcut to perform an action, or a hint about a feature that might make your work in Office quicker and easier.

✦ **Notes** give you some background or additional information about a feature, or advice about how to use the feature in your day-to-day activities.

As a bonus, three helpful appendixes are included that walk you through the creation of a newsletter in Word, an amortization table in Excel, and a presentation in PowerPoint. When you finish, you can begin using these items in your work right away!

The *Office 97 Visual Learning Guide* is so easy to use, you should be up and running with Office 97 in no time. Enjoy!

PART I
Getting Started

1 Welcome to Office 97

As confusing as computers are today, not understanding the basic elements you see onscreen can be frustrating. What's a dialog box? Where is that pop-up menu coming from? The good thing about Microsoft Office products is that the elements are the same in each program. Throughout Part 1, you will learn the common ways you can approach tasks, regardless of the Office program you are using or the document in which you are working. The basic premise of each *Visual Learning Guide* is that people learn best by doing. In this chapter, you'll learn how to:

✦ Start and exit an Office 97 program

✦ Identify common screen elements

STARTING A PROGRAM

Starting a *program* (also called *application*) is simple to do—and it's the first, most necessary, step toward getting anything done. Because computers can be set up differently, you might not see the icons on your Desktop or the menu choices on the Programs menu that you see in this example.

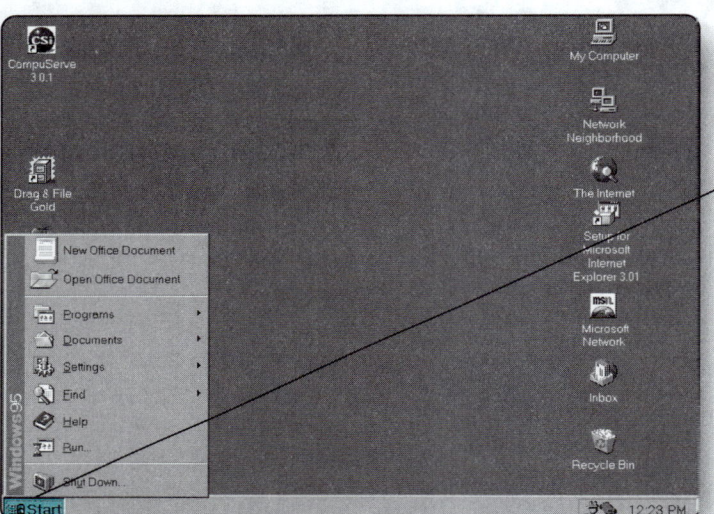

1. **Click** on the **Start button** on the Windows 95 Taskbar with the left mouse button. A pop-up menu will appear.

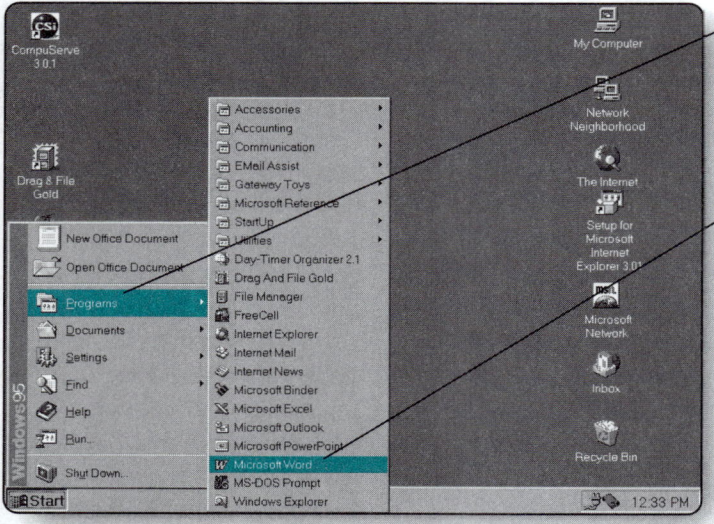

2. **Move** the **mouse pointer** up the menu to **Programs** to highlight it. The Programs pop-up menu will appear.

3. **Move** the **mouse pointer** to the right and **click** on the **program** you want to start. The Welcome screen for the program will appear briefly before the main program window opens.

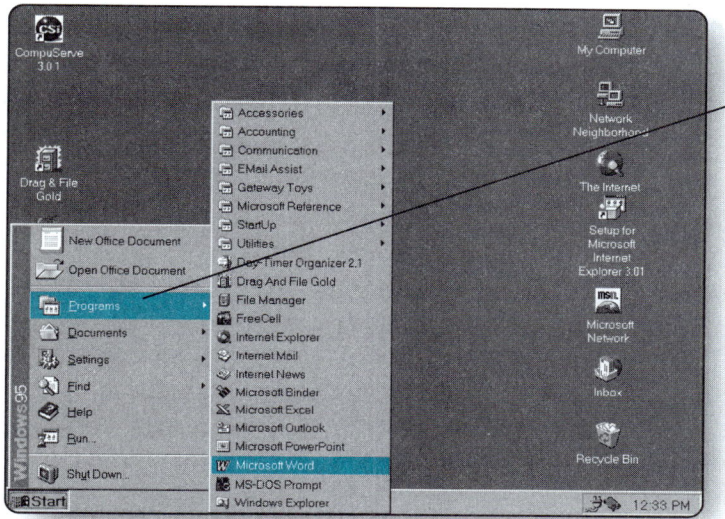

NOTE

You may have installed all of your Office programs in a folder. If you don't see the program you want to start, highlight the folder on the Programs pop-up menu most likely to contain the program you want to use. A third pop-up menu will appear with additional choices.

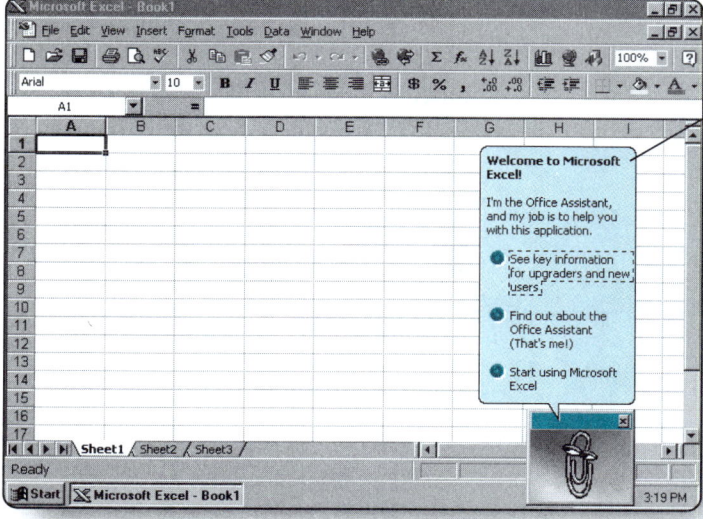

TIP

If this is your first time using a program, the Office Assistant appears with a balloon welcoming you. For example, if you are using Excel for the first time, the balloon says, "Welcome to Excel." Click on the blue button next to "Start using Microsoft Excel" (or the appropriate program name). If you're asked for a user name, type your name and initial in the dialog box and click on OK. For more information about working with Office Assistant, see Chapter 4, "Getting Help."

IDENTIFYING COMMON SCREEN ELEMENTS

All Office 97 programs contain common screen elements. You'll learn more about the following elements as you work in individual programs in this book:

✦ A title bar shows the name of the program and the name of the document that is currently open.

✦ A menu bar

✦ Window control buttons

✦ At least one (possibly more than one) toolbar

✦ The working area (also called the *document area*)

✦ A horizontal scroll bar

✦ A vertical scroll bar

✦ A status bar

✦ The insertion point

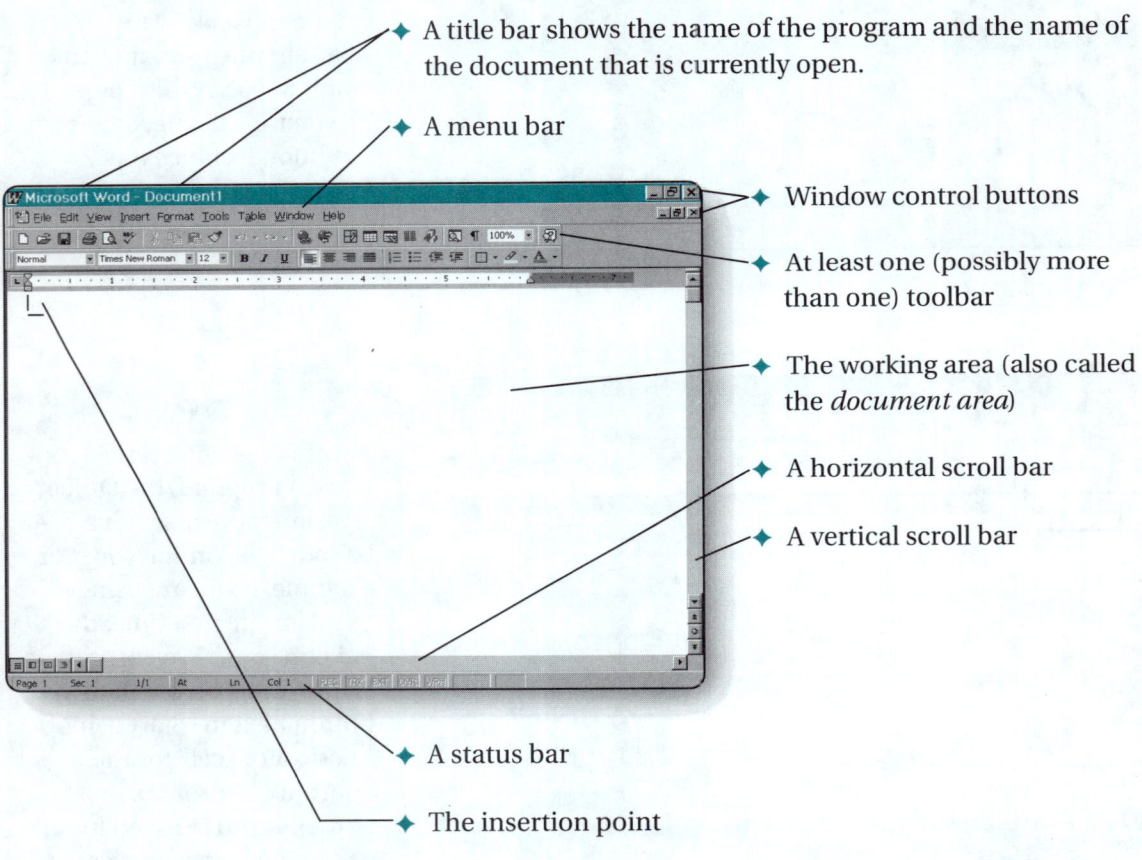

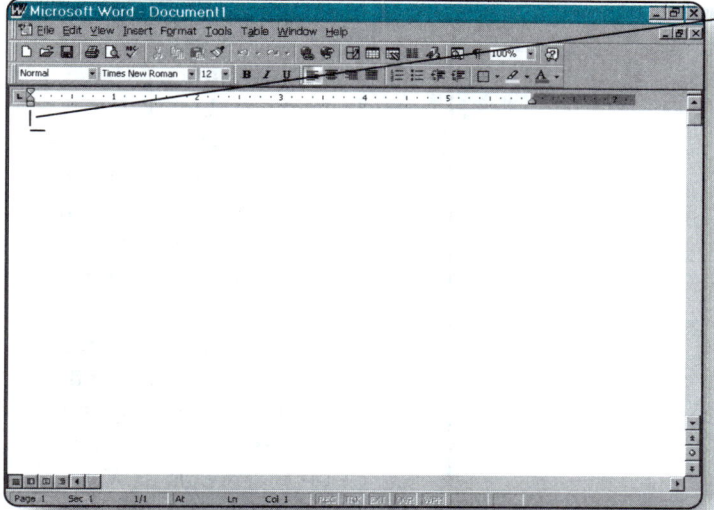

The insertion point appears in different locations in the various Office programs. On your screen, it flashes. The insertion point represents the location at which text will appear when you start typing. As you type, the insertion point moves to the right.

> **NOTE**
> You also might see the Windows 95 Taskbar onscreen.

EXITING A PROGRAM

When you no longer want to work in a program, you should follow the proper procedures for exiting the program to ensure that you don't damage files.

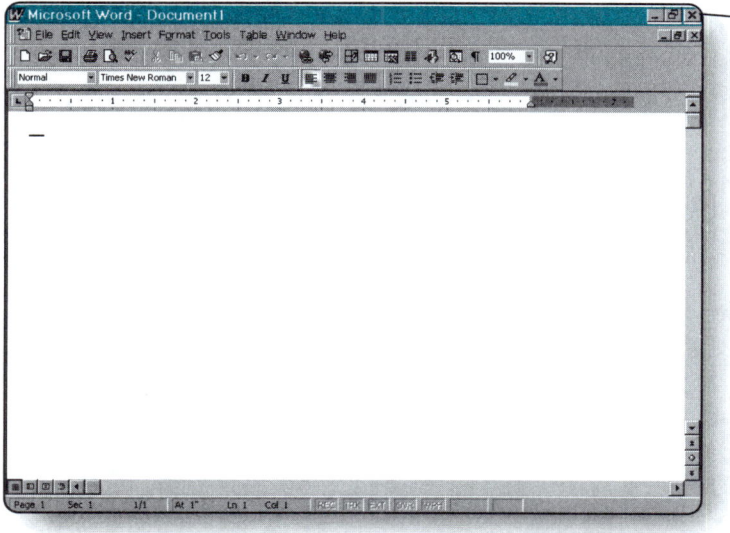

1. **Click** on the **Close button** (X). The program will close.

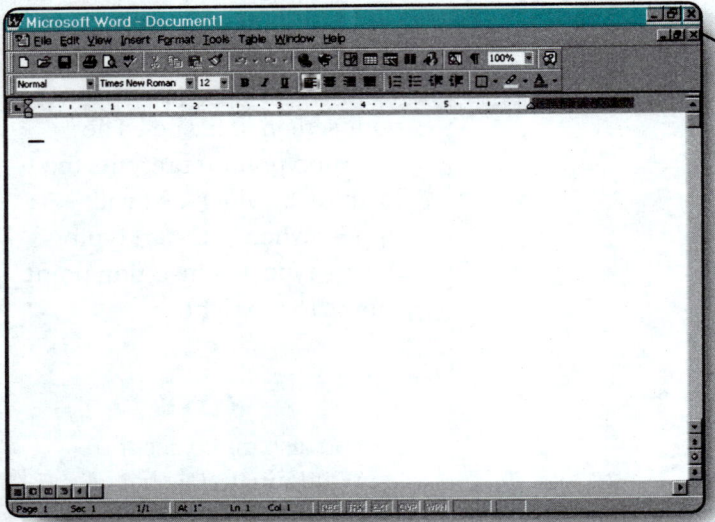

2 Choosing Commands

You use commands to communicate with programs—commands are your way of telling a program what you want it to do. Most often, you issue commands by choosing them from menus, but you also can issue commands using toolbars and shortcut menus. In this chapter, you'll learn how to:

✦ Use the menu bar and keyboard to choose commands

✦ Work with shortcut menus and toolbars

USING THE MENU BAR

Each Office 97 program contains a menu bar at the top, immediately below the title bar. You open menus to see the commands they contain and choose commands. If you previously closed Word, follow the steps in Chapter 1 to reopen Word.

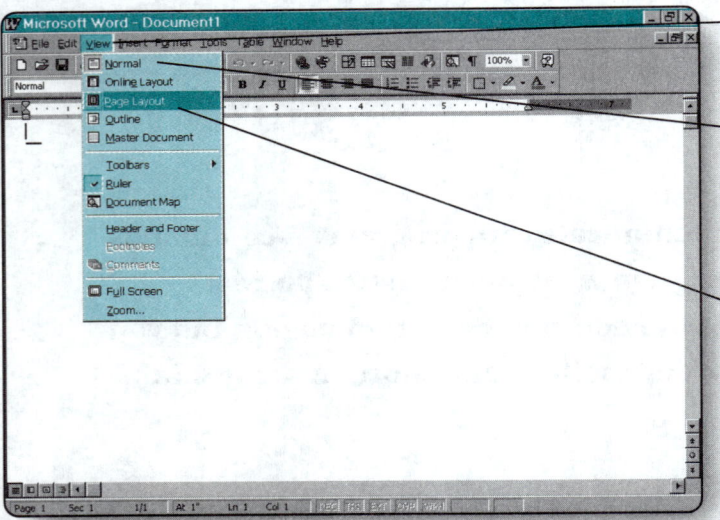

1. Click on **View**. The View menu will appear.

In the figure, Word appears in Normal view. Notice that the icon to the left of the Normal command appears "pressed."

2. Click on **Page Layout**. Word will switch to Page Layout view.

TIP

If you change your mind and don't want to choose a command, press the Esc key until the menu closes or click anywhere in the working area outside the menu.

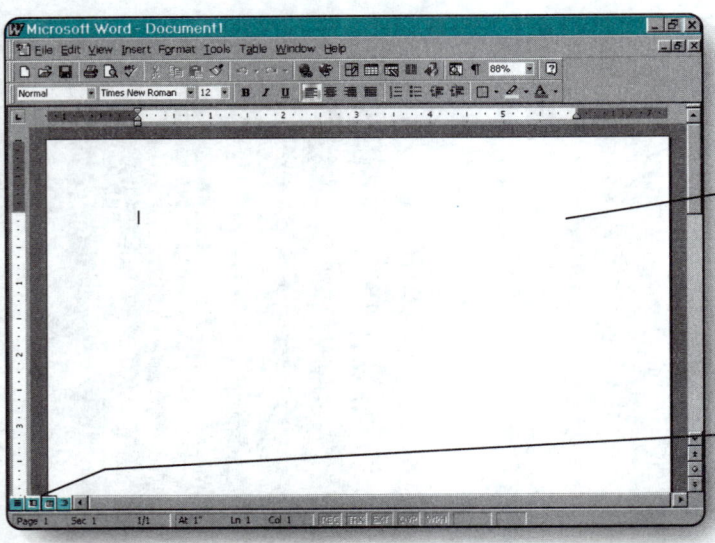

In Page Layout view, you can see the page (and any text on it) exactly as it will appear when you print it.

TIP

To switch between views, you can use the buttons at the left edge of the status bar.

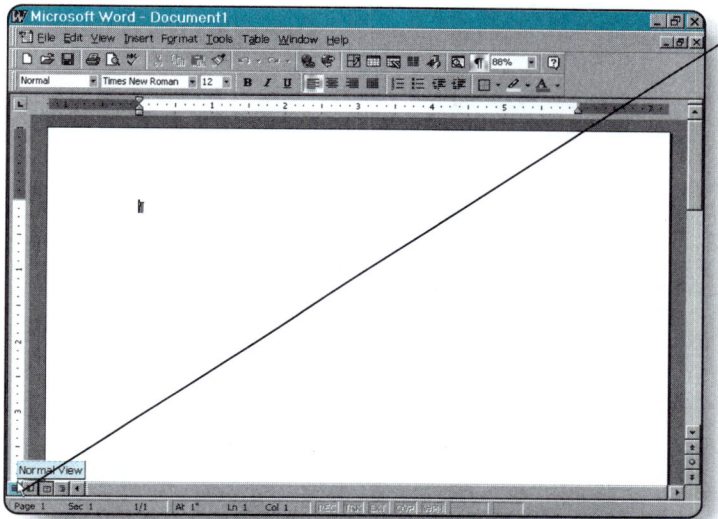

3. **Click** on the **Normal View button**. Word will switch to Normal view.

USING THE KEYBOARD TO CHOOSE COMMANDS

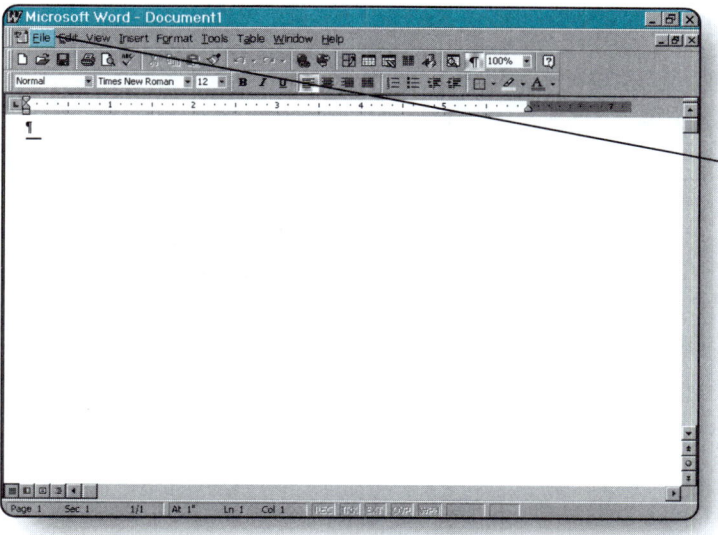

You can open menus and choose commands using the keyboard.

1. **Press** the **Alt key** on your keyboard. The menu bar will become active and a gray box will appear on the File menu.

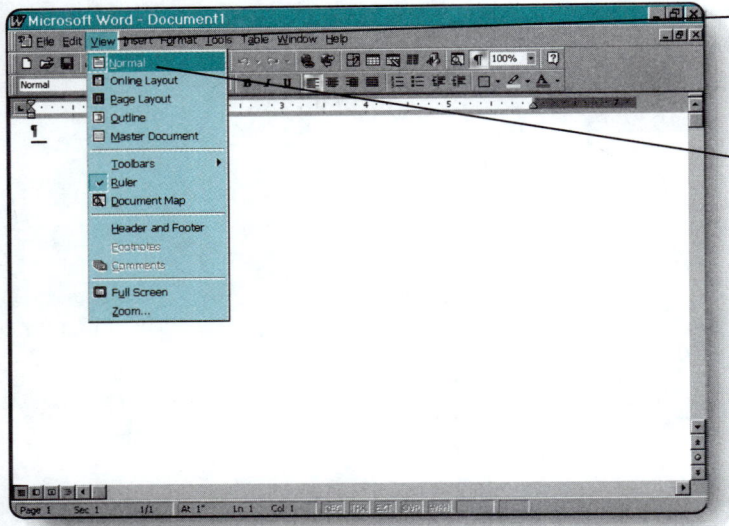

2. **Press** the **underlined letter** of a menu name. The menu will appear.

3. **Press** the **underlined letter** of a command name. The command will execute.

NOTE

The action you take next depends entirely on the command you chose.

USING SHORTCUT MENUS

Shortcut menus contain a limited number of commands. The commands you see on a shortcut menu depend on what you're doing at the time you open the shortcut menu. You always press the *right* mouse button to open a shortcut menu.

1. **Move** the **mouse pointer** into the working area. The pointer will appear as an I-beam.

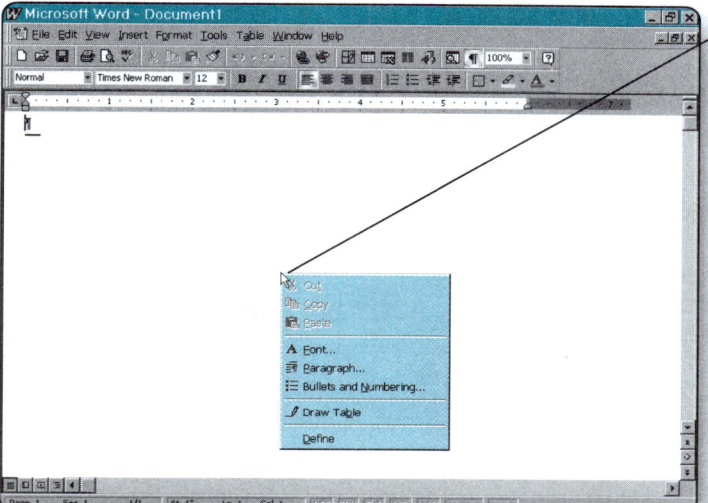

2. Press the **right mouse button** (*right-click*). The mouse pointer will change to an arrow and the shortcut menu for regular text will appear in the working area of the document.

TIP

Press the Esc key or click on the working area to close a shortcut menu without choosing a command.

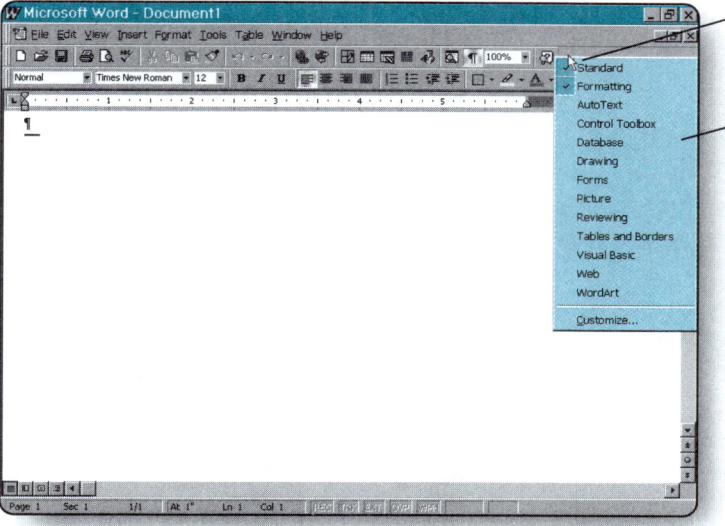

3. Move the **mouse pointer** to the right edge of a toolbar.

4. Right-click the **mouse button**. The shortcut menu for displaying toolbars will appear (a displayed toolbar has a ✔ next to its name).

5. Close the **shortcut menu** without choosing a command.

USING TOOLBARS

Toolbars contain buttons that act as shortcuts for choosing menu commands. For example, you can create a numbered list by opening a menu and choosing a command or by clicking on a toolbar button. You must use the mouse to choose a toolbar button.

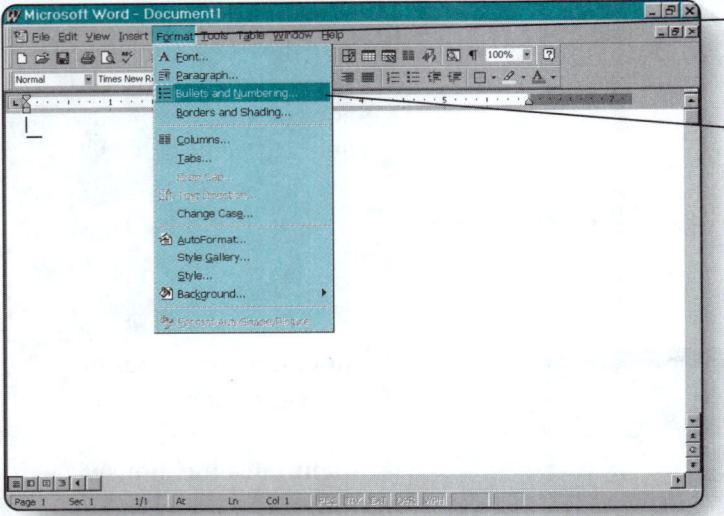

1. Click on **Format**. The Format menu will appear.

2. Click on **Bullets and Numbering**. The Bullets and Numbering dialog box will open.

NOTE

Ordinarily, you would start by placing the insertion point anywhere in the first paragraph you want numbered.

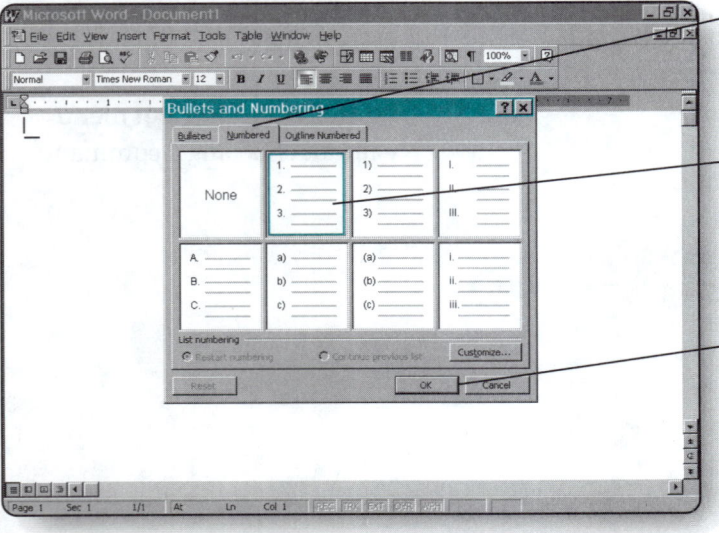

3. Click on the **Numbered tab**. The available numbering formats will appear.

4. Click on the **second box** of the top row. A border will appear around the box to indicate you selected it.

5. Click on **OK**. The Bullets and Numbering dialog box will close.

Word will display "1." in your document.

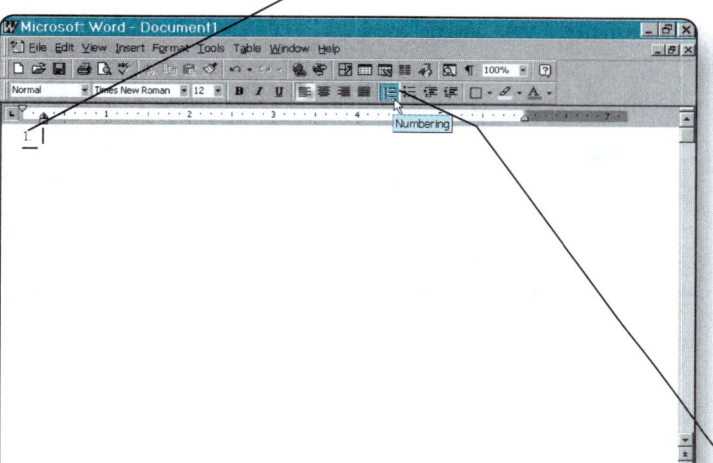

6. **Click** on the **Numbering button**. The number will disappear from the paragraph onscreen.

3 Common Ways to Work in Documents

Some of the tasks you perform while working in documents are the same, regardless of the program in which you are working. And, Office 97 programs let you perform these tasks in the same way, regardless of the program in which you are working. In this chapter, you'll learn how to:

- ✦ Preview a document before printing
- ✦ Print, save, and close a document
- ✦ Open an existing document
- ✦ Start a new document
- ✦ Fix mistakes

PREVIEWING A DOCUMENT

Print Preview is available in Word and Excel (in PowerPoint, you can view slides as you create them) and is most helpful when you're trying to make sure information is aligned as you want it.

What you see (and the rest of the tasks we cover in this chapter) would be more meaningful if you had some text onscreen, so we'll start by letting Word add some random text.

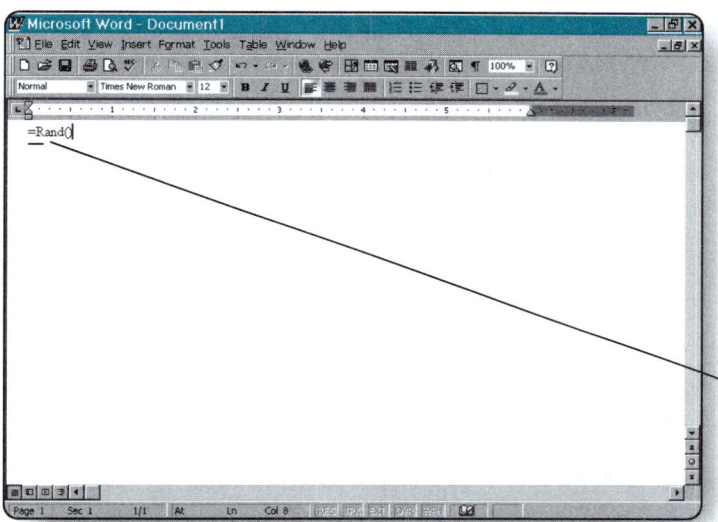

1. **Type** =**Rand**(). The insertion point will move to the right as you type.

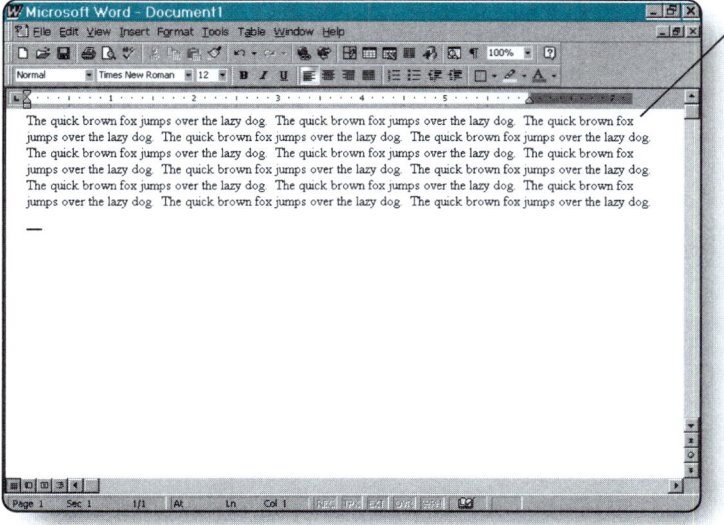

2. **Press** the **Enter key.** The text you typed will be replaced with several copies of the sentence "The quick brown fox jumps over the lazy dog."

NOTE

The text you typed was actually a formula that Word 97 recognizes as meaning "enter some sample text."

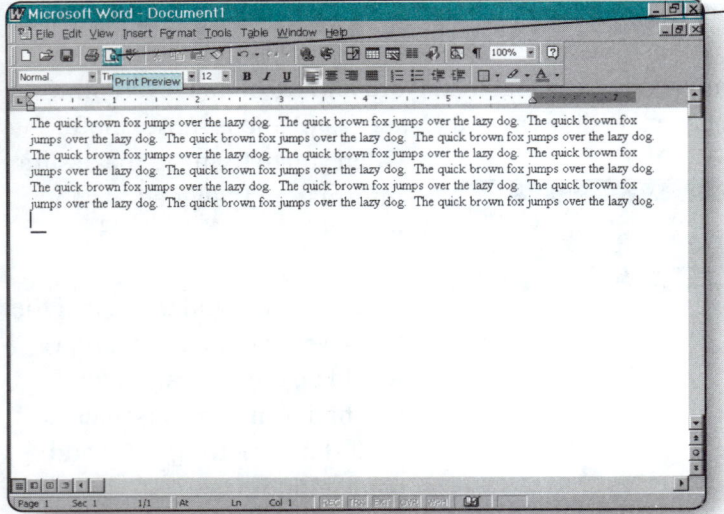

3. **Click** on the **Print Preview button**. Word will switch to Print Preview mode, in which you can see the layout and appearance of your document as it will appear when printed.

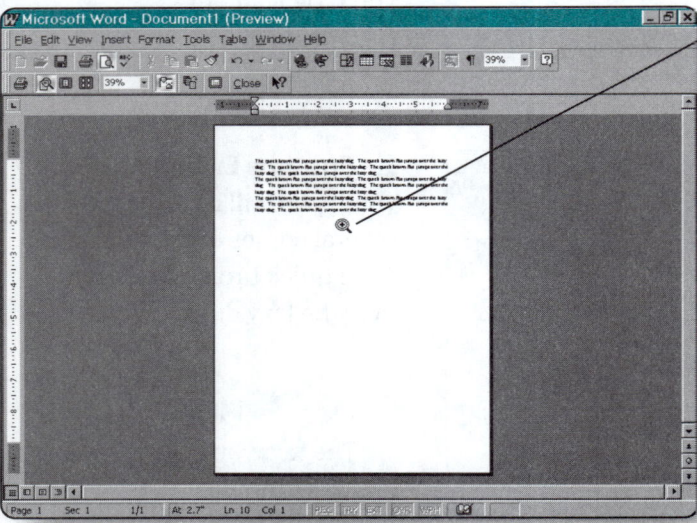

4. **Move** the **mouse pointer** over the document onscreen. The pointer will change to a magnifying glass.

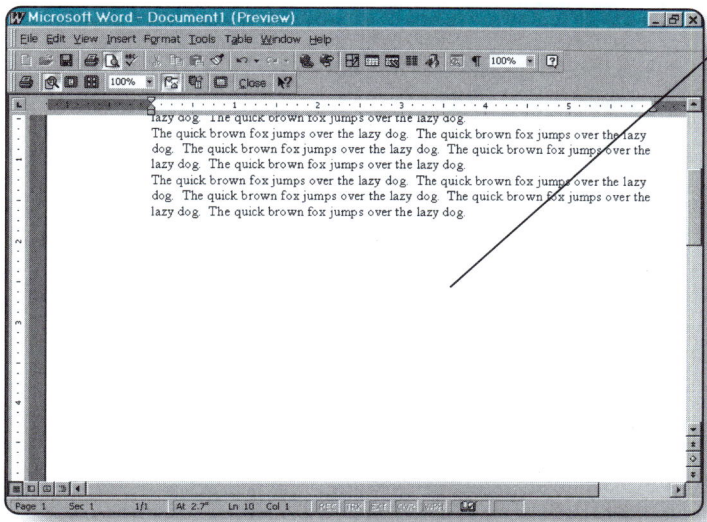

5. **Click** on the **document**. It will enlarge (zoom) so you can actually read the text.

6. **Click** on the **document** again to return the document to regular size.

PRINTING A DOCUMENT

Each Office 97 program contains a Print button on the Standard toolbar that makes printing easy. In addition, you can print from Print Preview in both Word and Excel.

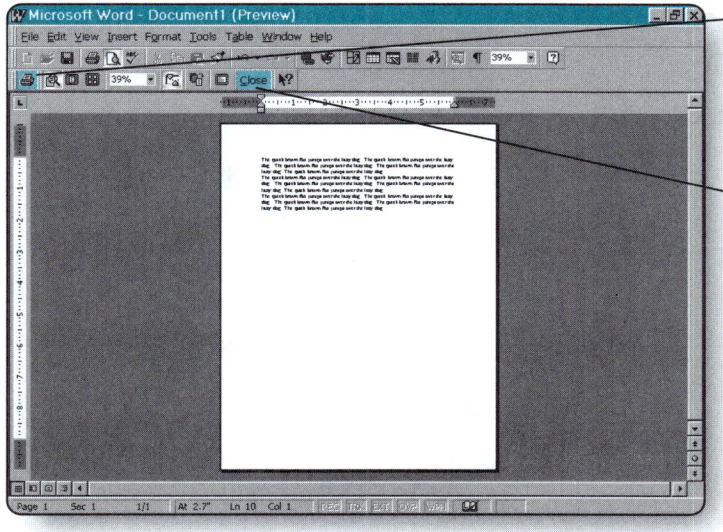

1. **Click** on the **Print button** on the Print Preview toolbar. The document will be printed from Print Preview.

2. **Click** on the **Close button**. You will return to Normal view.

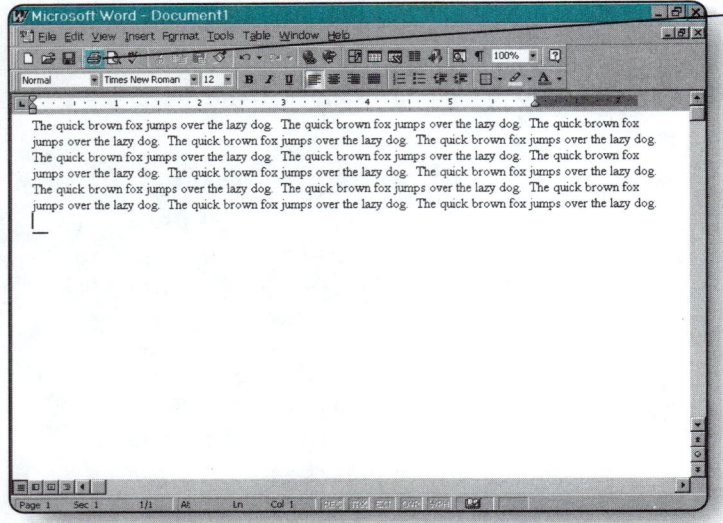

3. **Click** on the **Print button**. The document will be printed from Normal view.

SAVING A DOCUMENT

The first time you save a document, you must supply a name. Each subsequent time you save, the program will simply use the name you already supplied and write over the document. It replaces the original version with the new, updated version.

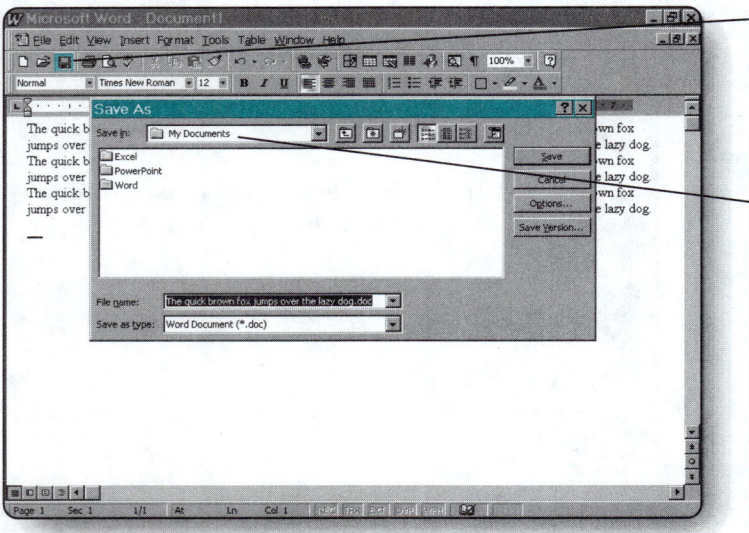

1. **Click** on the **Save button**. The Save As dialog box will open.

NOTE

While you can store all documents in the My Documents folder, I chose to use Windows Explorer to create additional folders inside the My Documents folder to separate Word, Excel, and PowerPoint documents.

2. **Double-click** on the **Word folder**. The folder will open.

In the File name: list box, you should see some highlighted text, which represents the name Word is proposing for this document.

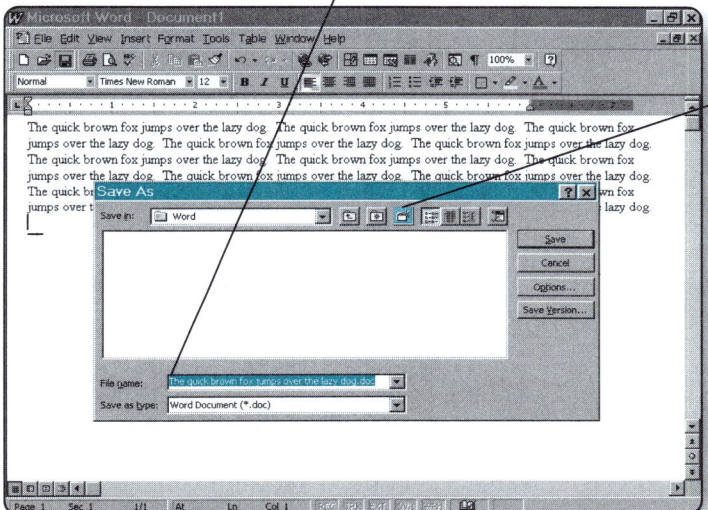

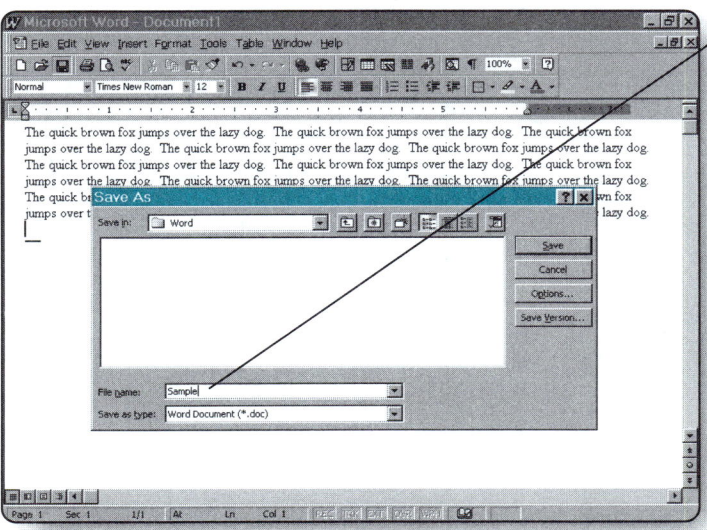

3. **Type** the **name** you want to assign to this document. The name will replace the highlighted text.

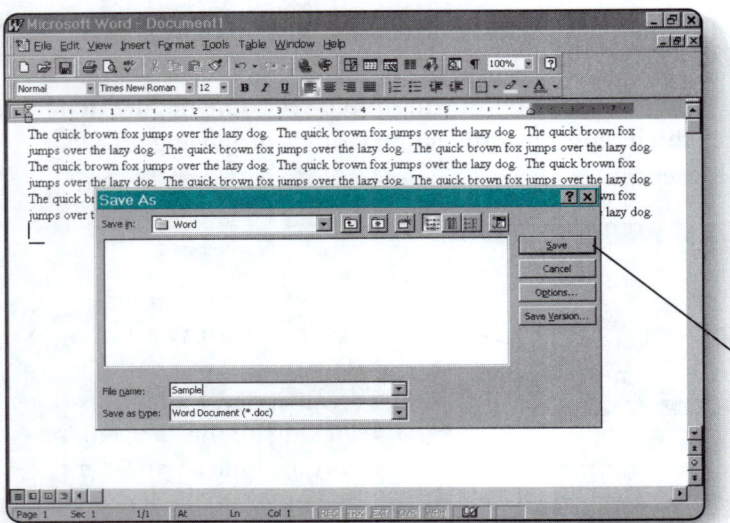

4. **Click** on the **Save button**. The Save As dialog box will close and the document will be saved.

The name you provided for the document will appear in the title bar. It will replace Document1, which appeared before the document was saved. Your title bar might not show the .doc extension; the appearance of this information depends on the settings you established for Windows.

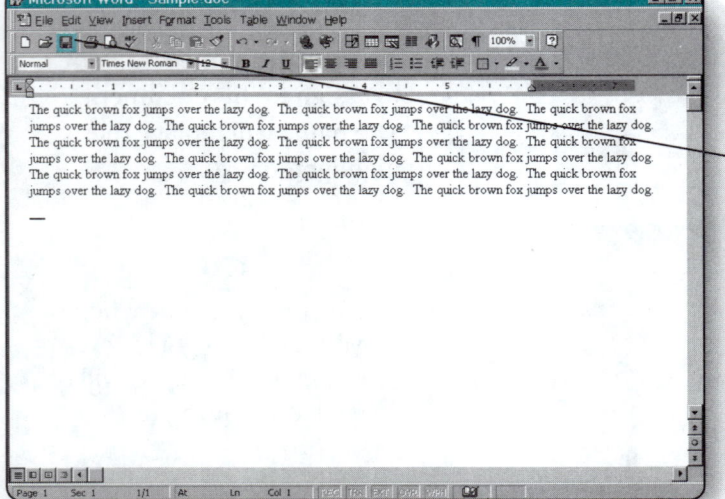

The next time you click on the Save button while working in this document, the Save As dialog box will not open. Instead, the program will simply save the document. Watch the status bar to see the program saving the document.

CLOSING A DOCUMENT

When you finish working in a document, you can remove it from your screen by closing it. Closing a document *does not* close the program; therefore, you can keep working in the program by either opening another document or by starting a new document.

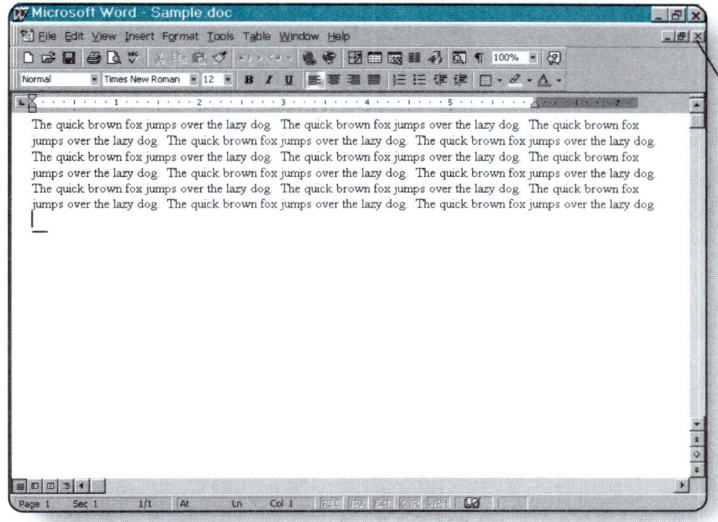

1. **Click** on the **document's Close button** (☒).

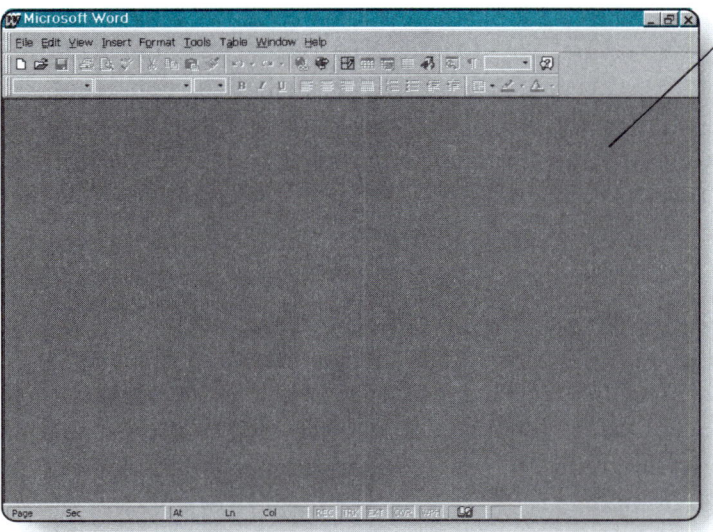

If you made no changes since you last saved the document and you have no other documents open, the document will close.

If you made changes and you did not save them, a dialog box will open to remind you.

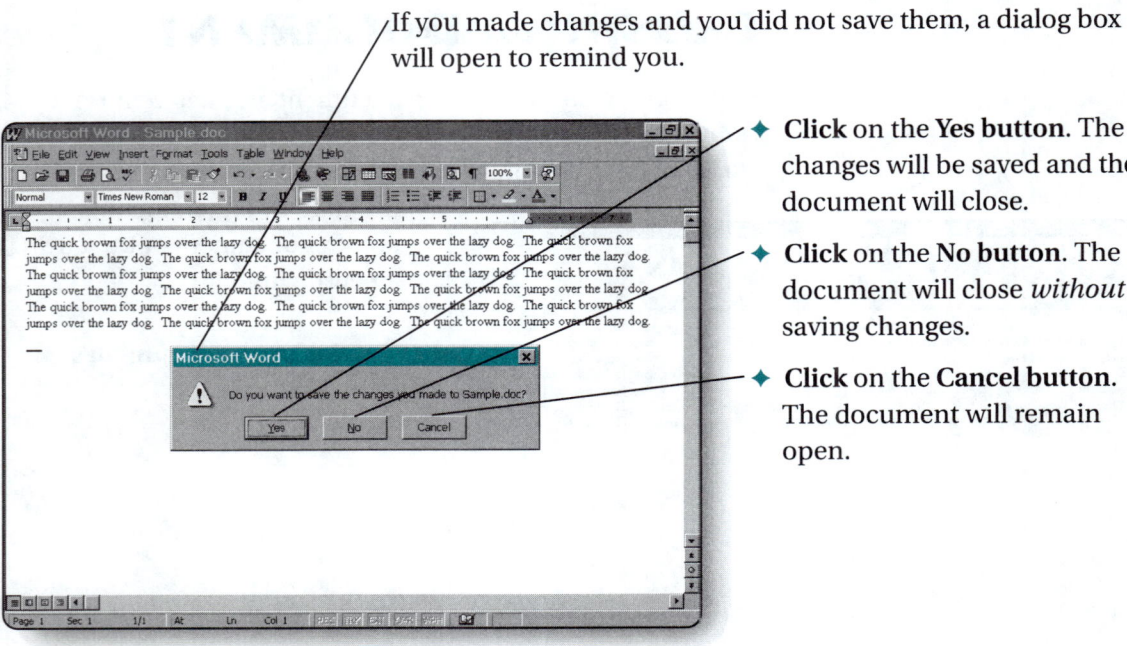

◆ **Click** on the **Yes button**. The changes will be saved and the document will close.

◆ **Click** on the **No button**. The document will close *without* saving changes.

◆ **Click** on the **Cancel button**. The document will remain open.

OPENING AN EXISTING DOCUMENT

There are several ways to open an existing document. If you're already working in the program that created the document, you can open the document from inside the program. If you haven't started the program, you can use either the Documents menu or the Start menu to start an Office 97 program and open a specific document.

From Inside a Program

If you're already working inside a program and you want to open a document created by that program, you may be able to use the program's File menu, or you can use the program's Open command.

Reopening a Recently Opened Document

Documents you recently worked on appear at the bottom of the File menu. You can open any document you see on the File menu by choosing it.

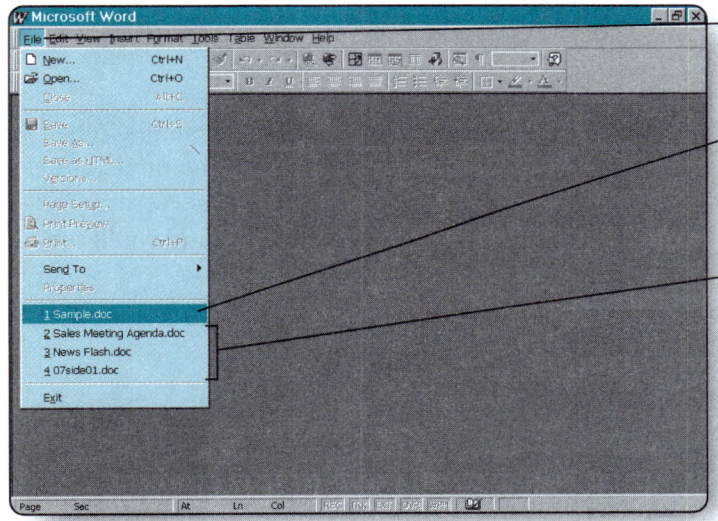

1. **Click** on **File**. The File menu will appear.

2. **Click** on a **document** at the bottom of the File menu. The document will open.

If you recently worked on a document, its filename will appear at the bottom of the File menu.

TIP

You can close this document by clicking on the document's Close button or by choosing Close from the File menu.

Using the Open Button

If the document you want to open does not appear at the end of the File menu, use the Open button.

1. **Click** on the **Open button**. The Open dialog box will open.

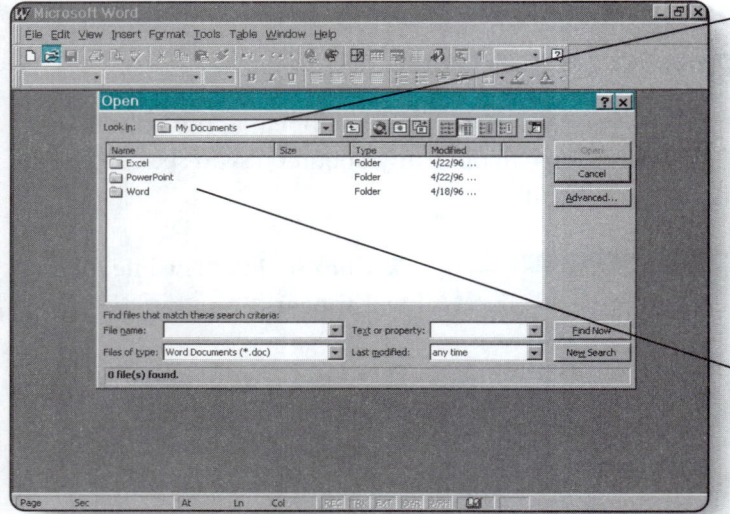

If you just started a program session, you will see the My Documents folder, which may contain folders for each of the individual programs. The My Documents folder will appear until you look in a different folder to save or open a document.

2. **Double-click** on the **folder** containing the document you want to open, if necessary. The folder will open and you'll see its contents.

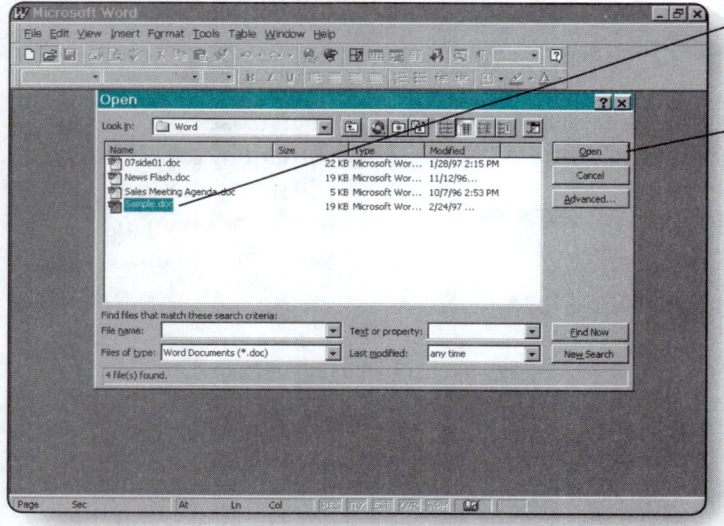

3. **Click** on the **document** you want to open.

4. **Click** on the **Open button**. The Open dialog box will close and the document will appear.

Using the Documents Menu

Suppose you haven't started a program yet, but you know exactly which document you want to open. You might find that document on the Documents menu. Windows stores the last 15 documents you opened on the Documents menu. Only Windows 95 programs can make entries on the Documents menu, so you might not always see recently opened documents on the Documents menu.

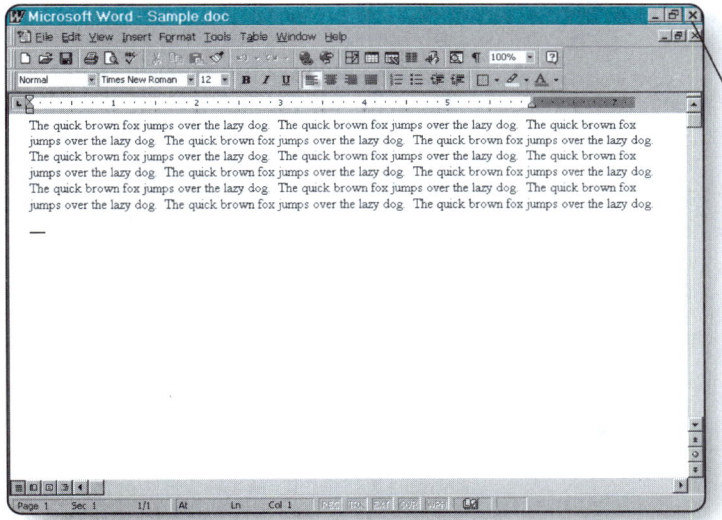

1. **Click** on the **program Close button** (☒). The program will close and you will return to the Windows 95 Desktop.

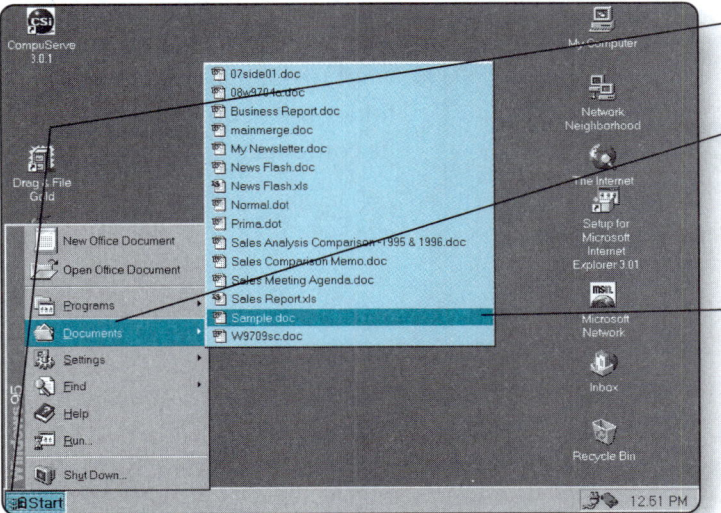

2. **Click** on the **Start button**. The Start menu will appear.

3. **Move** the **mouse pointer** to **Documents**. Documents will be highlighted and the Documents menu will appear.

4. **Click** on the **document** you want to open. The program will open and then the document will appear.

Using the Start Menu

Office 97 makes it easy to open any Office 97 document (and program), even while working in another program. This method is most efficient when you are working in one Office 97 program and want to open a document created in another Office 97 program.

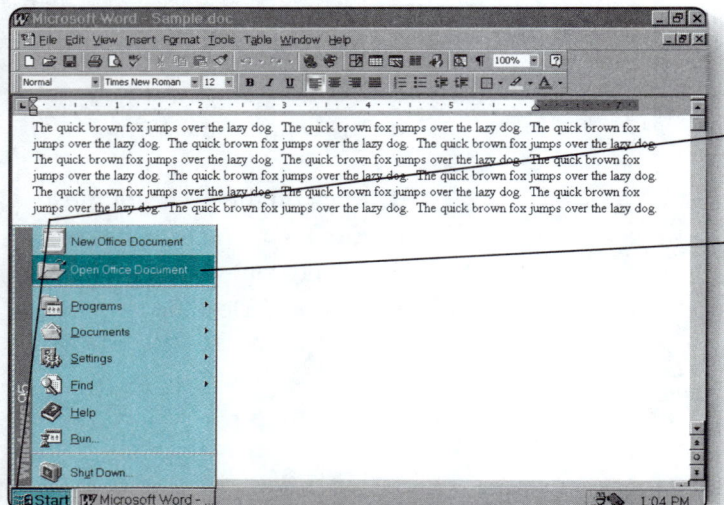

1. **Click** on the **Start button**. The Start menu will appear.

2. **Click** on **Open Office Document**. The Open dialog box will open, showing you the contents of the My Documents folder.

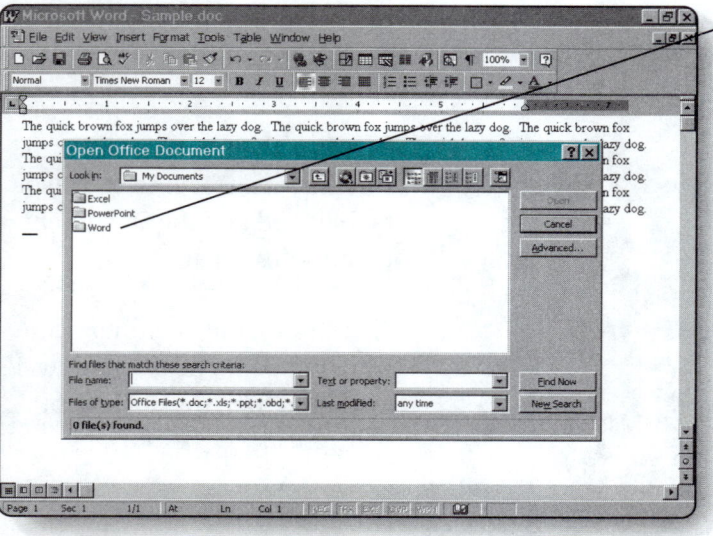

3. **Double-click** on the **folder** containing the document you want to open, if necessary. The folder will open and you'll see its contents.

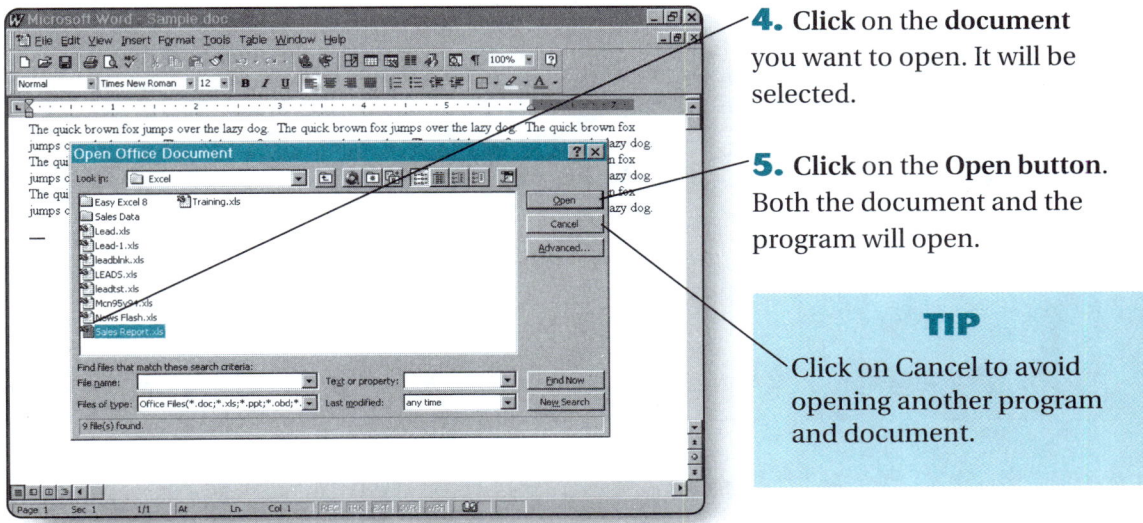

4. Click on the **document** you want to open. It will be selected.

5. Click on the **Open button**. Both the document and the program will open.

STARTING A NEW DOCUMENT

Again, you have a few ways of creating a new Office 97 document. You can work from inside the program or you can work from the Start menu.

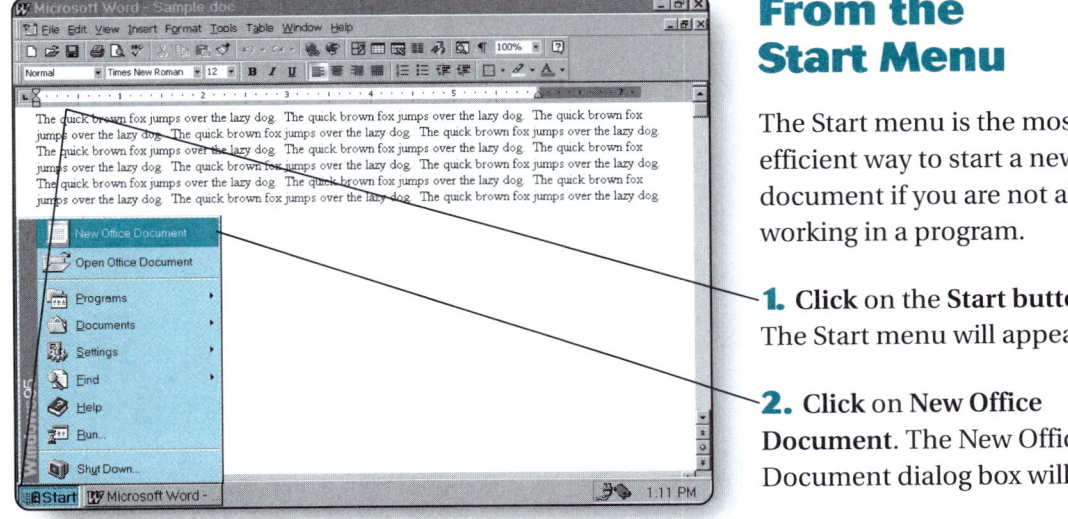

From the Start Menu

The Start menu is the most efficient way to start a new document if you are not already working in a program.

1. Click on the **Start button**. The Start menu will appear.

2. Click on **New Office Document**. The New Office Document dialog box will open.

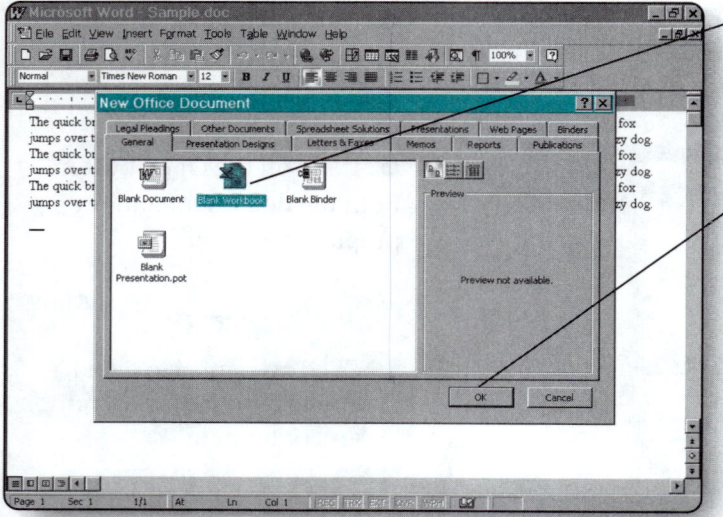

3. **Click** on **Blank Workbook**, the type of new document you want to start. The icon will be selected.

4. **Click** on **OK**.

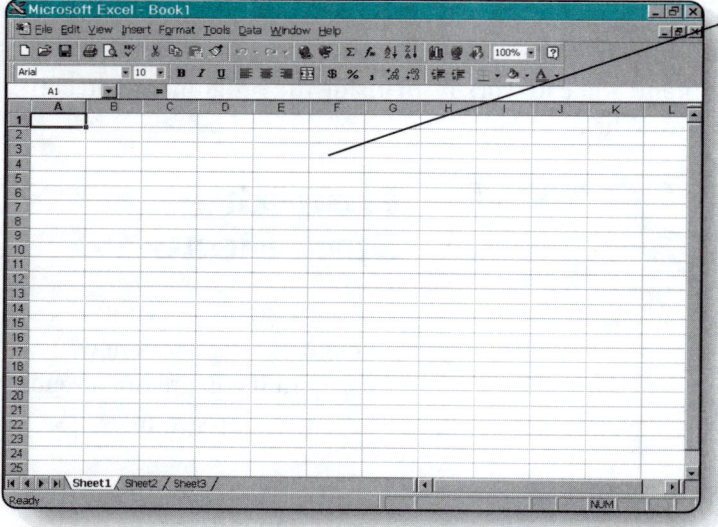

The program will start and a new blank document for that program will appear.

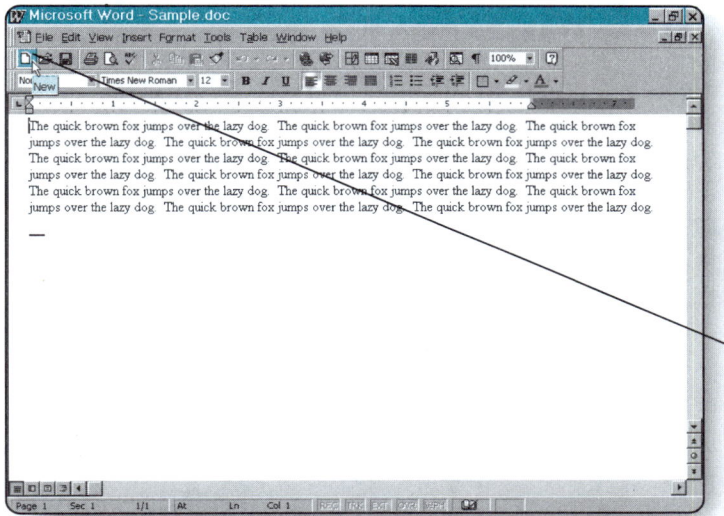

Using the Standard Toolbar

If you're already working inside an Office 97 program and you want to start another document in that same program, use the program's New command.

1. **Click** on the **New button**. A new document will appear.

The name of the new document usually contains the number 2. For example, in Word, the document would be called "Document2;" in Excel, the document would be called "Book2."

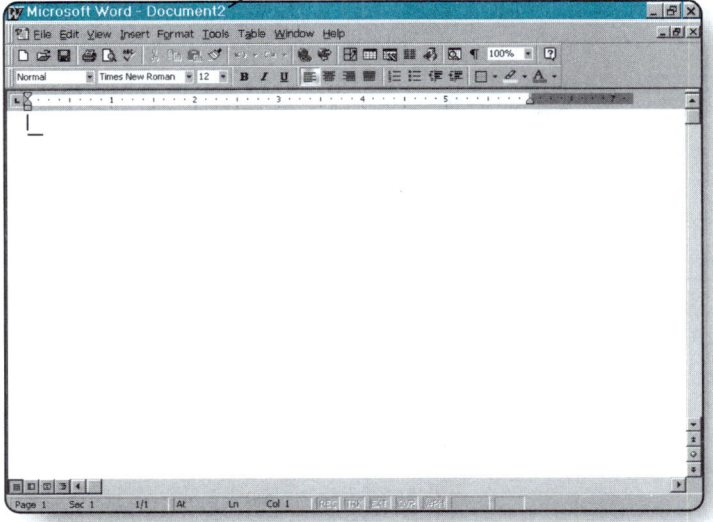

FIXING MISTAKES

Because we're human, we all make mistakes. Many of the mistakes you make can easily be repaired in any of the Office 97 programs by using the Undo command. The Undo command tells the program to reverse the last action you took. The following steps are done in Word.

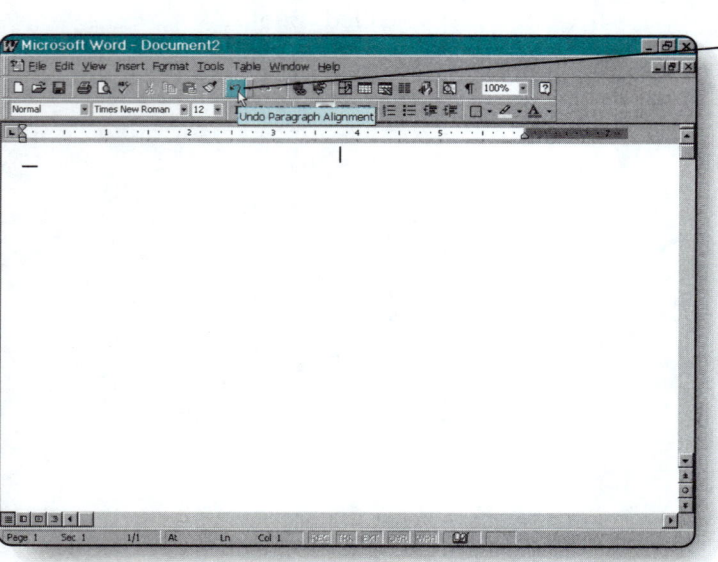

1. **Click** on the **Center button**. The insertion point will move to the center of the current line.

NOTE

If the line already contained text, the insertion point would not move; the text would simply align around a center-aligned tab.

2. **Click** on the **Undo button**. The paragraph alignment will be reversed. The text will realign with the left margin—its original alignment.

TIP

The first time you click on the Undo button, the program reverses the last action you took. You can continue clicking on the Undo button to reverse prior actions in the order in which you originally performed them.

4 Getting Help

As you might expect, getting help in each of the Office 97 programs is a similar process. There are several different ways to get help. In this chapter, you'll learn how to:

+ **Use Office Assistant**

+ **Identify screen parts**

+ **Search the Help file**

+ **Get help on the Web**

USING OFFICE ASSISTANT

Office Assistant is an animated help tool that searches for answers to questions you formulate. Sometimes, Office Assistant will appear as you work, even if you didn't ask for help. Office Assistant is available in *all* Office 97 programs, and is, in fact, the same Office Assistant in each program.

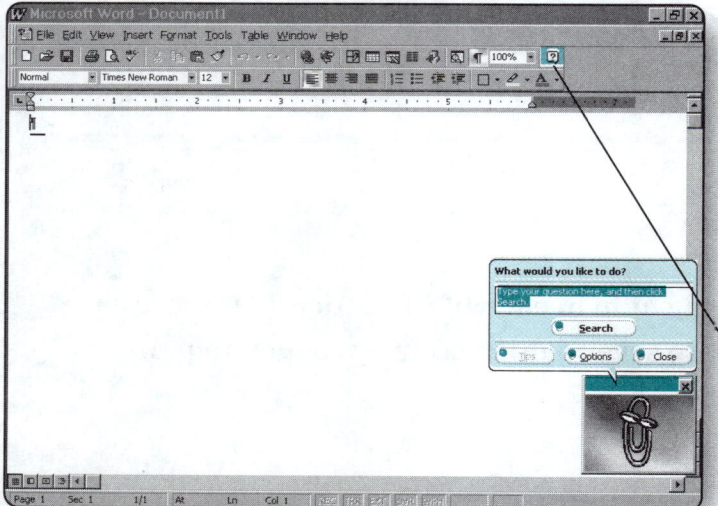

Asking for Help

1a. **Press** the **F1 key**. Office Assistant will appear.

OR

1b. **Click** on the **Office Assistant button**. Office Assistant will appear.

NOTE

You might see a light bulb in the Office Assistant window or on the Office Assistant button. When you do, click on the light bulb, and Office Assistant will display a tip about performing an action in a more efficient way.

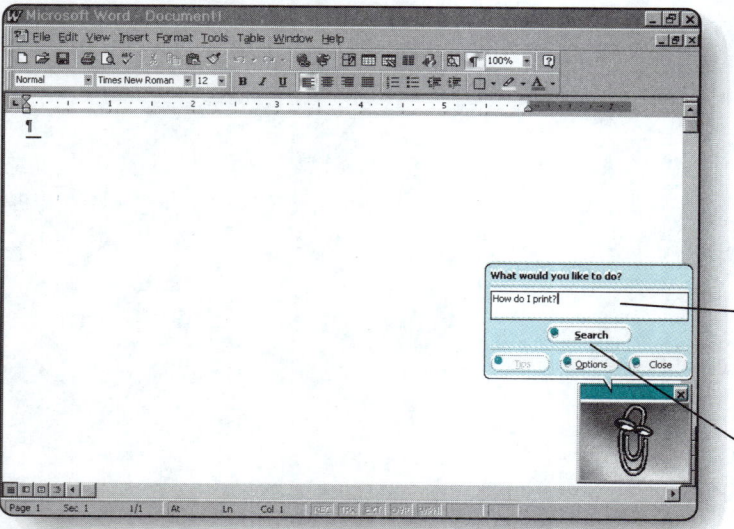

2. **Type** a **question**. The question will appear in Office Assistant's bubble.

3. **Click** on **Search**. Office Assistant will display possible topics for you to read.

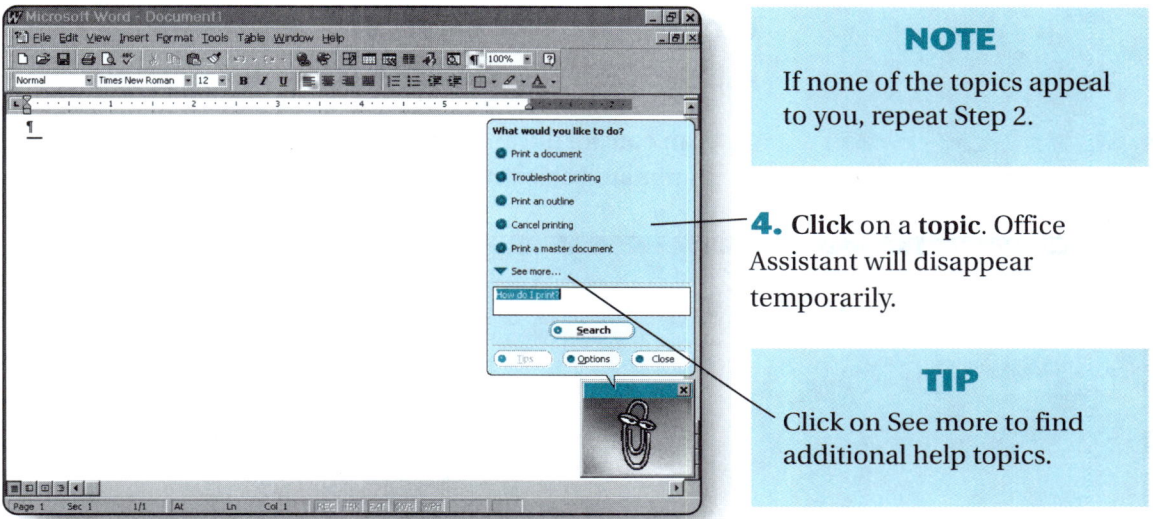

4. **Click** on a **topic**. Office Assistant will disappear temporarily.

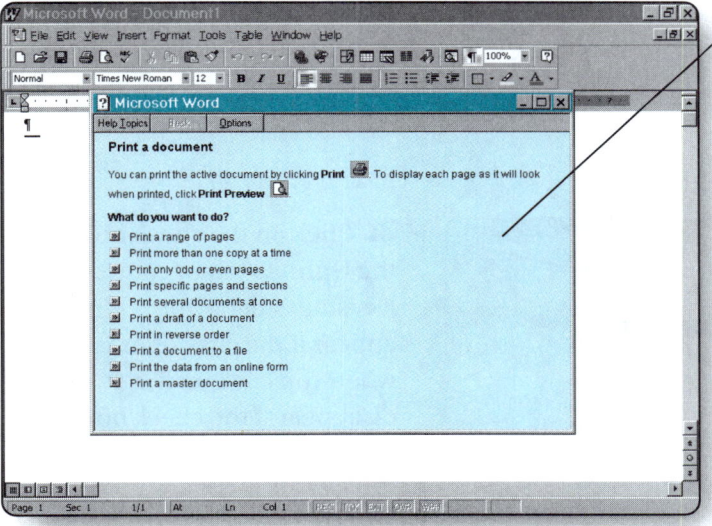

The Help information for the topic you chose will appear.

Controlling Office Assistant's Behavior

You can control the appearance of Office Assistant (there are nine animated characters from which to choose) and when it will appear. Remember, Office Assistant is a common tool for all Office 97 programs. Therefore, if you change the appearance or behavior of Office Assistant while working in Word, Office Assistant will appear and function that way in PowerPoint, Excel, and Outlook as well.

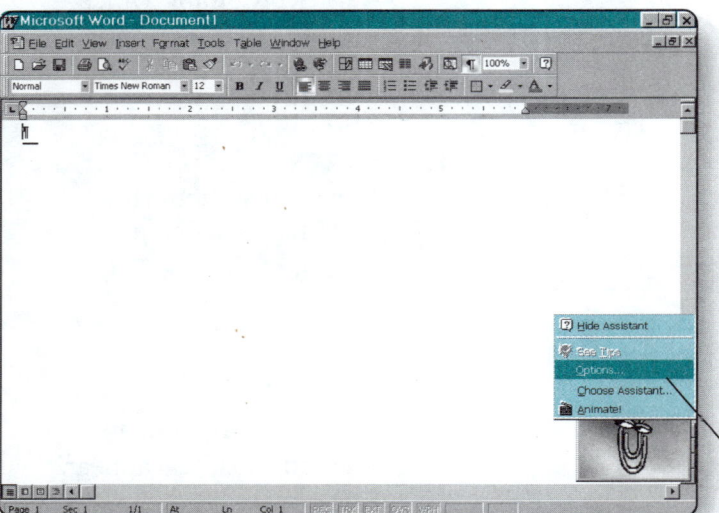

1. **Right-click** on the **Office Assistant window**. A shortcut menu will appear.

2. **Click** on **Options**. The Office Assistant dialog box will open.

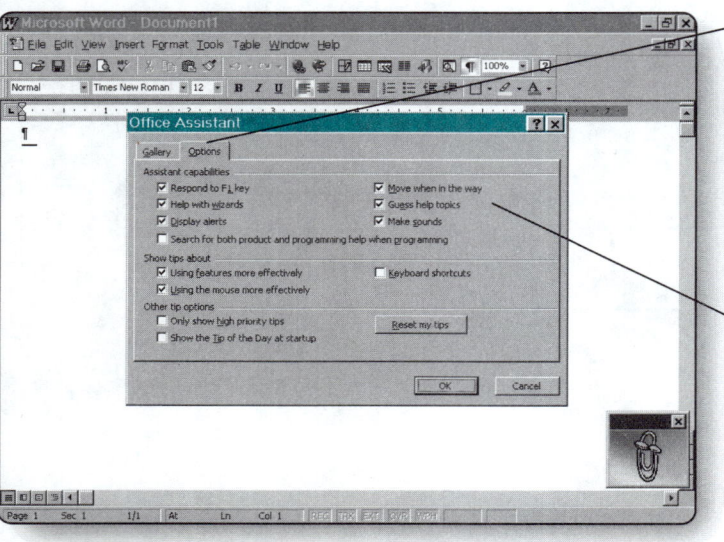

3. **Click** on the **check boxes** on the **Options tab** to control Office Assistant's behavior. A ✔ will appear if the check box is empty when you click on it; a ✔ will disappear if the check box already has a ✔ in it.

The check boxes in the Assistant capabilities section control what Office Assistant will do.

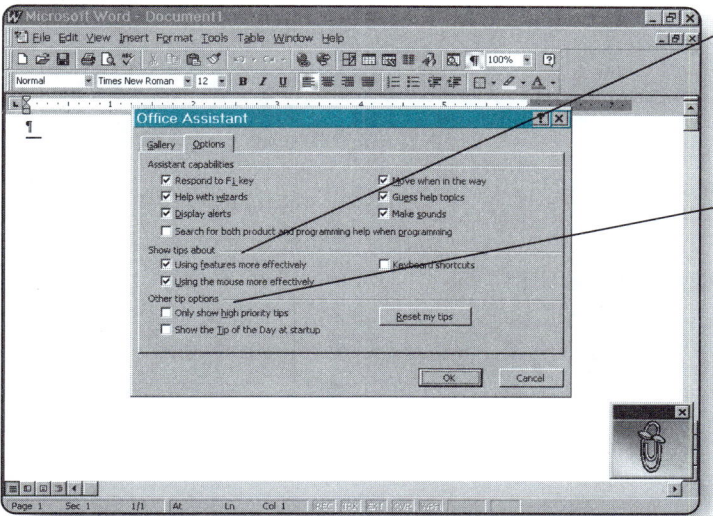

The check boxes in the Show tips about section control the kind of information Office Assistant displays.

The check boxes in the Other tip options section control miscellaneous options and reset Office Assistant's tips. If you reset tips, you might see tips that you have seen in the past.

TIP

If you don't want Office Assistant to appear unless you ask for help, remove the ✔ from the Guess help topics check box.

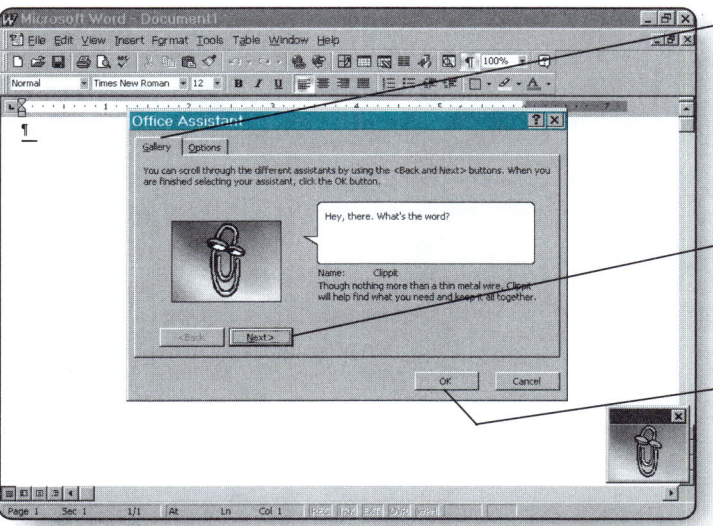

4. **Click** on the **Gallery tab**. The tab will come to the front. From this tab, you will be able to control Office Assistant's appearance.

5. **Click** on **Next**. Word will display the first of the available images for Office Assistant.

6. **Click** on **OK** after you make your choice. The changes will appear.

TIP

Depending on the way Office was installed, you may be prompted to insert the installation CD when you click on OK. Follow any instructions you see onscreen.

USING WHAT'S THIS? TO GET HELP

There will be times when you see something onscreen that you just don't recognize. For example, you might point at a toolbar button, see its ScreenTip, and still not know its function. In cases like this, use What's This?

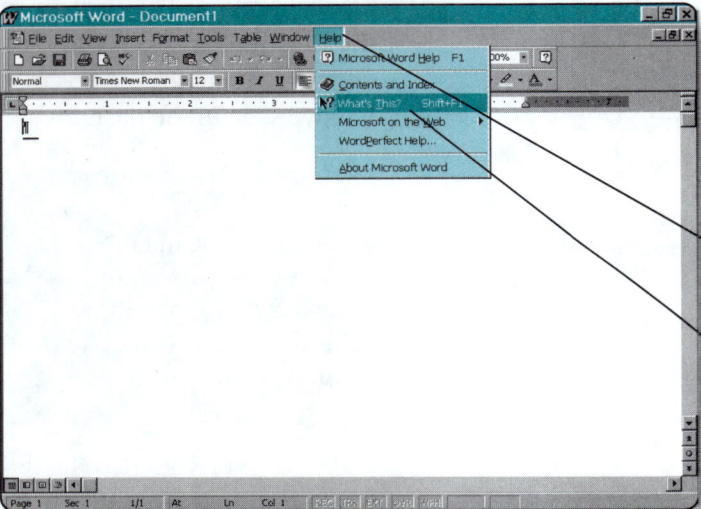

1. **Click** on **Help.** The Help menu will appear.

2. **Click** on **What's This?** The mouse pointer will change to a pointer with a question mark attached.

TIP

As a shortcut, you can press the Shift and F1 keys at the same time.

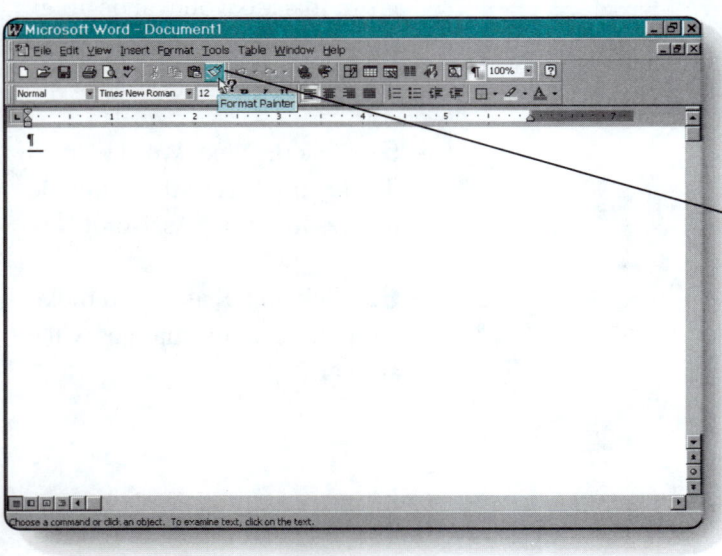

3. **Point** at the **item** that you want information about.

TIP

You can click on any part of the screen for information.

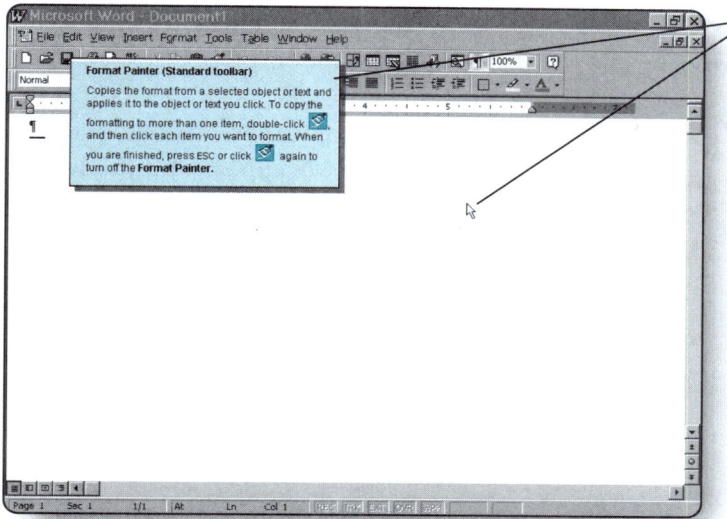

4. **Click** on the **item**. The mouse pointer will return to its normal shape and an explanation of the item on which you clicked will appear.

SEARCHING THE HELP FILE

You can directly search the Help file in three ways using the Contents and Index command.

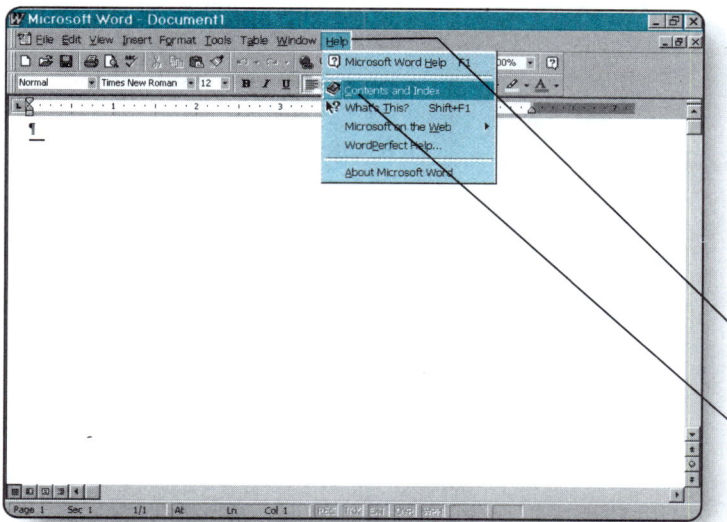

Using the Contents Tab

From the Contents tab, you can search the Help file the same way you would use the table of contents of a book—by subject.

1. **Click** on **Help**. The Help menu will appear.

2. **Click** on **Contents and Index**. The Help Topics dialog box will open.

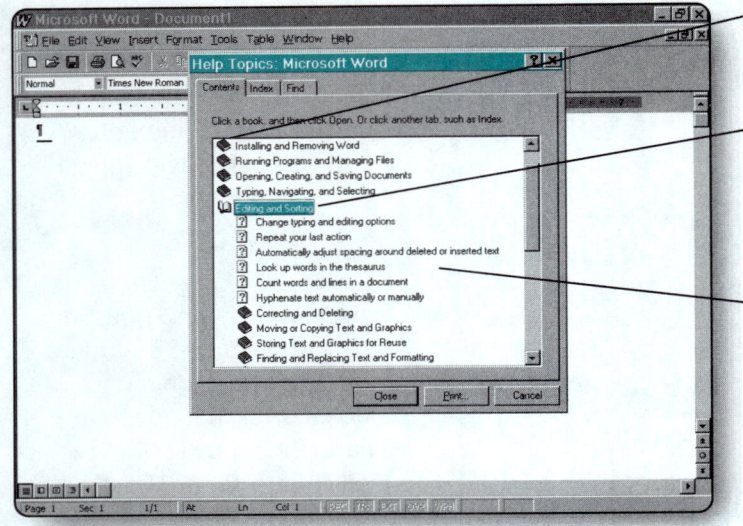

3. **Double-click** on a **book** in the Contents tab.

The topics contained in that book will appear, and you will see more books that you can double-click on.

4. **Double-click** on a **topic**. A Help topic similar to the one displayed by Office Assistant will appear.

Using the Index Tab

From the Index tab, you can search the Help file the same way you would use the index of a book—alphabetically by topic. This method is particularly useful if you are familiar with the terminology of a program. If the Help Topics dialog box doesn't appear onscreen, follow steps 1 and 2 of the preceding task.

1. **Click** on the **Index tab**. The available index entries will appear.

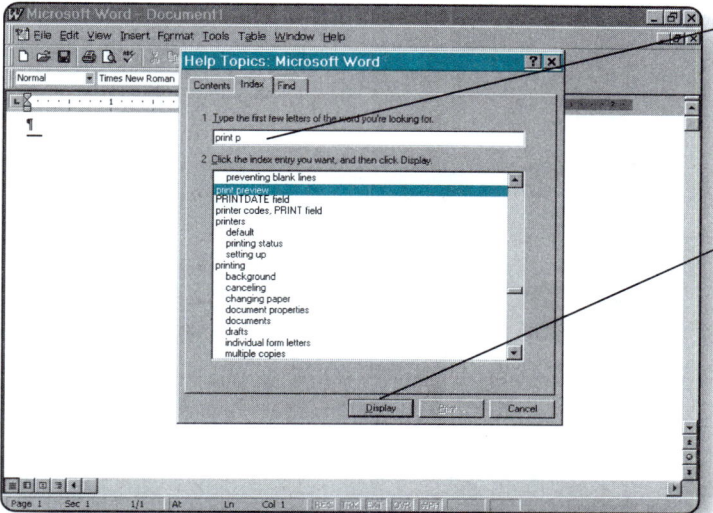

2. **Type** the **first few letters** of the item on which you want to search. The index entries in the box will scroll to match the characters you type.

3. **Click** on **Display**. A Help topic similar to the one displayed by Office Assistant will appear.

You might see the Topics Found dialog box displaying a breakdown of the topic you selected. If you see the Topics Found dialog box, select a topic and then click on Display.

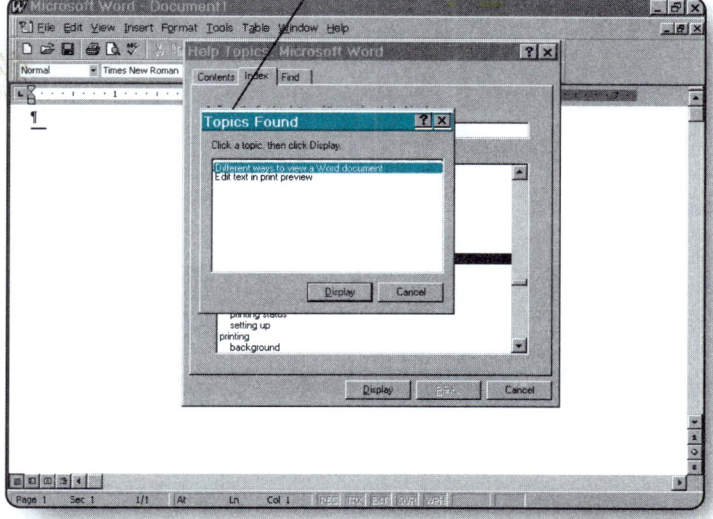

Using the Find Tab

From the Find tab, you can search the Help file similar to the way you use the Index tab—but you don't need to know the terminology of the program. The Find tab lists *all* words in the Help system, even if they aren't listed in the Index. If the Help Topics dialog box doesn't appear onscreen, click on Help, and then click on Contents and Index.

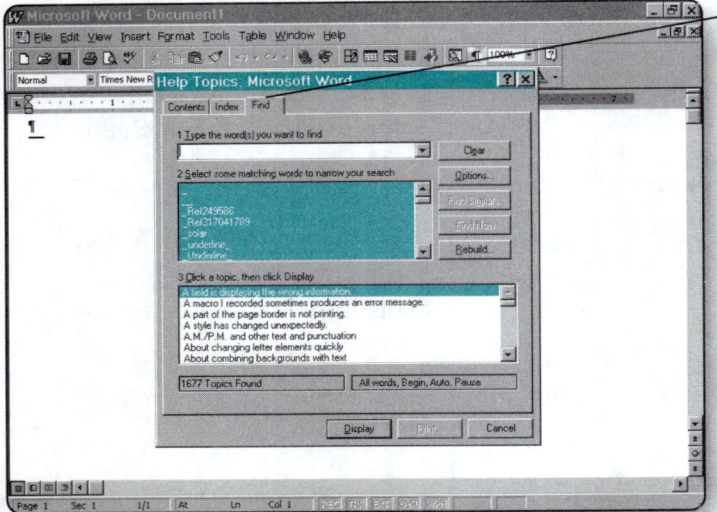

1. **Click** on the **Find tab**. The available index entries will appear.

NOTE

The first time you click on the Find tab, the Find Setup Wizard will appear. Just click on Next, and then click on Finish. The Find Setup Wizard takes a few seconds to create a list of the words available in the Help system.

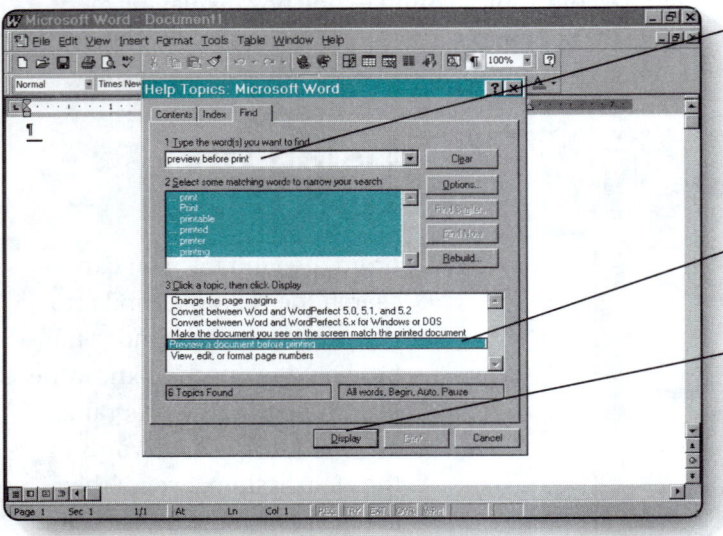

2. **Type** a **term** or **phrase** for which you want to search. All Help topics that contain the word(s) you type will appear in the Select some matching... box.

3. **Click** on a **topic**. The item will be selected.

4. **Click** on **Display**. A Help topic similar to the one that appeared when you used Office Assistant will appear.

GETTING HELP ON THE WEB

With Office 97, you no longer need to start your Web browser to access the Internet. In fact, you can get help about Office 97 products from inside any Office program.

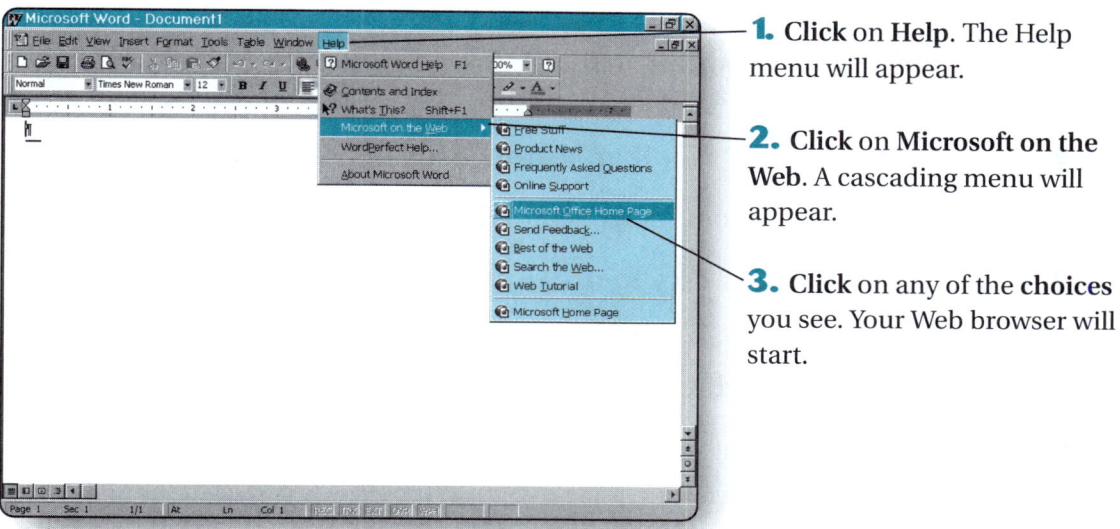

1. **Click** on **Help**. The Help menu will appear.

2. **Click** on **Microsoft on the Web**. A cascading menu will appear.

3. **Click** on any of the **choices** you see. Your Web browser will start.

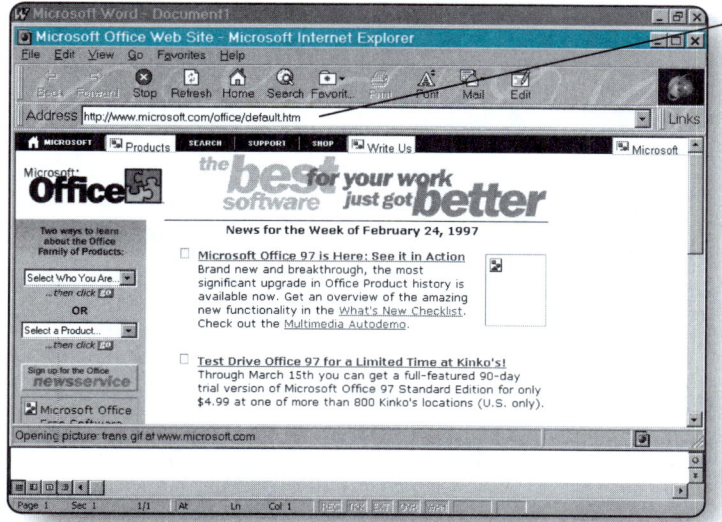

When you connect to the Internet, you will see a Web page—the Web page you see will depend on the command you selected.

PART I REVIEW QUESTIONS

1. How do you start any Office 97 program? *See Chapter 1*

2. How do you exit from any Office 97 program? *See Chapter 1*

3. How do you display a shortcut menu? *See Chapter 2*

4. Explain the value of a toolbar button. *See Chapter 2*

5. How do you give a document a name? *See Chapter 3*

6. What toolbar button do you use to save a document? *See Chapter 3*

7. How do you close a document? *See Chapter 3*

8. Name the two methods you can use to start a new document. *See Chapter 3*

9. Name the three methods you can use to open a previously saved document. *See Chapter 3*

10. Name the three methods of help available in any Office program. *See Chapter 4*

PART II
Word

mar

jumps

ice D

Excel

Excel 8
s Data
ad.xls
ead-1.xls
leadblnk.xls
LEADS.xls
leadtst.xls
Mcn95v94.xls
News Flash.xls
Sales Report.xls

5 Learning the Basics

When you first start any Office program, including Word, you need to learn how to enter and manipulate information. If you don't have Word open on your screen, follow the steps in Chapter 1 to open Word. In this chapter, you'll learn how to:

✦ Type, delete, and select text

✦ Change fonts and font sizes

✦ Format text to make it appear **bold**, *italic*, or <u>underlined</u>

✦ Move around a document

✦ Align text horizontally and vertically

✦ Move and copy text

✦ Create a bulleted list and a numbered list

TYPING TEXT

When you first open Word, you will be working in Document1, and you will see the insertion point flashing in the working area. The *insertion point* is a vertical bar that marks where text will appear when you type. As you type, the insertion point moves to the right. If you make a typing mistake, press the Backspace key; each time you press it, Word will delete the character immediately to the left of the insertion point.

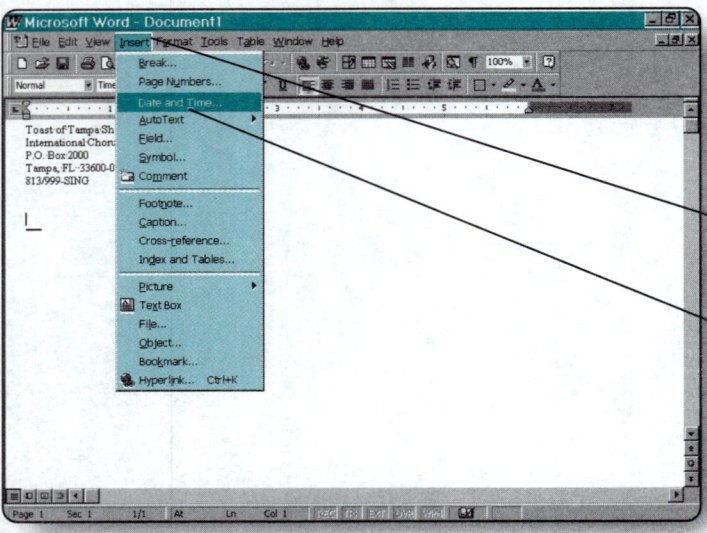

1. **Type** the **information** that would typically appear in your letterhead. This information could include your company name, address, city, state, zip code, and phone number.

NOTE

This data would typically appear on separate lines. As you reach the end of each line of the address, press the Enter key to begin a new line.

2. **Click** on **Insert**. The Insert menu will appear.

3. **Click** on **Date and Time**. The Date and Time dialog box will open.

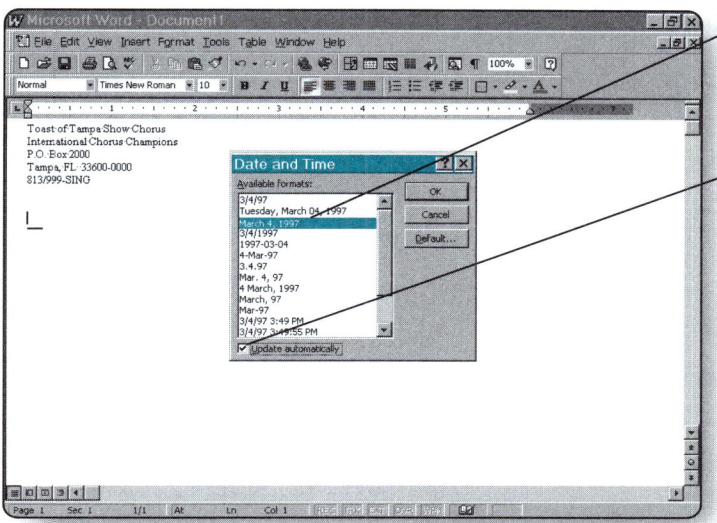

4. **Click** on a **format** for the date in the Available formats: list. The item will be selected.

5. **Click** on **Update Automatically**. A ✔ will appear in the check box.

6. **Click** on **OK**. The dialog box will close and the date will appear in the document at the insertion point.

NOTE

If you press the left arrow key or click anywhere in the date, you'll notice that its background is shaded and appears gray. You actually inserted a *date field*; which is a date that will change to match your computer's date. If you open this letter tomorrow, you'll see tomorrow's date.

TIP

If you moved the insertion point into the date, press the End key on your keyboard to return the insertion point to the end of the line containing the date.

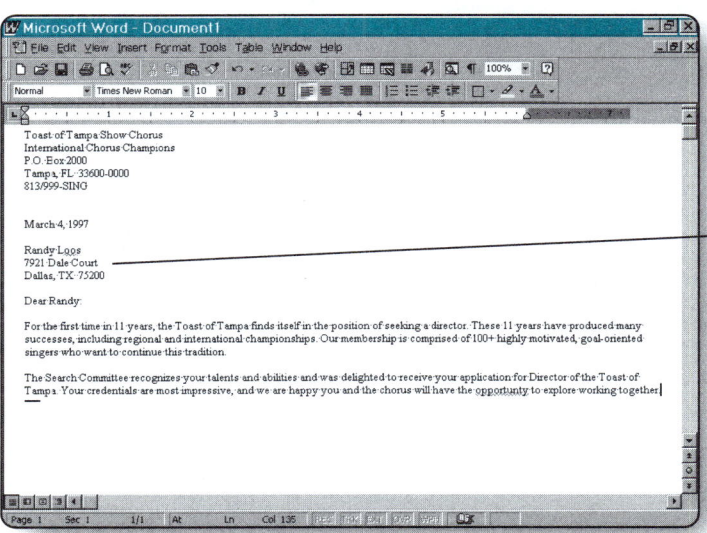

7. **Press** the **Enter key twice**.

8. **Type** an **inside address**. Be sure to press the Enter key after each line.

9. **Press** the **Enter key twice**.

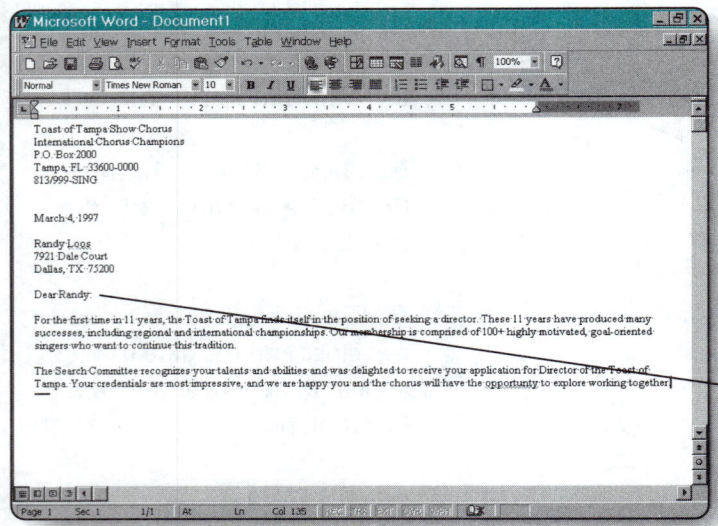

10. Type a **salutation**.

11. Press the **Enter key twice**.

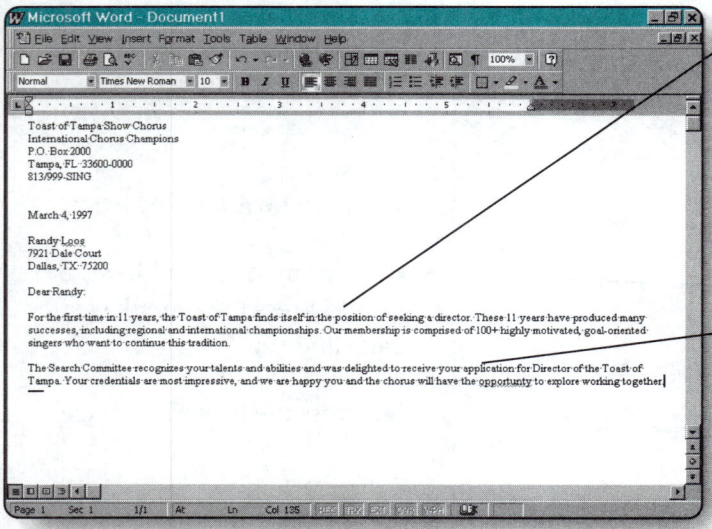

12. **Type** some **text** for the first paragraph. Do *not* press the Enter key as the insertion point approaches the end of a line. Word will automatically create a new line for you as you type.

13. Press the **Enter key twice**.

14. **Type** some **text** for the second paragraph.

For the purpose of this exercise, you might want to type a paragraph with deliberate spelling mistakes.

DISPLAYING NON-PRINTING CHARACTERS

Typists often like to see visual representations for non-printing characters, such as tabs and the spaces between words.

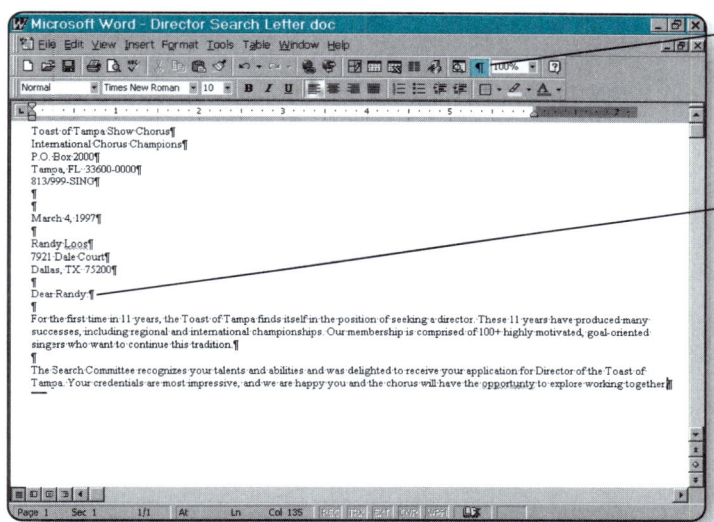

1. **Click** on the **Show/Hide (Paragraph) button**. Non-printing characters will appear in your document.

When you display non-printing characters, Word shows dots between words to represent spaces and paragraph marks at the end of each line where you pressed the Enter key. When you press the Tab key, you'll see a right-pointing arrow representing the tab.

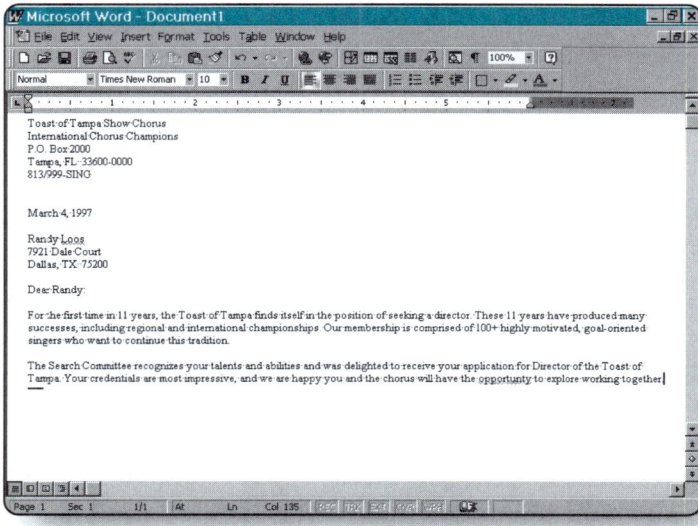

Turning Off Non-Printing Characters

The Show/Hide (Paragraph) button works like an On/Off Switch.

1. **Click** on the **Show/Hide (Paragraph) button**. The non-printing characters will be hidden.

SELECTING TEXT WITH THE MOUSE

You often need to select text before you can perform an action. *Selecting* text is the process of identifying text on which you want Word to operate. Regular text appears onscreen as black letters on a white background. When you select text, it appears as white letters highlighted by a black bar—this appearance is often called *reverse video*. To select text, you can drag using the mouse.

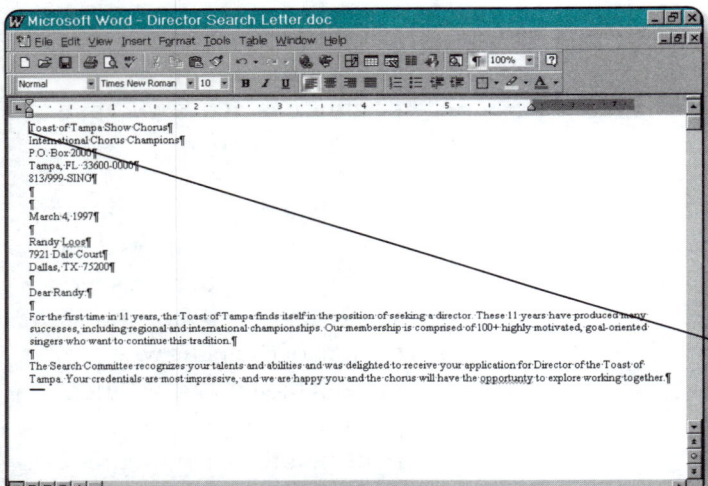

1. **Click** at the **beginning** of the document. The insertion point will appear to the left of the first letter in the document.

2. **Press** and **hold** the **mouse button** and **drag** the **mouse pointer** over the words in the first line of the document.

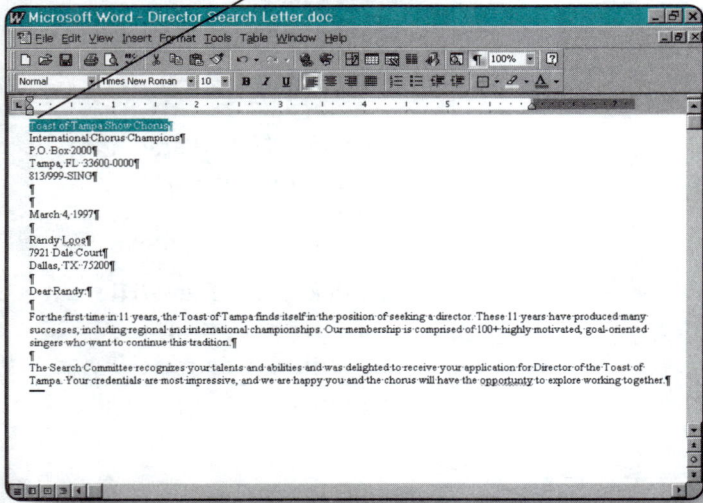

3. **Release** the **mouse button**. The words will appear in reverse video.

NOTE

The process described in step 2 is called *dragging*. Dragging means pressing and holding the mouse button while moving the mouse. When the letters you want appear in reverse video, releasing the left mouse button completes the process of dragging.

4. **Click anywhere** in the document. The selection will be canceled—the reverse video will disappear, but the text will remain.

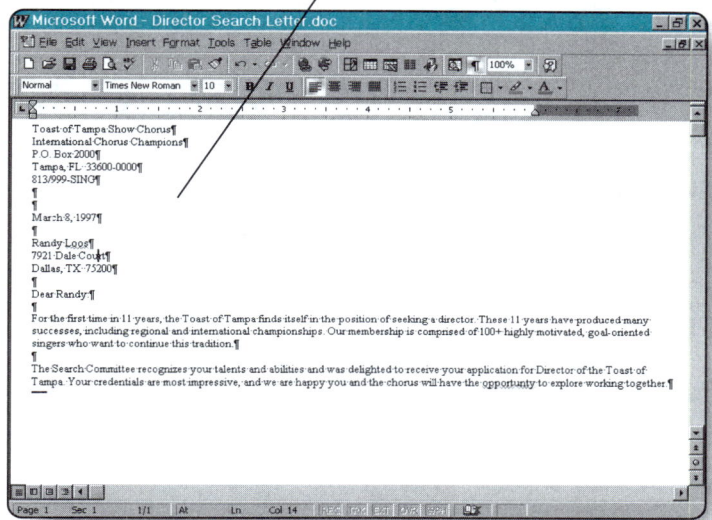

ENHANCING TEXT

Enhancing text is the process of changing its appearance. For example, you can change fonts or point sizes or add embellishments, such as boldface, italic, or underline.

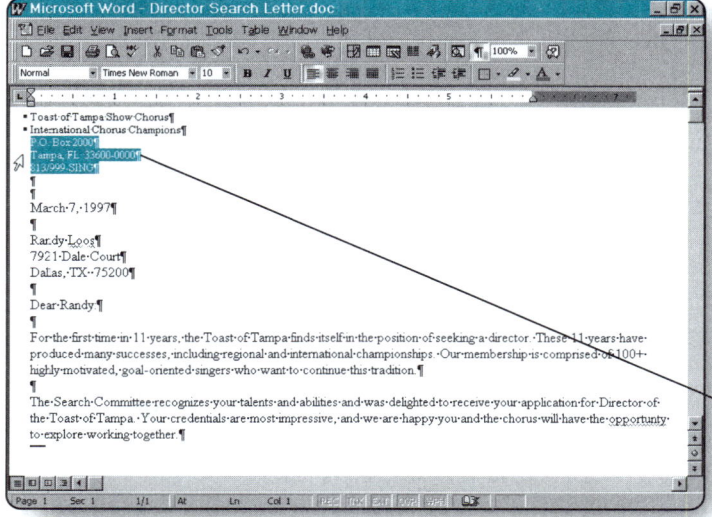

Changing the Font

The *font* is the typeface of the text. Windows comes with a variety of fonts, and Word adds some additional fonts. Other programs installed on your computer might also install fonts.

1. **Select** some **text** in the document.

TIP

To select multiple lines, move the mouse pointer in the left margin next to the top line. When the mouse pointer changes to an arrow pointing up and to the right, drag down.

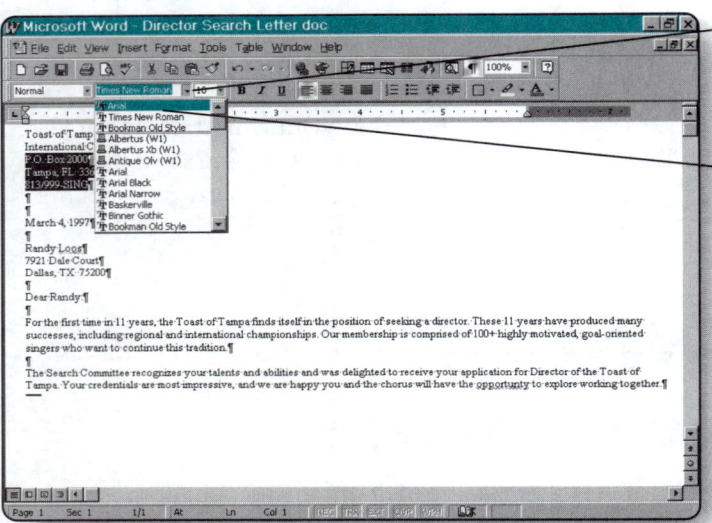

2. **Click** on the **arrow** (▼) next to the Font list box. A list of available fonts will appear.

3. **Click** on a **font name**. The font of the selected text will change.

Changing the Font Size

The *font size* controls how large the font appears.

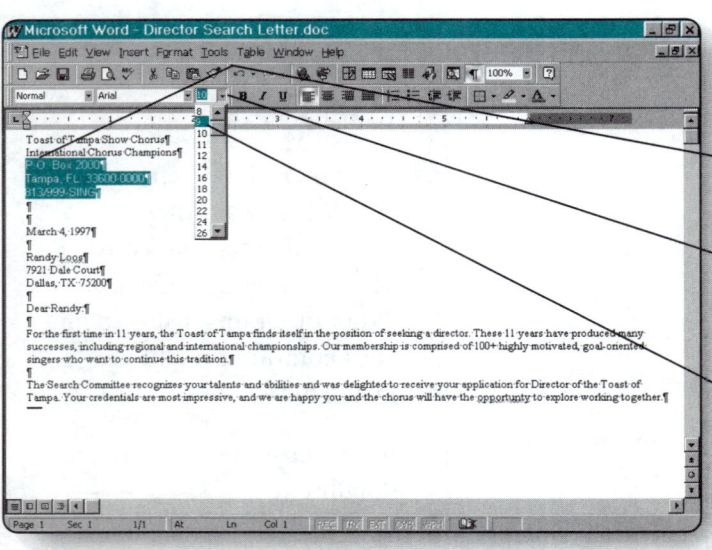

1. **Select** some **text** in the document.

2. **Click** on the **arrow** (▼) next to the Font Size list box. A list of available font sizes will appear.

3. **Click** on a **font size**. The size of the selected text will change.

4. **Select** some **different text** in the document.

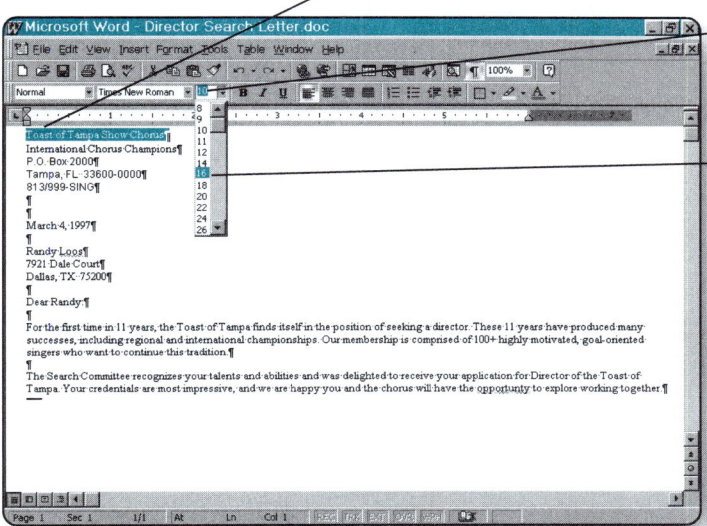

5. **Click** on the **arrow** (▼) next to the Font Size list box. A list of available font sizes will appear.

6. **Click** on a different **font size**. The size of the selected text will change.

TIP

To select a single line of text, move the mouse pointer in the left margin next to the line. When the mouse pointer changes to an arrow pointing up and to the right, click.

Adding Boldface and Italics

Boldface and italic type help draw attention to text.

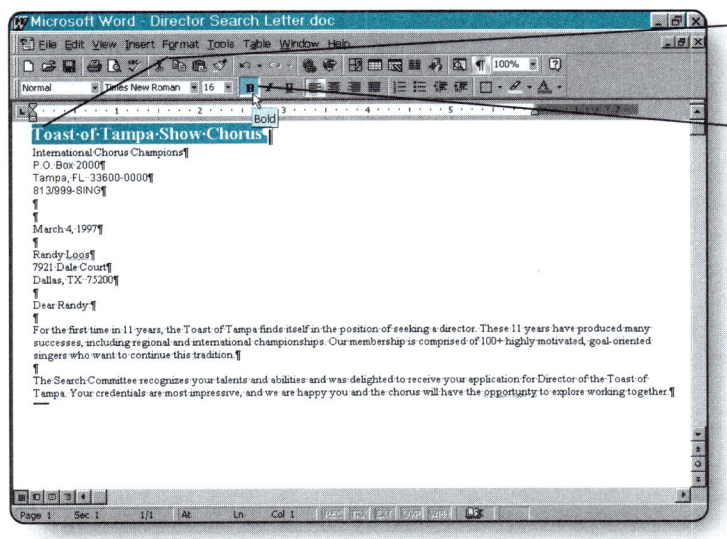

1. **Select** some **text** in the document.

2. **Click** on the **Bold button**. The appearance of the selected text will change.

TIP

To apply boldface to a single word, place the insertion point anywhere in that word and click on the Bold button.

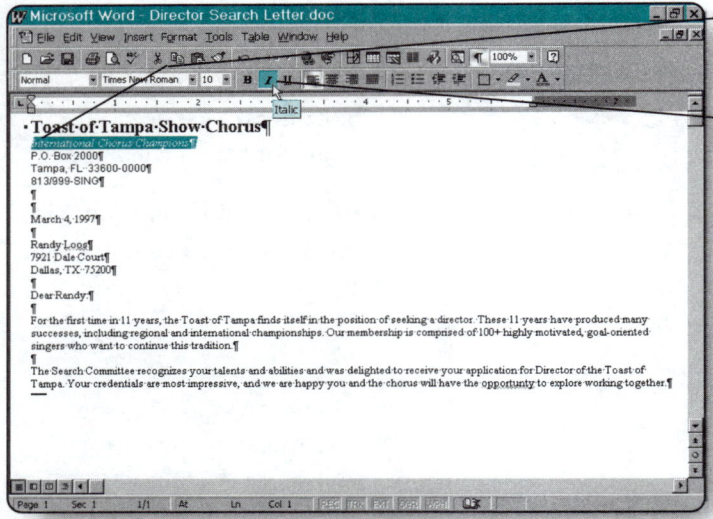

3. **Select** some different **text** in the document.

4. **Click** on the **Italic button**. The appearance of the selected text will change.

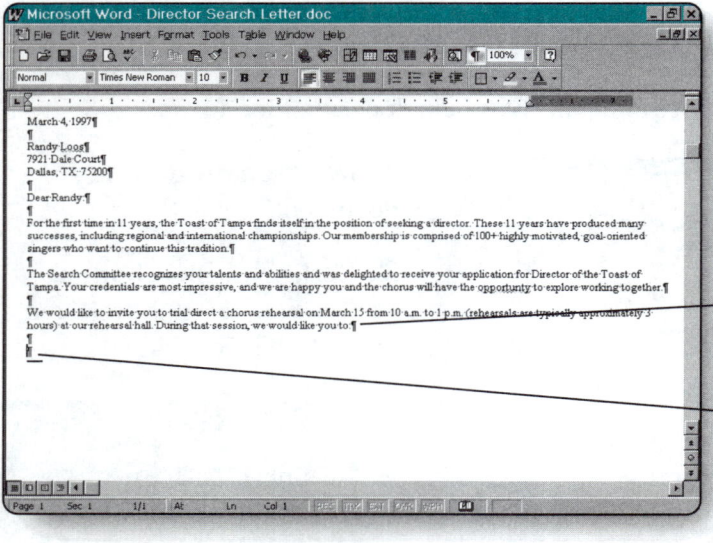

Creating a Numbered List

Numbering paragraphs is easy.

1. **Press** the **Enter key twice** at the end of the document.

2. **Type** some **text** that would lead in to a numbered list.

3. **Press** the **Enter key twice**.

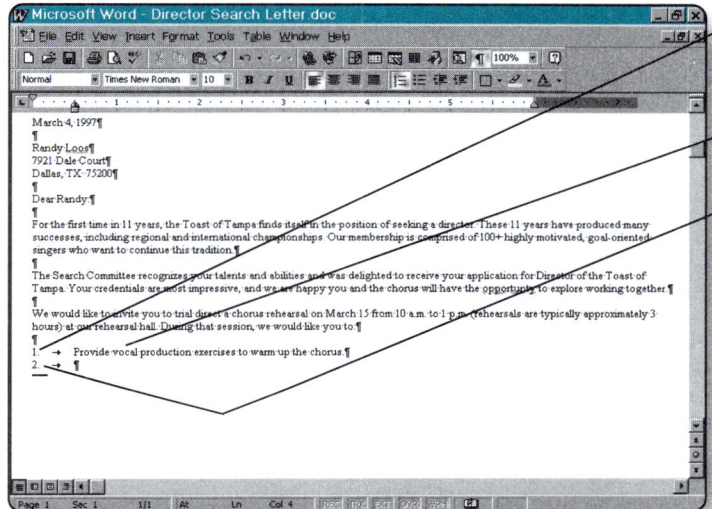

4. Type **1.** and **press** the **Tab key**.

5. Type some **text**.

6. **Press** the **Enter key**. Word will automatically insert "2." and a tab character.

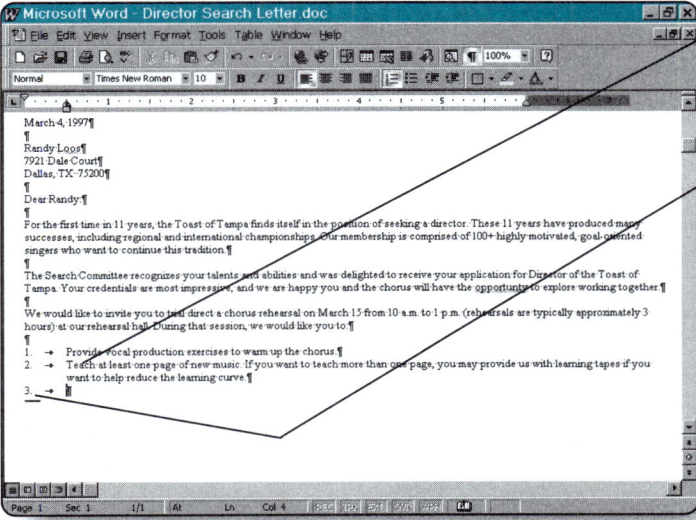

7. **Type** some **text**. As you type, the text will automatically align with the tab.

8. **Press** the **Enter key**. Word will automatically insert "3." and a tab character.

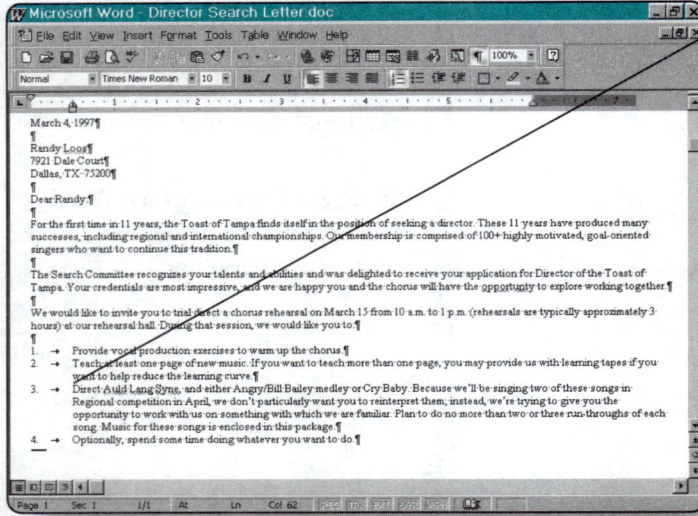

9. **Type** some **text**.

10. **Press** the **Enter key**. Word will automatically insert "4." and a tab character.

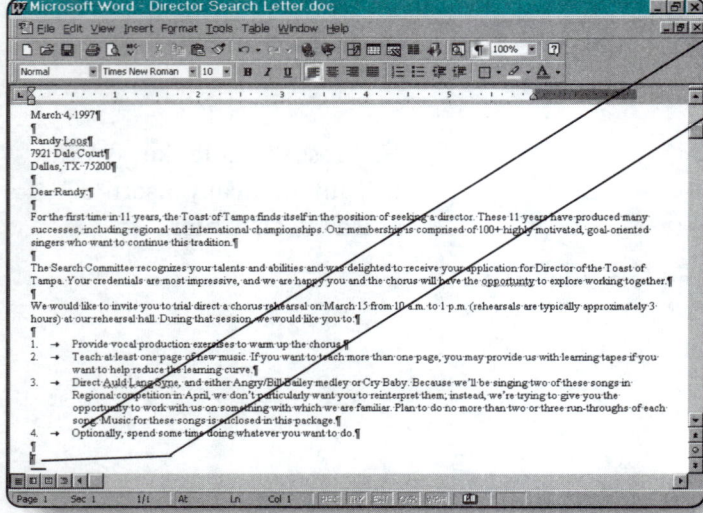

11. **Type** some **text**.

12. **Press** the **Enter key twice** after number 4. Word will insert the number 5 after you press the Enter key once, but will remove it and stop numbering paragraphs after you press the Enter key the second time.

Creating a Bulleted List

You can create a bulleted list as easily as you created a numbered list. You can also convert existing text into a bulleted list.

Creating a Bulleted List from Scratch

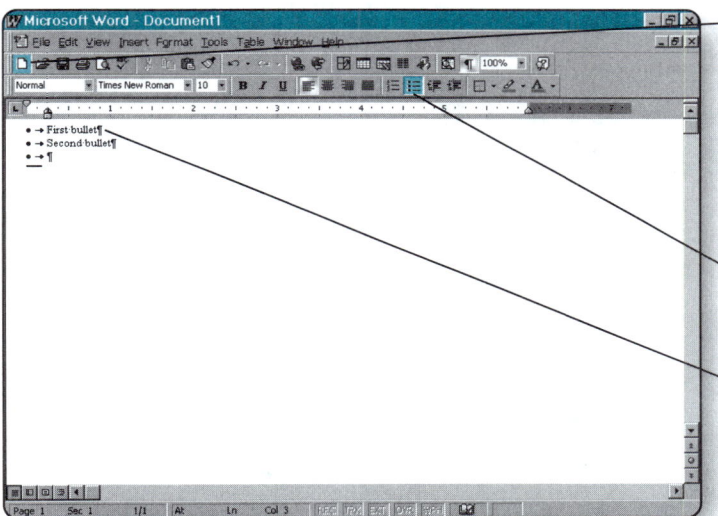

1a. **Click** on the **New button**. A new document will appear.

OR

1b. **Place** the **insertion point** where the list will begin.

2. **Click** on the **Bullets button**. A bullet will appear.

3. **Type** some **text**.

4. **Press** the **Enter key**. Word will insert another bullet.

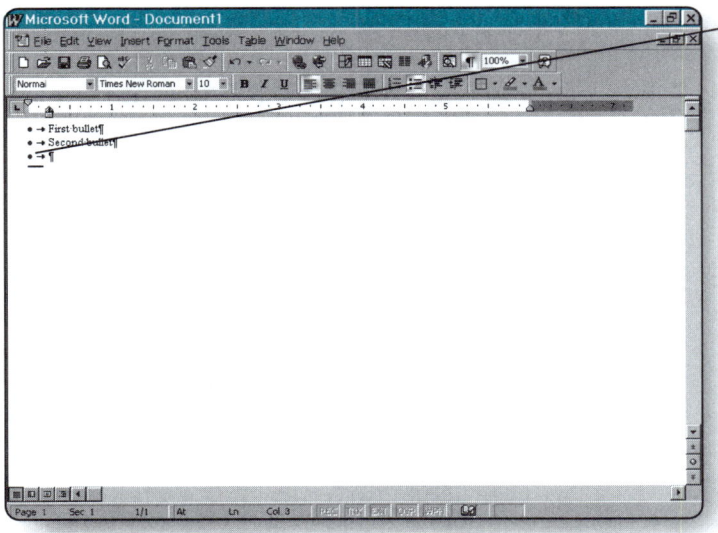

Word will operate as it did when you created a numbered list—it will insert another bullet after you type text and press the Enter key. When you press the Enter key twice, Word will end the bulleted list.

TIP

If you started a new document, use the Window menu to switch back to the document in which you were originally working for the next task.

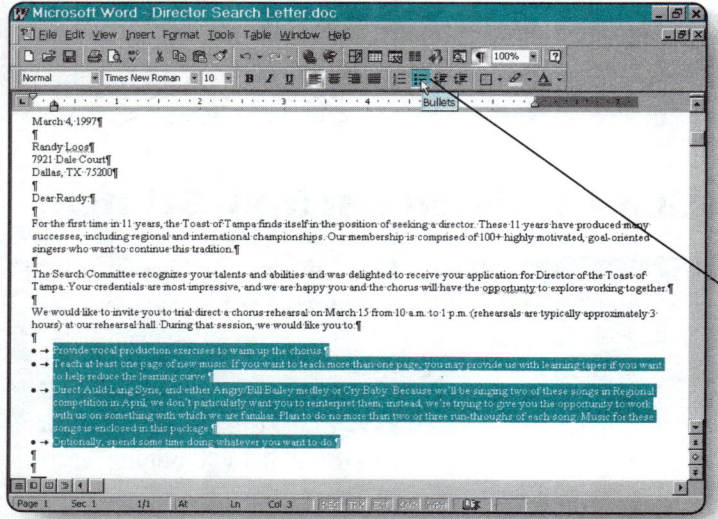

Creating a Bulleted List from Existing Text

1. **Select** the **text** you want to convert to a bulleted list (such as the numbered list).

2. **Click** on the **Bullets button**. The numbers will change to bullets. If you selected text that did not contain numbers, Word will add bullets and align the text with tabs.

NOTE

If you started a new document to create a bulleted list from scratch, use the Window menu to switch back to it and select that bulleted list for the next task.

Removing Bullets and Numbering

1. **Select** the **bulleted** or **numbered list** that you want to remove.

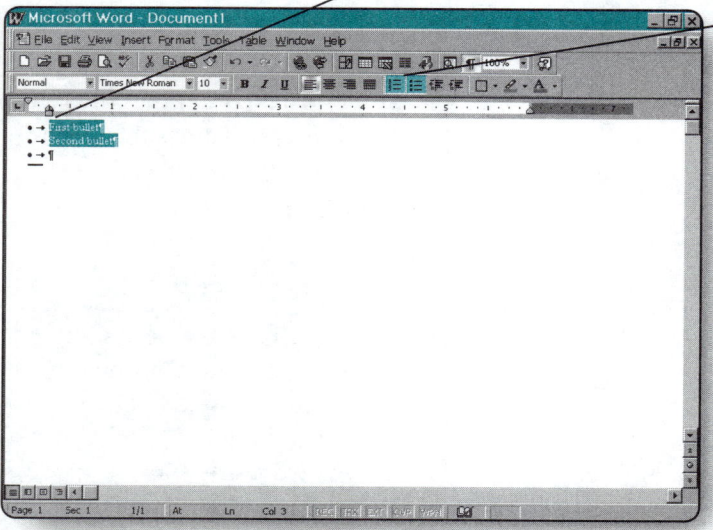

2. **Click** on the **Bullets** or **Numbering button**. The formatting will disappear.

Both the Bullets and the Numbering buttons act like On/Off switches. Clicking once adds bullets or numbers; clicking a second time removes bullets or numbers; clicking a third time adds bullets and numbers; and so on.

MOVING AROUND IN A DOCUMENT

To edit a document, you will need to move the insertion point. You can use the horizontal and vertical scroll bars to view the area in which you want to work and then click the mouse to move the insertion point. You can also use the key combinations listed in the table in this section.

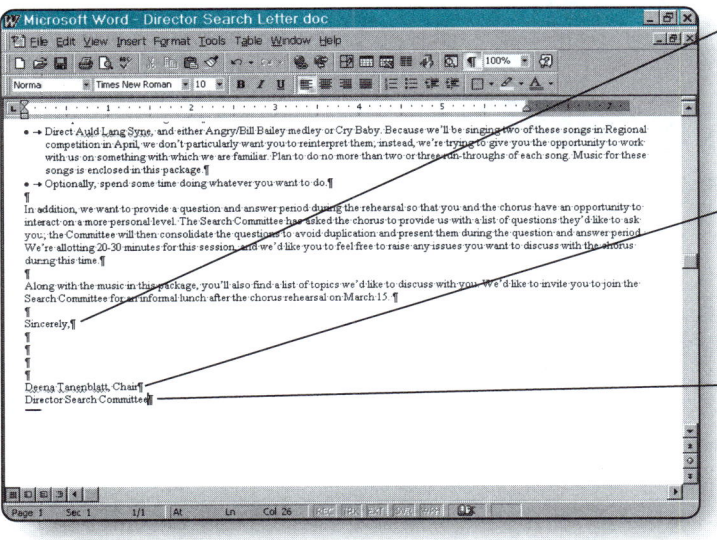

1. **Type** at least **two paragraphs** to finish the letter. (Press the Enter key twice between paragraphs.) For some of the later steps in this task to make sense, you'll need a letter at least as long as the one in the figure.

2. **Press** the **Enter key twice**.

3. **Type** a **closing**.

4. **Press** the **Enter key four times**.

5. **Type** the **name** of the person who will sign the letter.

6. **Press** the **Enter key**.

7. **Type** the **title** of the person who will sign the letter.

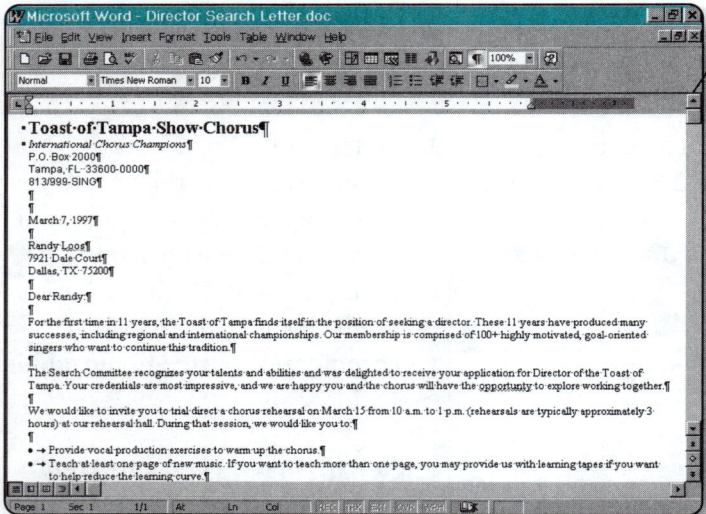

8. **Click** on the **arrow** (▲) at the top of the vertical scroll bar until the scroll box appears immediately beneath the scroll arrow. You will be able to see the beginning of the document, but you will not be able to see the insertion point.

TIP

The horizontal scroll bar works the same way as the vertical scroll bar; use it to move from side to side in a document.

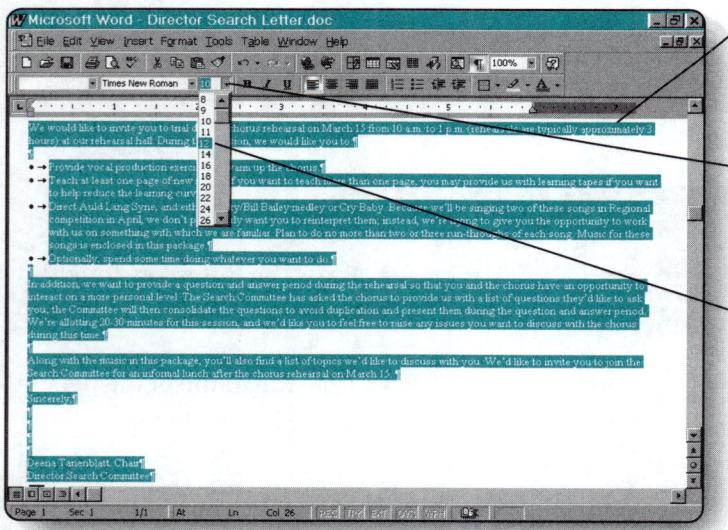

9. **Select all text** in the document from the date to the end of the document.

10. **Click** on **arrow** (▼) next to the Font Size list box. A list of available font sizes will appear.

11. **Click** on a larger **font size**, such as 12 point. The font of the body of the letter will change.

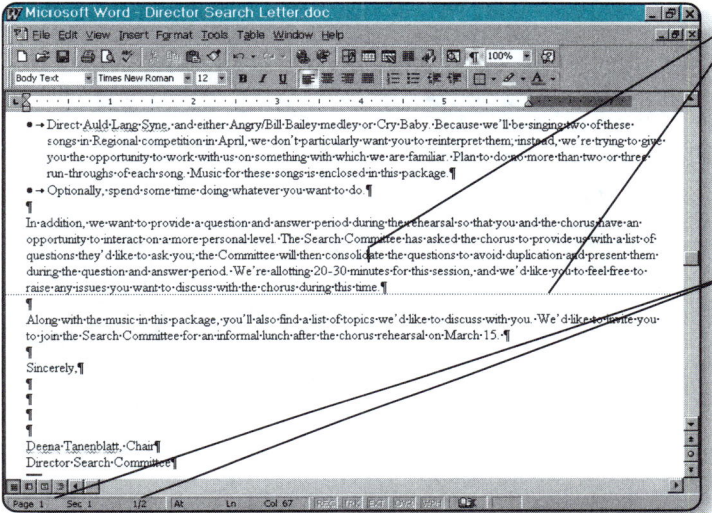

12. **Click anywhere** in the letter. The selection will be canceled. The dotted line you see represents a page break Word inserted because Page 1 filled with text.

The status bar shows you the current location of the insertion point. You can see that the insertion point appears on Page 1 in Section 1. The 1/2 you see represents page 1 of 2.

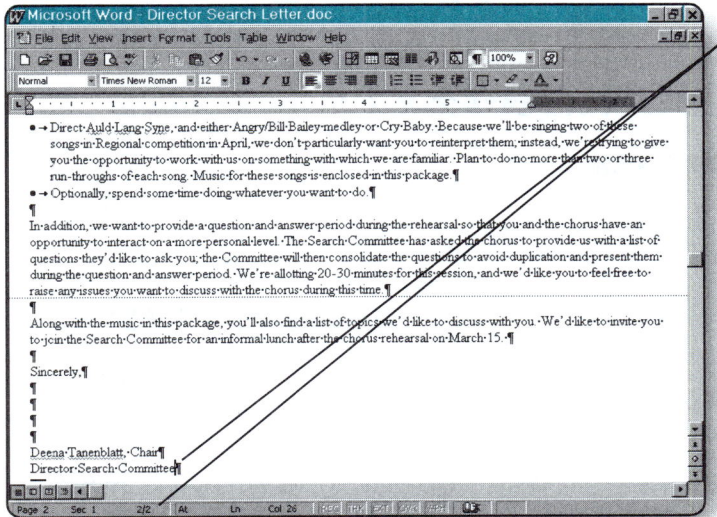

13. **Press** the **Ctrl and End keys** at the same time. The insertion point will move to the bottom of the document. Notice the changes in the status bar.

Use the key combinations in the following table to move around your document.

Press these keys	To move the insertion point
Left Arrow, Right Arrow	One character in the direction of the arrow key
Up Arrow, Down Arrow	One line in the direction of the arrow key
Ctrl+Left or Right Arrow	One word in the direction of the arrow
Ctrl+Up or Down Arrow	One paragraph in the direction of the arrow
Home	To the beginning of a line
End	To the end of a line
Ctrl+Home	To the beginning of the document
Ctrl+End	To the end of the document

TIP

If you press the Shift key and one of these key combinations, you will move the insertion point and select text. For example, pressing the Ctrl, Shift, and Right Arrow keys selects the rest of the current word and moves the insertion point to the beginning of the next word.

ALIGNING TEXT

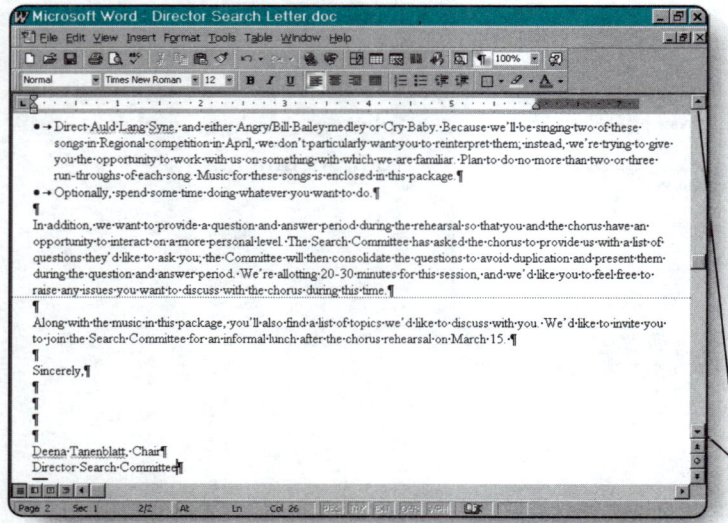

You can indent text, and you can align text horizontally and vertically.

Indenting Text

To draw the reader's attention to certain text, you sometimes want to indent that text so it doesn't line up with the left margin. You can indent text from both the left and the right margins.

1. Click on a **vertical scroll arrow** to find the bulleted list in your document.

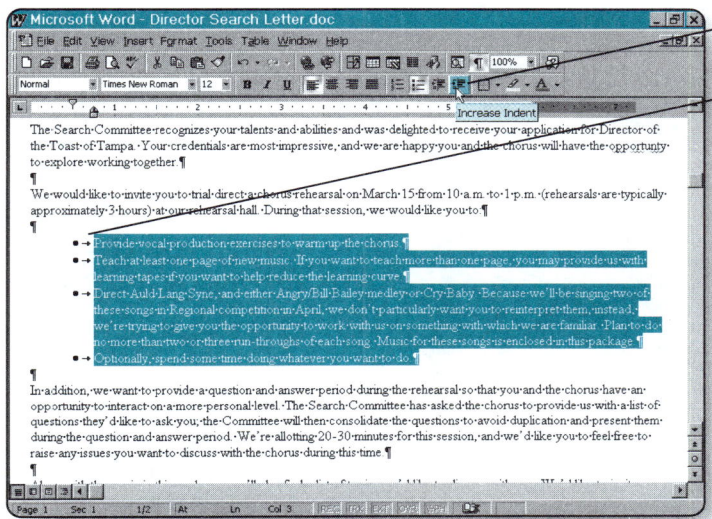

2. **Select** the **bulleted list**.

3. **Click** on the **Increase Indent button twice**. The selected text will align so the bullets appear ½ inch from the left margin.

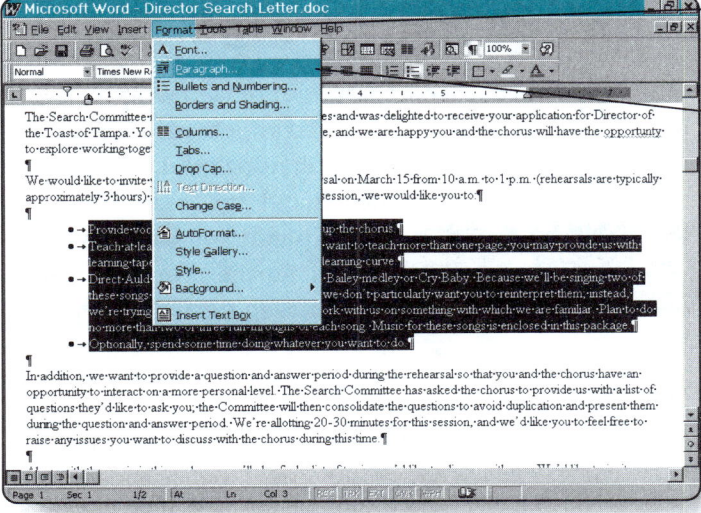

4. **Click** on **Format**. The Format menu will appear.

5. **Click** on **Paragraph**. The Paragraph dialog box will open.

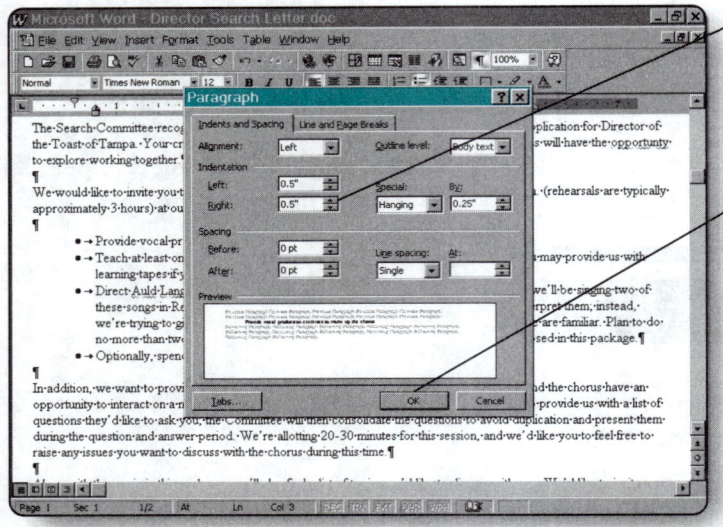

6. **Click** on the **arrow** (▲) next to the Right: text box in the Indentation section. The indentation will increase.

7. **Click** on **OK**. The dialog box will close, and the selected text will appear indented based on the settings you made in the dialog box.

TIP

Click anywhere in the document to cancel the selection.

Centering Text between the Left and Right Margins

By default, Word aligns all paragraphs at the left margin. In this case, the right margin has a ragged appearance. You can center the alignment of any paragraph horizontally between the left and right margins or align a paragraph with the right margin. Further, you can justify text between the margins so that neither the left or the right margin appear ragged.

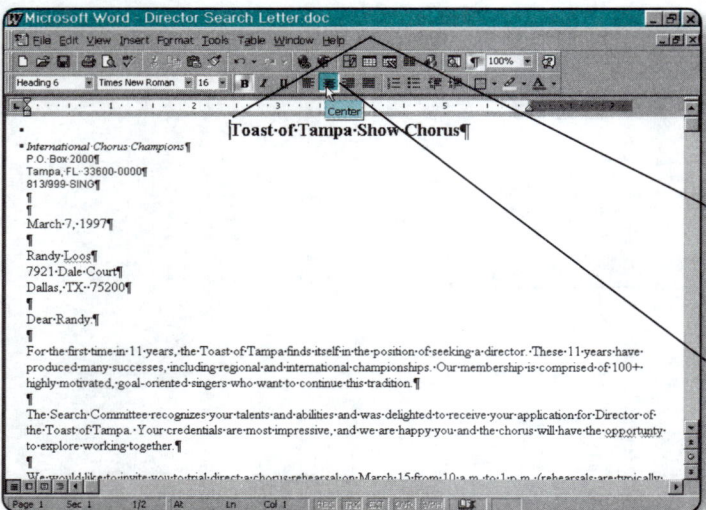

1. **Press** the **Ctrl and Home keys** at the same time. The insertion point will move to the beginning of the document.

2. **Click** on the **Center button**. The first line of text will be centered between the left and right margins.

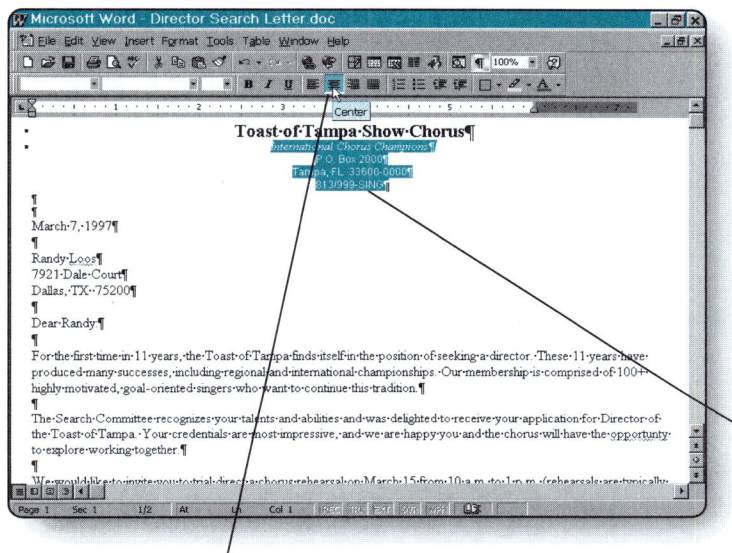

NOTE

When you change alignment while typing, Word continues using the selected alignment until you change it again. When you change alignment during editing, you select the text you want to align.

3. **Select** the rest of the **company address**.

4. **Click** on the **Center button**. The selected lines will be centered between the left and right margins.

Inserting a Page Break Manually

Suppose you decide that you don't want the page break to appear where Word puts it; insert a manual page break. If you plan to change settings for one page but not the other, make the page break function as a section break also. Word allows you to create different settings (such as margins or vertical alignment) for each section of a document.

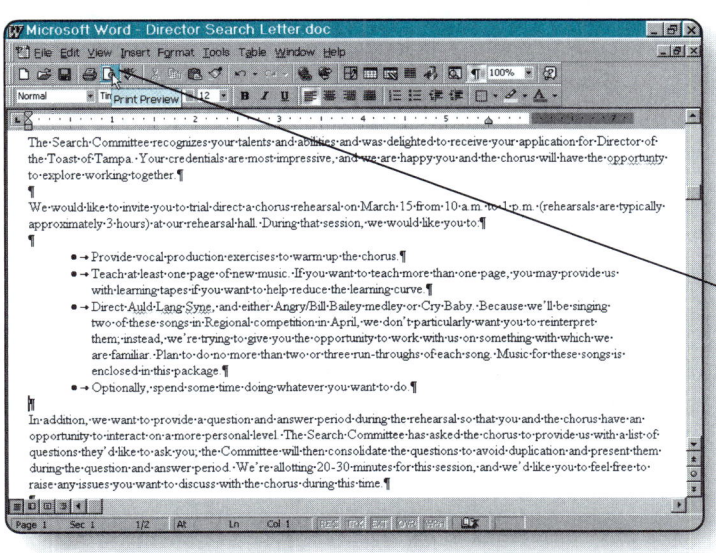

1. **Click** on the **Print Preview button**. The document will appear in Print Preview.

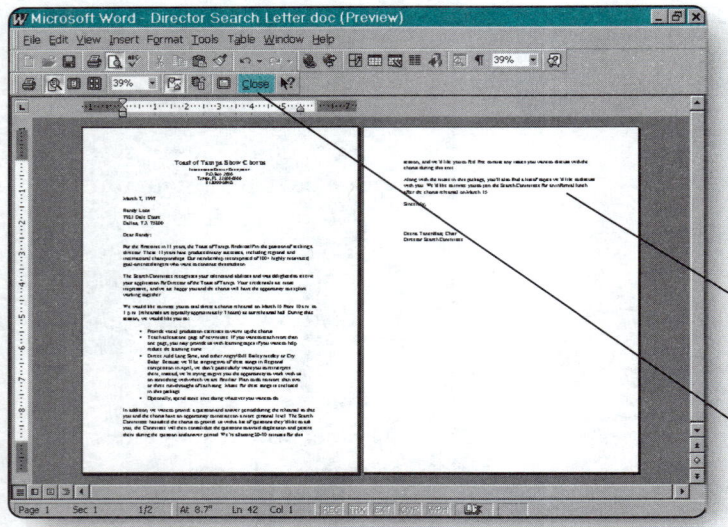

View the document in Print Preview to decide where you want to add a page break.

2. **Click** on the **Close button** (⊠). Print Preview will close.

3. **Click** to the **left** of the **paragraph mark** immediately before the place where you want to add a page break.

4. **Click** on **Insert**. The Insert menu will appear.

5. **Click** on **Break**. The Break dialog box will open.

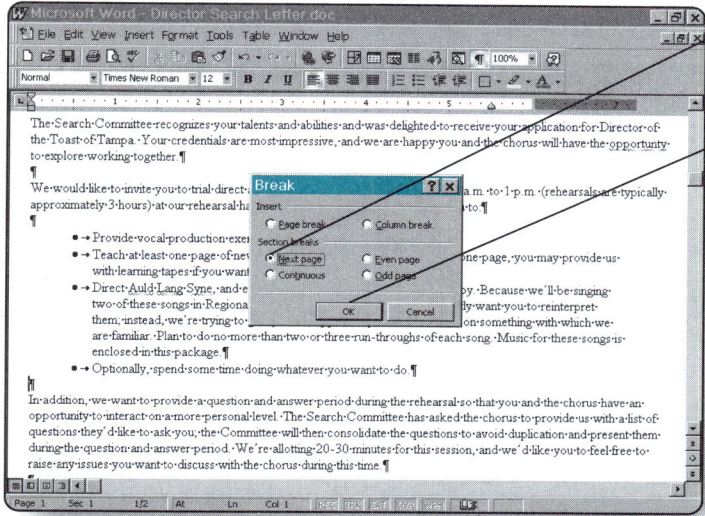

6. Click on **Next Page**. The option will be selected.

7. Click on **OK**. A section break will appear in the document.

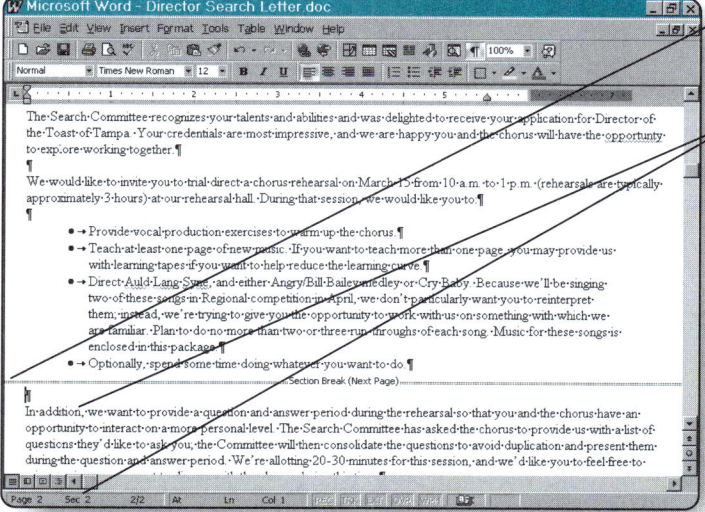

A *section break* divides the document into two sections.

The text below the insertion point will move to the next page. Also notice the status bar; the insertion point appears on Page 2 in Section 2 of the document.

TIP

If you only need to insert a page break (that is, you don't need to insert both a section and a page break), you can insert a page break by pressing the Ctrl and Enter keys at the same time.

Centering Text between the Top and Bottom Margins

By default, Word aligns text at the top of each page. However, you can change the vertical alignment of text. When you change vertical alignment, you affect the entire document unless the document is broken into sections. If a document contains sections, then you can set vertical alignment for only one section.

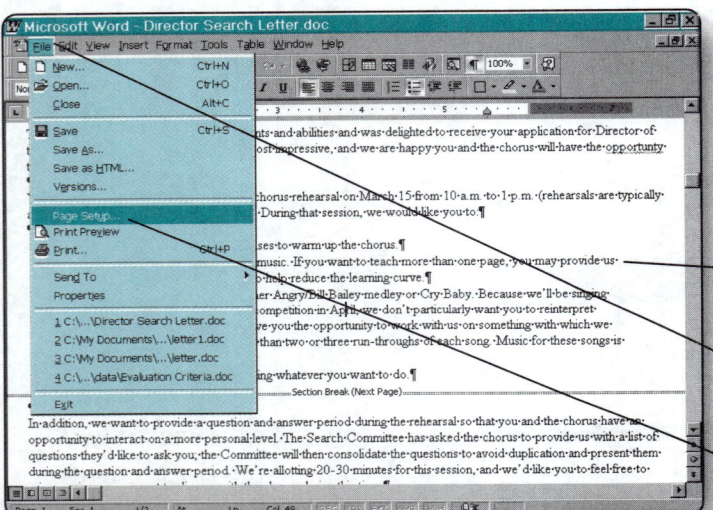

1. Click anywhere on Page 1 to set alignment for Section 1.

2. Click on **File**. The File menu will appear.

3. Click on **Page Setup**. The Page Setup dialog box will open.

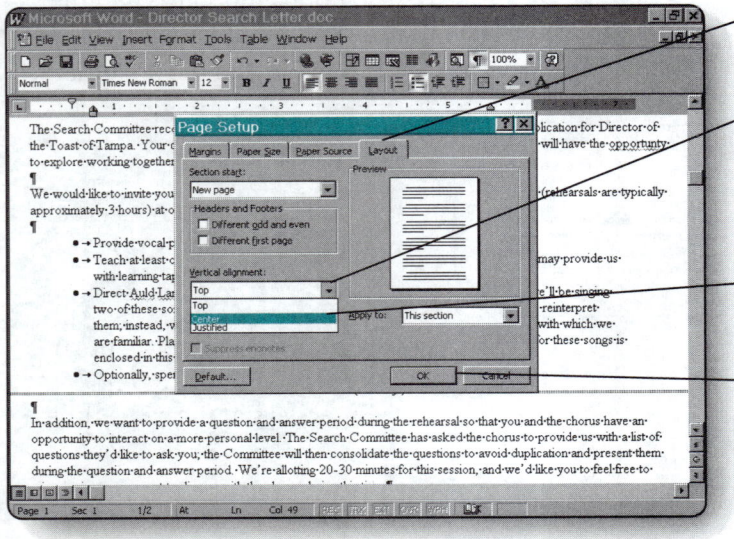

4. Click on the **Layout tab**. The tab will come to the front.

5. Click on the **arrow** (▼) next to the Vertical alignment: list box. A list of available alignments will appear.

6. Click on **Center**. The list box will close.

7. Click on **OK**. The dialog box will close.

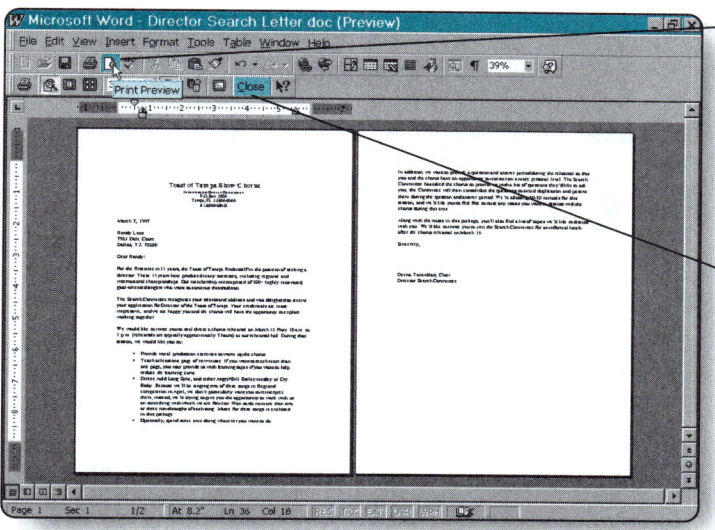

8. **Click** on the **Print Preview button**. The document will appear in Print Preview. The vertical alignment on Page 1 is centered; Page 2 remains aligned at the top of the page.

9. **Click** on the **Close button** ([X]). You will return to Normal view.

MOVING OR COPYING TEXT

You can make copies of text you've already typed, and you can move text.

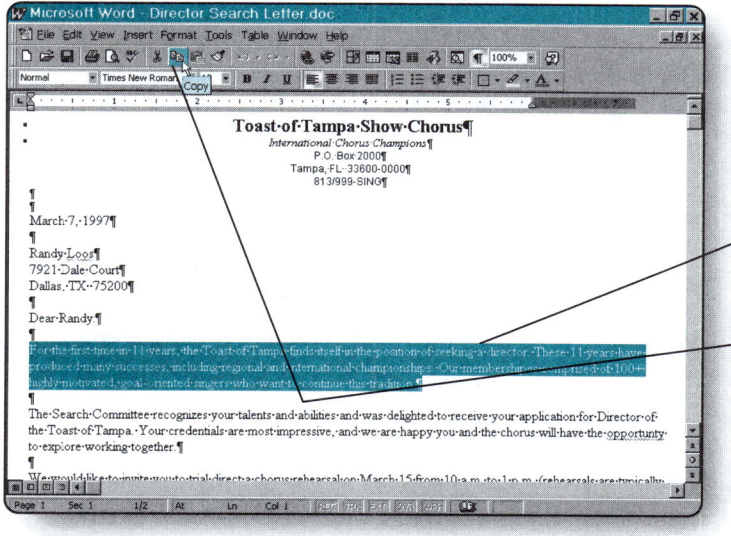

Copying Text

When you *copy* text, you make a duplicate of text. The original text is unaffected by your action.

1. **Select** the **text** you want to copy.

2. **Click** on the **Copy button**. A copy of the selected text will be placed on the Windows Clipboard.

3. Place the **insertion point** at the beginning of the location where you want the copied text to appear.

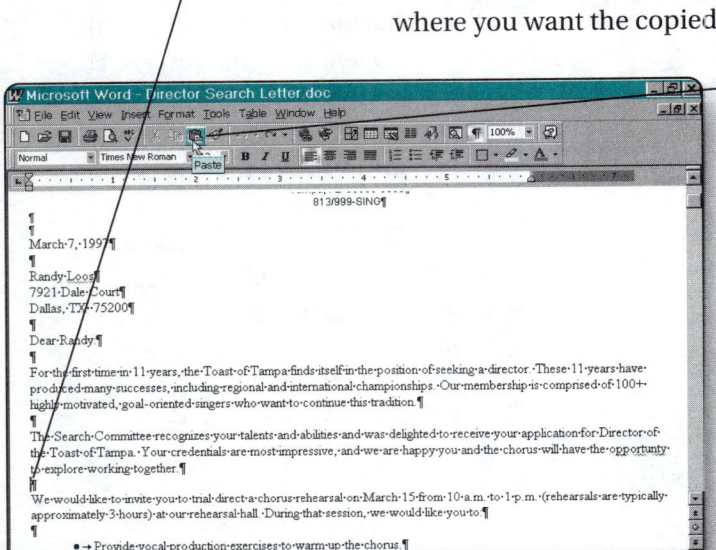

4. Click on the **Paste button**. The contents of the Windows Clipboard will be placed at the insertion point.

Moving Text

When you *move* text, you remove it from its original location and place it in a new location. The process of moving text is very similar to the process of copying text.

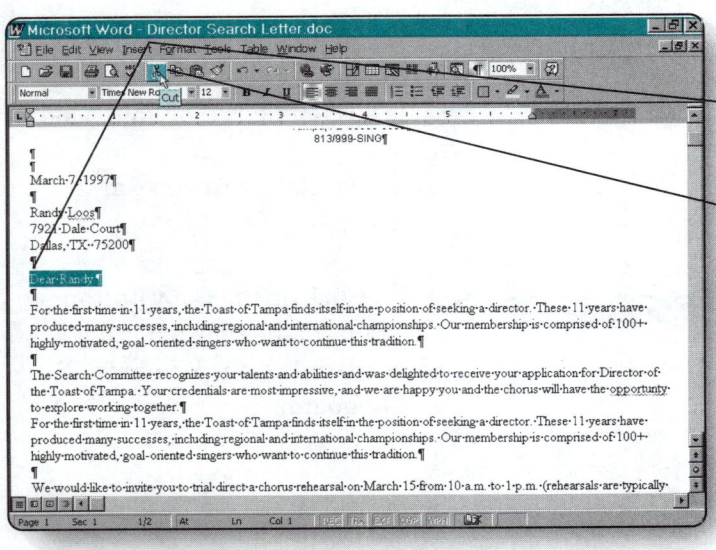

1. Select the **text** you want to move.

2. Click on the **Cut button**. The selected text will disappear from your screen and be placed on the Windows Clipboard.

3. **Place** the **insertion point** at the beginning of the location where you want the moved text to appear.

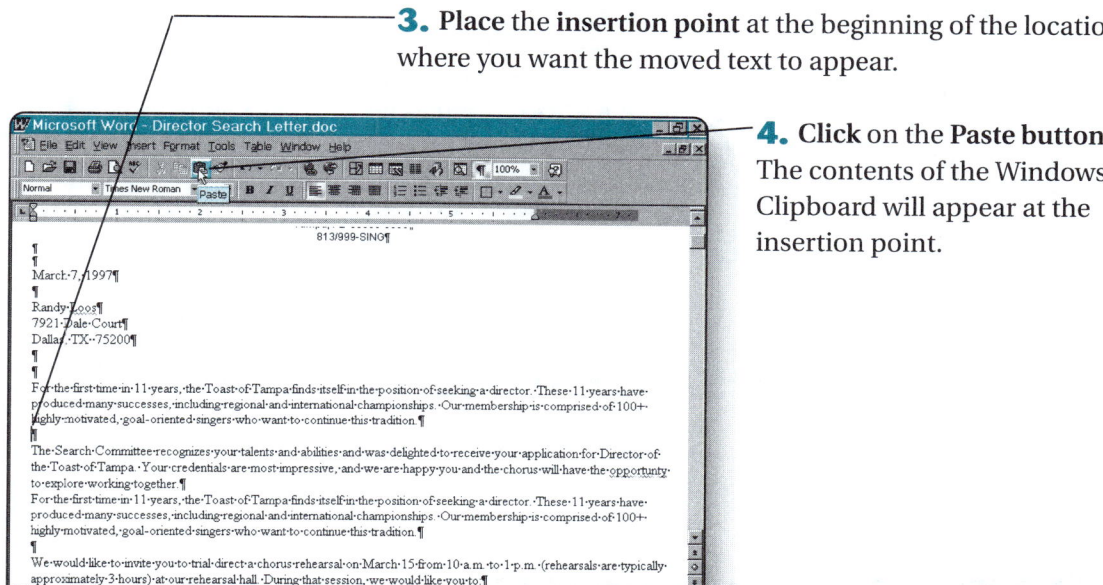

4. **Click** on the **Paste button**. The contents of the Windows Clipboard will appear at the insertion point.

UNDOING ACTIONS

Suppose you change your mind immediately after you take an action. Use the Undo feature to reverse your last action.

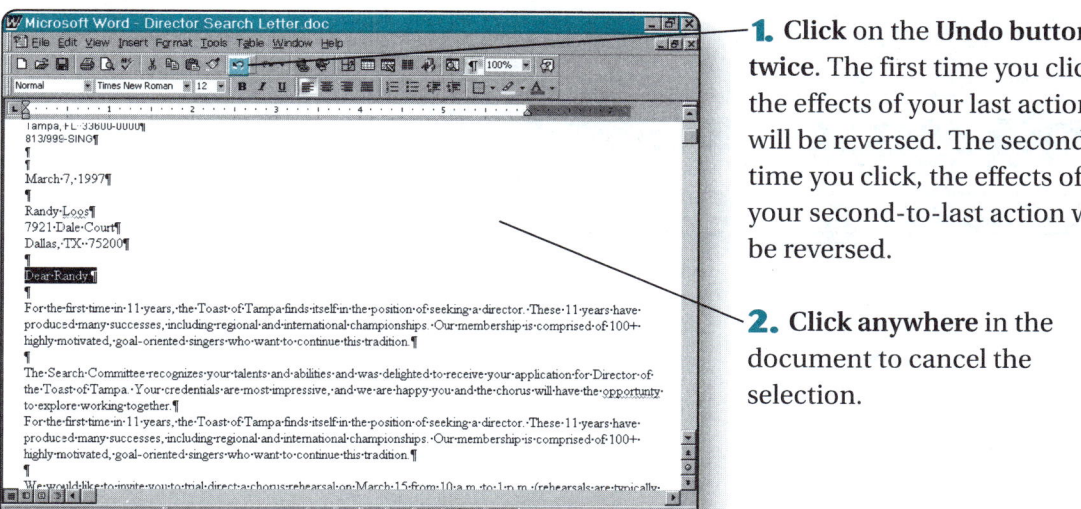

1. **Click** on the **Undo button twice**. The first time you click, the effects of your last action will be reversed. The second time you click, the effects of your second-to-last action will be reversed.

2. **Click anywhere** in the document to cancel the selection.

DELETING BLOCKS OF TEXT

You may decide that you need to delete a large amount of text.

1. Select the **text** you want to delete.

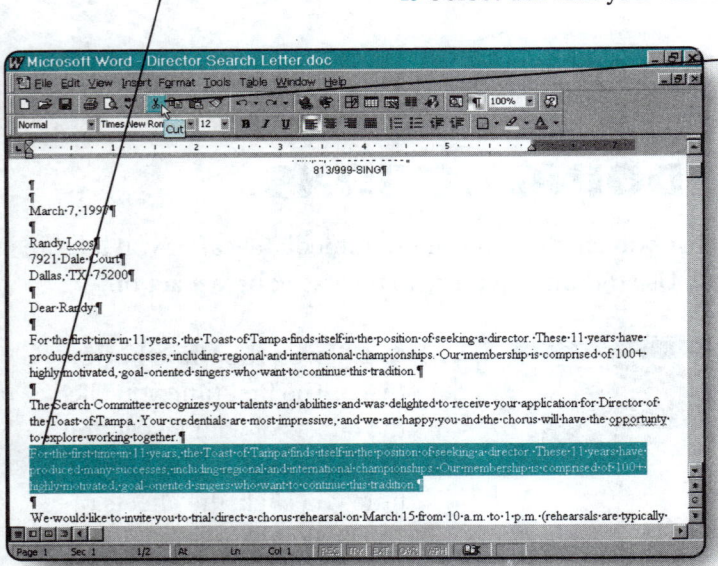

2a. Click on the **Cut button**. The text will disappear.

OR

2b. Press the **Delete key** or the **Backspace key**. The selected text will be removed from your screen.

6 Improving Your Writing

Word contains tools you can use to improve your writing. In this chapter, you'll learn how to:

✦ Use the thesaurus

✦ Find and replace text

✦ Identify words you want automatically corrected if you misspell them

✦ Check spelling and grammar

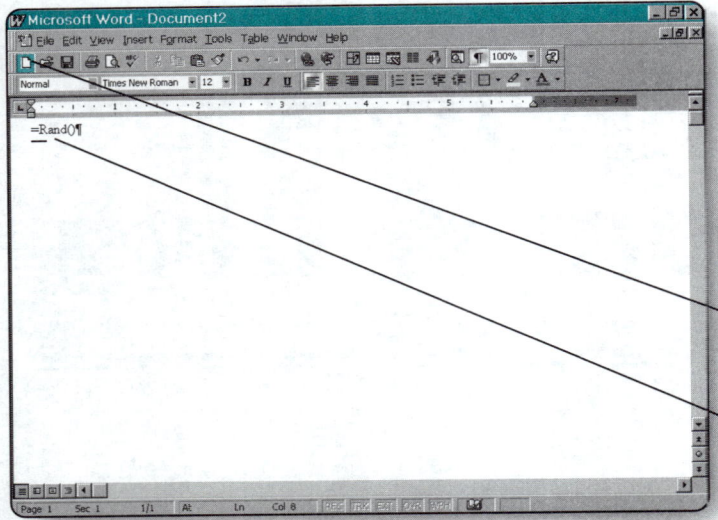

USING THE THESAURUS

Occasionally, you may find that you just can't think of the "right word" while you're working. Use Word's Thesaurus to help you.

1. **Click** on the **New button.** A new document will appear.

2. **Type** =**Rand**().

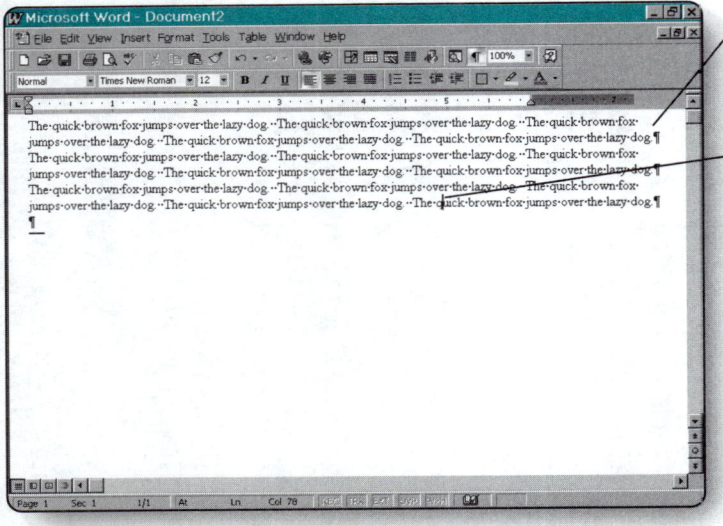

3. **Press** the **Enter key.** Random text will appear in your document.

4. **Place** the **insertion point** in the word for which you want to find a synonym.

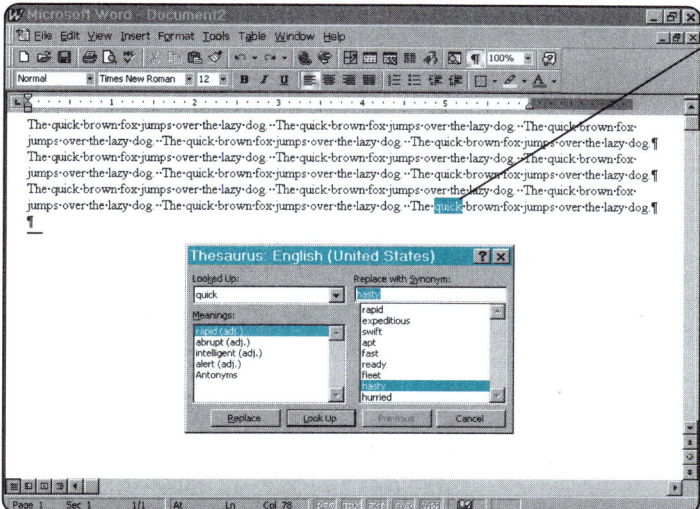

5. **Press** the **Shift** and **F7 keys** at the same time. Word will select the word containing the insertion point and open the Thesaurus dialog box.

NOTE

You can use the menus to open the Thesaurus dialog box by clicking on Tools, highlighting Language, and then clicking on Thesaurus.

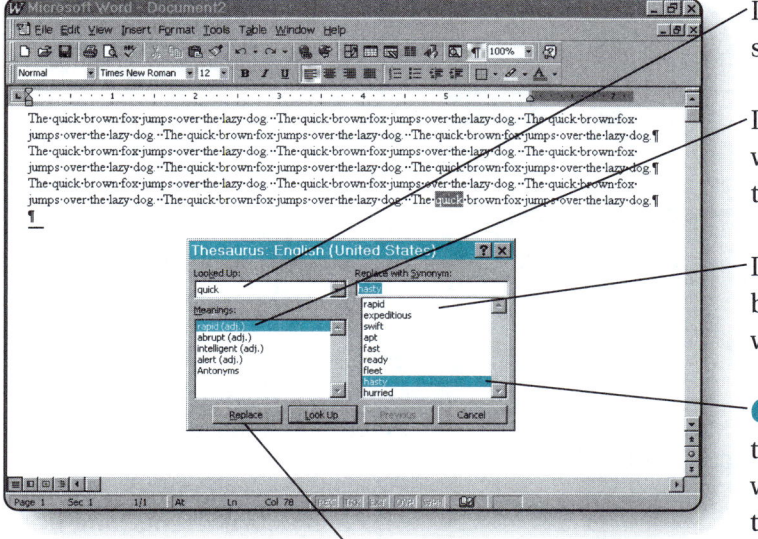

In the Looked Up: list box, you'll see the word being looked up.

In the Meanings: box, you'll see words with similar meanings that you can look up.

In the Replace with Synonym: box, you'll see synonyms for the word you looked up.

6. **Click** on the **word** you want to use to replace the selected word. The word will appear in the Replace with Synonym: box.

7. **Click** on **Replace**. The dialog box will close, and Word will change the selected word to the one you chose in the dialog box.

FINDING AND REPLACING

Finding and replacing text can be one of the speediest ways to correct a "global" mistake in a document. Word will begin searches at the insertion point and search forward in your document to the end. If you don't move the insertion point to the beginning of the document before you start the search, Word will continue the search from the top of the document until it reaches the insertion point.

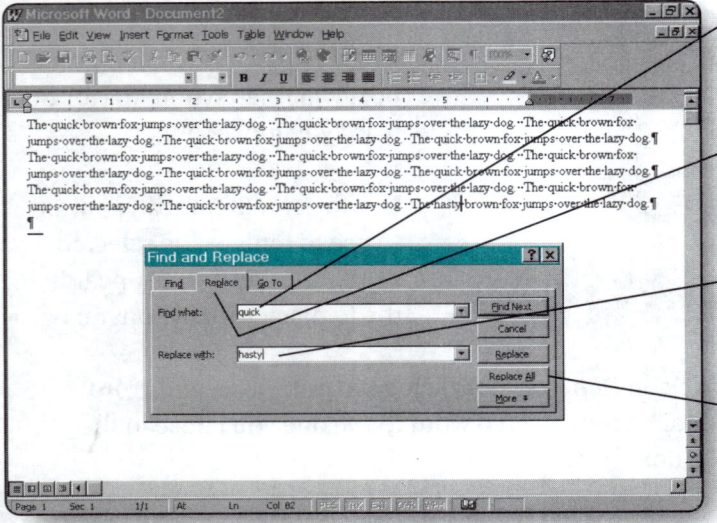

1. Click on the **Select Browse Object button** at the bottom of the vertical scroll bar. A pop-up graphic menu will appear.

2. Click on the **Binoculars button**. The Find and Replace dialog box will open.

3. Type the **word** for which you want to search in the Find what: list box.

4. Click on the **Replace tab**. The dialog box will expand to include a Replace with: list box.

5. Click in the **Replace with: list box** and **type** the **replacement word**.

6. Click on **Replace All**. Word will replace all occurrences of the first word with the second word.

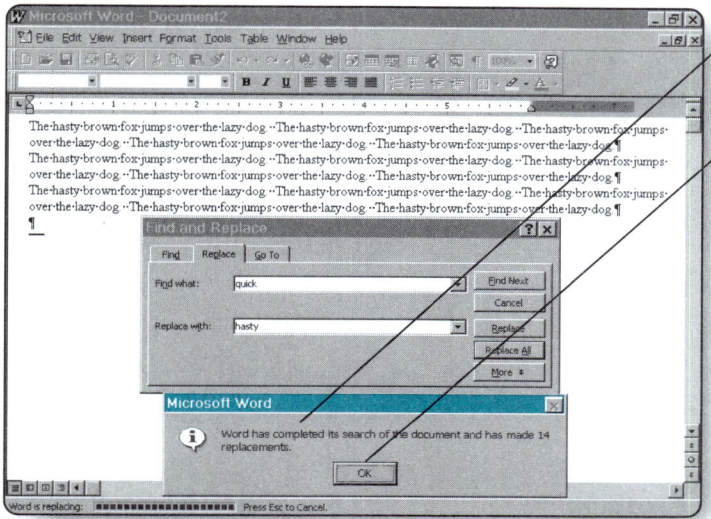

A dialog box will show you how many replacements were made.

7. **Click** on **OK.** The dialog box will close and the Cancel button in the Find and Replace dialog box will change to the Close button.

8. **Click** on **Close.** You will return to the document.

USING AUTOCORRECT

Everyone has this problem—you type certain words wrong all the time. You can tell Word to fix those words for you. Word already knows about some common mistakes, such as replacing "teh" with "the."

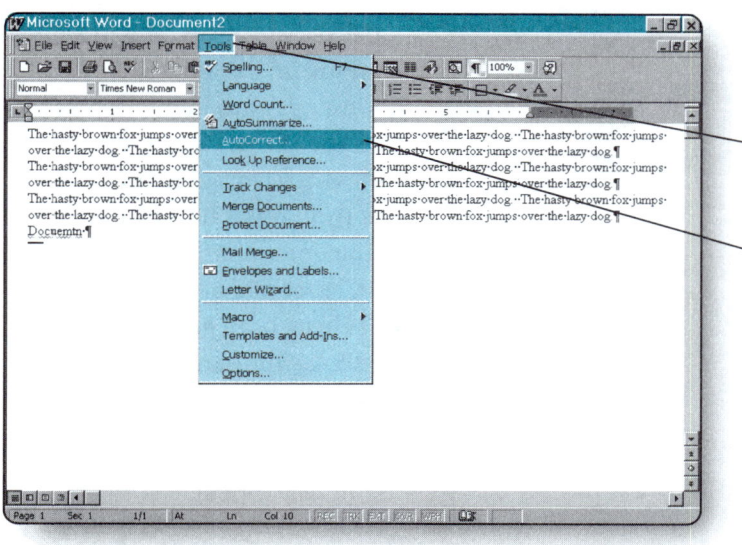

1. **Click** on **Tools.** The Tools menu will appear.

2. **Click** on **AutoCorrect.** The AutoCorrect dialog box will open.

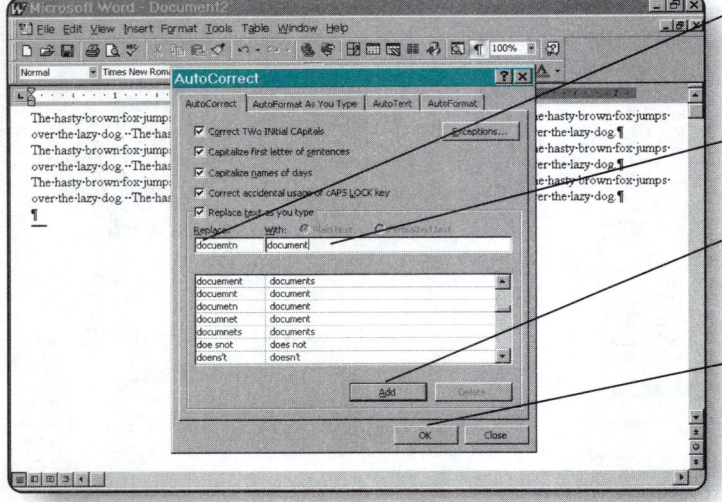

3. **Type** a **word you commonly misspell or mistype** in the Replace: text box.

4. **Type** the **correct spelling of that word** in the With: text box.

5. **Click** on **Add**. Word will add the set to the list at the bottom of the dialog box.

6. **Click** on **OK**. The dialog box will close.

NOTE

To test AutoCorrect, press the Ctrl and End keys at the same time (commonly notated as Ctrl+End) to move the insertion point to a blank line at the end of the document. Then, type the commonly misspelled word and press the spacebar. The word will be capitalized and then its spelling will be corrected.

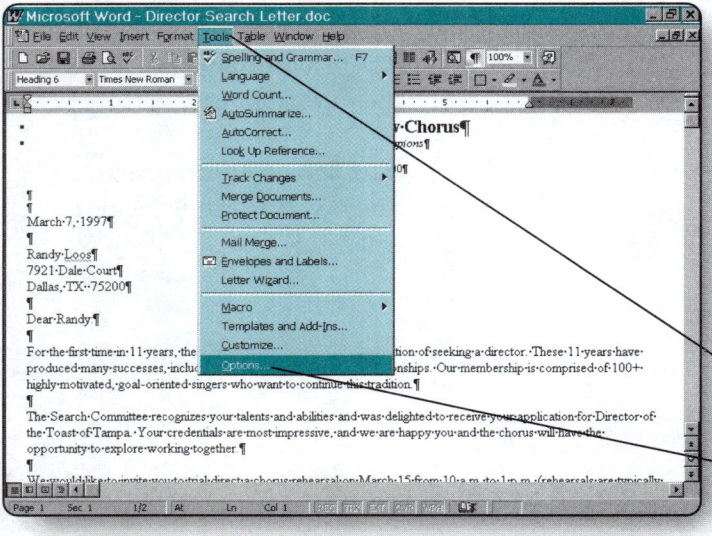

CHECKING SPELLING & GRAMMAR

As you type, you might notice some wavy underlined words—these are words whose spellings Word doesn't recognize. Reopen, if necessary, the letter you were working on in Chapter 5 or another document and press the Ctrl and Home keys at the same time (Ctrl+Home) to move the insertion point to the beginning of the document. In this task, you'll first make sure that Word will check both grammar and spelling simultaneously; then you'll perform the check.

1. **Click** on **Tools**. The Tools menu will appear.

2. **Click** on **Options**. The Options dialog box will open.

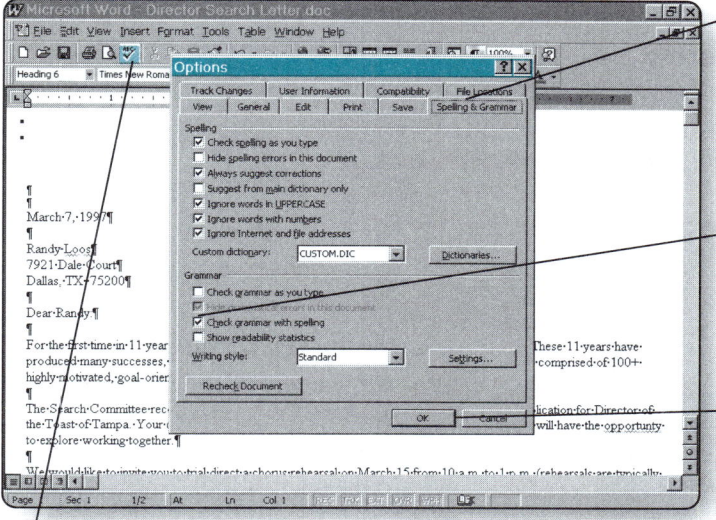

3. **Click** on the **Spelling & Grammar tab**. The operating options for both the Spelling and Grammar checkers will appear.

4. **Click** on the **check box** next to Check grammar with spelling, if you don't see a ✔ already in the box.

5. **Click** on **OK.** The Options dialog box will close and you will return to the document.

TIP

You can also start the Spelling and Grammar checker by clicking on the Spelling and Grammar button on the Standard toolbar. The button appears immediately to the right of the Print Preview button.

NOTE

As with searching, Word will start looking for misspelled words and grammar mistakes at the insertion point and search forward until it reaches the end of your document.

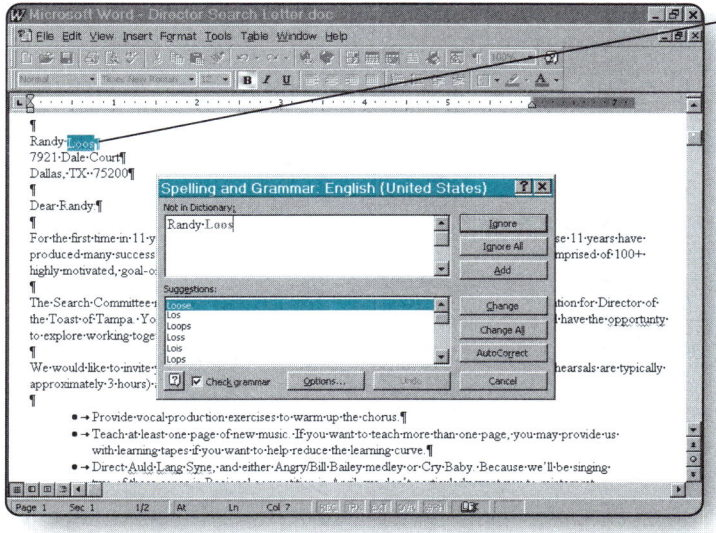

6. **Press** the **F7 key**. Word will highlight the first wavy underlined word and the Spelling dialog box will open.

NOTE

If the Grammar checker is not installed, all the options for Grammar will appear gray.

The highlighted word in the document will appear in red in the dialog box.

Suggestions you can use to replace the highlighted word appear at the bottom of the dialog box.

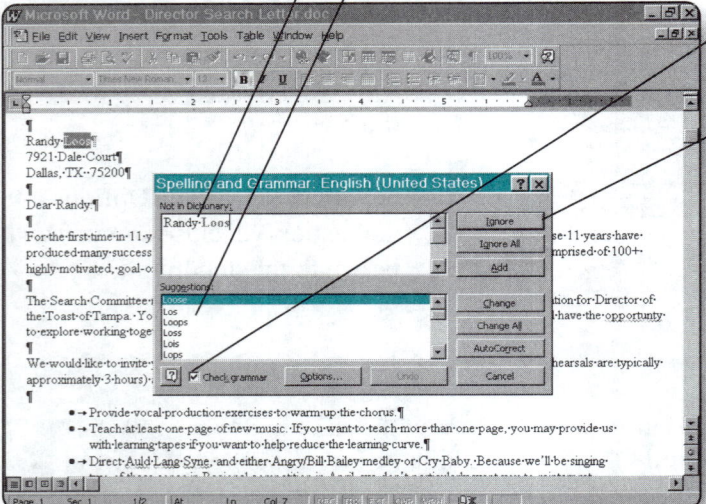

Notice that Word is checking both spelling and grammar.

7. **Click** on **Ignore**, if Word finds a word that is spelled correctly such as a person's name. Word will highlight the next word and make suggestions.

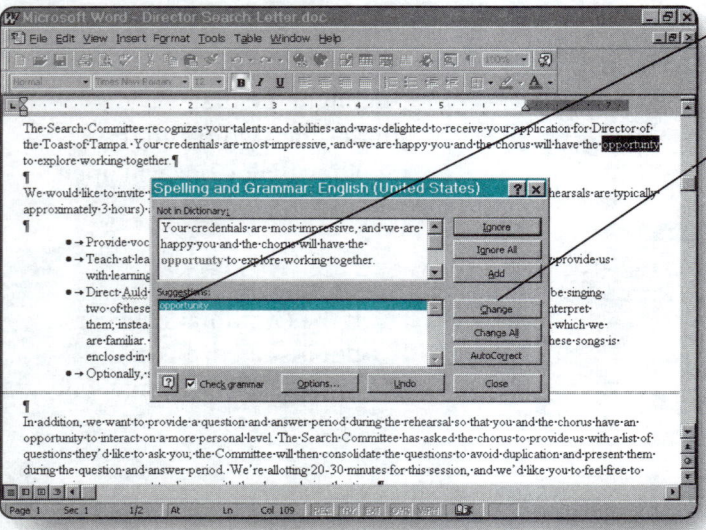

8. **Click** on **a word** in the Suggestions: box.

9. **Click** on **Change**. Word will change the misspelled word to the suggested word and search for the next misspelling.

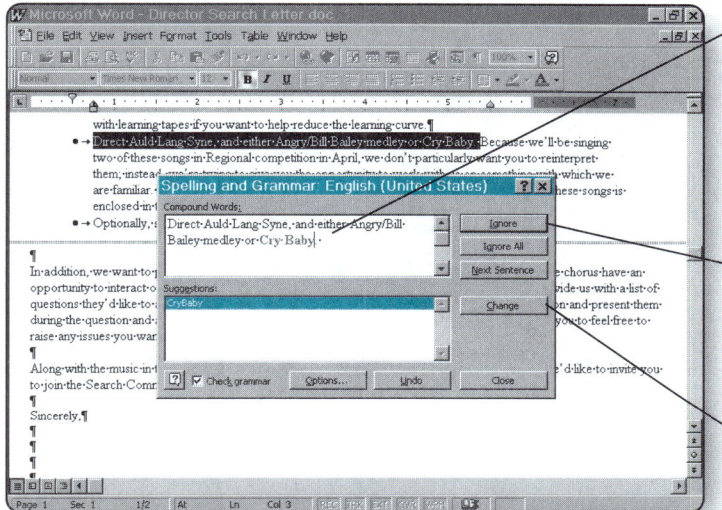

10. **Continue responding** to the misspellings Word finds using step 7 or steps 8 and 9. If Word displays a grammar suggestion, it will appear highlighted in green.

11a. **Click** on **Ignore** to ignore a grammar rule that doesn't apply.

OR

11b. **Click** on **Change.** Word will continue checking your document; respond as necessary using either step 7 or steps 8 and 9. Eventually, you will see a dialog box telling you that the spelling and grammar check is complete.

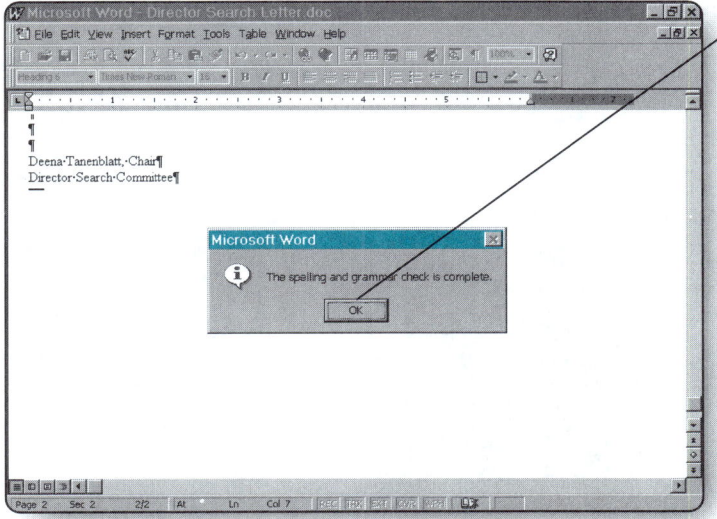

12. **Click** on **OK.** The dialog box will close.

7 Formatting Word Documents

Much of the time you spend in a word processor is spent making documents look the way you want them to look. In this chapter, you'll learn how to:

+ Add a header

+ Use styles

+ Highlight text

+ Use revision marking

+ Add and view comments

+ Accept and reject revisions

ADDING A HEADER

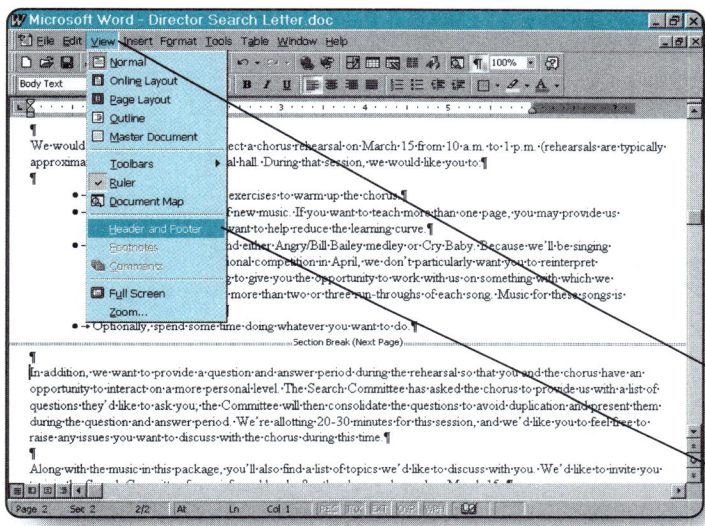

You can add headers (or footers) to any section of a document; different sections can have different headers and footers. For example, in a letter, you typically want to add a header to page 2 that doesn't print on page 1.

1. **Click anywhere** on Page 2 of a document.

2. **Click** on **View**. The View menu will appear.

3. **Click** on **Header and Footer**. Word will switch to Page Layout view and the Header and Footer toolbar will appear. In addition, your text will appear gray.

NOTE

You add footers to a document the same way you add headers. To add a Footer, click on the Switch Between Header and Footer button.

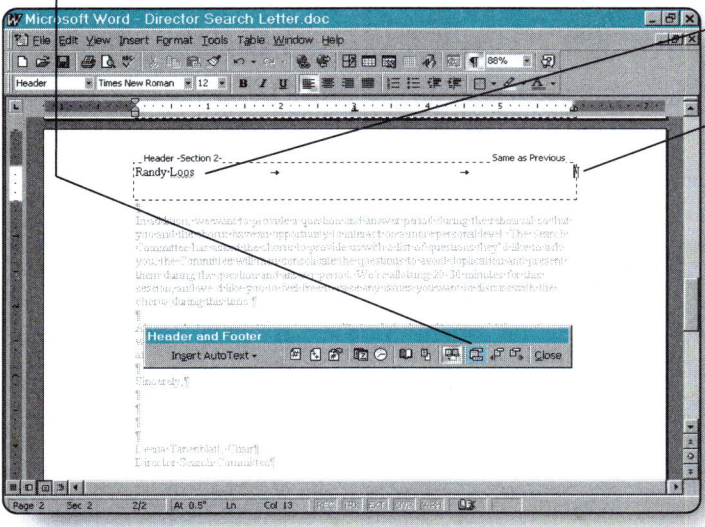

4. **Type** the **name** of the letter's recipient in the Header box.

5. **Press** the **Tab key twice**.

TIP

Headers and footers contain two preset tabs; the first is a center-aligned tab, and the second is a right-aligned tab.

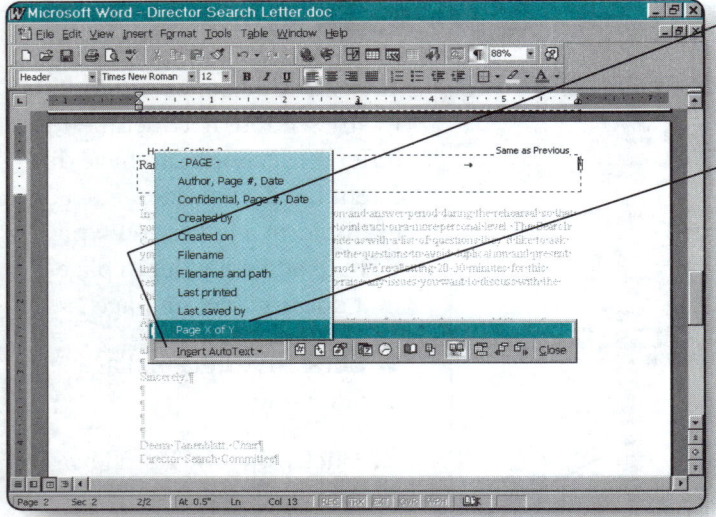

6. **Click** on the **Insert AutoText button**. A pop-up menu will appear.

7. **Click** on **Page X of Y**. The words "Page 1 of 2" will appear.

NOTE

The numbers you see are actually fields, like the date you inserted previously. These numbers update if the page moves. If you happen to see Page 2 of 1, press the Left Arrow key once and then press the F9 key. Word will update the page number so it appears correctly.

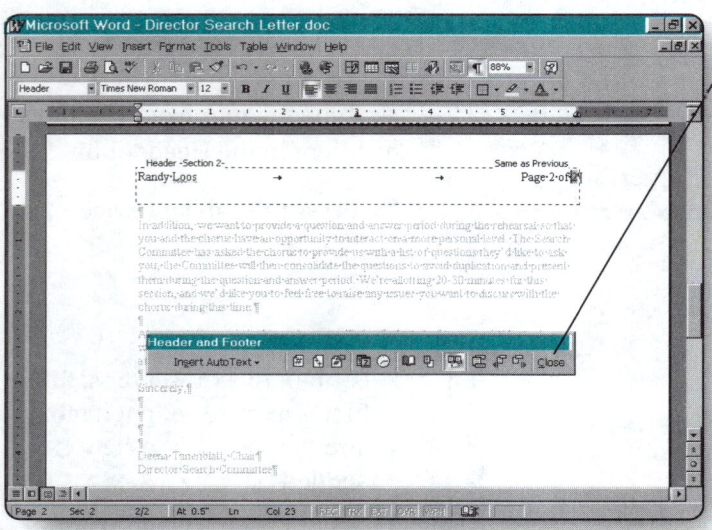

8. **Click** on **Close.** The Header and Footer toolbar will close and you will return to Normal view—where headers and footers are not visible.

TIP

Headers and footers are visible in Page Layout view and in Print Preview.

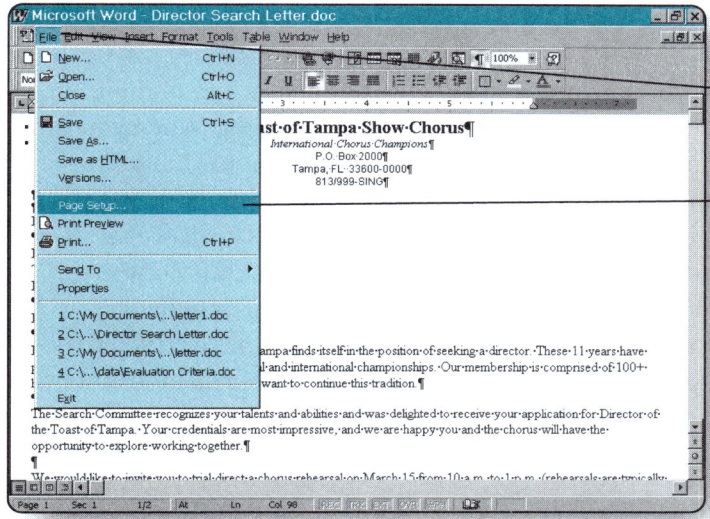

9. **Click anywhere** on Page 1.

10. **Click** on **File**. The File menu will appear.

11. **Click** on **Page Setup**. The Page Setup dialog box will open.

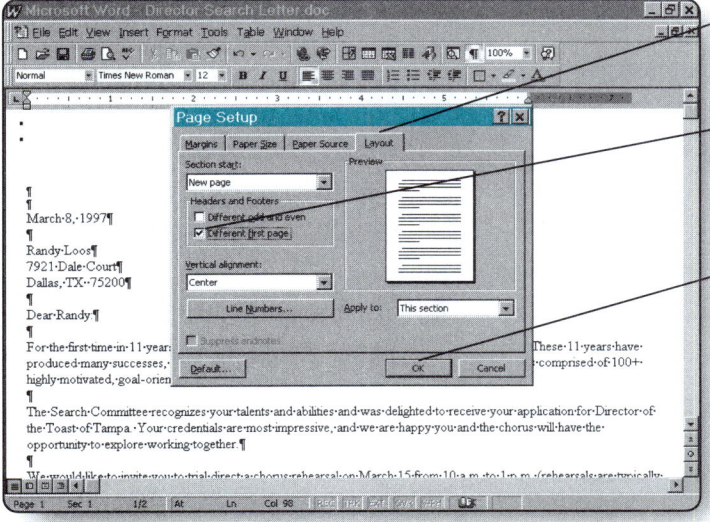

12. **Click** on the **Layout tab**. The tab will come to the front.

13. **Click** on the **check box** next to Different first page. A ✔ will appear in the box.

14. **Click** on **OK**. The dialog box will close.

NOTE

The preceding six steps ensure that the header you created appears only on pages after page 1.

USING STYLES

Styles contain appearance settings, such as indentation, bullets, boldface type, and paragraph spacing. When you store this information in a style, you can easily apply the settings to any paragraph by applying the style. Word contains two types of styles: paragraph and character. *Character styles* can contain only character formatting. Setting fonts, font sizes, and boldface type can be accomplished with character formatting. *Paragraph styles* can contain both character and paragraph formatting. *Paragraph formatting* includes such formatting as line spacing and indentation.

Displaying the Style Area

While working in Normal view, you can display the style area so you can see what styles are applied to the various paragraphs of your document.

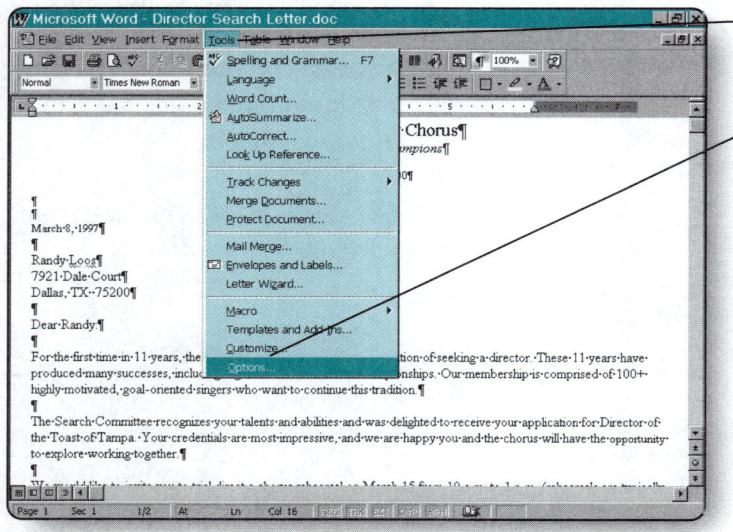

1. **Click** on **Tools**. The Tools menu will appear.

2. **Click** on **Options**. The Options dialog box will open.

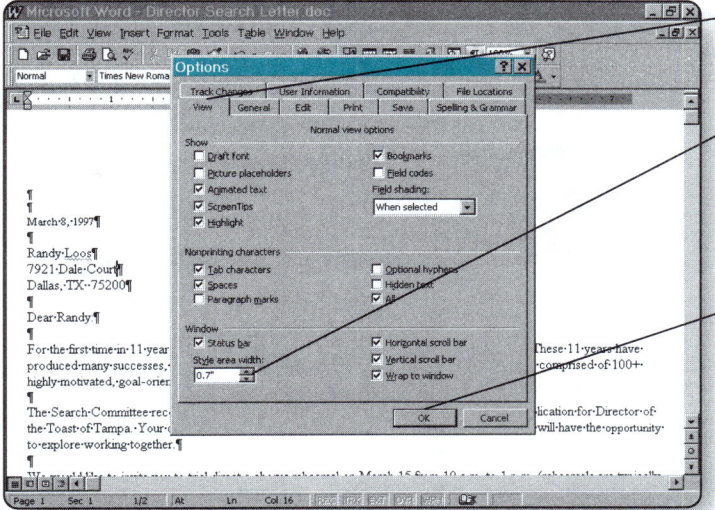

3. **Click** on the **View tab**. The tab will come to the front.

4. **Click** on the **spinner box arrows** (◆) of the Style area width: text box to apply a different width.

5. **Click** on **OK**. Word will redisplay your document.

TIP

Set the Style area width to at least .7 for the best results.

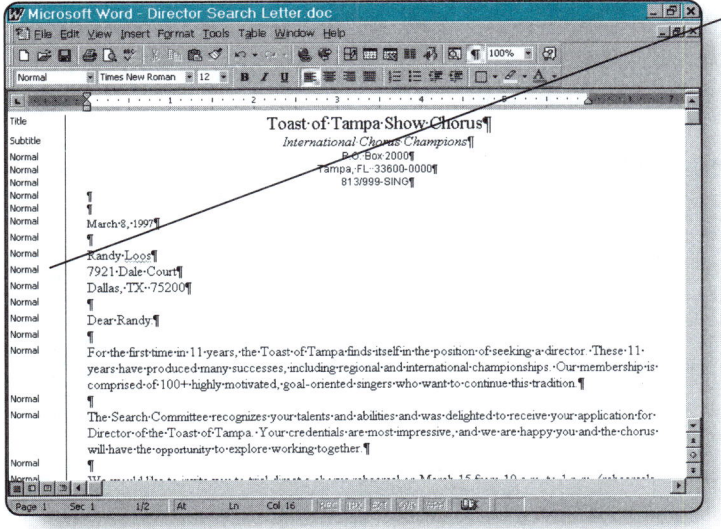

The style area appears at the left edge of the document.

Applying an Existing Style

Word comes with predefined styles you can use.

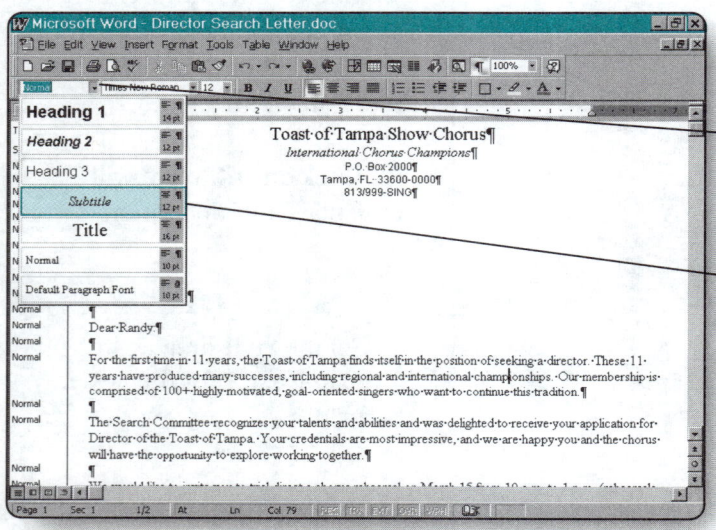

1. **Click** on **a paragraph** to apply a style.

2. **Click** on the **arrow** (▼) next to the Style list box. A list of available styles will appear.

3. **Click** on a **style**. A border will appear around the selected style.

Word will apply the settings of the style you selected to the paragraph containing the insertion point.

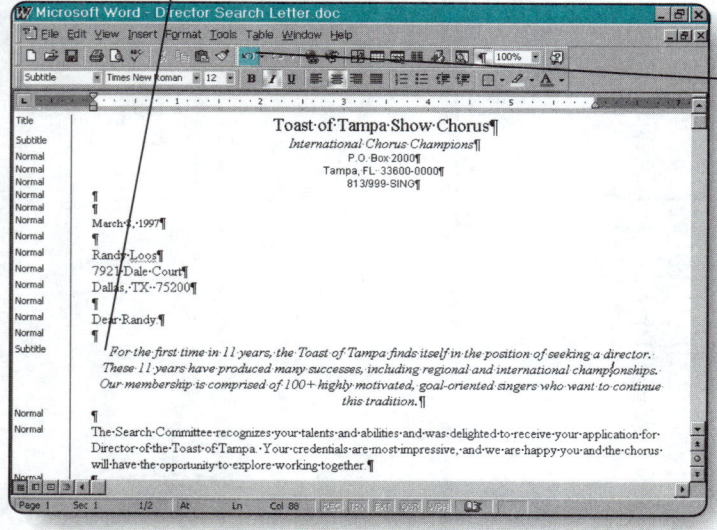

TIP

If you change your mind, click on the Undo button to remove the style settings or apply a different style using the steps in this task.

Creating Your Own Style

The easiest way to create your own style is to format text the way you want it to appear in the style and then create a style "by example." In this task, we'll create a Bulleted List style using the bulleted list we made in Chapter 5.

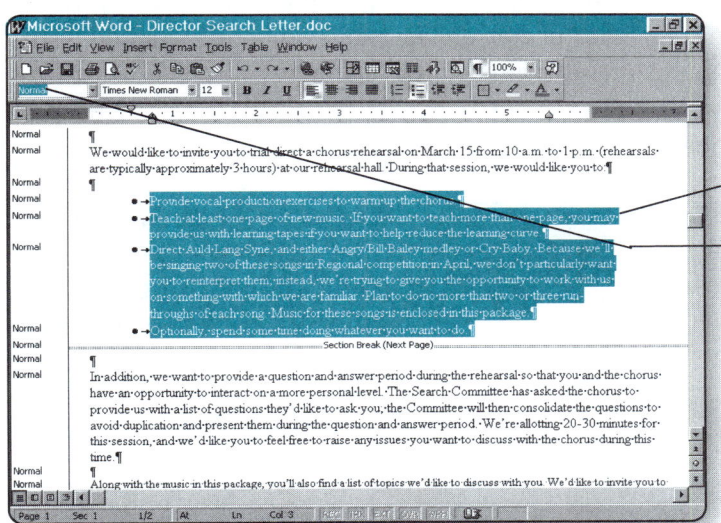

1. Select a **bulleted list**.

2. **Click** in the **Style list box**. Word will select the name of the current style.

3. **Type** a **name** for the style you want to define.

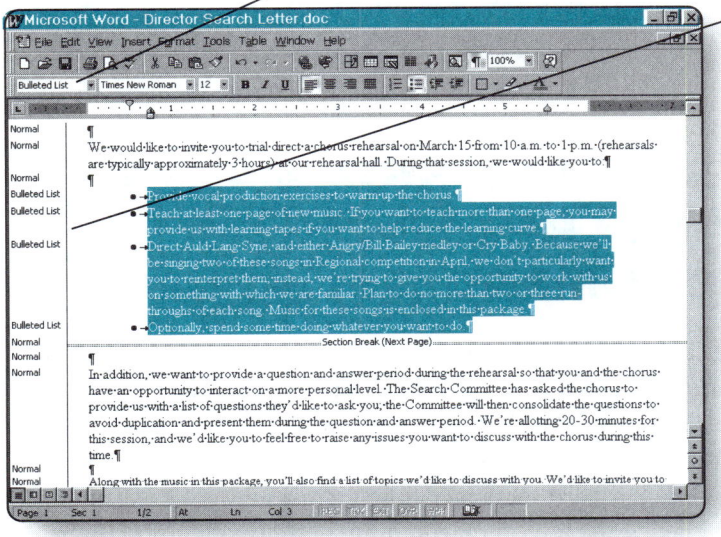

4. **Press** the **Enter key**. The style for the selected paragraphs will change to the new style you just defined.

TIP

You can now apply this style to any paragraph in the document. Simply place the insertion point in any paragraph, click on the arrow (▼) next to the Style list box, and click on the name of the new style.

HIGHLIGHTING TEXT

Highlighting text is a great way to call attention to it. Think of highlighting as using a highlighter pen to mark text on a printout. Be aware, however, that highlighted text in Word will print as a shade of gray on black and white printers; you need a color printer to print colored highlighting.

1. **Select** some **text** to highlight.

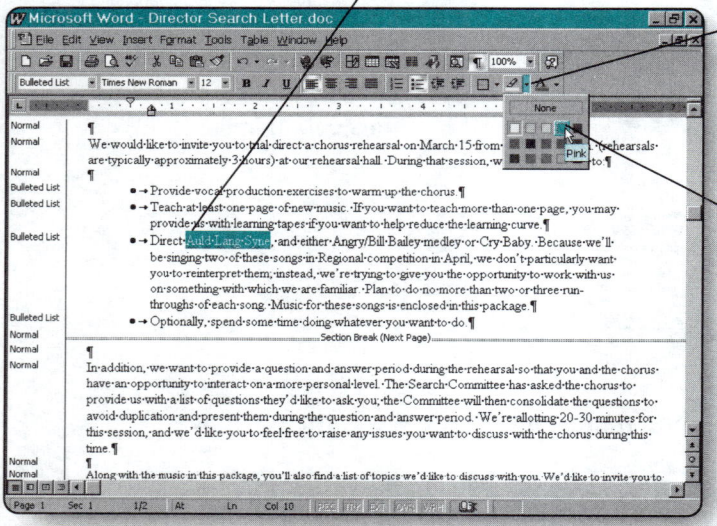

2. **Click** on the **arrow** (▼) next to the Highlight button. A color palette will appear, from which you can choose a highlight color.

3. **Click** on a **color**. Word will highlight the selected text in the color you chose.

TIP

To remove highlighting, click on the Undo button to undo your action or reopen the Highlight color palette and click on None.

USING REVISION MARKS WHILE REVIEWING A DOCUMENT

You can pass a document around from one reviewer to another and let each reviewer suggest changes. When you turn on revision marks, Word doesn't actually delete text; instead, it marks the text with strikethrough to indicate a suggested deletion. Similarly, new text appears in a new color. All changes you make appear with marks in the margin to identify them.

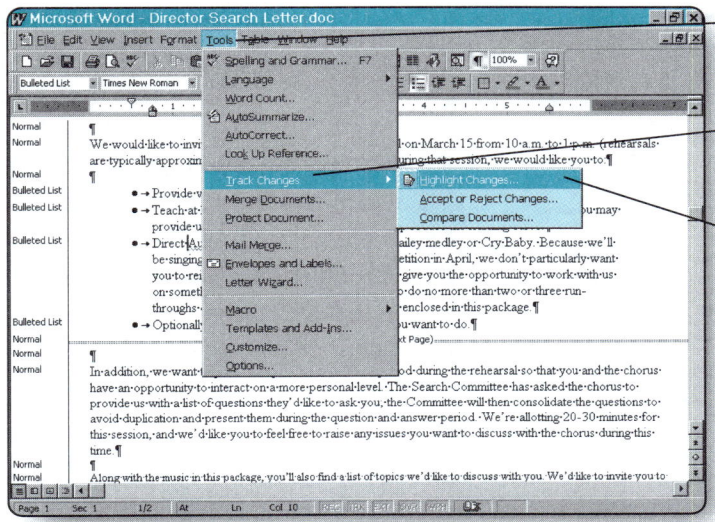

1. **Click** on **Tools**. The Tools menu will appear.

2. **Point** to **Track Changes**. A cascading menu will appear.

3. **Click** on **Highlight Changes**. The Highlight Changes dialog box will open.

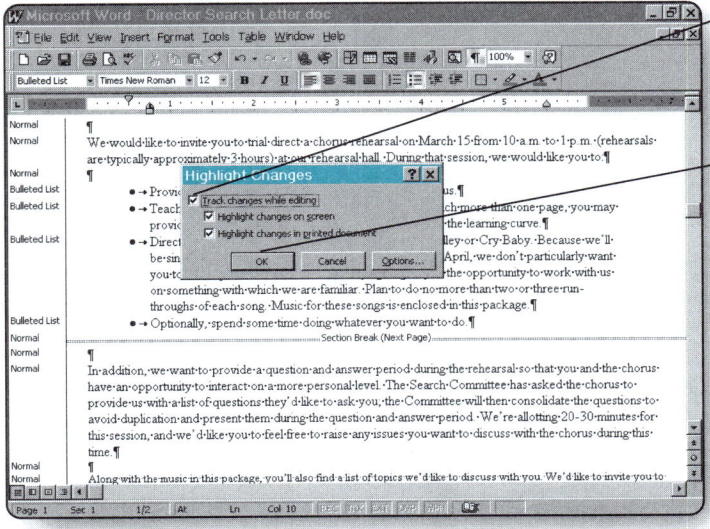

4. **Click** on **Track changes while editing check box**. A ✔ will appear in the check box.

5. **Click** on **OK**. Word will redisplay your document.

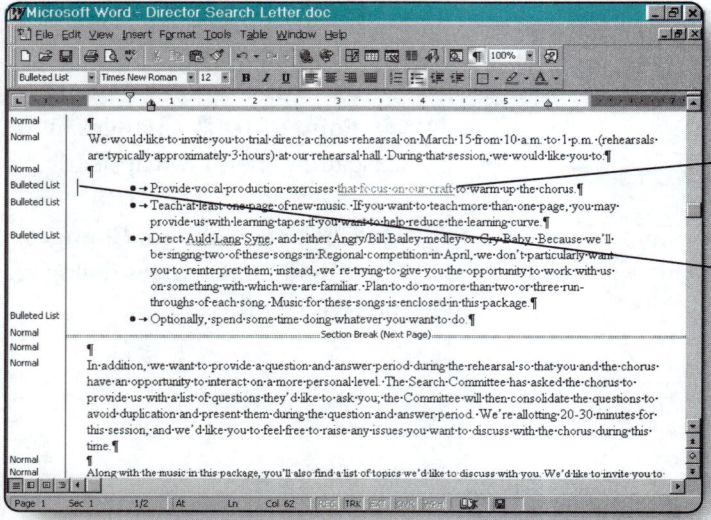

6. **Position** the **insertion point** where you want to make a change.

7. **Type** some **text**. The new text will appear in a different color.

Word also places a vertical bar in the left margin to indicate a change has been made to the line.

TIP

Move the mouse pointer over the new text and Word will display a tip showing who added the text and when.

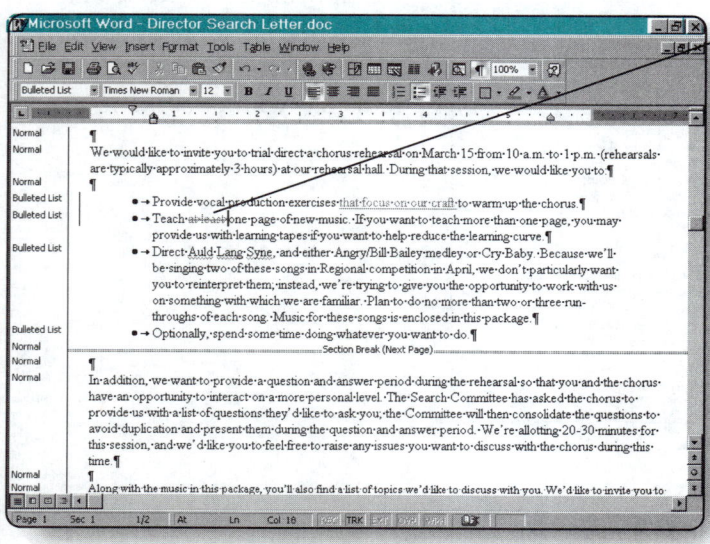

8. **Delete** some **text**. Word will strike through the text you delete, but the text will not be removed from the document. Again, Word will place a vertical bar in the left margin to indicate a change has been made to the line.

USING COMMENTS

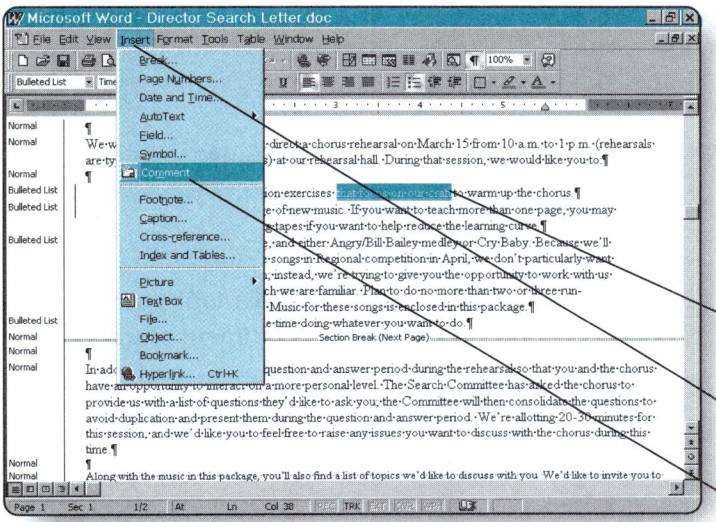

You can use Word's Comment feature to add ideas and insights while reviewing a document.

Adding Comments to a Document

1. **Select** the **text** about which you want to comment.

2. **Click** on **Insert**. The Insert menu will appear.

3. **Click** on **Comment**. Word will apply yellow highlighting to the selected text and open the Comment pane.

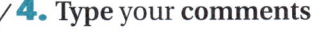

4. **Type** your **comments**.

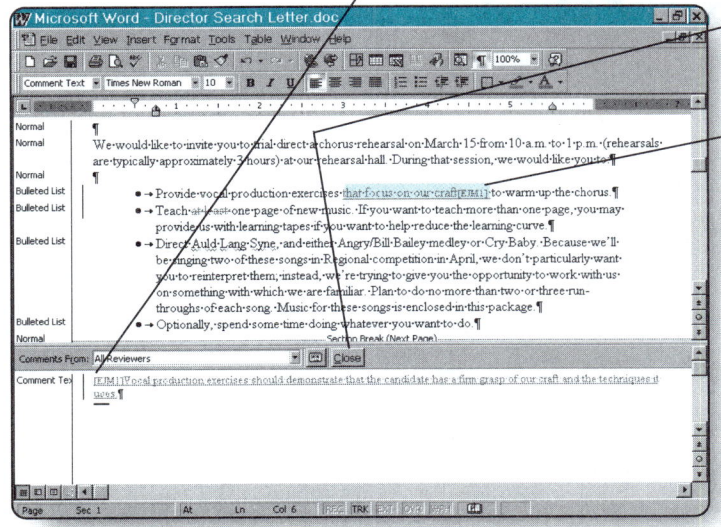

5. **Click** on **Close**. The Comment pane will disappear.

Your initials, followed by the number 1, will appear highlighted in the document, indicating a comment exists.

Viewing and Deleting Comments

If you receive a document containing comments, you'll see notations containing the reviewer's initials in the document that represent the comment.

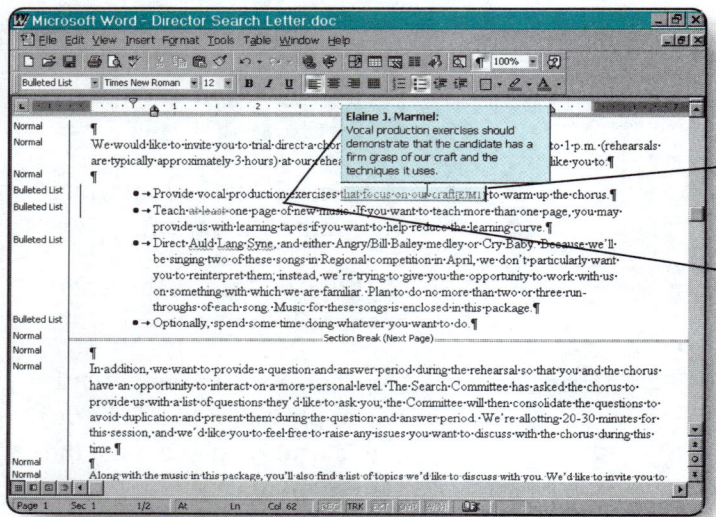

1. **Scroll** through your **document** until you see a comment.

2. **Move** the **mouse pointer** over the comment marker.

A ScreenTip will appear showing the comment.

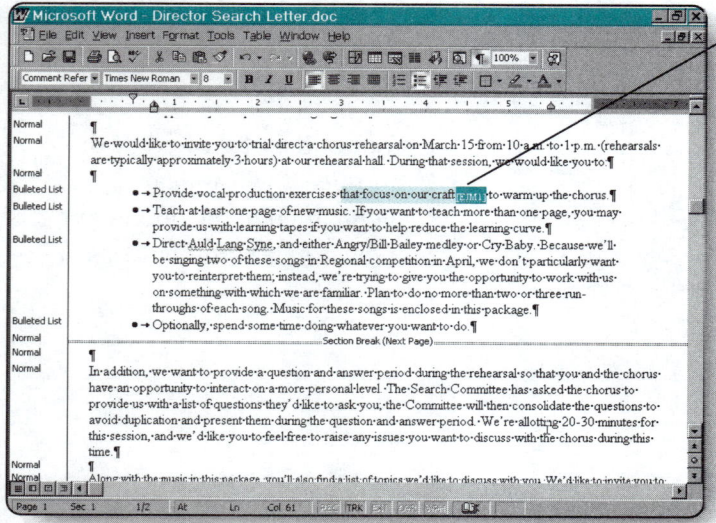

3. **Select** a **comment marker** in the document.

4. **Press** the **Delete key**. The comment and its highlighting will disappear and the text that was highlighted when the comment was inserted will remain.

ACCEPTING OR REJECTING REVISIONS

When you receive a document containing revisions marks, you can choose to accept or reject the revisions.

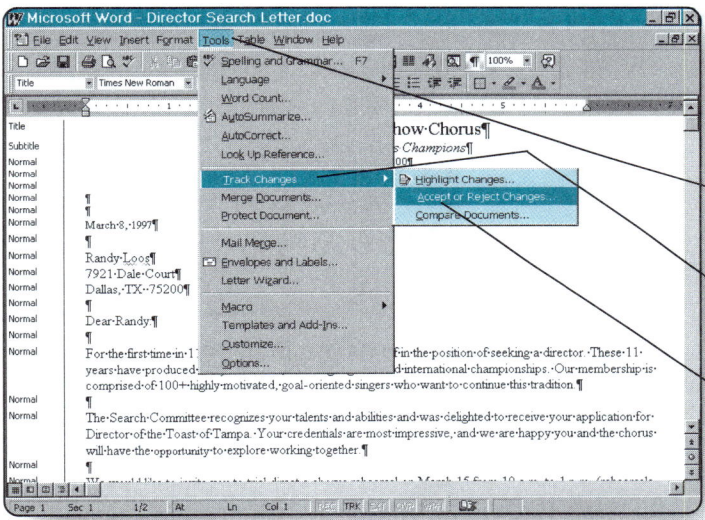

1. **Press** the **Ctrl and Home keys** at the same time**.** The insertion point will move to the beginning of the document.

2. **Click** on **Tools**. The Tools menu will appear.

3. **Point** at **Track Changes**. A cascading menu will appear.

4. **Click** on **Accept or Reject Changes**. The Accept or Reject Changes dialog box will open.

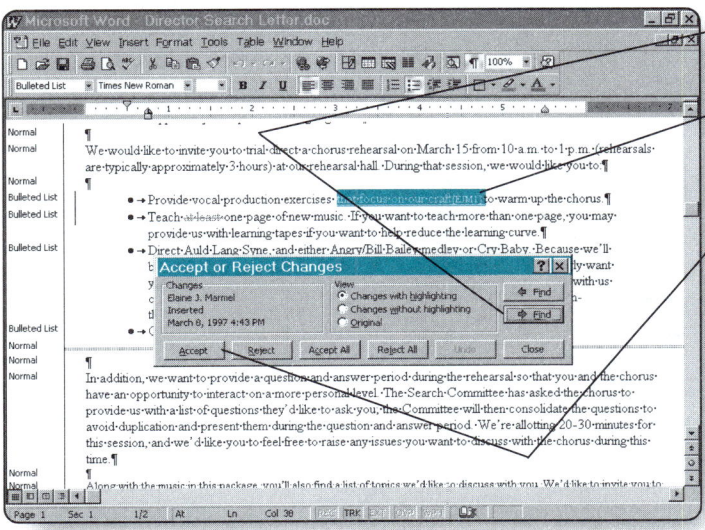

5. **Click** on the **Find button**.

Word will highlight the first change it finds in the document.

6. **Click** on the **Accept button**. Word will accept the change, remove the revision marks from the document, and automatically find the next change.

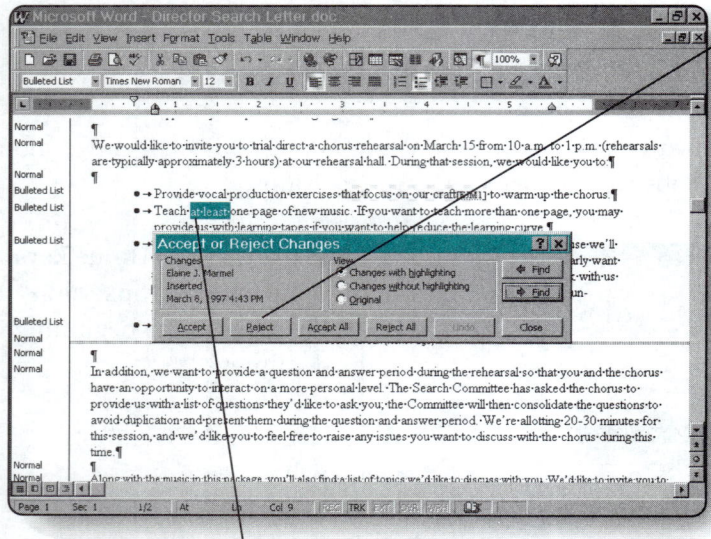

7. **Click** on the **Reject button**. Word will ignore the change.

Word will also return the text to its original appearance and remove the revision marks.

When Word finds no more revisions, a dialog box will open.

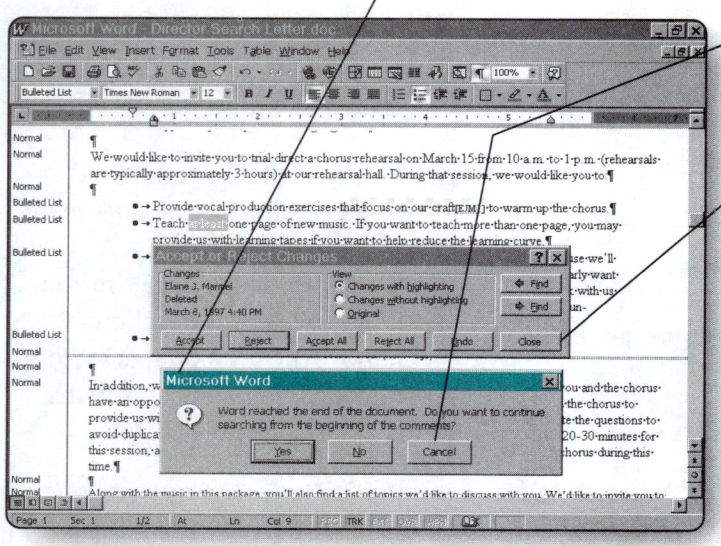

8. **Click** on **Cancel**. The Accept or Reject Changes dialog box will reappear.

9. **Click** on **Close**. Word will redisplay the document.

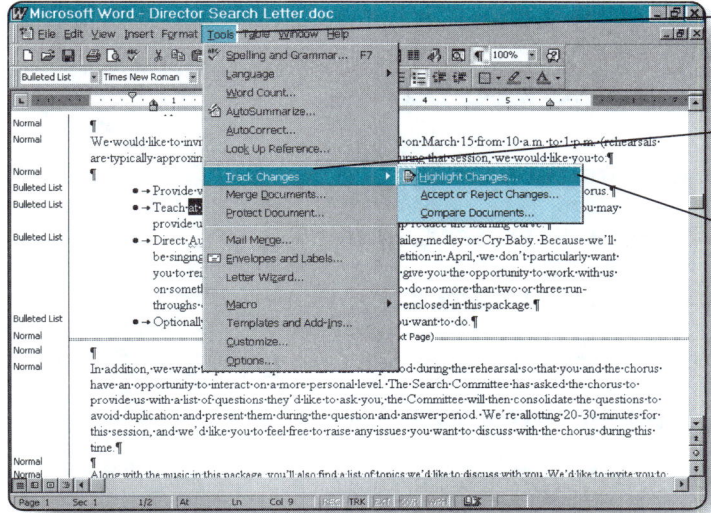

10. **Click** on **Tools**. The Tools menu will appear.

11. **Point** at **Track Changes**. A cascading menu will appear.

12. **Click** on **Highlight Changes**. The Highlight Changes dialog box will appear.

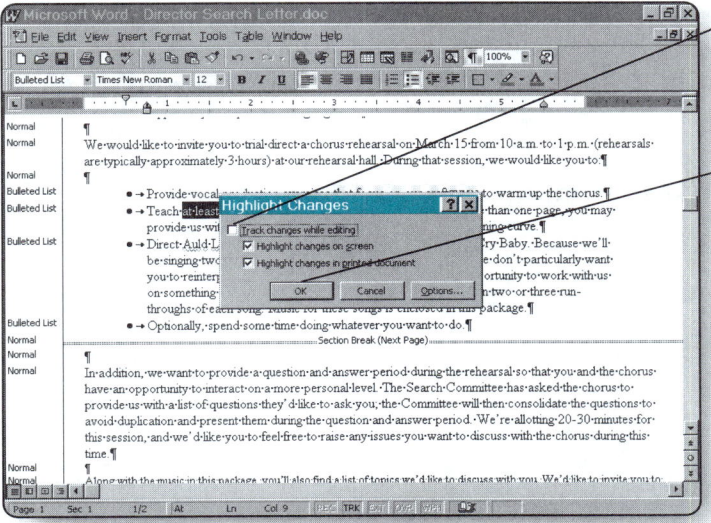

13. **Click** on the **Track changes while editing check box**. The ✔ will be removed.

14. **Click** on **OK**. Word will redisplay your document and apply revision marks to the changes you made.

PART II REVIEW QUESTIONS

1. How do you select text with the mouse? *See Chapter 5*

2. Describe the process of moving text. *See Chapter 5*

3. How do you make text bold? *See Chapter 5*

4. How do you change the font and font size? *See Chapter 5*

5. How do you create a numbered list? *See Chapter 5*

6. How do you indent text? *See Chapter 5*

7. How do you center text between the left and right margins? The top and bottom margins? *See Chapter 5*

8. How do you insert a page break? *See Chapter 5*

9. Describe the tools available in Word to help you improve your writing. *See Chapter 6*

10. How do you apply a style to a paragraph? *See Chapter 7*

P A R T   I I I

Excel

man

jumps

ice Do

Excel

Excel 8
s Data
ad.xls
ead-1.xls
leadblnk.xls
LEADS.xls
leadtst.xls
Mcn95v94.xls
News Flash.xls
Sales Report.xls

8 Learning Excel Basics

Just like when you first started Word, you need to learn how to enter and manipulate information when you first start Excel. If you don't have Excel open on your screen, follow the steps in Chapter 1 to open Excel. In this chapter, you'll learn how to:

✦ **Understand the Excel window**

✦ **Enter text and numbers**

✦ **Correct cell entries**

✦ **Move around the worksheet**

✦ **Select cells**

✦ **Automatically fill cells with information**

✦ **Copy and move information**

UNDERSTANDING THE EXCEL WINDOW

As you learned in Chapter 1, many elements in Office 97 programs are common. You'll find the title bar, menu bar, toolbars, and window size control buttons on the Excel window, but it also contains some different elements.

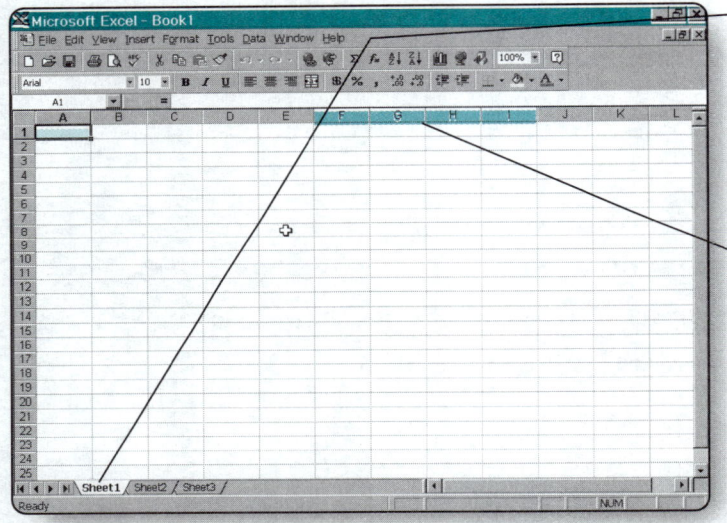

An Excel document is called a *workbook* and each workbook is made up of *worksheets*. By default, a new workbook contains three worksheets, but you can add or delete sheets.

The Excel window contains rows that are numbered and columns headed by letters. You'll find 255 columns and 65,536 rows. Column letters run from A to Z and then begin with AA, AB, AC, and continue to IV.

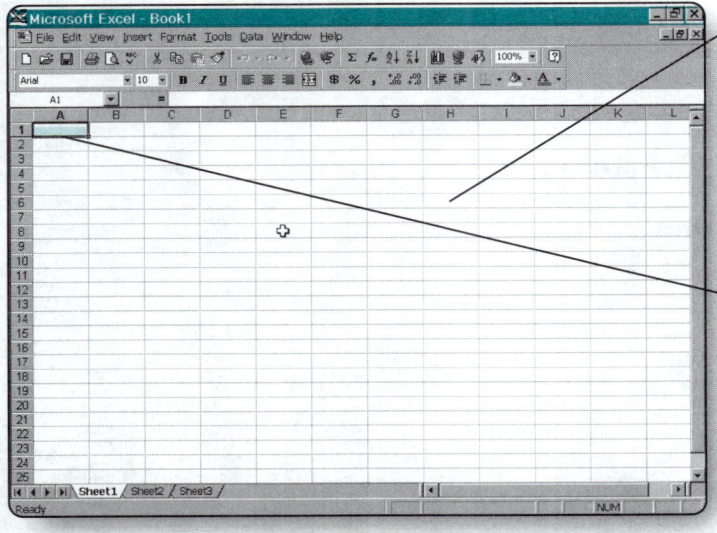

The intersection of a column and row is called a *cell*. You refer to a cell by its column letter and row number. When you type a cell's column letter and row number, the result is a *cell address*.

The *selected cell* is the one that appears surrounded by the *cell pointer*, a dark border. The selected cell will be affected if you enter information or perform a command.

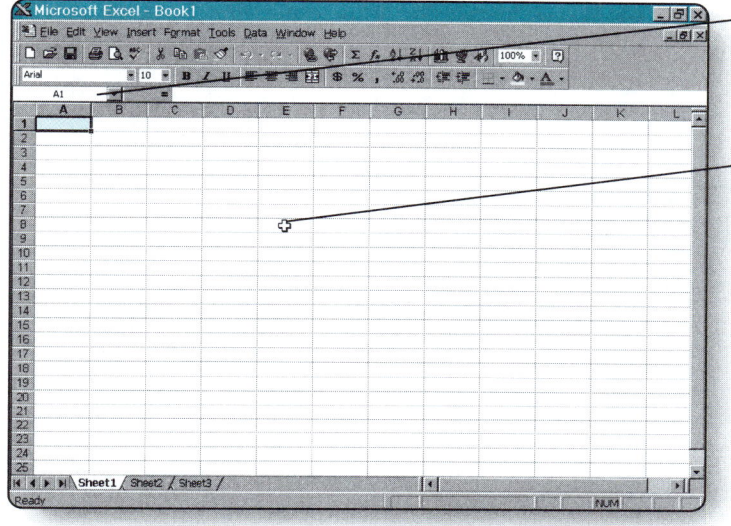

You can identify the current location of the cell pointer by looking at the Name list box.

The typical mouse pointer in Excel has the shape of a plus sign, reminiscent of the Red Cross symbol. The mouse pointer shape will change as you perform actions, but this pointer is the one you'll see most often.

TIP

As you type, you'll see an insertion point in the cell. If you make a mistake while typing, press the Backspace key to delete the character immediately to the left of the insertion point.

ENTERING TEXT AND NUMBERS

Most of the entries you'll make in Excel will be number entries. These kinds of entries are called *values*. Values include all kinds of numeric information: calculations, dollars, dates, and times.

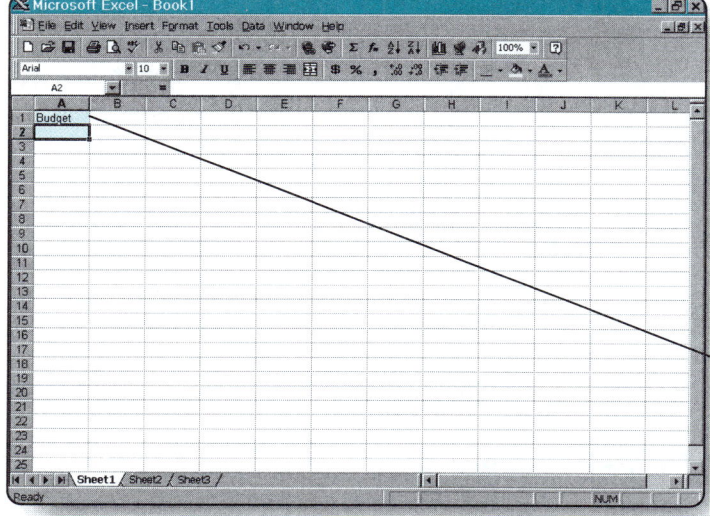

The other type of entry you'll make in Excel will be a text entry; these are called *labels*. Although you can enter information in any order, you might find it most useful to enter labels before you enter values, so you can be sure you enter values in the correct cells.

1. **Type Budget** and **press** the **Enter key.** Excel will store the information in A1 and move the cell pointer down one cell to A2.

2. **Press** the **Down Arrow key twice**. The cell pointer will move to A4.

3. **Type Rent** and press the **Enter key**. The cell pointer will move to A5.

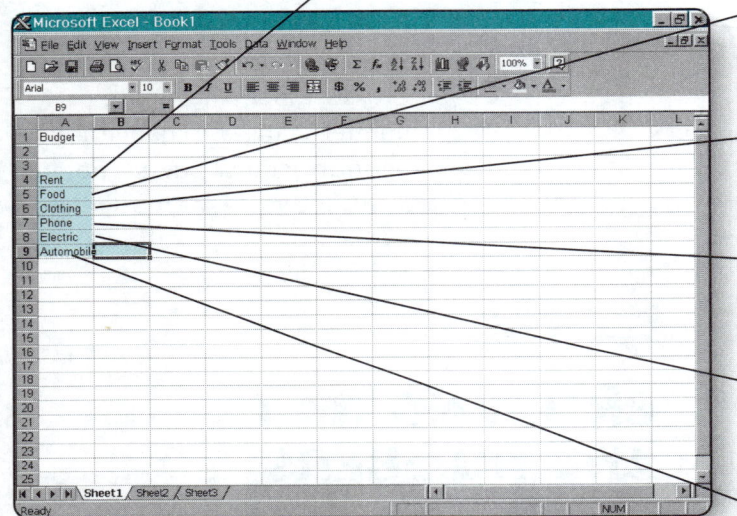

4. **Type Food** and **press** the **Enter key**. The cell pointer will move to A6.

5. **Type Clothing** and **press** the **Enter key**. The cell pointer will move to A7.

6. **Type Phone** and **press** the **Enter key**. The cell pointer will move to A8.

7. **Type Electric** and **press** the **Enter key**. The cell pointer will move to A9.

8. **Type Automobile** and **press** the **Right Arrow key**.

9. **Press** the **Up Arrow key five times**. The cell pointer will move to B4.

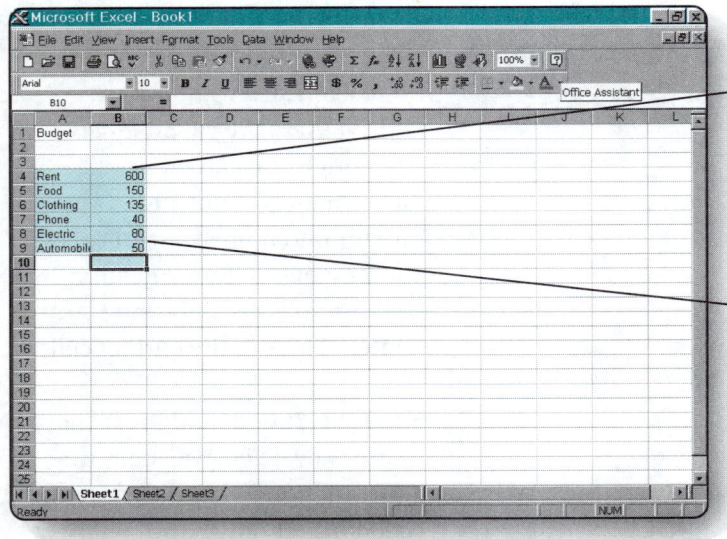

10. **Type** the **following numbers** in column B and **press** the **Enter key** after each number: **600, 150, 135, 40, 80, and 50.**

By default, labels align at the left edge of a cell and values align at the right edge of a cell.

CORRECTING A CELL ENTRY

You can correct cell entries by simply typing over them, by undoing previous actions, or by editing cells.

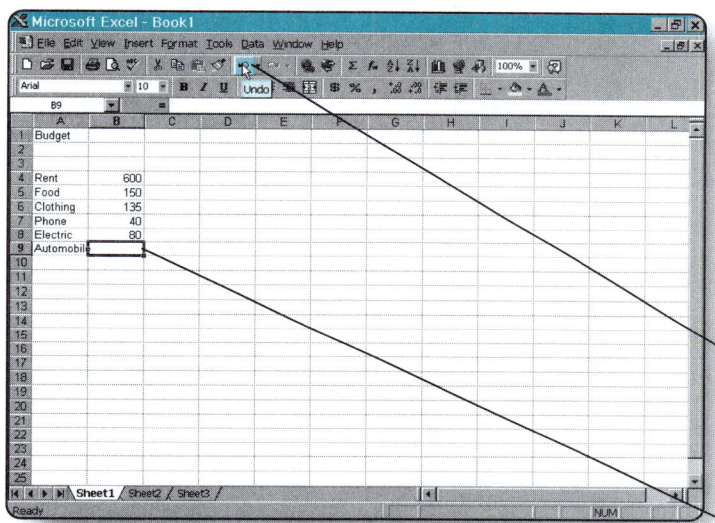

Using Undo

As in Word, you can undo your last 16 actions in Excel. Suppose that you want to increase the automobile budget number from 50 to 60. Since the last action you took was entering 50, you can undo it.

1. **Click** on the **Undo button**. Excel will remove the number 50 from B9 and place the cell pointer in B9.

2. **Type 60** and **press** the **Enter key.** The new number will be entered.

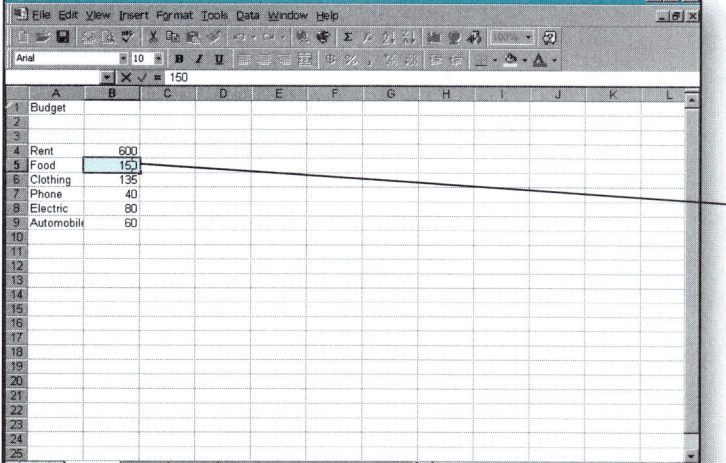

Editing a Cell

You might find that you need to edit a cell long after you entered information into it.

1. **Click** on **B5.** The cell will be selected.

2. **Press** the **F2 key.** An insertion point will appear to the right of the information in B5.

3. **Press** the **Left Arrow key.** The insertion point will move to the right of the 5 in 150.

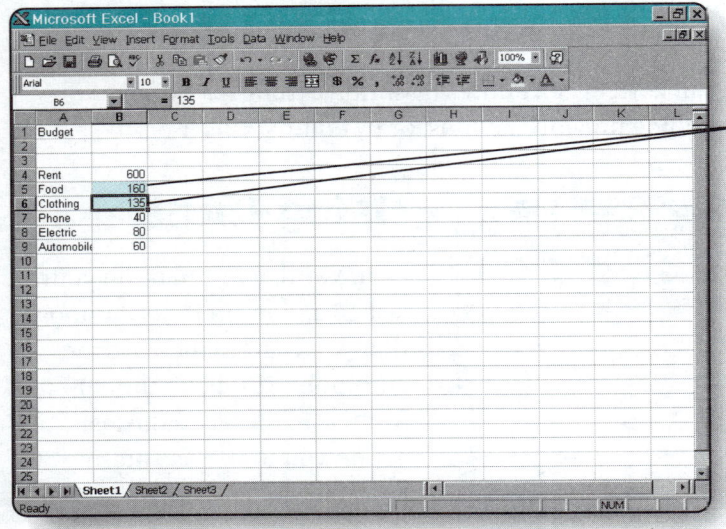

4. **Press** the **Backspace key**. The 5 will be deleted.

5. **Type 6** and **press** the **Enter key**. Excel will store 160 in cell B5 and move the cell pointer to B6.

MOVING AROUND A WORKSHEET

As you have already seen, you can move the cell pointer around the worksheet using the arrow keys.

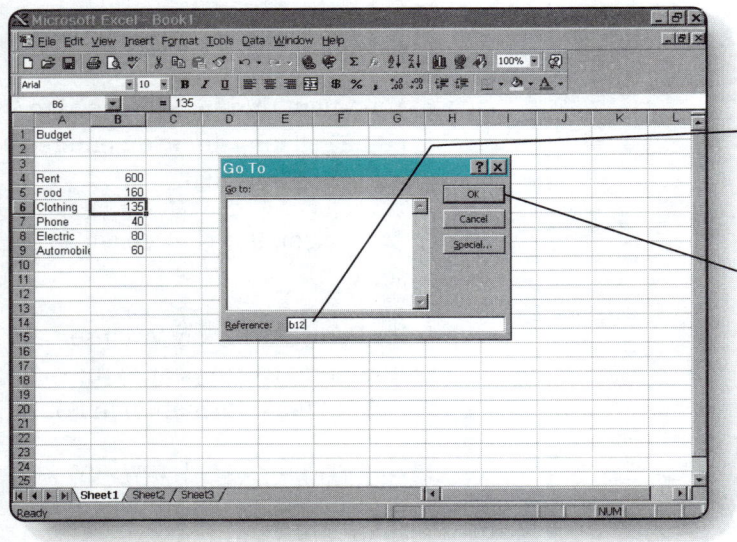

1. **Press** the **F5 key**. The Go To dialog box will open.

2. **Type** the **cell address** to which you want to move the cell pointer.

3. **Click** on **OK**. The cell pointer will move to the address you typed.

Use the following table to help you navigate around a worksheet.

Press these keys	To move the cell pointer
Left Arrow, Right Arrow	One cell in the direction of the arrow key
Up Arrow, Down Arrow	One row in the direction of the arrow key
Ctrl+an arrow key	To the last cell containing information in the direction of the arrow
Home	To Column A in the current row
Ctrl+Home	To A1
Ctrl+End	To the last cell in the worksheet that contains information

SELECTING CELLS

Most of the commands and options in Excel operate on the selected cell. You can select a single cell, as you have already seen, or you can select a group of cells—a group of cells is called a *range*. The cell address for a range of cells is the cell address of the upper-left corner of the range and the lower-right corner of the range, separated by a colon. For example, the worksheet in the figure currently contains numbers in cells B4:B9—that is, cells B4, B5, B6, B7, B8, and B9.

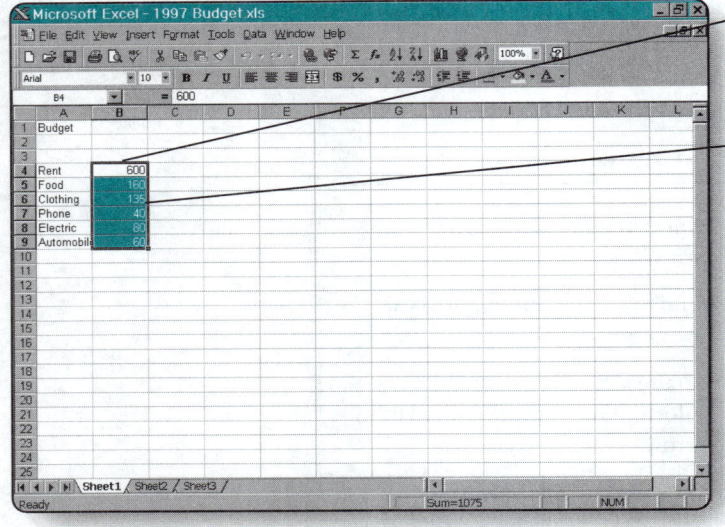

1. **Click** on the **cell** that will be the upper-left corner of the selected range.

2. **Press** and **hold** the **mouse button** and **drag** the **mouse pointer** down until you have selected all the cells you want in the range.

3. **Release** the **mouse button**. The range will be selected.

4. **Click anywhere** in the worksheet to cancel your selection.

TIP

You can also hold down the Shift key and press the Down Arrow key as many times as necessary to select the cells in a range.

AUTOMATICALLY FILLING CELLS WITH INFORMATION

Excel makes some time-consuming tasks very easy. For example, you often use months as column labels. Instead of typing each month, let Excel do it for you. To fill cells automatically, you enter the first value of the series into a cell. Excel learns by example.

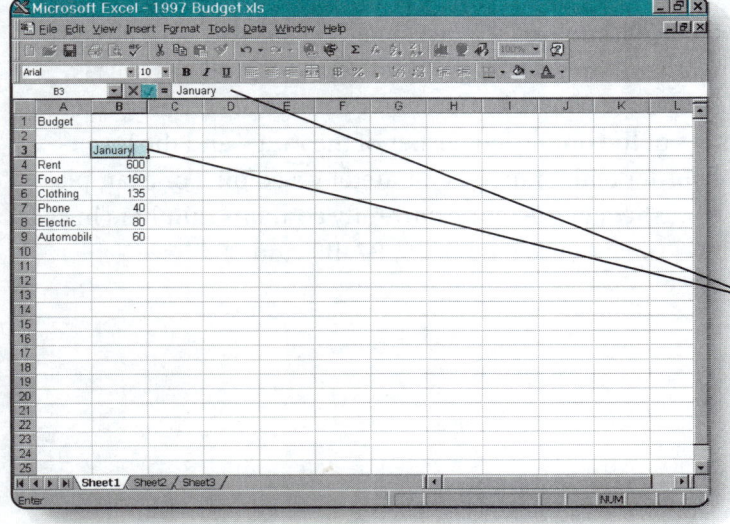

1. **Click** on the **first cell** of the range you want to fill.

2. **Type January**. As you type, notice that information will appear both in the cell and in the Formula bar.

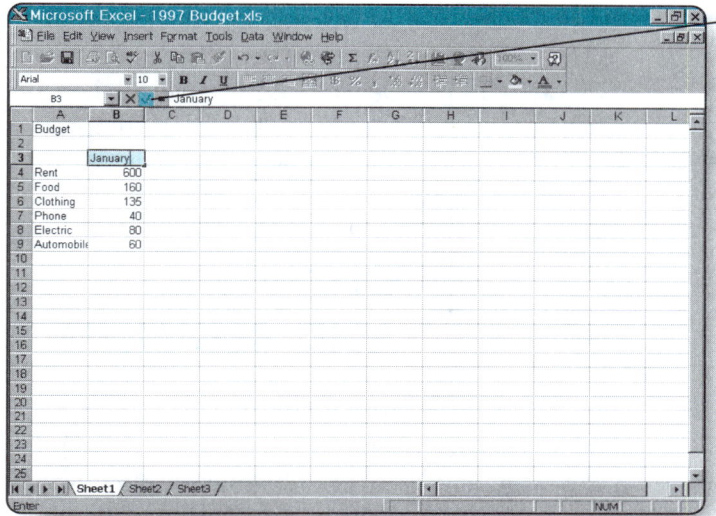

3. **Click** on the **Check Mark** (✔) **button** in the Formula bar. Excel will store the information and leave the cell pointer in the selected cell. To fill by example, the cell pointer must appear in the cell containing the first value.

TIP

Cells show the results of what you type, while the Formula bar displays what you actually typed.

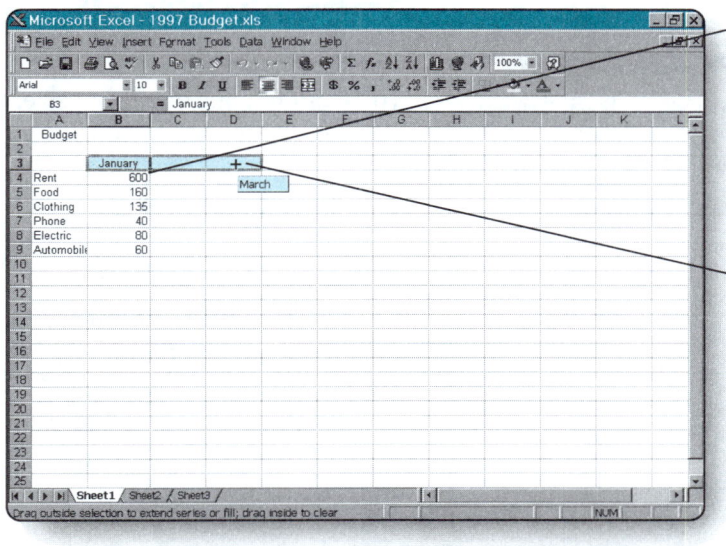

4. **Move** the **mouse pointer** over the square (fill handle) that appears in the lower-right corner of the selected cell. The shape of the mouse pointer will change to a solid black plus sign.

5. **Drag** the **mouse** to the right. As you drag, you'll see ScreenTips containing month names.

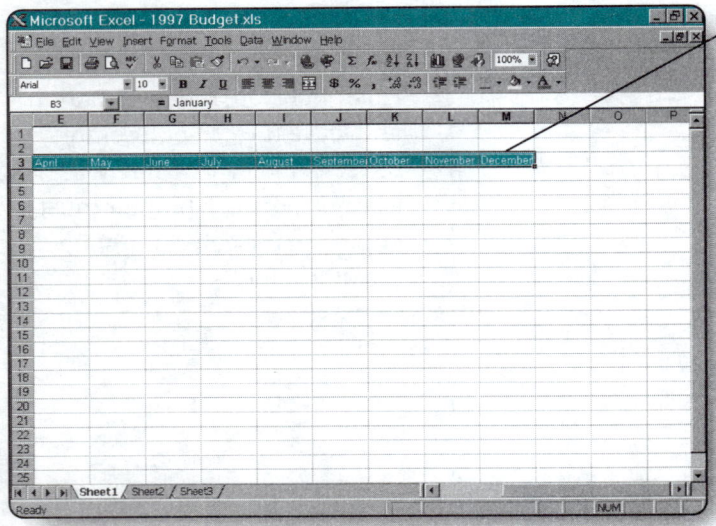

6. **Release** the **mouse button** when you see a ScreenTip for December. Excel will fill the selected cells with the months for one year.

COPYING AND MOVING

You can move and copy information in Excel using two different methods: drag-and-drop, or the traditional method of cut or copy, and paste. The traditional method places information on the Windows Clipboard, while the drag-and-drop method does not.

TIP

If you were moving the information, you wouldn't press the Ctrl key.

Drag-and-Drop

Use this method when the range you want to copy equals, in size, the range you are copying.

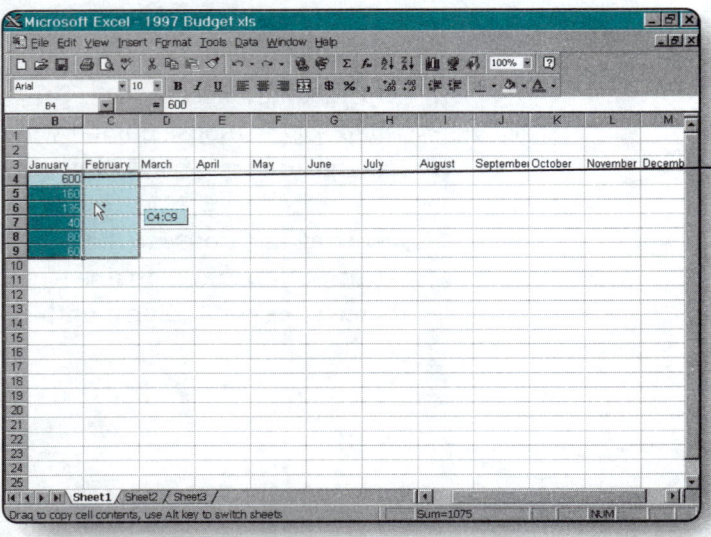

1. **Select** a **range of cells**.

2. **Press** the **Ctrl key** and position the **mouse pointer** on **one** of the **outside boundaries** of the selected range. The shape of the mouse pointer will change to an arrow with a small plus sign attached.

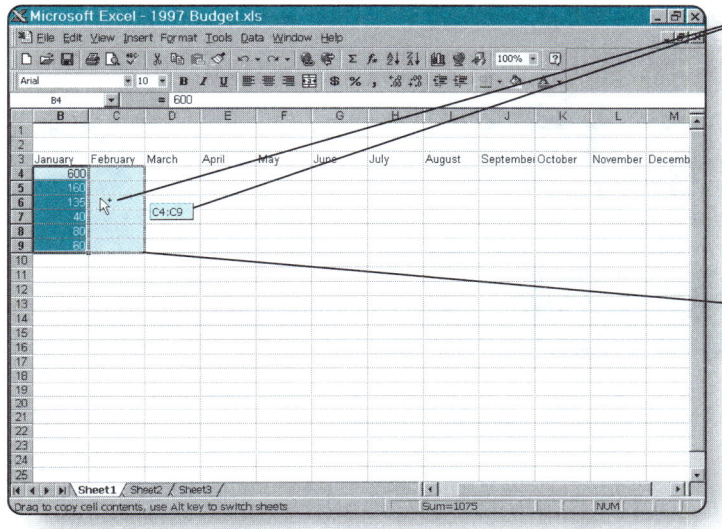

3. Drag the **mouse pointer** to the right to outline the cells into which you want to copy. As you drag, you'll notice a ScreenTip showing you the range where the information will appear if you release the mouse button.

4. **Release** the **mouse button**. The range of cells will be copied to a new location.

Copy and Paste

To copy information to and from ranges that are not equal in size, use the traditional cut or copy, and paste method.

1. **Select** a **range of cells** to copy.

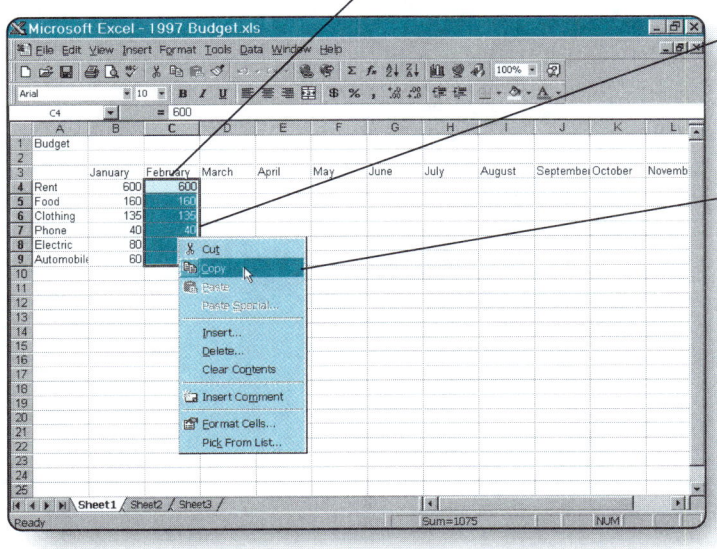

2. **Move** the **mouse pointer** over the selected range and **right-click**. A shortcut menu will appear.

3. **Click** on **Copy**. Excel will place the selected information on the Windows Clipboard.

TIP

If you were moving the range, you would click on Cut.

Excel will also display an animated border around the selected range.

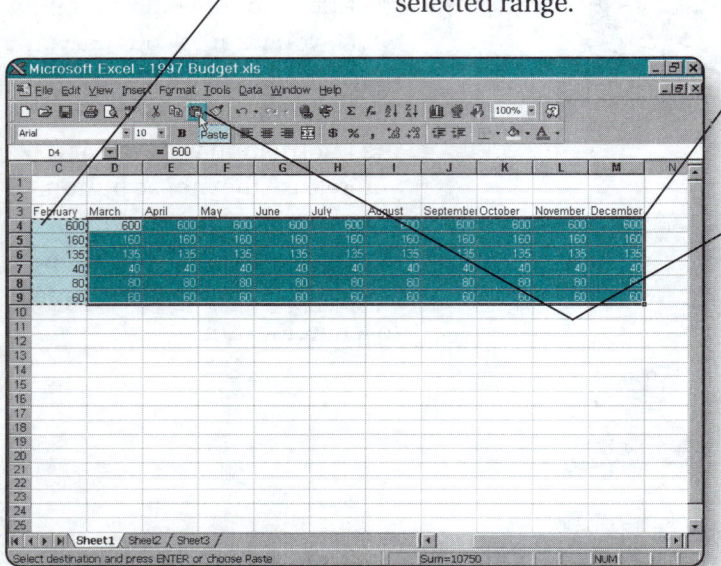

4. **Select** a **range of cells** in which to place the copied information.

5. **Click** on the **Paste button**. The information you copied in step 3 will appear in the selected cells.

6. **Press** the **Esc key** to finish the process. The animated border will disappear.

9 Working with Ranges

Most of the work you do in Excel will be with ranges of cells. Typically, you will work on a single cell at a time when entering information only. In this chapter, you'll learn how to:

✦ **Automatically format a range to make it attractive**

✦ **Align text in cells**

✦ **Format number entries in cells to make them more meaningful**

✦ **Specify the number of decimal places you want appearing in a number entry**

AUTOMATICALLY FORMATTING A RANGE

Although you can manually format cells to improve the appearance of your worksheet, you also can let Excel format a worksheet for you in one of several different styles.

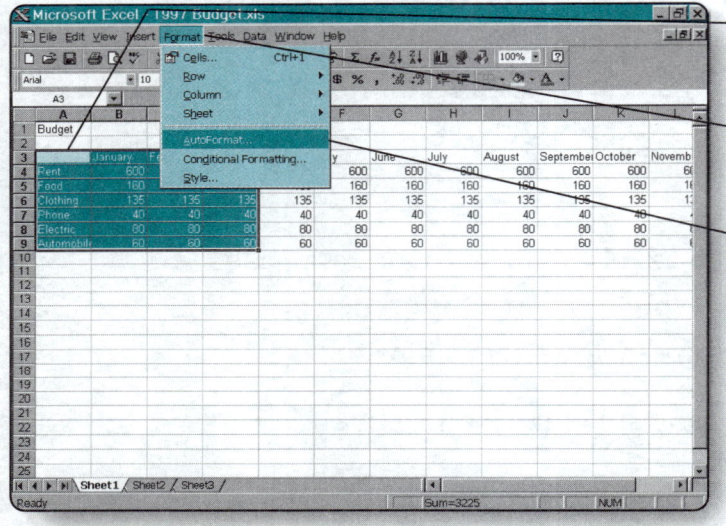

1. Select the **range of cells** you want to format.

2. Click on **Format**. The Format menu will appear.

3. Click on **AutoFormat**. The AutoFormat dialog box will open.

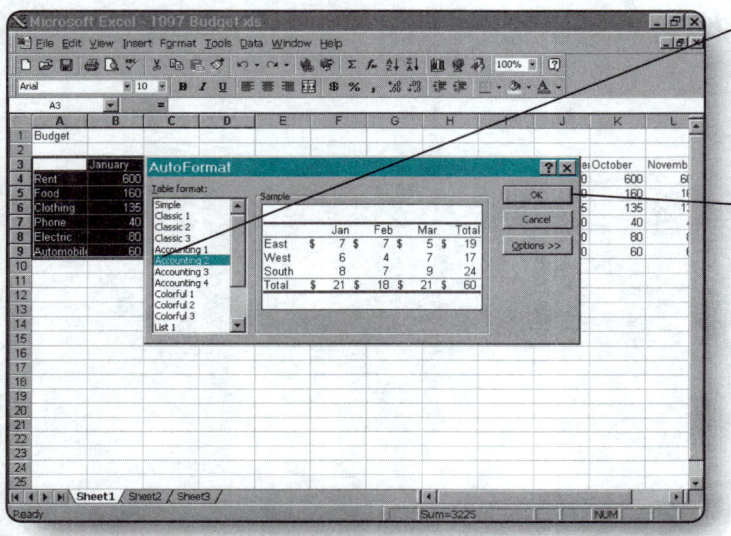

4. Click on a **Table Format** in the Table format: list. The Sample box will show a preview of the formatting.

5. Click on **OK**. Excel will apply the formatting to your document.

6. **Click anywhere** in the worksheet to cancel the selection. You will be able to see the formatting Excel applied.

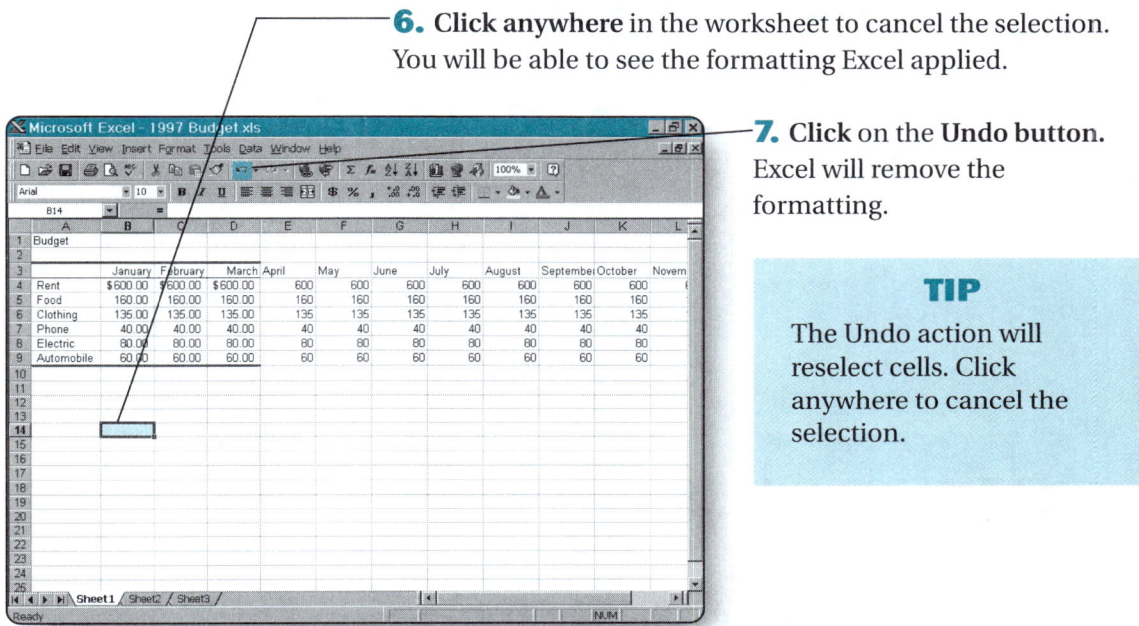

7. **Click** on the **Undo button.** Excel will remove the formatting.

TIP

The Undo action will reselect cells. Click anywhere to cancel the selection.

ALIGNING TEXT

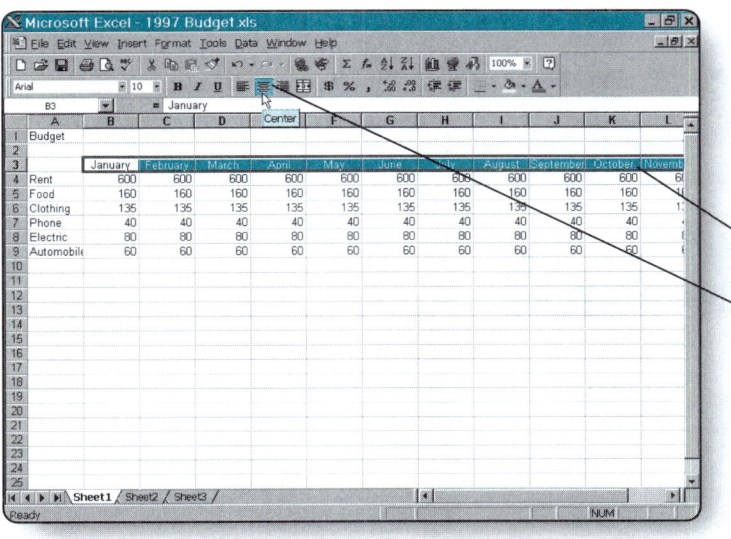

As you saw earlier, text automatically aligns at the left edge of a cell and numbers align at the right edge. You can change this alignment.

1. **Select** some **cells.**

2. **Click** on the **Center button.** The contents of the cells will align in the centers of the selected cells.

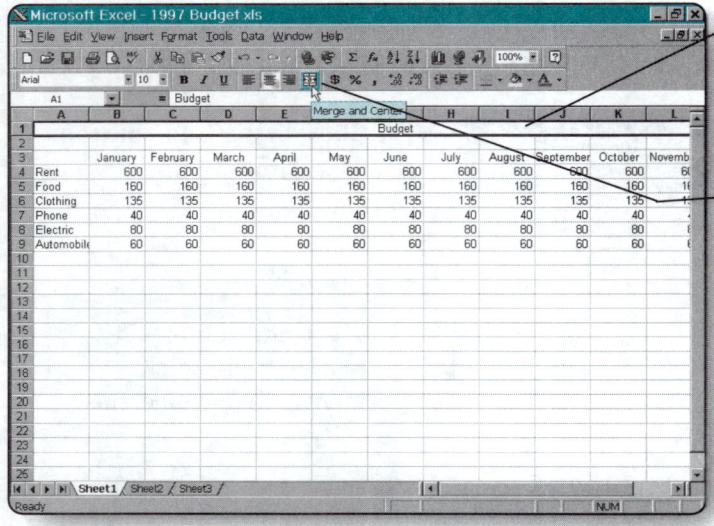

3. **Select** a different **range of cells**, preferably one you want to use as a title for the worksheet.

4. **Click** on the **Merge and Center button**. Excel will merge the selected range into one cell and center its contents.

FORMATTING NUMBER ENTRIES

You can add decimals and dollar signs to your numbers.

1. **Select** a **range of cells**.

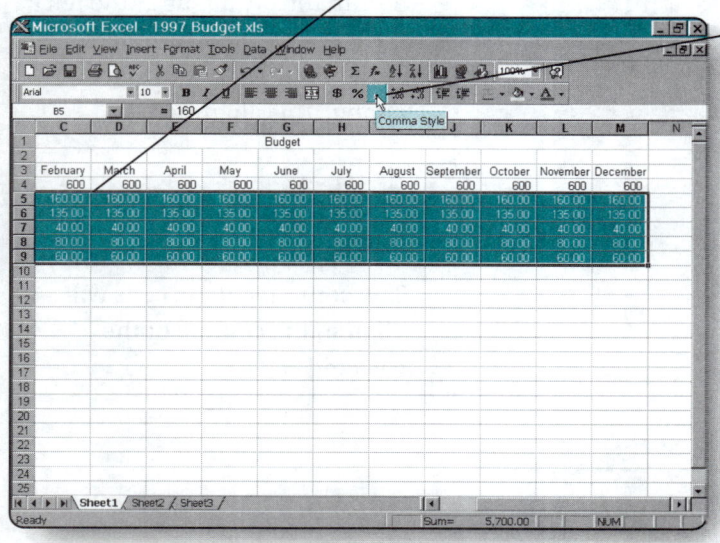

2. **Click** on the **Comma Style button**. Excel will change the selected cells so that they contain a decimal place and two zeros after the decimal. If any of the numbers exceed 1,000, Excel will also include commas at the appropriate locations.

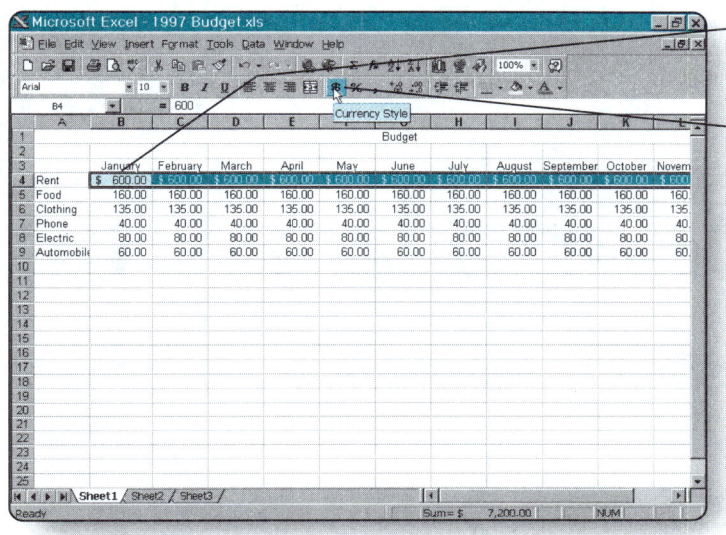

3. Select a different **range of cells**.

4. Click on the **Currency Style button**. Excel will change all the number formats so they include a dollar sign and two places after the decimal.

SPECIFYING DECIMAL PLACES

Suppose you decide you don't want to see two decimal places, but you want to leave the rest of the formatting.

1. Select a **range of cells**.

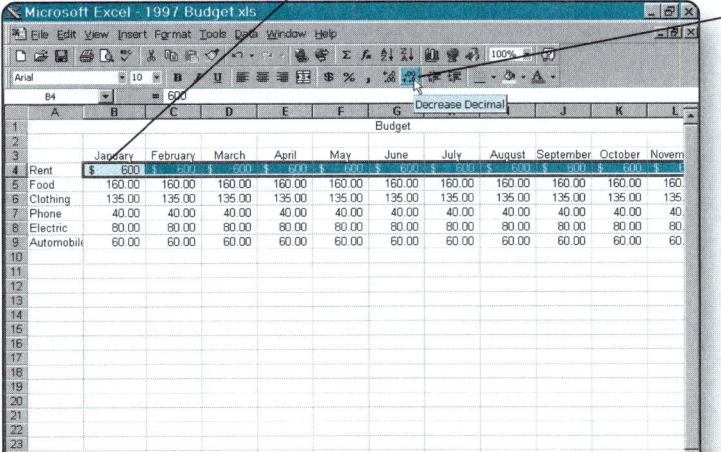

2. Click on the **Decrease Decimal button twice**. Excel will change all the number formats so they include a dollar sign and no decimal places.

10 Doing Math

Why use a spreadsheet program, if not to do math? You can perform mathematical calculations on any cell containing a value. Obviously, numbers are values, but, in Excel, dates and times can also be values. The format of information determines whether Excel views the information as a label or a value, so the distinction between labels and values becomes important when you calculate. In this chapter, you'll learn how to:

+ **Use formulas to add, subtract, multiply, and divide**

+ **Total cells quickly**

+ **Calculate an average**

+ **Use the AutoCalculate feature**

+ **Copy a formula**

USING FORMULAS TO ADD NUMBERS

In Excel, you use formulas to add, subtract, multiply, and divide. These formulas will remind you of your high school days. The major difference is that you can (and should, whenever possible) use cell addresses instead of numbers in your formulas. That way, if you change the value of a cell, Excel will automatically update any formula that included that cell.

When you add, use a plus sign (+); to subtract, use a minus sign (−); to multiply, use an asterisk (*); and to divide, use a slash (/).

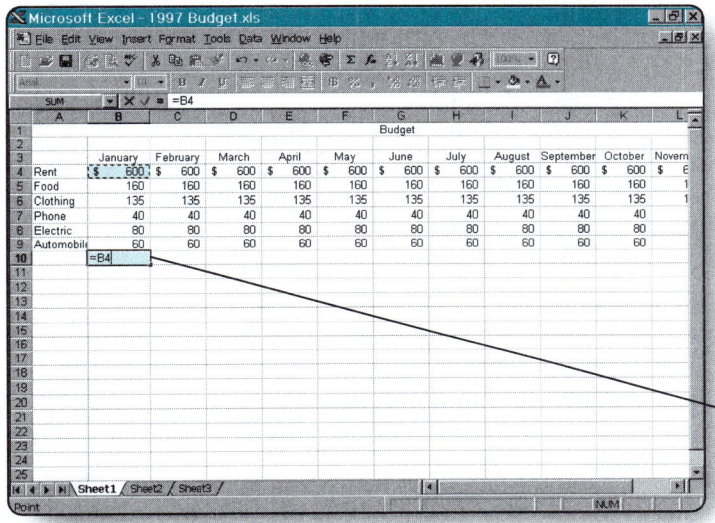

1. Click on the **cell** where you want to place a formula.

2. Type = (**equal sign**). Beginning a cell entry with an equal sign lets Excel know that you're entering a formula.

3. Click on the **first cell** you want to include in the formula. Excel will surround the cell with an animated border, and the cell's address will appear as part of the formula.

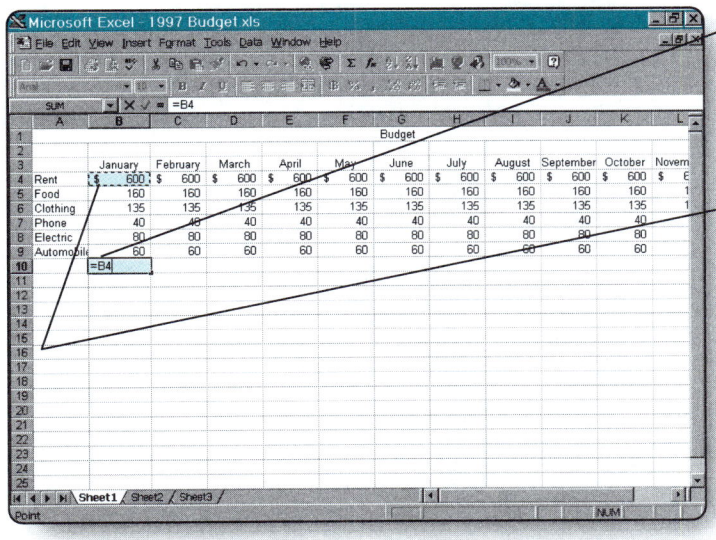

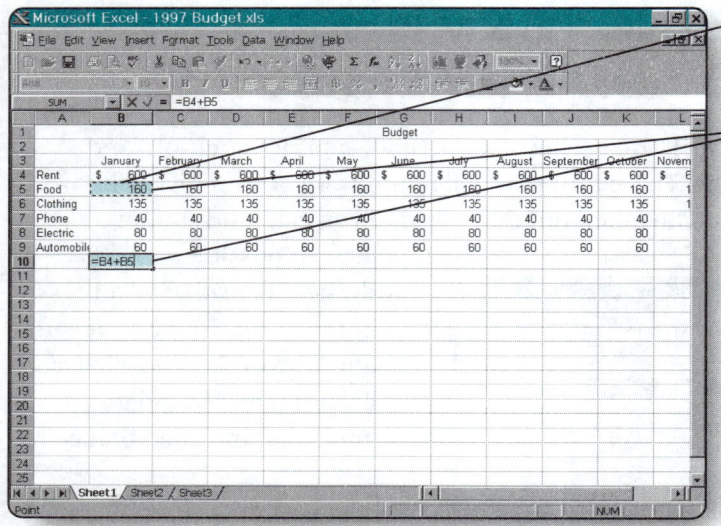

4. **Press** the **+ key (plus sign)**. It will be added to the formula.

5. **Click** on the **next cell** you want to include in the formula. Excel will surround the cell with an animated border, and the cell's address will appear as part of the formula.

> **NOTE**
>
> By default, Excel uses the rules you learned in high school when determining the order in which it calculates: Excel performs multiplication and division before performing addition and subtraction. To change the order in which Excel calculates, use parentheses. Excel will perform calculations that appear in parentheses before performing all other calculations. For example, 3+4*2=11 or (3+4)*2=14.

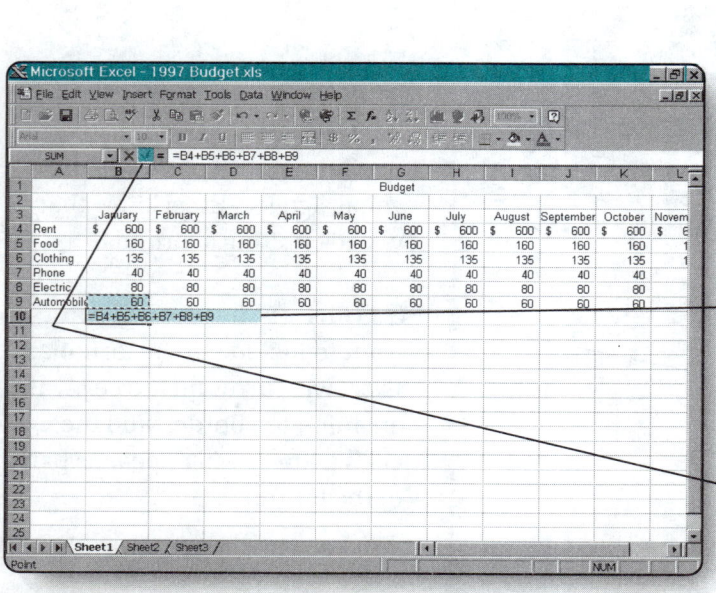

6. **Repeat steps** 4 and 5 until you complete the formula, changing the cell you click on in step 5.

7. **Click** on the **Check Mark (✔) button** in the Formula bar. The formula will be accepted.

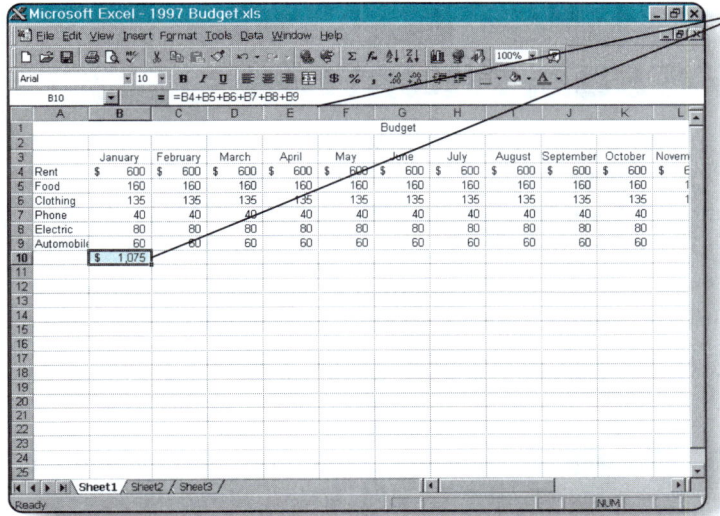

Notice that the result of the formula appears in the cell that contains the formula, but the actual formula appears in the Formula bar.

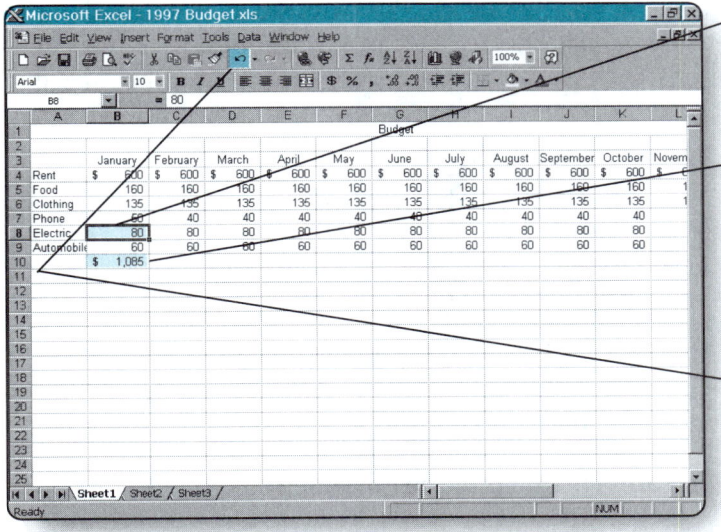

8. **Click** on a **cell** referenced in the formula. The cell will be selected.

9. **Type** a different **number** and **press** the **Enter key**. Excel will update the sum in the cell containing the formula to reflect the change.

10. **Click** on the **Undo button**. The cell you changed will return to its original value.

TOTALING CELLS WITH THE SUM FUNCTION

Well, that worked, but it was somewhat cumbersome. "There *must* be an easier way," you say. And, for sums, there is an easier way. Note, however, that the steps you're about to use will work only when you're adding a column of numbers. For subtraction, multiplication, or division, you must use the steps in the preceding task. Of course, the good news is that most of the math you'll do using Excel will involve adding columns of numbers.

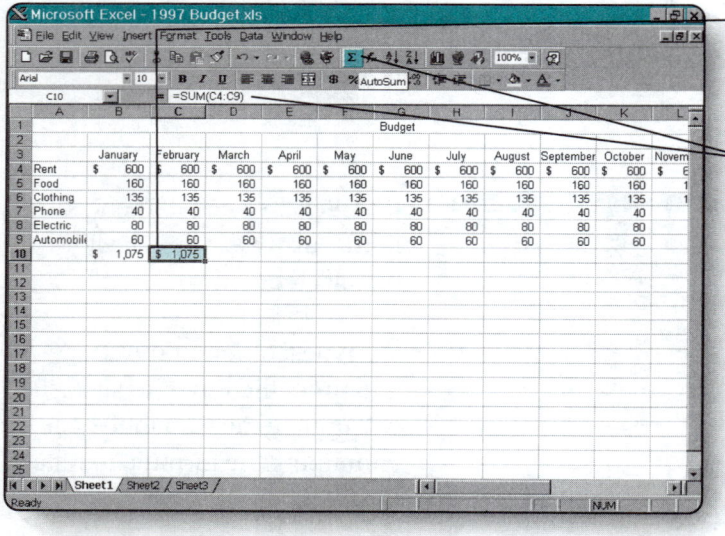

1. **Click** on a **cell** at the bottom of a range of numbers. The cell will be selected.

2. **Double-click** on the **Auto-Sum button**. The sum of the range will appear in the selected cell, but the SUM function will appear in the Formula bar.

Functions are a shortcut for creating formulas in Excel, and the SUM function is the function you use when you want to add a column (or row) of numbers.

Excel assumes you want to add the contiguous cells immediately above the cell pointer that contains values.

All functions contain three basic elements:

◆ An equal sign (=) that tells Excel a calculation follows

◆ The name of the function (in this case, SUM)

◆ A set of parentheses that contains *arguments*, which are instructions that describe how Excel should carry out the function. In this case, the argument identifies the range of cells Excel should include in the calculation.

TIP

If you single-click the AutoSum button, you'll see the function in the cell. You'll then need to press the Enter key to accept the function.

Excel contains more than 200 functions to help you calculate everything from simple sums to the future value of an investment. You'll explore a few more functions in this chapter.

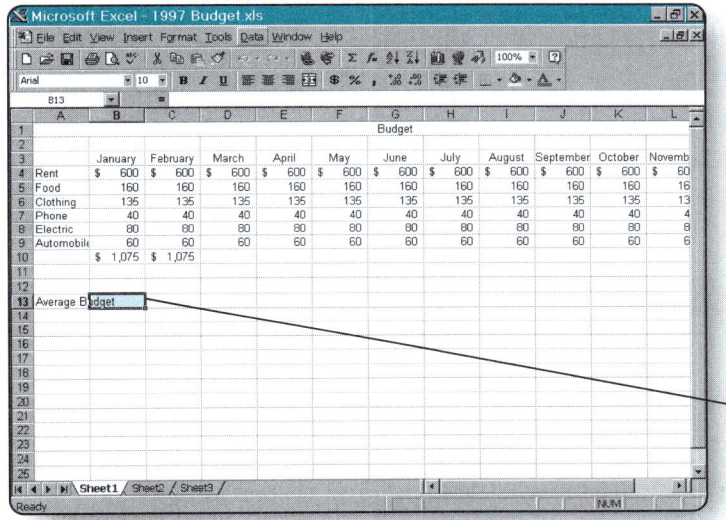

CALCULATING AN AVERAGE

Suppose you want to calculate the monthly average of your budget—use the AVERAGE function.

1. **Click** on a **cell**. The cell will be selected.

2. **Type** a **label** to identify what you intend to calculate, such as "Average Budget," and **press** the **Right Arrow key**.

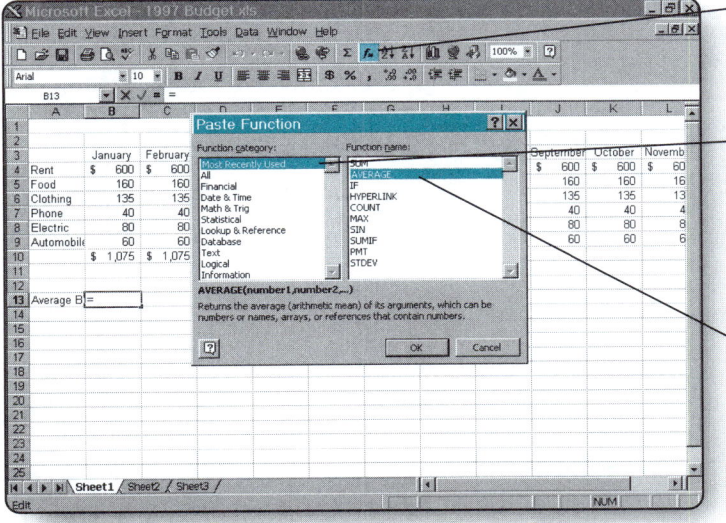

3. **Click** on the **Paste Function button**. The Paste Function dialog box will open.

4. **Click** on an **item** in the Function category: list on the left. You will see the functions available for that category in the Function name: list on the right.

5. **Click** on a **function** in the Function name: list. To calculate an average, **click** on **AVERAGE**. The description at the bottom of the box will change to describe the selected function.

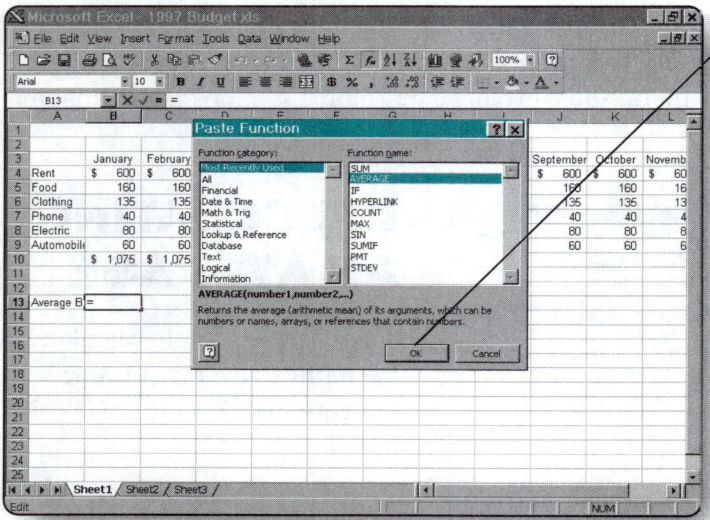

6. **Click** on **OK**. Excel will display a suggested formula in the Formula bar and a box immediately below the Formula bar in which you can make changes to the formula.

You may need to change the formula so that the average you're calculating will not include any totals (that would distort the average).

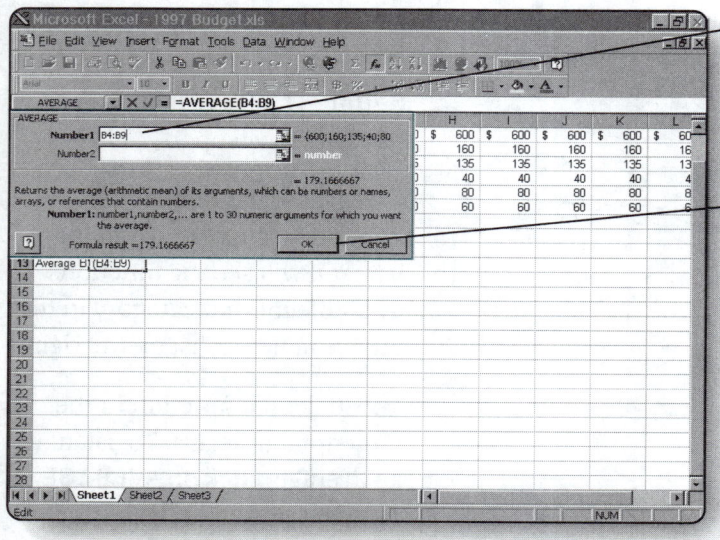

7. **Click** in the **Number 1 text box** and **change** the **range** so that it doesn't include any cells that have totals.

8. **Click** on **OK**. Excel will display the average of the range in the cell you selected in step 1.

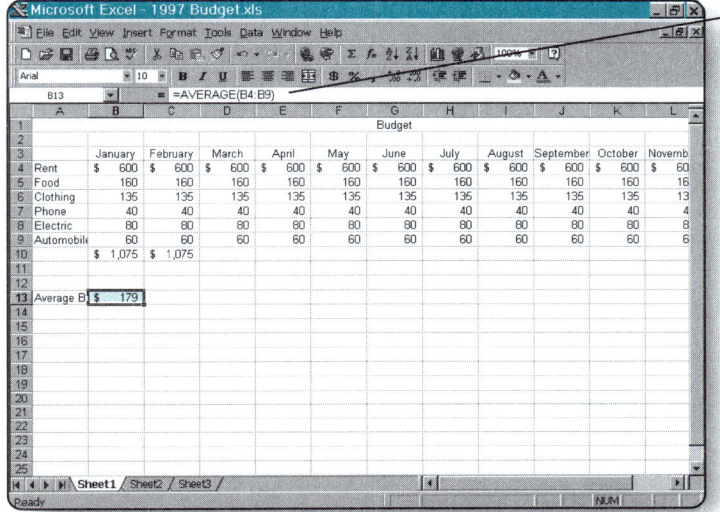

You'll see the formula in the Formula bar.

USING AUTOCALCULATE

You might find occasions when you need to know a sum or an average "at the moment," but you don't really need to store the number in a worksheet cell. For cases like these, use the AutoCalculate feature.

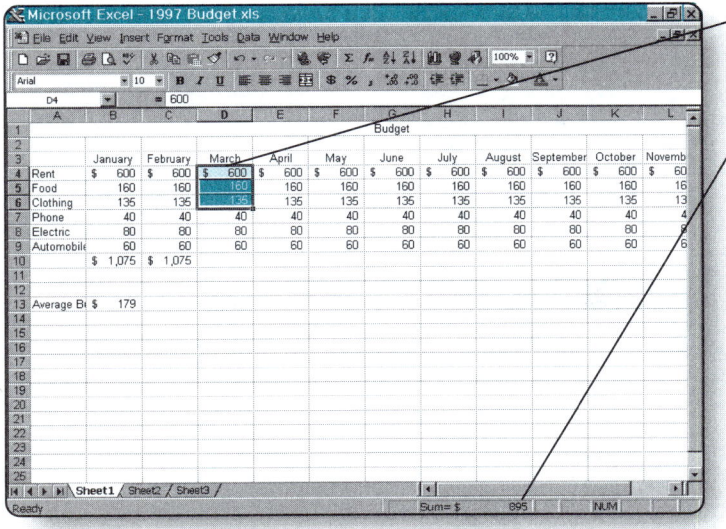

1. **Select** the **range of cells** you want to total.

Notice the sum of the selected cells appears in the status bar.

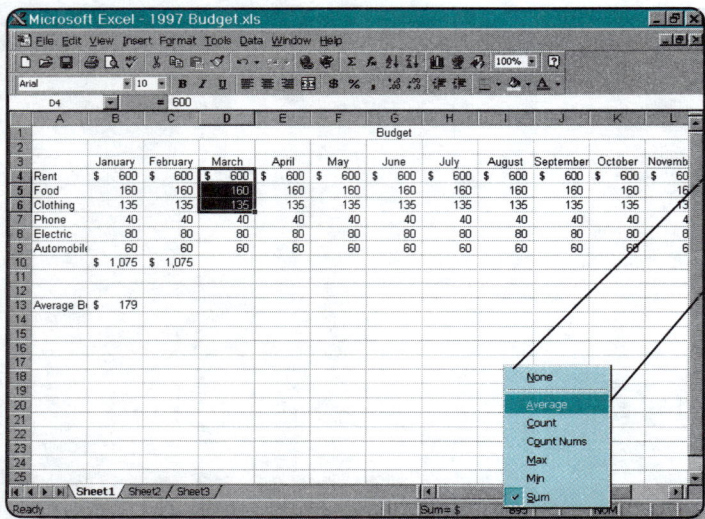

2. **Move** the **mouse pointer** to the status bar.

3. **Right-click**. A shortcut menu will appear.

4. **Click** on the **calculation** you want Excel to perform.

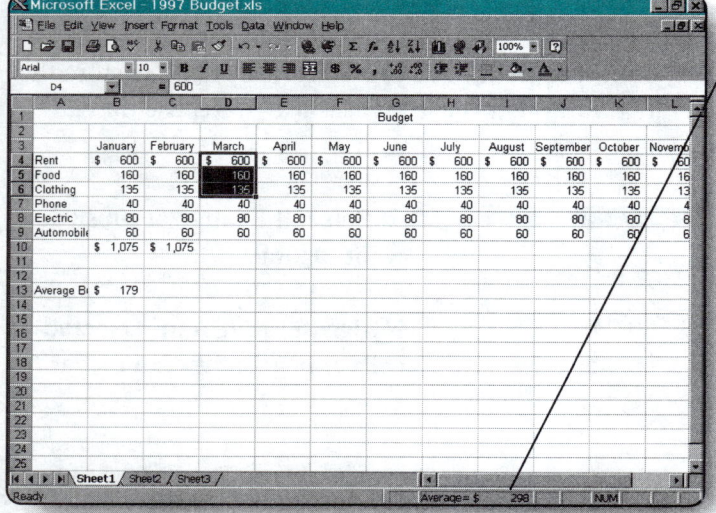

The new calculation now appears in the status bar.

COPYING A FORMULA

Because Excel uses *relative cell addressing*, you can copy formulas from one cell to another, saving you hours of typing. Relative cell addressing means that, by default, Excel adjusts a formula you copy so that the cells in the original formula refer to its new location.

You can see how this works by copying the SUM function; in this example, the SUM function appears in C10, and you'll copy it to D10. To make this example meaningful, first click on D7 and type any other number. By changing the value of D7, you'll be able to see that the formula you copy from C10 to D10 will, indeed, add column D, because the sum of column D will be different from the sum of column C.

1. **Click** on the **cell** containing the formula you want to copy. Notice that the formula in the Formula bar refers to the range summed by the formula; in the example, the formula bar refers to C4:C9.

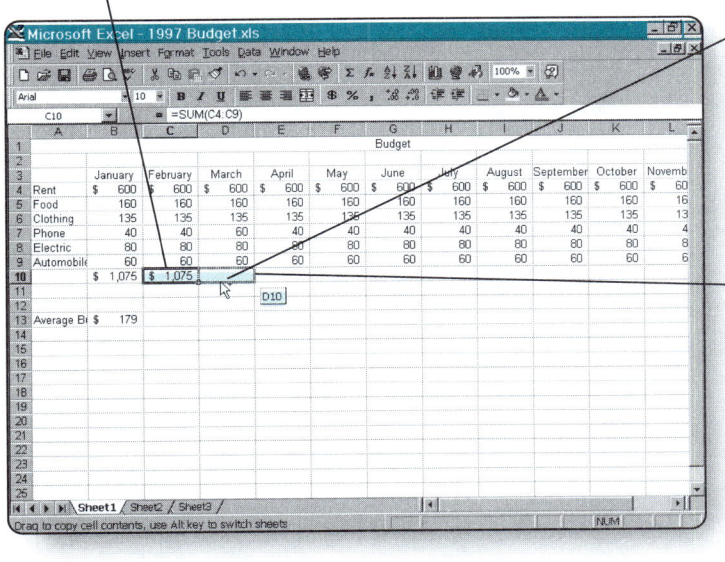

2. **Press** and **hold** the **Ctrl key** while **moving** the **mouse pointer** over one of the borders of the cell. The mouse pointer will change to an arrow with a plus sign attached.

3. **Drag** the **contents** of the **selected cell**, C10, to the location where you want the same formula to appear. In the example, I dragged to D10.

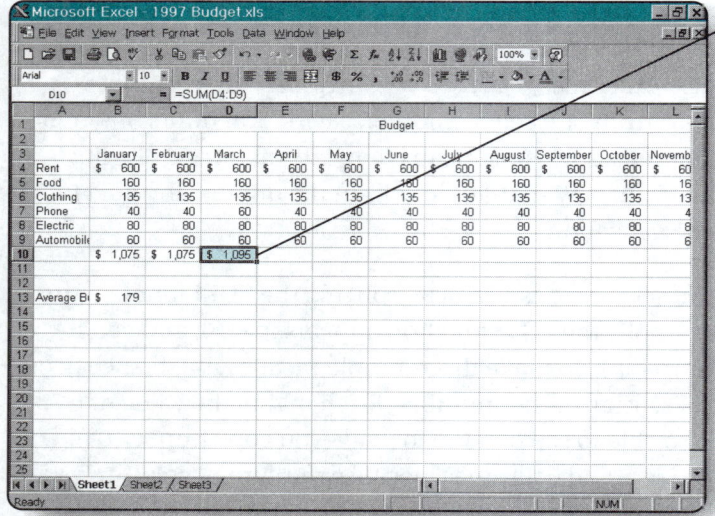

4. **Release** the **mouse button**. Excel will copy the formula.

In the example, the sum of column D will be $1,095, not $1,075, which is the sum of column C. In addition, as you can see in the Formula bar, Excel adjusted the formula you copied from C10 when you placed it in D10 to include D4:D9.

NOTE

You just used the drag-and-drop method of copying, but the results would have been the same if you had used the Copy and Paste buttons.

11 Changing the Structure and Appearance of Worksheets

Nobody makes a worksheet look exactly the way it ought to look the first time around. Think of your worksheet as a "work in progress." You'll want to change both its structure and appearance after you enter the basic information. In this chapter, you'll learn how to:

✦ Rename, add, and move worksheets

✦ Insert and delete rows

✦ Hide and redisplay columns

✦ Change the size of a column

✦ Change fonts

✦ Add boldface and italics

✦ Shade cells and add borders

✦ Add extra information to cells with comments

MODIFYING SHEETS

You can change the name of the worksheets in your workbook and you can add, move, and delete sheets.

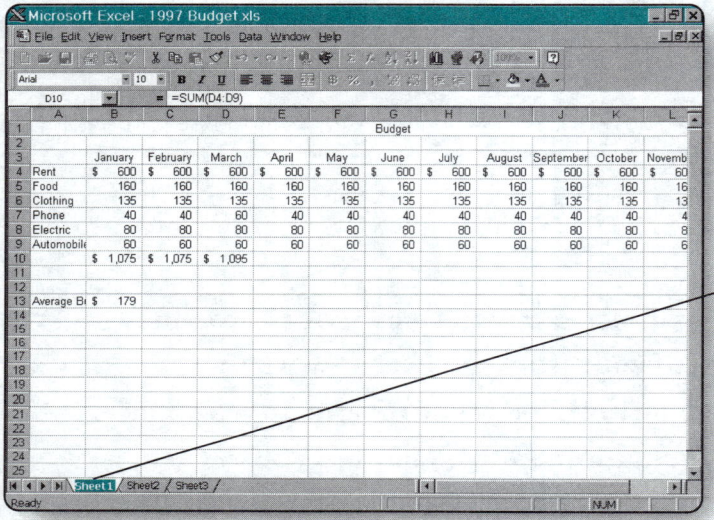

Renaming Sheets

You'll probably want to change the name of a sheet to make it more meaningful.

1. Double-click on the **Sheet1 Sheet tab**. The name of the Sheet tab will be selected.

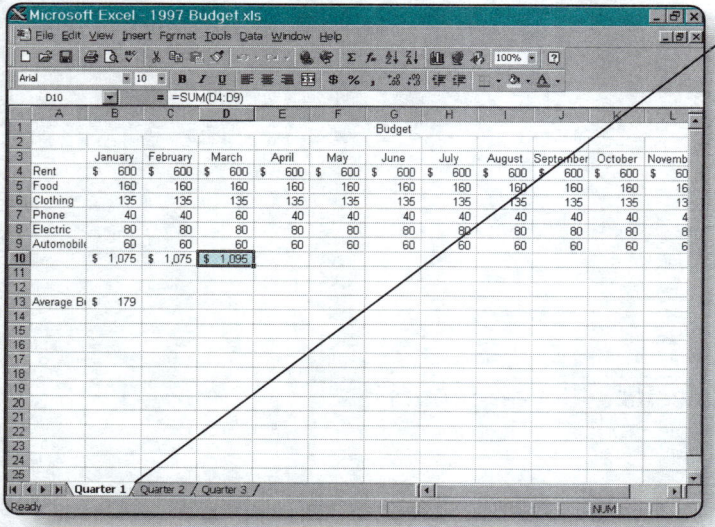

2. Type the **name** you want to give the sheet.

3. Press the **Enter key**. The name will change.

4. Repeat steps 1 and **2** for the other two sheets.

NOTE

When you double-click on a Sheet tab to change its name, the sheet is also displayed.

Adding Sheets

Suppose you decide you want to make a budget workbook and you want to break up your budget information so it appears on four sheets—one for each quarter of the year. By default, Excel only supplies three sheets so you'll need to add a sheet.

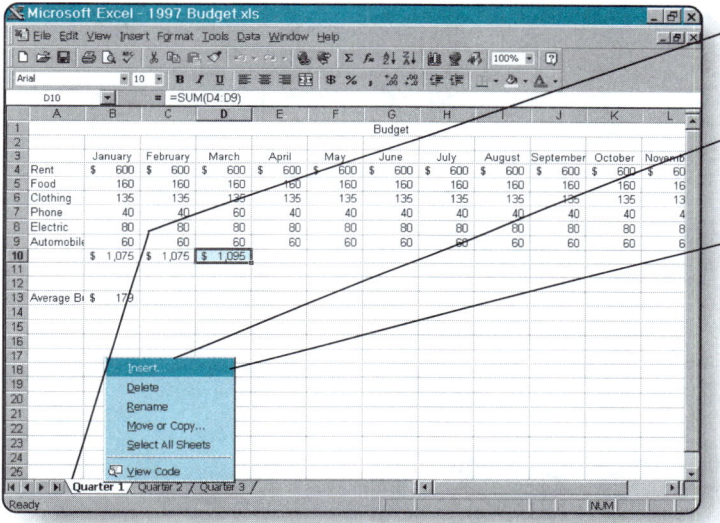

1. **Click** on the **first Sheet tab**. The worksheet will be displayed.

2. **Right-click** on the **Sheet tab**. A shortcut menu will appear.

3. **Click** on **Insert**. The Insert dialog box will open.

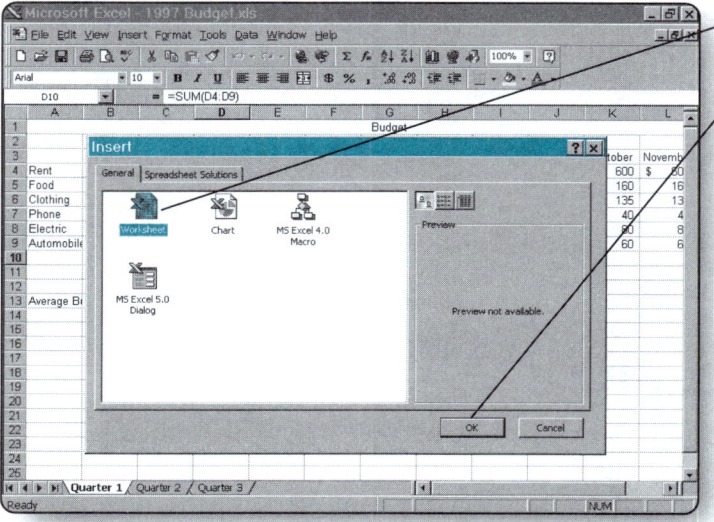

4. **Click** on **Worksheet**.

5. **Click** on **OK**. Excel will insert a new blank sheet labeled Sheet4.

NOTE

Excel always adds sheets in front of the selected sheet. You will be unable to add a new sheet at the end of the workbook but you'll learn how to move sheets to reorder them in the next section.

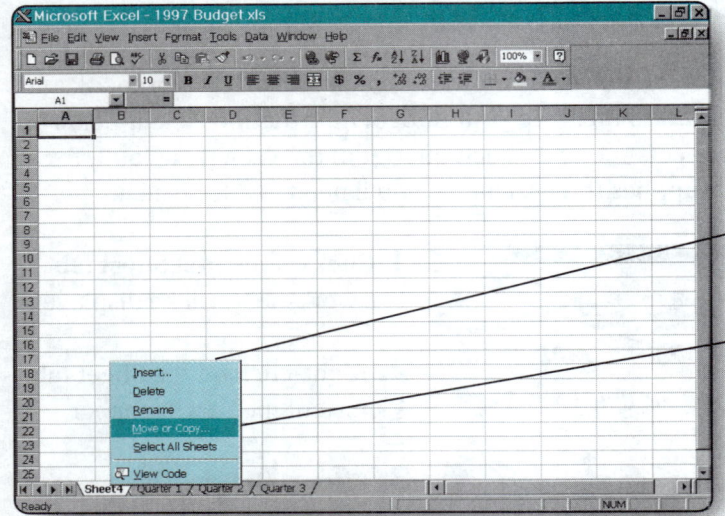

Moving Sheets

You can move Sheet4 to the end of the workbook and then rename it.

1. **Right-click** on the **Sheet4 tab**. A shortcut menu will appear.

2. **Click** on **Move or Copy**. The Move or Copy dialog box will open.

3. **Click** on (**move to end**) in the Before sheet: box.

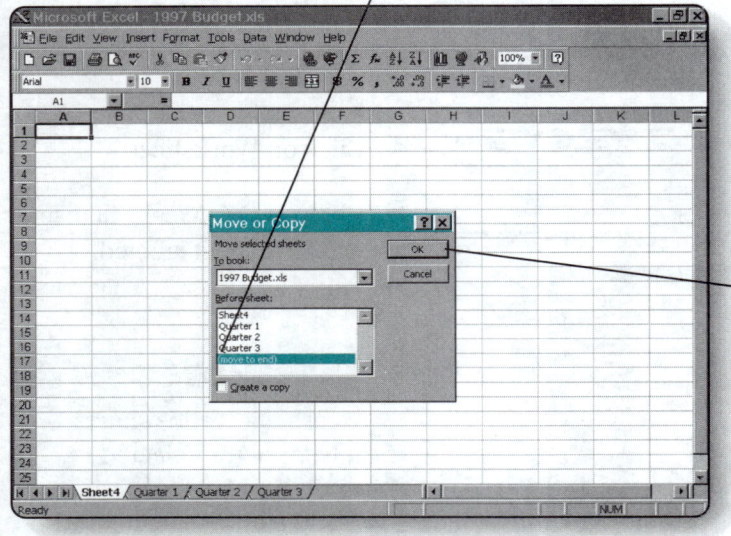

NOTE

Notice that you can copy a sheet instead of moving it. Just place a ✔ in the Create a copy check box.

4. **Click** on **OK**. Excel will move Sheet4 to the end of the workbook.

TIP

You also can move sheets between workbooks. First, open both workbooks. Right-click on the sheet you want to move and click on Move or Copy. In the Move or Copy dialog box, click on the arrow (▼) next to the To book: list box. Then click on the other workbook option and select a location from the Before sheet: box.

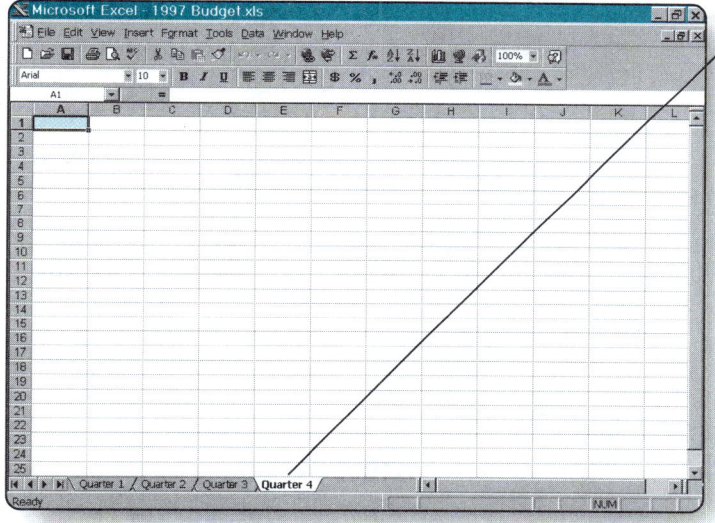

5. Double-click on Sheet4 and type a new name.

6. Press the Enter key. Excel will rename Sheet4 to the new name.

Copying Information between Sheets

1. Click on the sheet that contains the information you want to copy.

2. Select the range of cells you want to copy.

3. Click on the Copy button. Excel will copy the information to the Windows Clipboard and display an animated border around the selection.

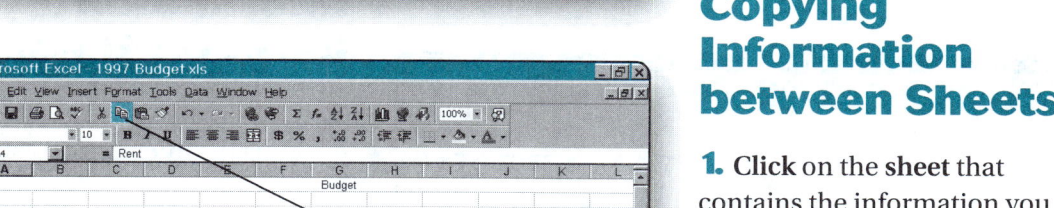

4. **Click** on the **sheet** where you want to place the copied information.

5. **Click** on the **first cell** that should contain the information you are copying. In the example, I clicked on A4.

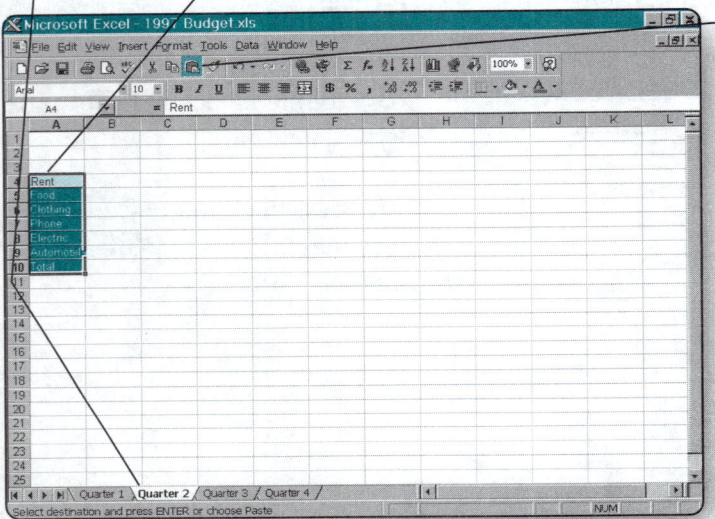

6. **Click** on the **Paste button**. Excel will copy the information stored on the Windows Clipboard to the selected location.

7. **Repeat steps** 5 through 7 as often as necessary.

8. **Press** the **Esc key** when you are finished copying.

Moving Information between Sheets

1. **Click** on the **sheet** that contains the information you want to move.

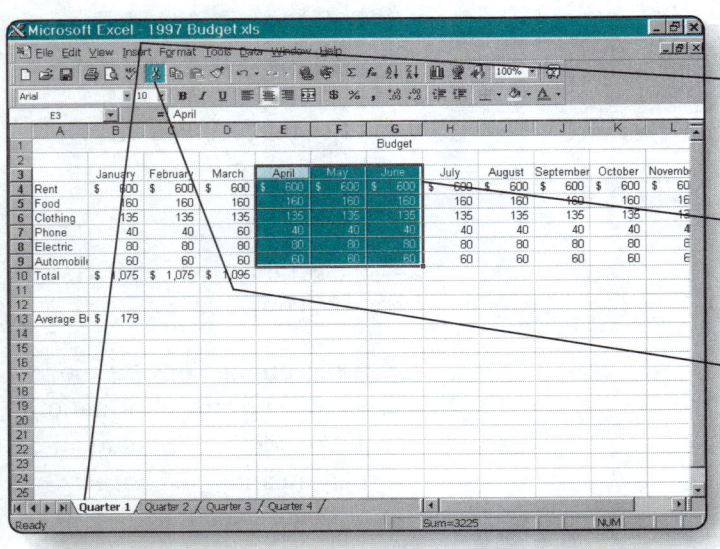

2. **Select** the **range of cells** that contain the information you want to move to another sheet.

3. **Click** on the **Cut button**. Excel will copy the information to the Windows Clipboard and display an animated border around the selection.

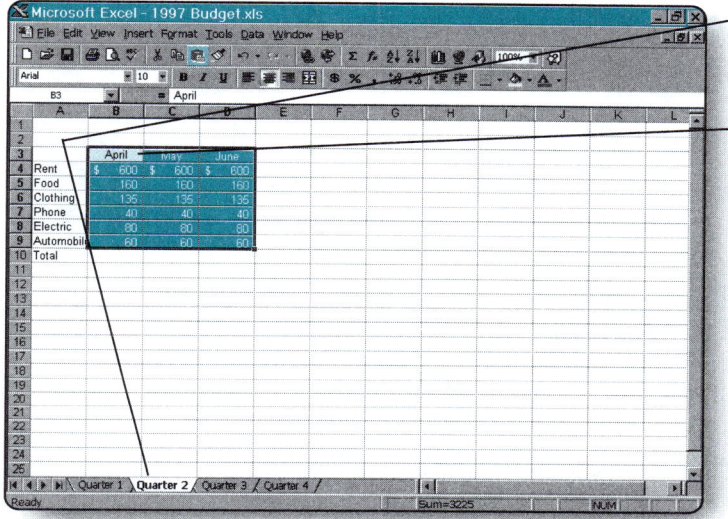

4. **Click** on the **sheet** to which you want to move information.

5. **Click** on the **first cell** that should contain the information you are moving. In the example, I clicked on B3.

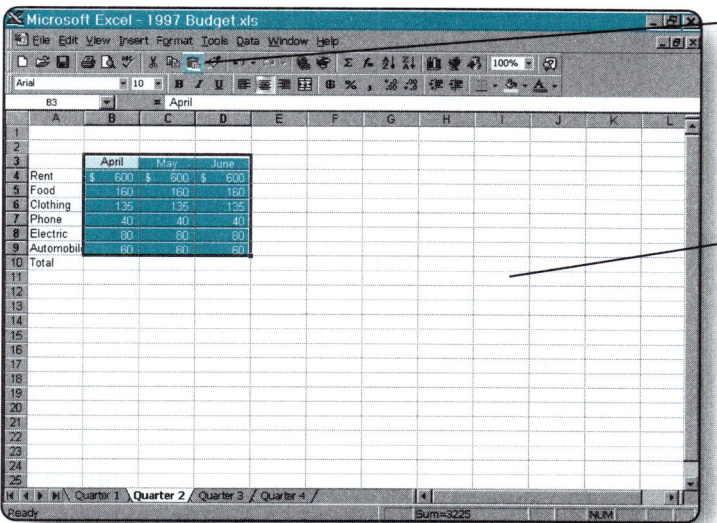

6. **Click** on the **Paste button**. Excel will copy the information stored on the Windows Clipboard to the selected location.

7. **Click anywhere** to cancel the selection.

TIP

You can delete any sheet at any time. Select the sheet, right-click on the Sheet tab, and click on Delete. Excel will warn you that the selected sheet will be deleted permanently. Click on OK to delete the sheet or Cancel to keep the sheet.

INSERTING AND DELETING ROWS AND COLUMNS

It's difficult to remember everything you want in a worksheet while you're setting it up. To modify the structure of your worksheet, you can insert and delete rows and columns.

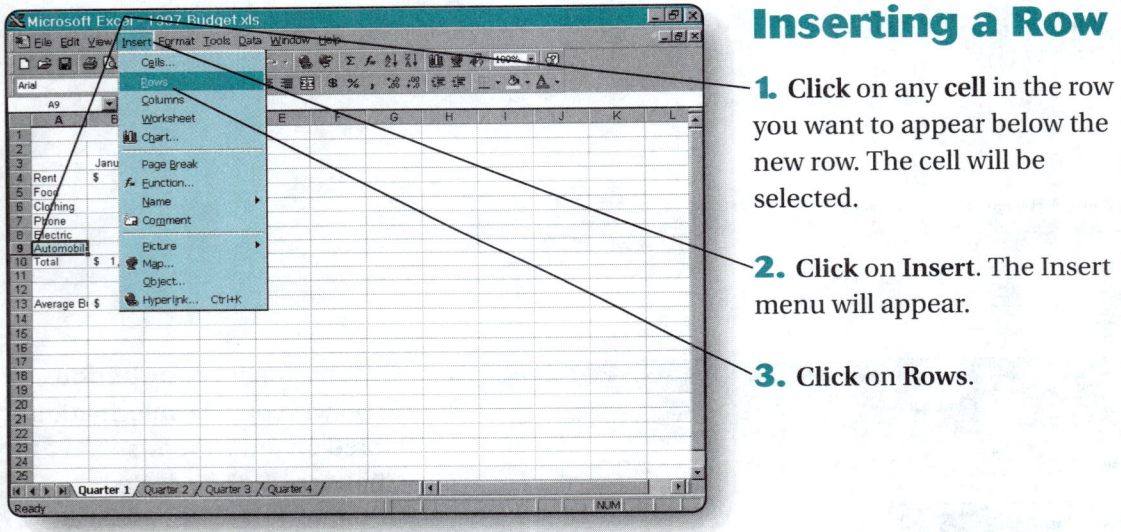

Inserting a Row

1. **Click** on any **cell** in the row you want to appear below the new row. The cell will be selected.

2. **Click** on **Insert**. The Insert menu will appear.

3. **Click** on **Rows**.

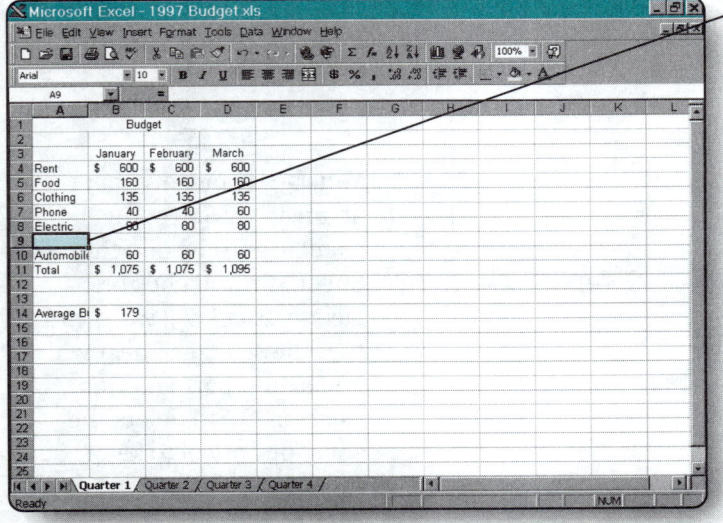

Excel will add a row to your worksheet above the selected row.

TIP

Excel will insert new columns to the left of the selected column. To insert a column, select the column you want to appear to the right of the new column and then click on Insert. On the Insert menu, click on Columns.

Deleting a Row or Column

1. **Click** on any **cell** in the row or column you want to delete. The cell will be selected.

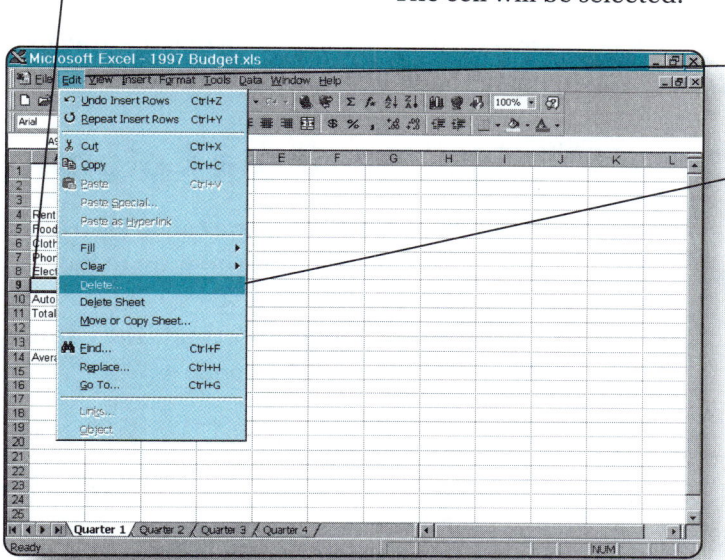

2. **Click** on **Edit**. The Edit menu will appear.

3. **Click** on **Delete**. The Delete dialog box will open.

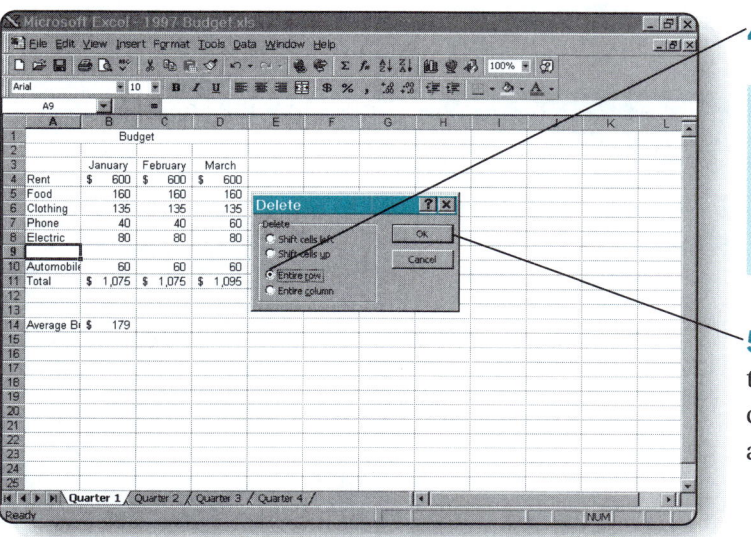

4. **Click** on **Entire Row**.

NOTE

If you were deleting a column, you would click on Entire Column.

5. **Click** on **OK**. Excel will delete the selected row or column and close the space between the adjacent rows or columns.

HIDING AND DISPLAYING COLUMNS

Sometimes you want information in your worksheet, but you don't want that information to appear onscreen or to be available for printing. You can hide columns or rows so they aren't visible.

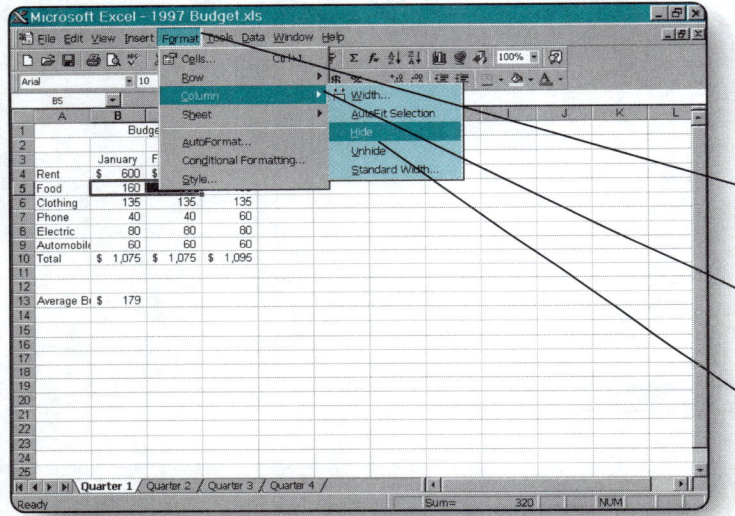

Hiding a Column

1. **Click** on **one cell** in each of the columns you want to hide.

2. **Click** on **Format**. The Format menu will appear.

3. **Click** on **Column**. A cascading menu will appear.

4. **Click** on **Hide**. Excel will hide the columns containing the selected cells.

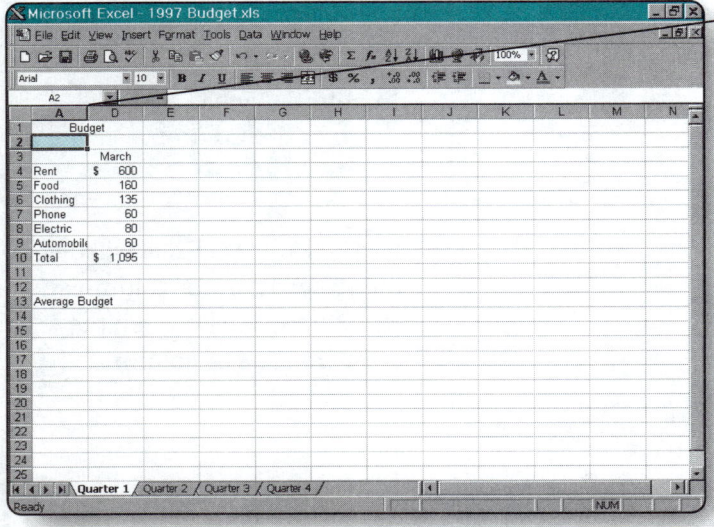

Notice that the column letters for B and C are missing.

NOTE

You can hide rows using these steps with slight modifications. Select a cell in each row you want to hide and click on Row in step 3.

NOTE

You can redisplay rows using these steps with slight modifications. Select cells that span across hidden rows and click on Row in step 3.

Displaying Hidden Columns

Eventually, you'll probably want to redisplay columns or rows you previously hid.

1. **Select cells** that span across the hidden columns.

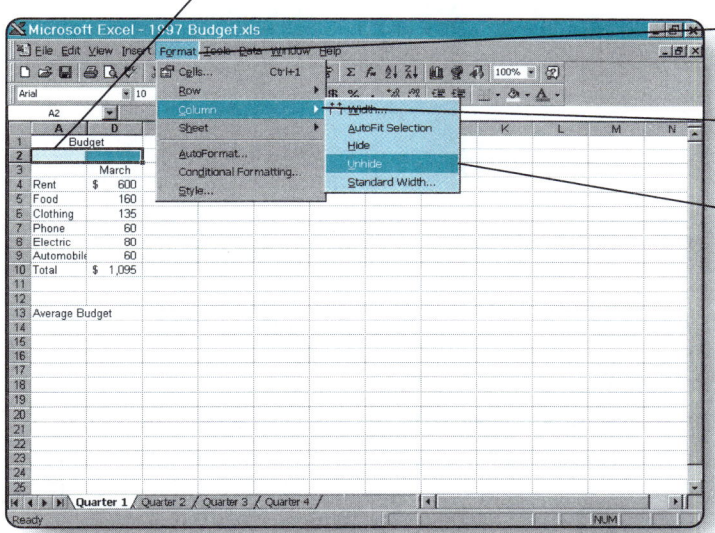

2. **Click** on **Format**. The Format menu will appear.

3. **Click** on **Column**. A cascading menu will appear.

4. **Click** on **Unhide**. Excel will redisplay the hidden columns.

CHANGING COLUMN WIDTH

Most of the time, Excel will automatically adjust column widths or row heights for you, but occasionally, you will need to change the width of a column or the height of a row.

1. **Click** on any **cell** in the column you want to widen. The cell will be selected.

2. **Move** the **mouse pointer** to the column header area, where the column letters appear, to the right of the column you want to widen. The shape of the mouse pointer will change.

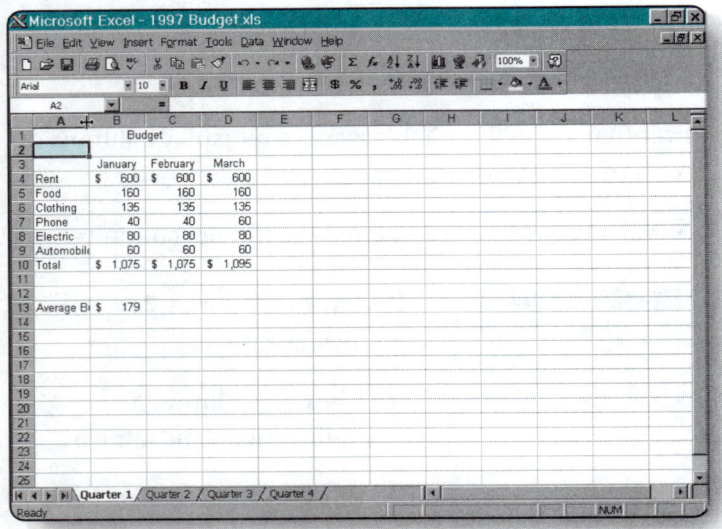

3. Double-click. Excel's AutoFit feature will automatically adjust the column's width to fit the widest entry in the column.

You can also use an alternative method that lets you control the size of the column.

4. Click on the **sheet** with which you want to work.

5. Move the **mouse pointer** to the column header area, where the column letters appear, to the right of the column you want to widen. The shape of the mouse pointer will change.

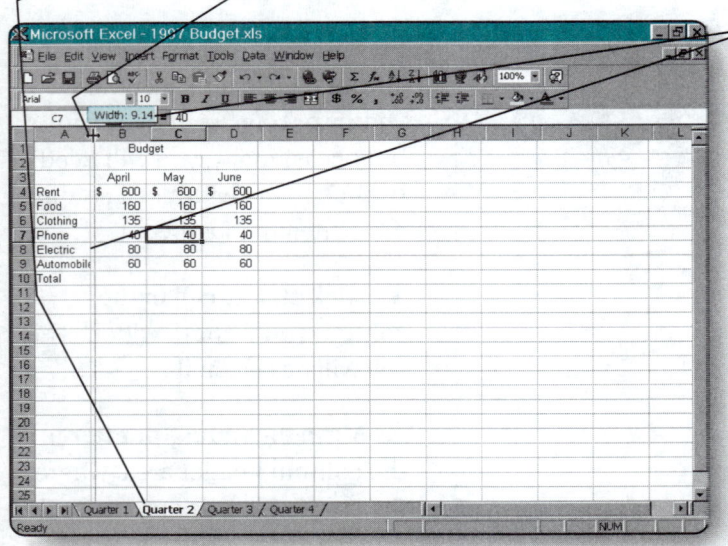

6. Drag the **mouse** to the right. You will see a line indicating the column's border and a ScreenTip indicating the column's width in characters.

7. Release the **mouse button**. The column's width will change.

TIP

Both of these techniques will work to change row height. Move the mouse pointer to the row header area at the bottom of the row you want to adjust and then double-click or drag up or down.

IMPROVING THE APPEARANCE OF A WORKSHEET

You can perform the same kinds of enhancements to your worksheet that you can perform on a Word document—and many of the methods you use are the same.

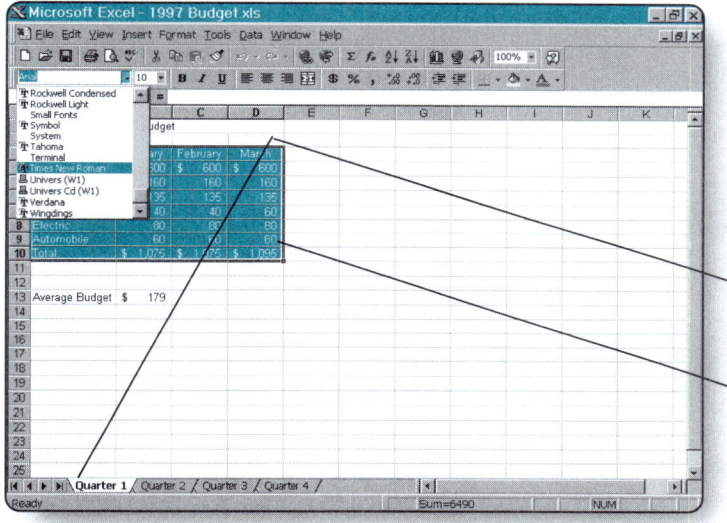

Changing Fonts and Font Sizes

You can change the fonts and font sizes in any or all cells in a worksheet.

1. **Click** on the **sheet** with which you want to work.

2. **Select** a **range of cells** to modify.

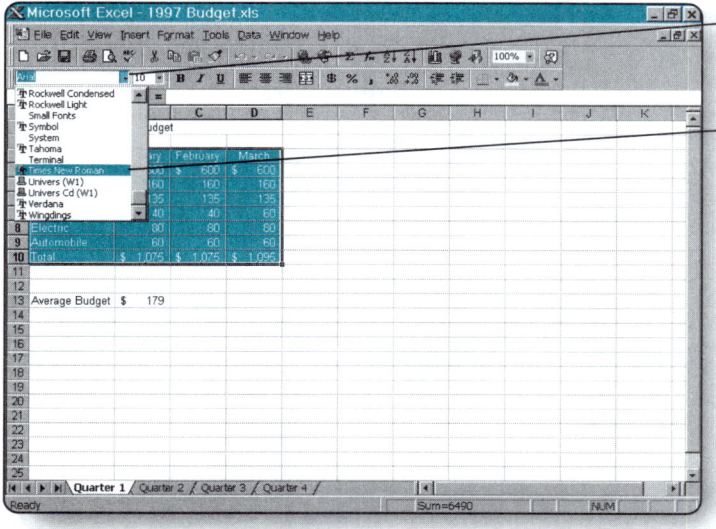

3. **Click** on the **arrow** (▼) next to the Font list box.

4. **Click** on the **font** you want to use in the selected cells. The font in the selected cells will change.

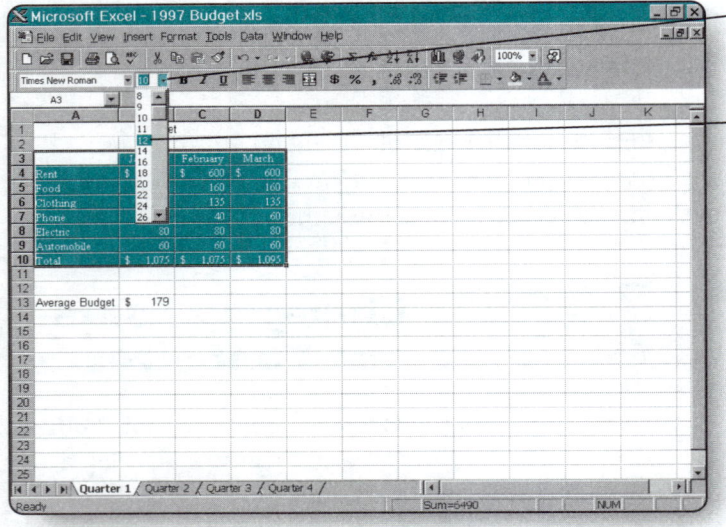

5. **Click** on the **arrow** (▼) next to the Font Size list box.

6. **Click** on the **font size** you want to use. The font size in the selected cells will change.

Enhancing Fonts

You can enhance fonts by adding boldface, italics, or underlining to them.

1. **Click** on a **cell**. The cell will be selected.

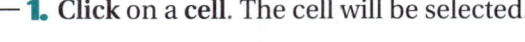

2. **Click** on the **Bold button**. The text in the cell will appear bold.

3. **Change** the **font size**, if necessary, using the steps in the preceding task.

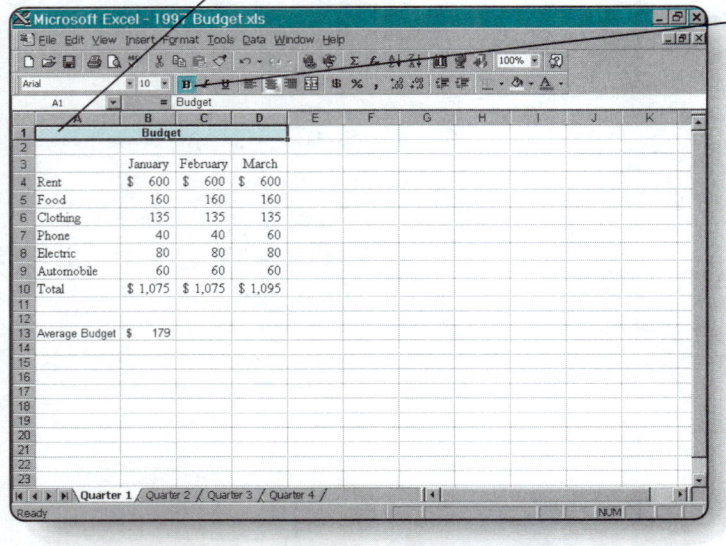

4. Select a **range of cells**.

5. **Press** and **hold** the **Ctrl key** while **selecting** a different **range of cells**. Excel will select two ranges at the same time.

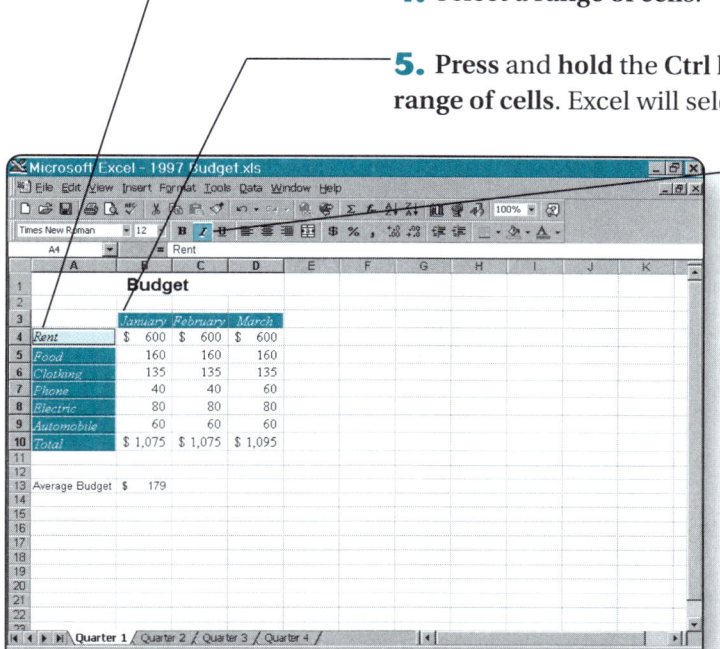

6. **Click** on the **Italics button**. Excel will add italics to the selected ranges.

Shading Cells

Shading adds visual interest to a worksheet. You can also use shading to draw attention to certain cells.

1. Select a **range of cells** to shade.

2. **Click** on the **arrow** (▼) next to the Fill Color button. A color palette will appear.

3. **Click** on the **color** you want to use for shading.

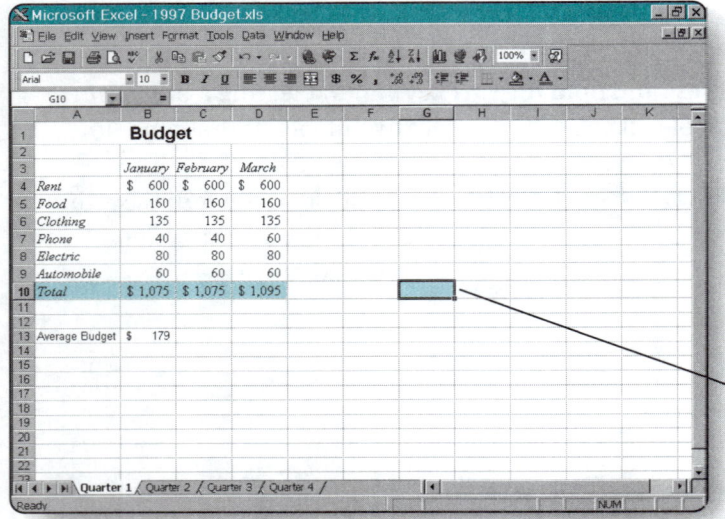

If you have access to a color printer or intend to view the worksheet on a monitor, you can choose any color. If you intend to print the worksheet on a black and white printer, use shades of gray—particularly lower percentages. That way, your information will still be visible even though it's shaded.

4. Click on **any cell** in the worksheet. Excel will cancel the selection and you will see the shading.

Adding Borders

Borders also add visual interest and call attention to cells.

1. Select the **range of cells** to which you want to add a border.

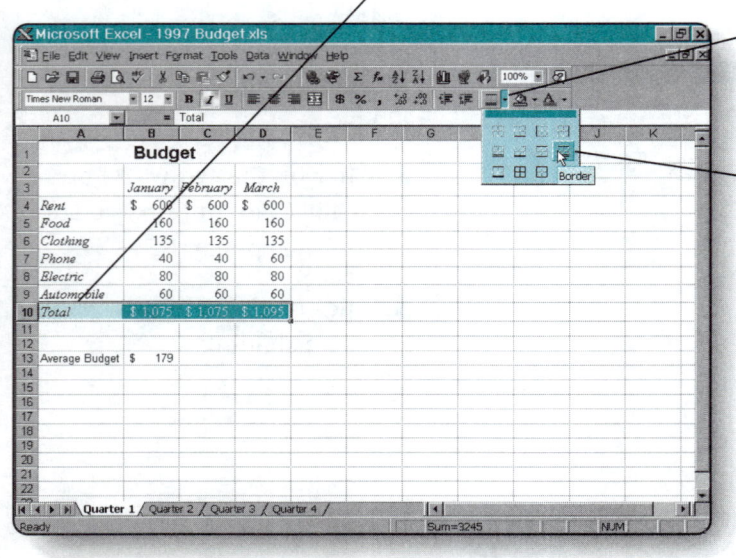

2. Click on the **arrow** (▼) next to the Borders button. A palette will appear.

3. Click on a **border style**. The style will be applied.

4. Click on any **cell** in the worksheet. Excel will cancel the selection.

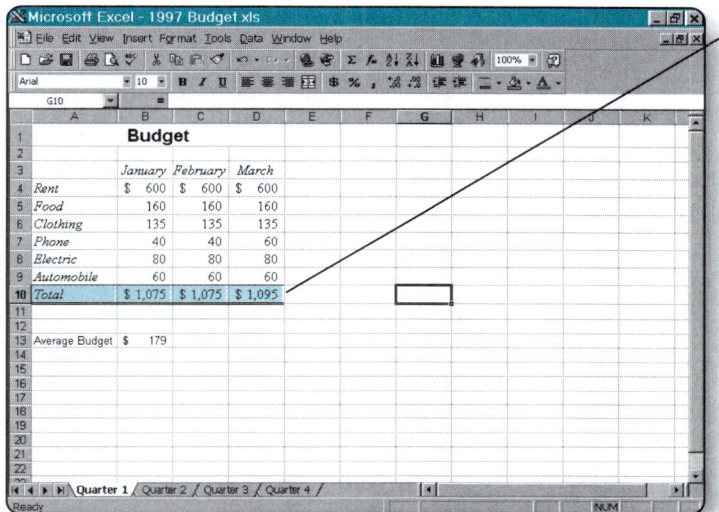

The border you added will appear around the cells you selected.

ADDING COMMENTS TO CELLS

Cell comments can explain information to a viewer.

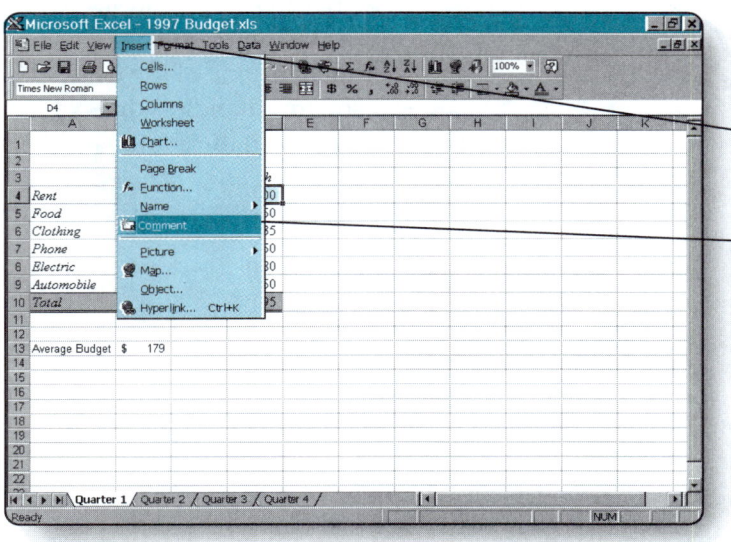

1. **Click** on the **cell** for which you want to add a comment.

2. **Click** on **Insert**. The Insert menu will appear.

3. **Click** on **Comment**. A box will appear in which you can type the comment you want to attach to the selected cell.

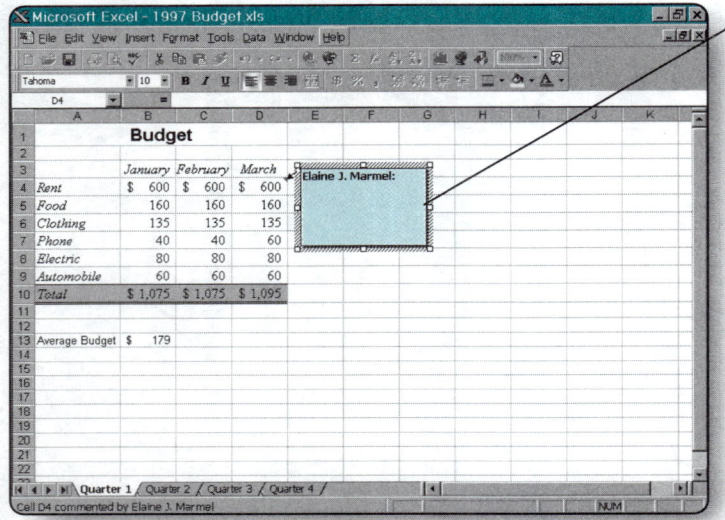

An insertion point also appears in the box—if you're using standard Windows colors, the insertion point is a very light shade of gray.

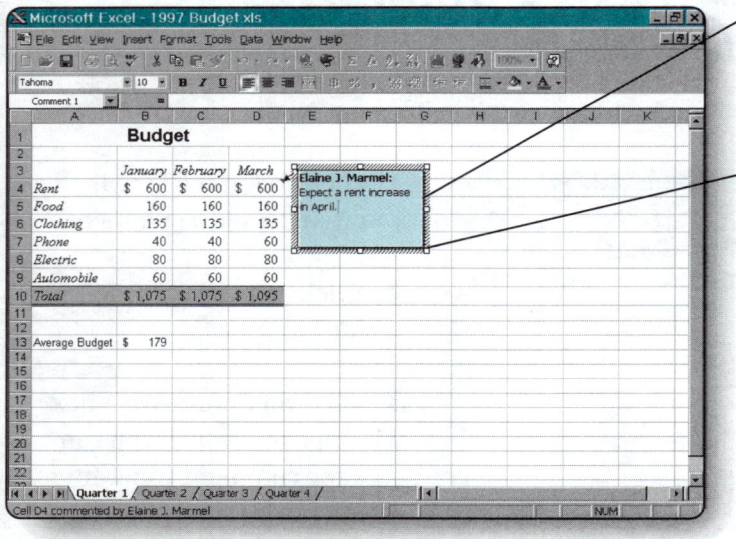

4. **Type** some **comment text**.

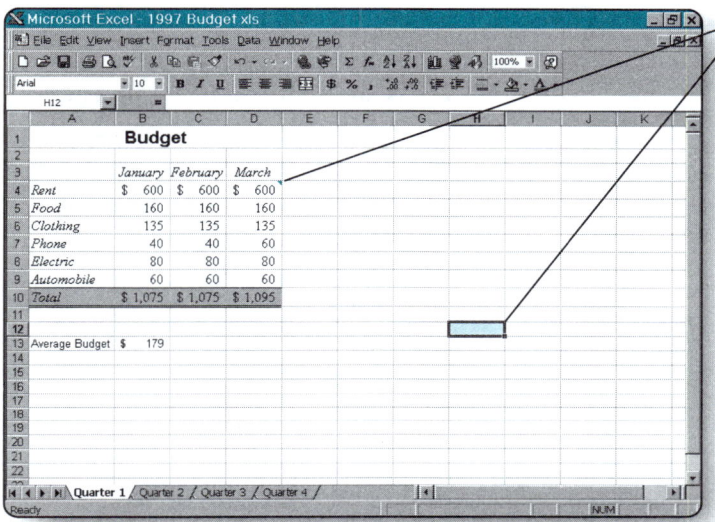

5. **Click** in **any cell** in the worksheet. The comment box will close and a small red marker will appear in the upper-right corner of the cell containing the comment.

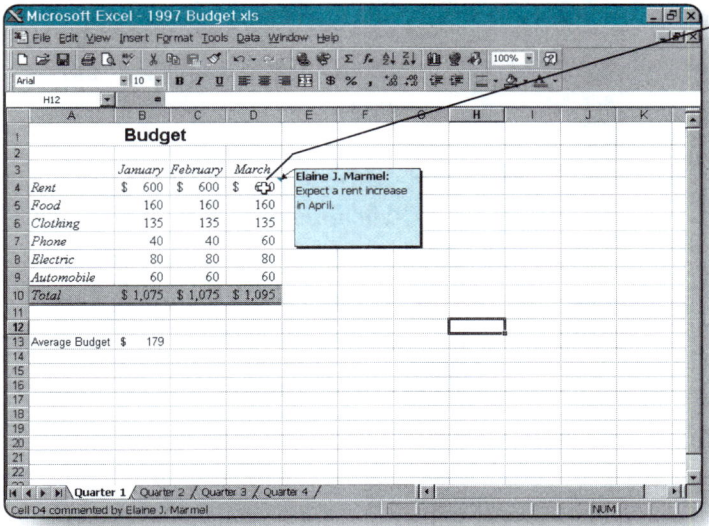

6. **Move** the **mouse pointer** over the **cell** containing the comment. The cell comment will appear.

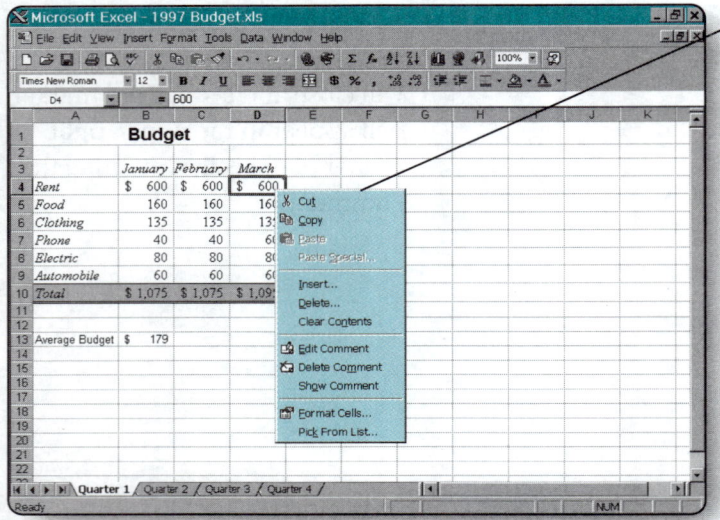

7. Right-click the **mouse** over the cell containing the comment. A shortcut menu will appear, from which you can choose to edit or delete the comment, or make the comment visible at all times instead of just when you point at the cell.

PRINTING COMMENTS

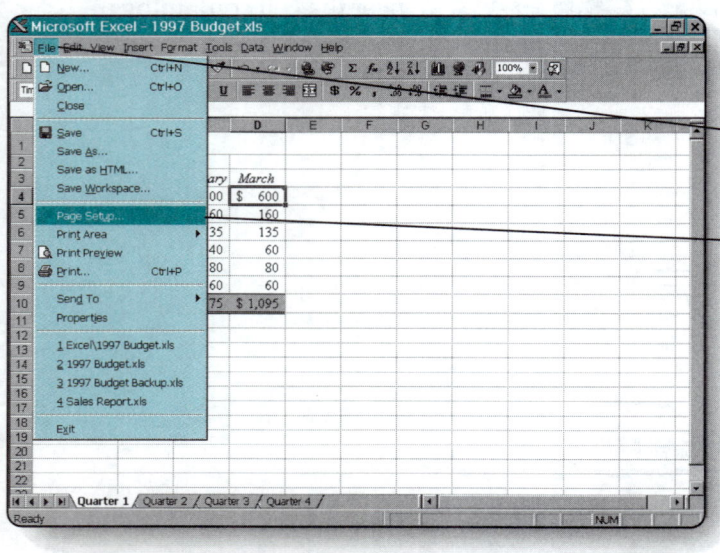

You can print comments along with your worksheet.

1. Click on **File**. The File menu will appear.

2. Click on **Page Setup**. The Page Setup dialog box will open.

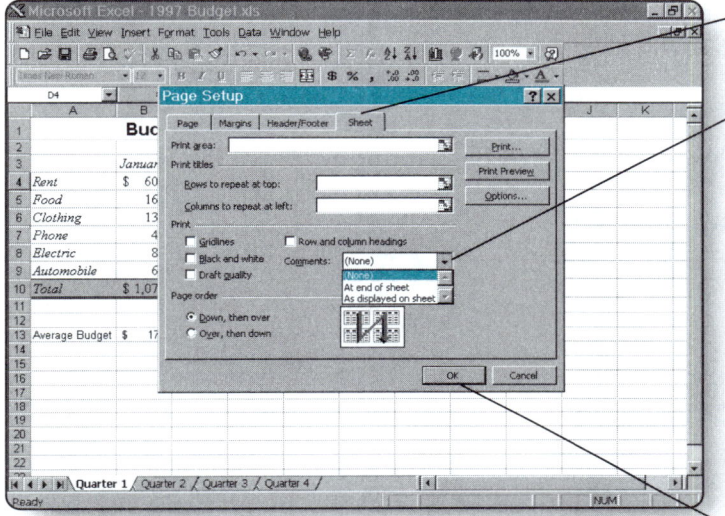

3. **Click** on the **Sheet tab**. The tab will come to the front.

4. **Click** on the **arrow** (▼) next to the Comments: list box. A list of available choices will appear.

5. **Choose** where you want to **print comments**.

If you choose to print comments where they appear on the sheet, you must display comments on the worksheet using step 7 in the preceding task.

6. **Click** on **OK**. When you print the worksheet, the comments will print in the format you selected.

CREATING A CHART

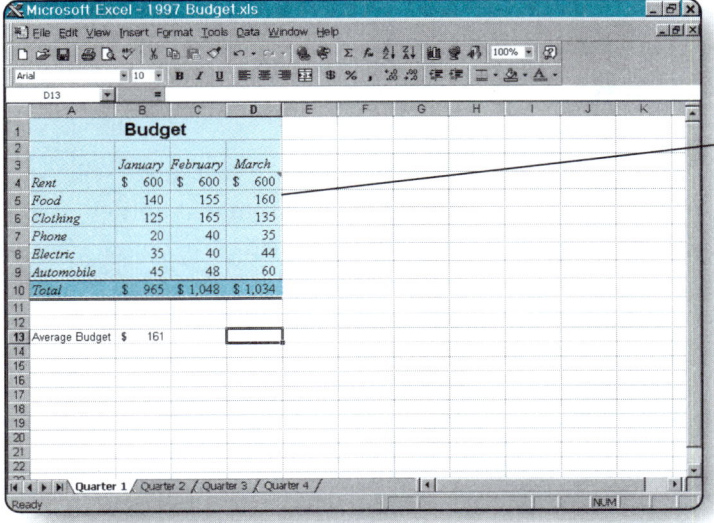

A picture is worth 1,000 words, or so the adage goes. Excel certainly makes it easy for you to display your worksheet information in chart form. For the example in this task, change the data in the worksheet so it matches the data in the figure. By following along, the chart you create will be meaningful.

1. **Click** on the **cell** representing the upper-left corner of the range you want to chart.

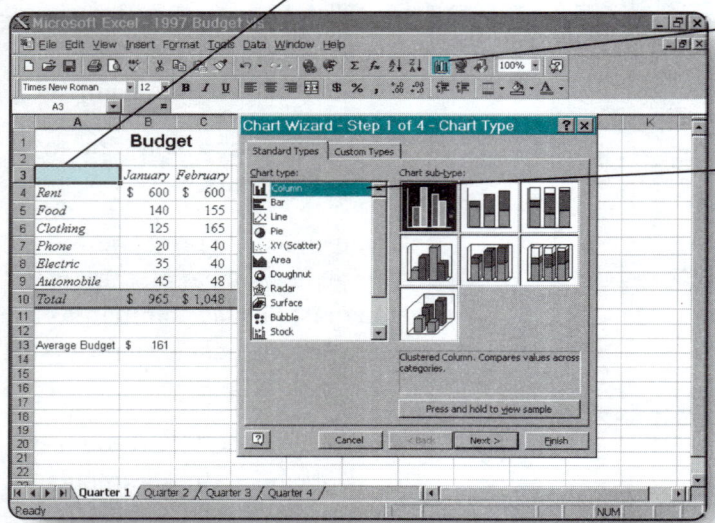

2. **Click** on the **Chart Wizard button**. The Chart Wizard – Step 1 of 4 dialog box will open.

3. **Select** a **chart type** from the Chart type: list. Depending on the type you choose, the chart sub-types on the right will change.

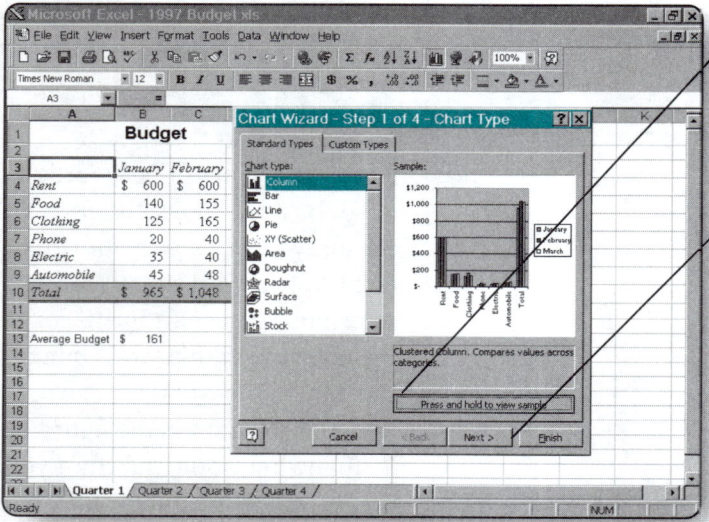

4. **Click** on the **Press and hold to view sample button.** You will see a preview of your data in the chart type you chose.

5. **Click** on **Next**. Excel will place an animated border around the data in your worksheet that it intends to chart and the Chart Wizard – Step 2 of 4 dialog box will open.

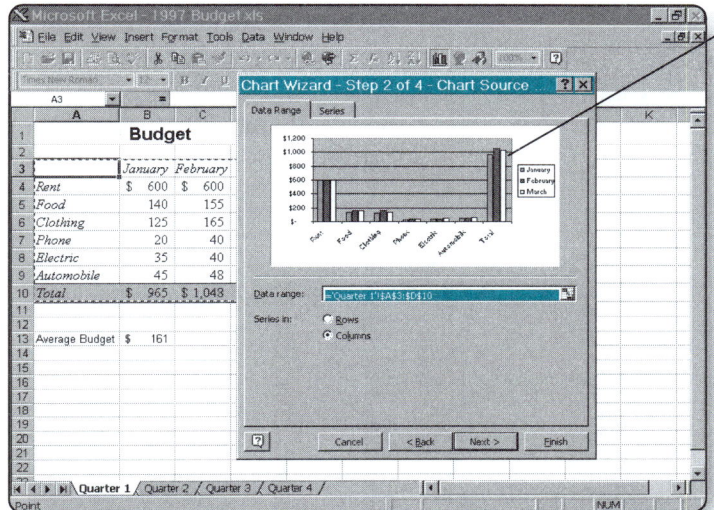

In the second Chart Wizard dialog box, Excel will display your data charted by columns—the legend shows months.

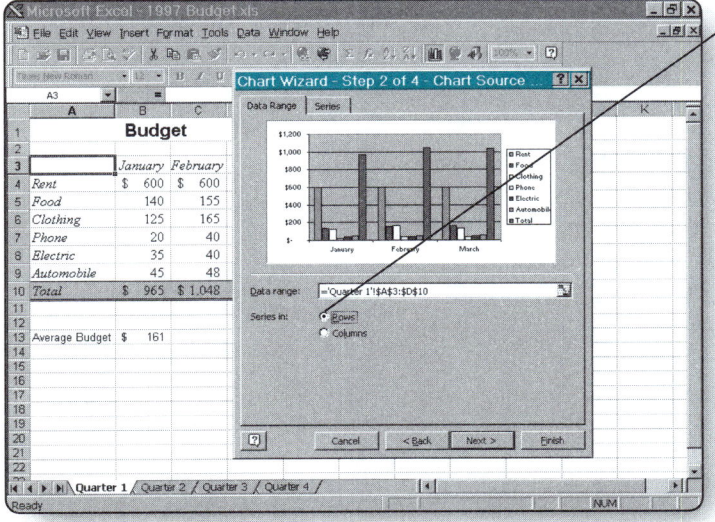

6. Click on **Rows**. Excel will redisplay your data charted by row.

NOTE

If you have a Total row in your data, Excel will include it in the chart. You should exclude that row from the range you intend to chart because it usually isn't meaningful in a chart.

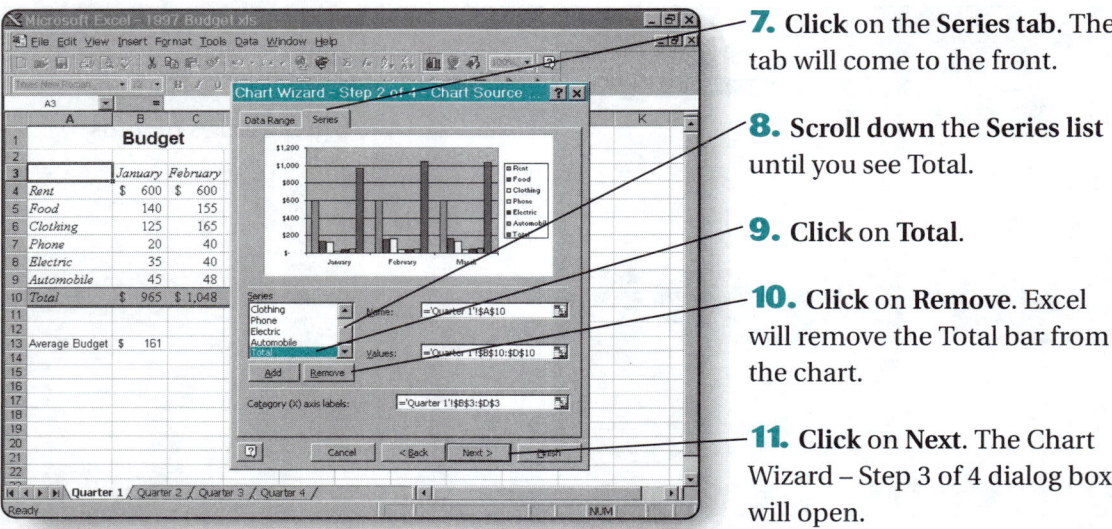

7. **Click** on the **Series tab**. The tab will come to the front.

8. **Scroll down** the **Series list** until you see Total.

9. **Click** on **Total**.

10. **Click** on **Remove**. Excel will remove the Total bar from the chart.

11. **Click** on **Next**. The Chart Wizard – Step 3 of 4 dialog box will open.

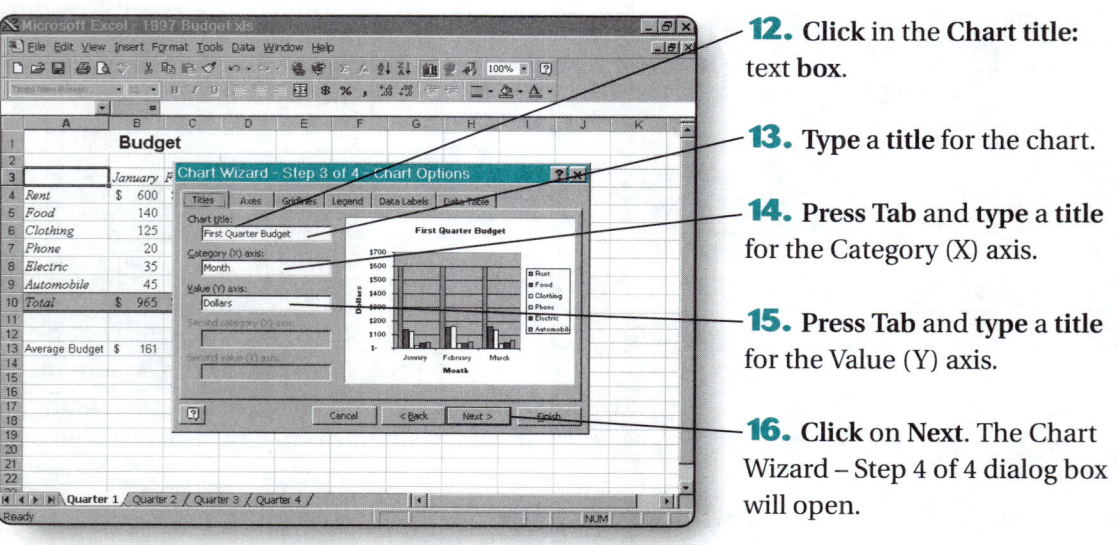

12. **Click** in the **Chart title: text box**.

13. **Type** a **title** for the chart.

14. **Press Tab** and **type** a **title** for the Category (X) axis.

15. **Press Tab** and **type** a **title** for the Value (Y) axis.

16. **Click** on **Next**. The Chart Wizard – Step 4 of 4 dialog box will open.

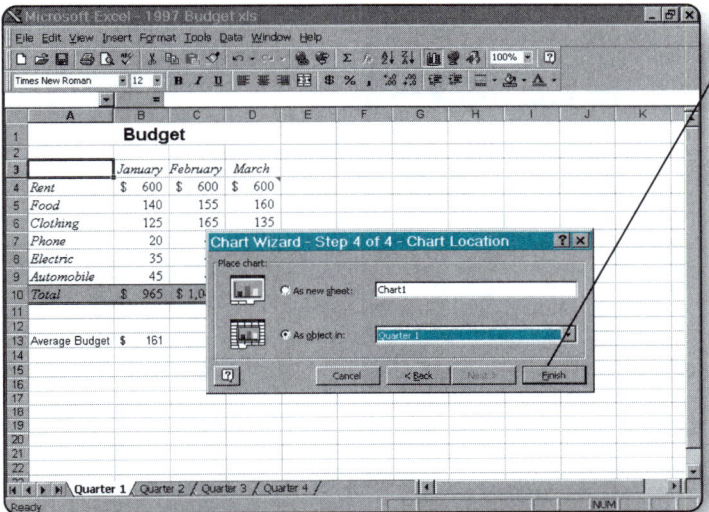

17. Click on **Finish.** The chart will appear in your worksheet along with your data.

Excel will display the chart and the Chart toolbar.

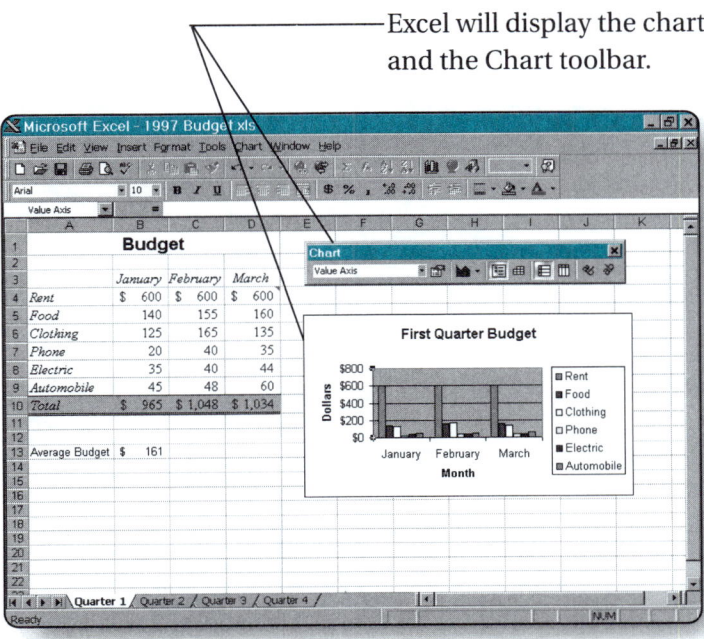

TIP

To move the chart so it doesn't cover your data, click on the chart to select it—you'll see small black squares, called *handles*, surrounding it. Move the mouse pointer inside the selected chart (you'll see a ScreenTip that says, "Chart Area") and then drag the chart to wherever you want it to appear. You can resize the chart by dragging any handle.

You can move the Chart toolbar by dragging its title bar. You can click anywhere in the worksheet to cancel the selection of the chart and to hide the Chart toolbar.

PART III REVIEW QUESTIONS

1. **What is a cell?** *See Chapter 8*

2. **How do you copy cells using drag-and-drop?** *See Chapter 8*

3. **How do you align text within a cell?** *See Chapter 9*

4. **How do you make cell entries appear like dollars?** *See Chapter 9*

5. **How do you multiply two cells?** *See Chapter 10*

6. **How do you sum a column of numbers?** *See Chapter 10*

7. **How do you rename a worksheet?** *See Chapter 11*

8. **How do you insert a row?** *See Chapter 11*

9. **How do you add boldface or italics to cells?** *See Chapter 11*

10. **How do you create a chart?** *See Chapter 11*

PART IV

PowerPoint

Excel 8
es Data
ed.xls
ead-1.xls
leadblnk.xls
LEADS.xls
leadtst.xls
Mcn95v94.xls
News Flash.xls
Sales Report.xls

12 Creating and Viewing Presentations

You use PowerPoint to create presentations. Each PowerPoint presentation file consists of *slides* that contain information you want to convey to an audience. Think of PowerPoint slides as pages of your presentation. Don't confuse PowerPoint presentation slides with 35 mm slides, which are only one of the ways you can store (and present) your presentation. You can also store your PowerPoint presentation slides on overhead transparencies, or you can simply print them on paper and give them to your audience. And, if you prefer, you can create a computer slide show in PowerPoint as well.

PowerPoint creates each presentation file based on a *template*. A template contains predefined information, such as text and colors. Some templates contain more information that may help you, such as sample text. In this chapter, you'll learn how to:

✦ Create a presentation using a template

✦ Change views

CREATING A PRESENTATION

1. **Start PowerPoint**. The PowerPoint dialog box will open, and you will choose a method to start working in PowerPoint.

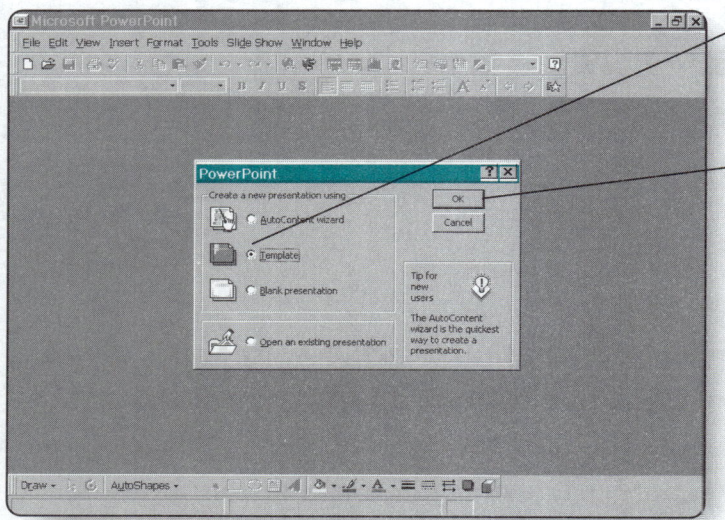

2. **Click** on **Template**. The option button will be selected.

3. **Click** on **OK**. The New Presentation dialog box will open.

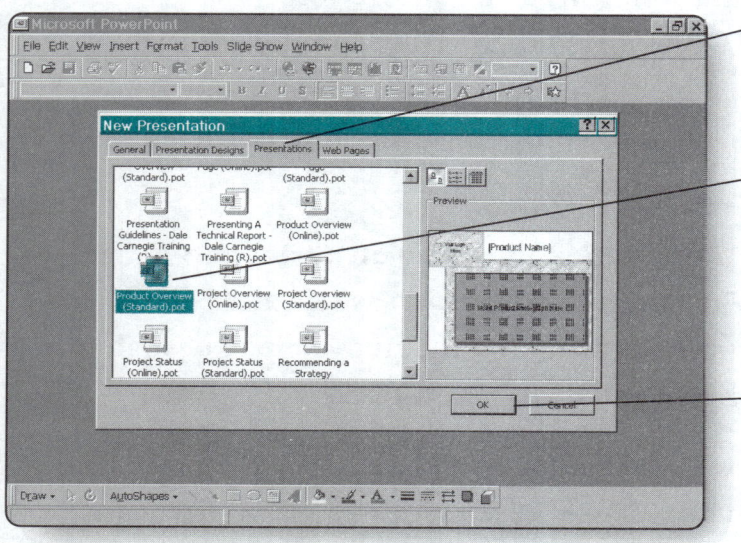

4. **Click** on the **Presentations tab**. The tab will come to the front.

5. **Click** on the **template** on which you will base your presentation. You will see a preview of the template on the right side of the dialog box.

6. **Click** on **OK**.

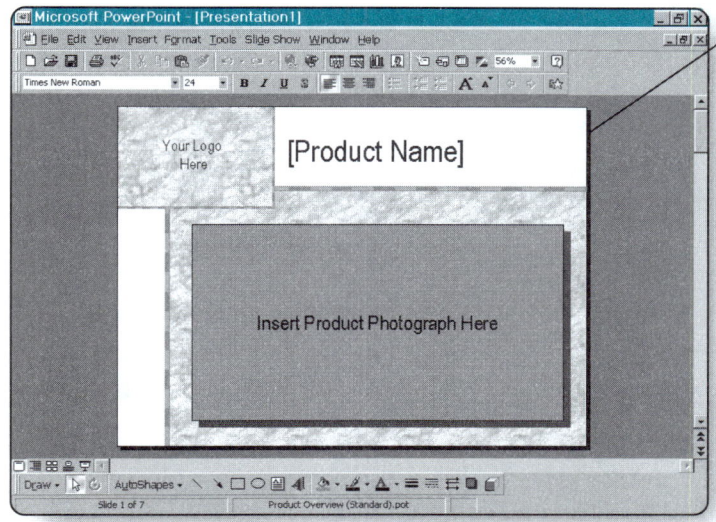

PowerPoint will display your new presentation in Slide view.

SWITCHING VIEWS

You can display your presentation in one of five views in PowerPoint. In the following task, you will explore each of the views in PowerPoint and see how you move from slide to slide in each view.

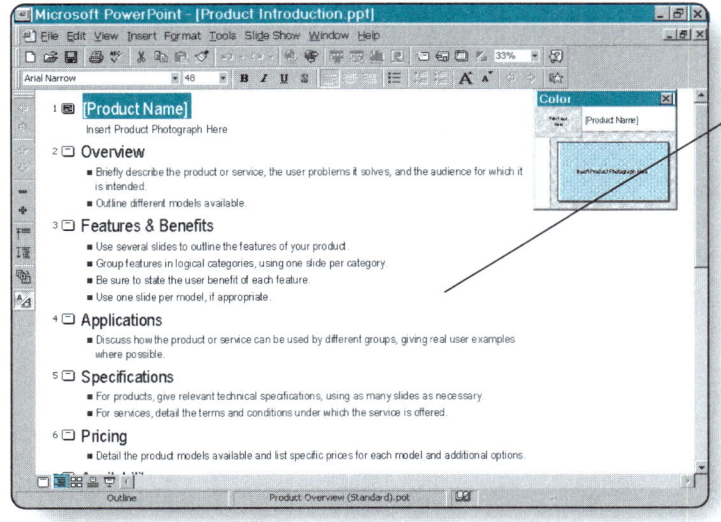

Outline View

In Outline view, your presentation appears like an outline you would use when organizing your thoughts. Use Outline view to help you organize your presentation's information. In the default Outline view, you can see all the information on each slide; the title of each slide appears as a heading, and the information on the slide appears below.

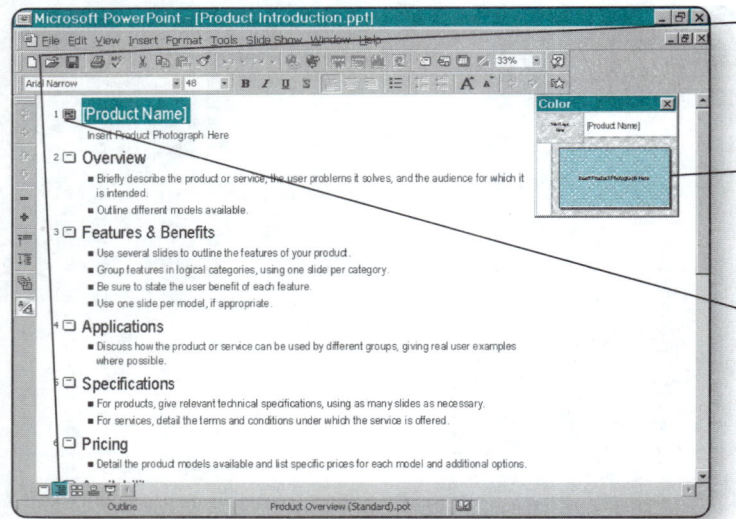

1. **Click** on the **Outline View button**. PowerPoint will switch the presentation to Outline view.

In Outline view, you will also see a window showing a miniature version of your slide.

A number and an icon will appear to the left of each slide. You can click on an icon to select that slide.

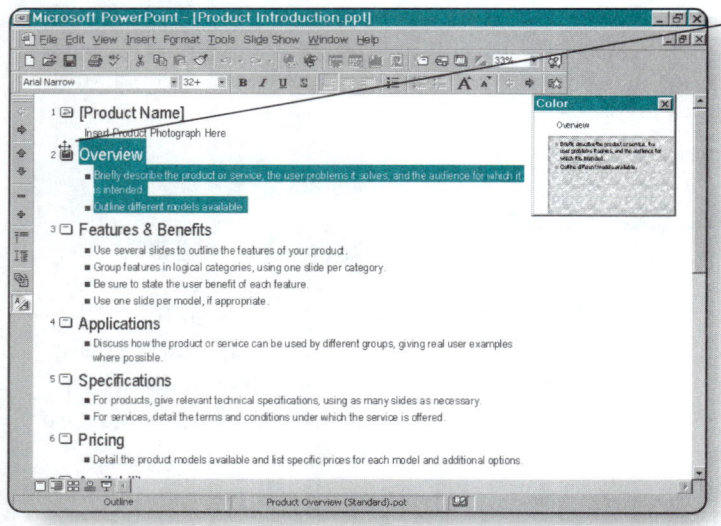

2. **Click** on a **slide icon**. As you move the mouse pointer over the slide icon, the shape of the mouse pointer will change to a four-headed arrow, and PowerPoint will select all the information for that slide.

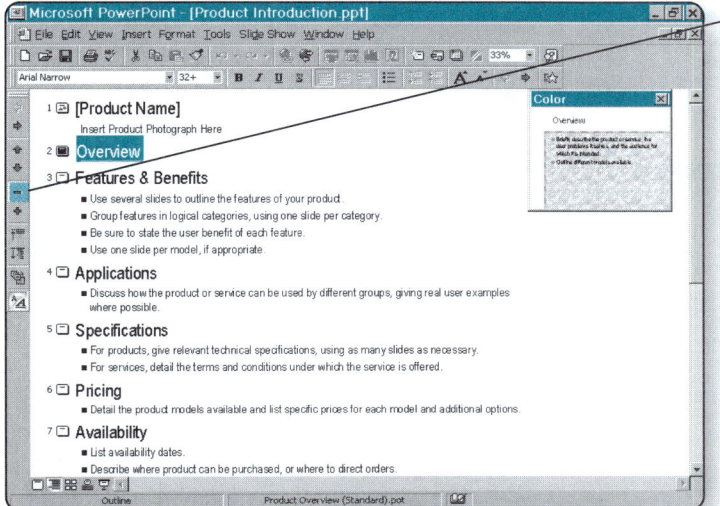

3. **Click** on the **Collapse button**. PowerPoint will hide the contents of the selected slide.

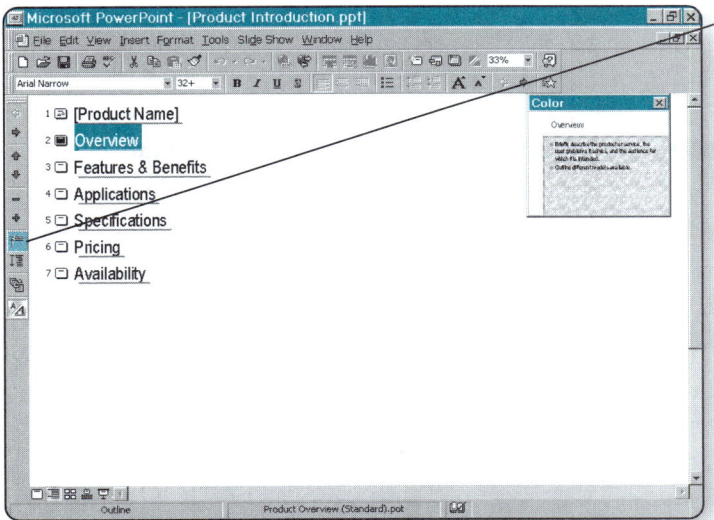

4. **Click** on the **Collapse All button**. PowerPoint will hide the contents of all slides.

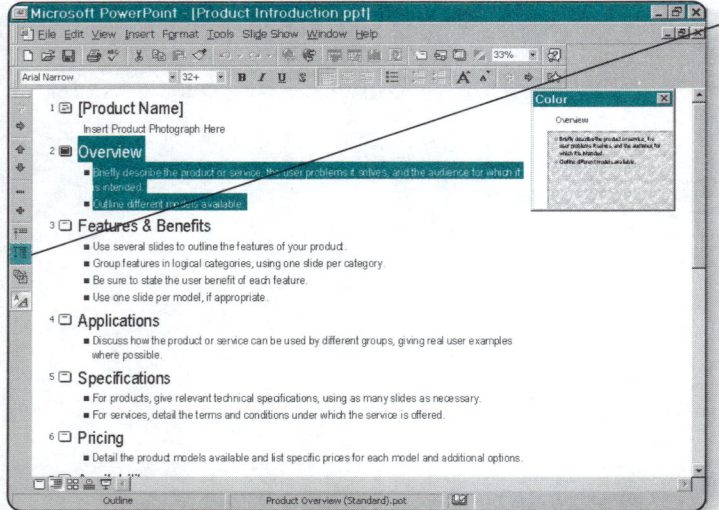

5. **Click** on the **Expand All button**. PowerPoint will display the contents of all slides.

Slide View

Slide view shows you a close-up image of your slide the way it will appear when you print it.

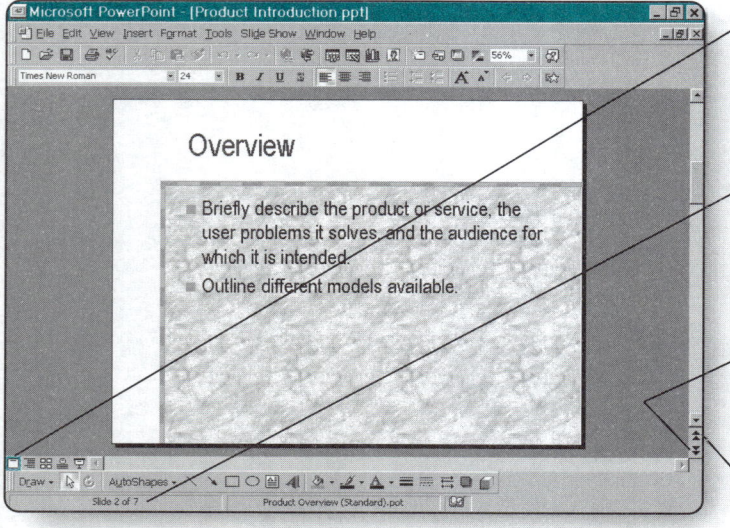

1. **Click** on the **Slide View button**. You will see a single slide—the one you previously selected in Outline view.

In Slide view, the status bar tells you the number of slides in your presentation and which slide you are viewing.

2. **Click** on the **Next Slide button**. The next slide in the presentation will appear.

Similarly, clicking on the Previous Slide button will display the previous slide in the presentation.

Slide Sorter View

Use Slide Sorter view to see a miniature view of each slide in the presentation. Slide Sorter view provides an easy way to view the overall effects of your presentation and check for variety in slide appearance—variety helps keep your audience awake. You can't edit slides in Slide Sorter view, but you can change the order in which slides appear in Slide Sorter view.

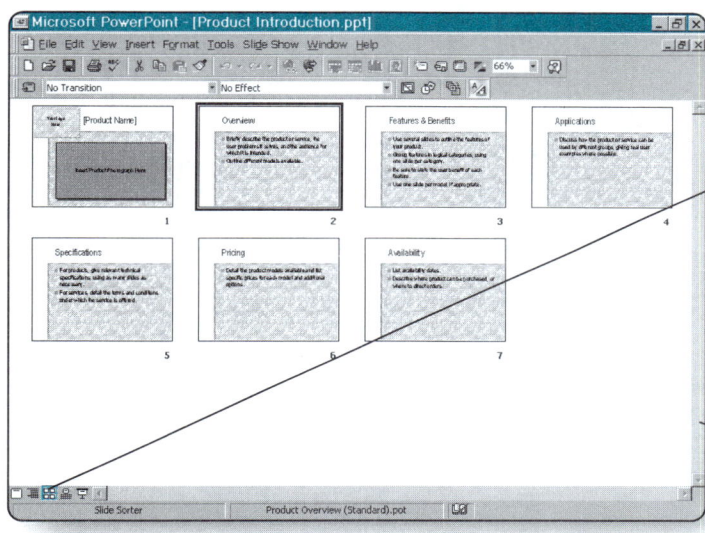

1. **Click** on the **Slide Sorter View button**. You will see all the slides in your presentation. A dark border will appear around the selected slide.

TIP

If you can't see all the slides in your presentation, use the vertical scroll bar to scroll down and view additional slides.

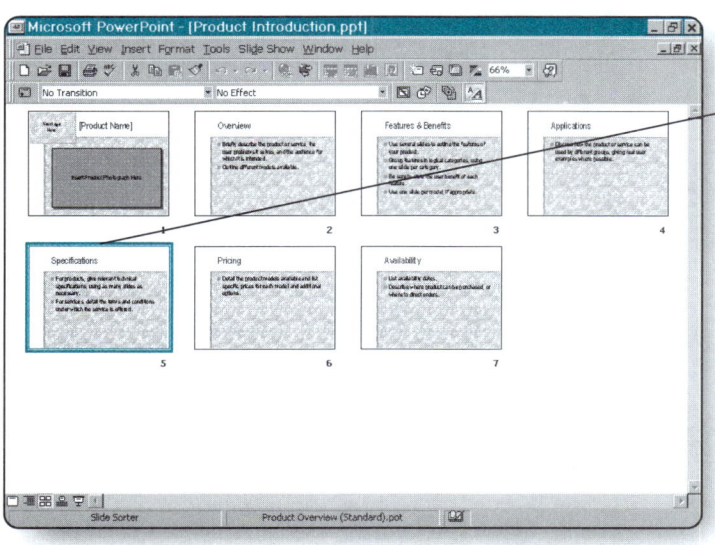

2. **Click** on a **slide**. PowerPoint will select the slide, and the black border will appear around the slide.

Notes Page View

You can create speaker notes—notes to remind yourself of what you want to say when a slide appears. You store these notes in Notes Page view. In Chapter 13, you'll learn how to print these notes.

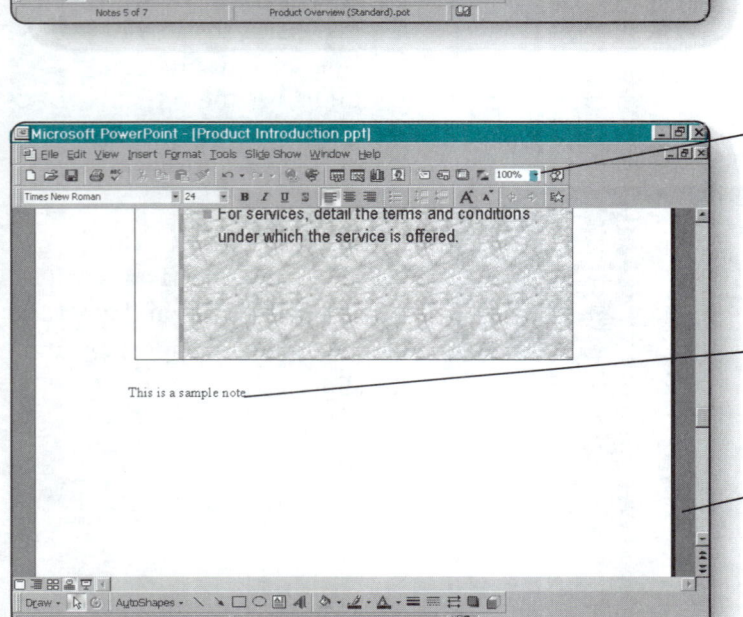

1. Click on the **Notes Page View button**. The selected slide will appear onscreen, at the top portion of an 8½ x 11 page. You can add notes for the slide on the bottom portion of the page.

2. Click in the **Notes** part of the page. A flashing insertion point will appear inside a graphics box.

3. Click on the **arrow** (▼) of the Zoom list box. A list of available zoom percentages will appear.

4. Click on a **Zoom Size**.

5. Type the **text** you want to store as a note for the selected slide.

6. Click anywhere in the gray area onscreen. PowerPoint will accept the changes to the graphics box.

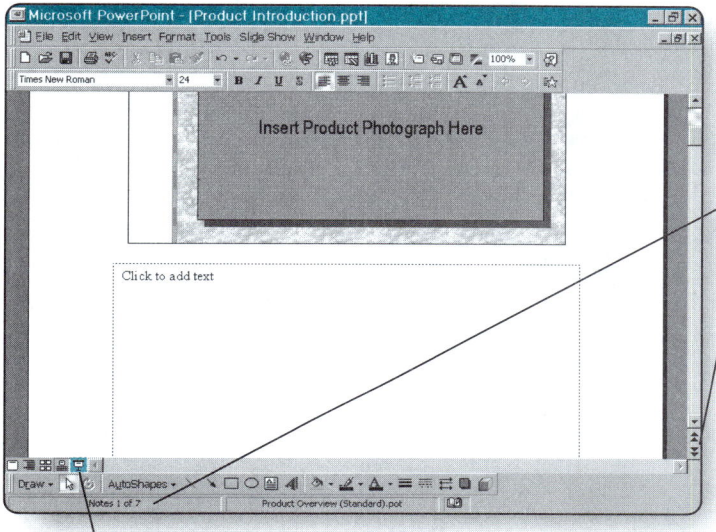

Slide Show View

Use Slide Show view to display your presentation onscreen.

1. **Click** on the **Previous Slide button repeatedly**, if you're still in Notes Page view, until you see the first slide of the presentation.

2. **Click** on the **Slide Show button**. All screen elements will disappear, and the image of the first slide will fill your screen.

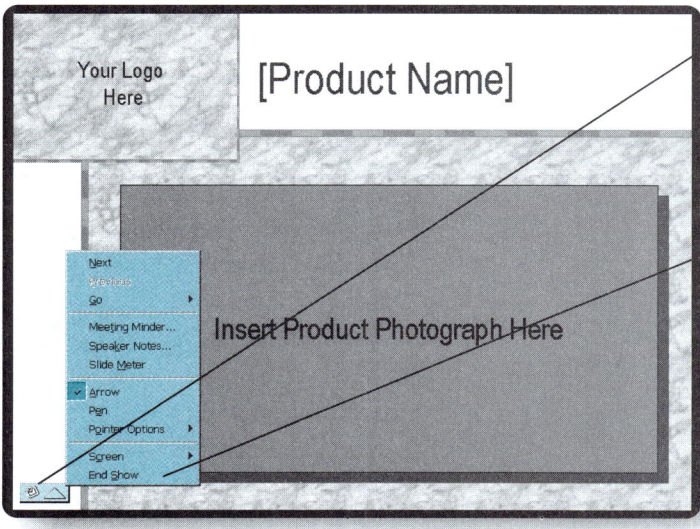

3. **Click** on the **button** in the lower-left corner. A shortcut menu will appear—use this menu to control the behavior of the slide show.

4. **Click** on **End Show**. You will return to PowerPoint.

> **TIP**
>
> You can press the spacebar to advance the slide show by one slide, and you can press the Esc key to end the slide show at any time.

13 Editing a Presentation

Although PowerPoint's templates provide some rather impressive slides, you'll need to make modifications to any presentation you create. In this chapter, you'll learn how to:

- ◆ Add and delete slides
- ◆ Rearrange the order of slides
- ◆ Change a presentation's background appearance
- ◆ Change a slide's layout
- ◆ Edit text on a slide
- ◆ Print a slide

ADDING AND DELETING SLIDES

You'll be working in the presentation you created in Chapter 12. If it is not open onscreen, use the techniques you learned in Chapter 3 to open it.

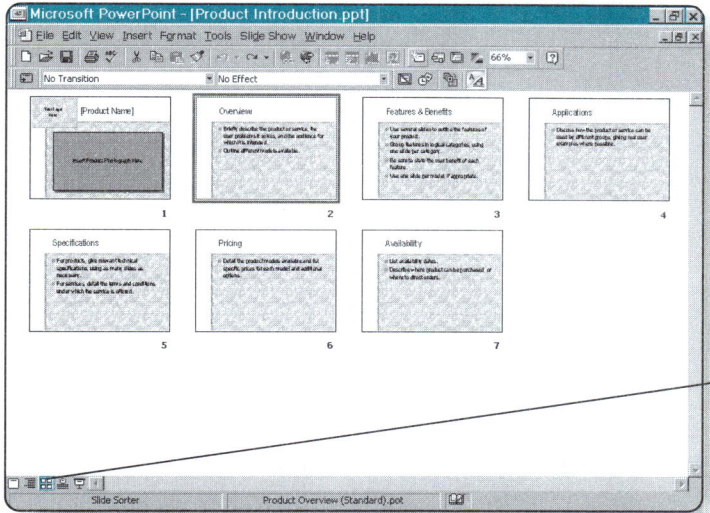

Adding Slides

You can add a slide to a presentation at any time. In this task, you will learn how to add a slide that contains bullets. PowerPoint will add slides immediately after the selected slide.

1. Click on the **Slide Sorter View button**. You will see all the slides in the presentation.

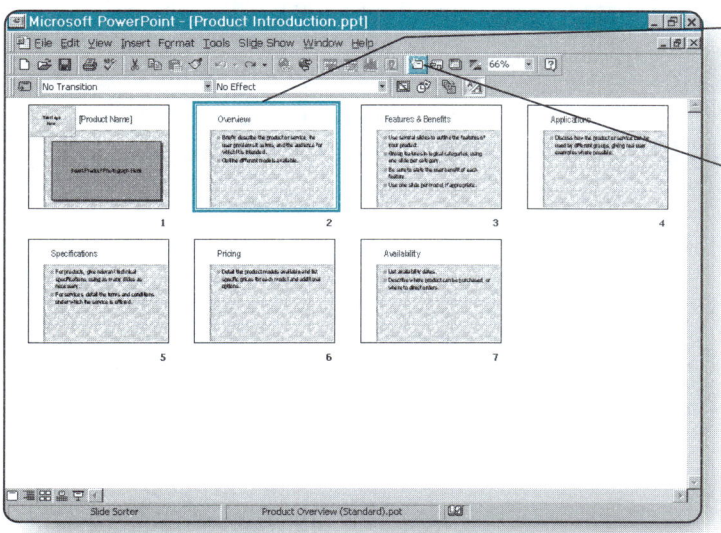

2. Click on a **slide**. The new slide will appear after the selected slide.

3. Click on the **New Slide button**.

The New Slide dialog box will open with the Bulleted List slide layout suggested.

4. Click on **OK**.

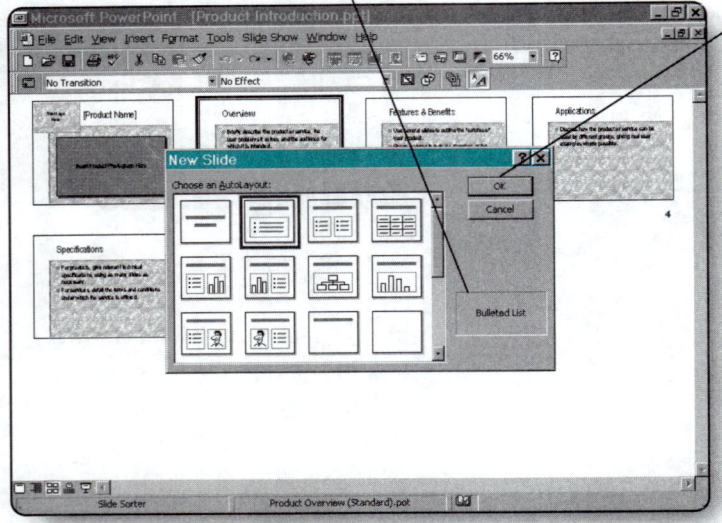

PowerPoint will add a blank slide formatted to receive bullets after the slide you selected. The new slide will be selected.

5. Click on the **Slide View button**. It will be much easier to add text to the new slide in Slide view.

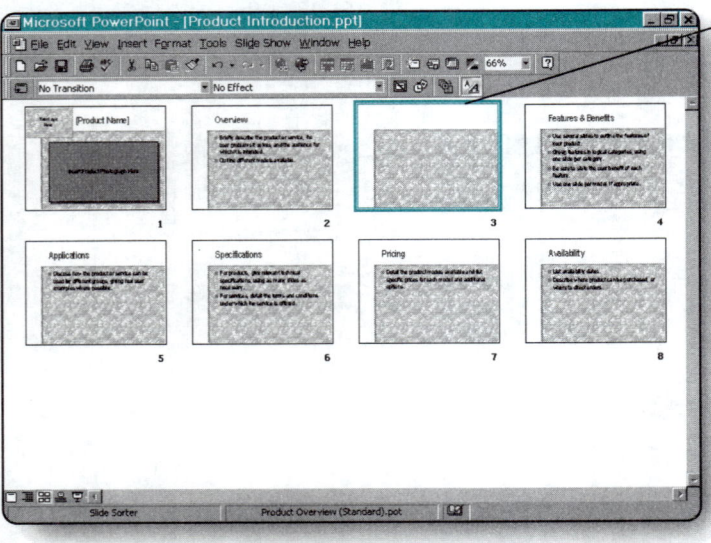

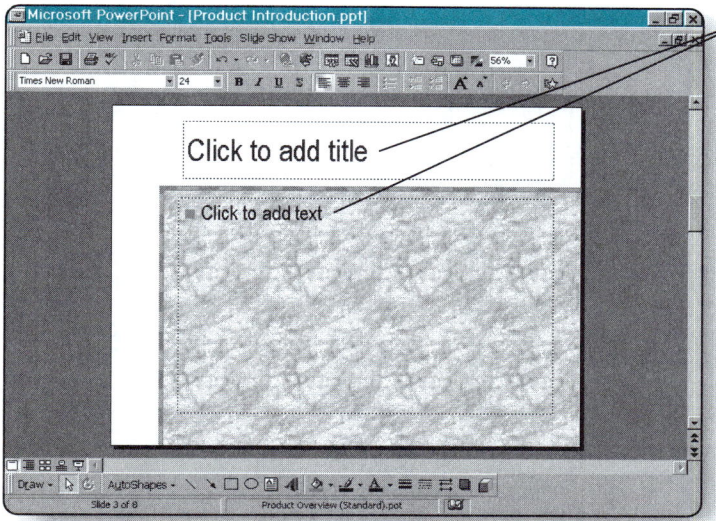

PowerPoint will redisplay the new blank slide. Notice that it contains instruction blocks that you didn't see in Slide Sorter view.

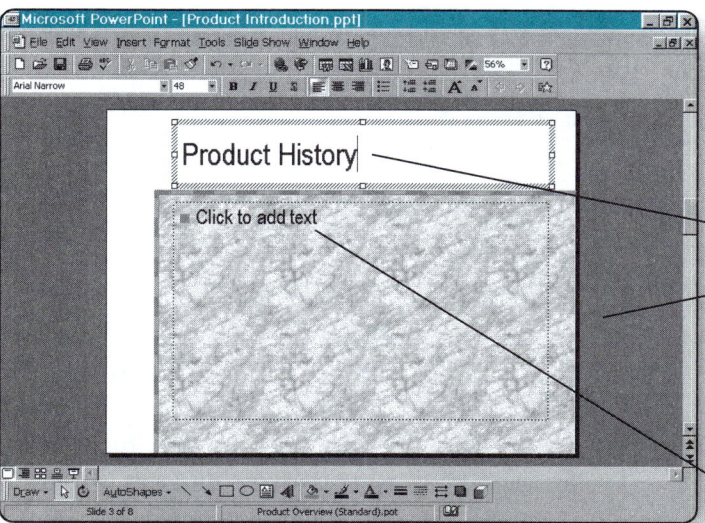

6. **Click** on **Click to add title**. Those words will disappear and will be replaced by a text object box containing an insertion point.

7. **Type** a **title** for the slide.

8. **Click** on the **gray area** onscreen. Both the insertion point and the handles that surrounded the text object box will disappear.

9. **Click** on **Click to add text**. Those words will disappear and will be replaced by a text object box containing an insertion point.

NOTE

Clicking on the gray area indicates that you are done typing and ready to take some other action.

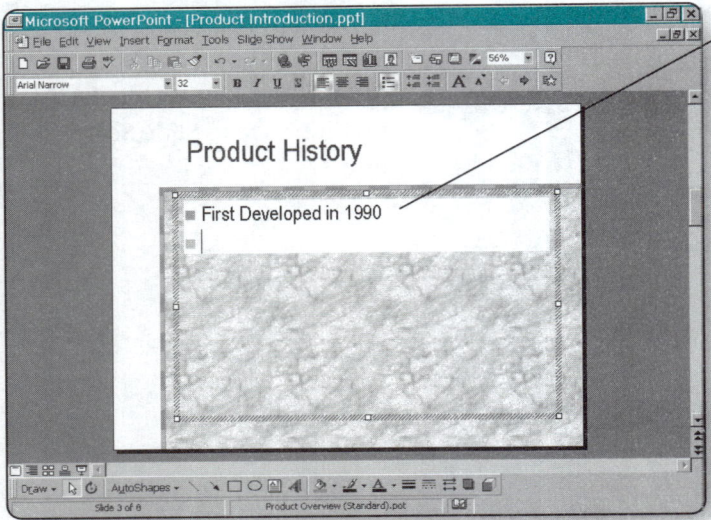

10. **Type** some **text** and **press** the **Enter key**. PowerPoint will start a new line preceded by a bullet.

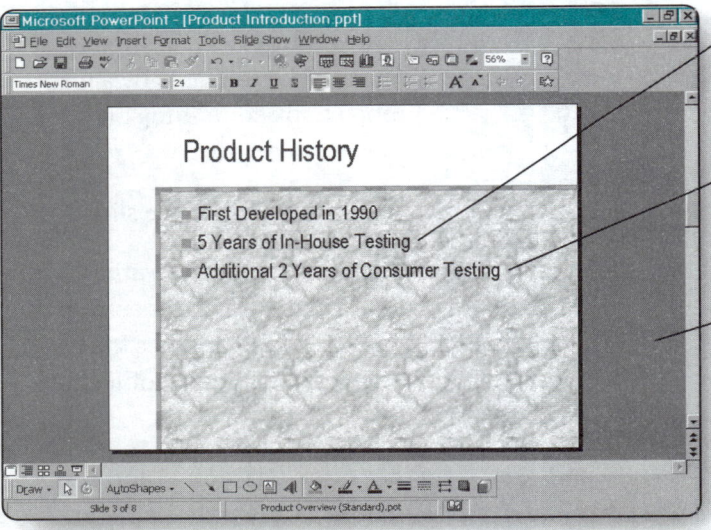

11. **Type** more **text** and **press** the **Enter key**. An additional bullet will appear.

12. **Type text** for each bullet you need until you finish typing the last bullet.

13. **Click** on the **gray area** onscreen. The insertion point and the handles that surrounded the text object box will disappear and you will see the bullets you typed onscreen.

Deleting Slides

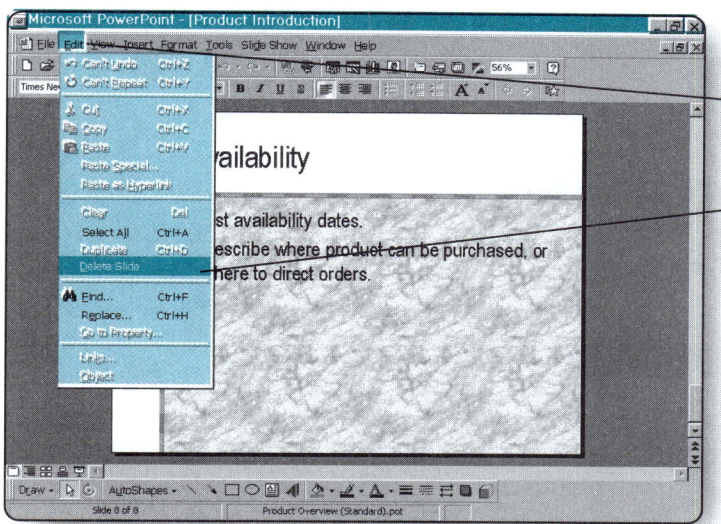

1. **Select** a **slide** to delete.

2. **Click** on **Edit**. The Edit menu will appear.

3. **Click** on **Delete Slide**. PowerPoint will delete the selected slide.

TIP

PowerPoint will display the slide that appeared immediately before the slide you deleted.

REARRANGING SLIDES

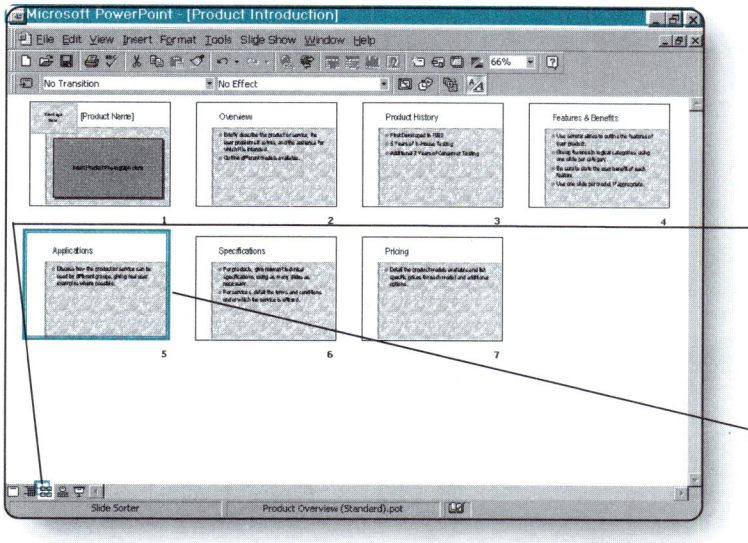

You might decide that you'd rather display slides in an order other than the one you originally created. Use Slide Sorter view to rearrange slides.

1. **Click** on the **Slide Sorter View button**. All the slides in your presentation will appear. A dark border will appear around the selected slide.

2. **Click** on the **slide** you intend to move. The slide will be selected.

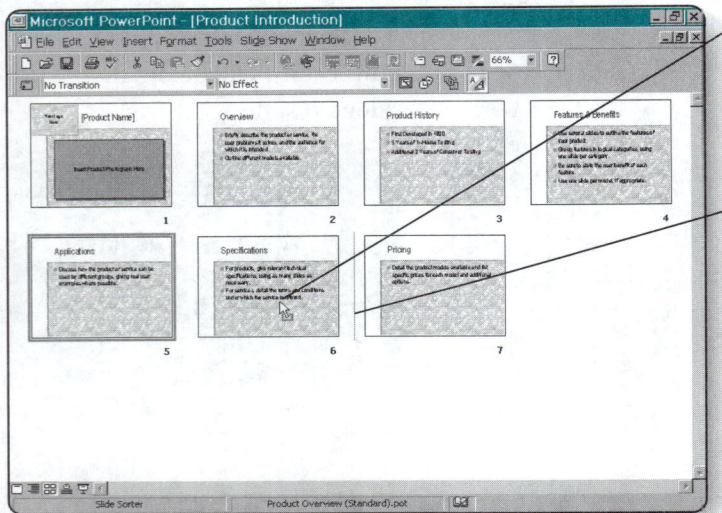

3. Drag the selected slide to its new location. The mouse pointer shape will change slightly as you drag.

You will see a large gray vertical bar as you drag. This bar represents the location where the new slide will appear when you drop the slide.

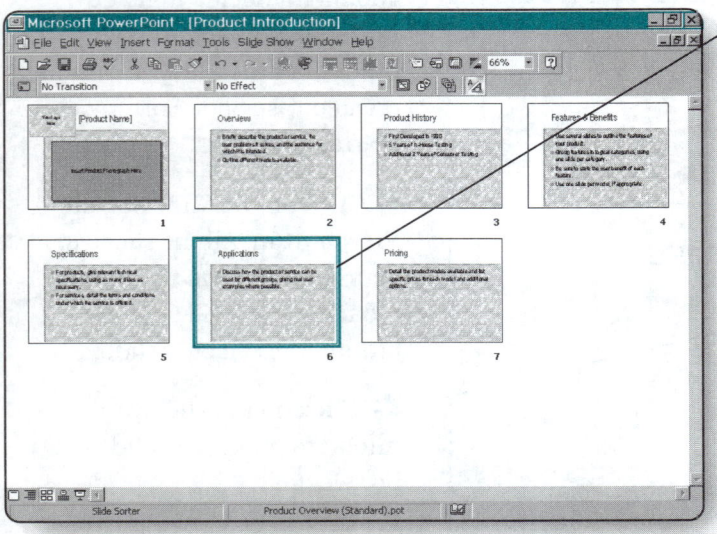

4. Release the mouse button. The slide will appear in its new position.

CHANGING PRESENTATION DESIGNS

If you don't really like the background appearance of your presentation, you don't need to start over; you can simply change the presentation design.

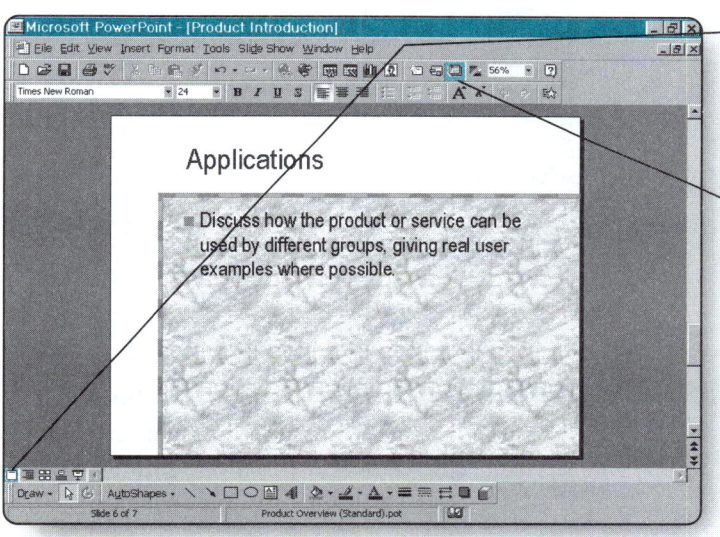

1. **Click** on the **Slide View button**. You will be able to see the appearance of the slides better in Slide view.

2. **Click** on the **Apply Design button**. The Apply Design dialog box will open.

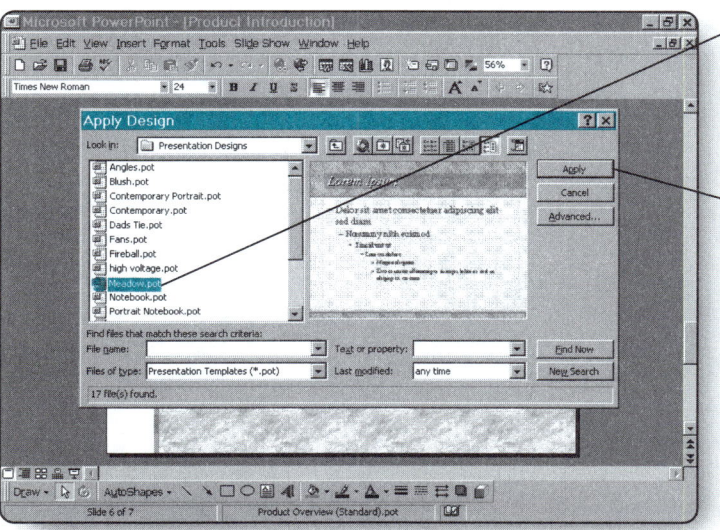

3. **Click** on a **design** in the list on the left side of the dialog box. A sample of the design will appear to the right.

4. **Click** on **Apply**.

TIP
You can preview the appearance of any design by clicking on it.

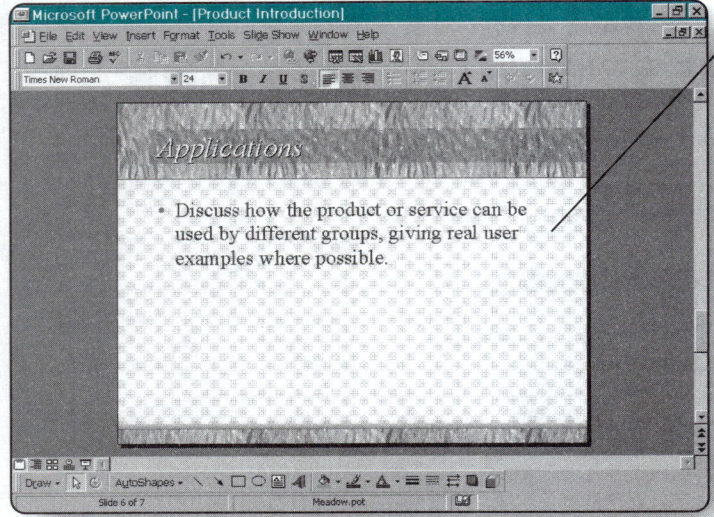

PowerPoint will redisplay the selected slide in your presentation using the design you chose.

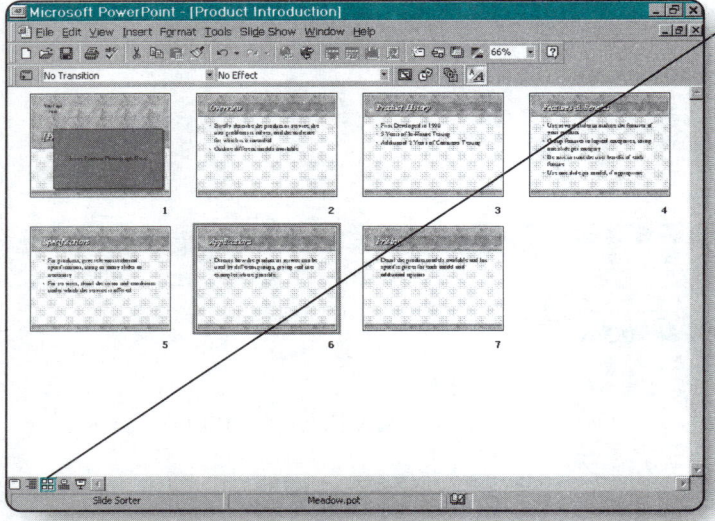

5. **Click** on the **Slide Sorter View button.** You will see that PowerPoint applied the new design to all slides in your presentation.

CHANGING SLIDE LAYOUTS

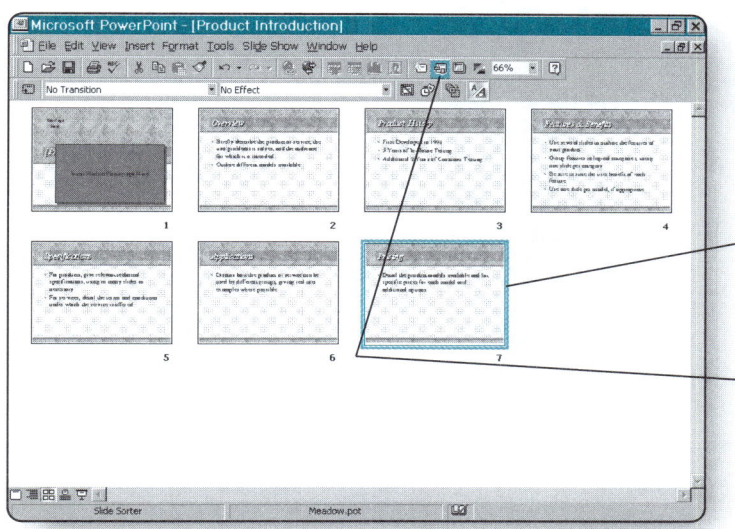

You might find that you need to change the layout of a slide. For example, you may need to change a bullet layout to a table layout.

1. **Click** on the **slide** whose layout you want to change. The slide will be selected.

2. **Click** on the **Slide Layout button**. The Slide Layout dialog box will open.

On the left side of the dialog box, you will see visual represen-tations of possible slide layout styles. In the lower-right corner, you will see a description of the selected layout that you can use to make sure you select the correct slide layout.

3. **Click** on a **layout**.

4. **Click** on **Apply**. The layout of the selected slide will change to the layout you chose. You will not notice the change in Slide Sorter view.

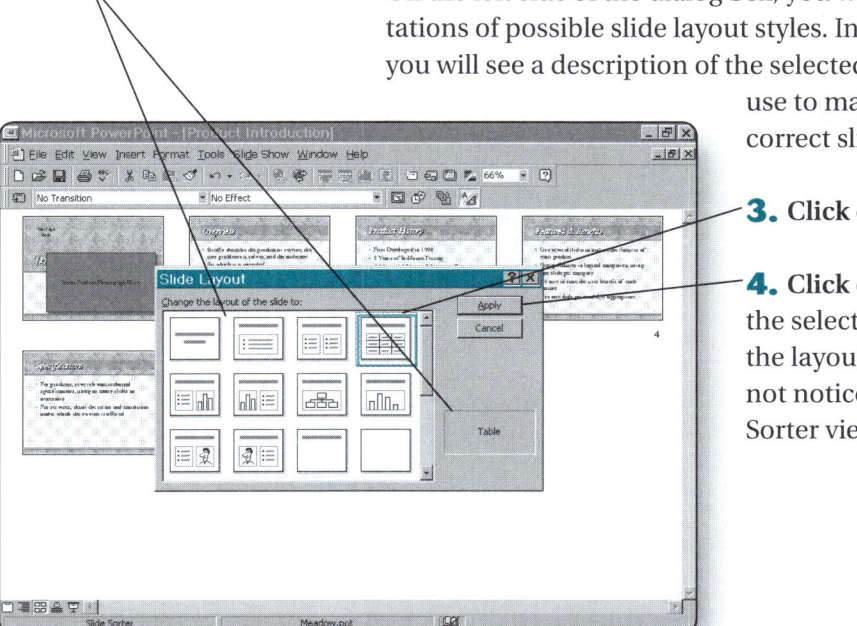

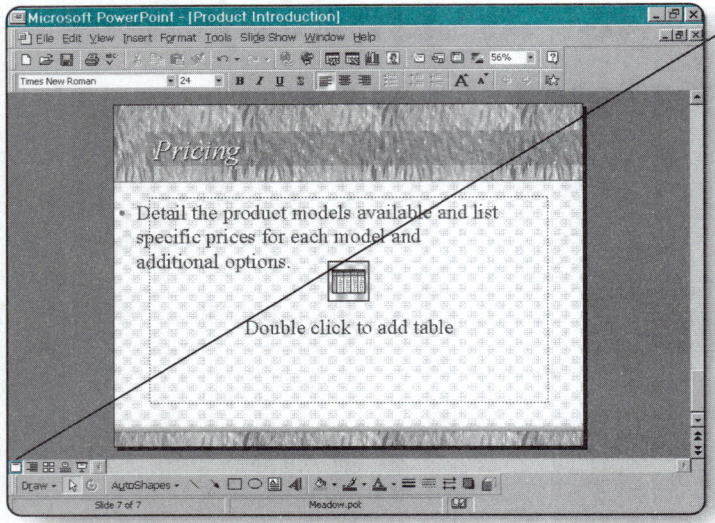

5. **Click** on the **Slide View button**. The selected slide will reappear with instructions for using the new layout.

EDITING TEXT OBJECTS

You can edit the text that appears on your slides in a variety of ways. You'll find working from either Slide view or Outline view easiest.

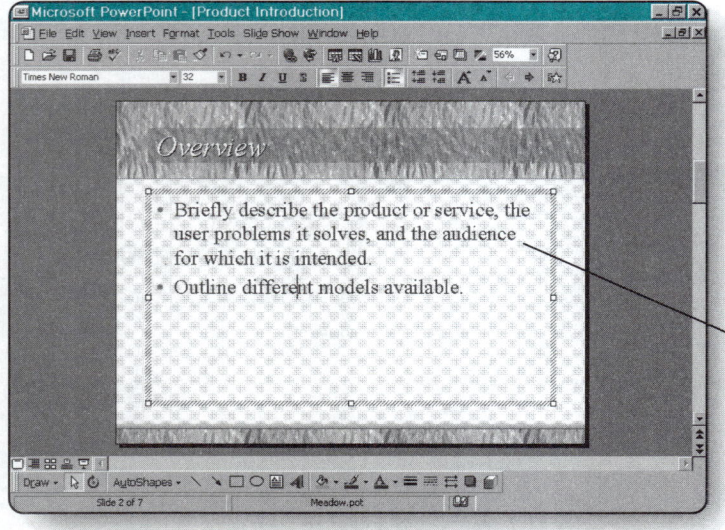

Changing Text

You'll want to change sample text that appears automatically on slides.

1. **Click** on a **slide** that contains sample text.

2. **Click** on the **sample text** that appears on the slide. PowerPoint will display the text in a text object box.

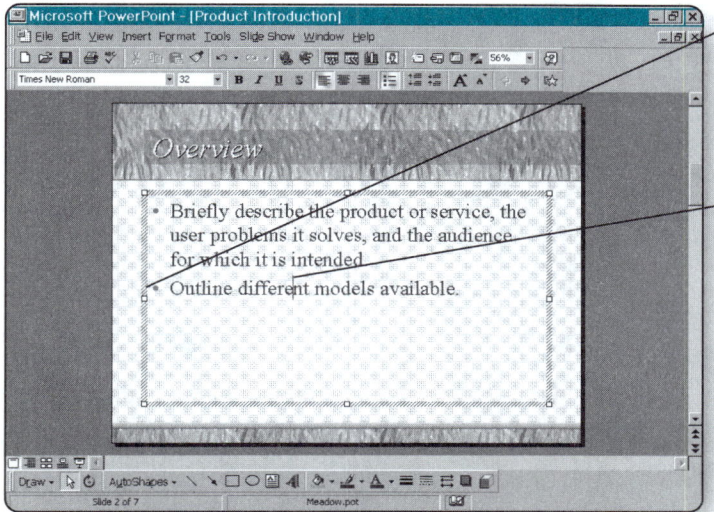

Text object boxes appear surrounded by a border that contains small white squares called *handles*.

You will also see an insertion point in the text object box.

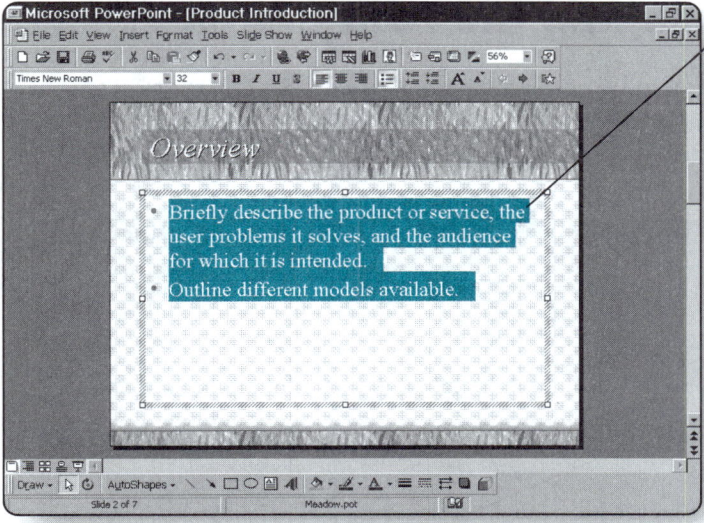

3. **Select all** of the **text** in the box. Use the same technique to select text that you used when selecting text in Word.

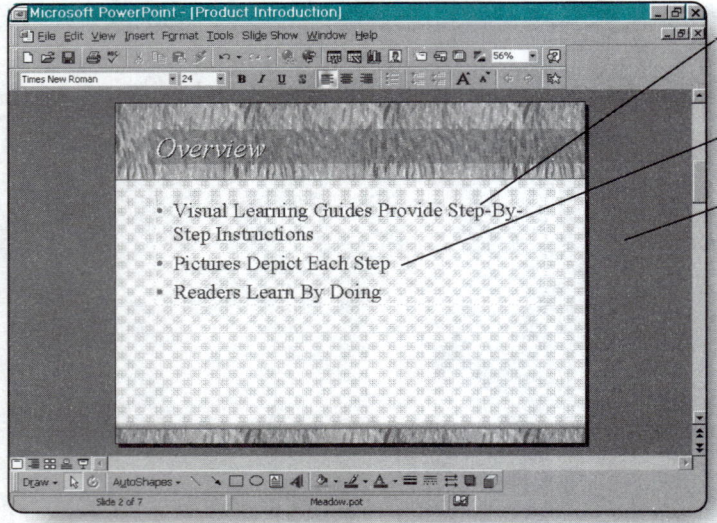

4. **Type text** to replace the sample text and **press** the **Enter key**.

5. **Type** more **text**, if necessary.

6. **Click** on the **gray area** onscreen. Your text changes will be accepted.

TIP

If you're more comfortable working in a word processing environment, switch to Outline view and make your changes to text in that view.

Changing the Font

You might want to change the font of text in a slide. In the previous task, you changed text in Slide view. In this task, you'll change the font in Outline view.

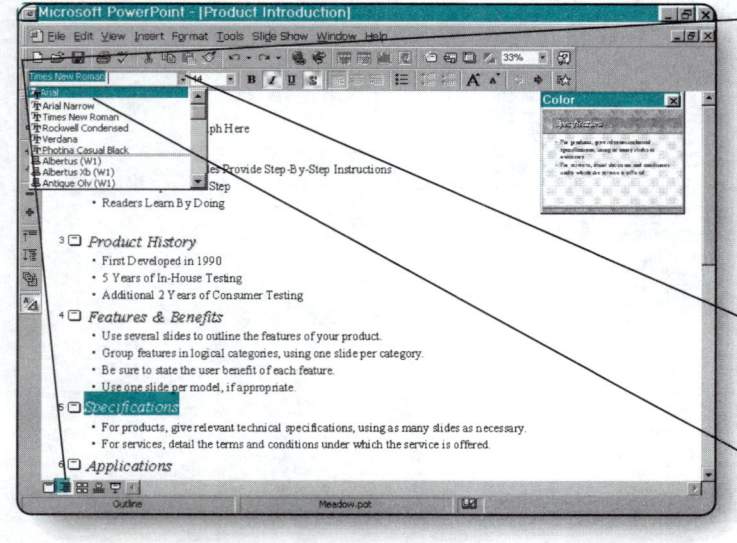

1. **Click** on the **Outline View button**. The presentation will appear in Outline view, and the title for the current slide will be selected.

2. **Select** the **text** you want to change.

3. **Click** on the **arrow** (▼) next to the Font list box. A list of available fonts will appear.

4. **Click** on the **font** you want to use.

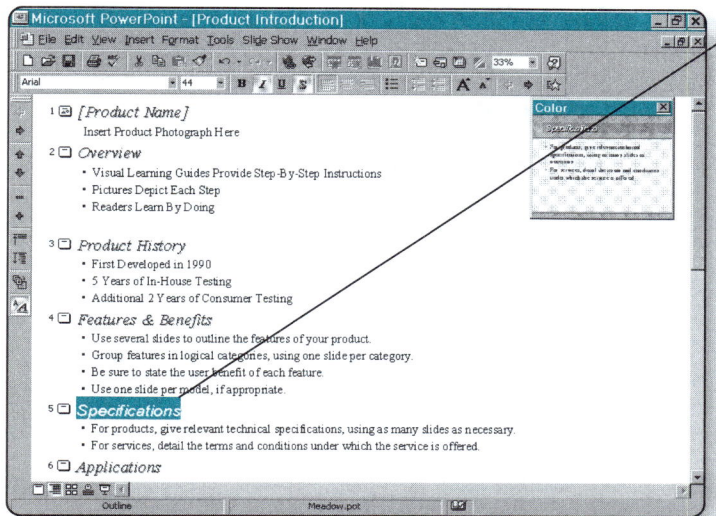

The font of the selected text will change.

TIP

You can change font size using the following steps. In step 3, click on the arrow (▼) next to the Font Size list box and in step 4, click on the font size you want to use.

Sizing a Text Object Box

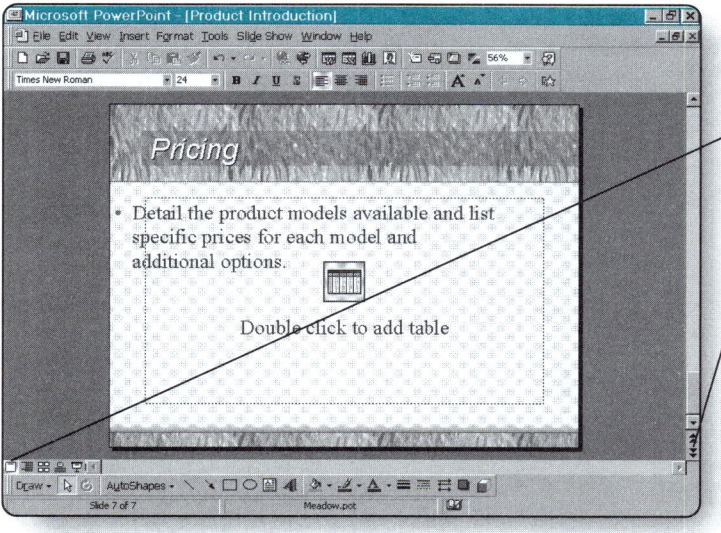

You might need to change the size of a text object box.

1. **Click** on the **Slide View button**. The presentation will appear in Slide view.

2. **Click** on the **Next Slide button** to select a slide.

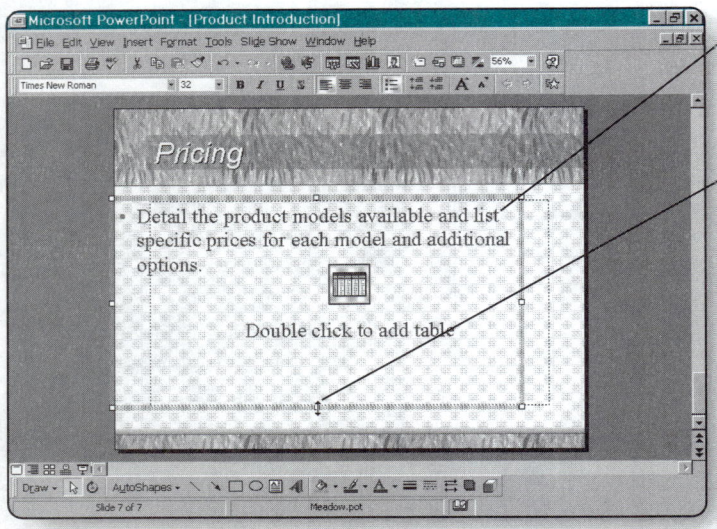

3. **Click** on a **text object**. Handles will appear around the object.

4. **Move** the **mouse pointer** over any handle. The shape of the mouse pointer will change to a two-headed arrow.

5. **Drag** the **mouse pointer** up.

The mouse pointer will change to a plus sign and the boundary of the text object box will shrink.

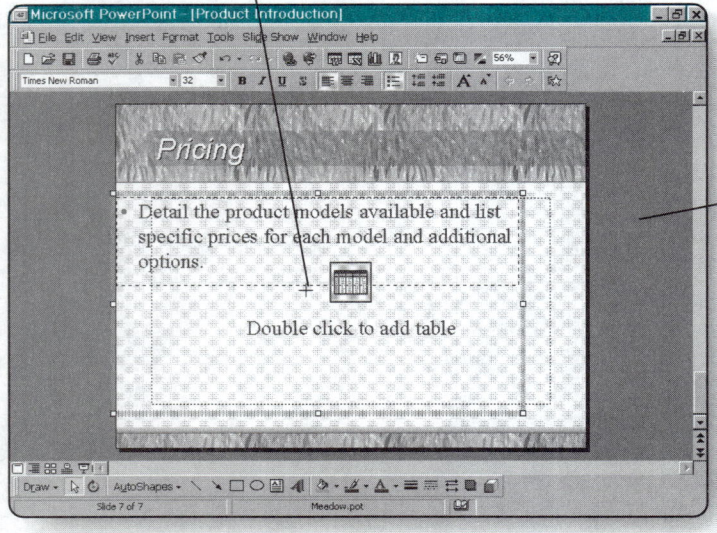

6. **Release** the **mouse button** when the boundary appears immediately below the last line of text in the box.

7. **Click** on the **gray area** onscreen. The change will be made.

TIP

You might see the mouse pointer change to a four-headed arrow. When the mouse pointer appears as a four-headed arrow, dragging will move the text object.

Deleting a Text Object

You might find that you need to delete a text object on a slide without deleting the slide.

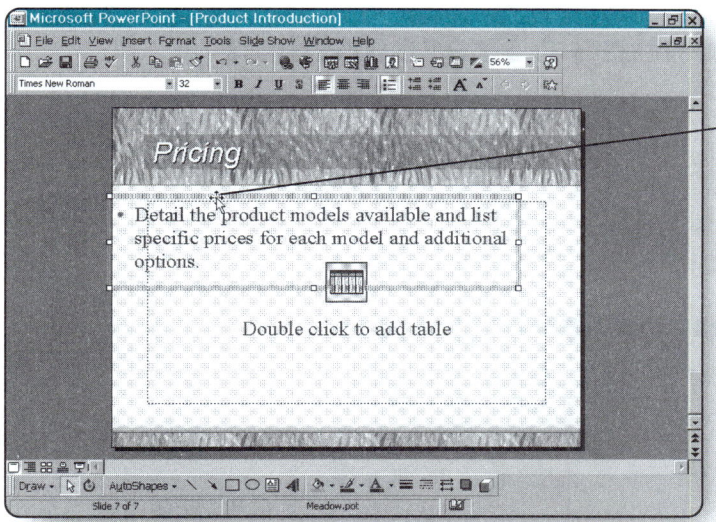

1. **Click** on the **text object** you want to delete.

2. **Click** on the **border** of the text object. As the mouse pointer passes over the border, you will see a four-headed arrow.

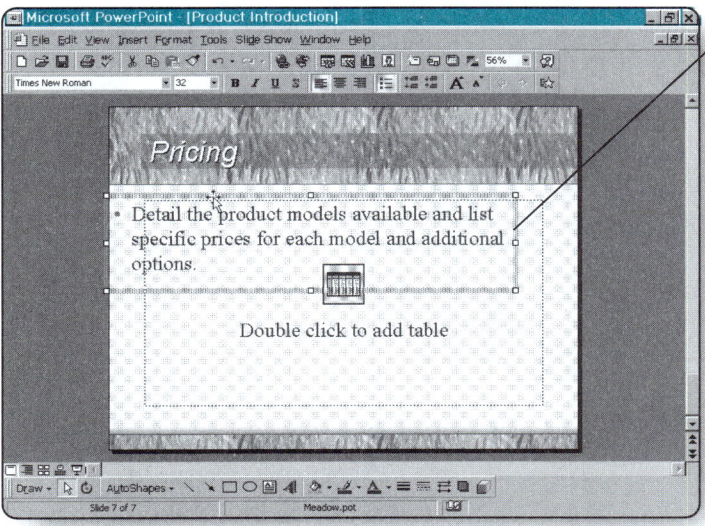

After you click on the border, the border will change from lines to dots.

3. **Press** the **Delete key**. The text object will disappear.

PRINTING IN POWERPOINT

You can print a presentation and you can print any notes you created for slides.

Printing a Presentation

You can print your presentation on paper or on overhead transparencies (which you can use to display the presentation on an overhead projector). The steps you follow to print are the same, regardless of the medium to which you choose to print; just place the correct medium in your printer.

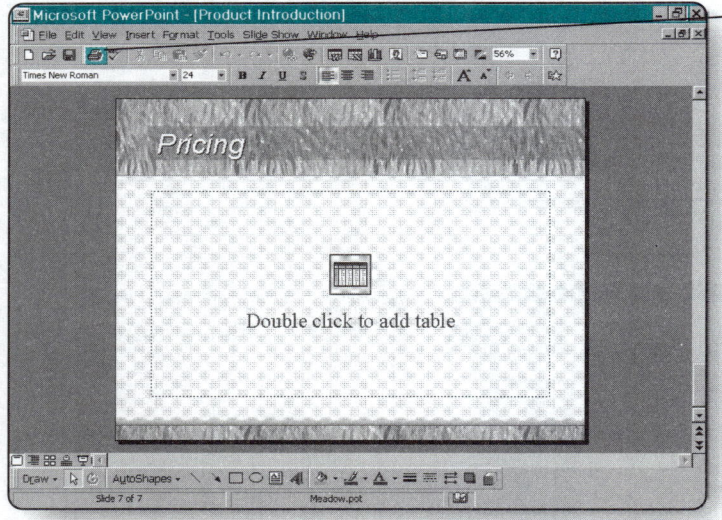

1. **Click** on the **Print button**. Your presentation slides will print.

NOTE

Your printer should be able to support graphics if you expect to get good quality printouts.

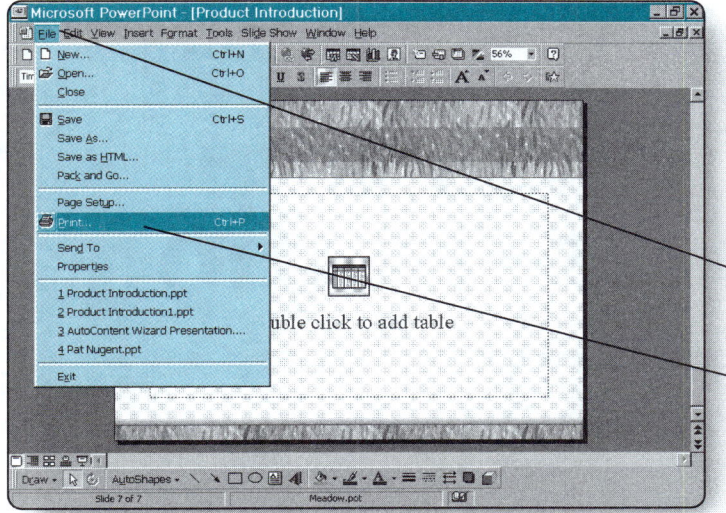

Printing Speaker Notes

If you created notes for any slides, you can print those for your own use.

1. **Click** on **File**. The File menu will appear.

2. **Click** on **Print**. The Print dialog box will open.

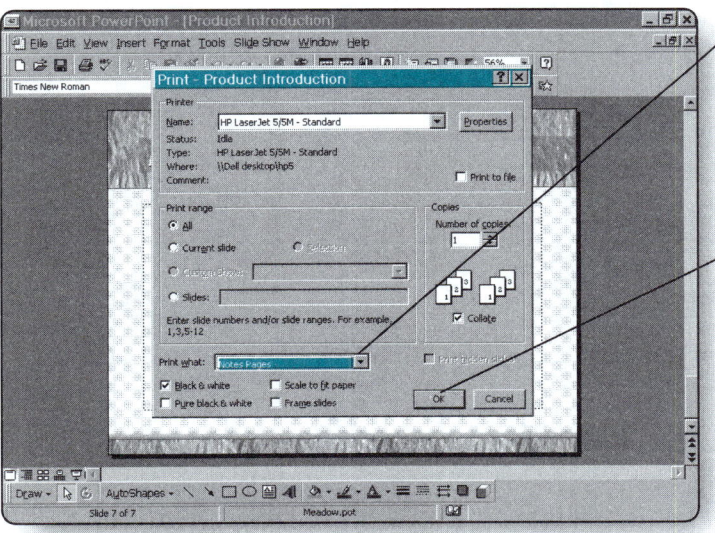

3. **Click** on the **arrow** (▼) next to the Print what: list box. A list of choices will appear.

4. **Click** on **Notes Pages**.

5. **Click** on **OK**. All your slides and any notes you created for those slides will print. The printed pages will look similar to the slides in Notes Page view.

14 Working with Special Effects in a Presentation

Adding special effects to a presentation is, perhaps, the most fun part of creating a presentation. And, special effects can enhance the effectiveness of your presentation if you use them in moderation. In this chapter, you'll learn how to:

✦ Add tables to a slide

✦ Insert charts

✦ Import Word documents

✦ Work with clip art

✦ Add transitions between slides

✦ Animate slides

✦ Add music to a presentation

ADDING TABLES

In the last chapter, we modified a slide so that it could include a table. In this task, use that slide or use the steps in the last chapter to create a slide that contains a table. When you add a table to a slide in PowerPoint, you actually insert a Microsoft Word table.

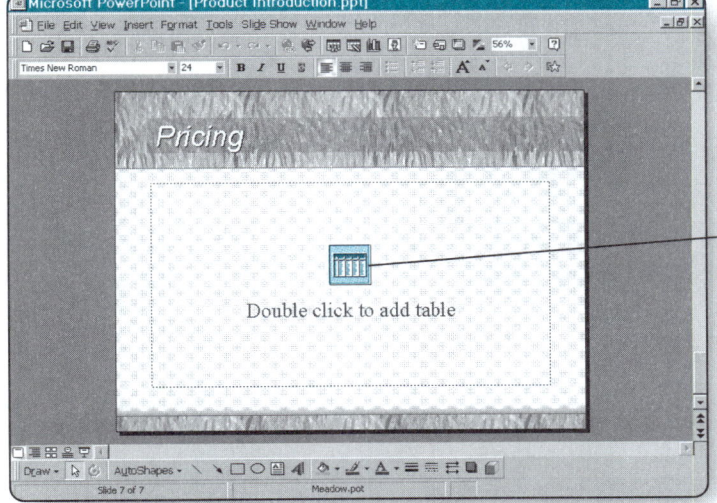

1. **Click** on the **slide** to which you will add a table. The slide will be selected.

2. **Double-click** on the **button** in the center of the slide. The Insert Word Table dialog box will open, suggesting a table of two columns and two rows. You only need to change the number of columns or rows if you need more or less than suggested.

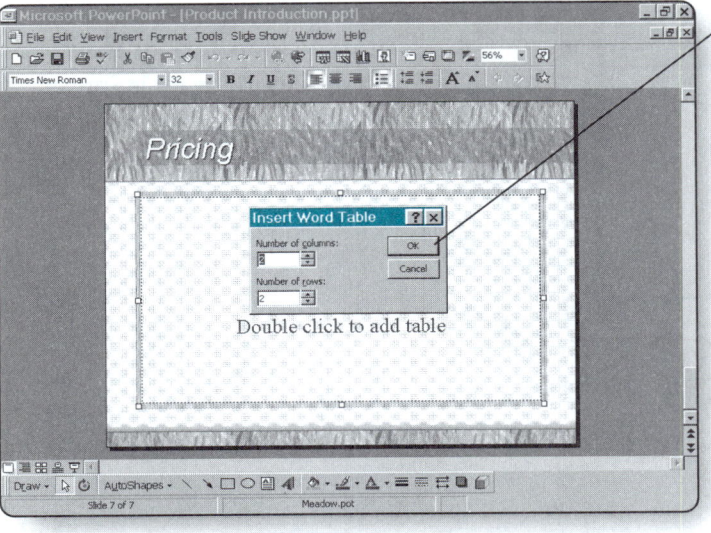

3. **Click** on OK. After a few moments, a table will appear on your slide.

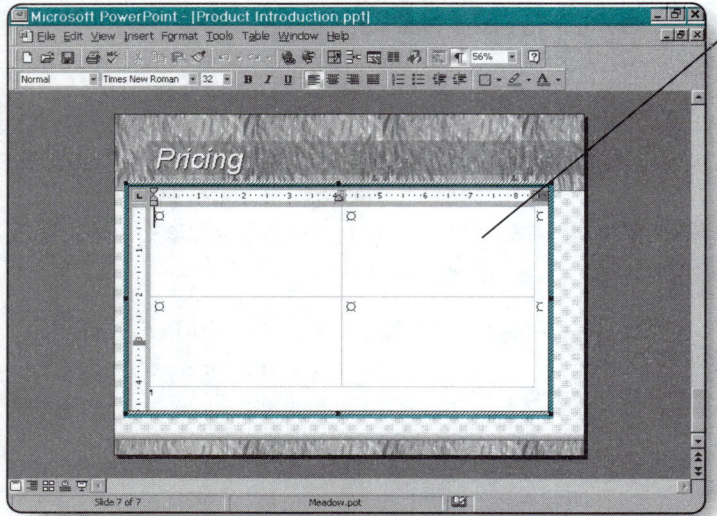

The table may look very large onscreen; don't worry, PowerPoint will adjust the size when you finish entering the table information.

4. Type a **heading** for the first column and **press** the **Tab key.**

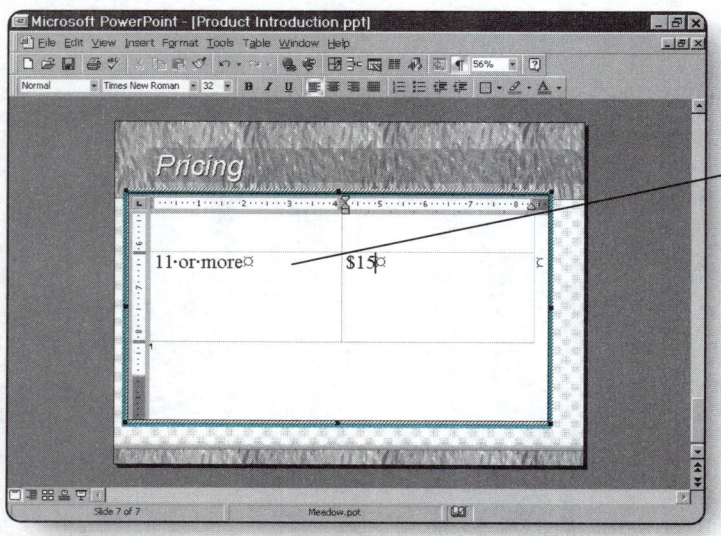

5. Type a **heading** for the second column and **press** the **Tab key.**

6. Type some **text** for the rest of the cells in the table (press the Tab key to move from cell to cell).

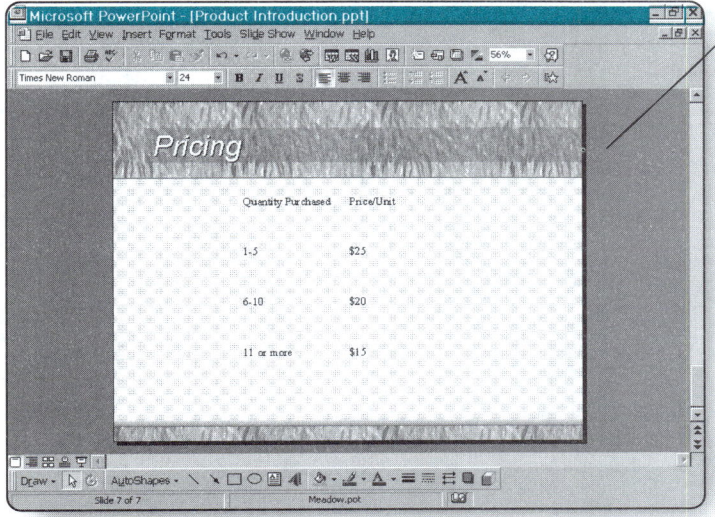

7. **Click** on the **gray area** outside the slide. PowerPoint will adjust the size of the table so that it fits on the slide.

INSERTING CHARTS

You can insert charts in PowerPoint in two ways: you can create the chart in PowerPoint or you can import a chart you created in Excel.

Using PowerPoint

You can add a slide that contains a chart using PowerPoint. PowerPoint will add a new slide immediately after the currently selected slide, so make sure you are viewing the slide you want to appear before the new slide.

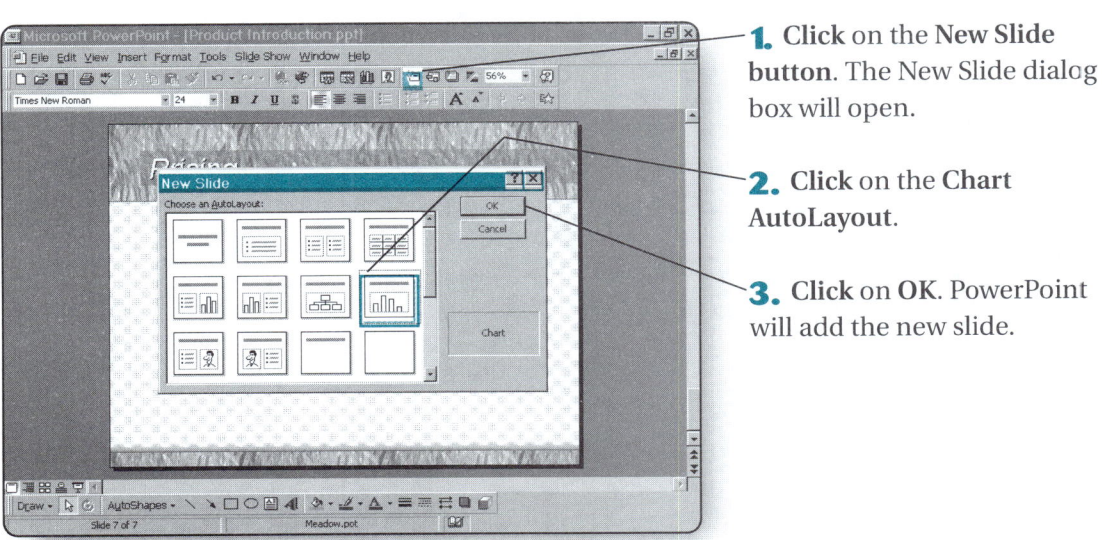

1. **Click** on the **New Slide button**. The New Slide dialog box will open.

2. **Click** on the **Chart AutoLayout**.

3. **Click** on **OK**. PowerPoint will add the new slide.

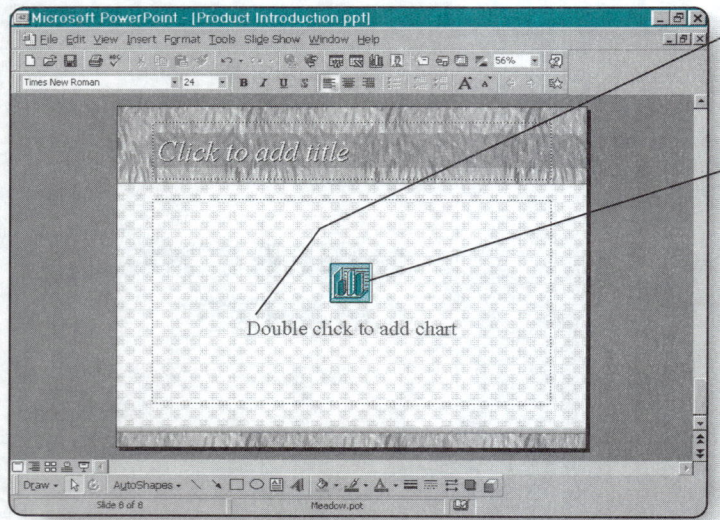

You'll see a prompt in the middle of the slide telling you how to start to add a chart.

4. **Double-click** on the **button** in the center of the slide.

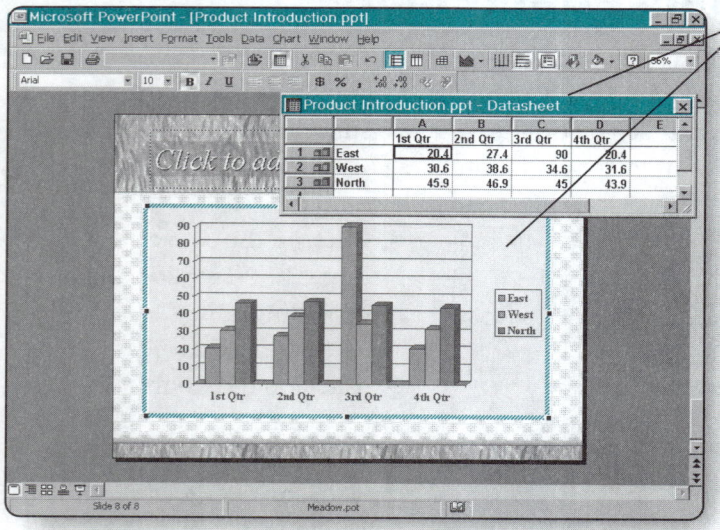

PowerPoint will display a sample chart and a Datasheet window containing the data used in the sample chart. You'll make changes in the Datasheet window to make changes to the chart. The menus will change so you can manipulate the chart and its data.

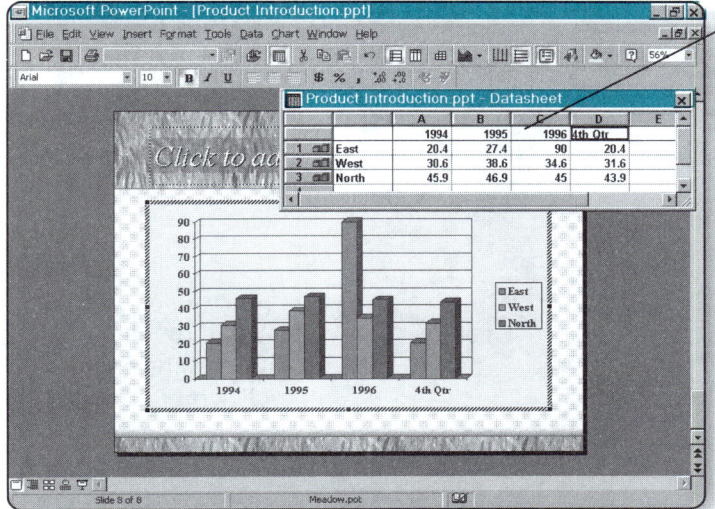

5. **Change** the **text** and **values** in the cells of the Datasheet as needed.

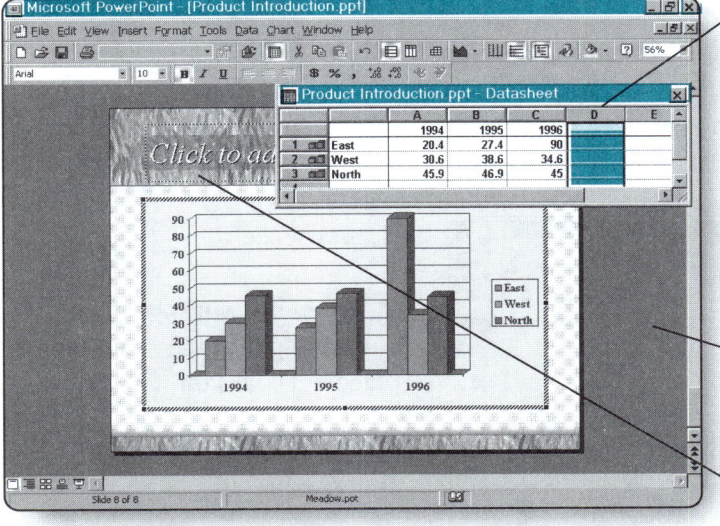

6. **Click** on the letter **D**. The entire column in the Datasheet will be selected.

7. **Press** the **Delete key**. All the data in the column will disappear, and the chart will adjust itself to display only data for the first three columns.

8. **Click** on the **gray area** outside the slide. The changes to the chart will be accepted.

9. **Click** on **Click to add title** in the slide.

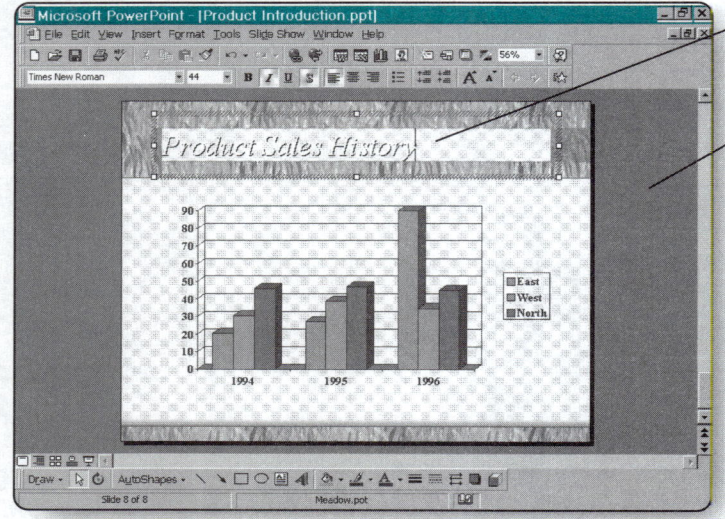

10. Type a **new title** for the slide.

11. **Click** on the **gray area** outside the slide. The changes to the chart will be accepted.

Inserting an Excel Chart

To insert a chart you created in Excel, you need to open the Excel worksheet in which you created the chart so that you can copy the chart to the Windows Clipboard. Then, you will paste the chart into a PowerPoint slide.

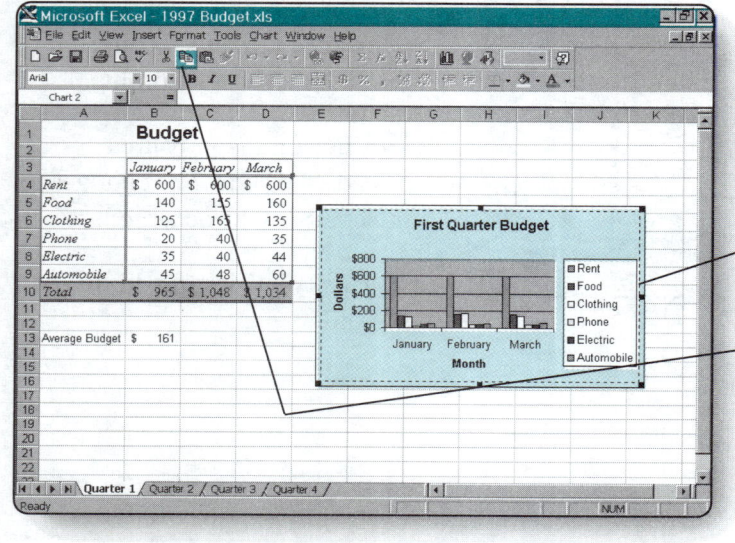

1. Start Excel.

2. **Open** the **worksheet** containing the chart you want to place in PowerPoint.

3. **Click** on **the edge of the chart** once to select it.

4. **Click** on the **Copy button.** Excel will copy the chart to the Windows Clipboard.

TIP

You can switch to PowerPoint by clicking on the program in the Windows Taskbar.

5. **Switch** to **PowerPoint**.

6. **Click** on the **New Slide button**. The New Slide dialog box will open.

7. **Click** on the **Title Only AutoLayout**.

8. **Click** on **OK**. The New Slide dialog box will close and the new slide will appear onscreen.

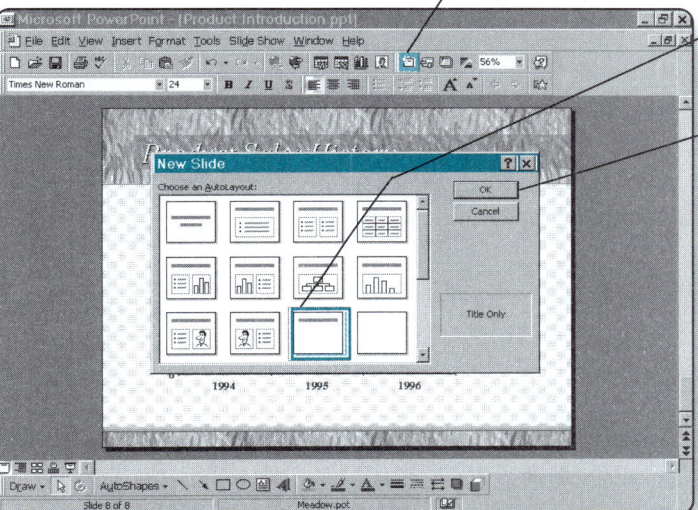

TIP

You can place the chart on an existing slide: click on the Next Slide or Previous Slide buttons until you see the slide on which you want to place the chart.

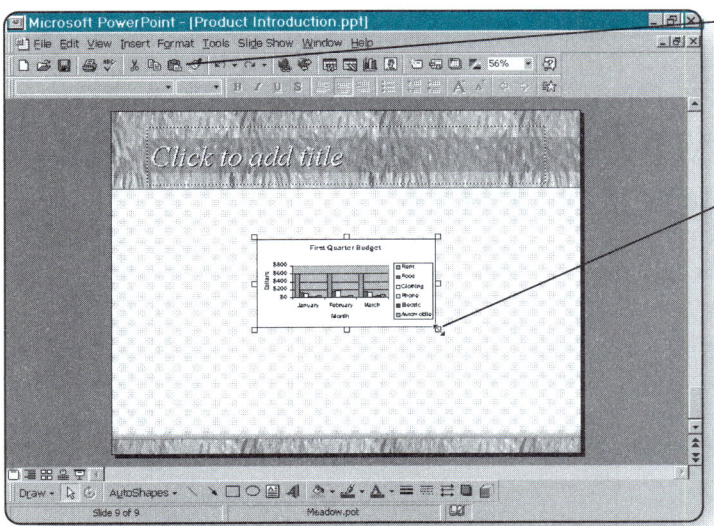

9. **Click** on the **Paste button**. A copy of the Excel chart will appear with handles, indicating it is selected.

10. **Drag** a **chart handle** outward to make the chart larger.

TIP

Dragging on a corner handle allows you to resize the chart in both directions (length and width) simultaneously and maintain the chart's proportions.

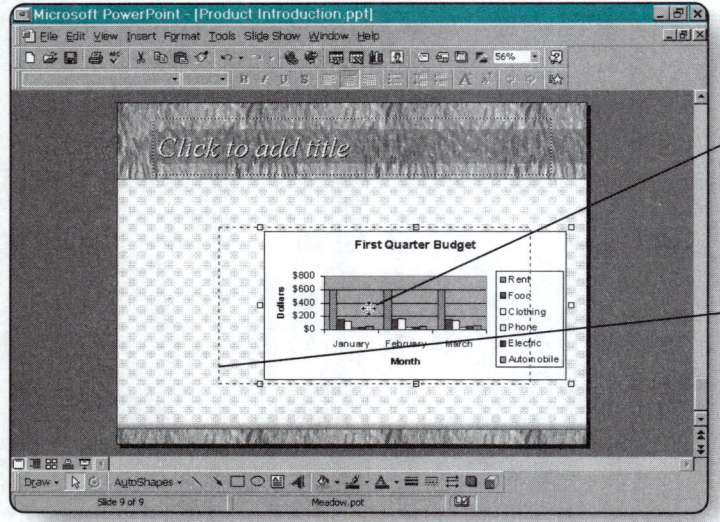

11. **Release** the **mouse button**. The chart will be resized.

12. **Move** the **mouse pointer** over the chart. The mouse pointer will change to a four-headed arrow.

13. **Drag** the **chart** to a different location on the slide.

14. **Release** the **mouse button**. The chart will be moved.

15. **Click anywhere** on the gray area. PowerPoint will cancel the selection.

16. **Close Excel**.

NOTE

The chart you just inserted will not be updated if you make any changes to the version in Excel. To update this slide, you will need to delete the chart in the slide (select it and press the Delete key) and then perform the steps in this section again.

NOTE

If you want, you can use a Word document that you have already created for this task. If you do, skip steps 1 through 4.

IMPORTING WORD DOCUMENTS

You can use a Word document to create a PowerPoint presentation. For example, suppose you have a meeting agenda you want to turn into a PowerPoint presentation. To complete this task, you will first create an agenda in Word. Then, we'll import it into our presentation in PowerPoint.

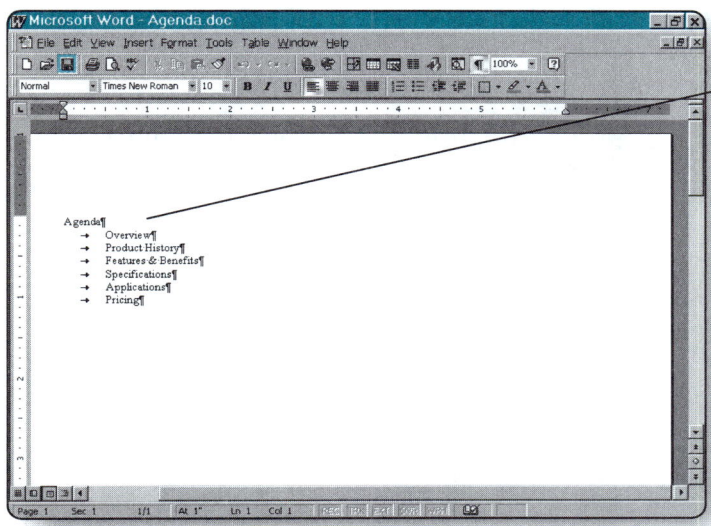

1. Start Word.

2. **Type** an **agenda** for a meeting.

3. **Save** the **document**.

4. **Close** Word.

5. **Switch** to a **PowerPoint presentation**.

6. **Click** on the **Outline View button**. PowerPoint will display the presentation in Outline view.

7. **Click** at the **end** of the **slide** you want to appear before the new slide.

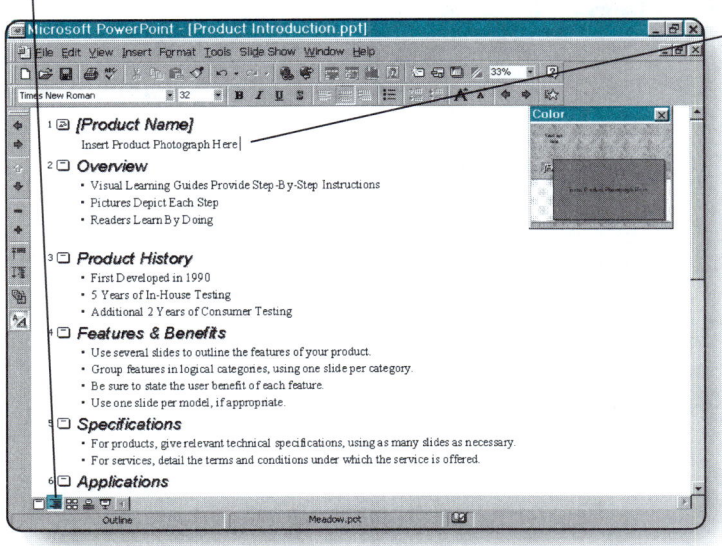

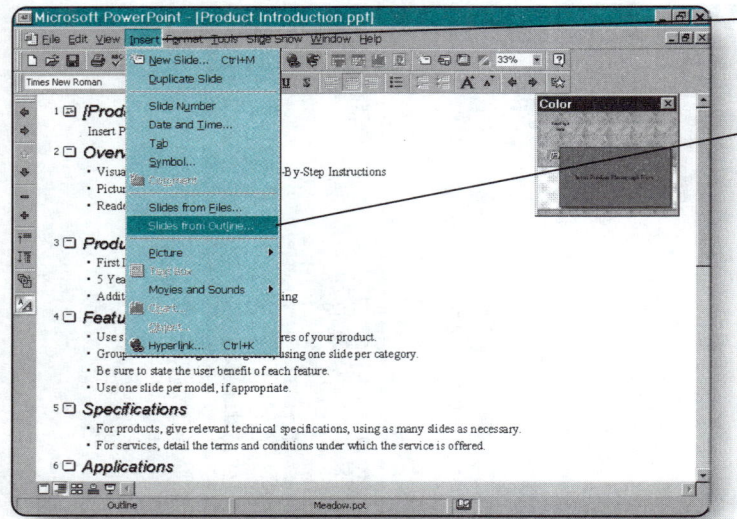

8. Click on **Insert**. The Insert menu will appear.

9. Click on **Slides from Outline**. The Insert Outline dialog box will open.

10. Click on the **arrow** (▼) of the Look in: list box. A list of available drives and folders will appear.

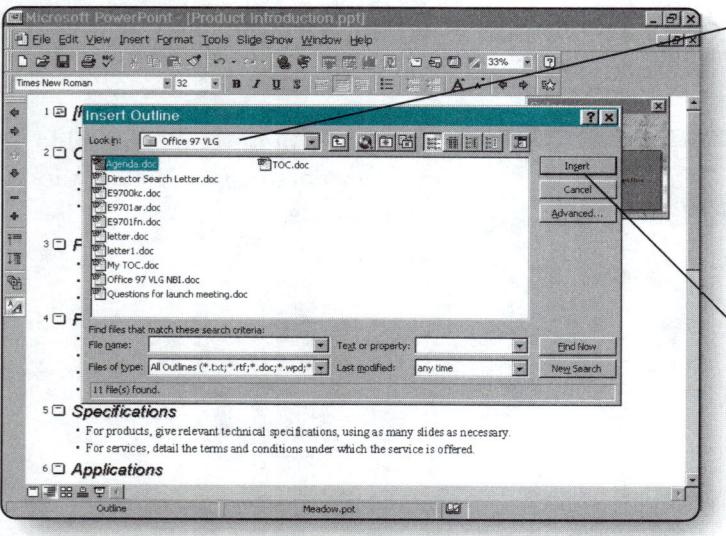

11. Navigate, using the Look in: list box, to the **folder** containing the document you want to import.

12. Click on the **document** you want to import. The document will be selected.

13. Click on **Insert**. The Insert Outline dialog box will close.

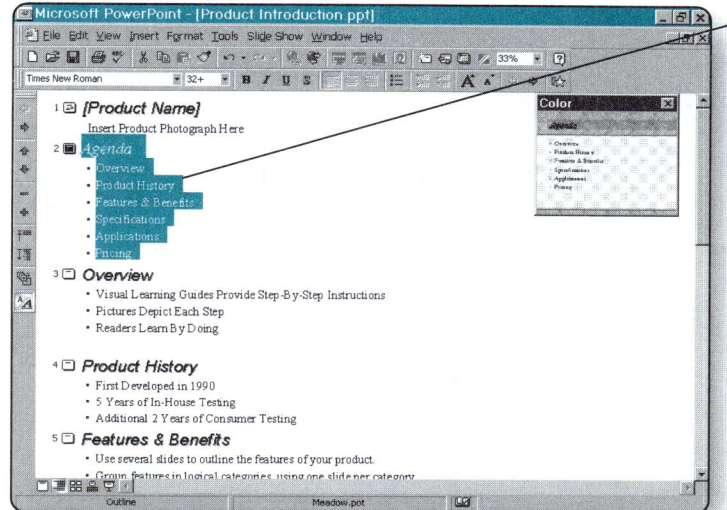

PowerPoint will insert the text in the Word document immediately after the slide containing the insertion point.

WORKING WITH CLIP ART

You can add visual interest to your slides by using clip art. When Office 97 was installed, some clip art was copied to your hard drive. However, you'll find additional clip art on the Office 97 CD-ROM, so insert it before you begin this section.

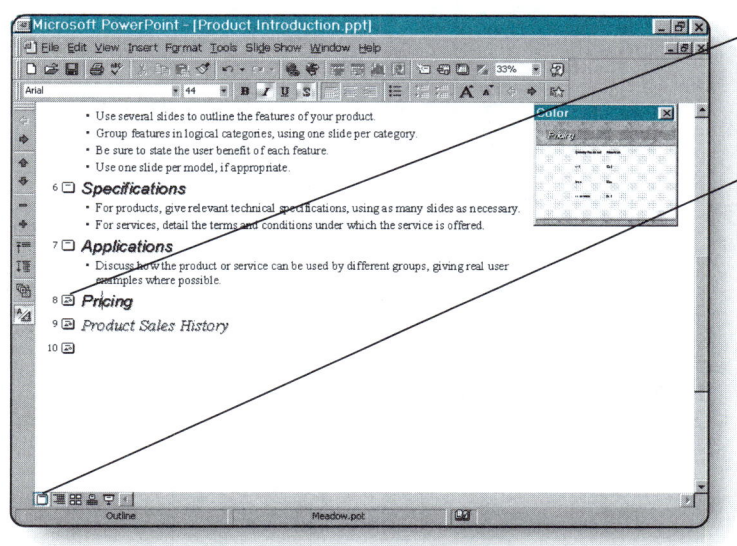

1. **Click** on the slide to which you want to add clip art. The slide will be selected.

2. **Click** on the **Slide View button.** PowerPoint will switch to Slide view.

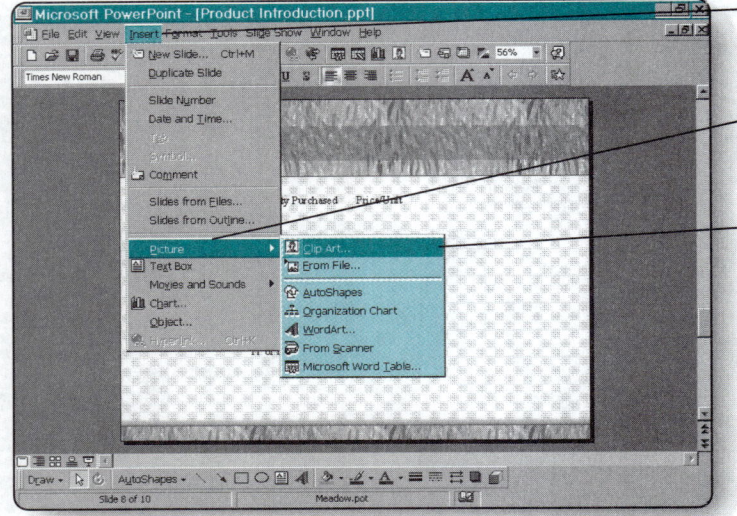

3. **Click** on **Insert**. The Insert menu will appear.

4. **Click** on **Picture**. A cascading menu will appear.

5. **Click** on **Clip Art**. Graphic handles will appear on the slide and the Microsoft Clip Gallery 3.0 dialog box will open.

6. **Click** on a **category** in the list on the left. The Preview box in the center of the dialog box will change to show only those images related to the category you chose.

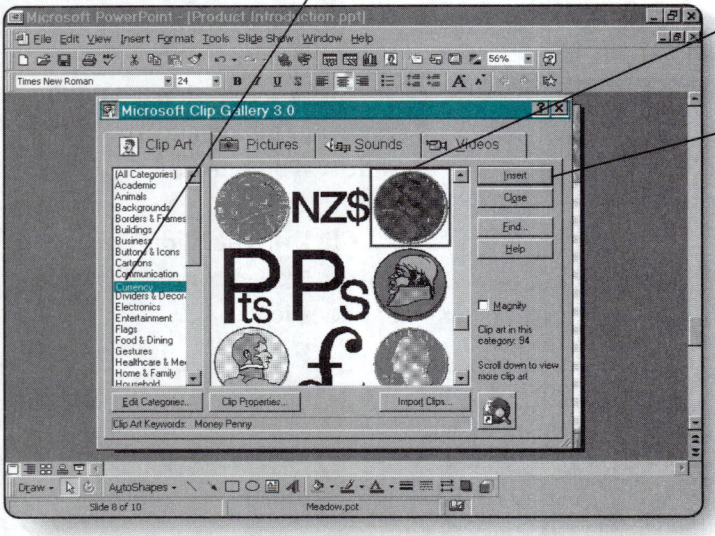

7. **Click** on the **image** you want to use.

8. **Click** on **Insert**. The Microsoft Clip Gallery 3.0 dialog box will close.

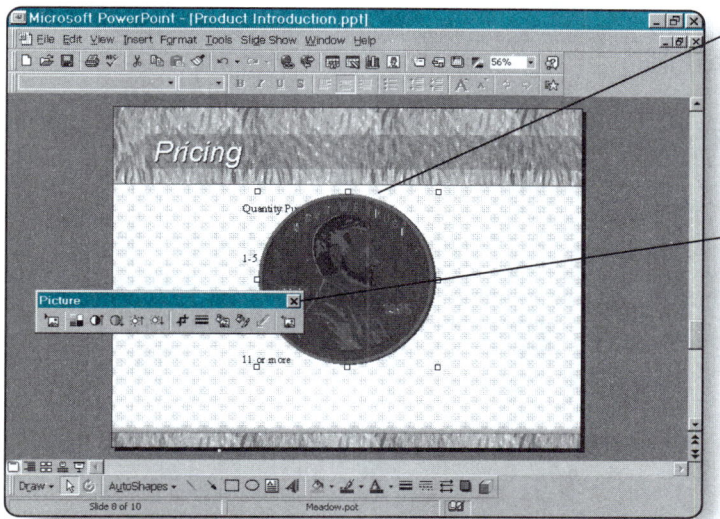

The image will appear in the center of the slide. Use the next three steps to resize the image.

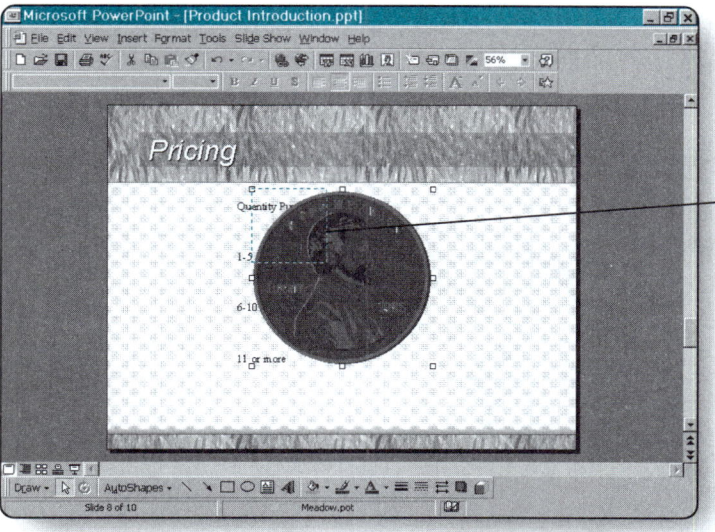

9. **Move** the **mouse pointer** over one of the handles. The mouse pointer will change to a two-headed arrow.

10. **Press** and **hold** the **mouse button** and **drag** the **handle** to resize the image.

11. **Release** the **mouse button**. The image will be resized.

12. **Move** the **mouse pointer** to the center of the image. The mouse pointer will change to a four-headed arrow.

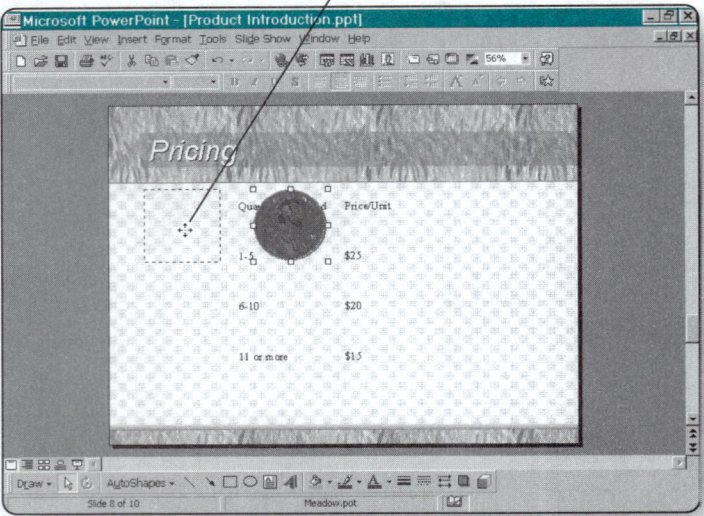

13. **Drag** the **image** to a new location.

TIP

See "Inserting an Excel Chart" earlier in this chapter for additional examples of resizing and moving an object.

14. **Release** the **mouse button**. The image will be moved.

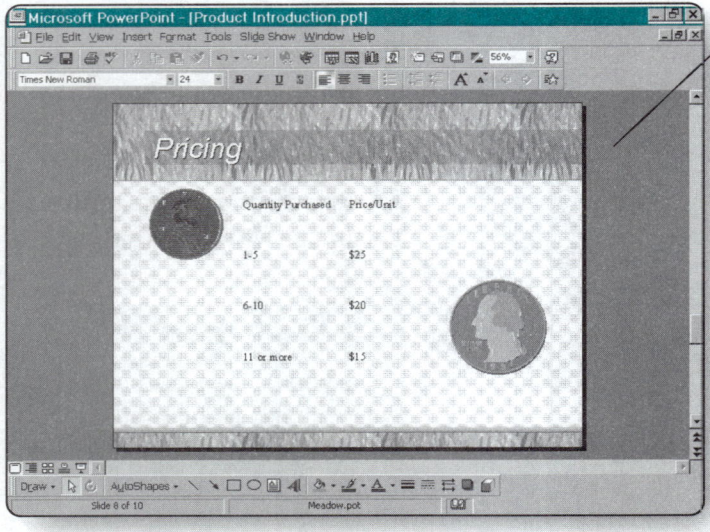

15. **Click** on the **gray area** outside the slide. PowerPoint will cancel the selection of the image.

TIP

Use only one type of transition, or possibly two, for each presentation but don't choose more than that. If you use more, the audience will be distracted from your presentation.

ADDING TRANSITIONS

Transitions are special effects you can use if you're creating a presentation you intend to show as a slide show on a computer. Transitions make the change between slides appear smoother by fading, wiping, or dissolving slides.

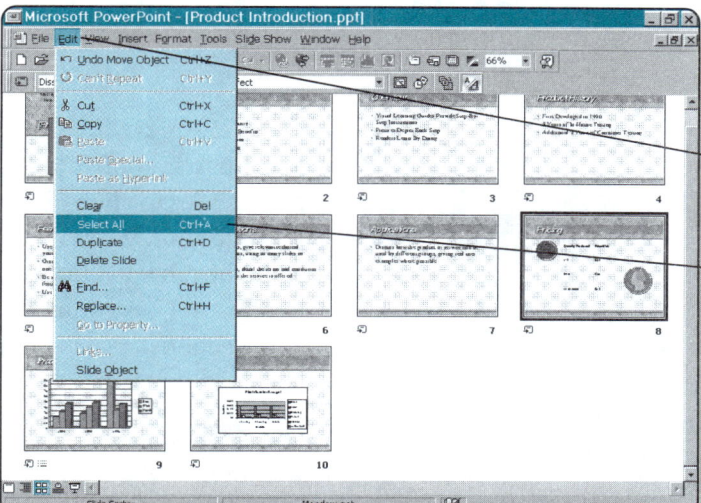

1. **Click** on the **Slide Sorter View button**. PowerPoint will switch to Slide Sorter view.

2. **Click** on **Edit**. The Edit menu will appear.

3. **Click** on **Select All**. PowerPoint will select all slides in the presentation.

NOTE

The transition you choose will apply to all slides in the presentation. If you want the transition to apply only to certain slides, select just those slides by holding down the Shift key while clicking on each slide.

4. **Click** on **Slide Show**. The Slide Show menu will appear.

5. **Click** on **Slide Transition**. The Slide Transition dialog box will open.

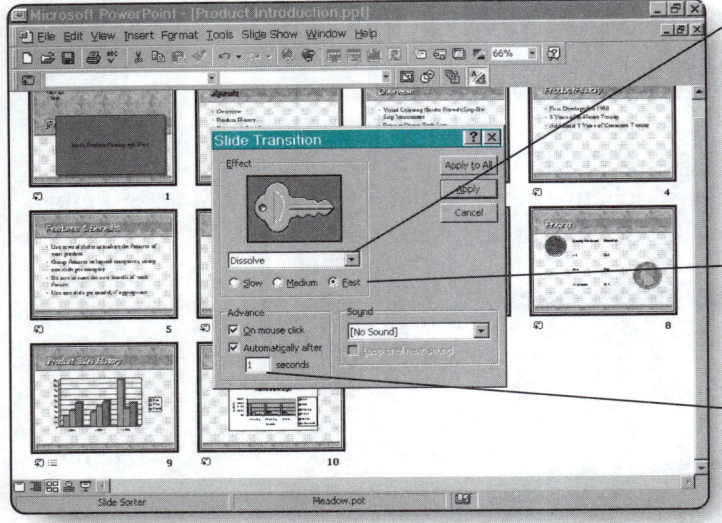

6. **Click** on the **arrow** (▼) below the picture. A list of available effects will appear.

7. **Click** on an **effect.** The effect will be selected.

8. **Click** on a **speed** (Slow, Medium, or Fast). You will see how the effect works.

9. **Click** on a **check box** in the Advance group to identify how you want the slides to change during the slide show. A ✔ will appear in the box. If you choose Automatically After, also supply a number of seconds.

TIP

You'll need to experiment with the effects to find the best one for your presentation. An effect such as Dissolve works well if you have design elements in the background of each slide. Dissolve keeps the background steady while dissolving only text.

NOTE

Placing a ✔ in both boxes in the Advance box tells PowerPoint to advance slides automatically after the number of seconds you specify *unless* you click the mouse before the time elapses. In that case, PowerPoint will advance the slide when you click the mouse.

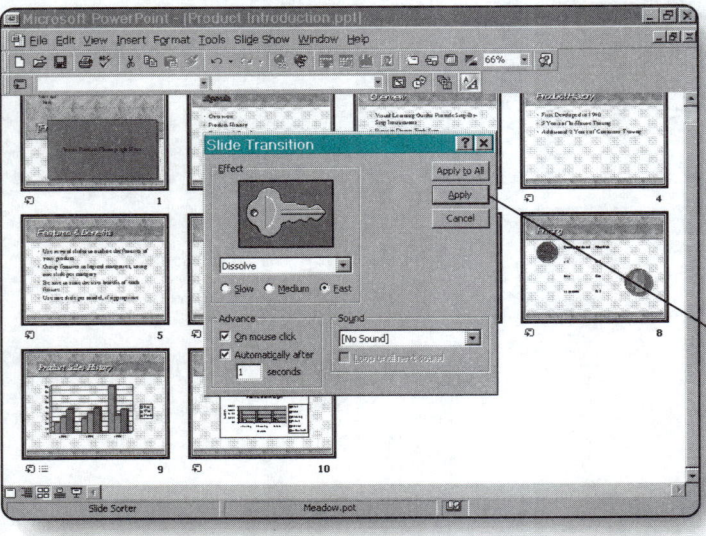

10. **Click** on **Apply.** PowerPoint will apply the settings to all selected slides.

ANIMATING SLIDES

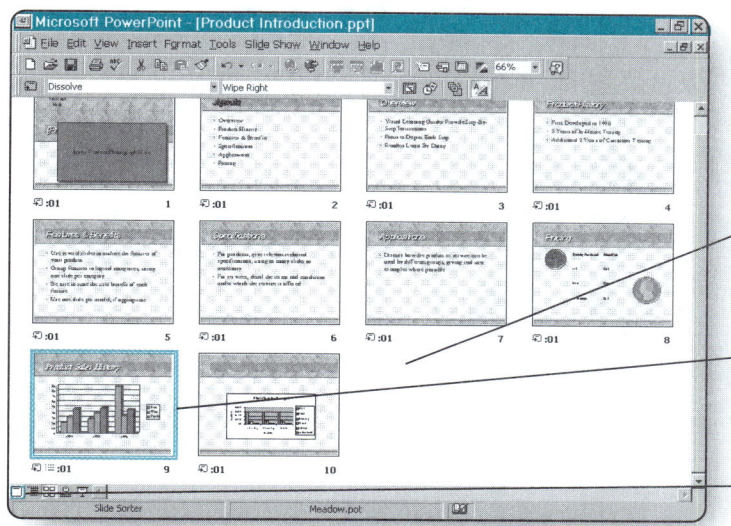

Animations are transitions you apply to elements on a slide, not to the entire slide. For example, you can use an animation to make a chart fade in or out.

1. **Click** on any **white space**. PowerPoint will cancel the selection of all slides.

2. **Click** on the **slide** containing the element you want to animate.

3. **Click** on the **Slide View button**.

4. **Click** on the **object** you want to animate. Handles will surround the object.

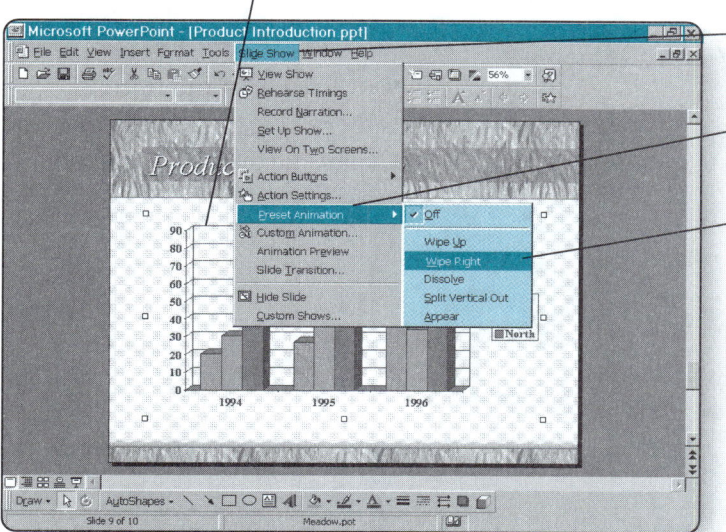

5. **Click** on **Slide Show**. The Slide Show menu will appear.

6. **Click** on **Preset Animation**. A cascading menu will appear.

7. **Click** on the **effect** you want to use. PowerPoint will apply the effect to the selected object. You'll see the effects of the animation when you run the slide show.

NOTE

The animation effects that appear on the cascading menu change depending on the type of object you select.

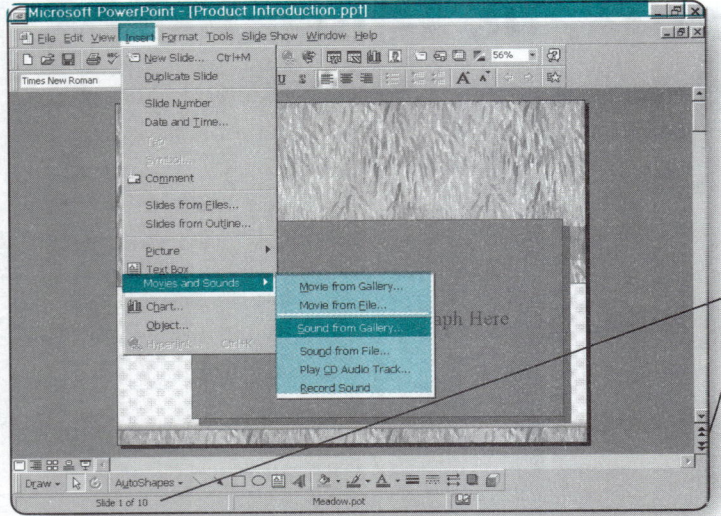

ADDING MUSIC

Sometimes, adding music to a presentation can be very effective.

1. **Click** on the **Next Slide button** or the **Previous Slide button** until you see the slide where you want music to begin playing.

2. **Click** on **Insert**. The Insert menu will appear.

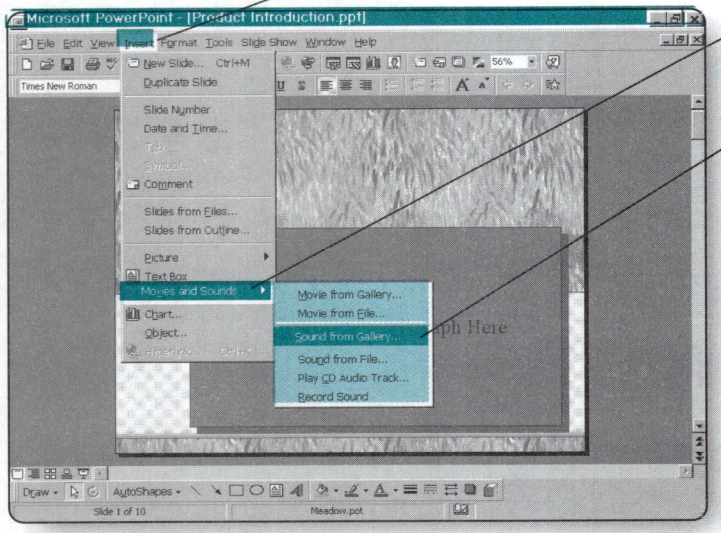

3. **Click** on **Movies and Sounds**. A cascading menu will appear.

4. **Click** on **Sound from Gallery**. The Microsoft Clip Gallery 3.0 dialog box will open.

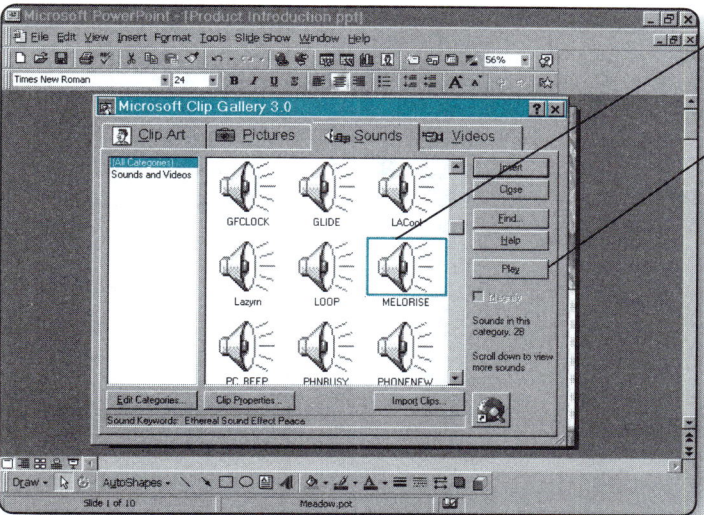

5. Click on a **sound** in the middle of the box.

6. Click on **Play** to hear the sound before you actually add it to your slide.

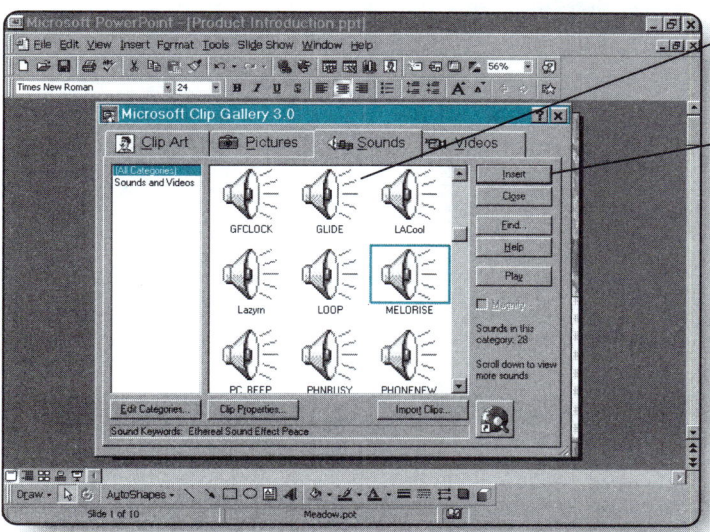

7. Click on the **sound** you want to add to your presentation.

8. Click on **Insert**. The Microsoft Clip Gallery 3.0 dialog box will close and you will see the selected slide.

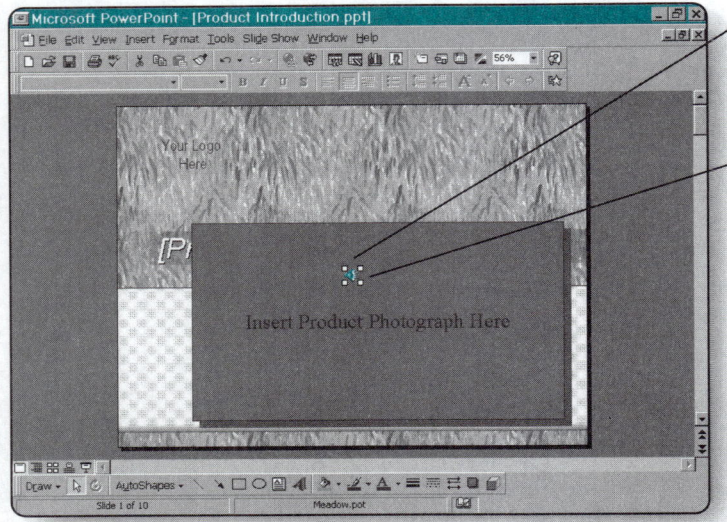

You will see a small megaphone (a sound icon) on the slide, representing the sound.

9. **Click** on the **sound icon.** Handles will appear around the icon.

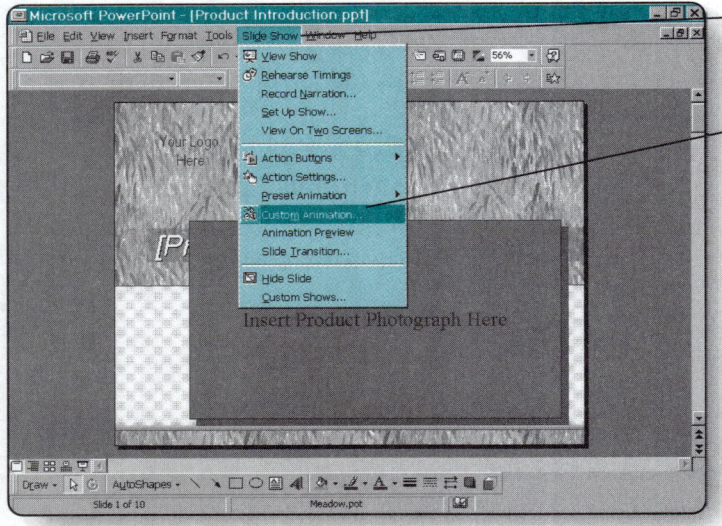

10. **Click** on **Slide Show.** The Slide Show menu will appear.

11. **Click** on **Custom Animation.** The Custom Animation dialog box will open.

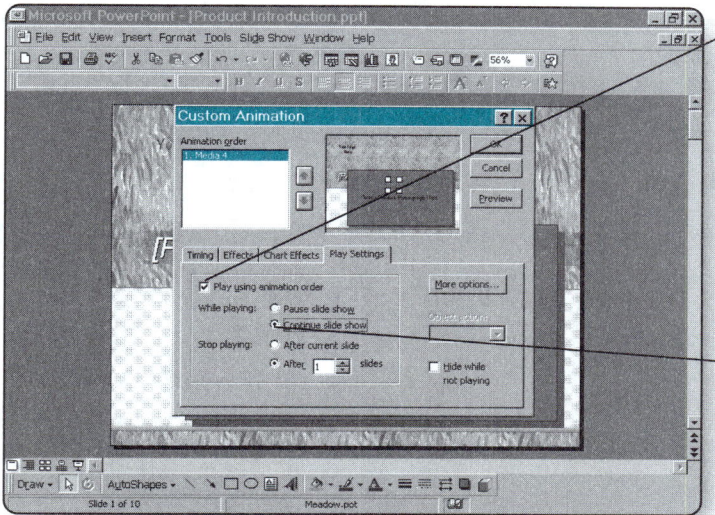

12. Click on the **Play using animation order check box**. A ✔ will appear in the box.

13. Click on **an option button** for While playing:. These option buttons specify how the sound will behave during a slide show.

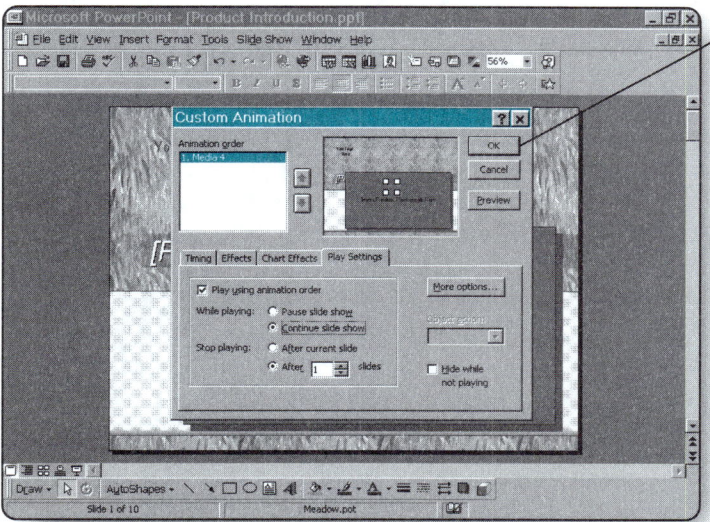

14. Click on **OK**. The Custom Animation dialog box will close.

PART IV REVIEW QUESTIONS

1. What do you call the items that comprise a PowerPoint presentation? *See Chapter 12*

2. Name the different views available for a presentation? *See Chapter 12*

3. Describe the process of adding and deleting a slide. *See Chapter 13*

4. What view do you use to rearrange slides? *See Chapter 13*

5. What is the difference between a presentation design and a slide layout? *See Chapter 13*

6. Can you change your presentation's design? *See Chapter 13*

7. How do you add a table to a slide? *See Chapter 14*

8. How do you add a chart to a slide? *See Chapter 14*

9. How do you add Clip Art to a slide? *See Chapter 14*

10. How do you add transitions to a slide show? *See Chapter 14*

PART V
Outlook

jump:
ice D

Exce

Excel 8
s Data
ad.xls
ead-1.xls
leadblnk.xls
LEADS.xls
leadtst.xls
Mcn95v94.xls
News Flash.xls
Sales Report.xls

15 Getting Started with Outlook

Outlook is the "information organizer" of Office 97—you can send and receive e-mail, store names and addresses, maintain a calendar, keep track of things you need to do, review a history of the things you've done, and keep notes. Microsoft has designed Outlook so that you can use it as an information center; you can even use Outlook to open Office documents. Start using Outlook by understanding the Outlook window. In this chapter, you'll learn how to:

✦ **Understand the Outlook window**

✦ **Display the Folder List in Outlook**

✦ **Add a folder**

✦ **Add a shortcut to the Outlook bar**

✦ **Reorder shortcuts on the Outlook bar**

✦ **Move a shortcut to a different group**

✦ **Add an Outlook group**

TIP

You might be asked to choose a Profile; accept whatever profile is suggested by clicking on OK.

UNDERSTANDING THE OUTLOOK WINDOW

In Outlook, you store information in folders. You open a folder in Outlook by clicking on a shortcut for the folder that appears in the Outlook bar. On the Outlook bar, shortcuts are organized into groups.

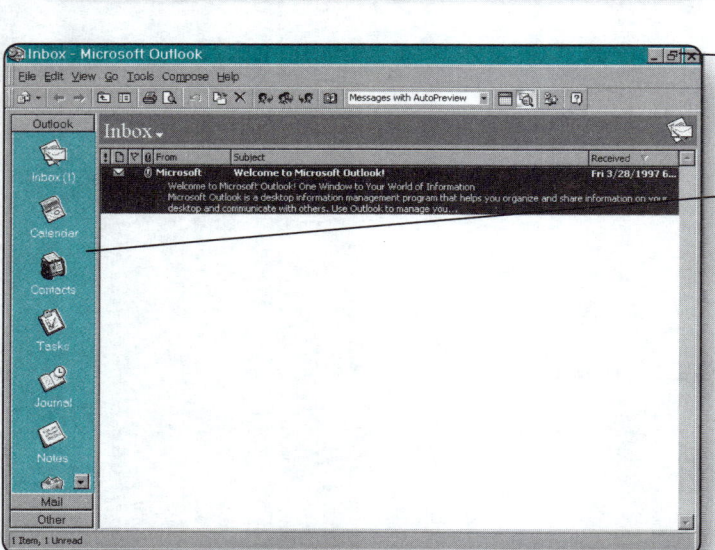

1. **Start Outlook** by double-clicking on the icon on your Desktop. The Outlook window will open and Office Assistant will offer help with Outlook.

2. **Click** on the **Show these choices at startup check box** to remove the ✔.

3. **Click** on **OK**. Office Assistant will close.

4. **Click** on the **Maximize button**. Windows will enlarge the Outlook window.

Along the left side of the screen, you will see the Outlook bar, which contains shortcuts to folders. The shortcuts you see initially are to folders that are created by default in Outlook. You can add shortcuts to the Outlook bar to organize information in Outlook in a way that suits your work style.

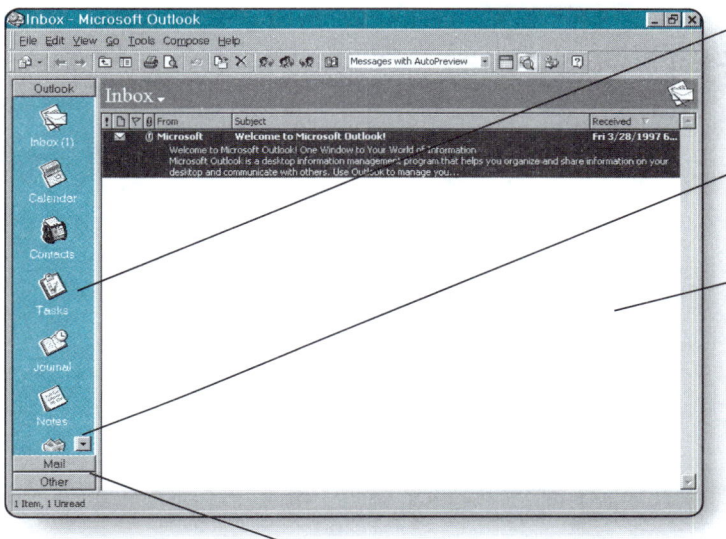

You will learn about each shortcut you see here in subsequent chapters.

Use the arrows to scroll through the shortcuts on the Outlook bar.

The right side of the window shows the contents of the folder that is currently selected on the left side of the window. When you first start Outlook, you will see the contents of the Inbox, which stores e-mail.

Notice on the left side of the window that Outlook organizes shortcuts into groups. The default group that appears is the Outlook group.

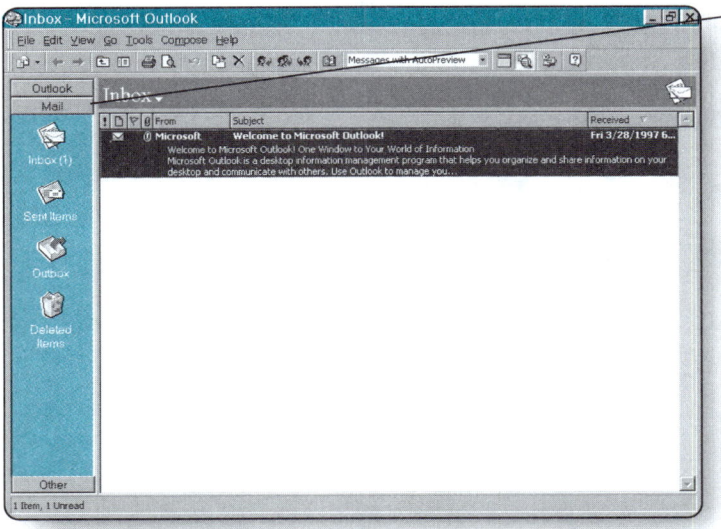

By clicking on the group icon, you can switch to the Mail group. In the Mail group, you can see only those shortcuts related to mail tasks.

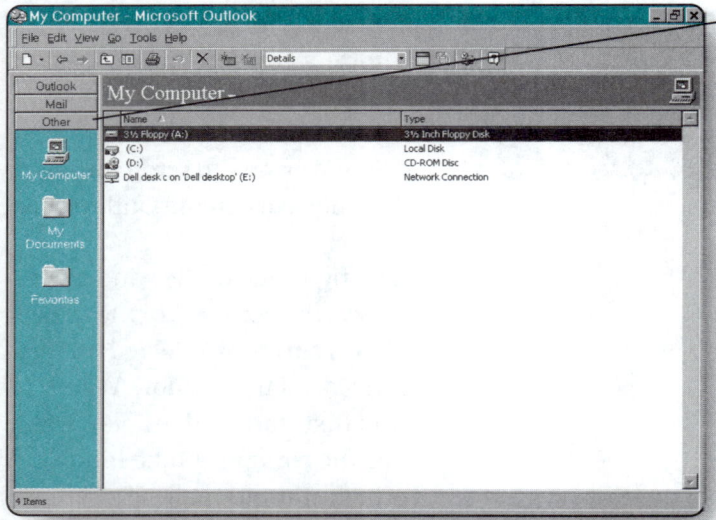

You can also switch to the Other group, which contains shortcuts that let you open folders on your computer or on any attached network drive.

DISPLAYING OUTLOOK FOLDERS

The Outlook bar contains shortcuts to folders; it doesn't contain the actual folders. However, you can display the folders as part of the Outlook window. As you'll learn later in this chapter, you can add folders that don't have shortcuts in the Outlook bar or you can create shortcuts in the Outlook bar for folders you add.

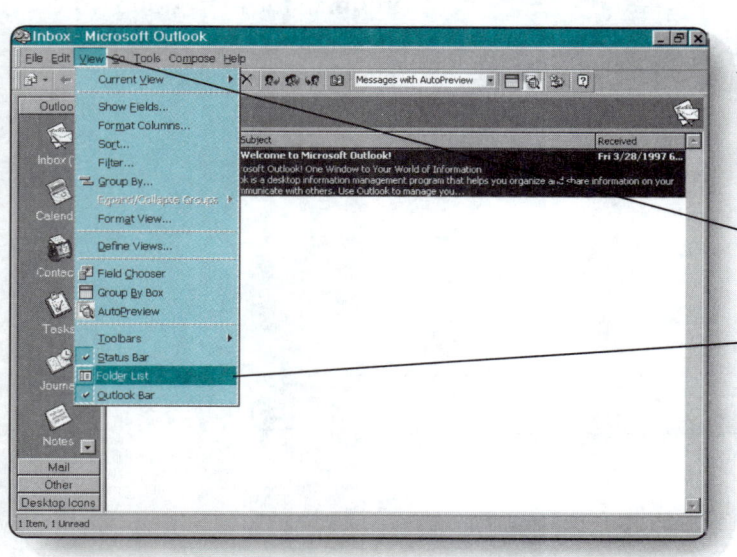

1. **Click** on **View**. The View menu will appear.

2. **Click** on **Folder List**.

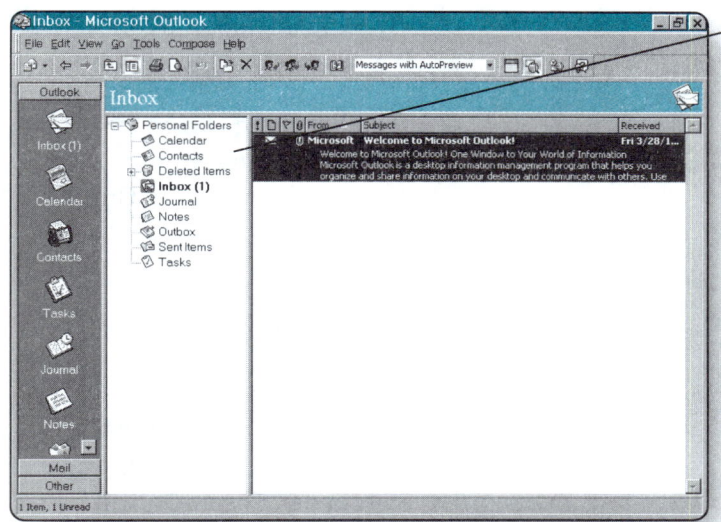

The Folder List will appear. Initially, the folders in the Folder List match the shortcuts that appear in the Outlook bar.

ADDING A FOLDER IN OUTLOOK

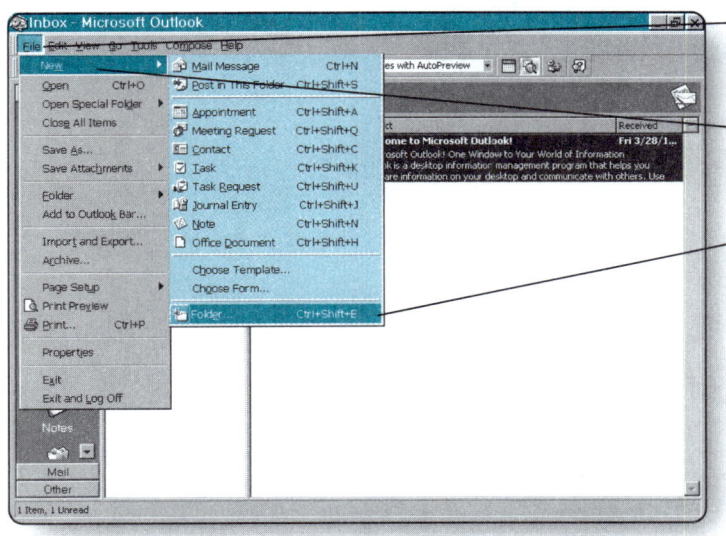

1. **Click** on **File**. The File menu will appear.

2. **Click** on **New**. A cascading menu will appear.

3. **Click** on **Folder**. The Create New Folder dialog box will open.

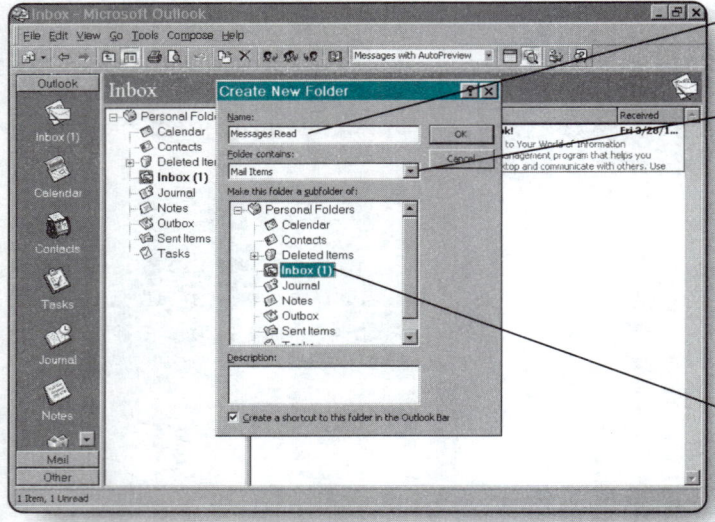

4. Type the **folder name** in the Name: text box.

5. Click on the **arrow (▼)** of the Folder contains: list box. A list of items you can track in Outlook will appear.

6. Click on the **type of information** the new folder will contain.

7. Click on the **folder** inside which you want to place the new folder. The folder will be selected.

8. Click on **OK**. The Create New Folder dialog box will close.

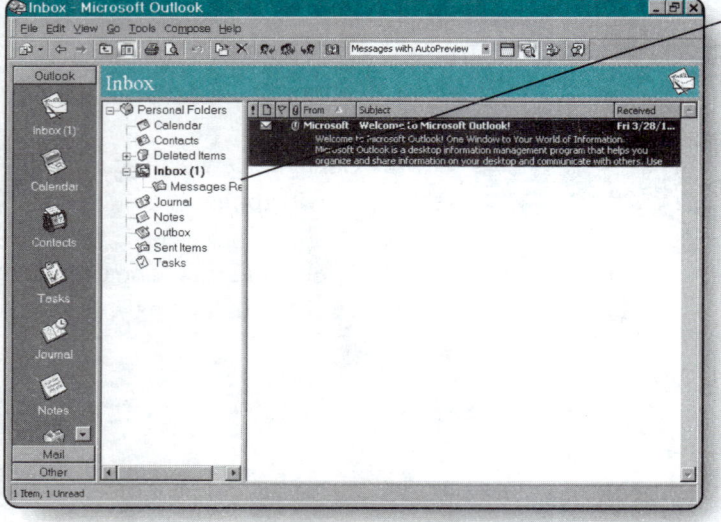

The new folder will appear in the Folder List.

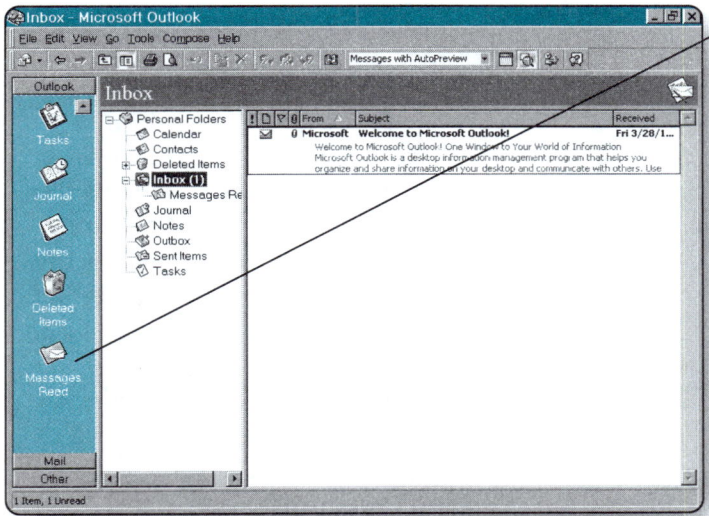

If you scroll to the bottom of the Outlook bar, you'll also find a shortcut for the folder you just added.

TIP

You might want to add folders to Outlook to help you organize the e-mail you receive.

ADDING A SHORTCUT TO THE OUTLOOK BAR

You can use Outlook as an information center from which you open documents. The default Outlook bar already contains a shortcut to the My Documents and Favorites folders. You can add an Outlook bar shortcut that will display all the shortcuts that currently appear on your Desktop.

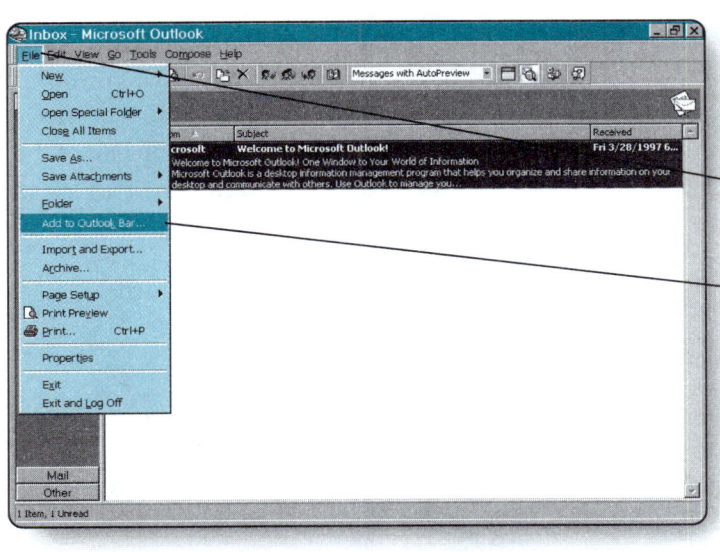

1. Click on **File**. The File menu will appear.

2. Click on **Add to Outlook Bar**. The Add to Outlook Bar dialog box will open.

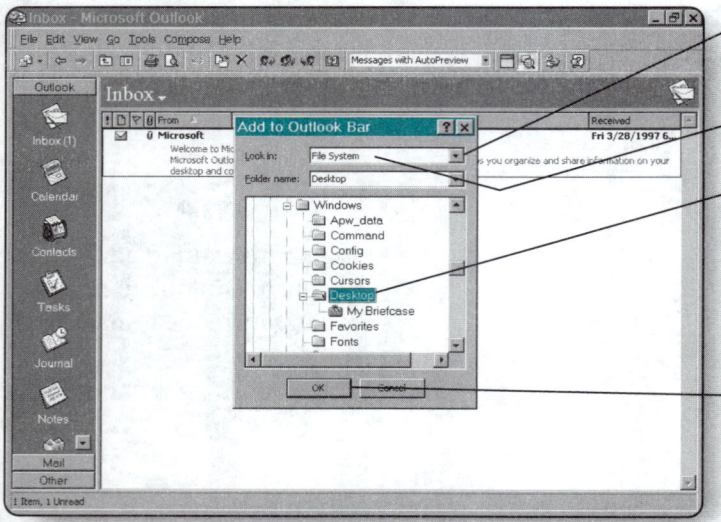

3. **Click** on the **arrow** (▼) next to the Look in: list box.

4. **Click** on **File System**.

5. **Double-click** on the **folder** containing the shortcut you want to add to the Outlook bar (Desktop shortcuts are stored in the \Windows\Desktop folder).

6. **Click** on **OK**. The folder containing the shortcut will appear at the bottom of the Outlook bar.

NOTE

You will need to double-click on the My Computer icon to see the drives on your computer. Then, double-click on the drive that contains Windows 95 (probably your C drive). Finally, double-click on the Windows folder to find the Desktop folder.

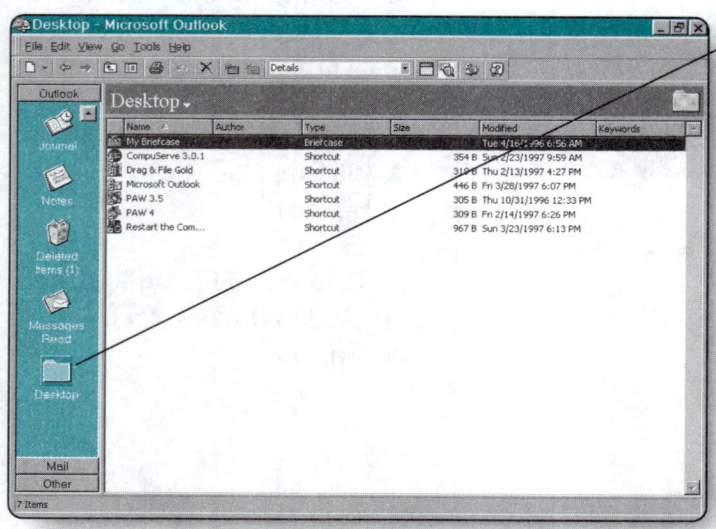

7. **Click** on the **shortcut** you just added to the Outlook bar. You will see the shortcuts stored in the folder on the right side of the Outlook window.

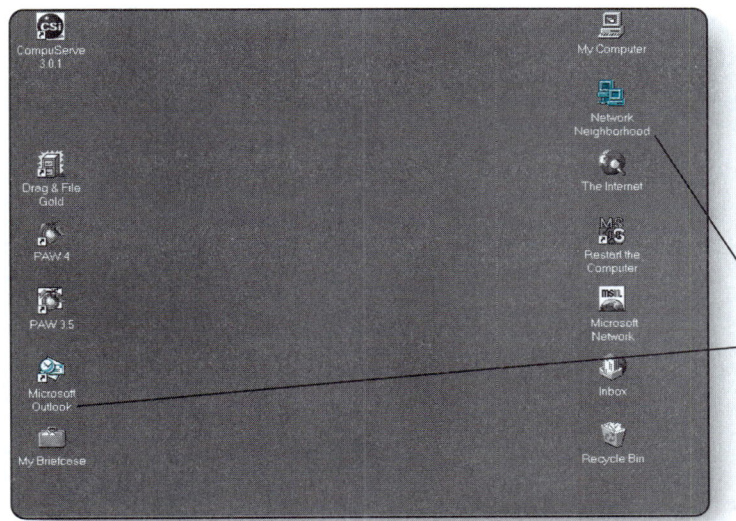

NOTE

Only *shortcuts* are stored in the Desktop folder. You can identify a Desktop shortcut by paying close attention to the icon— shortcut icons contain a small arrow.

The Microsoft Outlook icon is a shortcut, but the Network Neighborhood icon is not.

TIP

You can add items that appear in the Programs folder on the Windows Start menu using these steps. In step 5, open the \Windows\Start Menu\Programs folder and find the folder containing the program you want to add to the Outlook bar. All the shortcuts in that folder will be added to the folder that appears on the Outlook bar.

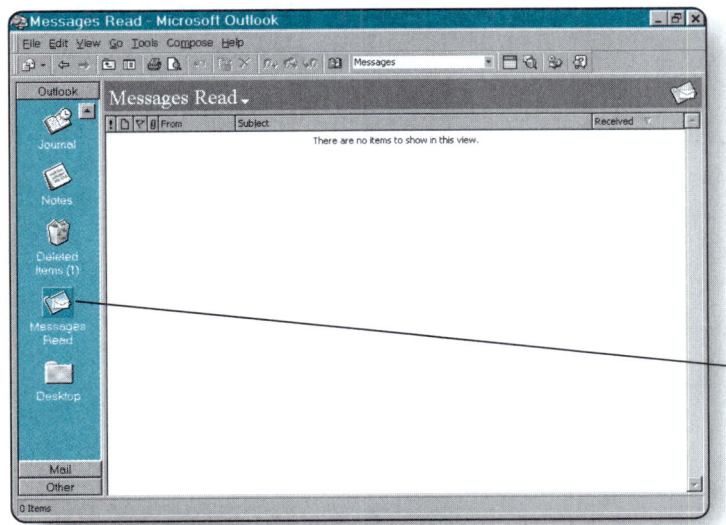

CHANGING THE ORDER OF OUTLOOK BAR SHORTCUTS

You can move a shortcut up or down on the Outlook bar.

1. **Point** at the **shortcut** you want to move. A square will appear around the shortcut.

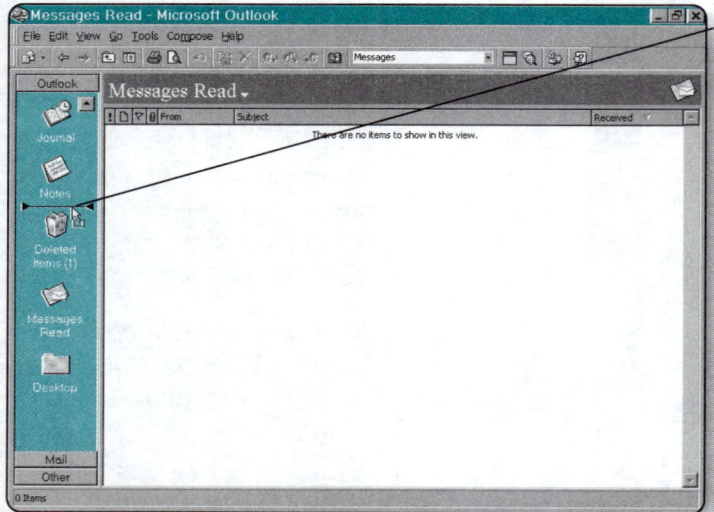

2. **Drag** the **shortcut** up or down in the list. A black marker will appear between existing shortcuts as the mouse pointer moves over an acceptable spot.

TIP

If the shortcut isn't appearing at an acceptable spot, you'll see the international "not" symbol—the circle with the line in it.

3. **Release** the **mouse button**. The shortcut will appear in its new location.

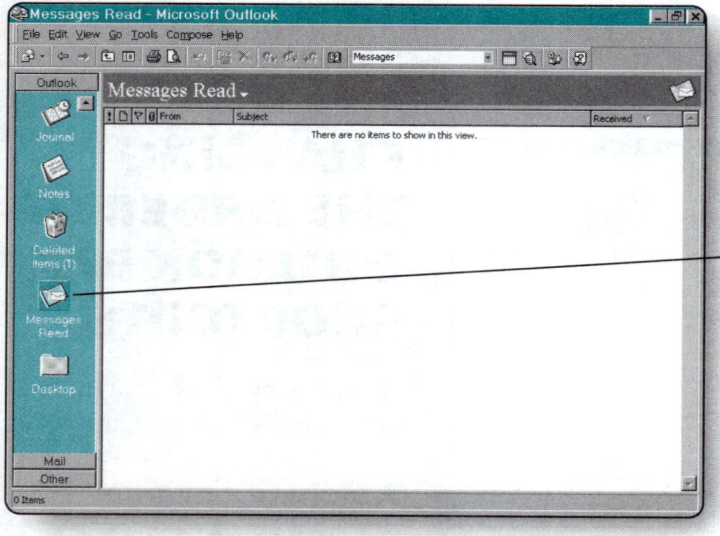

MOVING A SHORTCUT TO A DIFFERENT GROUP

1. **Point** at the **shortcut** you want to move. A square will appear around the shortcut.

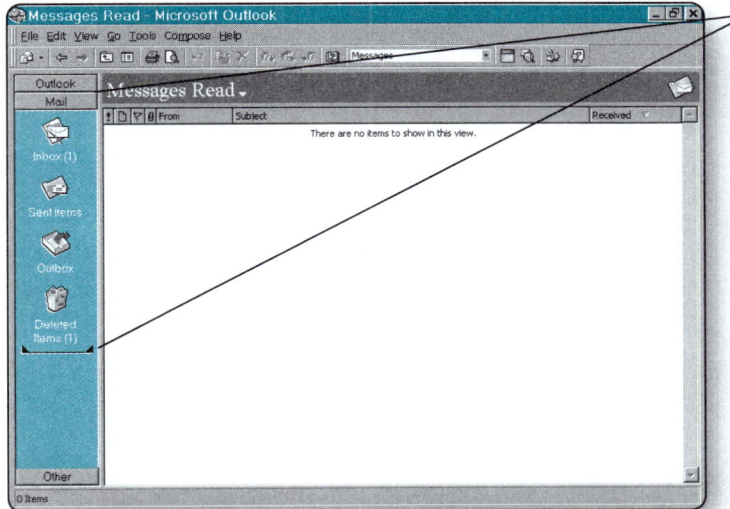

2. **Drag** the **shortcut** onto the group name in which you want to place it. Outlook will automatically open that group, and the shortcut's position will be either at the top or the bottom of the group. Do *not* release the mouse button yet.

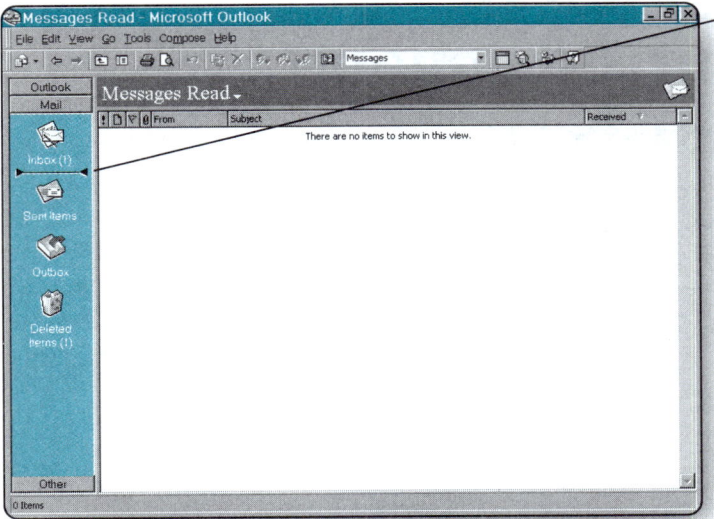

3. **Drag** the **shortcut** up or down in the list. As you move the pointer to an acceptable spot, a black marker will appear between existing shortcuts.

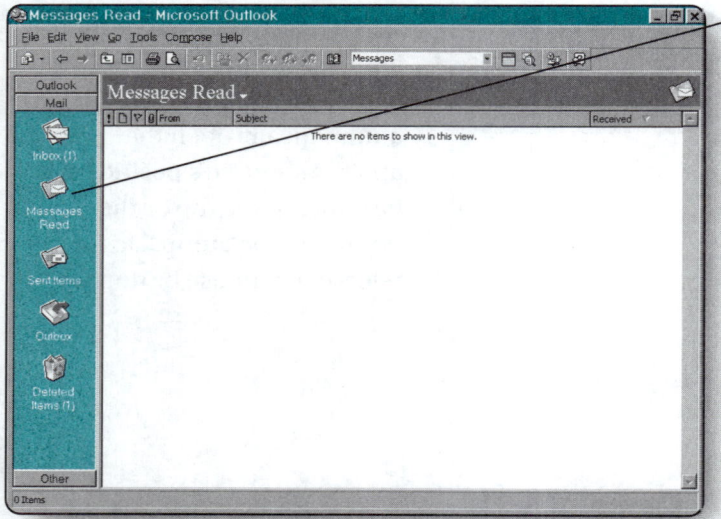

4. **Release** the **mouse button**. The shortcut will appear at its new location.

ADDING AN OUTLOOK GROUP

You can create a new group for the Outlook bar.

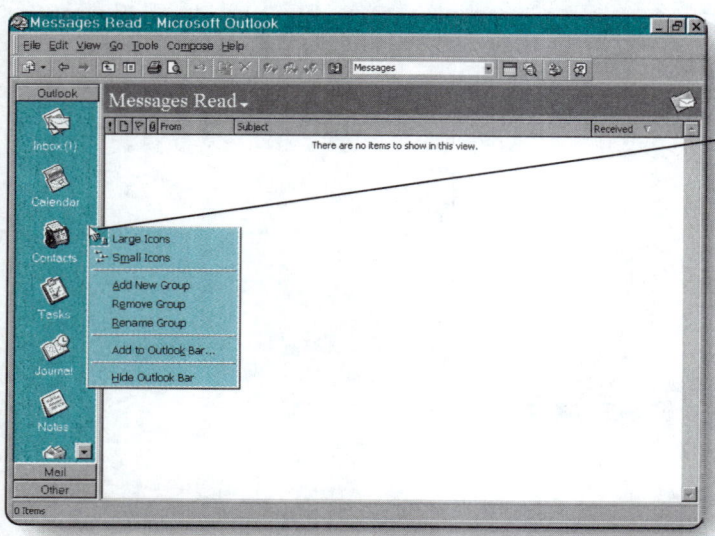

1. **Right-click** on the **Outlook bar**, making sure the mouse pointer is not pointing at an existing folder. A shortcut menu will appear.

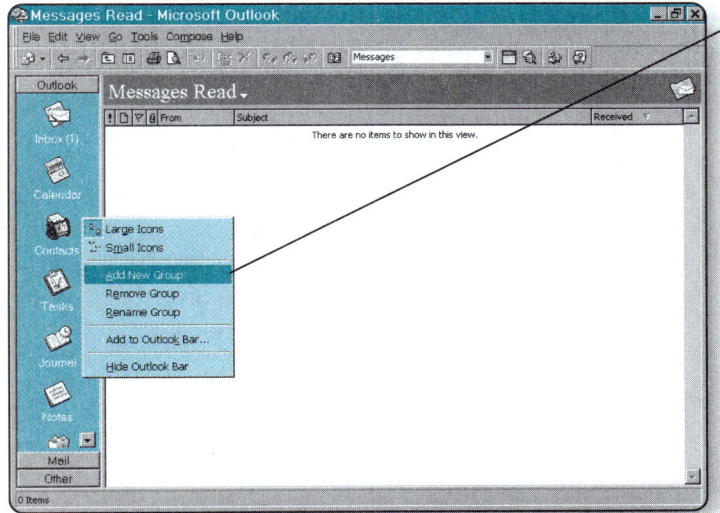

2. **Click** on **Add New Group**.

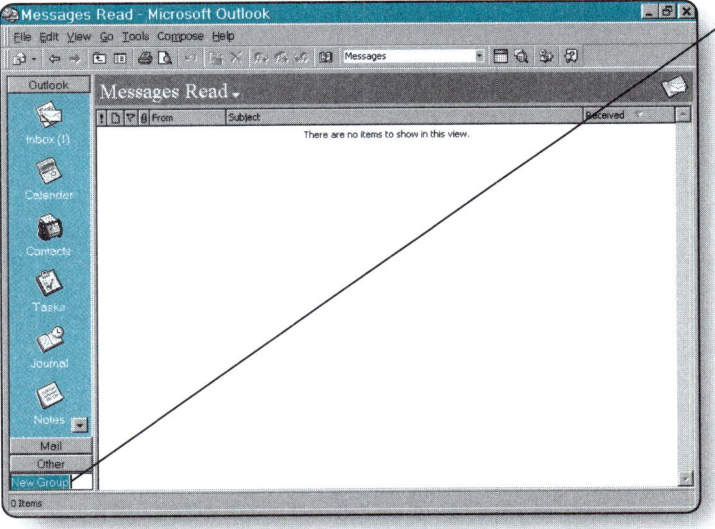

A button named New Group will appear at the bottom of the Outlook bar.

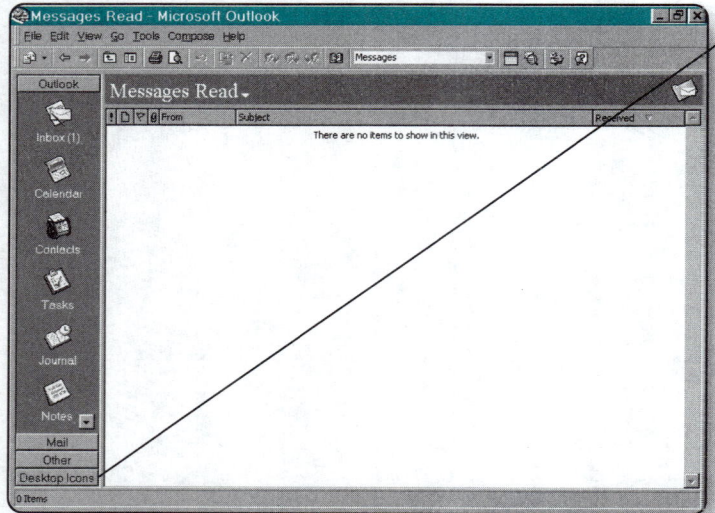

3. Type the **name** of the new group and **press** the **Enter key**.

TIP

If you want, you can drag existing shortcuts into the new group using the steps in "Moving a Shortcut to a Different Group."

16 Working with the Address Book

Outlook contains an address book that you can use to maintain a variety of information about business and personal contacts. You can use the address book to print a phone or address list, telephone a contact, or send e-mail to a contact. In this chapter, you'll learn how to:

✦ **Add an address book entry**

✦ **Print a contact list**

✦ **Telephone a contact from Outlook**

ADDING AN ADDRESS BOOK ENTRY

The address book in Outlook is ready and waiting for you to add entries.

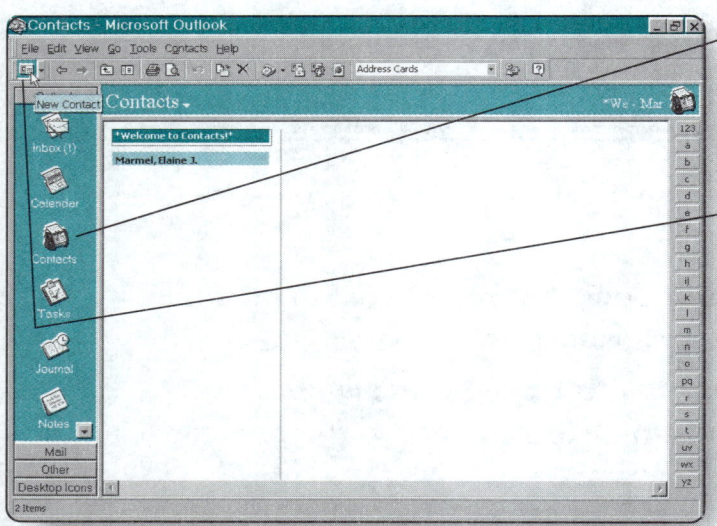

1. **Click** on the **Contacts shortcut**. Your list of entries will appear (initially, the contact list will contain only you).

2. **Click** on the **New Contact button**. The Contact window will appear.

NOTE

The New button in Outlook is context-sensitive. When you're viewing the Inbox, clicking on New will start a new mail message. When you're viewing Contacts, clicking on New will start a new contact.

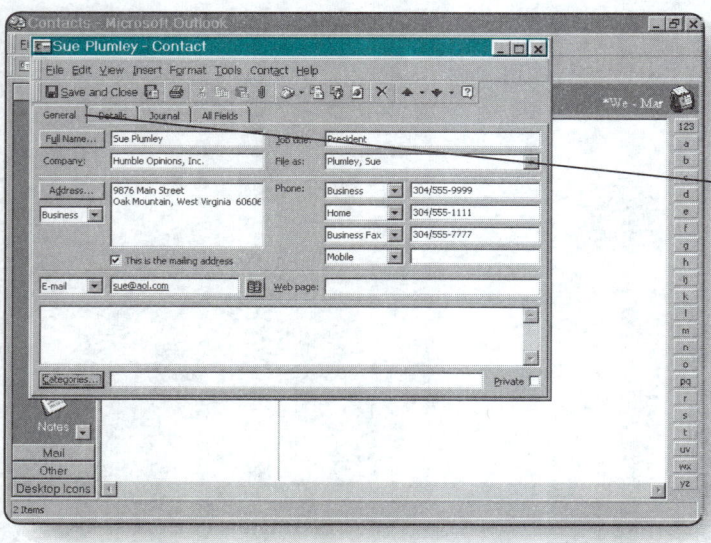

3. **Type information** in each box on the General tab.

4. **Press** the **Tab key** to move from box to box.

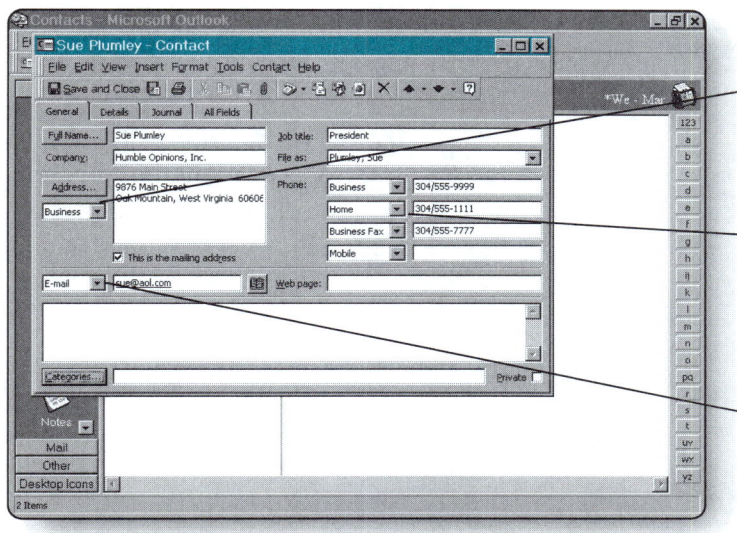

NOTE

You can enter up to three addresses by clicking on the arrow (▼) below the Address button.

You can enter up to 19 phone numbers by clicking on any of the arrows (▼) next to the Phone number list boxes.

You can enter up to three e-mail addresses by clicking on the arrow (▼) next to the E-mail list box.

5. **Click** on the **Categories button**. The Categories dialog box will open.

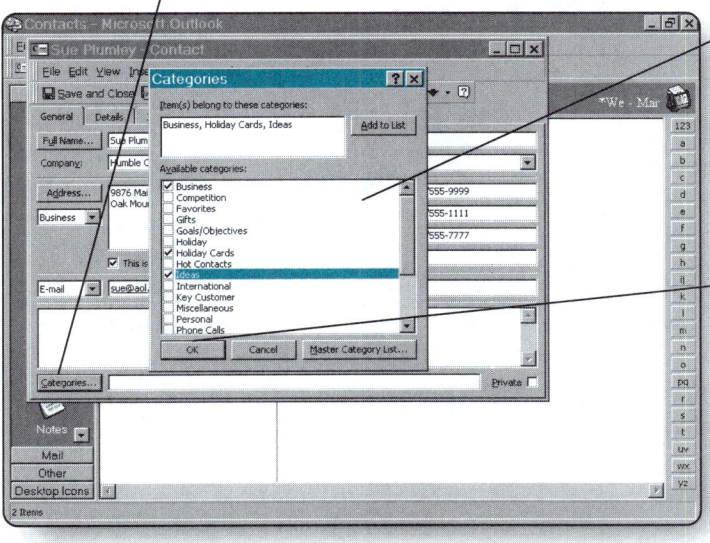

6. **Click** on **any** of the **available categories** to assign the contact to categories that you can use to produce telephone or mailing lists of contacts with similar characteristics.

7. **Click** on **OK**. The Categories dialog box will close.

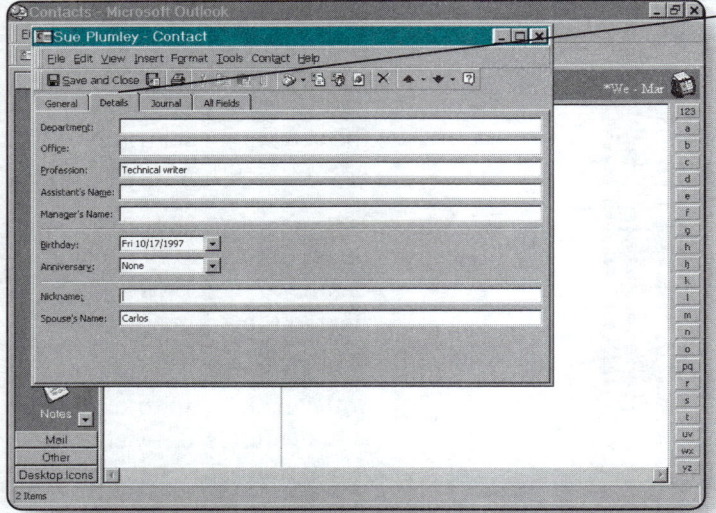

8. **Click** on the **Details tab**. The tab will come to the front.

9. **Type** any **additional information** about the contact that you would like to keep track of.

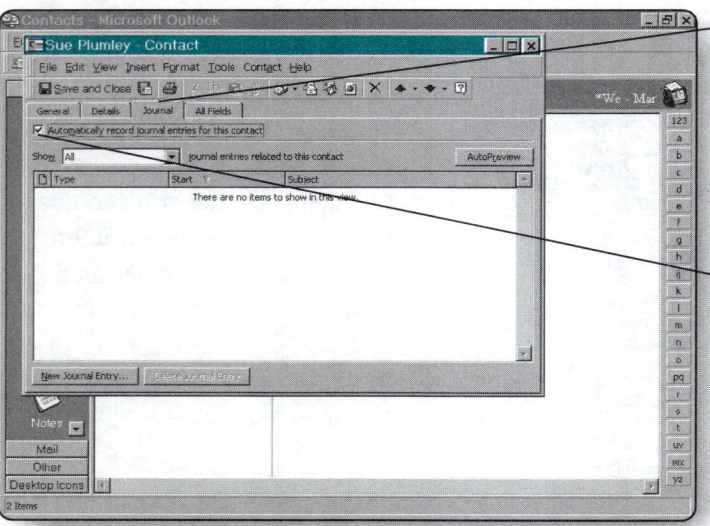

10. **Click** on the **Journal tab**. You will see a list of recorded contacts you have made with this person, such as meetings you have scheduled or e-mail you have sent or received.

11. **Click** on the **Automatically record journal entries for this contact check box**. A ✔ will appear in the box, telling Outlook to automatically track contacts for this entry.

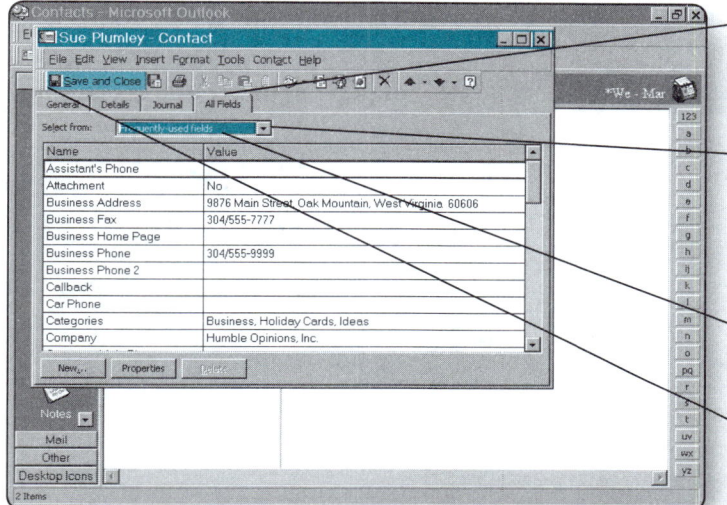

12. Click on the **All Fields tab**. You will see information about the contact in tabular form.

13. Click on the **arrow (▼)** next to the Select from: list box. A list of types of information will appear.

14. Click on the **type of information** you want to see.

15. Click on the **Save and Close button**. Outlook will save this entry.

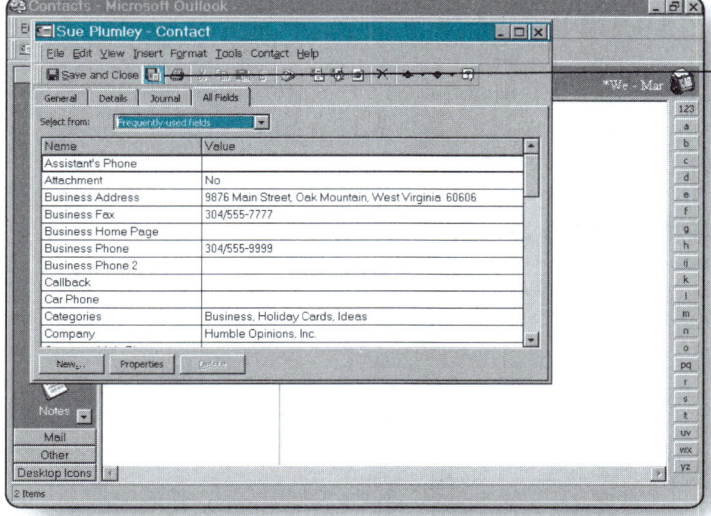

NOTE

You can click on the Save and New button to save the current entry and start a new entry.

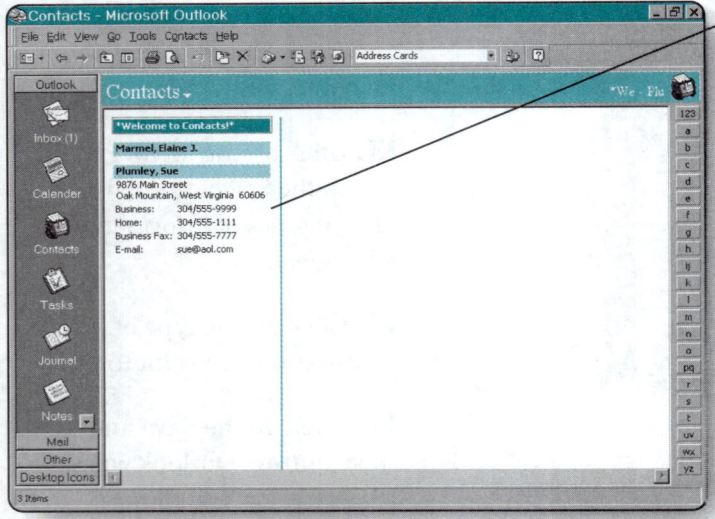

After you enter a new contact, you'll see information about the contact in the Contacts window.

TIP

To open and edit any contact's information, double-click on the contact's name.

IMPORTING ADDRESSES FROM WORD

Suppose you've already created an address book with entries in another program, such as Word. You don't need to rekey these addresses in Outlook—you can import them.

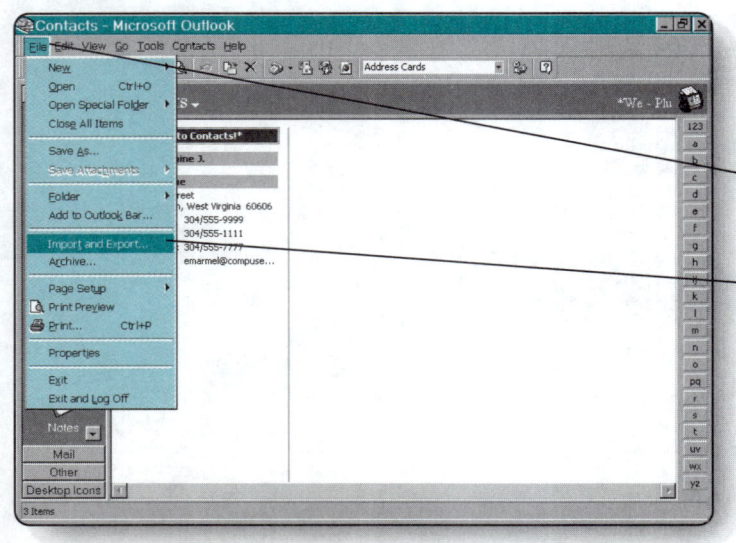

1. Click on the **Contacts shortcut**. You'll see your list of entries.

2. Click on **File**. The File menu will appear.

3. Click on **Import and Export**. The Import and Export Wizard will open.

TIP

You can import addresses from a variety of places, including Schedule+, Excel files, and Access databases. In this book, you'll walk through importing addresses stored in your Personal Address Book, which is also used by Microsoft Exchange. To import from other programs, the steps are basically the same, but the process is more complex and beyond the scope of this book.

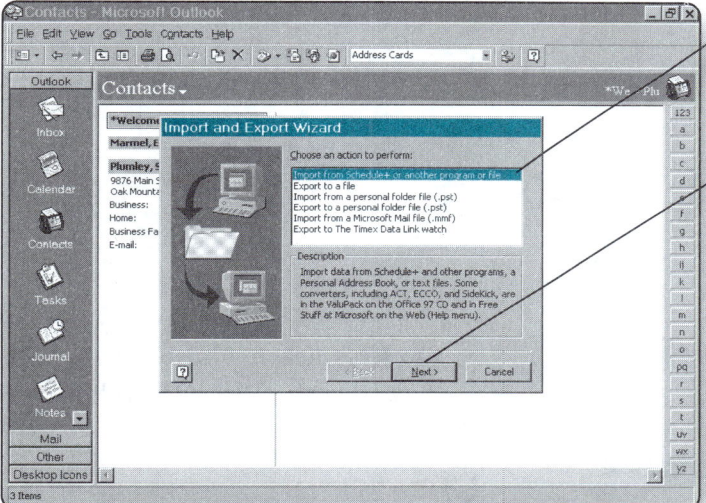

4. Click on **Import from Schedule+ or another program or file.**

5. Click on **Next.**

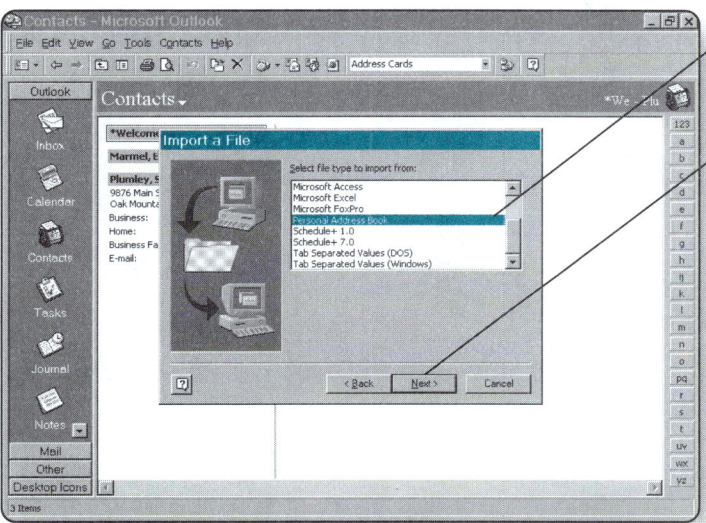

6. Click on **Personal Address Book.**

7. Click on **Next.**

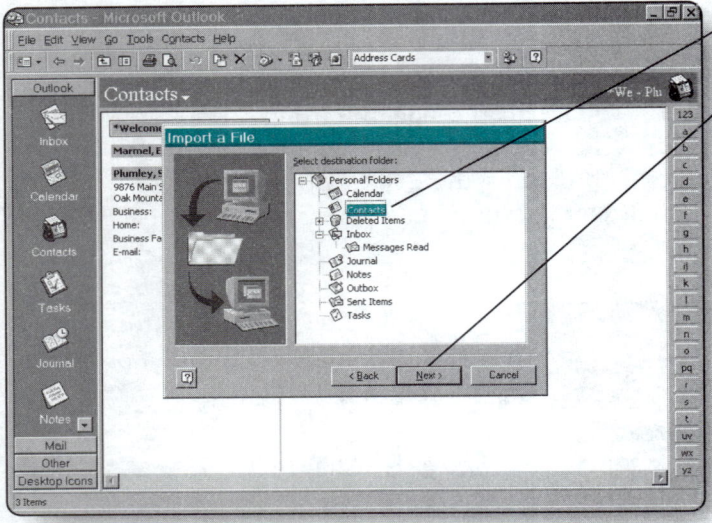

8. **Click** on **Contacts**.

9. **Click** on **Next**.

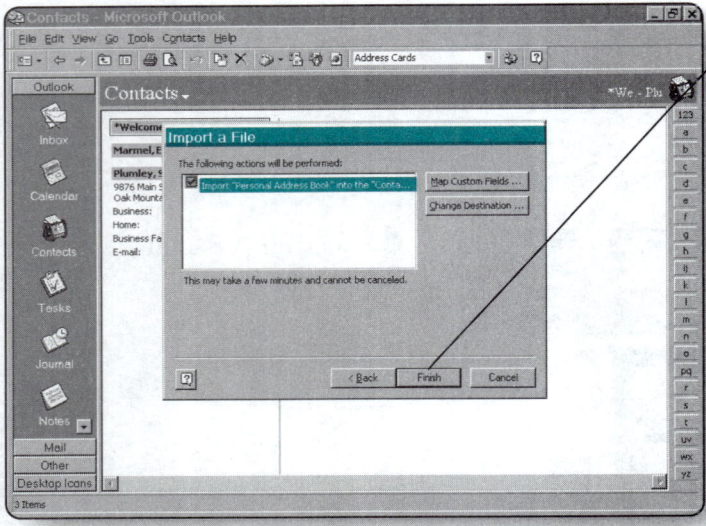

10. **Click** on **Finish**. The Import and Export Wizard will close.

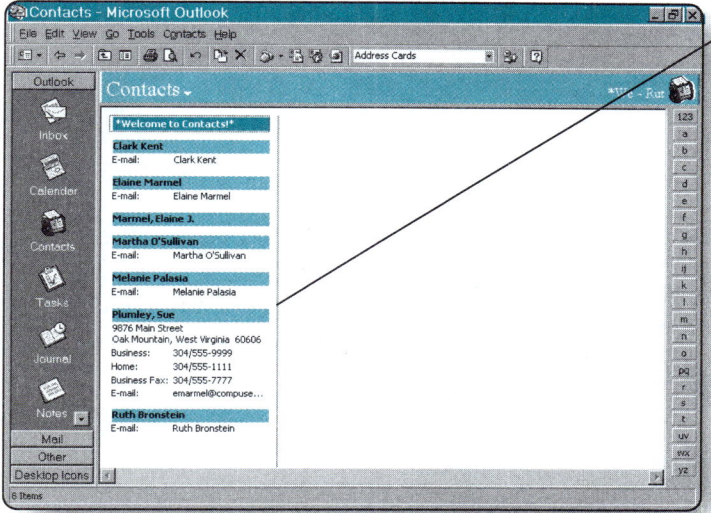

The name and address information stored in the Personal Address Book will appear in the Contacts window.

PRINTING A CONTACT LIST

You can print the information you store about your contacts in a variety of formats: Card Style, Small Booklet Style, Medium Booklet Style, Memo Style, and Phone Directory Style.

TIP

Click on the Preview button to see the output onscreen. In Preview mode, click on the Print button to redisplay the Print dialog box or click on the Close button (☒) to return to Outlook without printing.

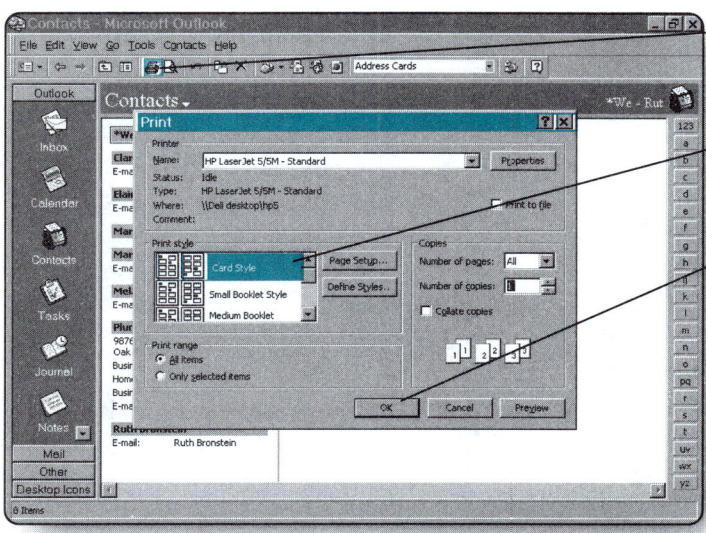

1. **Click** on the **Print button**. The Print dialog box will open.

2. **Click** on a **print style**. The item will be selected.

3. **Click** on **OK**. The contact list will print.

DIALING A CONTACT

If your computer is attached to a modem and you have a telephone on the same line, you can let Outlook dial the phone for you when you decide to call a contact.

1. **Click** on the **contact** you want to call.

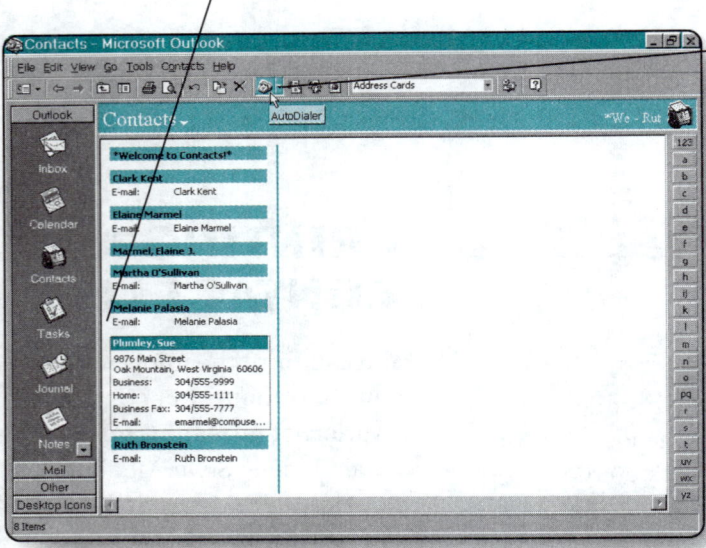

2. **Click** on the **AutoDialer button**. The New Call dialog box will open.

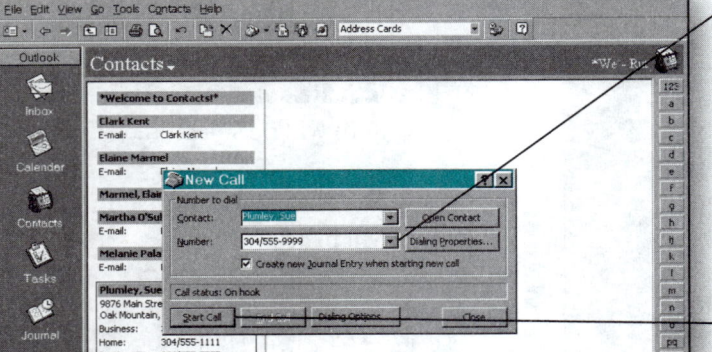

NOTE

Optionally, you can click on the arrow (▼) next to the Number: list box to display a list of phone numbers you have previously dialed and select a different number to dial than the one appearing in the Number: list box.

3. **Click** on **Start Call**. If you're tracking phone calls in the Journal, the Phone Call Journal Entry dialog box will open, along with the Call Status dialog box.

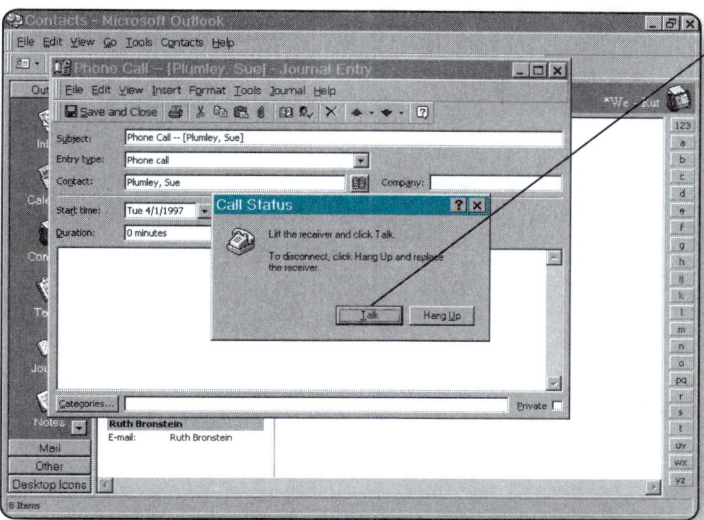

4. Lift the **telephone receiver** and **click** on **Talk** to speak to the party at the other end of the call.

TIP

If there's no answer, click on Hang Up to cancel the call.

5. **Hang up** the **telephone receiver** to complete the call just as you would complete any phone call.

6. Enter notes in the **Journal Entry window** if you're tracking phone calls in the Journal.

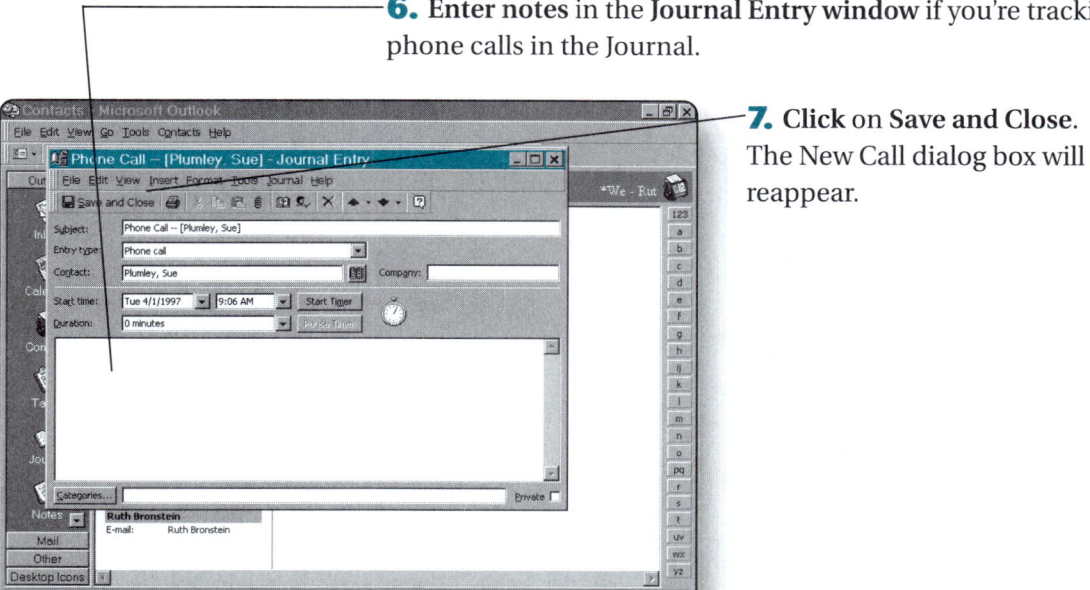

7. Click on **Save and Close**. The New Call dialog box will reappear.

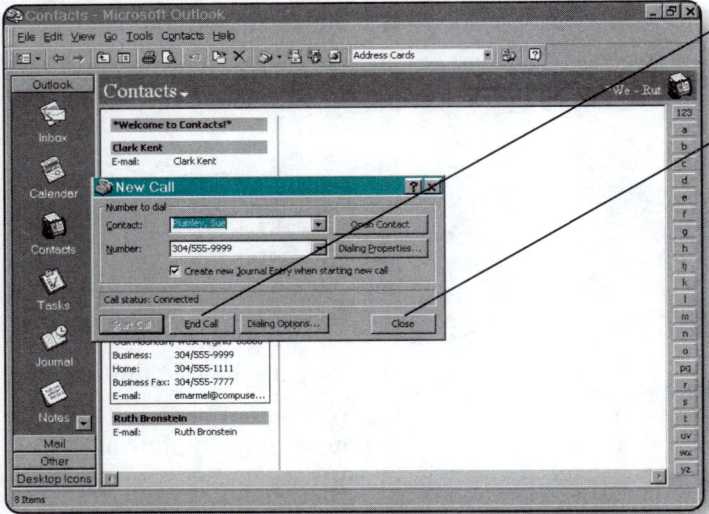

8. **Click** on **End Call** to complete the call in Outlook.

9. **Click** on **Close**. The New Call dialog box will close.

17

Using E-mail

Outlook enables you to use your existing e-mail or fax program to send and receive e-mail messages and faxes. You can also create an e-mail or fax message and check for new mail in Outlook. In this chapter, you'll learn how to:

✦ Send an e-mail message

✦ Respond to an e-mail message

SENDING AN E-MAIL MESSAGE

In Outlook, you can access your e-mail software to send e-mail messages.

TIP

You can also send faxes from Outlook.

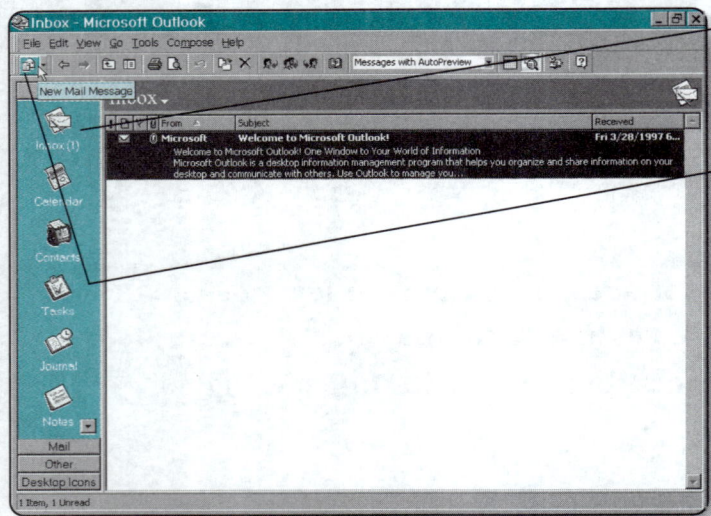

1. **Click** on the **Inbox shortcut** in the Outlook bar to display the Inbox.

2. **Click** on the **New Mail Message button**. A new mail message window will appear.

NOTE

If you don't want to use the Address Book, as steps 3 through 6 explain, you can type the recipient's e-mail address in the box next to the To button.

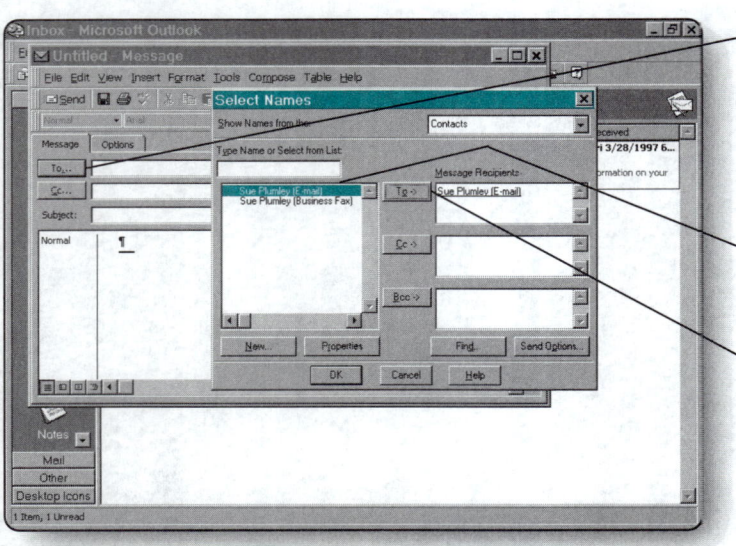

3. **Click** on the **To button**. The e-mail addresses you have stored in the Contact list will appear in the Select Names dialog box.

4. **Click** on the **recipient's name**.

5. **Click** on the **To button**. The recipient's name will appear in the Message Recipients box.

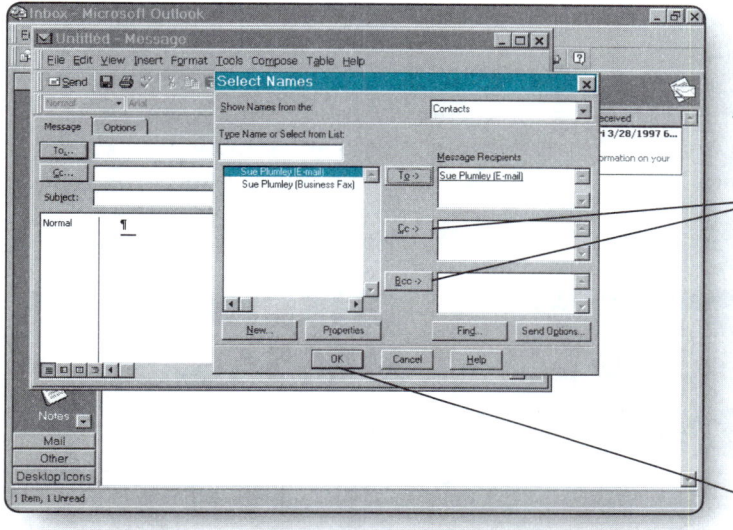

TIP

To send the message to more than one recipient, repeat steps 4 and 5.

To send copies of the message to a recipient, repeat the same steps, but click on the Cc button instead of the To button in step 5. Use the Bcc button to send blind copies of the message.

6. **Click** on **OK**. The Select Names dialog box will close.

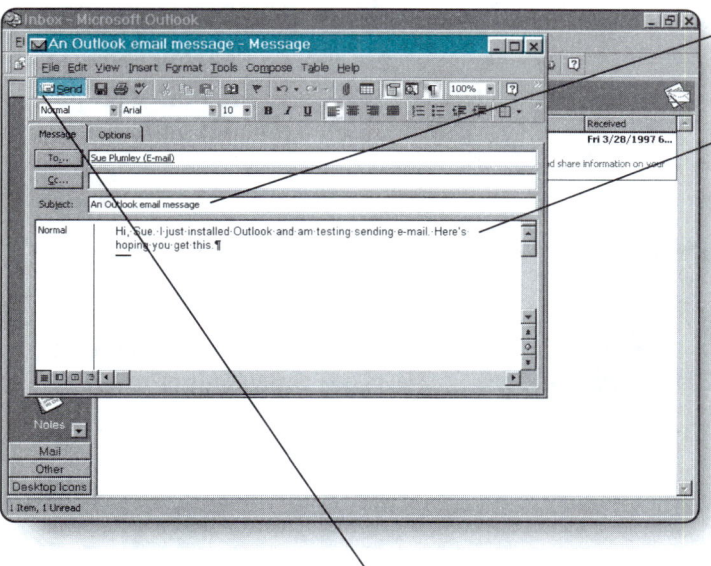

7. **Type** a **subject** for the message in the Subject: text box.

8. **Type** a **message**.

TIP

To send a file, click on the Insert File button (it looks like a paper clip). The Insert File dialog box will open. Navigate to the folder containing the file and choose the file. When you click on OK, you'll see an icon representing the file in your mail message.

9. **Click** on the **Send button**. The Message window will close and the Inbox window will appear.

TIP

Messages you send will appear in the Sent Items folder. A shortcut to this folder appears in the Mail group. You can double-click on items you send to open and view them.

NOTE

E-mail messages are sent immediately unless your e-mail software is configured to hold messages in the Outbox until you connect and send your messages.

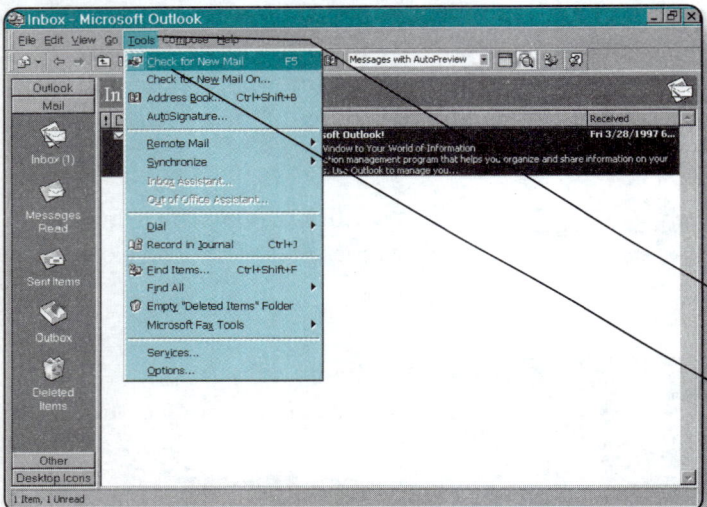

CHECKING FOR MESSAGES

You can check for new mail from inside Outlook; any e-mail you receive will appear in your Outlook Inbox.

1. **Click** on **Tools**. The Tools menu will appear.

2. **Click** on **Check for New Mail**. Your e-mail program will launch, and Outlook will check for messages.

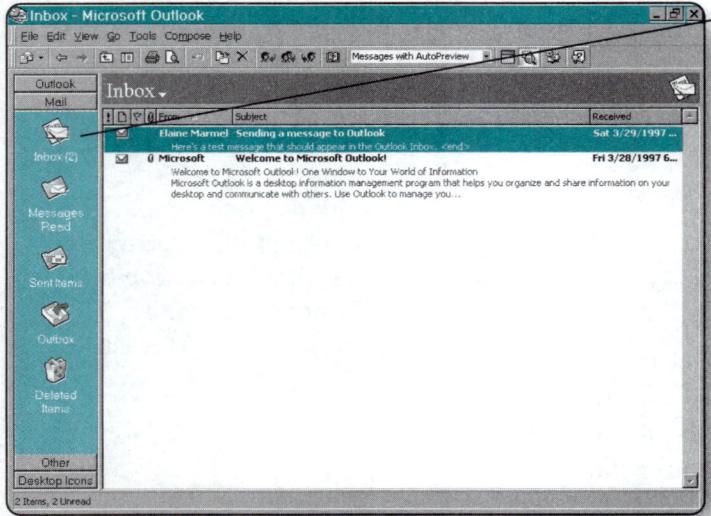

Any new messages you receive will appear in the Outlook Inbox.

The number of unread messages in your Inbox appears in parentheses after the Inbox shortcut.

TIP

If you are always connected to your e-mail system, messages will appear automatically in your Inbox and you won't need to check for messages.

RESPONDING TO A MESSAGE

You can respond to a message you receive in a number of ways: reply to the message, forward the message, delete the message, or close the message without answering.

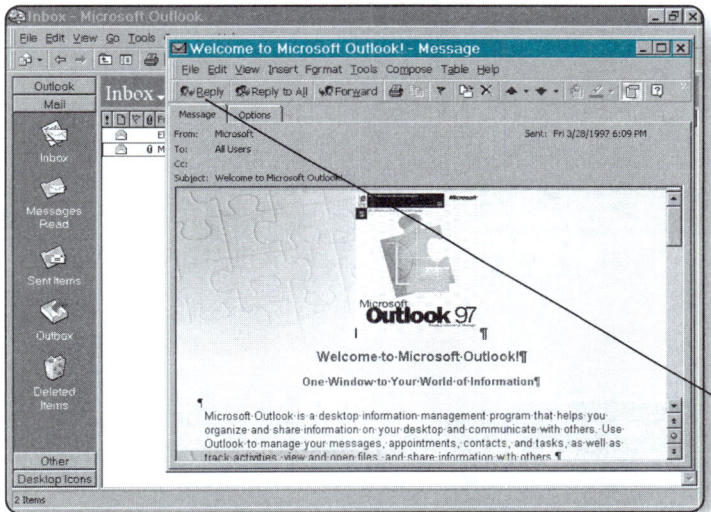

Replying to a Message

Most people consider it a common courtesy to respond to a message they receive.

1. **Double-click** on a **message**. The message will open so you can read it.

2. **Click** on the **Reply button**.

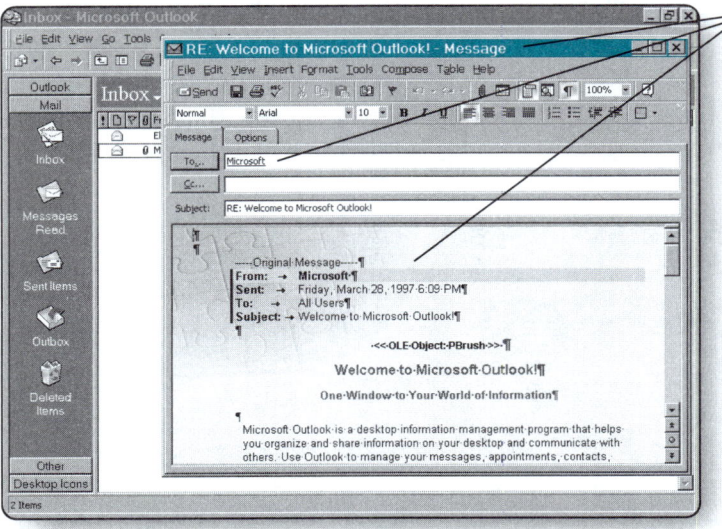

Outlook will add header information to the original message and allow you space to add information at the top of the message. Outlook will also fill in the To text box with the address of the original sender. Notice the title bar—it will indicate that you are replying to a message.

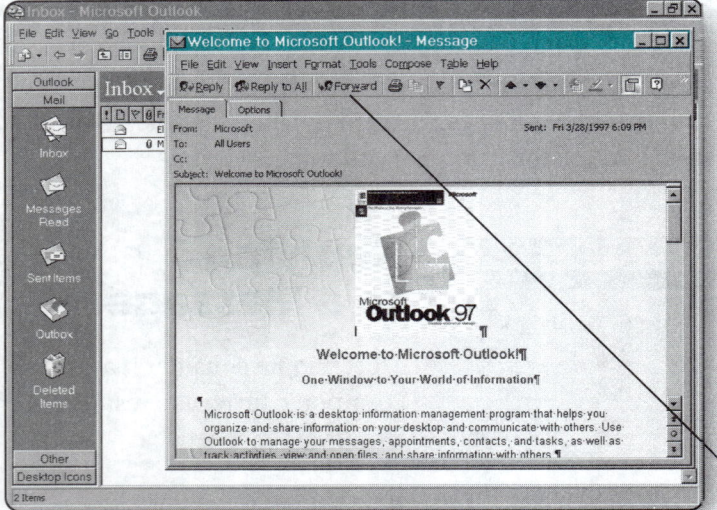

Forwarding a Message

On occasion, information might come to you via e-mail that you want to share with others. In these cases, you can forward the message.

1. **Double-click** on a **message**. The message will open so you can read it.

2. **Click** on the **Forward button**.

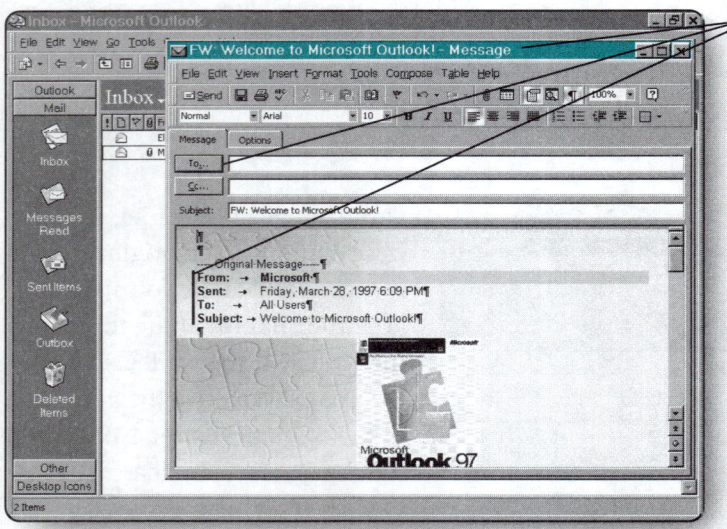

Outlook will add header information to the original message, allow you space to add information at the top of the message, and wait for you to click on the To button and address the message to another recipient. Notice the title bar— it will indicate that you are forwarding a message.

Deleting a Message

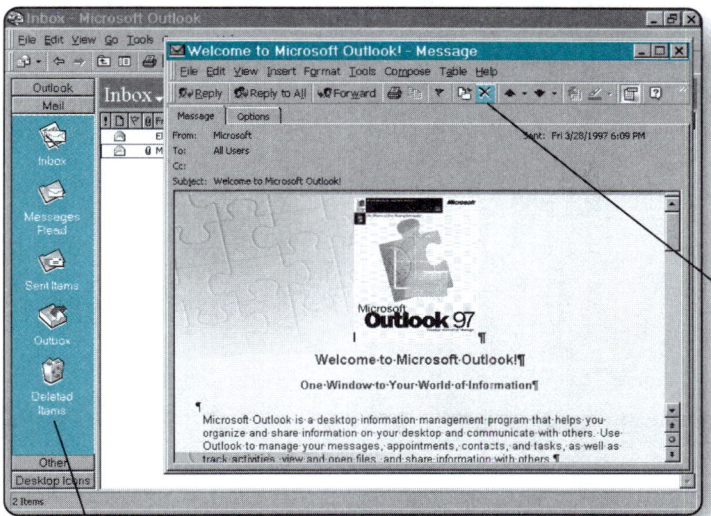

Some messages require no response and you don't need to keep them so you can delete them.

1. **Double-click** on a **message**. The message will open so you can read it.

2. **Click** on the **Delete button**.

Outlook will move the message from the Inbox to the Deleted Items folder. You can display the contents of that folder and see the deleted message.

TIP

Items remain in the Deleted Items folder until you delete them from that folder.

Using Folders to Manage Messages

In some cases, you might not be ready to respond to a message when you receive it. You might want to close it and answer it later. You might even want to create a "Pending" folder in which to store these messages.

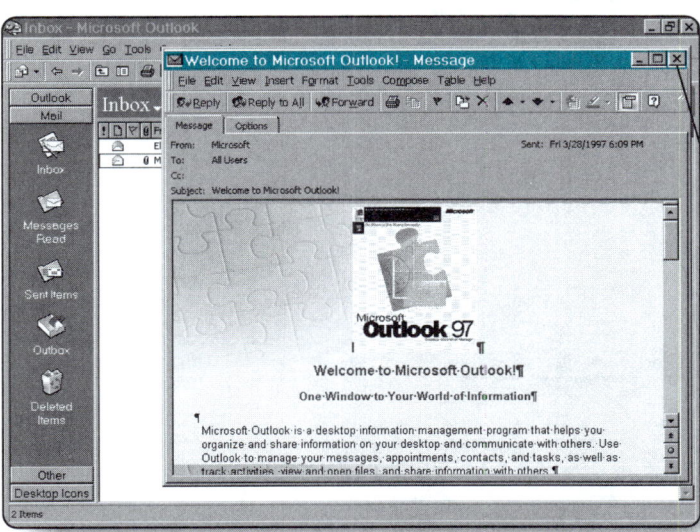

1. **Double-click** on a **message**. The message will open so you can read it.

2. **Click** on the **Close button** (✕) to close and keep the message without taking any action. Outlook will leave the message in the Inbox folder.

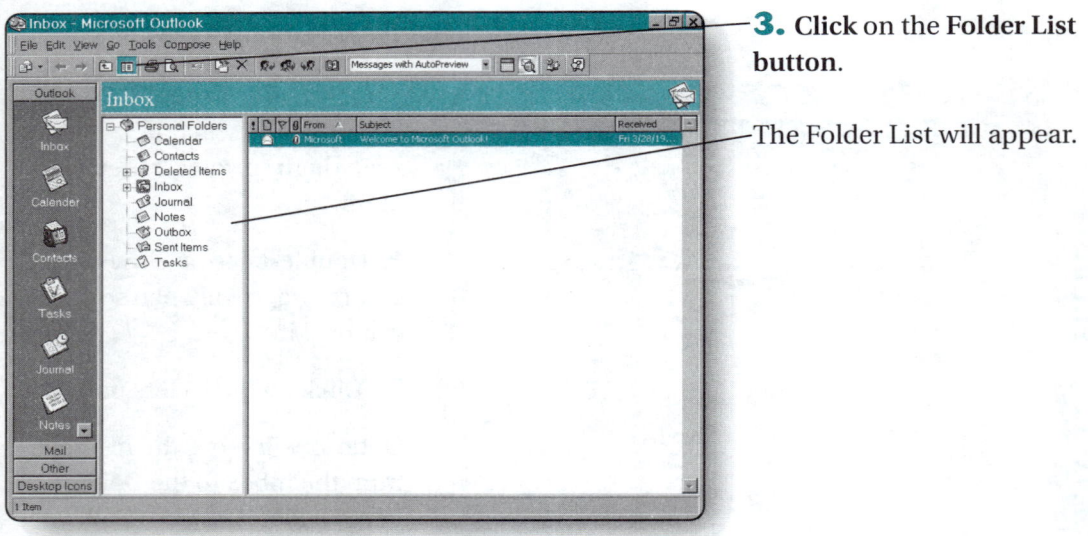

3. **Click** on the **Folder List button**.

The Folder List will appear.

4. **Click** on **File**. The File menu will appear.

5. **Click** on **New**. A cascading menu will appear.

6. **Click** on **Folder**. The Create New Folder dialog box will open.

7. **Click** on **Inbox** to tell Outlook where you want to place the new folder.

8. **Type** a **folder name** in the Name: text box.

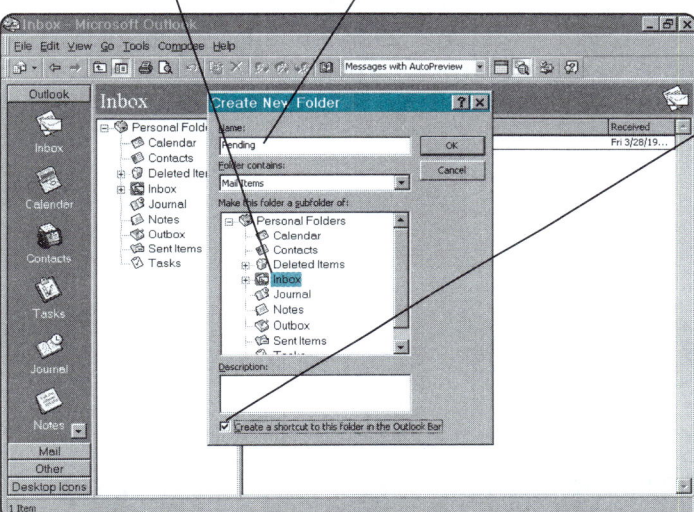

9. **Click** on **OK**. The Create New Folder dialog box will close.

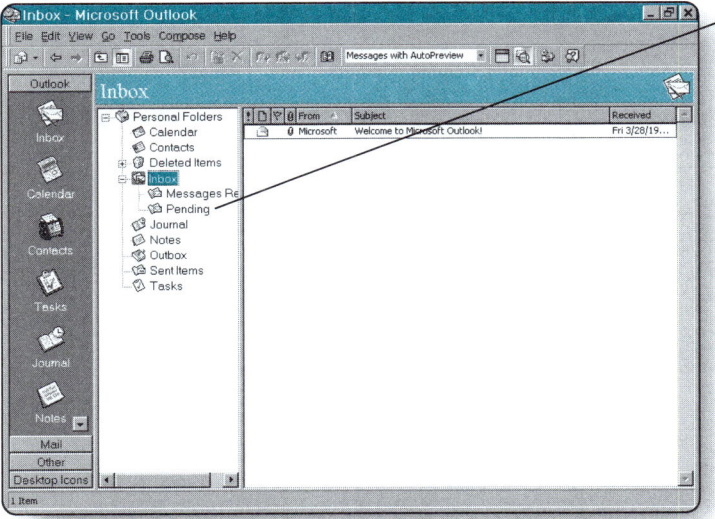

A new folder will appear under the Inbox in the Folder List, but the Inbox will still be the selected folder.

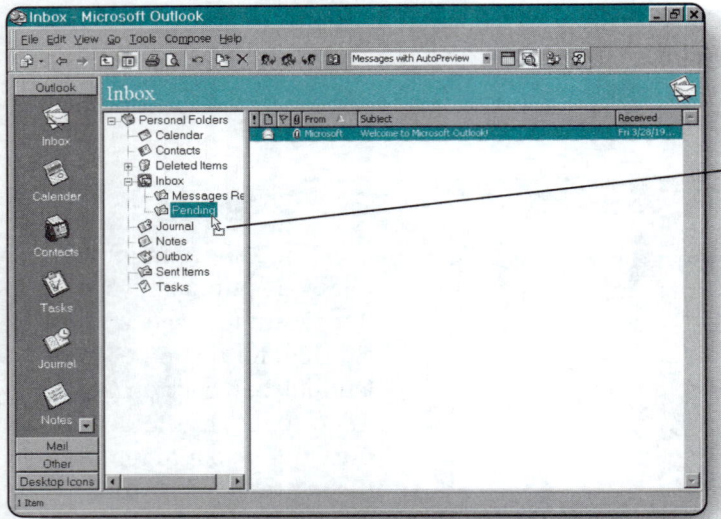

10. **Press** and **hold** the **mouse button** and **drag** a **message** from the Inbox to the new folder.

11. **Release** the **mouse button**. Outlook will move the message to the new folder.

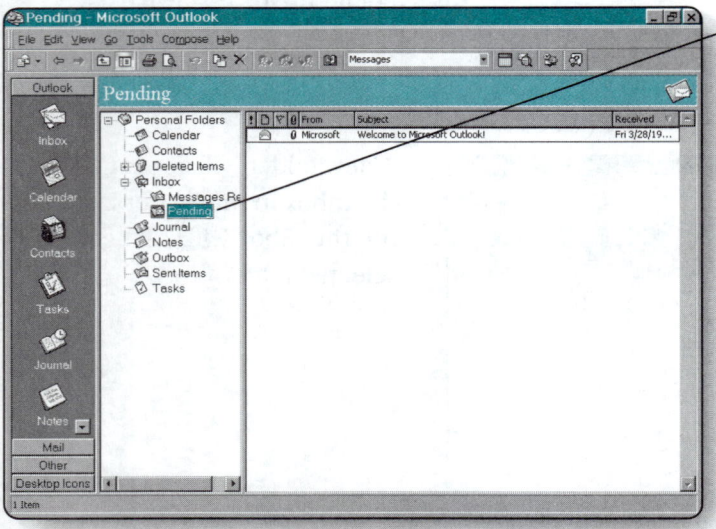

12. **Click** on the **new folder**. You will see the message you just moved in the window on the right.

18 Using the Calendar

You can use the Outlook Calendar to schedule appointments, meetings, and events. You can also use the Outlook Calendar for individual or group scheduling. In this chapter, you'll learn how to:

✦ **Make an appointment**

✦ **Change the Calendar's display**

✦ **Create a recurring appointment**

✦ **Schedule a meeting**

✦ **Create an event**

✦ **Print the Calendar**

VIEWING THE CALENDAR

You can view your Calendar from several different perspectives: one day at a time, one week at a time, one month at a time, and in a tabular format. You can switch to these views in a few different ways.

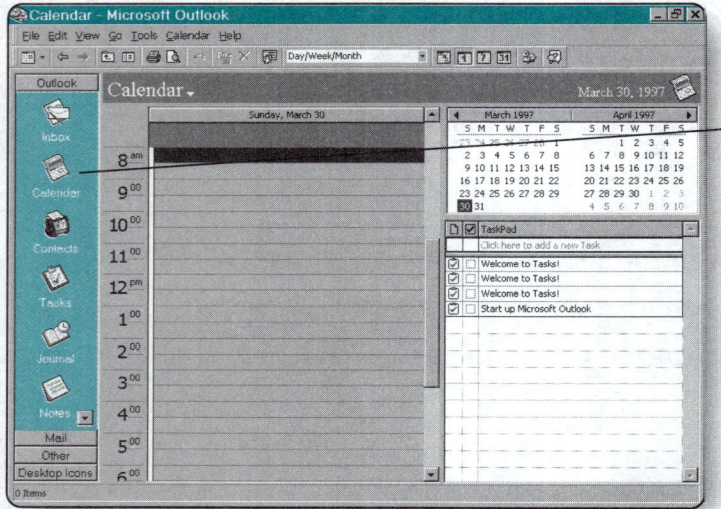

Changing the Calendar's View

1. **Click** on the **Calendar shortcut** in the Outlook bar. The Calendar will appear in the one-day-at-a-time view.

TIP

Times that appear gray are not "business hours"—no appointments can be scheduled during those times.

2. **Click** on the **Week button**. The Calendar view will change to display one week at a time.

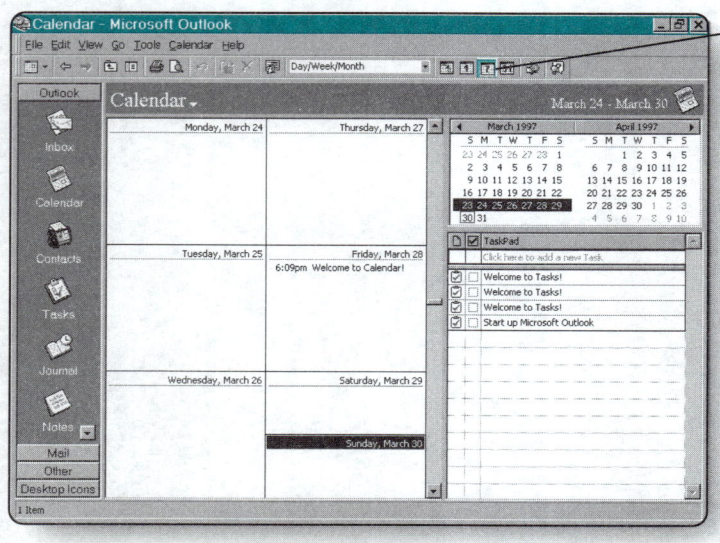

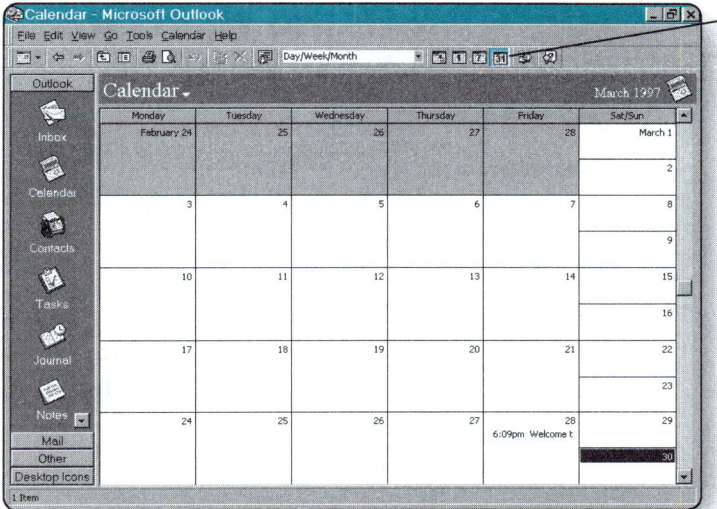

3. **Click** on the **Month button**. The Calendar view will change to display one month at a time.

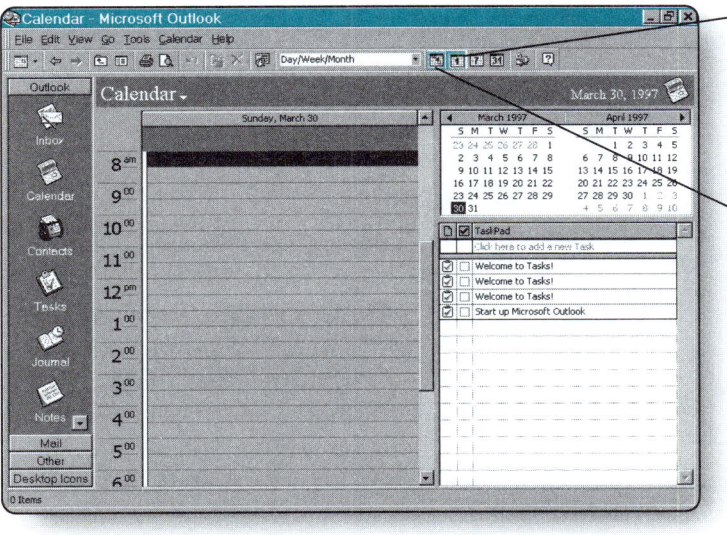

4. **Click** on the **Day button**. The Calendar view will redisplay the default view of one day at a time.

TIP

To quickly select "today" in the Calendar, click on the Go to Today button.

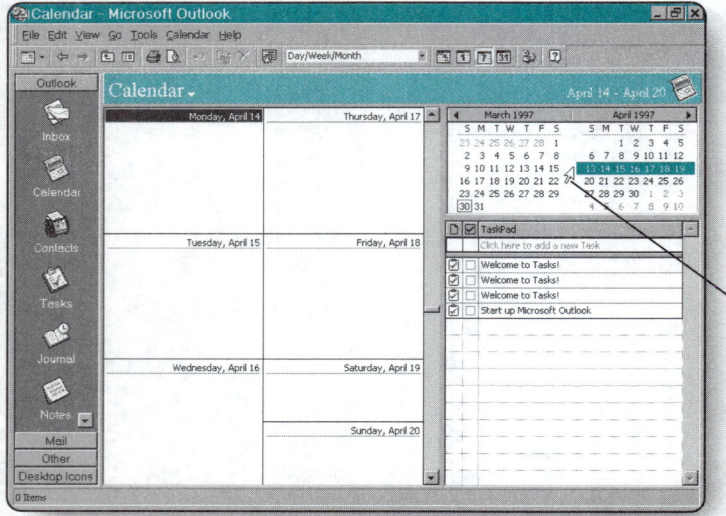

Using the Date Navigator

The Date Navigator helps you quickly switch between Calendar views and select days, weeks, or months to view.

1. **Click** to the **left of the Sunday of the week** you want to view. The Calendar view will display that week.

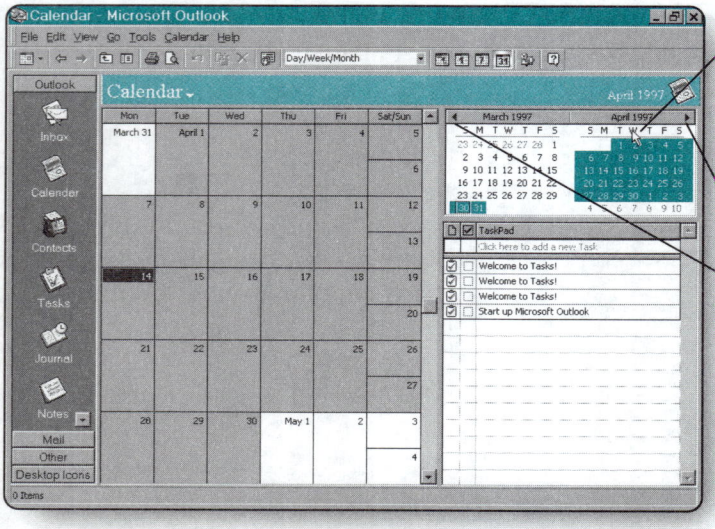

2. **Click anywhere** on the **day of the week headings** for the month you want to view. The Calendar view will display the month on which you clicked.

NOTE

If you need to see a different month, click on the arrows (◄►) that appear next to the month names.

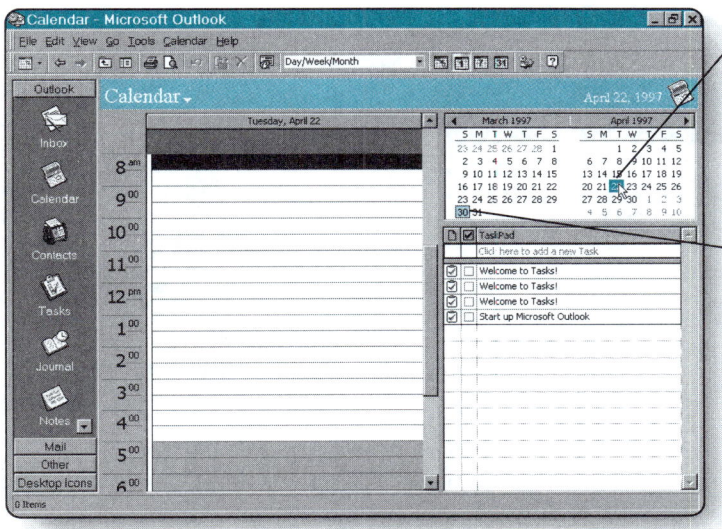

3. **Click** on the **day** you want to view. The Calendar view will show just the day on which you clicked.

Looking at the Calendar in Table View

Sometimes, seeing a list of appointments on the Calendar works better than any of the views.

1. **Click** on **View**. The View menu will appear.

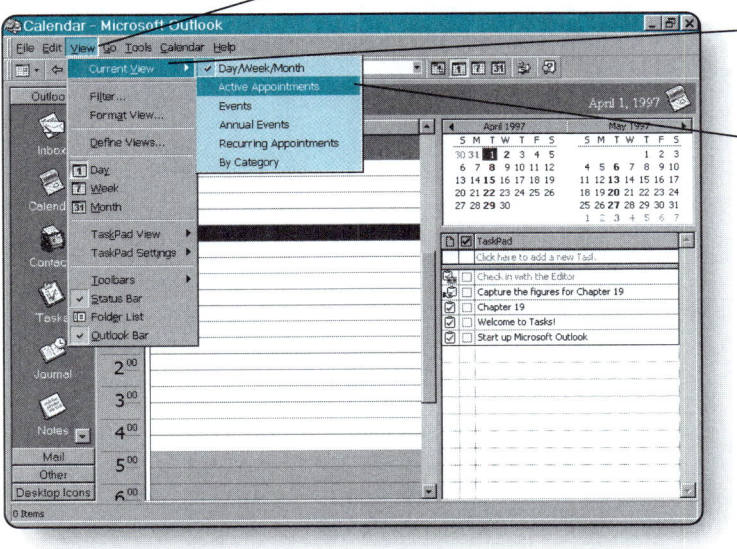

2. **Click** on **Current View**. A cascading menu will appear.

3. **Click** on **Active Appointments**.

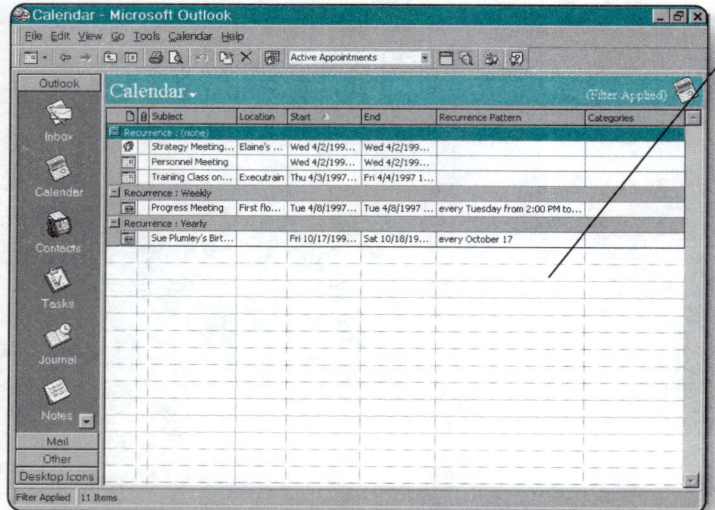

The table view of your Calendar will appear in the Calendar window.

TIP

You can print the table view of your Calendar—just switch to this view and then use the steps in the last task of this chapter.

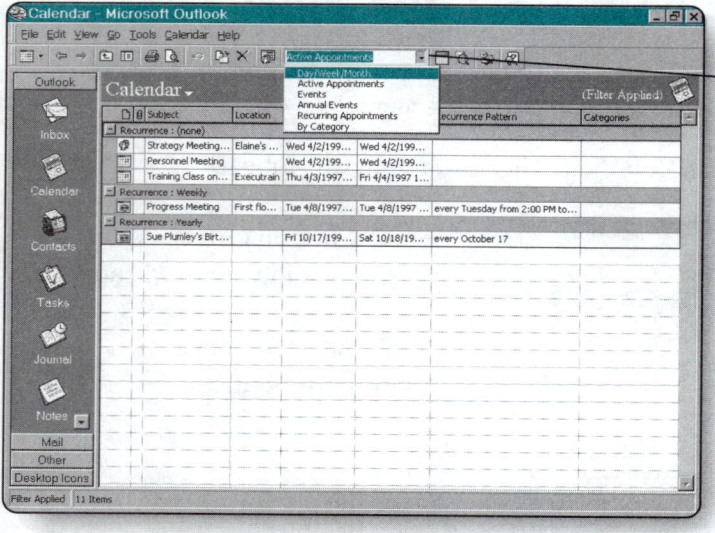

TIP

You can click on the arrow (▼) of the Current View box and choose Day/ Week/ Month to redisplay the original view of your Calendar.

MAKING AN APPOINTMENT

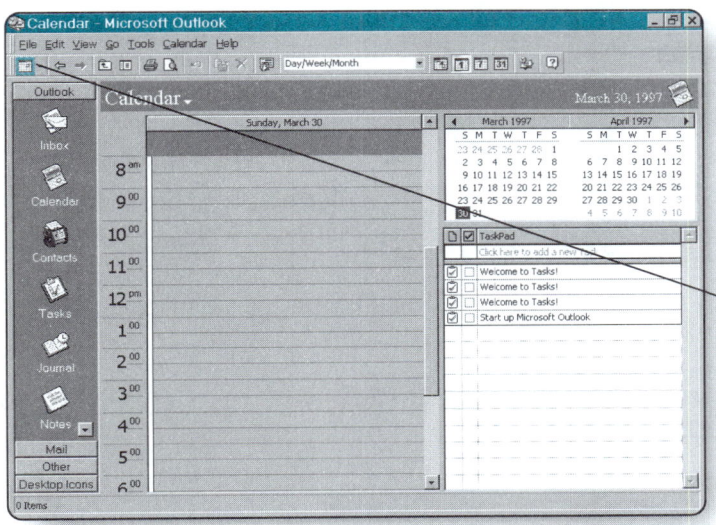

An *appointment* is an entry you make on the Calendar to reserve time for an activity; appointments do not include other people. To make a new appointment, make sure you are viewing the Calendar.

1. **Click** on the **New Appointment button**. The Appointment window will appear.

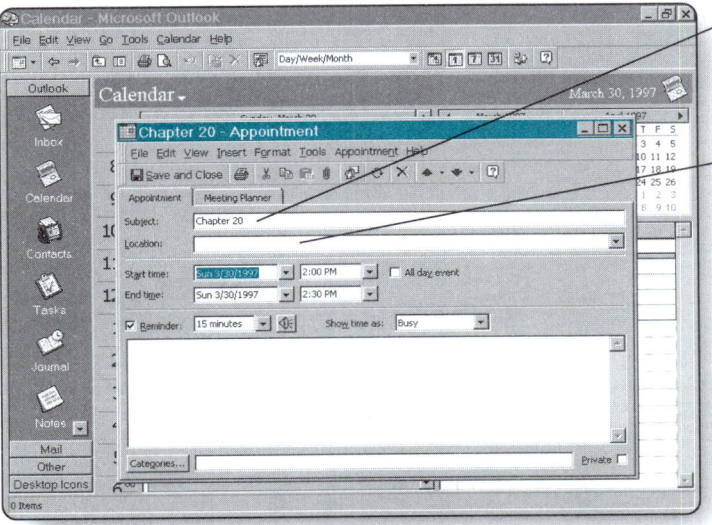

2. **Type** a **subject** for the appointment and **press** the **Tab key**.

3. **Type** a **location** for the appointment and **press** the **Tab key**. Typing a location is optional.

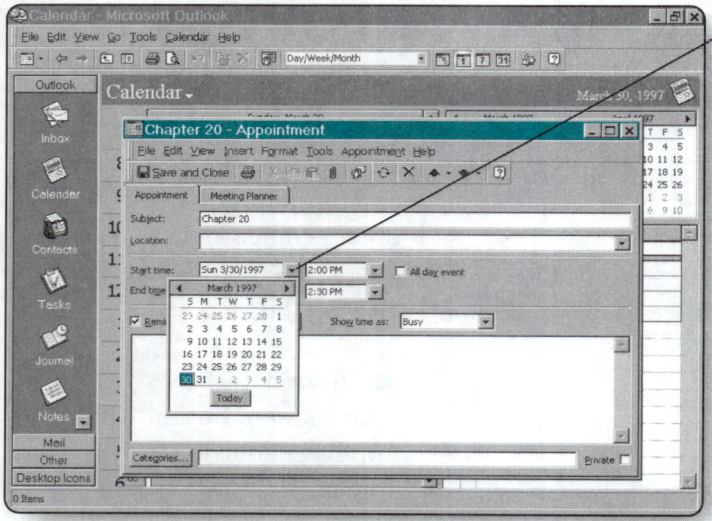

4. **Click** on the **arrow** (▼) next to the Start time: date box. A small calendar will appear, from which you can select a date for the appointment.

5. **Click** on the **date** for the appointment and **press** the **Tab key**. Outlook will insert the date into the Appointment window and close the small calendar.

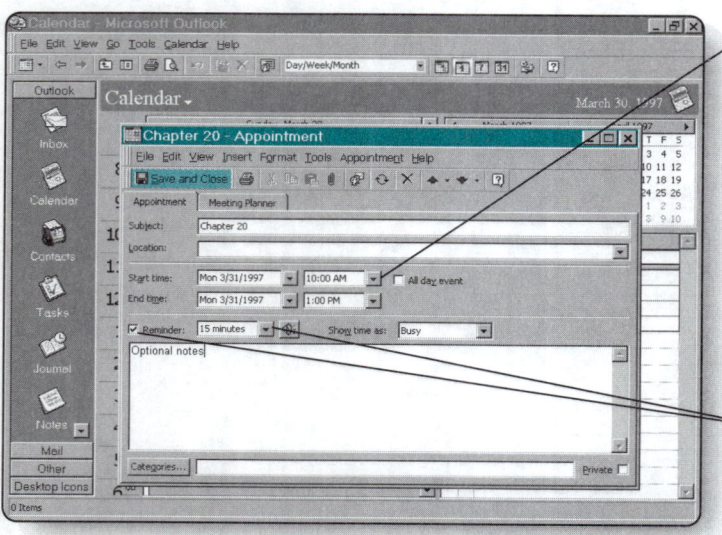

6. **Click** on the **arrow** (▼) next to the Start time: time box. A list of available times will appear.

7. **Select** a **start time** for the appointment.

NOTE

Place a ✔ in the Reminder: check box to tell Outlook to remind you of the appointment by playing a sound. If you do this, you can use the Reminder: list box to specify the amount of time prior to the appointment that Outlook will remind you.

TIP

To set an end time, repeat steps 6 and 7 using the arrows (▼) next to the End time: date and time boxes.

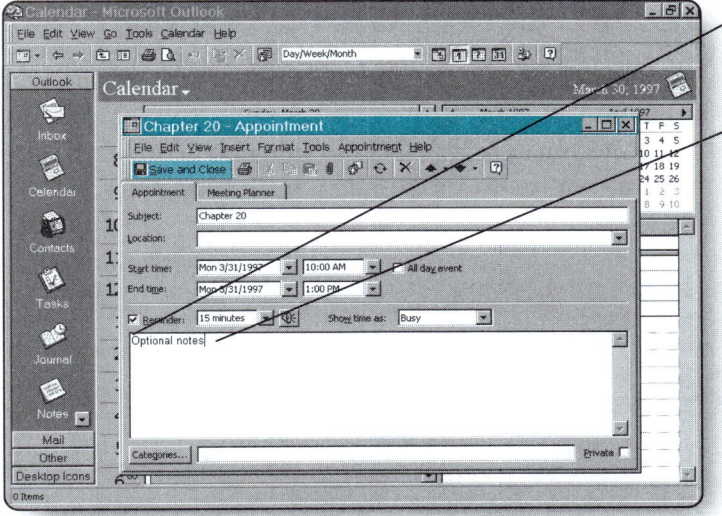

8. Click in the **box** at the bottom of the window.

9. Type any **notes** about the appointment. Typing a note is optional.

10. Click on the **Save and Close button**. Outlook will save the appointment on the day and at the time you scheduled it.

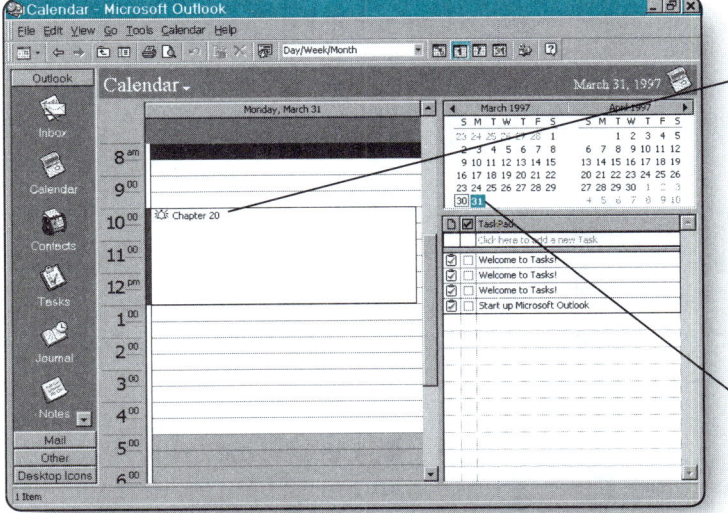

TIP

To view the appointment, switch to the scheduled day or to the week or month view containing the appointment. To edit the appointment, double-click on it.

NOTE

Notice, in the Date Navigator, that future dates containing appointments appear bold.

SCHEDULING A MEETING

Meetings are entries for which you schedule time and invite others to attend. When you invite others who are using Outlook, Outlook will let you look at their schedules and determine if they have free time at the proposed meeting time. When you schedule the meeting, you'll send an e-mail to each person and put a tentative activity on each person's Calendar.

If you want to invite someone who is not using Outlook, you won't be able to check for free time; however, if you have stored that person's e-mail address in your Outlook address book, you can send an e-mail requesting attendance.

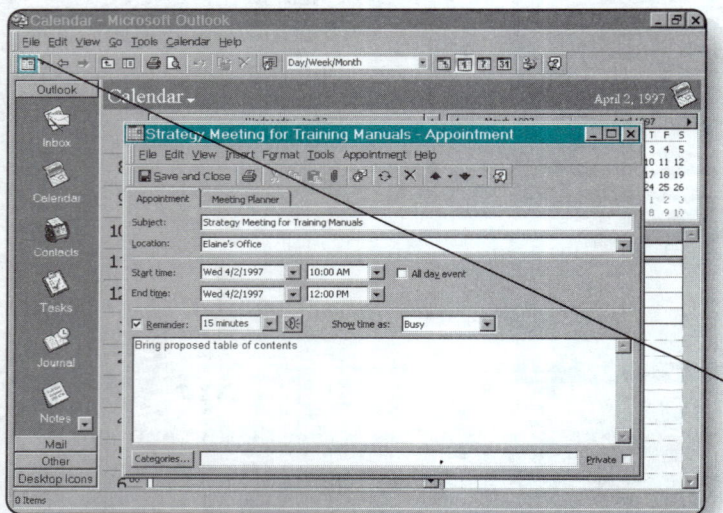

1. **Click** on the **New Appointment button**. A blank Appointment window will appear.

2. **Type** the **meeting information**.

3. **Click** on the **Meeting Planner tab**. The tab will come to the front.

4. **Click** on the **Invite Others button**. The Select Attendees and Resources dialog box will open.

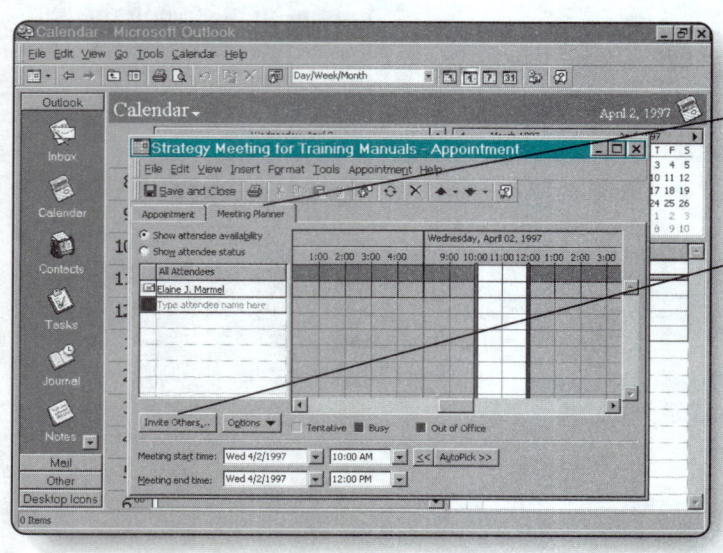

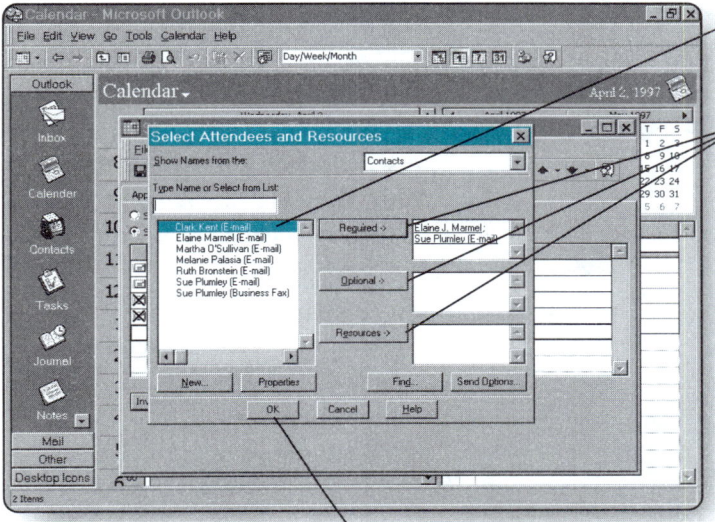

5. Click on the **name** of a proposed attendee.

6. Click on **Required**, **Optional**, or **Resources**, depending on the attendee's status at the meeting.

NOTE

Repeat steps 5 and 6 for each person to whom you want to send e-mail to invite to the meeting.

7. Click on **OK**. The dialog box will close and the Meeting Planner tab will be visible.

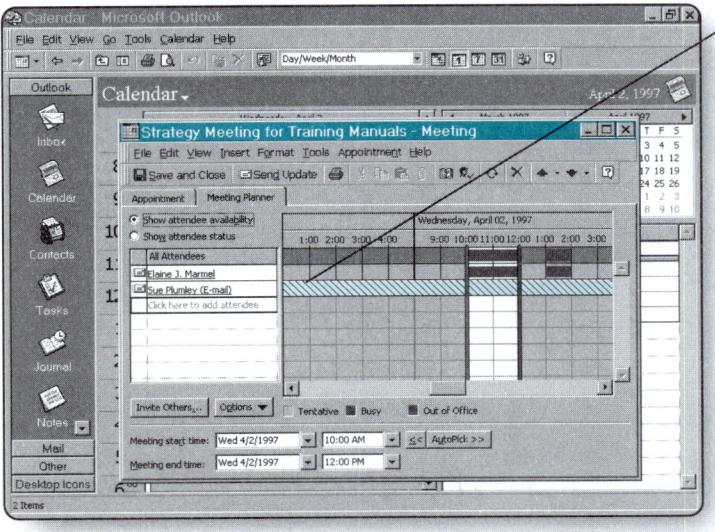

The people you selected will appear on the Meeting Planner tab. If their schedules are not available (either because they are not using Outlook or because they are not on the network), you'll see diagonal lines through their schedule.

You can invite people to attend a meeting even if you don't have an e-mail address for them; you simply tell Outlook not to send an e-mail message.

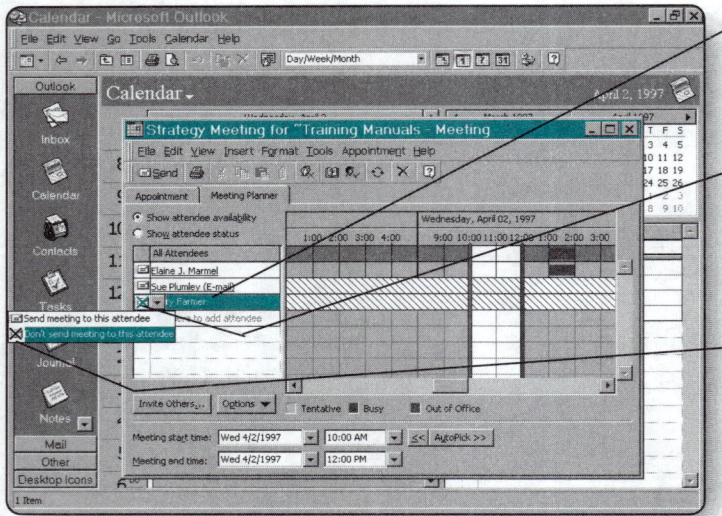

8. Type the **name** of a proposed attendee on the Meeting Planner tab and **press** the **Tab key**.

9. **Click** on the **envelope** next to the name of the person to whom you *do not* want to send e-mail. A list box will open.

10. **Click** on **Don't send meeting to this attendee** and **press** the **Tab key**.

Outlook will place an X over the envelope next to the attendee's name.

11. **Click** on **Send**. Outlook will send e-mail messages through your e-mail program to the proposed attendees.

CREATING AN EVENT

Events are entries that span more than one day, such as a conference. Events are very similar to appointments.

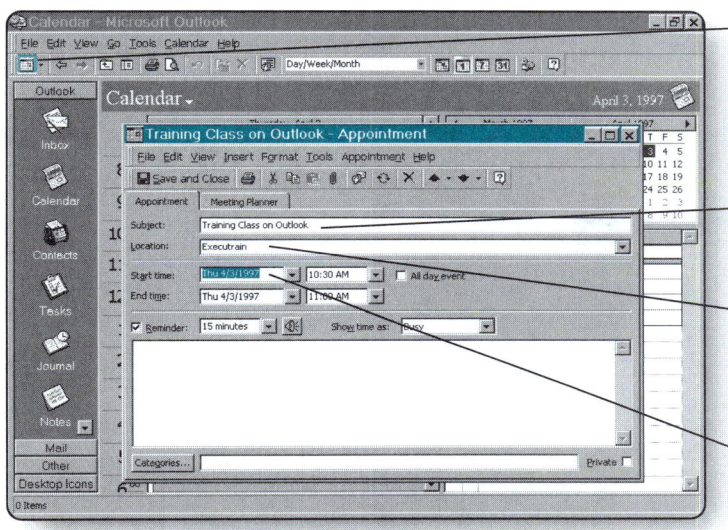

1. **Click** on the **New Appointment button**. The Appointment window will appear.

2. **Type** a **subject** for the event and **press** the **Tab key**.

3. **Type** a **location** for the event and **press** the **Tab key**. Providing a location is optional.

4. **Select** the **start date** for the event.

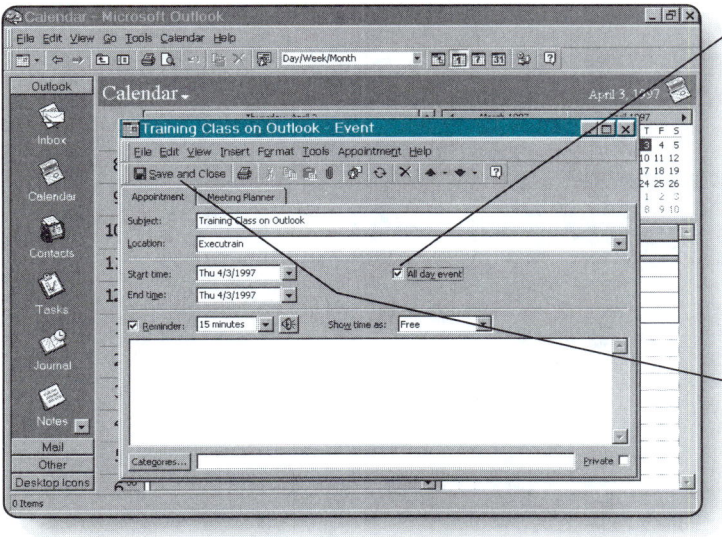

5. **Click** on the **All day event check box**. A ✔ will appear in the box and the list boxes where you could set a time will disappear.

6. **Type** the remaining **information** as you would for any appointment or meeting.

7. **Click** on the **Save and Close button**. Outlook will save the event at the top of day you scheduled it.

CREATING RECURRING ENTRIES

Recurring entries are useful for recording appointments, meetings, or events that occur on a regular basis. Weekly meetings are a good example of a recurring entry.

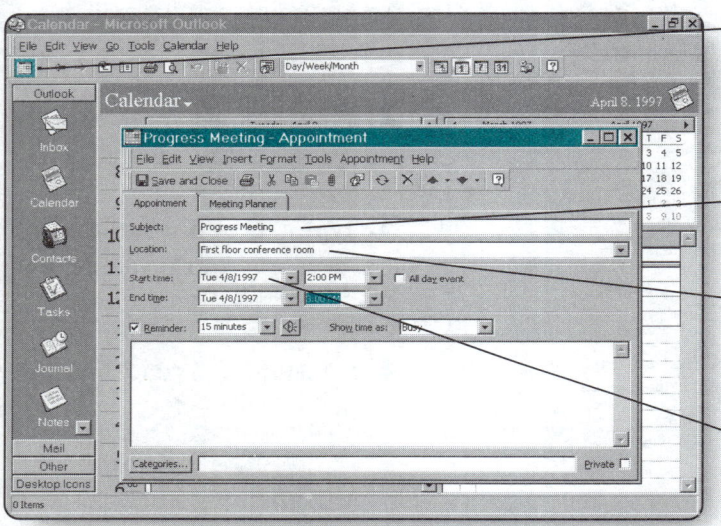

1. Click on the **New Appointment button**. The Appointment window will appear.

2. Type a **subject** and **press** the **Tab key**.

3. Type a **location** and **press** the **Tab key**. Providing a location is optional.

4. Select the **start date**.

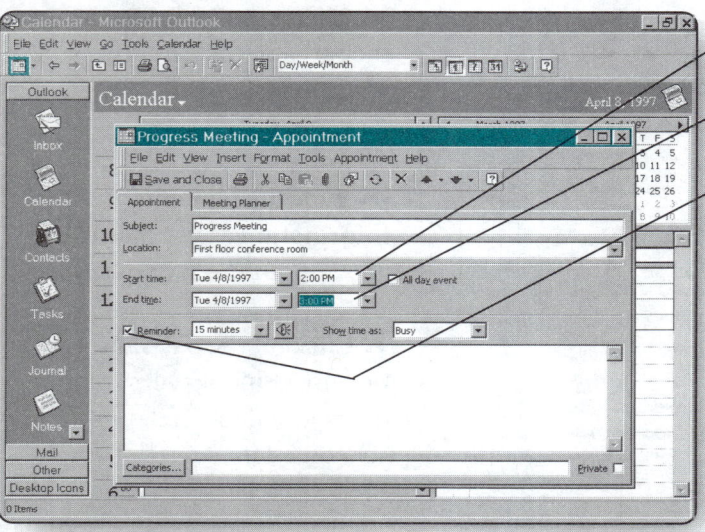

5. Select the **start time**.

6. Select the **end time**.

7. Set the **reminder** the way you want it.

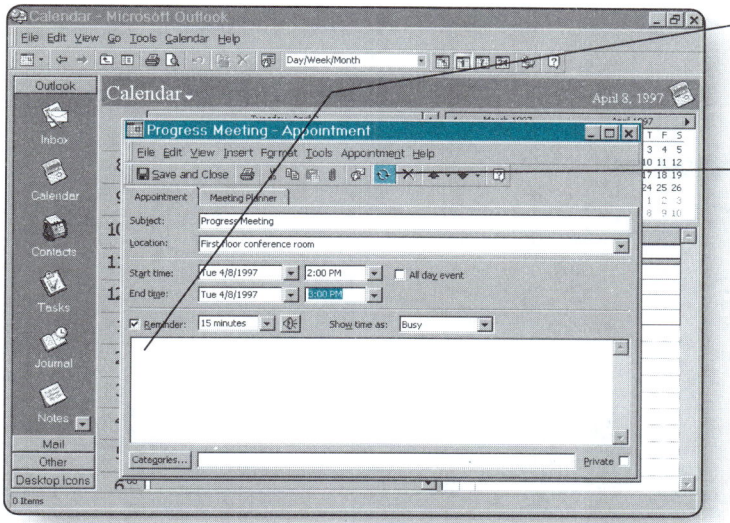

8. Type any **notes** for the entry in the box at the bottom of the window.

9. Click on the **Recurrence button**. The Appointment Recurrence dialog box will open.

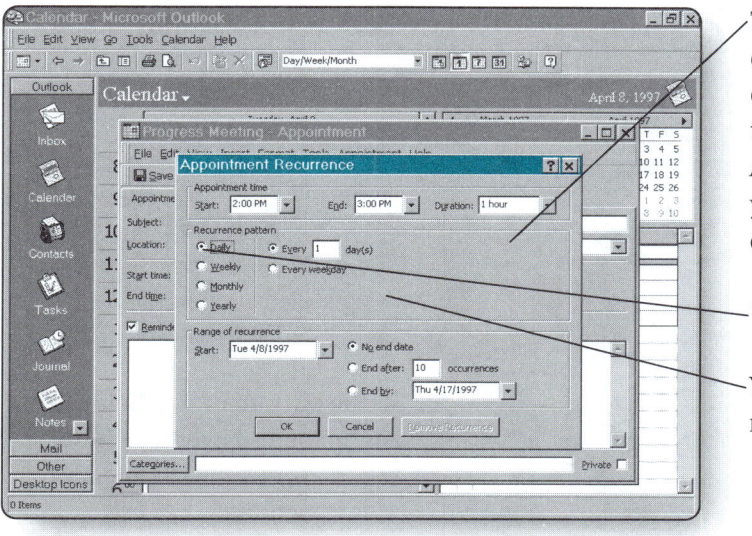

The Recurrence pattern choices on the right change, depending on the frequency you choose on the left side of the dialog box. After you choose a frequency, you must specify how often the entry will occur.

10. Click on **Daily**.

You will see the choices for daily recurrence.

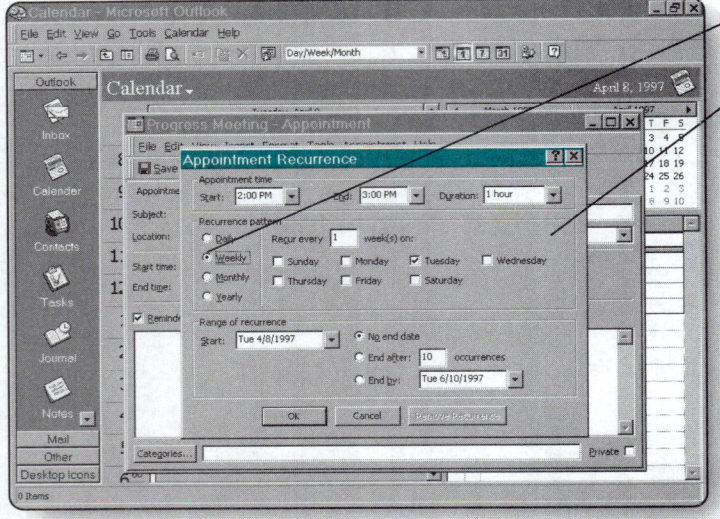

11. Click on **Weekly**.

You will see the choices for weekly recurrence.

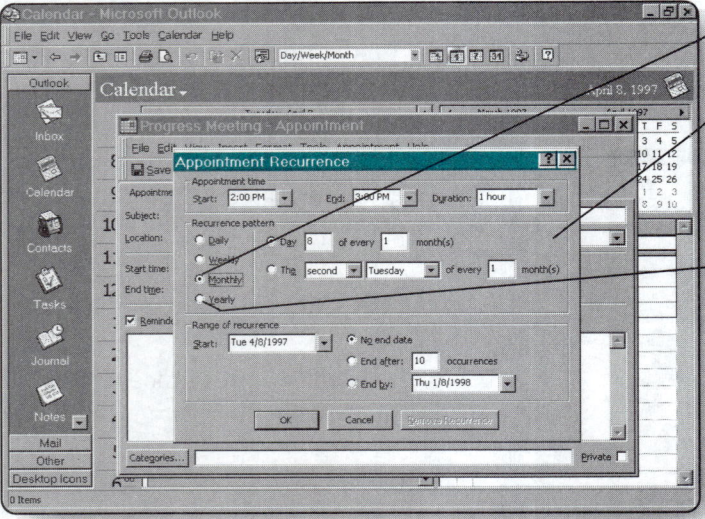

12. Click on **Monthly**.

You will see the choices for monthly recurrence.

NOTE

You can also click on Yearly for yearly recurrence.

At the bottom of the dialog box, set the period over which the recurring entry will appear on your Calendar.

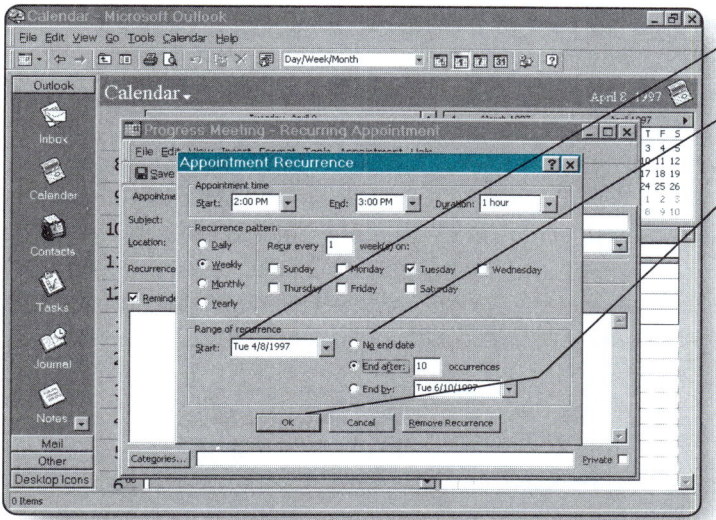

13. Select a **start date**.

14. Select an **end date**.

15. **Click** on **OK**. The Recurring Appointment window will reappear.

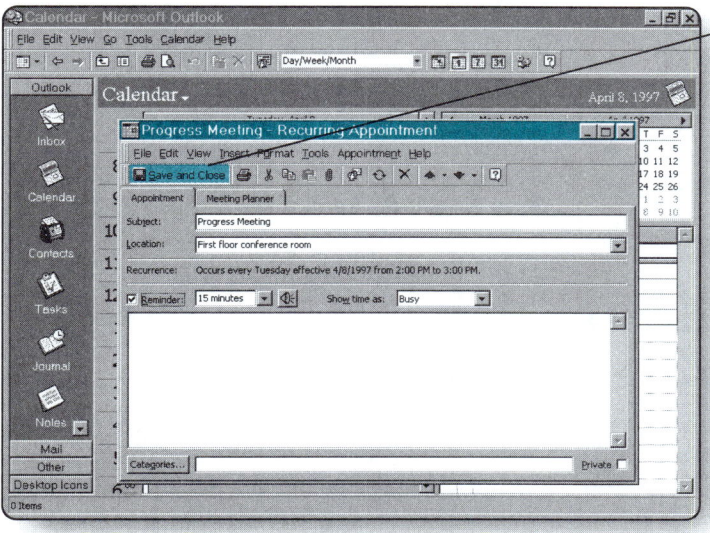

16. **Click** on **Save and Close**. The Appointment window will close and Outlook will display the recurring entry on your calendar.

NOTE

On the Date Navigator, all the dates for which you scheduled the recurring entry appear in bold.

PRINTING THE CALENDAR

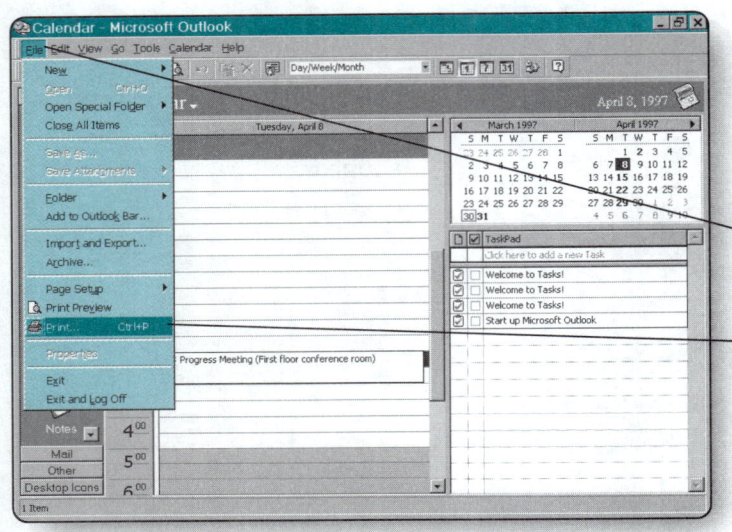

You can print a daily, weekly, monthly, or tri-fold Calendar. Be sure to start in the Calendar view (click on the Calendar shortcut on the Outlook bar).

1. **Click** on **File**. The File menu will appear.

2. **Click** on **Print**. The Print dialog box will open.

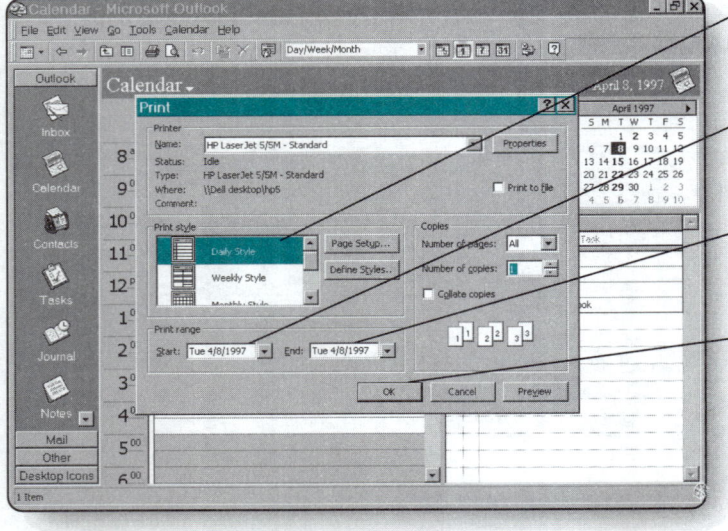

3. **Click** on a **Print Style** (Daily, Weekly, Monthly, or Tri-fold).

4. **Select** a **start date** for the Print range.

5. **Select** an **end date** for the Print range.

6. **Click** on **OK**. Your Calendar will print.

19 Using Outlook to Keep Organized

Using the Tasks folder, you can create a To Do list that you can use to make sure things don't "fall through the cracks." You can also use Outlook's Journal to keep an eye on what you have been doing. The Notes folder provides a place where you can store miscellaneous information—the kind of information you usually would place on a sticky note. In this chapter, you'll learn how to:

- ✦ **Create a task**
- ✦ **Assign a task to someone else**
- ✦ **Create a recurring task**
- ✦ **Print a To Do list**
- ✦ **Use the Journal to track information**
- ✦ **Use the Notes folder to store miscellaneous information**

CREATING A TASK

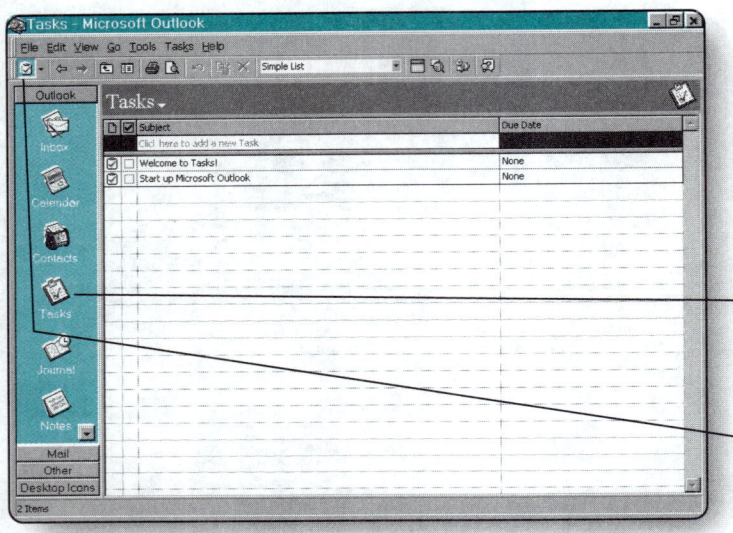

A *task* is something you need to get done. It doesn't necessarily have a due date, but it is something you want to get done and don't want to forget. All information on a task is optional except the subject.

1. **Click** on the **Tasks shortcut** on the Outlook bar. The Tasks window will appear.

2. **Click** on the **New Task button**. The New Task window will appear.

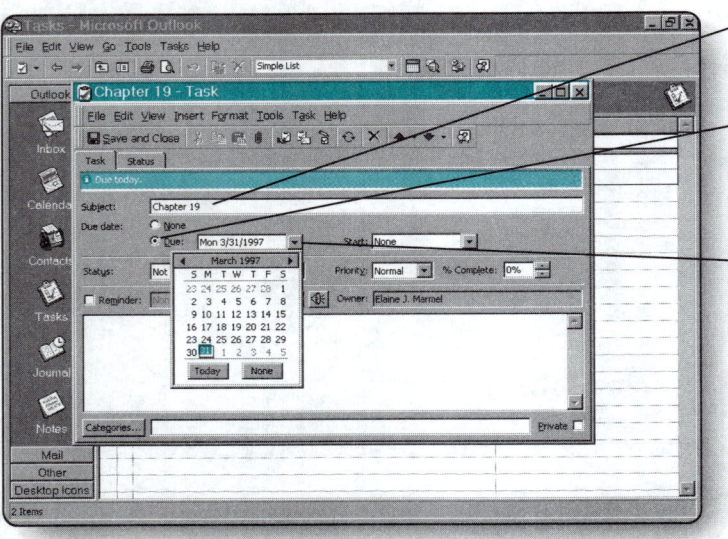

3. **Type** a **subject** for the task in the Subject: text box.

4. **Click** on the **Due option button**. Outlook will allow you to assign dates to the task.

5. **Click** on the **arrow** (▼) next to the Due: box. A small calendar will appear from which you can select a due date.

6. **Click** on a **date** on the calendar.

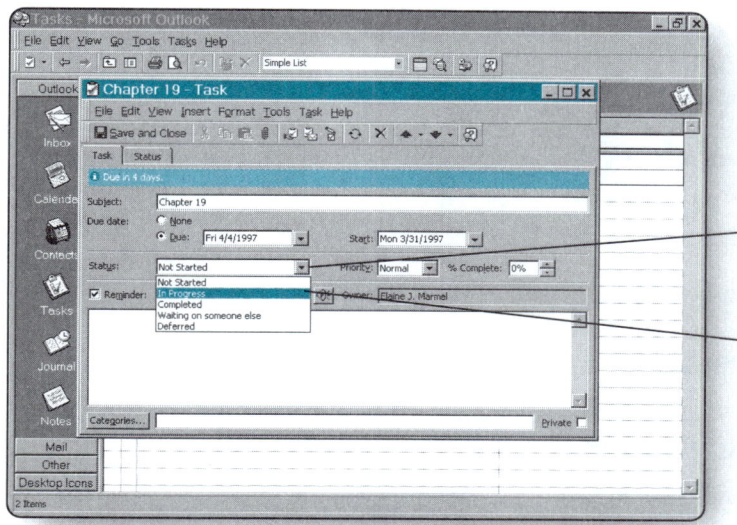

NOTE

Repeat steps 5 and 6 to assign a Start: date.

7. **Click** on the **arrow** (▼) next to the Status: list box.

8. **Click** on a **status** for the task.

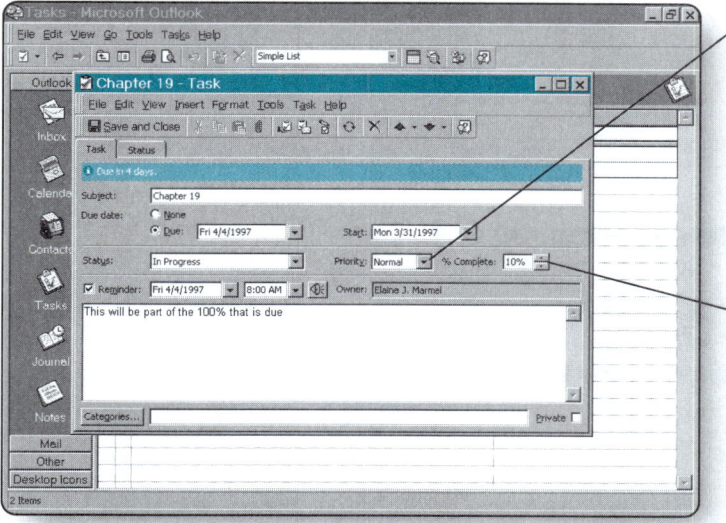

9. **Click** on the **arrow** (▼) next to the Priority: list box. A list of possible priorities will appear.

10. **Click** on a **priority** for the task. You can choose Normal, Low, or High.

11a. **Type** a **percentage** in the % Complete: text box.

OR

11b. **Click** on the **arrows** (♦) next to the % Complete: box to indicate how much of the task is finished.

TIP

If you want Outlook to remind you of the task by playing a sound, place a ✔ in the Reminder: check box. If you do this, you can use the Reminder: list boxes to select a date and time that Outlook will remind you.

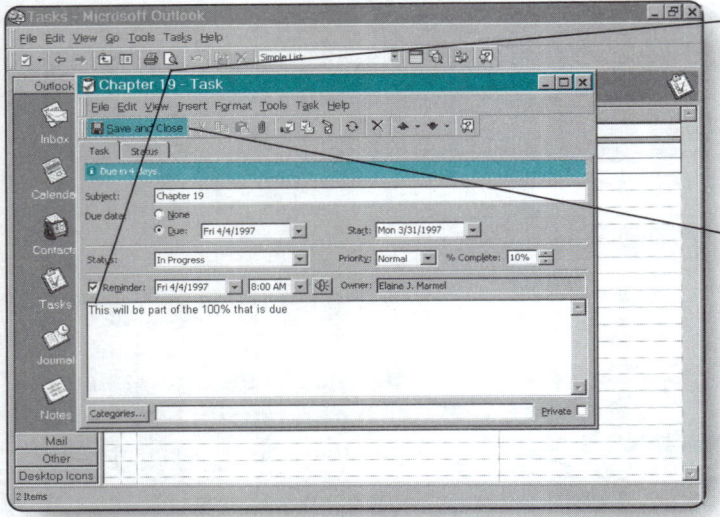

12. **Click** in the **box** at the bottom of the window.

13. **Type** any **notes** you want about the task.

14. **Click** on the **Save and Close button**. Your changes will be saved.

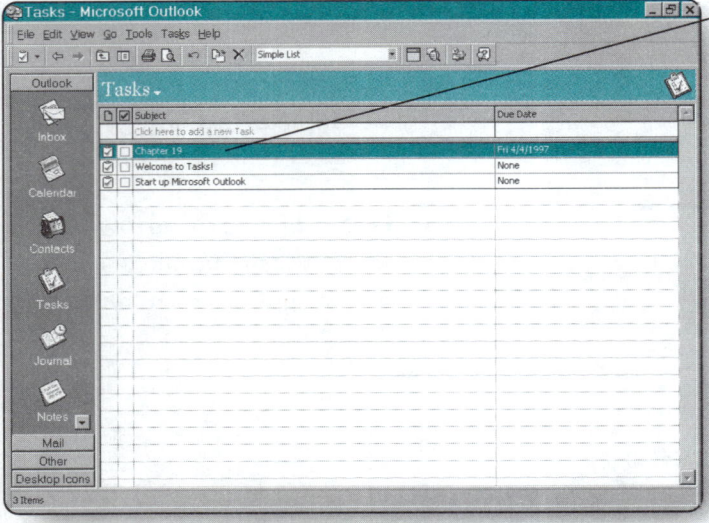

Outlook will save the task in the Task window.

TIP

Consider creating additional folders for the Task window and use each folder to organize tasks by project. Then, you can print several To Do lists, each one showing what you need to do for a specific project.

NOTE

To edit a task, double-click on it to open its window. To delete a task, click on it in the Task window and then press the Delete key. To complete a task, click on the check box to the left of the task name in the Task window.

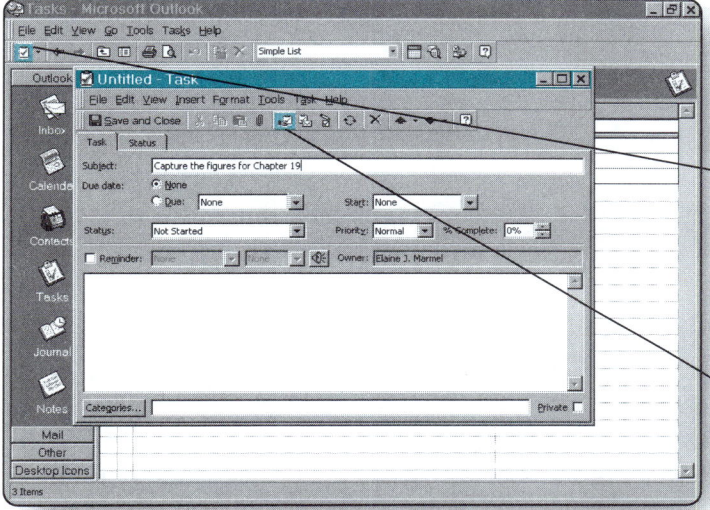

Assigning Tasks

You can create tasks and assign them to someone else.

1. **Click** on the **New Task button**. The Task window will appear.

2. **Type** the **information** needed to set up the task.

3. **Click** on the **Assign Task button**. Outlook will add an e-mail header area above the Subject: text box where you can supply an e-mail address for the person to whom you want to assign the task.

NOTE

You can simply type the e-mail address, or you can complete steps 4 through 7 to select recipients from your Address Book.

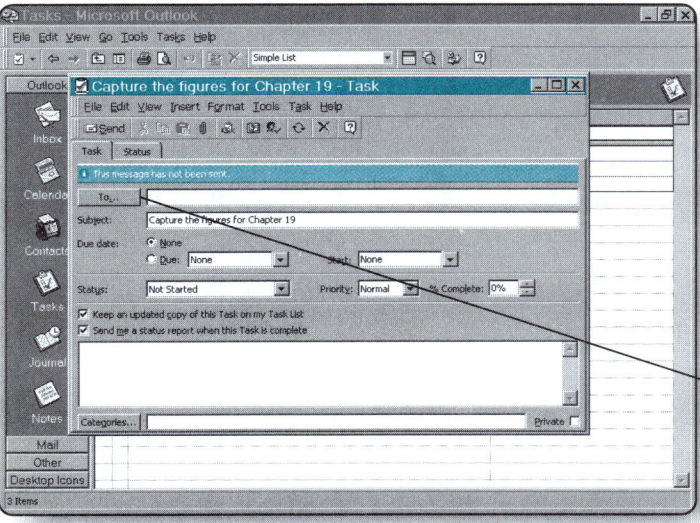

4. **Click** on the **To button**. The Select Task Recipient dialog box will open.

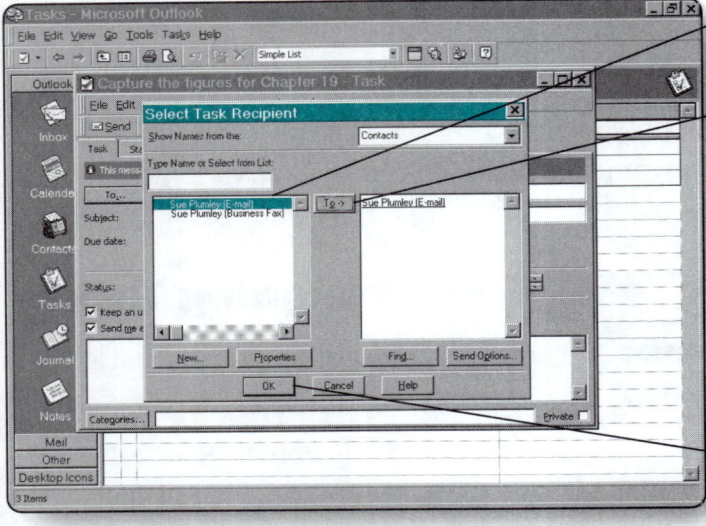

5. Click on a **name** in the left box.

6. Click on **To**. The name will appear in the right box.

7. Click on **OK**. The dialog box will close and the task will be visible.

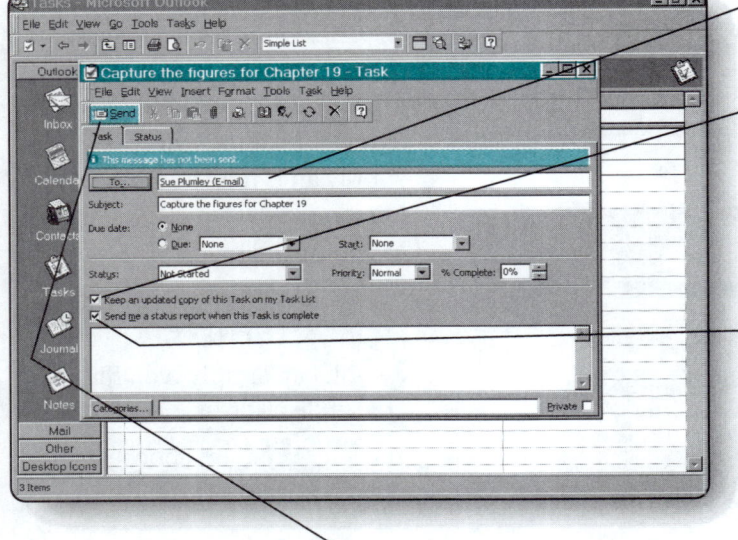

The names of the people you selected will appear on the task.

Use the Keep an updated copy of this task on my Task List check box to determine whether Outlook will keep a copy of the task on your Task List.

Use the Send me a status report when this Task is complete check box to determine whether Outlook will send you a status report when the recipient completes the task.

8. Click on **Send**. Outlook will send an e-mail message through your e-mail program, notifying the recipient(s) of the task assignment.

TIP

If someone assigns a task to you, you'll get an e-mail message and the task will appear both in your Inbox and on your Task List. When you open the task, you will see two buttons: Accept and Decline. Click on one of those buttons to send an e-mail message back to the originator to let them know if you will complete the task.

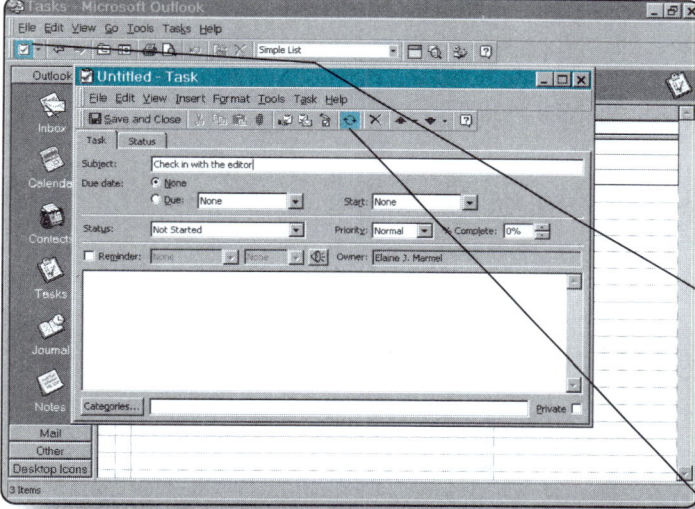

CREATING RECURRING TASKS

Sometimes, you need to do the same task at regular intervals, so set it up as a recurring task.

1. **Click** on the **New Task button**. The Task window will appear.

2. **Type** the **information** needed to set up the task.

3. **Click** on the **Recurrence button**. The Task Recurrence dialog box will open.

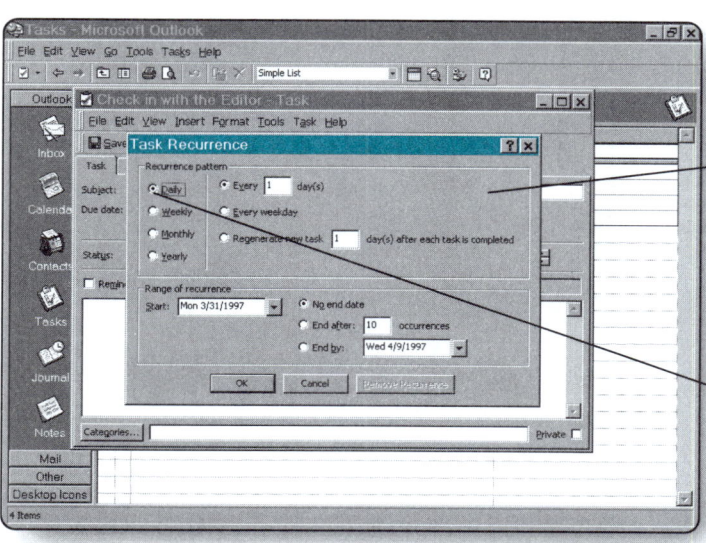

The Recurrence pattern choices on the right change depending on the frequency you choose on the left. After you choose a frequency, you must specify how often it will occur on the right.

4. **Click** on **Daily**. You will see the choices for a daily recurrence.

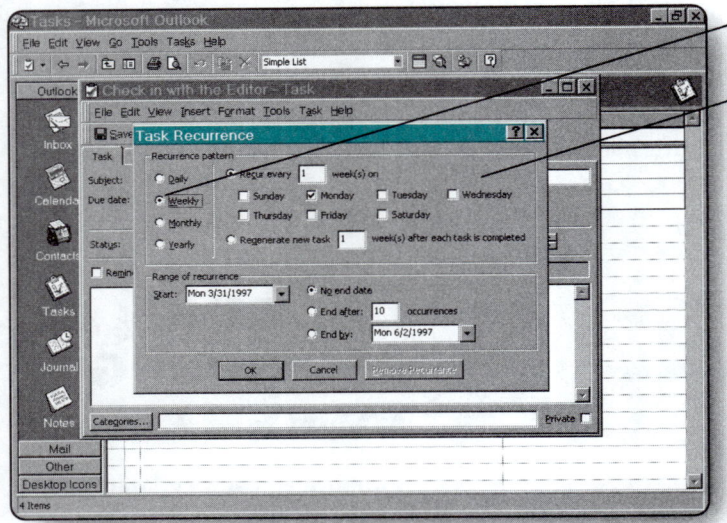

5. **Click** on **Weekly**.

You will see the choices for weekly recurrence.

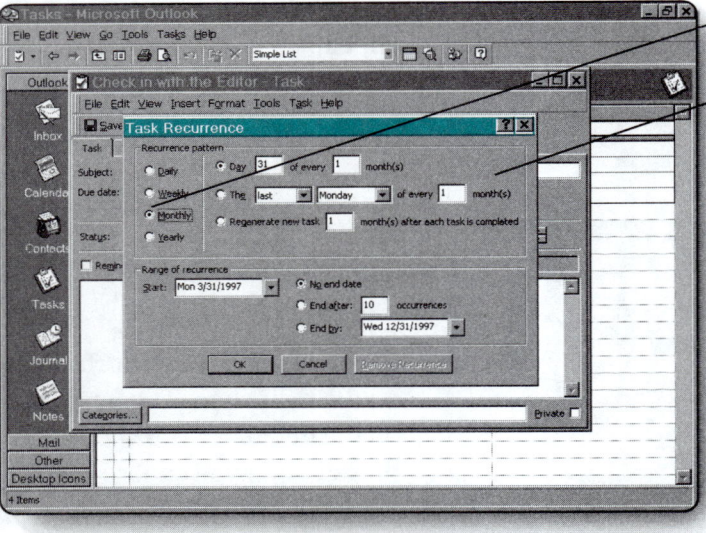

6. **Click** on **Monthly**.

You will see the choices for monthly recurrence.

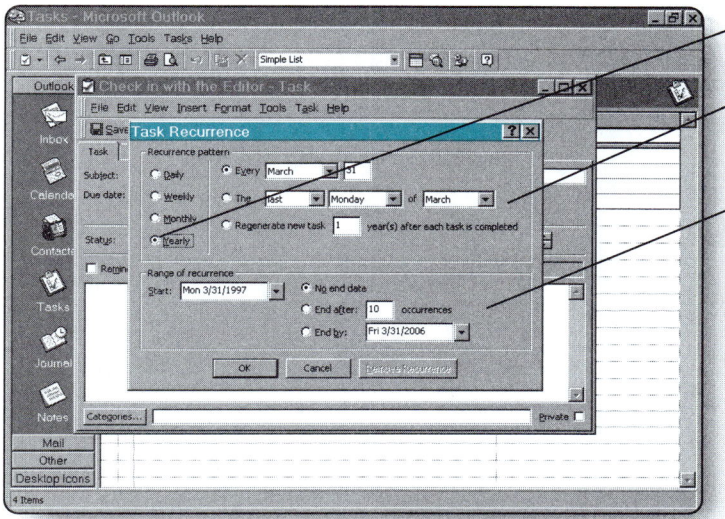

7. **Click** on **Yearly**.

You will see the choices for yearly recurrence.

At the bottom of the dialog box, you can set the period over which the recurring entry will appear on your calendar.

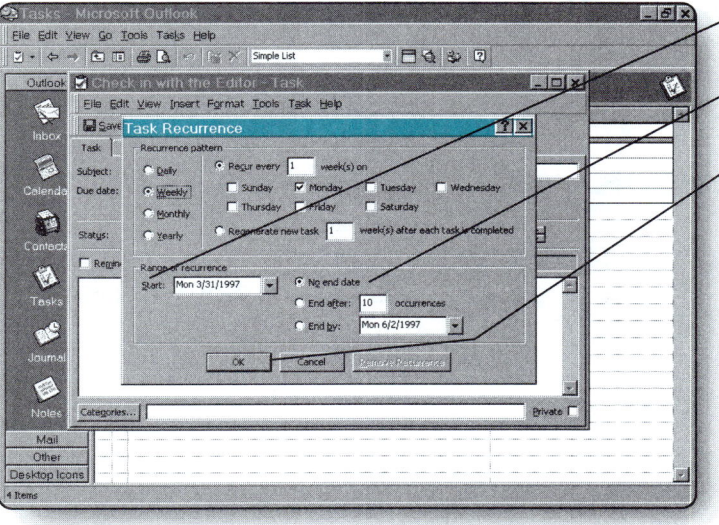

8. **Select** a **start date**.

9. **Select** an **end date**.

10. **Click** on **OK**. The Task window will reappear.

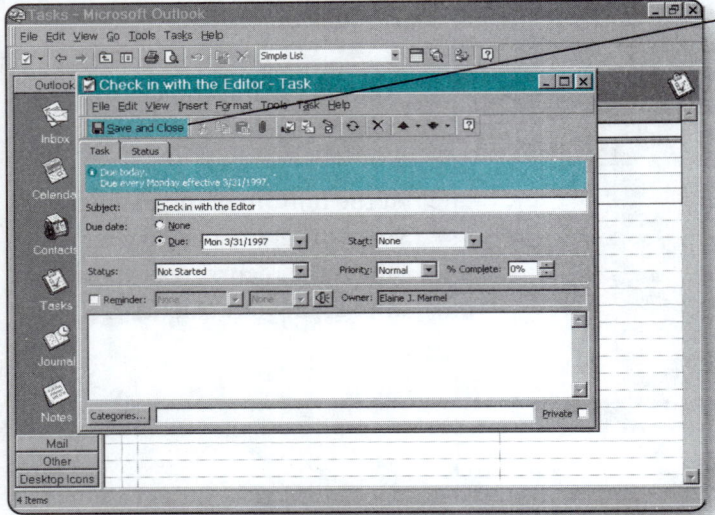

11. **Click** on **Save and Close**. Your changes will be saved.

PRINTING A TO DO LIST

When you print a To Do list, be sure to start in the Task view (click on the Task shortcut on the Outlook bar).

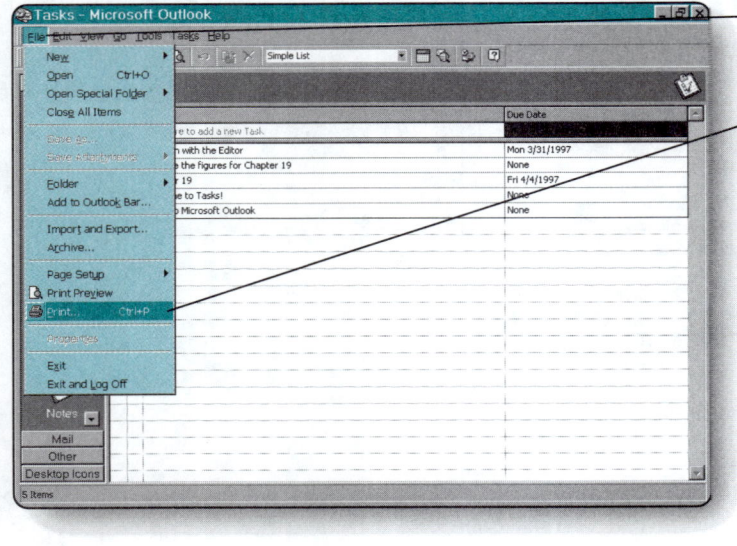

1. **Click** on **File**. The File menu will appear.

2. **Click** on **Print**. The Print dialog box will open.

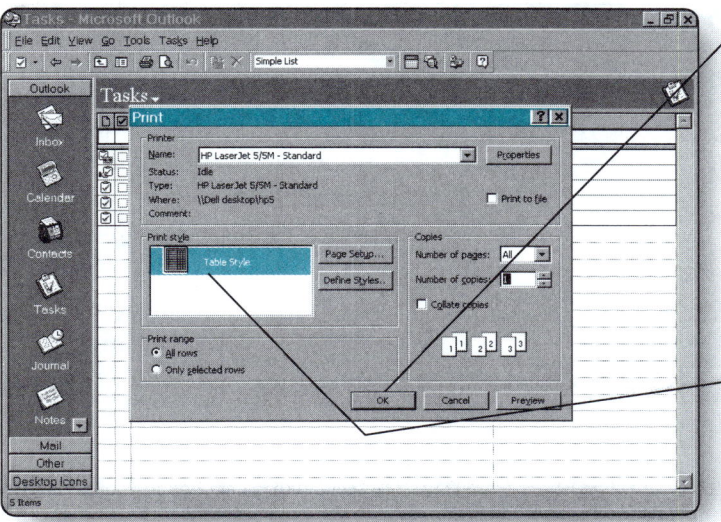

3. **Click** on **OK**. Your calendar will print.

TRACKING ACTIVITIES IN THE JOURNAL

The Journal in Outlook provides you with a record of what you've been doing.

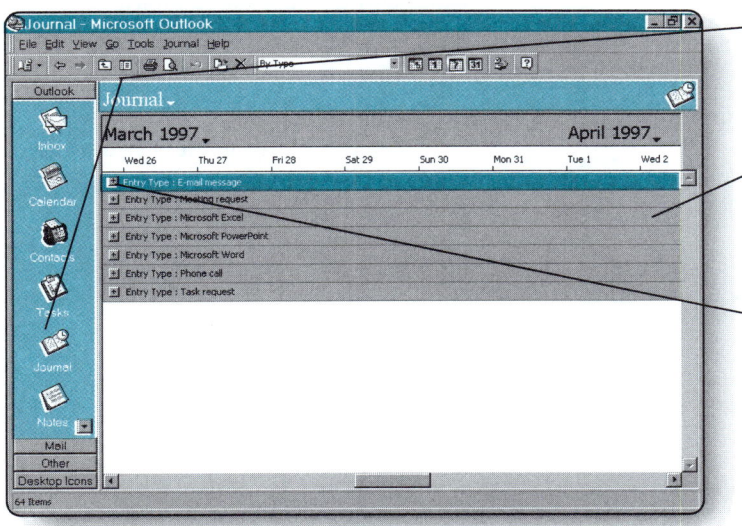

1. **Click** on the **Journal shortcut** on the Outlook bar. The Journal window will appear.

The types of entries being captured in the Journal will also appear.

2. **Click** on a + (**plus sign**) to the left of the entry type. You will see the activities associated with that entry type.

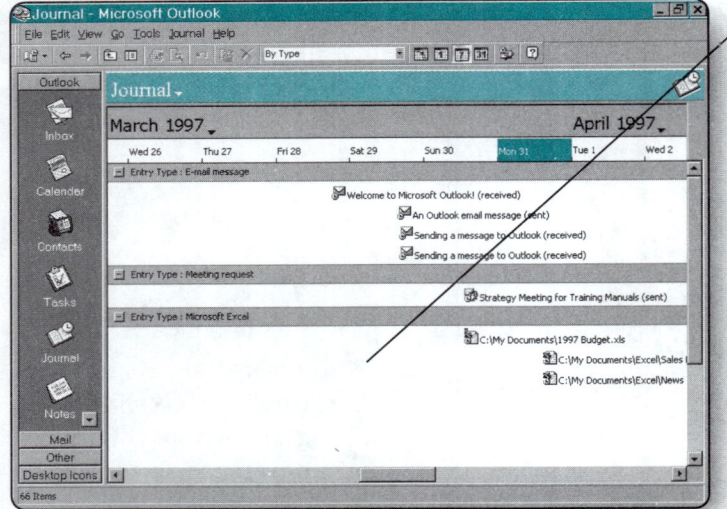

The default view of the Journal will show your activities in a timeline fashion, where entries are associated with dates. The Journal logs every Office document you open, even if Outlook isn't open at the time.

You can view the entries in the Journal in a variety of ways.

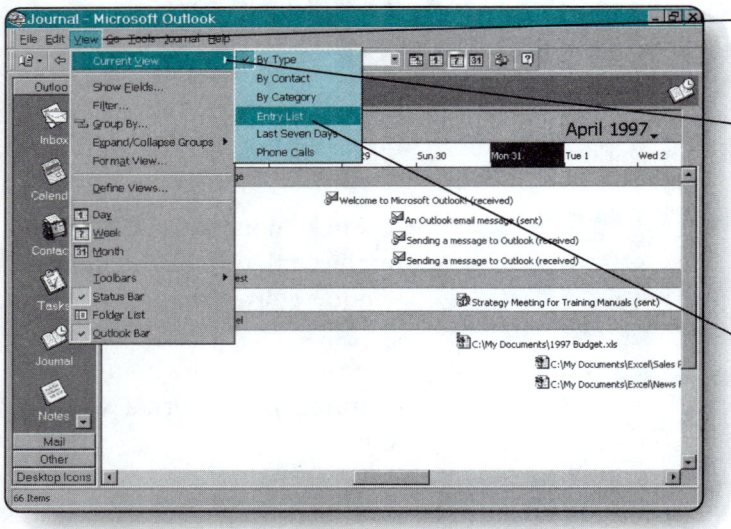

3. Click on **View**. The View menu will appear.

4. Click on **Current View**. A cascading menu will appear, and you will see the available views. The current view will have a ✔ next to it.

5. Click on the **view** you want to use. The new view will be applied.

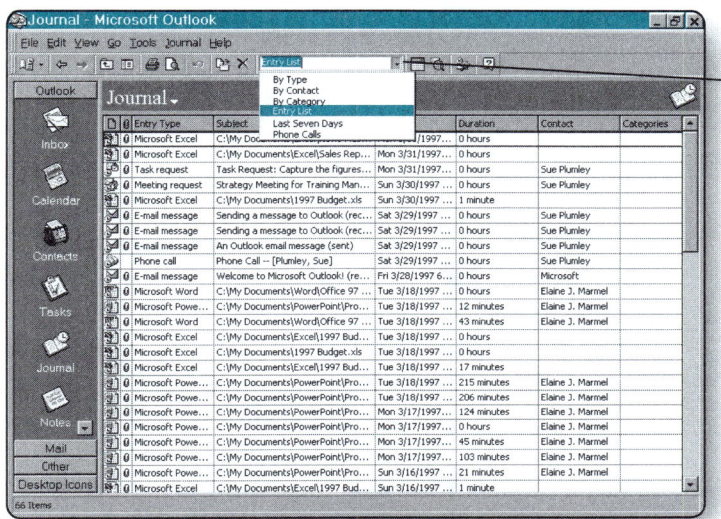

TIP

To quickly change views, click on the arrow (▼) next to the View list box and click on a view.

NOTE

If you double-click on any entry in the Journal window, it will open in Outlook, if it was created in Outlook, or in the Office application in which it was created.

MAKING NOTES

Think of the Notes window in Outlook as your electronic sticky notepad. Here you can record ideas you have, conversations you want to remember, and miscellaneous information that just doesn't fit in any other category.

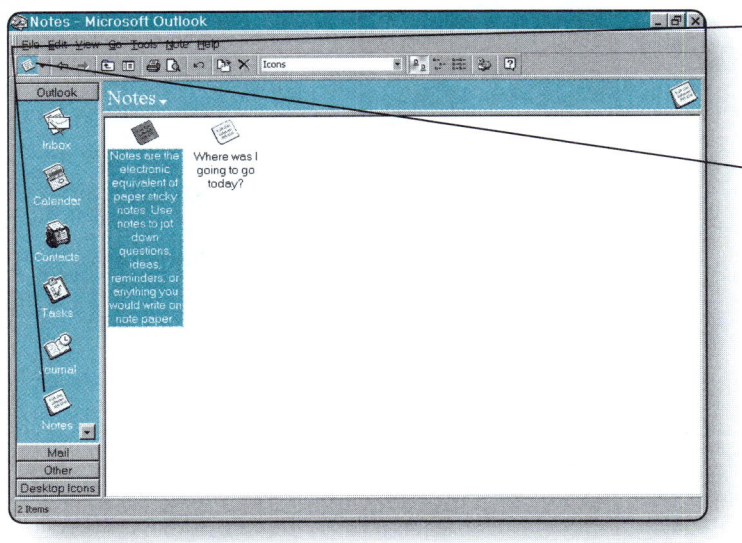

1. **Click** on the **Notes shortcut** on the Outlook bar. The Notes window will appear.

2. **Click** on the **New Note button**. A small window will appear.

NOTE

Depending on the type of display you're using, you may not be able to see the insertion point.

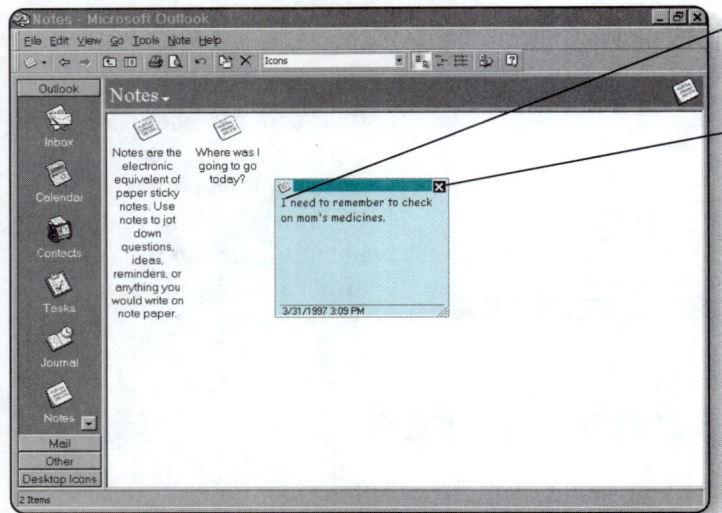

3. **Type** the **information** you want to store.

4. **Click** on the **Close button** ([×]) in the upper-right corner of the note's window.

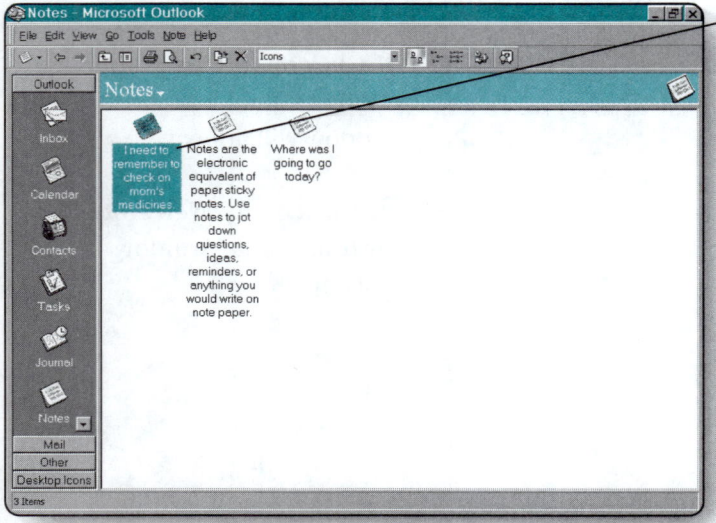

The note will appear in the Notes window.

TIP

To open a note, double-click on it. To delete a note, click on it once to select it and then press the Delete key.

PART V REVIEW QUESTIONS

1. Does the Outlook bar contain shortcuts or folders? *See Chapter 15*

2. How do you display Outlook folders? *See Chapter 15*

3. How do you add an entry to the Address Book? *See Chapter 16*

4. How do you print a contact list? *See Chapter 16*

5. How do you send an e-mail message? *See Chapter 17*

6. Name the three actions you can take to answer an e-mail message. *See Chapter 17*

7. What is the difference between an appointment, a meeting, and an event? *See Chapter 18*

8. Describe how to use the Date Navigator to switch calendar views and find a specific date. *See Chapter 18*

9. Describe how to assign a task to someone else. *See Chapter 19*

10. In the Journal, does Outlook automatically log Office documents you open? *See Chapter 19*

PART VI

Using
Office 97 Tools

20 Streamlining Office Activities

The Microsoft Office Shortcut Bar contains a series of toolbars that help speed up your work. For example, using these toolbars, you can quickly open Office documents or create new Office documents or access, from any Office program, a shortcut on your Desktop.

You can also speed up your work in Office 97 through the use of hyperlinks and e-mail for online document review. By using hyperlinks, you can work in one Office document and open another Office document with just one click. With e-mail, you can route documents that need review. In this chapter, you'll learn how to:

✦ Use the Microsoft Office Shortcut Bar

✦ Create and use hyperlinks in Office documents

✦ Use e-mail to send documents for review

WORKING WITH THE OFFICE SHORTCUT BAR

The Office Shortcut Bar provides you with quick access to the resources you use most often on your computer. When you first see the Office Shortcut Bar, it will appear at the top your screen, but you can move it. By default, the Office Shortcut Bar remains visible at all times, regardless of the program(s) in which you are working. However, you can hide it if you want, making it available but not always visible. You can close it as well.

Understanding and Using the Office Shortcut Bar

To use the Office Shortcut Bar, it must be installed. If it doesn't appear automatically when you start your computer, check for the Microsoft Office Shortcut Bar on the Programs menu. If you don't see it, use the Office 97 installation CD-ROM to add the Office Shortcut Bar. The installation will place the Microsoft Office Shortcut Bar in the Startup folder on your Programs menu. To start the Office Shortcut Bar, either restart your computer or select it from the Startup folder.

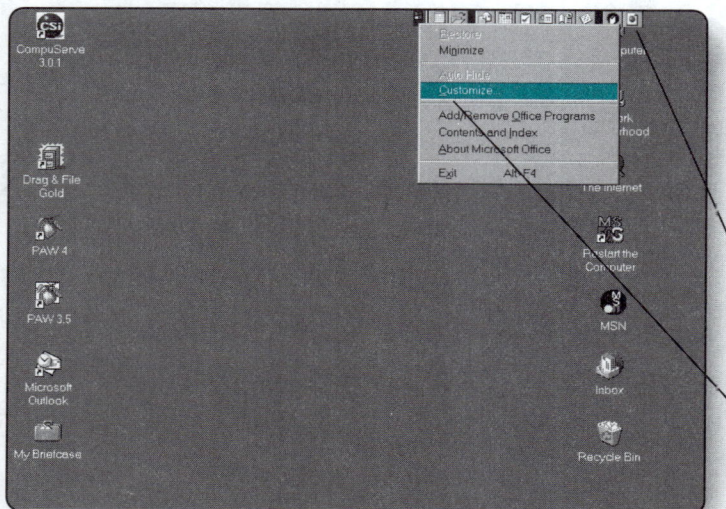

The Office Shortcut Bar will appear, by default, at the top of your screen. It automatically fits into the title bar of your programs. To make the Office Shortcut Bar easier to use, you can enlarge it.

1. **Right-click** on the Office Shortcut Bar control menu. A shortcut menu will appear.

2. **Click** on **Customize**. The Customize dialog box will open.

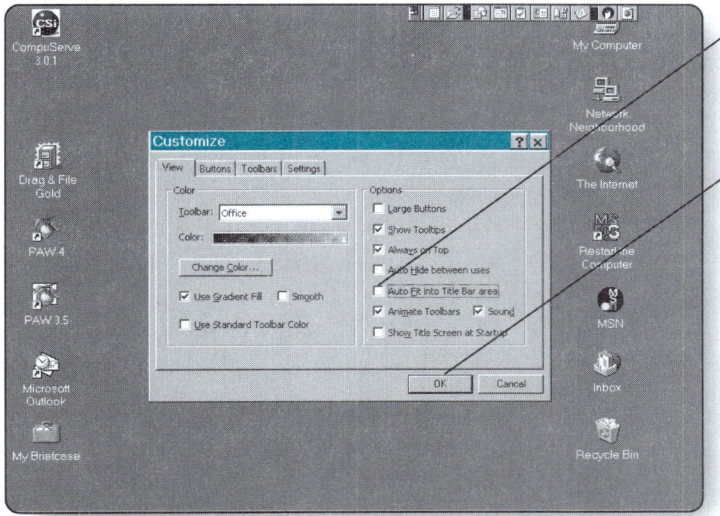

3. **Click** on **Auto Fit into Title Bar area**. The ✔ will disappear from the check box.

4. **Click** on **OK**. The shortcut bar will enlarge to fill the top of your screen.

The Office Shortcut Bar contains buttons to help you quickly get whatever you need.

Click on these buttons to create new Office documents and to open existing Office documents.

Click on these buttons to create new Outlook events.

Click on this button to open Microsoft Bookshelf Basics, which is a review of Microsoft Bookshelf.

Click on this button to go to a page on the Internet where Microsoft will describe how you can get results from Office 97.

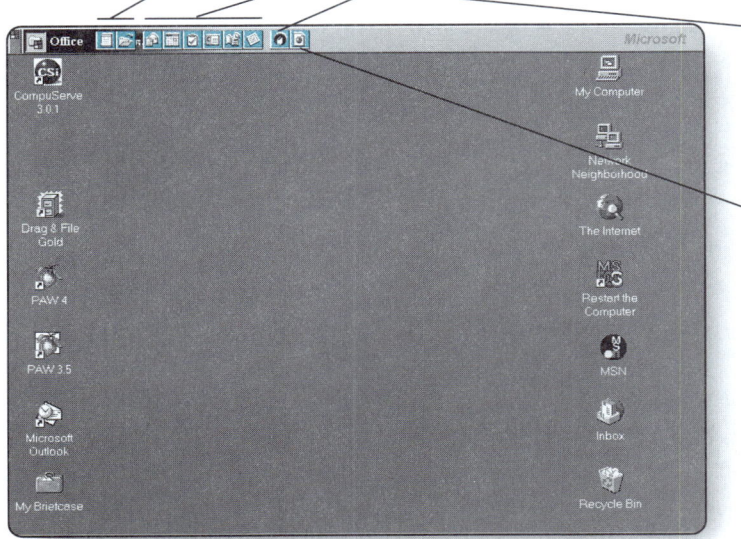

Moving the Office Shortcut Bar

You can place the Office Shortcut Bar anywhere onscreen.

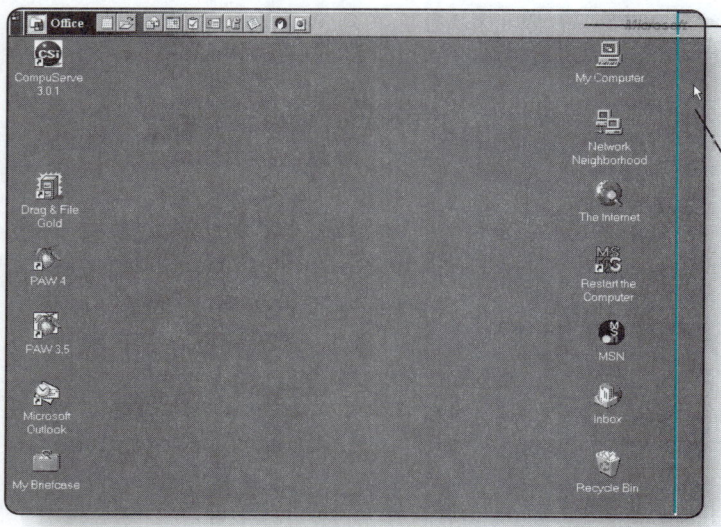

1. **Move** the **mouse pointer** onto a gray area on the shortcut bar. Make sure you're not pointing at any buttons.

2. **Drag** the **Office Shortcut Bar** to a new location. An outline representing the shortcut bar will appear.

3. **Release** the **mouse button**. The shortcut bar will appear wherever you drop it.

Hiding the Office Shortcut Bar

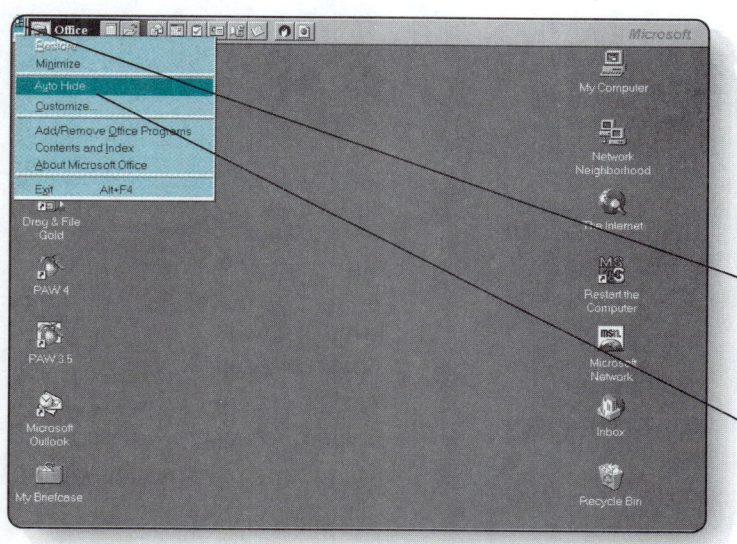

By default, the Office Shortcut Bar will appear onscreen all the time. If you aren't using Auto Fit and you don't want to see the shortcut bar all the time, you can temporarily hide it.

1. **Right-click** on the **Office Shortcut Bar menu**. The shortcut bar menu will appear.

2. **Click** on **Auto Hide**.

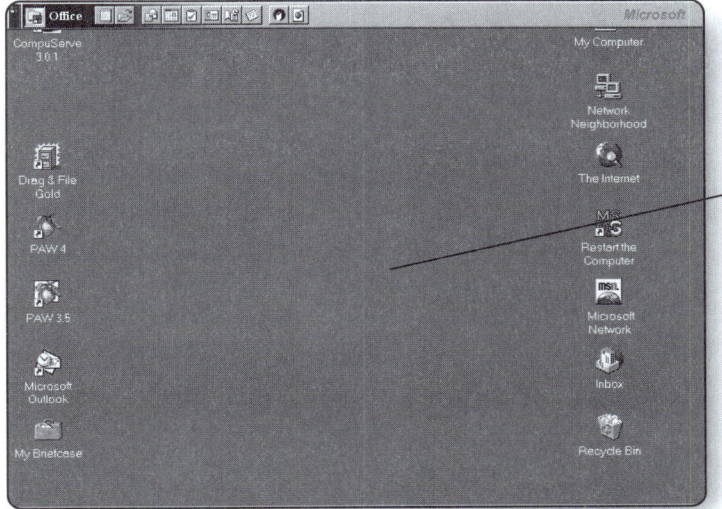

Your Desktop will adjust itself as though the Office Shortcut Bar were not there. Some shortcuts might not be entirely visible.

3. Click **anywhere** on the Desktop. The Office Shortcut Bar will roll up into an edge of the screen and disappear.

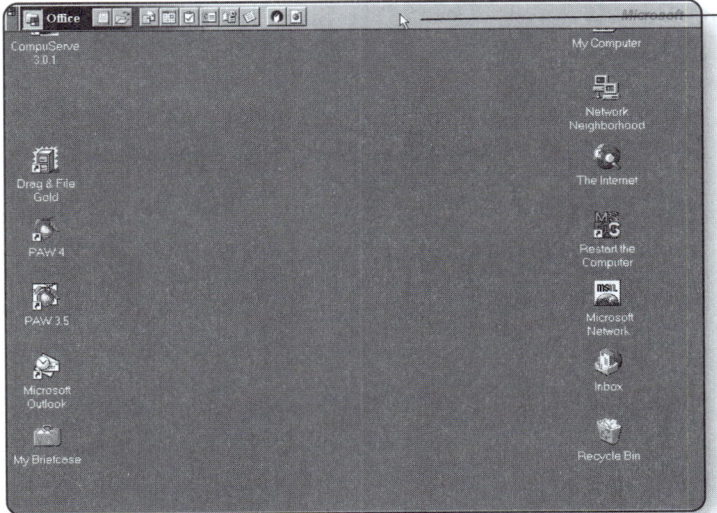

4. Move the **mouse pointer** to the location where the Office Shortcut Bar used to appear. The Office Shortcut Bar will reappear and remain visible as long as the mouse pointer stays somewhere over it.

NOTE

If you hide the Office Shortcut Bar, it will cover some portion of your screen when it reappears.

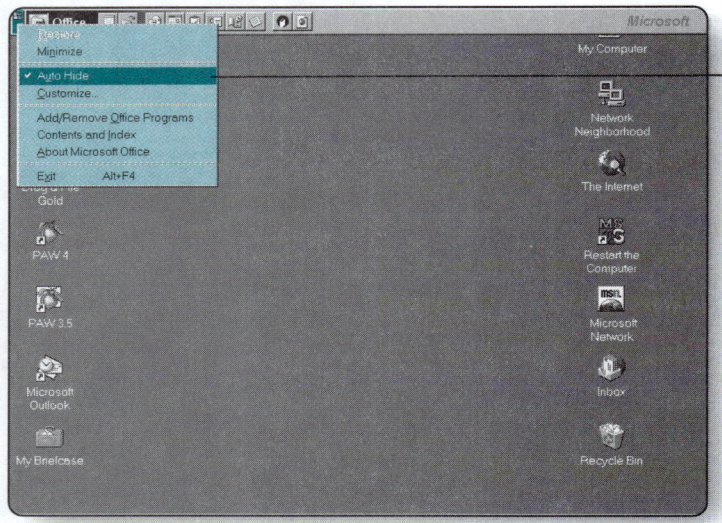

TIP

If you decide you prefer to see the Office Shortcut Bar at all times, move the mouse pointer to the edge of the screen so that you can see the Office Shortcut Bar. Then, repeat steps 1 and 2. When the Office Shortcut Bar menu appears in step 1, you'll see a ✔ next to Auto Hide. Repeating step 2 removes the ✔.

Closing the Office Shortcut Bar

1. **Right-click** on the **Office Shortcut Bar menu**. The Office Shortcut Bar menu will appear.

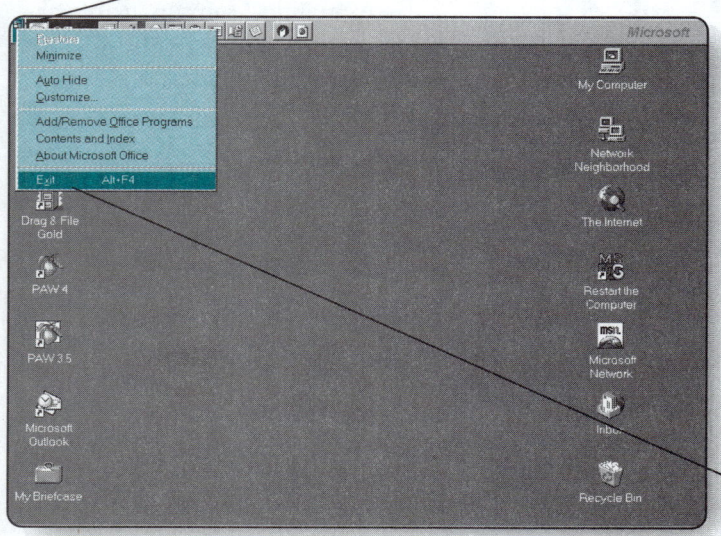

NOTE

The Office Shortcut Bar will automatically reappear when you restart your computer. To avoid this, either remove the shortcut for the Office Shortcut Bar from the Startup folder or use the Office 97 CD-ROM to remove the Office Shortcut Bar component.

2. **Click** on **Exit**. The Office Shortcut Bar will disappear.

TIP

You can restart the Office Shortcut Bar by clicking on the Start button, highlighting Programs, highlighting Startup, and clicking on Microsoft Office Shortcut Bar.

USING THE TOOLBARS ON THE OFFICE SHORTCUT BAR

The Office Shortcut Bar is actually a collection of toolbars. When you first see the Office Shortcut Bar, you will see only one toolbar, called *Office*. However, you can display and use any or all of the other toolbars on the Office Shortcut Bar.

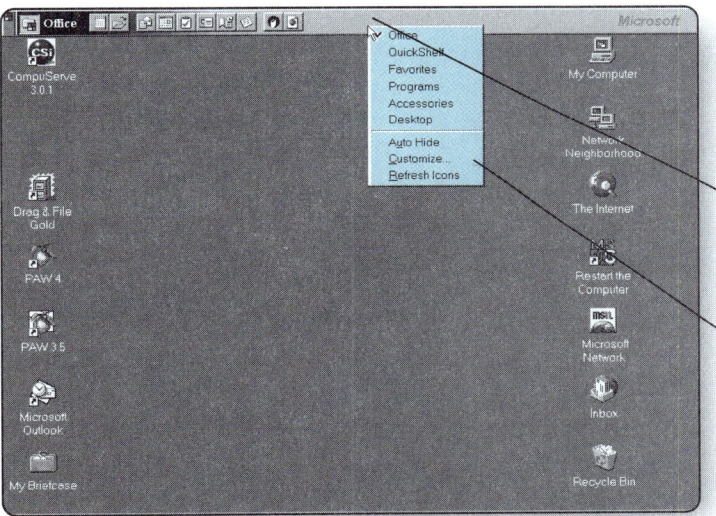

1. **Move** the **mouse pointer** anywhere onto the gray area of the Office Shortcut Bar.

2. **Right-click**. A shortcut menu will appear.

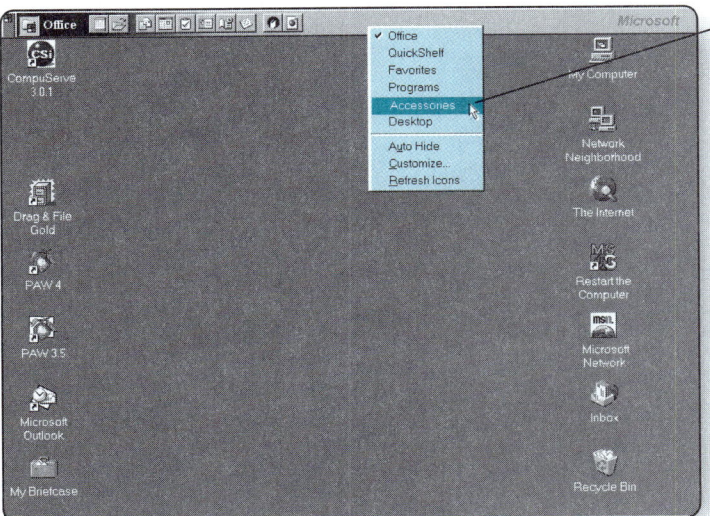

3. **Click** on the **toolbar** you want to display.

The toolbar you selected will replace the Office toolbar, but the Office toolbar will still be accessible.

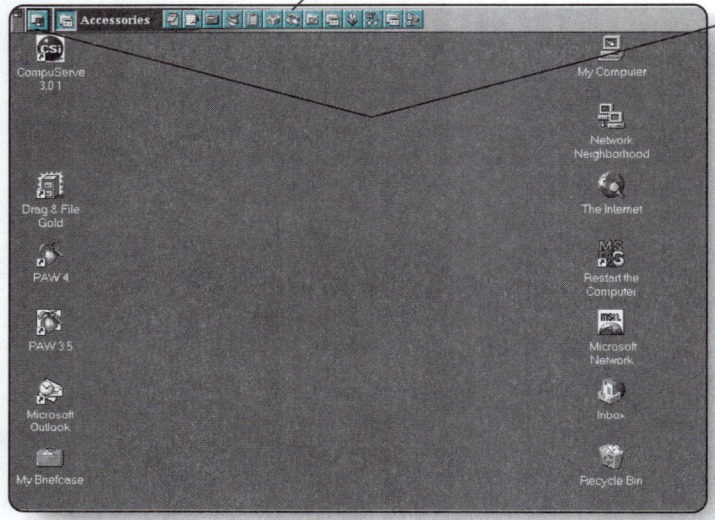

4. **Click** on the **Office toolbar icon.**

The Office toolbar will replace the other toolbar you displayed.

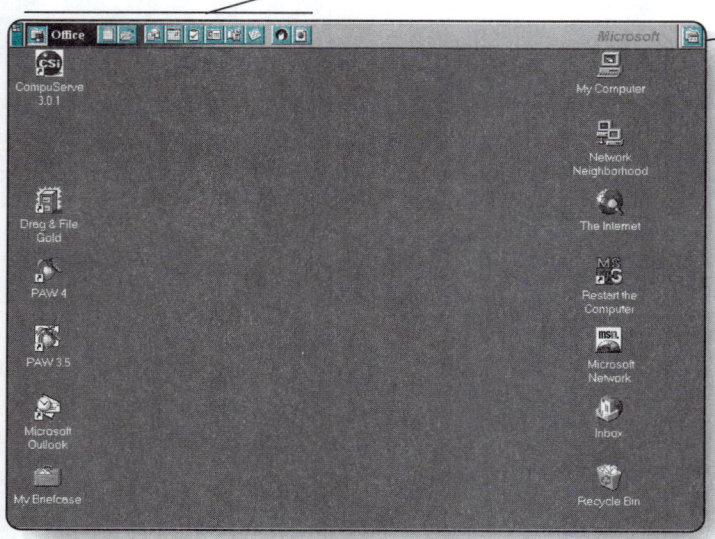

The other toolbar's icon will appear at the edge of the shortcut bar. You can switch between the toolbars by clicking on their icons.

TIP

To add another toolbar to the Office Shortcut Bar, repeat steps 1 through 3. To hide any toolbar, repeat steps 1 through 3 but, in step 3, select the toolbar you want to hide.

CUSTOMIZING THE OFFICE SHORTCUT BAR

Do you have something you use all the time that would be really convenient to have on one of the toolbars on the Office Shortcut Bar? You can add a button to a toolbar. To add a button to a toolbar, that toolbar must be visible. Use the steps in the previous task to display the toolbar on which you want to add a button.

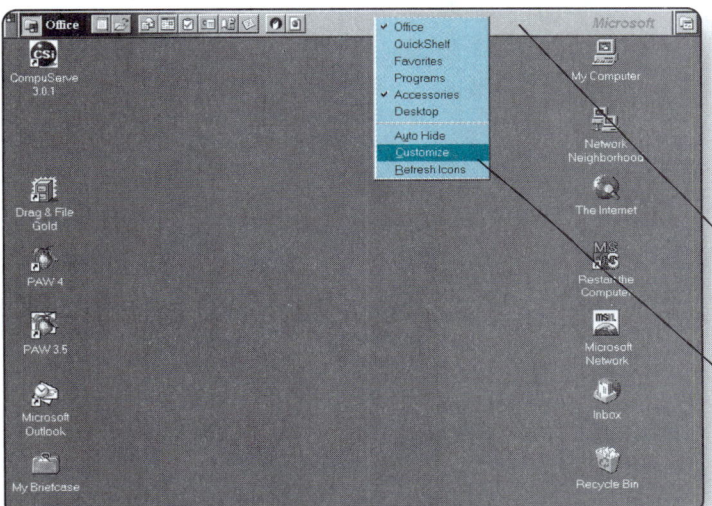

1. **Right-click** on the **gray area** of the Office Shortcut Bar. A shortcut menu will appear.

2. **Click** on **Customize**. The Customize dialog box will open.

3. **Click** on the **Buttons tab**. The tab will come to the front.

4. **Click** on the **arrow** (▼) next to the Toolbar: list box. A list of available toolbars will appear.

5. **Click** on the **toolbar** on which you want to add a button.

6. **Click** on **Add File**. The Add File dialog box will open.

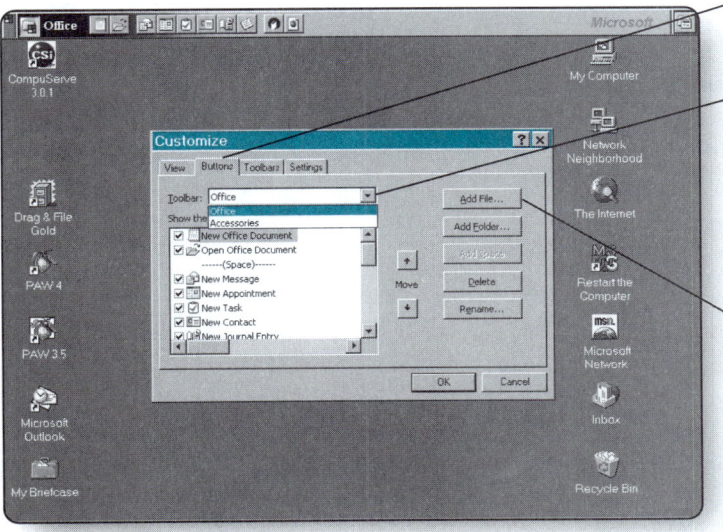

TIP

Buttons that appear on the selected toolbar have a ✔ next to them.

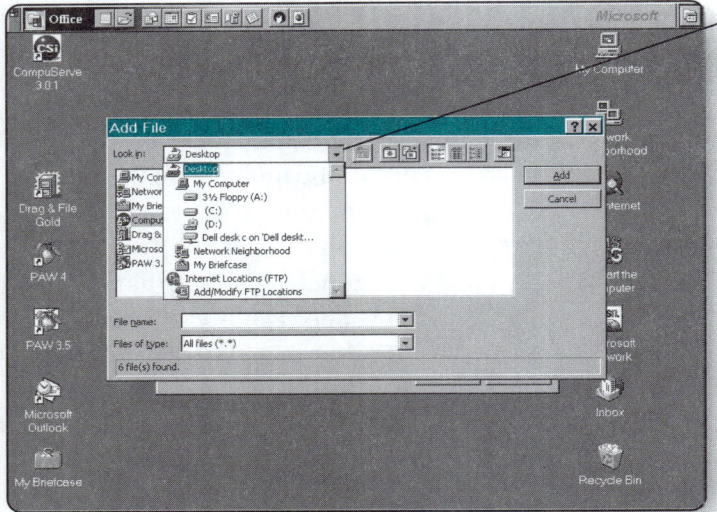

7. **Click** on the **arrow** (▼) next to the Look in: list box. A list of locations will appear.

8. **Navigate** to the **folder** containing the file for which you want to add a button.

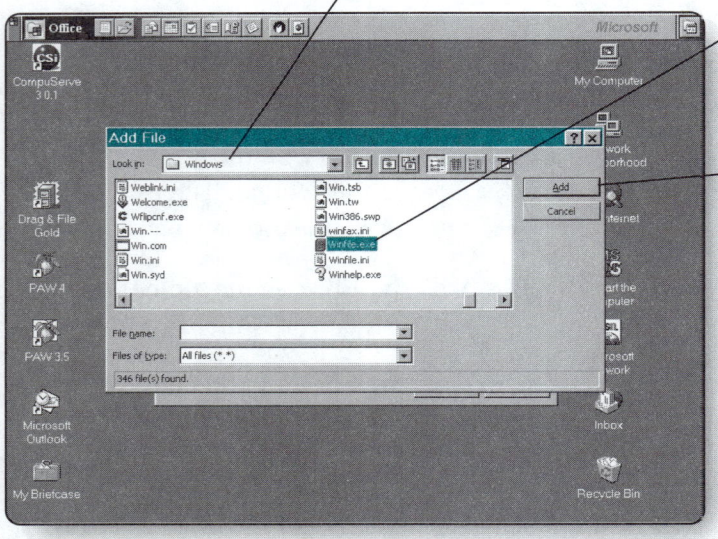

9. **Click** on the **file** for which you want to add a button. The file will be selected.

10. **Click** on **Add**. The Add File dialog box will close.

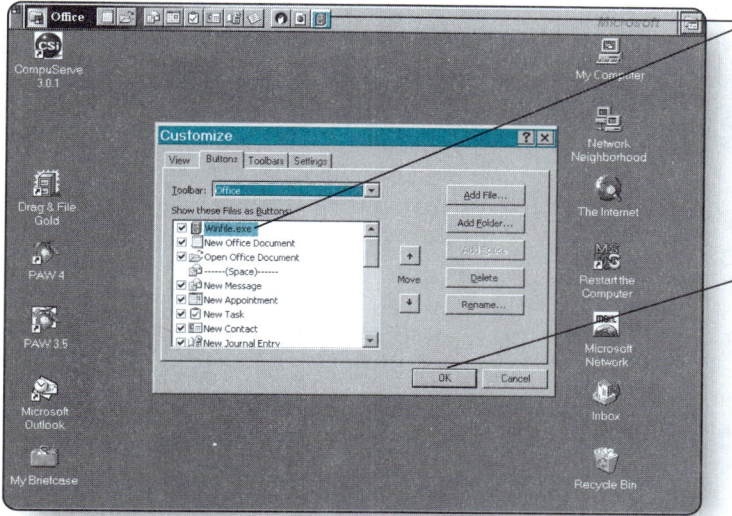

The Customize dialog box will reappear with the file you chose appearing as a button at the top of the list. A button for the file will also appear at the end of the toolbar.

11. Click on **OK**. The Customize dialog box will close, and you'll have a new button on the toolbar.

Renaming a Toolbar Button

The name you saw in the Customize dialog box in the previous task was the filename as it is stored on your computer. This is the name that will appear in the ScreenTip when you move the mouse pointer over the button. You can rename the button.

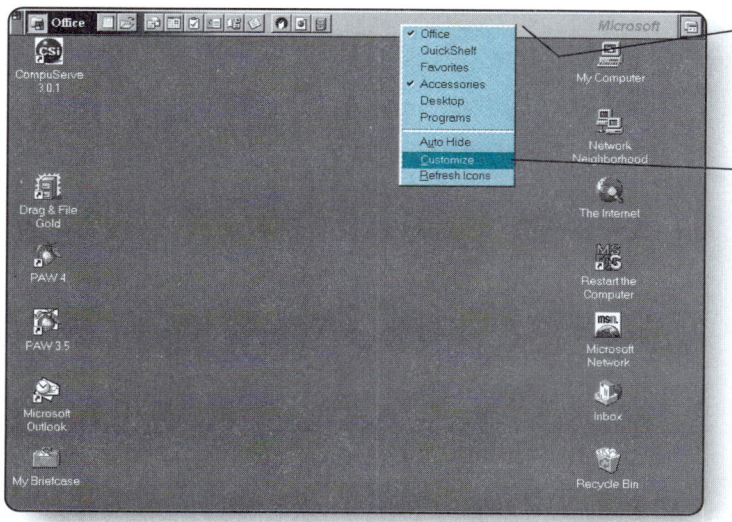

1. Right-click on the gray area of the Office Shortcut Bar. A shortcut menu will appear.

2. Click on Customize. The Customize dialog box will open.

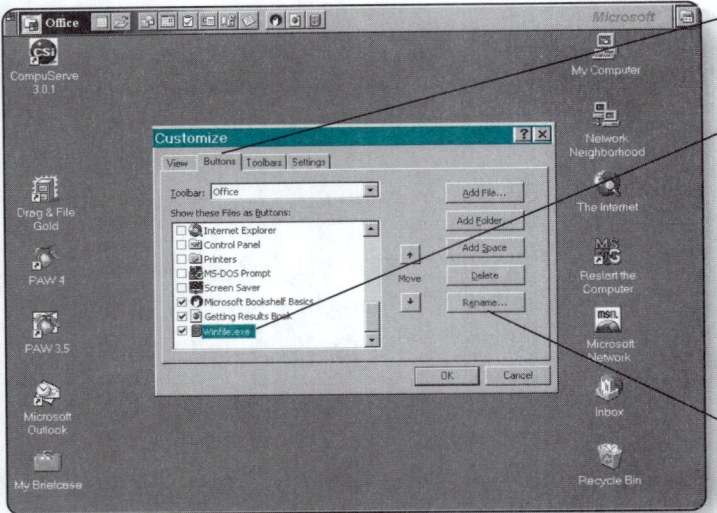

3. **Click** on the **Buttons tab**. The tab will come to the front.

4. **Click** on the **file** you want to rename. The file will be selected.

TIP
The file might appear at the end of the list.

5. **Click** on **Rename**. The Rename dialog box will open.

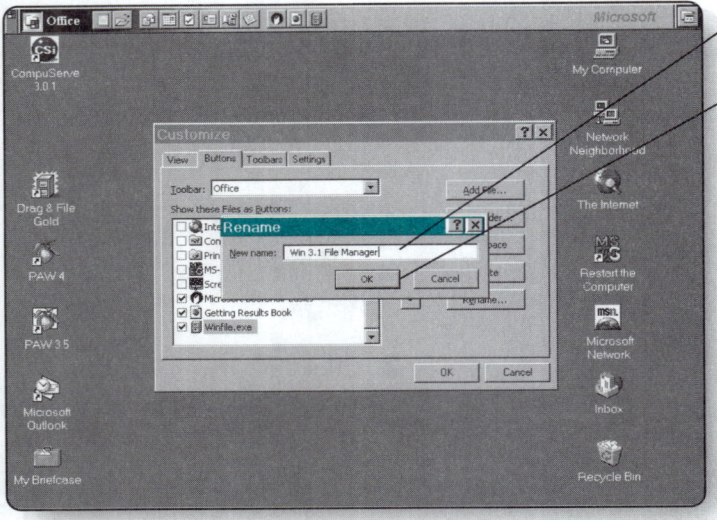

6. **Type** a **new name**.

7. **Click** on **OK**. The Rename dialog box will close.

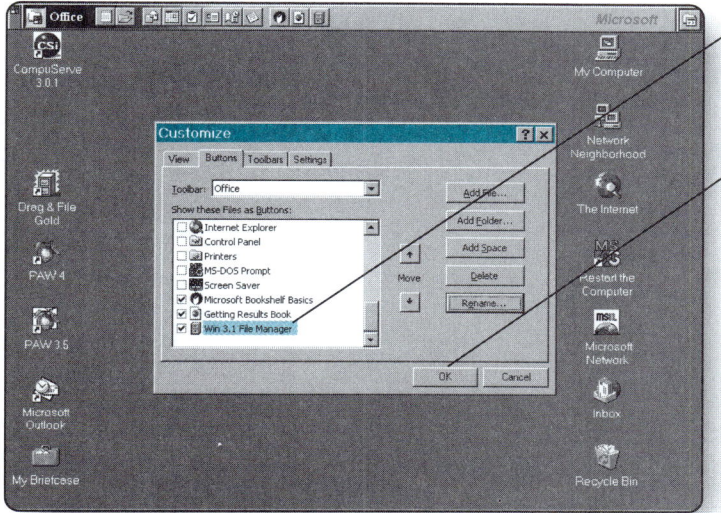

The Customize dialog box will reappear and the button will be renamed.

8. **Click** on **OK**. The Customize dialog box will close.

9. **Move** the **mouse pointer** over the button to see its ScreenTip. The ScreenTip will match the new name you supplied.

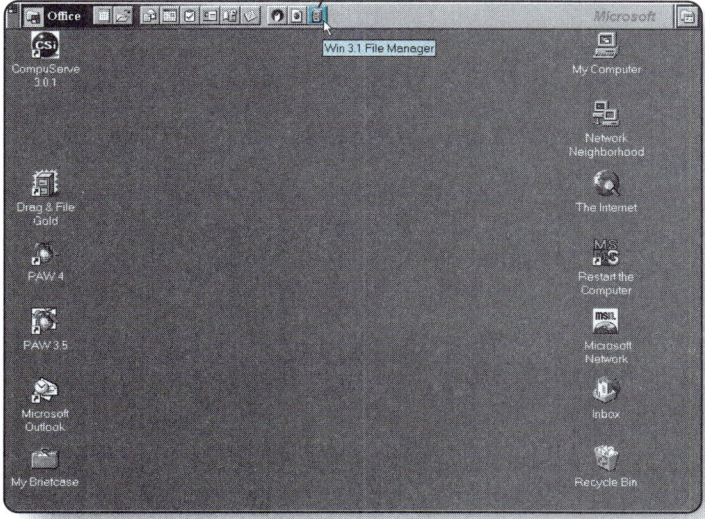

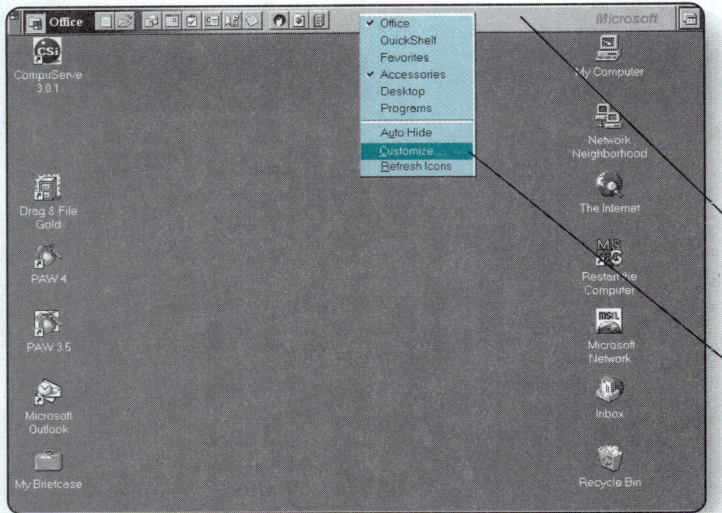

Moving a Toolbar Button

You can place toolbar buttons anywhere on the toolbar.

1. **Right-click** on the **gray area** of the Office Shortcut Bar. A shortcut menu will appear.

2. **Click** on **Customize**. The Customize dialog box will open.

3. **Click** on the **Buttons tab**. The tab will come to the front.

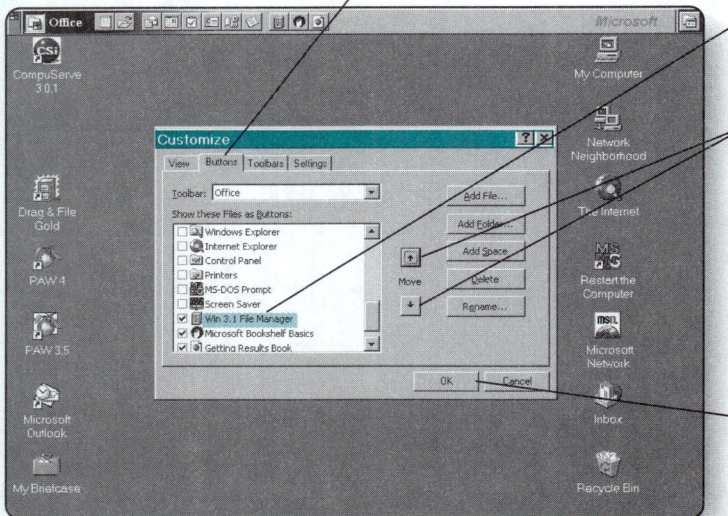

4. **Click** on the **file** whose button you want to move.

5. **Click** on the **Move arrows** in the direction you want to move. Each time you click, the button will move up or down (depending on which direction you choose) in the Customize dialog box and on the toolbar.

6. **Click** on **OK**. The Customize dialog box will close and the button will appear in its new location on the toolbar.

HYPERLINKS AND OFFICE DOCUMENTS

In Office 97, you can create hyperlinks to Office documents. These hyperlinks work just like the ones you use on the Internet, except they point to a document (probably on your network drive) and they open that document.

Creating a Hyperlink

Creating a hyperlink to an Office document is easy. Suppose you have a Word document that refers to an Excel workbook.

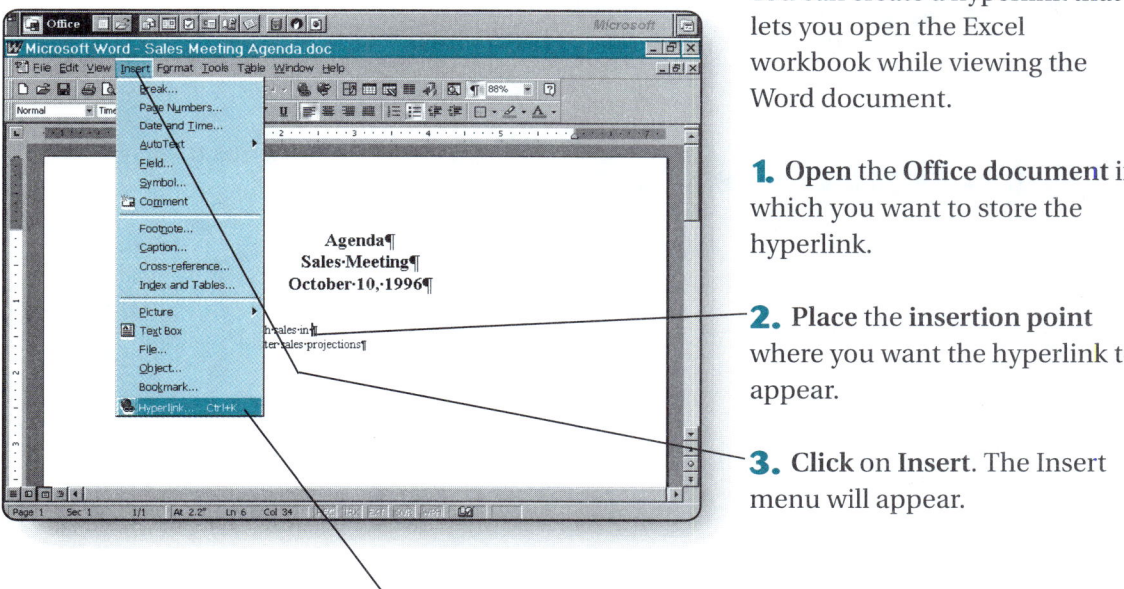

You can create a hyperlink that lets you open the Excel workbook while viewing the Word document.

1. **Open** the **Office document** in which you want to store the hyperlink.

2. **Place** the **insertion point** where you want the hyperlink to appear.

3. **Click** on **Insert**. The Insert menu will appear.

4. **Click** on **Hyperlink**. The Insert Hyperlink dialog box will open.

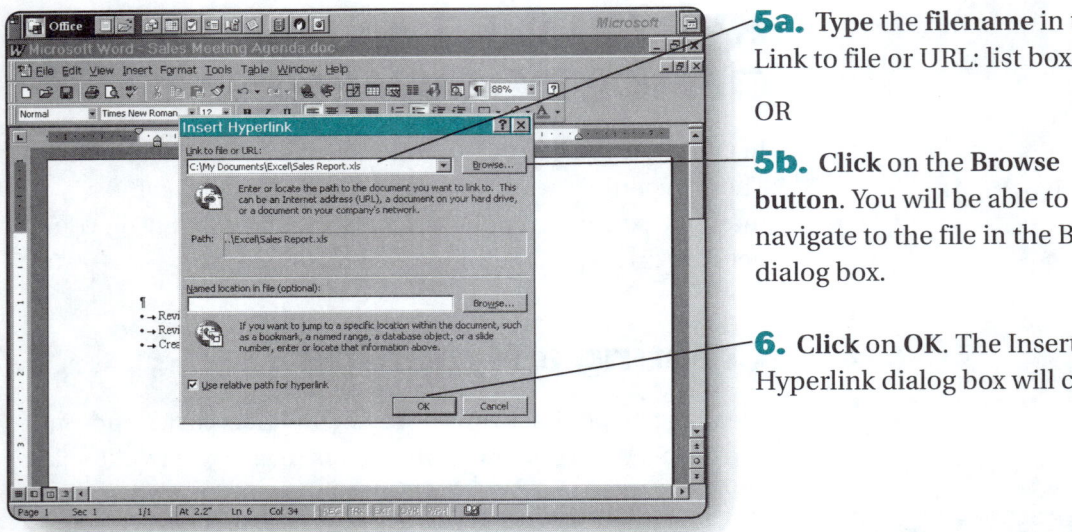

5a. Type the **filename** in the Link to file or URL: list box.

OR

5b. Click on the **Browse button**. You will be able to navigate to the file in the Browse dialog box.

6. Click on **OK**. The Insert Hyperlink dialog box will close.

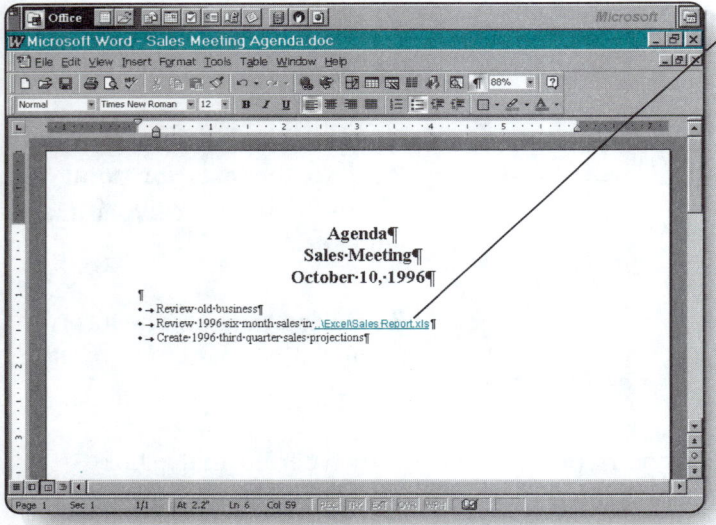

A hyperlink that displays the path to the document will appear in your document. The hyperlink will appear underlined and in blue print.

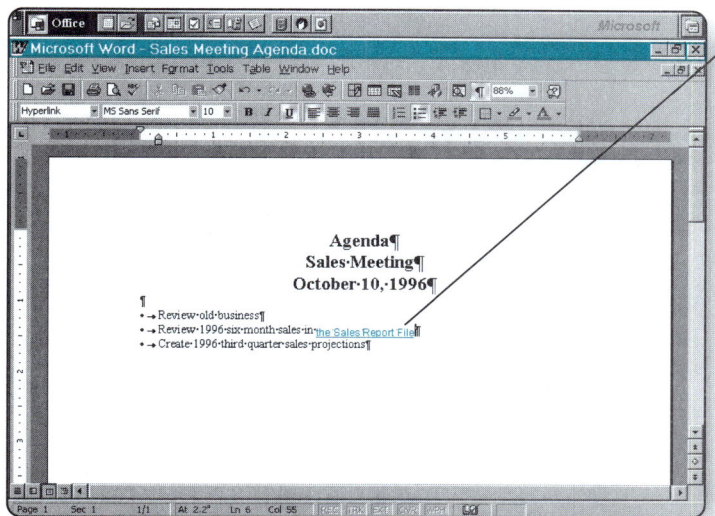

You can rename the hyperlink to make it more meaningful by selecting the hyperlink (use the keyboard to select it so that you don't click on the hyperlink) and typing a new name.

Using a Hyperlink

You can use a hyperlink to automatically open an Office document.

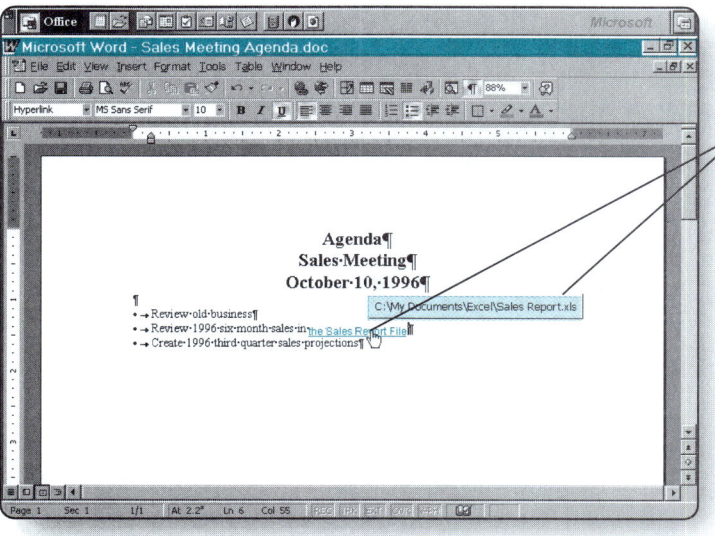

1. **Open** the **Office document** containing the hyperlink.

2. **Move** the **mouse pointer** over the hyperlink. The shape of the mouse pointer will change to the shape of a hand and you will see a ScreenTip that identifies the hyperlinked document's location.

3. **Click** on the **hyperlink**.

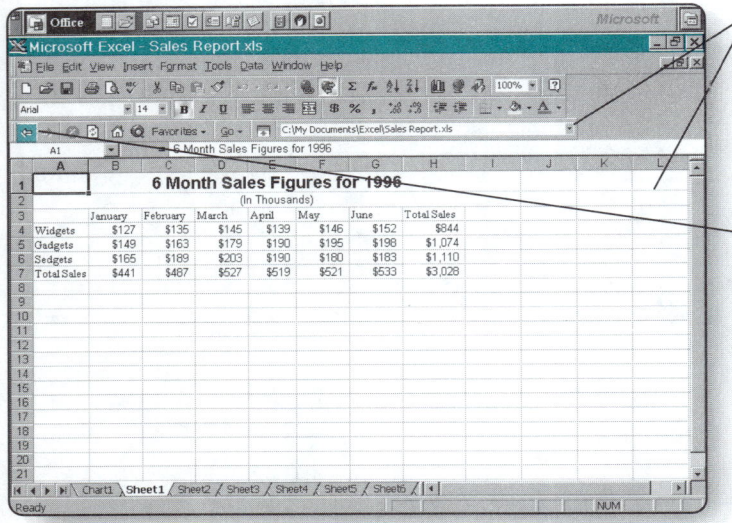

The document to which the hyperlink points will open and the Web toolbar will appear.

TIP

You can switch back to the original document by clicking on the Back button on the Web toolbar.

REVIEWING DOCUMENTS ONLINE

Suppose you decide that you want to send a document around for review and comments. You could use the traditional method—sometimes called the "sneakernet"—where you mail hard copies of the document to each person who should review it. Or, you could use e-mail. If you use e-mail, you can mail the document to all reviewers at the same time, or you can route the document for review.

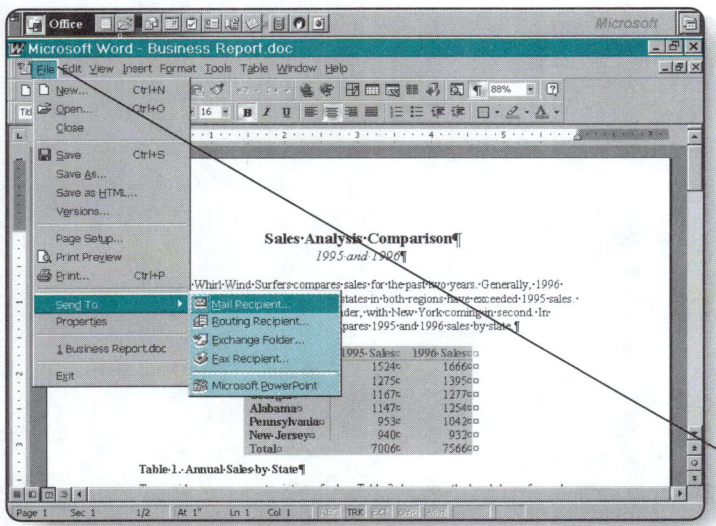

Mailing Documents for Review

1. Open the document you want to send for review.

2. Click on File. The File menu will appear.

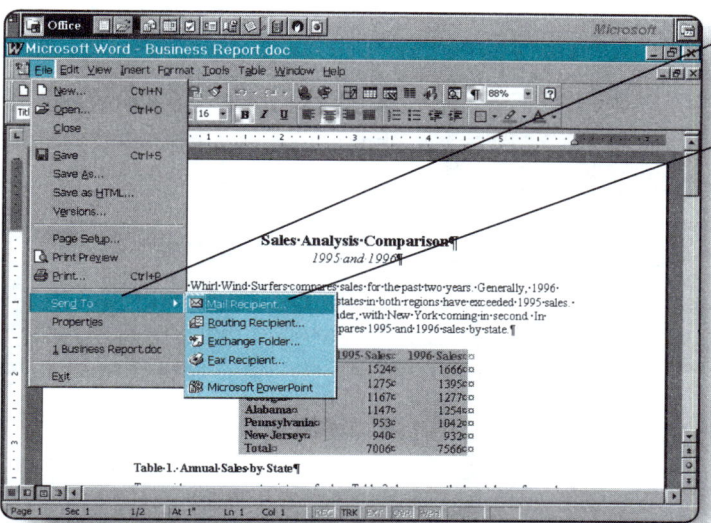

3. **Click** on **Send To**. A cascading menu will appear.

4. **Click** on **Mail Recipient**.

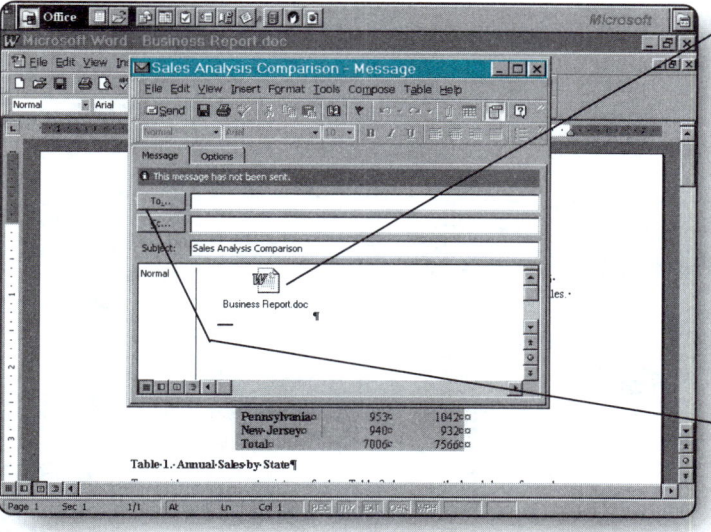

An e-mail message window will appear containing an icon that represents the document you opened in step 1.

5. **Click** on **To**. The Select Names dialog box will open.

6. Click on the **name** of a recipient in the left box.

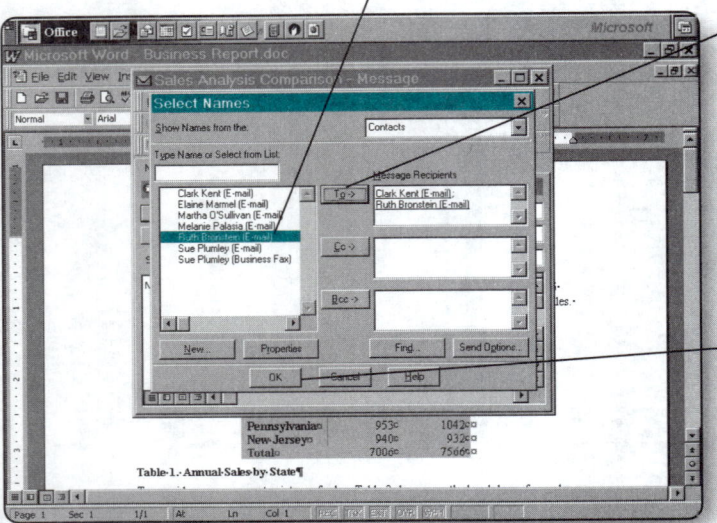

7. Click on **To**. The name of the recipient will appear in the Message Recipients box.

NOTE

Repeat steps 6 and 7 for each recipient.

8. Click on **OK**. The Select Names dialog box will close and the e-mail message window will reappear, containing the names of the recipients you selected.

9. Click in the **message portion** on the window and add any text you want the recipients to see when they receive the document.

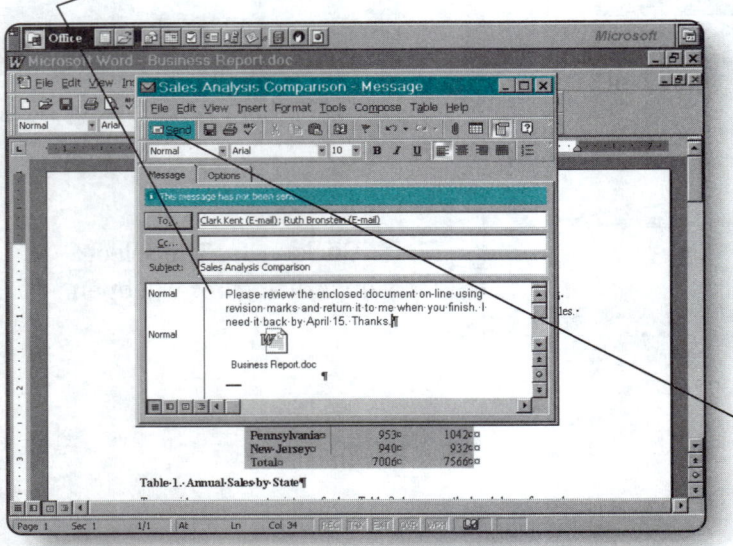

TIP

You might find it easiest to add text to the message if you press the Enter key once before typing, and then press the Ctrl and Home keys at the same time. The insertion point will move to its own line at the top of the mail message.

10. Click on **Send**. Depending on how your e-mail program is configured, the file will either be sent immediately or placed in your Outbox waiting to be sent.

Routing Documents for Review

When you route a document, you send the document around "in order." That is, when one person finishes with the document and mails it, it automatically goes to the next person on the list.

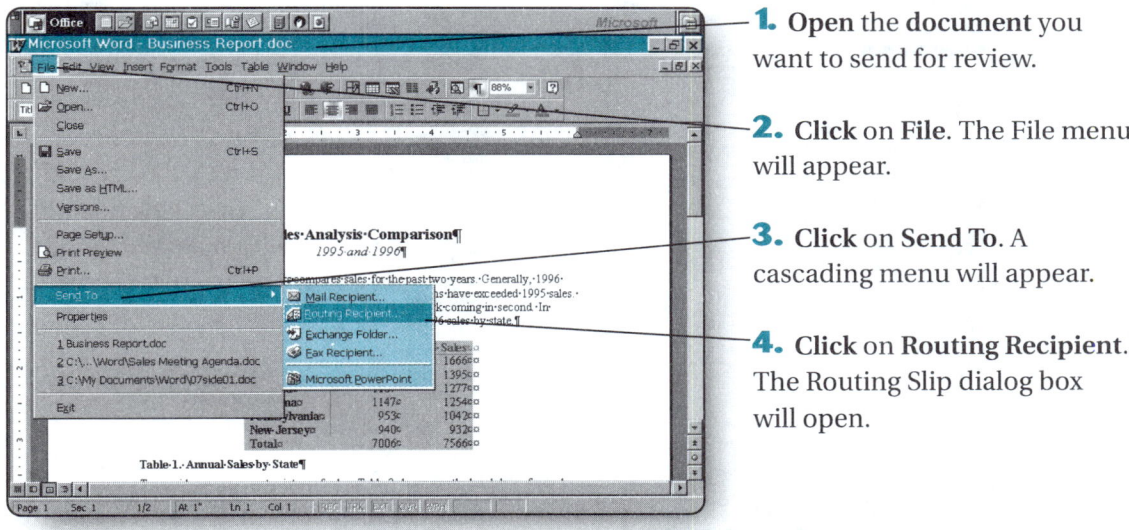

1. **Open** the **document** you want to send for review.

2. **Click** on **File**. The File menu will appear.

3. **Click** on **Send To**. A cascading menu will appear.

4. **Click** on **Routing Recipient**. The Routing Slip dialog box will open.

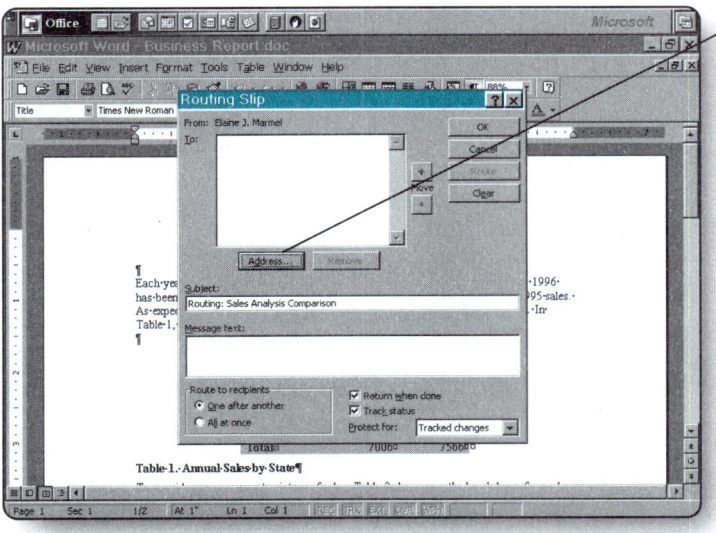

5. **Click** on **Address**. The Address Book dialog box will open.

6. Click on the **name** of a recipient in the left box.

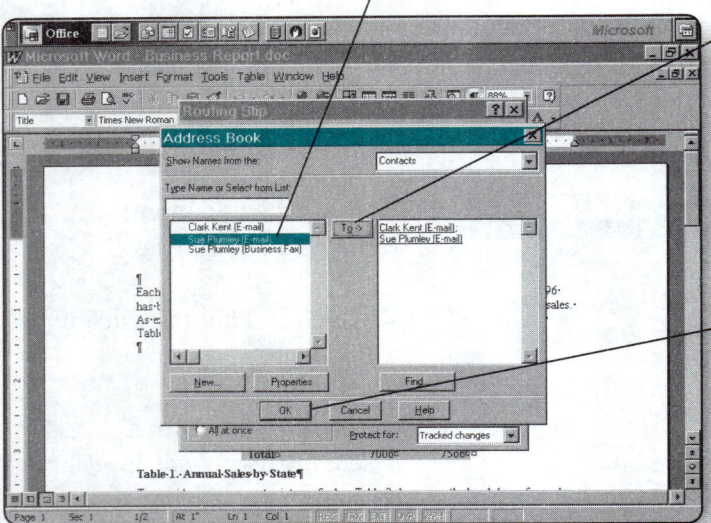

7. Click on **To**. The name will appear in the right box.

NOTE

Repeat steps 6 and 7 for each recipient.

8. Click on **OK**. The Address Book dialog box will close and the Routing Slip dialog box will reappear with the names of the recipients in the To: text box.

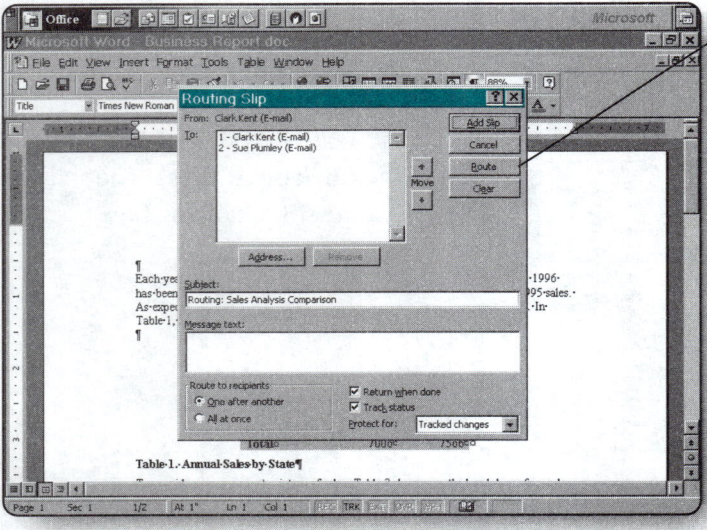

9. Click on **Route**. An e-mail message containing the document as an attachment will either be sent immediately or placed in your e-mail program's Outbox, depending on how your e-mail program is configured.

21 Using Binders

Most people believe that the computer age introduced an era where information is more easily accessed and organized. However, some people point out that the computer age introduced a new way for you, the user, to be disorganized. In addition to losing information in your file cabinet, now you can lose information on your computer too.

Microsoft Office Binder is a program that helps you organize files related to the same project. Think of Office Binder as an electronic version of a three-ring notebook. In the notebook, you would place printed copies of related work, regardless of how you created the documents. You use Office Binder to store related files, regardless of the program you used to create them. In this chapter, you'll learn how to:

+ Understand the Office Binder window
+ Create a binder
+ Add sections to a binder
+ Use documents stored in a binder
+ Unbind sections

UNDERSTANDING THE OFFICE BINDER WINDOW

The term Office Binder uses for an element you store in a binder is *section*. Therefore, a Word document, an Excel workbook, and a PowerPoint presentation are each sections when stored in a binder document. When you save a binder document that contains more than one section, you are still saving only one binder file. Microsoft Office Binder will appear on the Programs menu in Windows 95, if it was installed.

1. Start Microsoft Office Binder.

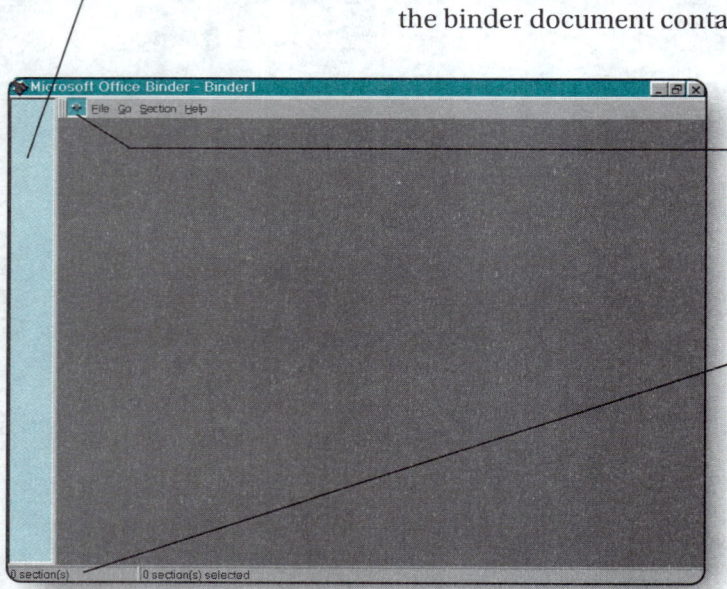

The Binder pane appears on the left side of the screen. When the binder document contains sections, you'll see icons representing those sections in the Binder pane.

Click on the Show/Hide Binder Pane button to make the Binder pane disappear. Click on the button again to make it reappear.

The status bar shows the number of sections in the binder.

SETTING UP A BINDER

You set up a binder by adding sections to it. You can add sections in two ways: add an existing file to a binder or create a new section while working in the binder.

Adding an Existing File to a Binder

Most often, you'll create documents first in their original applications and then decide to store them in a binder; therefore, you'll create the binder after you created the documents.

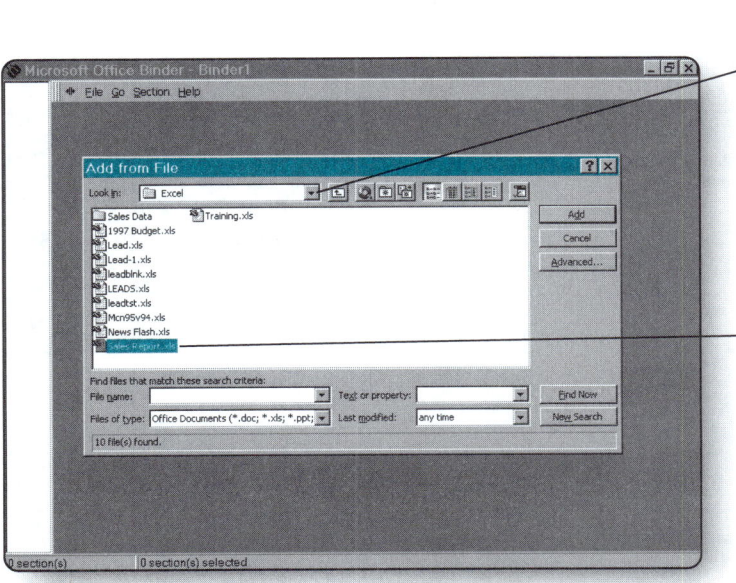

1. **Click** on **Section**. The Section menu will appear.

2. **Click** on **Add from File**. The Add from File dialog box will open.

The Add from File dialog box closely resembles the Open dialog box, and you use it the same way.

3. **Click** on the **arrow** (▼) next to the Look in: list box.

4. **Navigate** to the **file** you want to add as a section in a binder, using the Look in: list box and text box.

5. **Click** on the **file** you want to add.

6. **Click** on **Add**. Office Binder will add the file to the binder.

You will see a section icon for the document in the Binder pane.

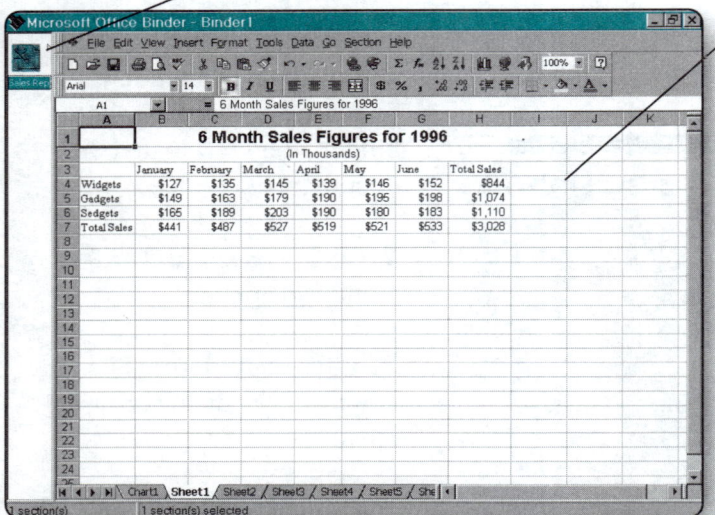

Because the section icon is selected, you can see the document in the Binder window. You can modify your document in any way you want from this window.

NOTE

Notice that the menus you see in Office Binder have changed. When you select a section from the Binder pane, you then see menus that look like modified versions of the menus you would ordinarily see if you opened the document in the application that created it.

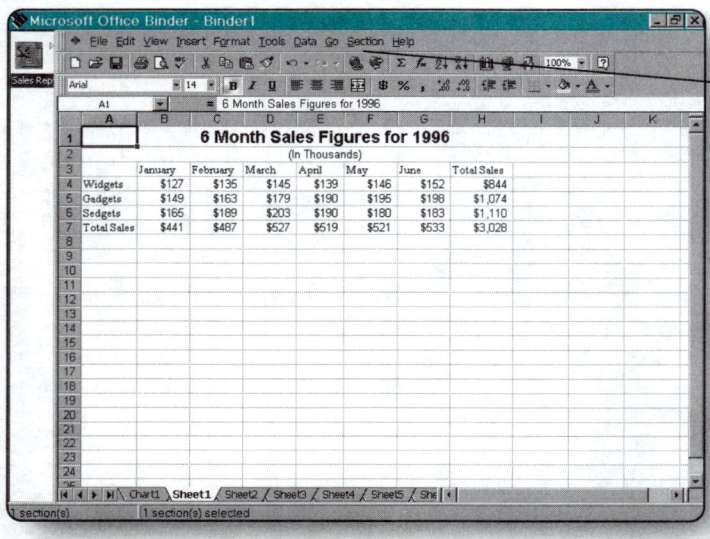

TIP

Repeat the previous steps to add additional files as sections to the binder. The Section menu appears immediately to the left of the Help menu.

Adding a New Section to a Binder

If you haven't already created the document you want to store in a binder, you don't need to open the originating application to create it; instead, you can create the document from inside the binder.

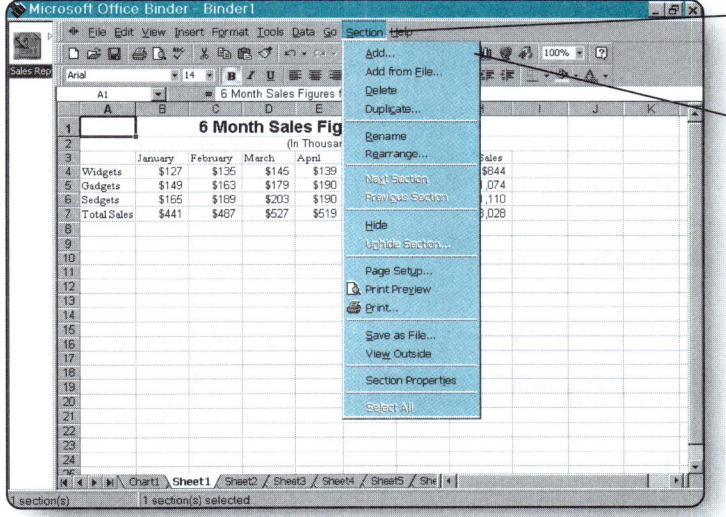

1. **Click** on **Section**. The Section menu will appear.

2. **Click** on **Add**. The Add Section dialog box will open.

The Add Section dialog box closely resembles the New dialog box for Office programs, and you use it the same way— you select a template on which to base your document.

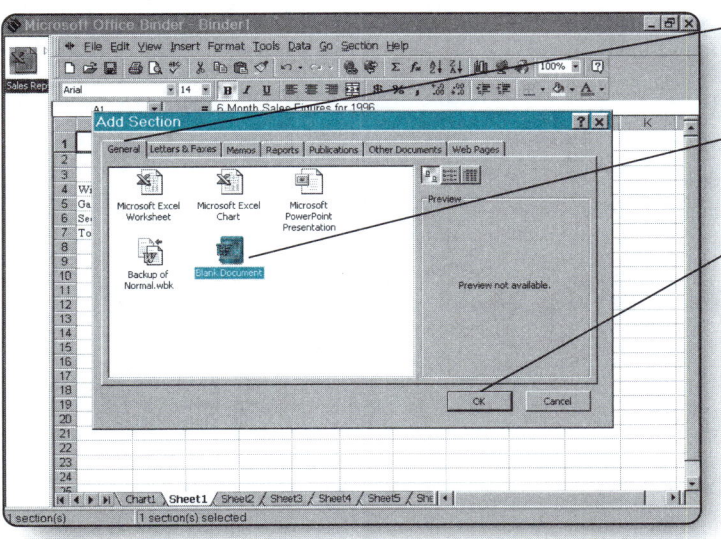

3. **Click** on the **tab** containing the template you want to use.

4. **Click** on the **template** you want to use.

5. **Click** on **OK**. The Add Section dialog box will close.

Office Binder will open a new

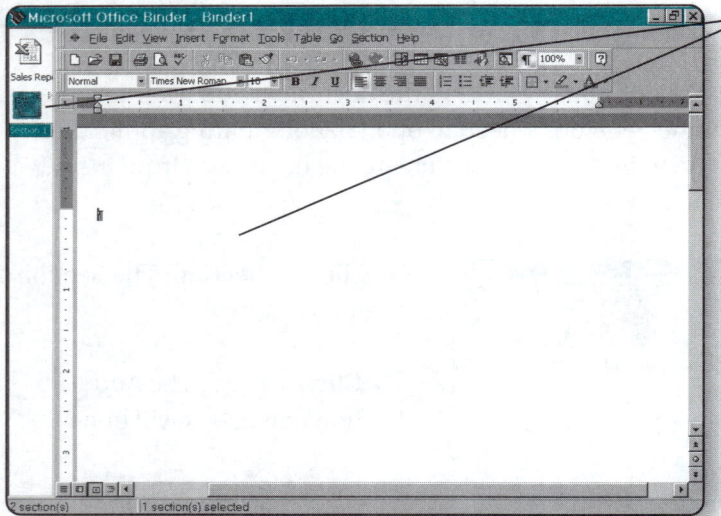

file in the application that uses the template you selected. Work in the application as you usually would.

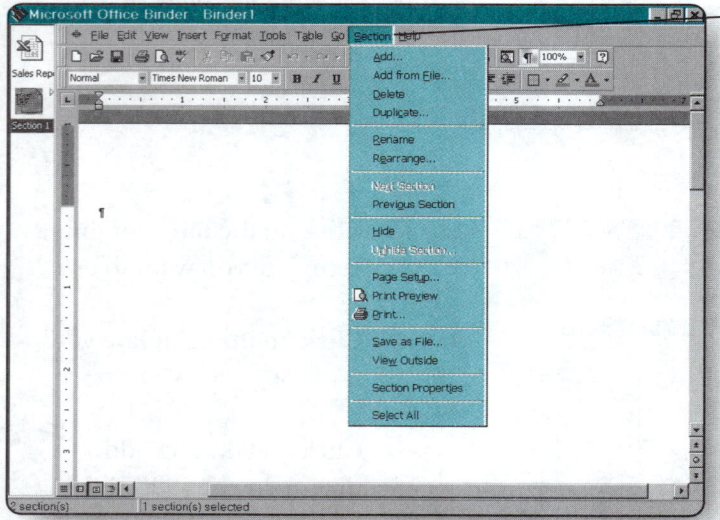

Since the Window menu has been replaced by the Section menu, you don't open multiple documents in the application simultaneously. Instead, you use the Section menu to add each document you need to the binder and then switch between binder sections.

WORKING WITH SECTIONS

As you know, sections are the documents that make up a binder. You can switch between sections within a binder, save a section as a separate document, and rename a section.

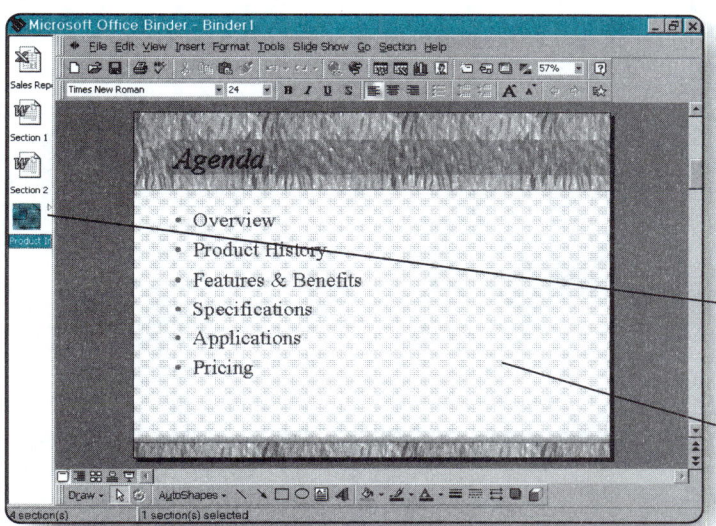

Switching between Sections

When you have more than one section in a binder, you can switch between sections to work on different documents in the binder.

1. **Click** on the **Binder pane icon** for the section on which you want to work.

The section you chose will appear in the Office Binder window, and you will be able to work on it.

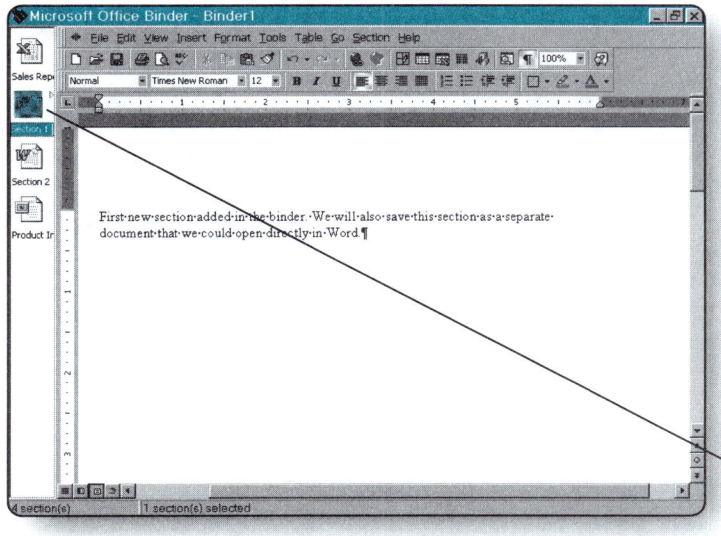

Saving a New Section

You don't need to save sections separately from binders, but you can. If you save a section only as part of a binder, then you will be able to access the section and work on it only from the binder. However, if you save the section as a separate file, you will be able to access it from the application that created it *and* from the binder.

1. **Click** on the **section** you want to save as a separate file.

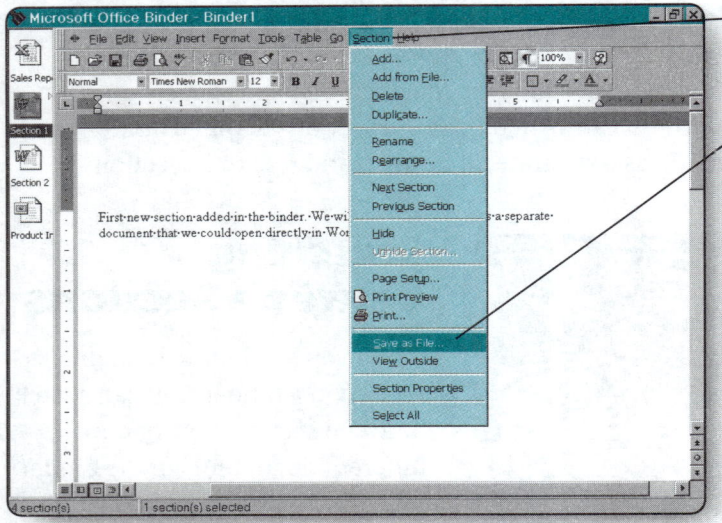

2. Click on **Section**. The Section menu will appear.

3. Click on **Save as File**. The Save As dialog box will open.

4. Click on the **arrow** (▼) next to the Save in: list box.

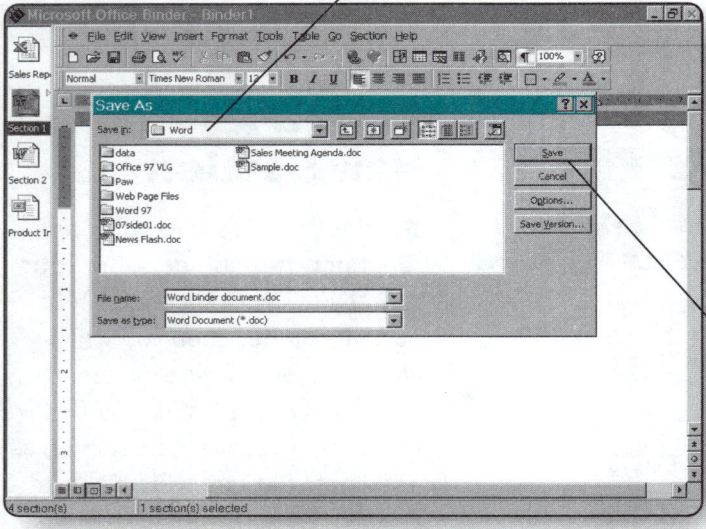

5. Navigate to the **folder** in which you want to save the document. For example, if you're saving a Word document, you might want to place it in the Word folder.

6. Type a **name** for the file in the File name: list box.

7. Click on **Save**. The Save As dialog box will close.

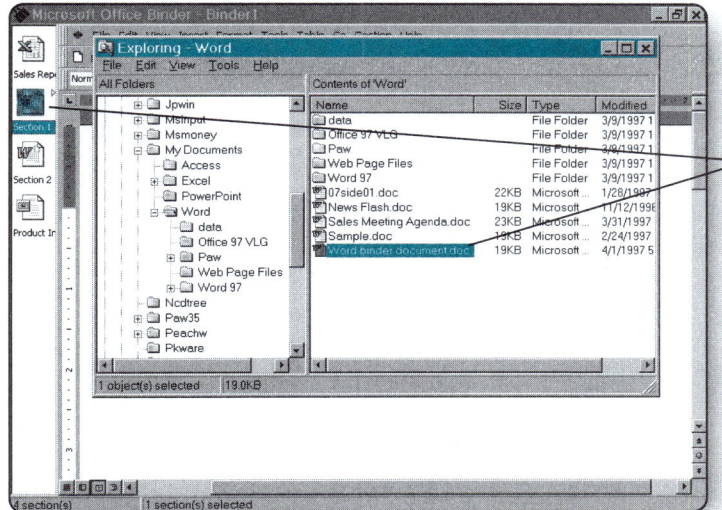

Office Binder will save the document to the folder you specified.

Note that saving the document did not affect the name for it that appears in the Binder pane.

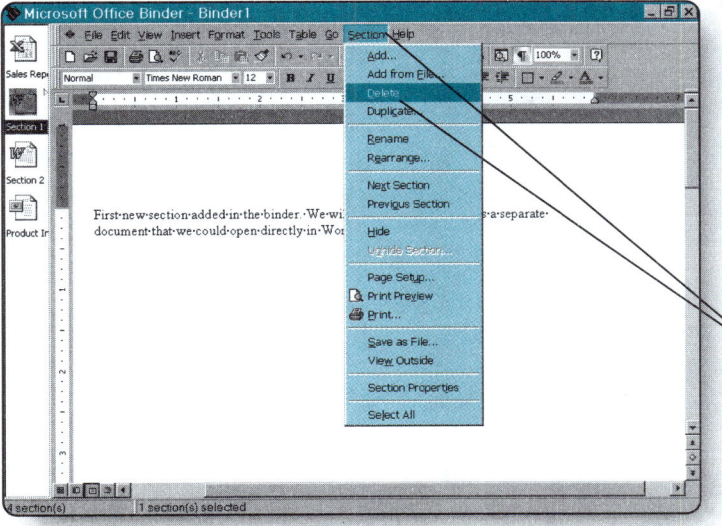

If you decide to save a section as a separate document, you might consider deleting the section from the binder so that you can avoid accidentally working on both versions of the document.

To delete a section, click on the section, click on Section, and finally, click on Delete. Office Binder will ask you to confirm that you want to delete a section.

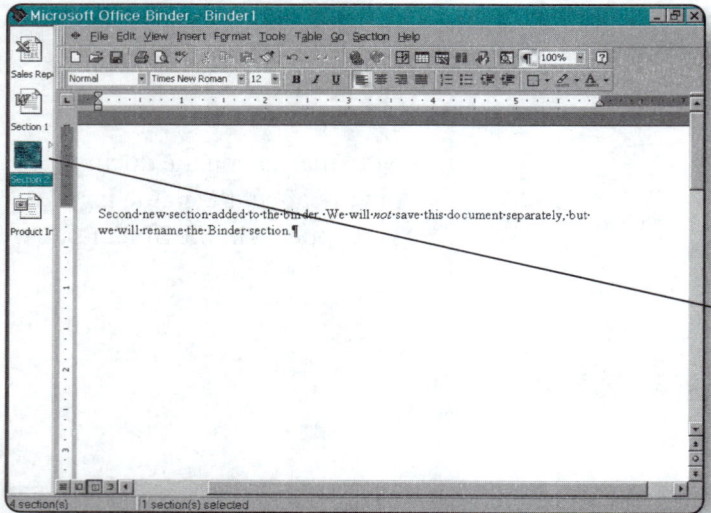

Renaming a Section

Generic names assigned to new sections you create while working in a binder are not particularly useful.

1. **Click** on the **icon** in the Binder pane for the section you want to rename.

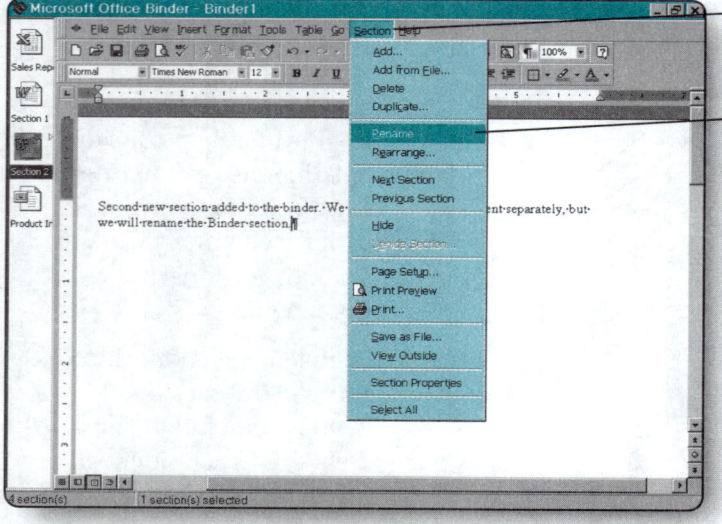

2. **Click** on **Section**. The Section menu will appear.

3. **Click** on **Rename**. Office Binder will select the name of the section in the Binder pane.

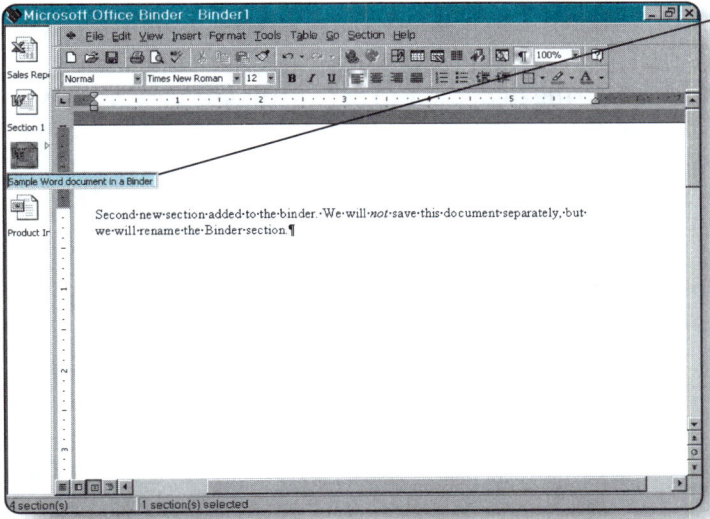

4. **Type** a **new name** for the section in the Binder pane.

5. **Press** the **Enter key**. Office Binder will change the name of the section and the portion of the section name that extends over the Binder pane will be hidden from view.

WORKING WITH BINDERS

Binders are files for the Office Binder program, and you can save and open them the same way you save and open other programs' files. You also can set a default folder where Office Binder will look each time you open or save a binder file.

NOTE

You will *not* find this section if you look in the Explorer because you did not save it as a separate file—you simply renamed it within the binder document.

Saving a Binder

Just as you would expect, you need to save binder documents as files if you want to use them again. And, if you don't save a binder document, any sections in them that are not saved as separate documents will be lost.

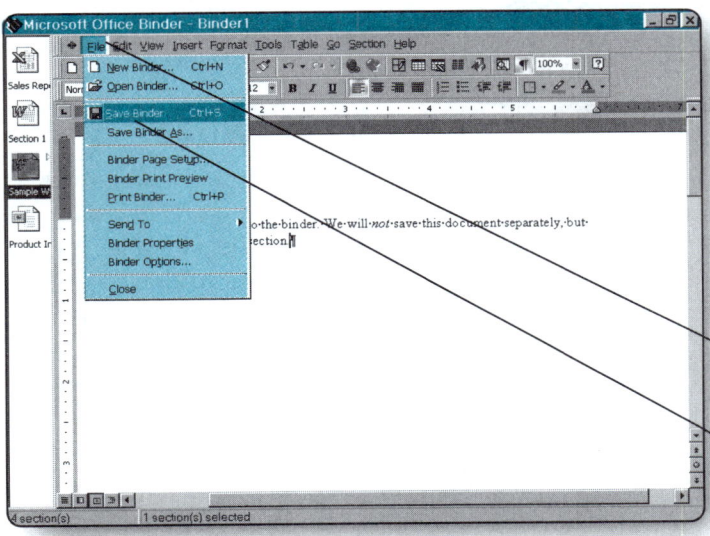

1. **Click** on **File**. The File menu will appear.

2. **Click** on **Save Binder**. The Save Binder As dialog box will open.

3. **Click** on the **arrow** (▼) next to the Save in: list box.

4. **Navigate** to the **folder** in which you want to save binders.

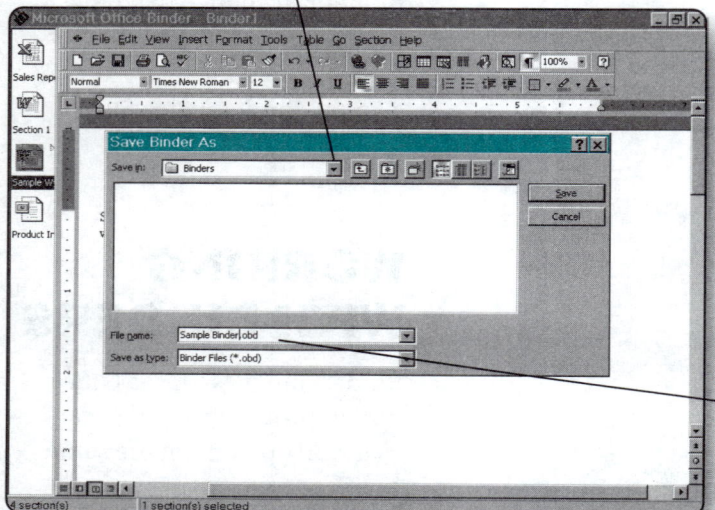

TIP

You might want to navigate to the New Documents folder and click on the New Folder button to create a folder just for binder documents. Then, double-click your new folder to store the binder.

5. **Type** a **name** in the File name: list box.

6. **Click** on **Save**. Office Binder will save the document as a file and the Save Binder As dialog box will close.

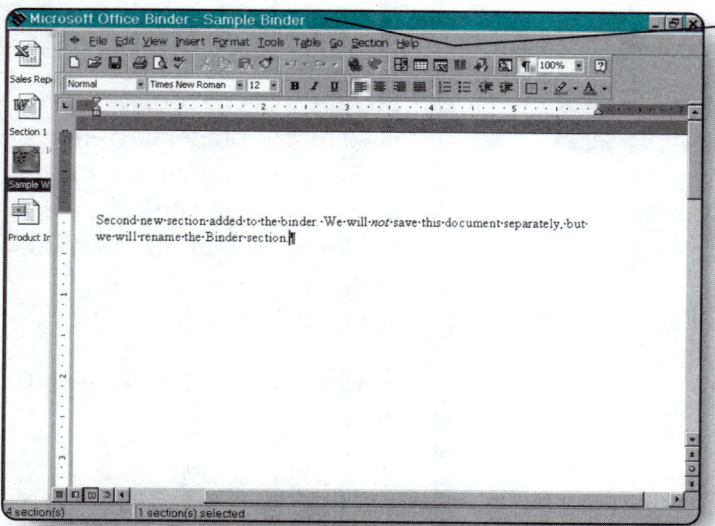

The title bar will change to reflect the name of the binder.

NOTE

If you check in the Windows Explorer, you *will* find a file for the binder, and files for any sections you saved separately. But, you won't find files for any sections you did not save separately.

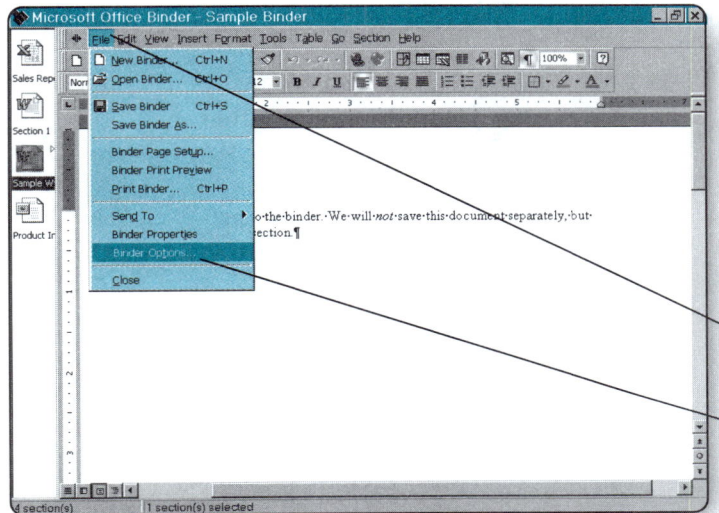

Setting Binder Defaults

You can set the location where Office Binder files are saved so you don't need to navigate there each time you want to open or save a binder.

1. **Click** on **File**. The File menu will appear.

2. **Click** on **Binder Options**. The Binder Options dialog box will open.

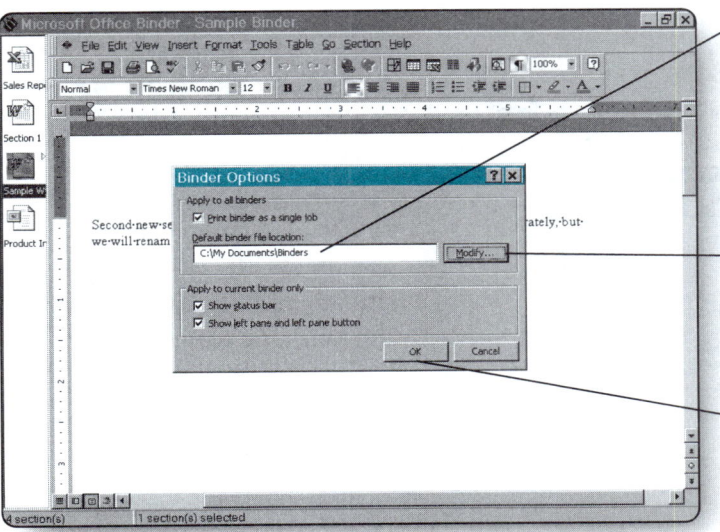

3. **Type** the **name** of the **folder** in which you want to save binders in the Default binder file location: text box.

> **TIP**
>
> Click on the Modify button to navigate to the folder you want to use.

4. **Click** on **OK**. The Binder Options dialog box will close. Each time you open or save a binder, Office Binder will automatically suggest the folder you selected in the Binder Options dialog box.

Opening a Binder

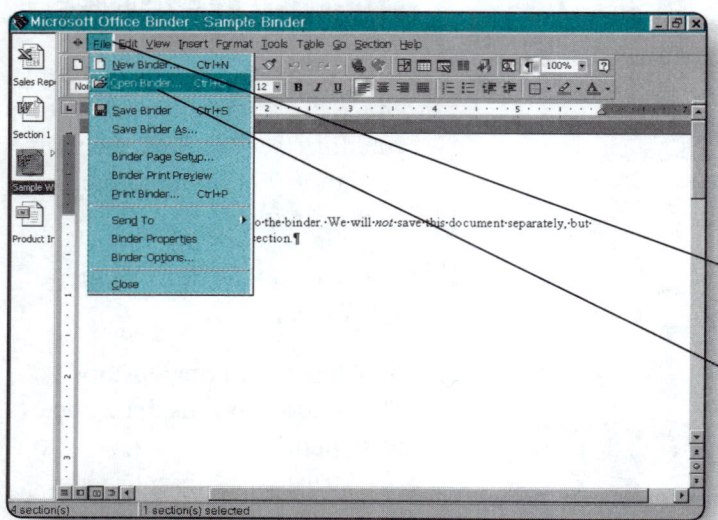

Each time you open a binder, you start another session of Office Binder. Suppose you started working on one binder and now want to work on another binder.

1. **Click** on **File**. The File menu will appear.

2. **Click** on **Open Binder**. The Open Binder dialog box will appear.

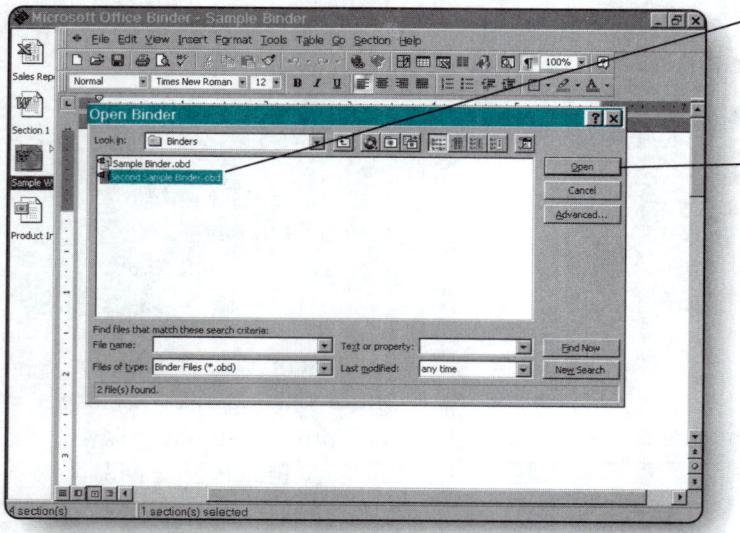

3. **Click** on the **binder** in which you want to work. The binder will be selected.

4. **Click** on **Open**. A new session of Office Binder will start and the binder you selected will appear in the window.

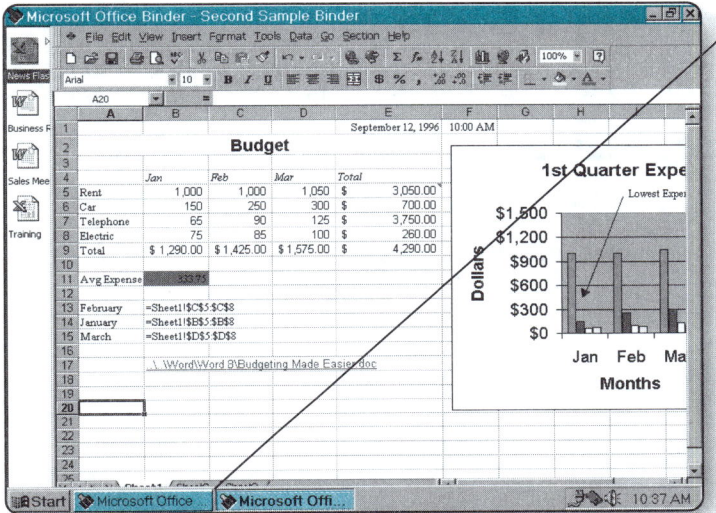

If you look at the Windows Taskbar, you'll see two sessions of Microsoft Office Binder running. You can switch between the sessions using the Taskbar.

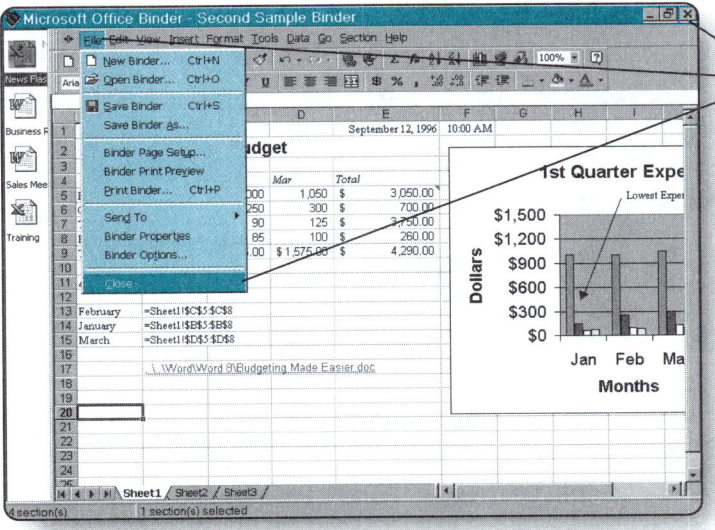

TIP

When you close a binder, you actually close the Office Binder program. Click on the Close button ([X]) in the upper-right corner of the Office Binder window or click on File, and then click on Close.

PRINTING

You can print the entire binder or you can print individual sections of the binder.

Printing a Section

1. **Click** on the **section** you want to print in the Binder pane.

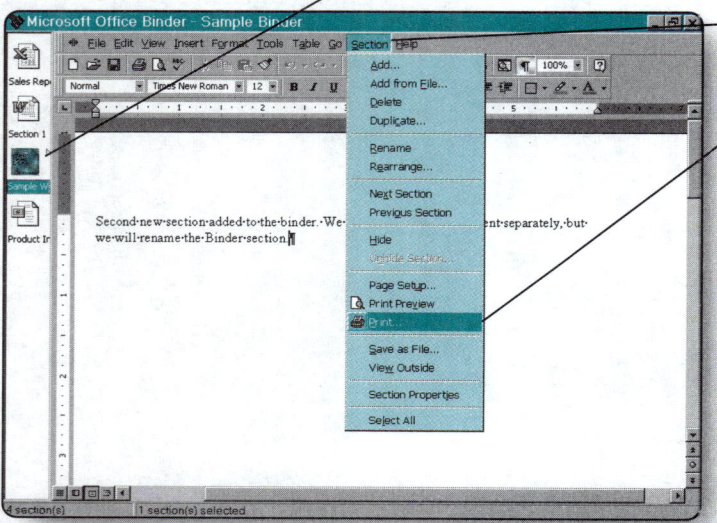

2. **Click** on **Section**. The Section menu will appear.

3. **Click** on **Print**. The Print dialog box will open.

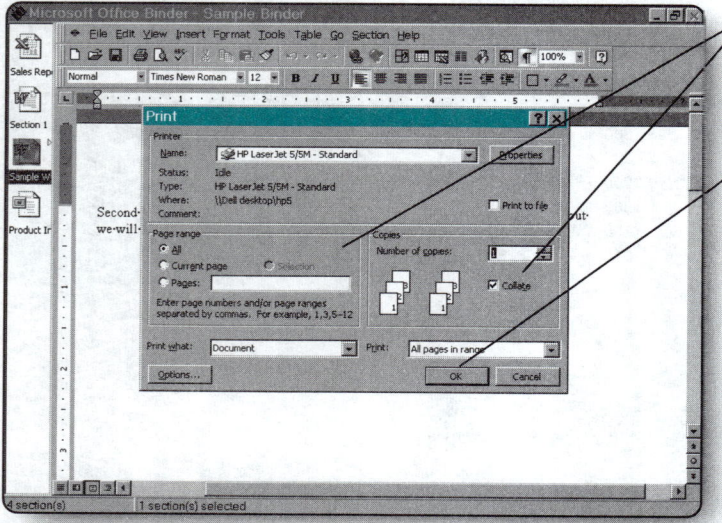

4. **Set** any **print options**, such as the Page Range or Number of copies.

5. **Click** on **OK**. The Print dialog box will close and the section will print.

TIP

The Print button on the toolbar that appears in each section will print that section without opening the Print dialog box.

Setting Binder Headers or Footers

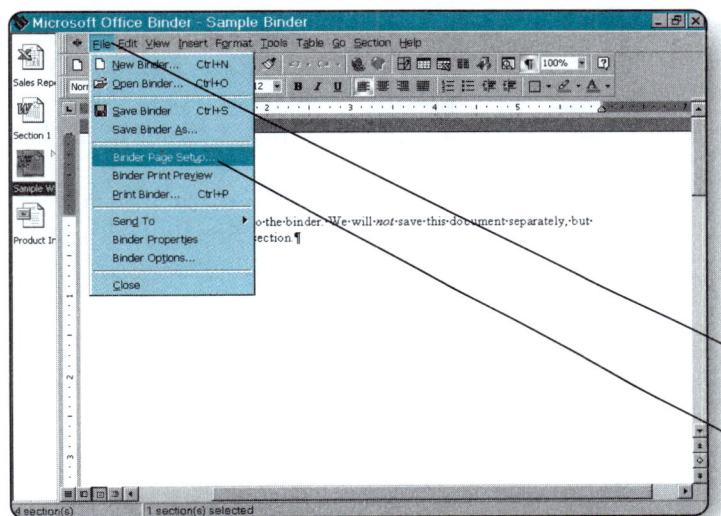

One advantage of using a binder is that you can use common headers and footers for documents created in different programs. For example, you might want to add a footer that includes a consecutive page number for each page in the binder.

1. Click on **File**. The File menu will appear.

2. Click on **Binder Page Setup**. The Binder Page Setup dialog box will open.

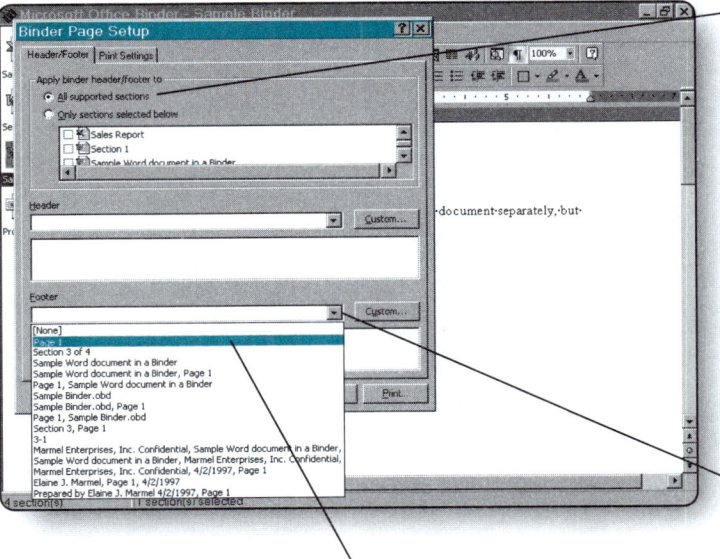

3. Click on **All supported sections**.

NOTE

All supported sections will include all Office 97 Word, Excel, or PowerPoint documents. Although you can include an Office 95 document in a binder, it is not considered a supported section.

4. Click on the **arrow** (▼) of the Footer list box. The list box will open.

5. Click on the **footer information** you want to print with the binder.

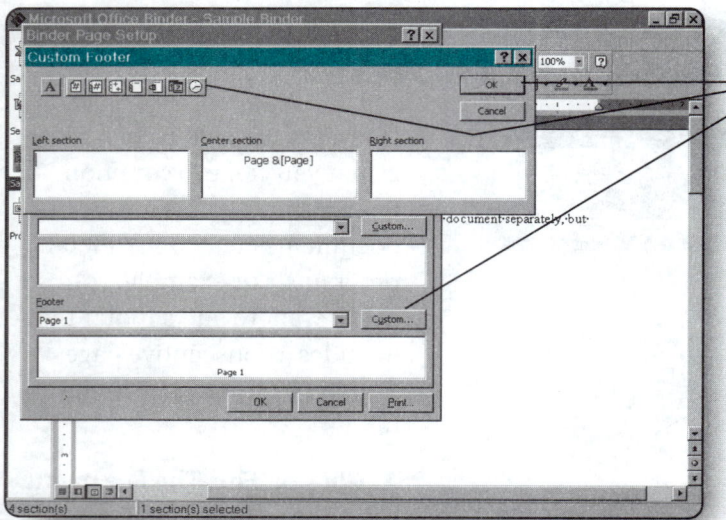

TIP

Click on Custom to open the Custom Footer dialog box and to set up a custom footer. Click in a section of the footer and then use the toolbar buttons in the dialog box to add footer information. Click on OK when you finish to return to the Binder Page Setup dialog box.

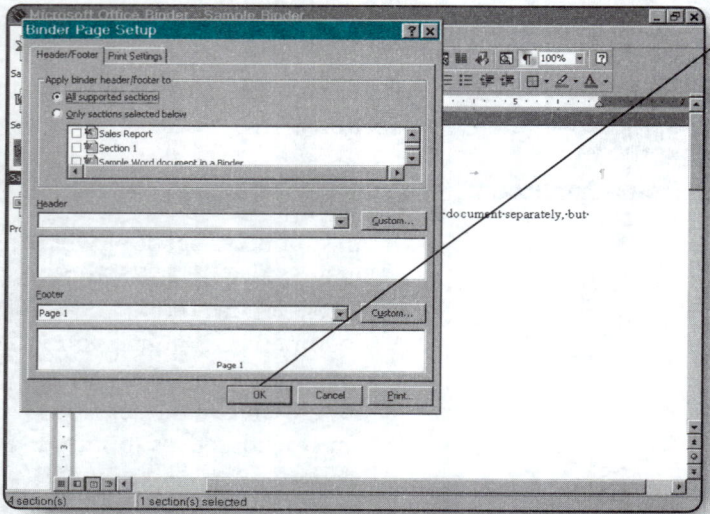

6. Click on **OK**. The Binder Page Setup dialog box will close.

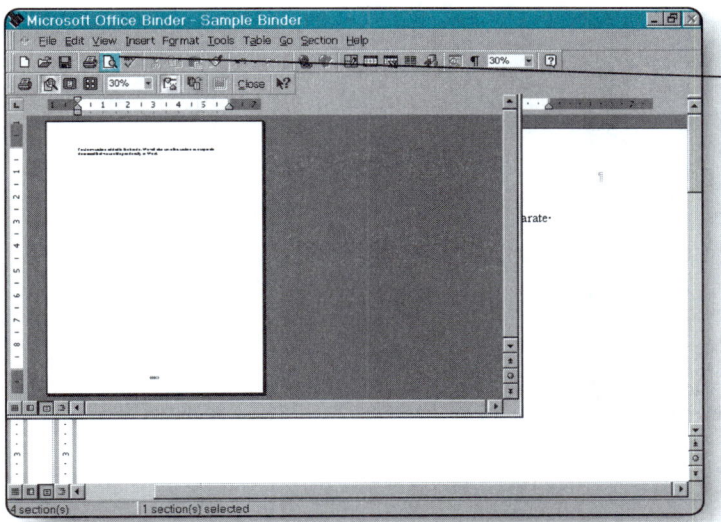

TIP

TIP

If you click on Print Preview in any section of the binder, you'll see the footer you added.

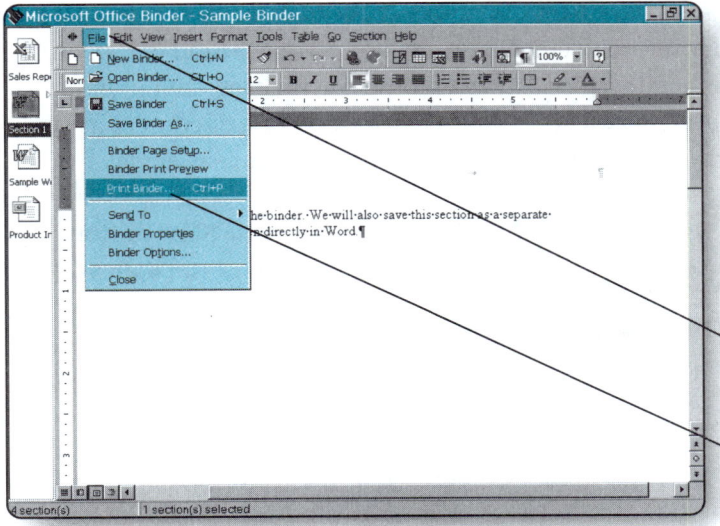

Printing the Binder

You might want to print the entire binder, particularly if you included page numbering that will consecutively number binder document pages.

1. **Click** on **File**. The File menu will appear.

2. **Click** on **Print Binder**. The Print dialog box will open.

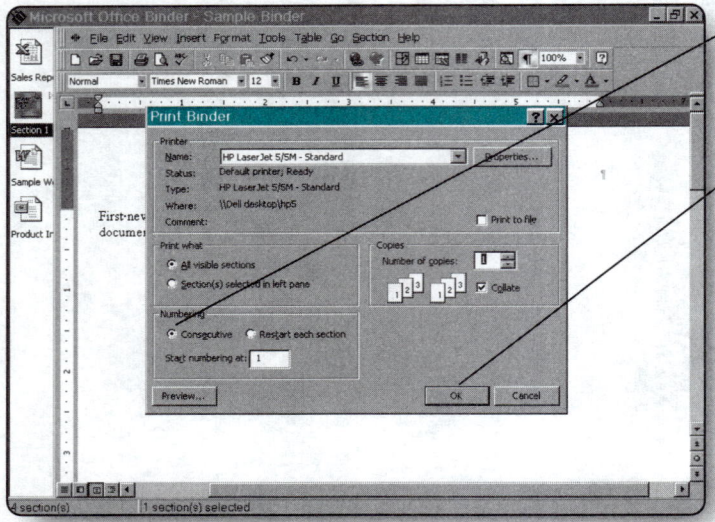

3. Change any **printing options** as needed, such as the way page numbering should occur.

4. Click on **OK**. The Print dialog box will close and the entire binder will print.

UNBINDING BINDERS

Suppose you decide you really don't want to bind documents together; instead, you want to work with each document separately. You could save each section as a document as you learned earlier in this chapter, but there's an easier way.

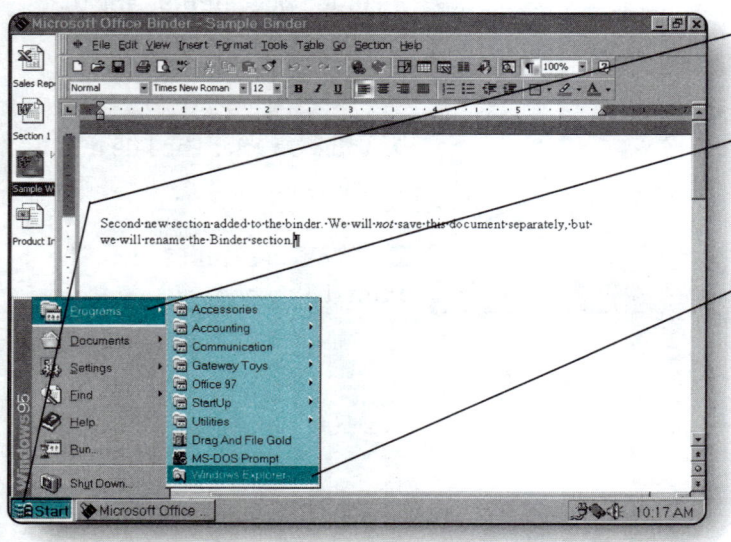

1. Click on the **Start button**. The Start menu will appear.

2. Move the **mouse pointer** to Programs. The Programs menu will appear.

3. Click on **Windows Explorer**. The Windows Explorer will appear.

4. **Navigate** to the **folder** containing the binder.

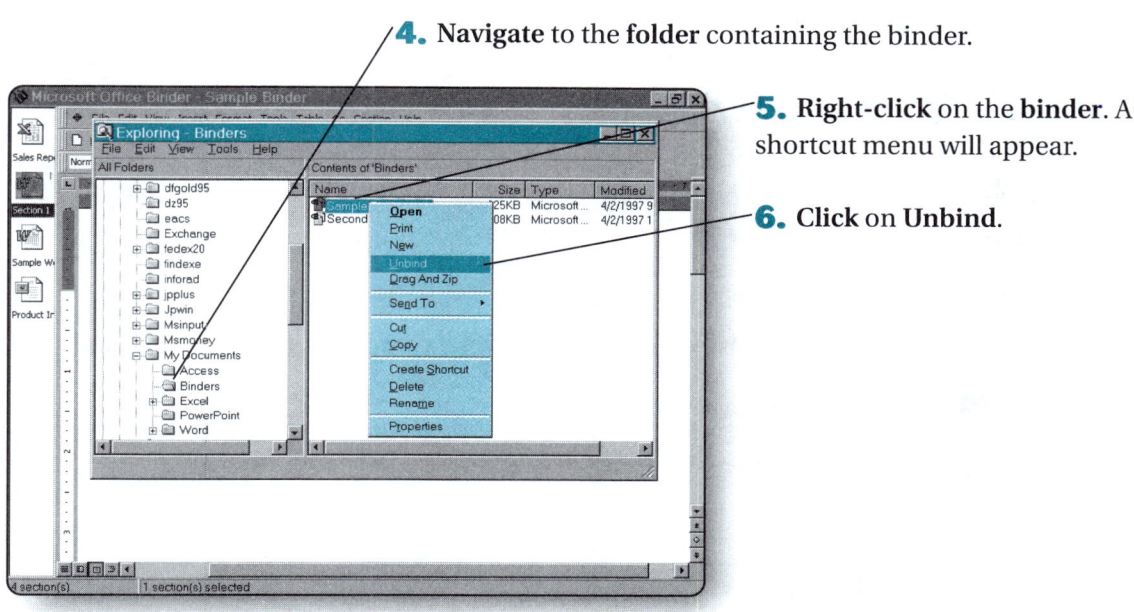

5. **Right-click** on the **binder**. A shortcut menu will appear.

6. **Click** on **Unbind**.

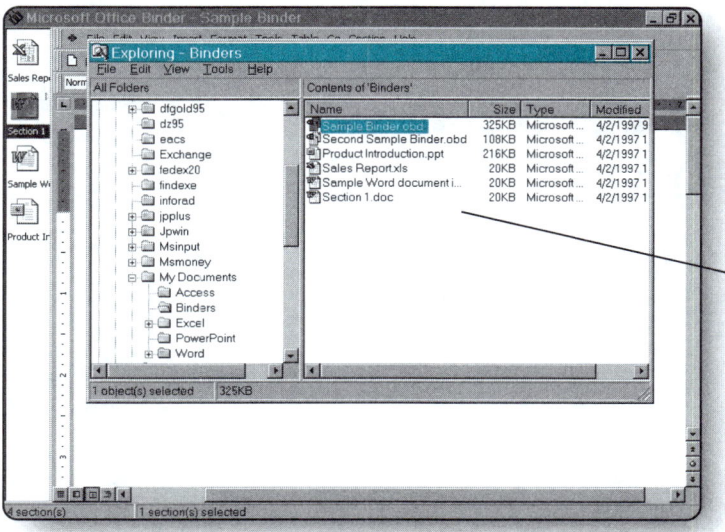

Each section in the binder will be saved as a separate document in the folder where the binder was saved, even sections that were not previously saved as separate documents.

The original binder will also remain intact.

PART VI REVIEW QUESTIONS

1. When you want to modify the Office Shortcut Bar in some way, do you right-click or left-click? *See Chapter 20*

2. When you want to use a tool on one of the Office Shortcut Bar toolbars, do you right-click or left-click? *See Chapter 20*

3. Describe how to move the Office Shortcut Bar. *See Chapter 20*

4. Can you add a toolbar button? *See Chapter 20*

5. Describe the process of creating a hyperlink. *See Chapter 20*

6. What is a binder? *See Chapter 21*

7. How do you add a section to a binder if the document already exists? *See Chapter 21*

8. How do you rename a section? *See Chapter 21*

9. Do you need to save a section as a separate document or can you just save it as part of the binder? *See Chapter 21*

10. Describe how to print a section and how to print a binder. *See Chapter 21*

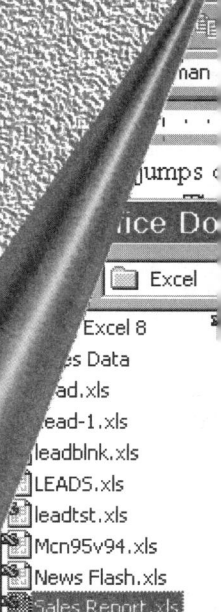

man

jumps

lice Do

📁 Excel

Excel 8
es Data
ad.xls
ead-1.xls
leadblnk.xls
LEADS.xls
leadtst.xls
Mcn95v94.xls
News Flash.xls
Sales Report.xls

22 Working on the Web

You can use most of your Office 97 applications—Word, Excel, and PowerPoint—to work on the World Wide Web. Each of these applications contains a Web toolbar that can launch your Web browser and take you to the Web sites you designate. And, you can get help on the Web from all the Office 97 programs, including Outlook and Office Binder. In this chapter, you'll learn how to:

- ✦ **Search the Web**
- ✦ **Display your start page**
- ✦ **Access a favorite Web site**
- ✦ **Access a specific Web site**
- ✦ **Get help on Office applications**

SEARCHING THE WEB

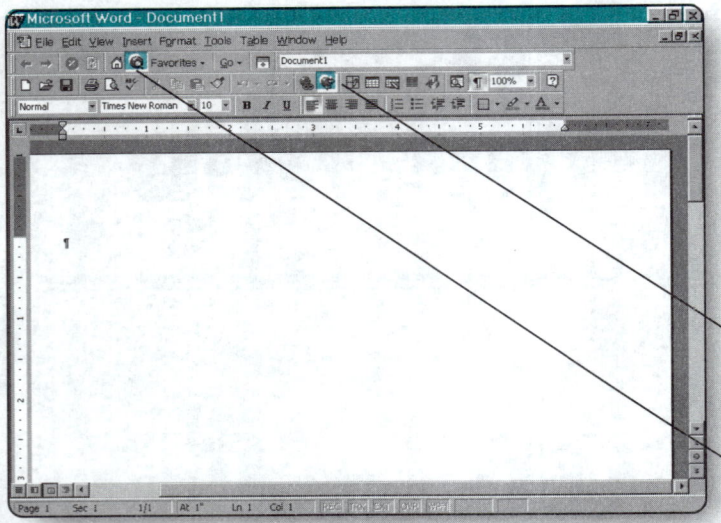

You can search the Web from an Office 97 application. The search page you will see is sponsored by Microsoft, and, from it, you will have access to the most popular search engines for the Web.

1. **Start** any **Office application**.

2. **Click** on the **Web Toolbar button**. The Web toolbar will appear.

3. **Click** on the **Search the Web button**.

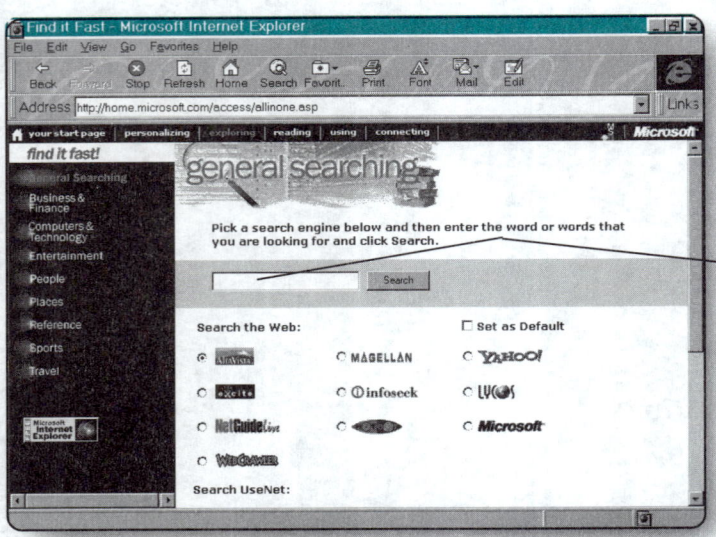

After you log on to the Internet through your Internet Service Provider, your Web browser will appear, showing the Microsoft-sponsored Web page, which looked like this on April 3, 1997.

4. **Click** in the **box** next to the Search button.

5. **Type** the **topic** for which you want to search.

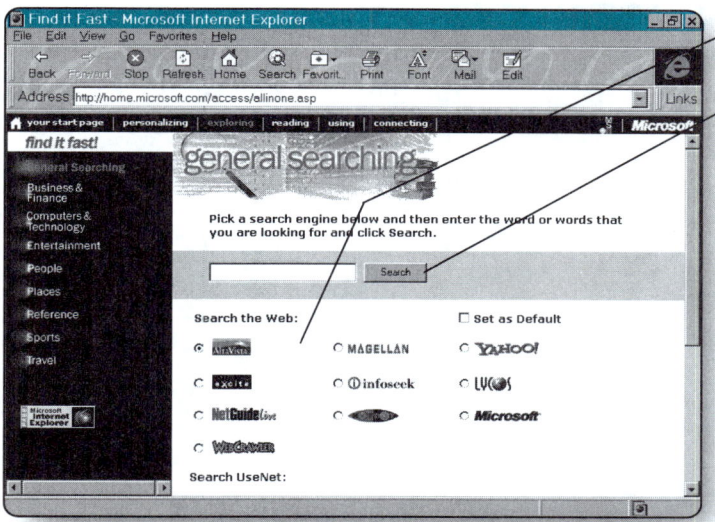

6. **Choose** a **search engine**.

7. **Click** on **Search**. The search engine will display the number of Web sites that contain information related to the word(s) for which you searched. Each response is referred to as a *hit*.

TIP

After you finish using the Web, you'll probably want to log off the Internet and return to work in your Office 97 application. Simply exit from your Web browser.

DISPLAYING YOUR START PAGE

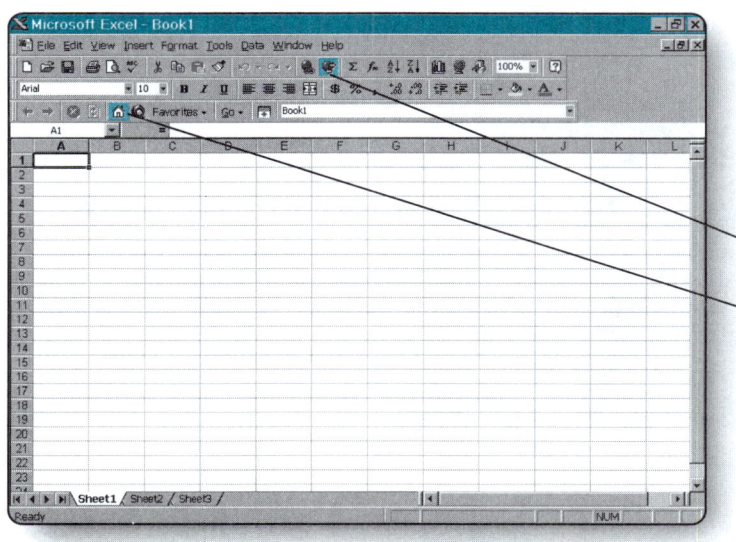

You can access your Internet start page (the page that opens first whenever you log on to the Internet) from inside an Office 97 application.

1. **Display** the **Web Toolbar**.

2. **Click** on the **Start Page** button.

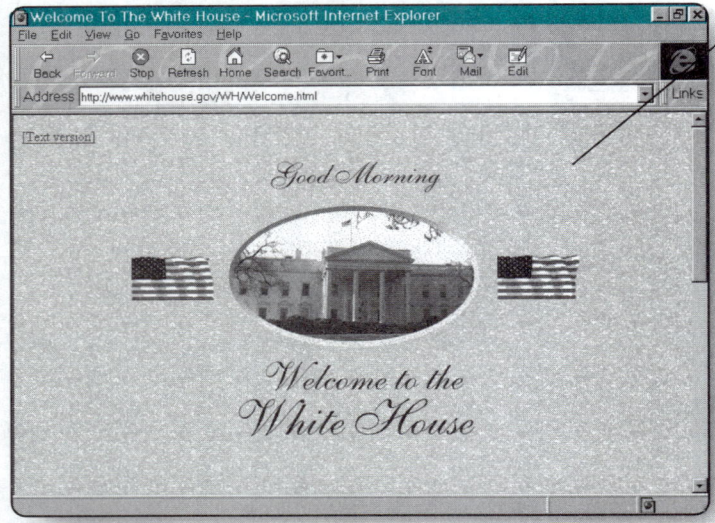

After you log on to the Internet through your Internet Service Provider, your Web browser will appear, showing your start page on the Internet.

VIEWING A FAVORITE PAGE

As you probably know from using your Web browser, you can store "favorite places" that you know you'll want to visit again. You can access a favorite Web site from within Office 97 applications.

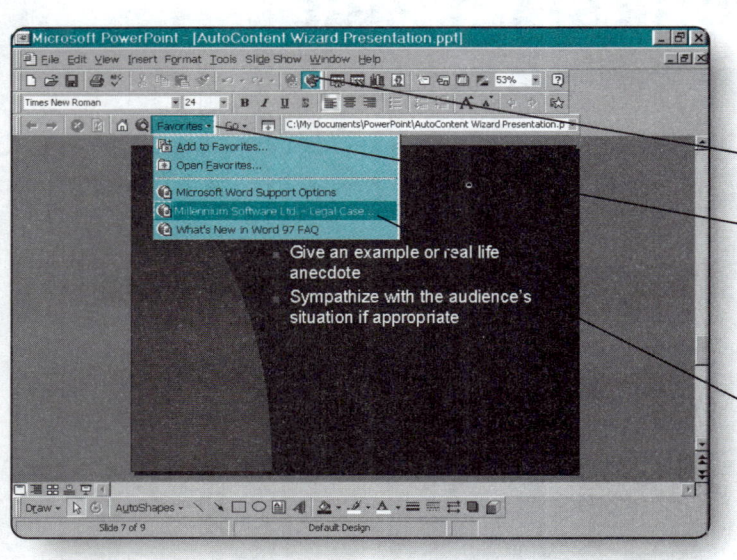

1. **Display** the **Web Toolbar**.

2. **Click** on the **Favorites list box button**. A list of favorites you have added to your computer will appear.

3. **Click** on the **page** you want to see.

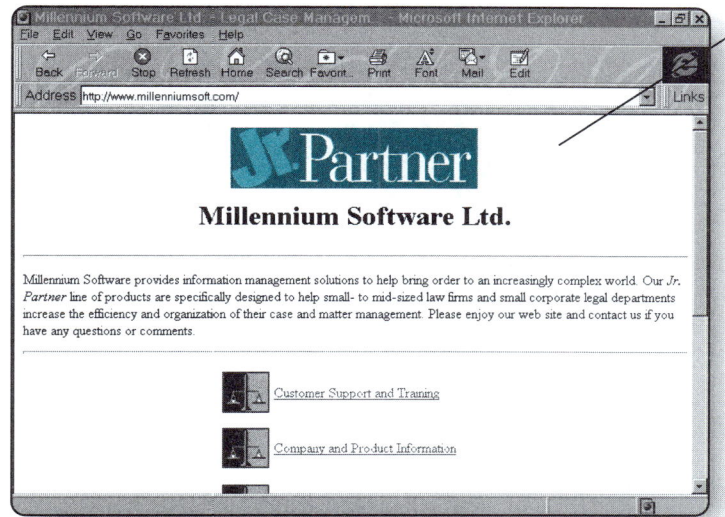

After you log on to the Internet through your Internet Service Provider, your Web browser will appear, showing the Internet page you chose from the Favorites list.

CHECKING OUT A SPECIFIC WEB ADDRESS

There you are, working in Word, and somebody comes along and says, "Check out this Web site." You can surf the Web without leaving Word.

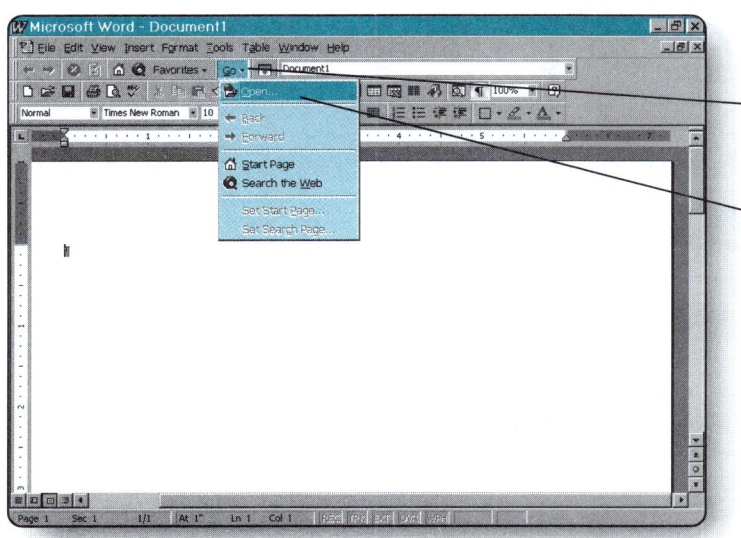

1. **Display** the **Web Toolbar**.

2. **Click** on the **Go list box button**. A menu will appear.

3. **Click** on **Open**. The Open Internet Address dialog box will open.

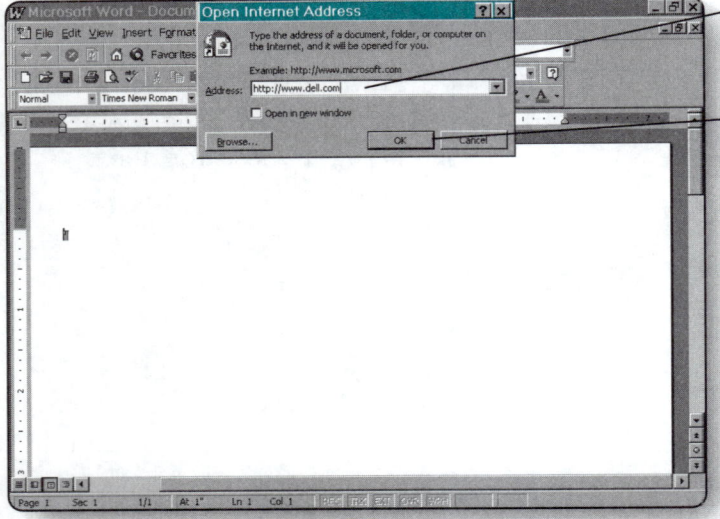

4. **Type** the **address** of the page you want to see.

5. **Click** on **OK**. The Open Internet Address dialog box will close.

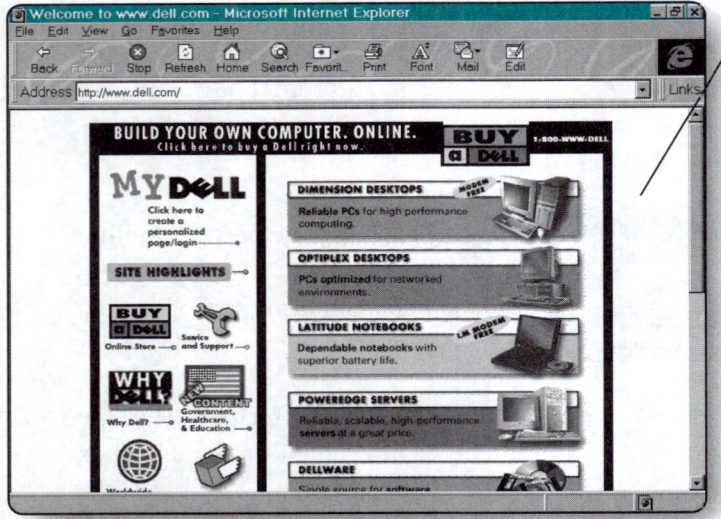

After you log on to the Internet through your Internet Service Provider, your Web browser will appear, showing the Internet page for which you typed the address.

USING THE WEB FOR HELP WITH OFFICE 97 APPLICATIONS

Need help with an Office 97 application? You can get it on the Web. And, you can access this help on the Web from all the Office 97 programs: Word, Excel, PowerPoint, Outlook, and Office Binder.

1. **Click** on **Help**. The Help menu will appear.

2. **Click** on **Microsoft on the Web**. A cascading menu will appear.

3. **Click** on the **type of help** you want.

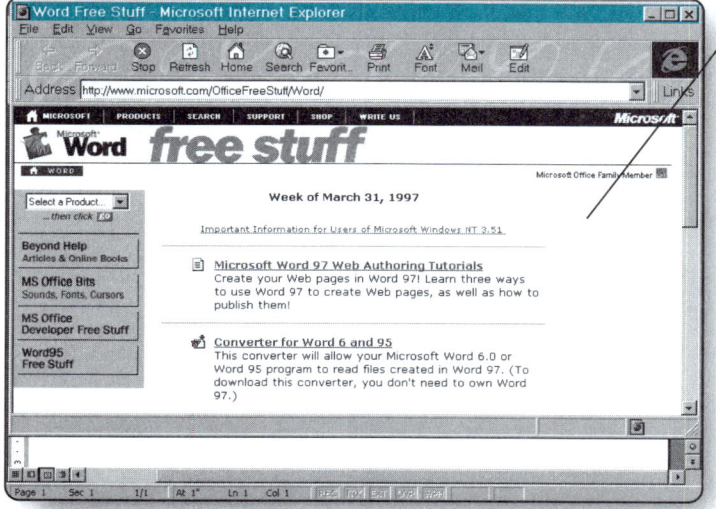

If you click on Free Stuff, you'll see a Web page like this one. You can see the many free items Microsoft makes available for you to use. For example, you can download templates and wizards to help you with common tasks in Word.

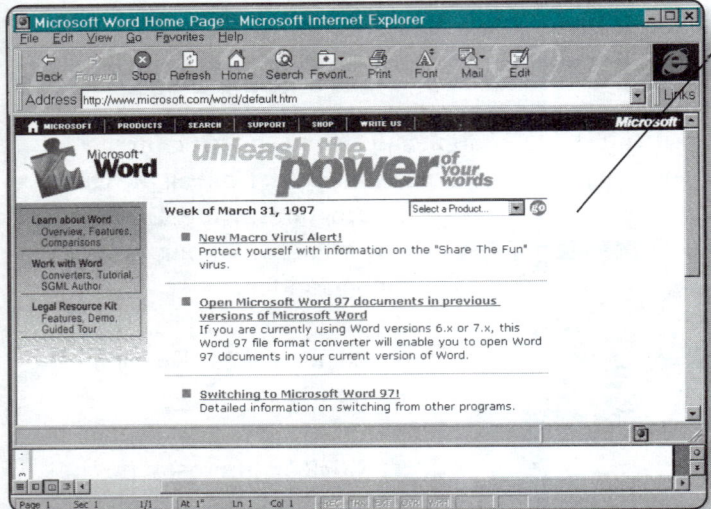

If you click on Product News, you'll see a Web page like this one. It always pays to periodically check this page; you might find out an update is available.

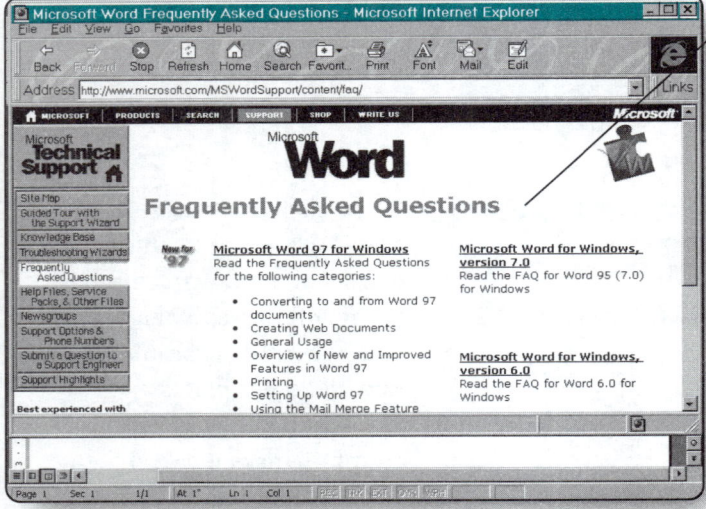

If you click on Frequently Asked Questions, you'll see a Web page like this one, where Microsoft posts questions asked frequently by Microsoft product users.

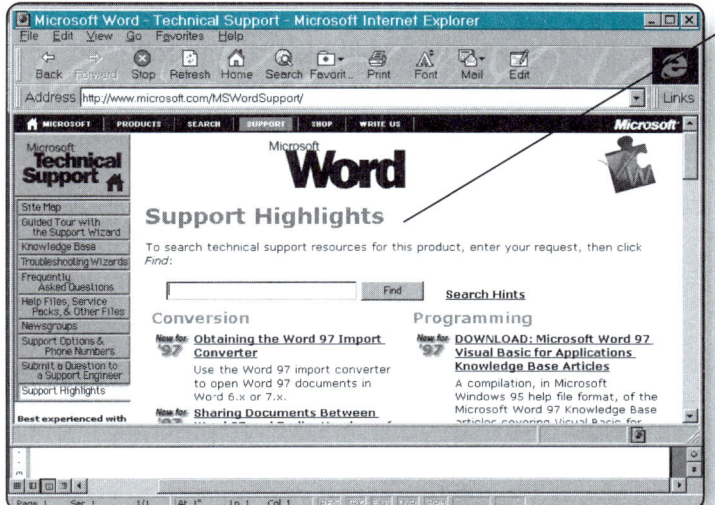

If you click on Online Support, you'll see a Web page where you can search for online support for the Office 97 product from which you accessed this page.

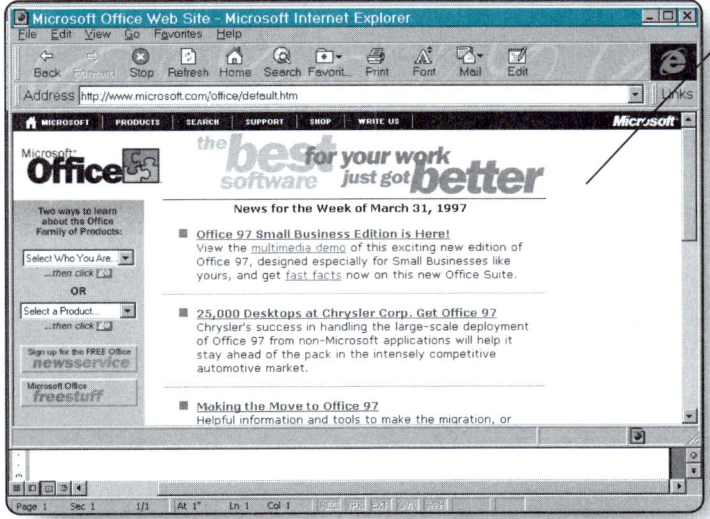

If you click on Microsoft Office Home Page, you'll see a Web page that provides information specifically about Office.

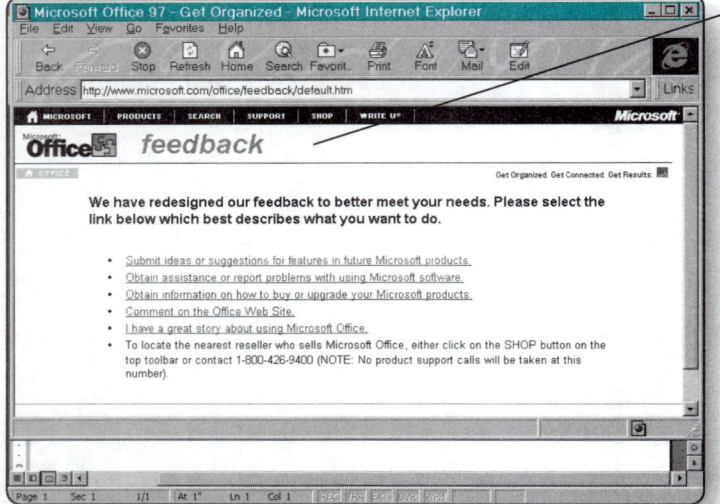

If you click on Send Feedback, you'll see a Web page like this one, where you can communicate with Microsoft about ideas or problems, provide stories, or get information about buying or upgrading products.

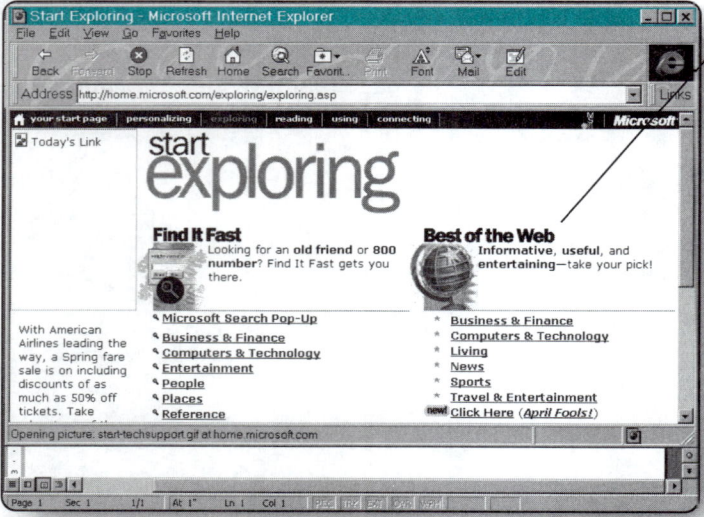

If you click on Best of the Web, you'll see a Web page like this one, from which you can jump to the Web pages that reflect, in the opinion of Microsoft, the best Web pages. If you're in the mood to surf, check out this page and use its hyperlinks to view Microsoft's Best of the Web.

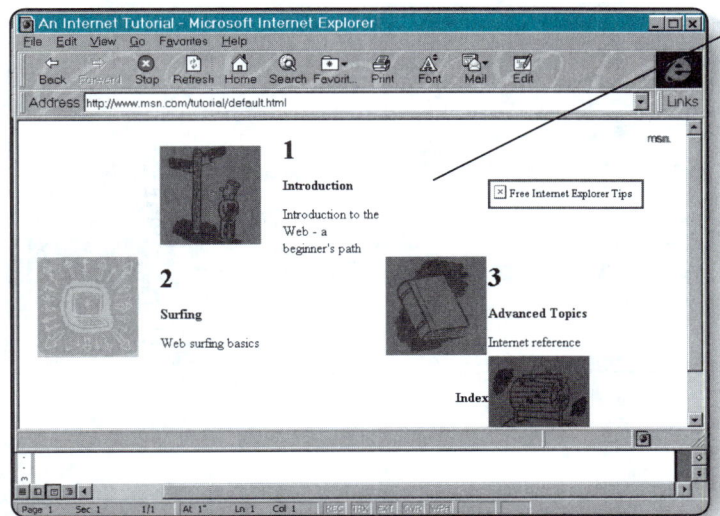

Are you new to the Web? Want some help? Choose the Web Tutorial provided by Microsoft.

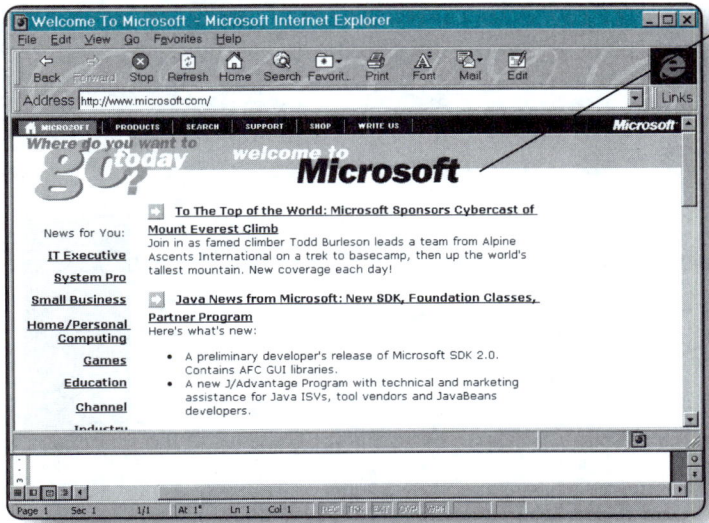

If you click on Microsoft Home Page, you'll see a Web page like this one, where you can learn about other Microsoft products besides Office.

23 Saving Office Documents as Web Documents

In Word, Excel, and PowerPoint, you can create documents that you can publish as Web documents. Web documents are documents that will appear on the Internet. They follow a different standard than the documents you typically create; to be able to read a document on the Internet, you must insert HTML tags. Since inserting HTML tags is cumbersome, you don't want to insert them while creating a document. So, Office programs let you create a document as you usually would and then, when you save the document as a Web document, the HTML tags are inserted. In this chapter, you'll learn how to:

✦ Save a Word document as a Web document

✦ Save an Excel workbook as a Web document

✦ Save a PowerPoint presentation as a Web document

SAVING A WORD DOCUMENT AS A WEB DOCUMENT

To save a Web document, you must have installed the Web Page Authoring (HTML) component of Office 97. Saving a Web document is different than publishing the document on the Web. You must have access to the Internet, the services of an Internet Service Provider, and some sort of Web server software (or access to such software) to actually publish a Web document.

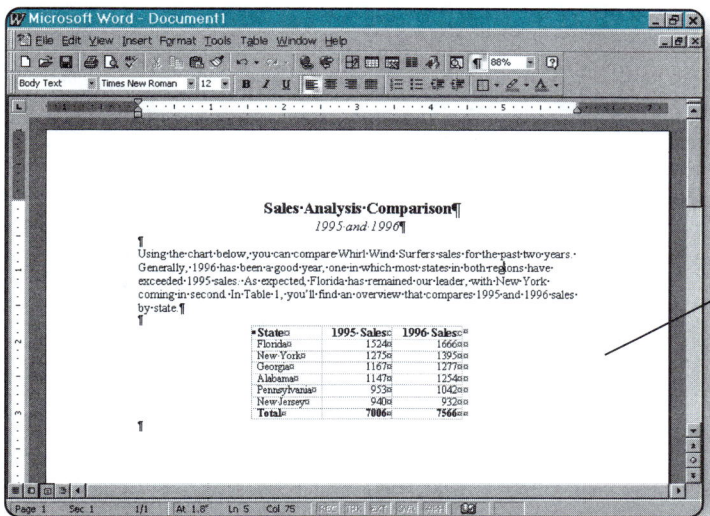

1. Open or **create** the **Word document** you want to save as a Web page.

2. Click on **File**. The File menu will appear.

3. Click on **Save as HTML**. The Save As HTML dialog box will open.

4. Click on the **arrow** (▼) next to the Save in: list box. The directory list will appear.

5. Navigate to the **folder** in which you want to save the Web document.

6. Type a filename.

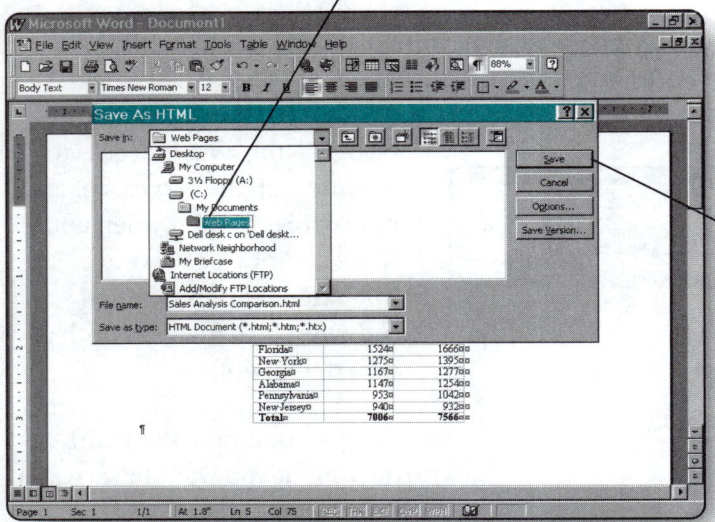

7. Click on **Save**. The Save As HTML dialog box will close.

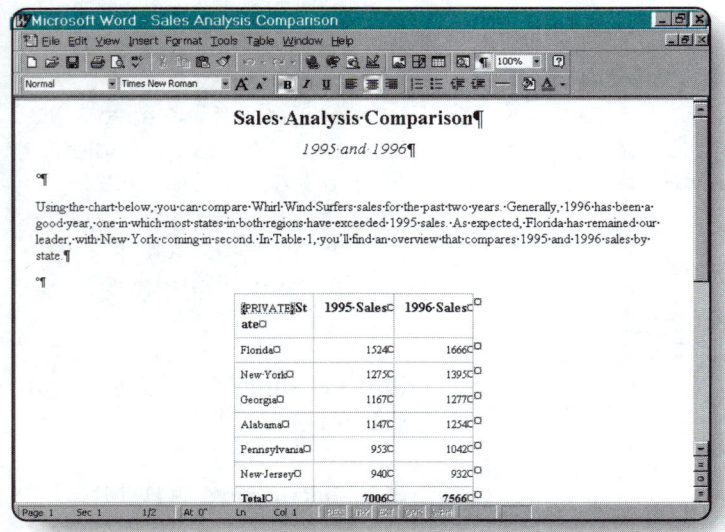

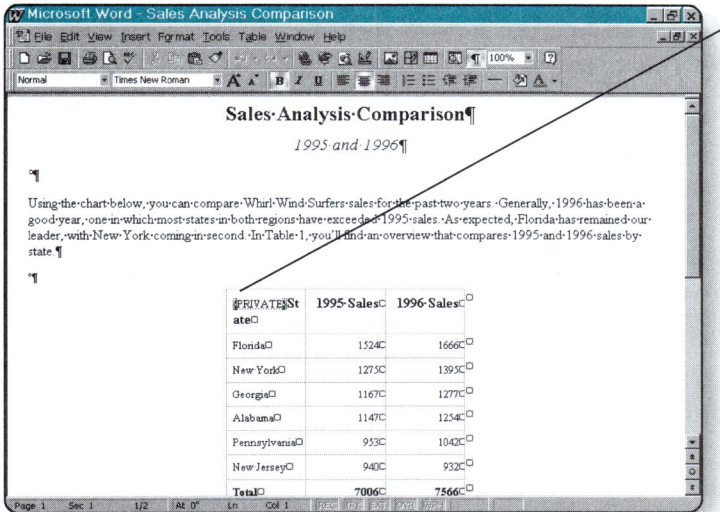

Word converts your document to HTML format and displays it onscreen. Notice that it contains HTML tags for Word features supported by HTML; other features not supported in HTML do not appear. The Standard toolbar changes to the HTML version.

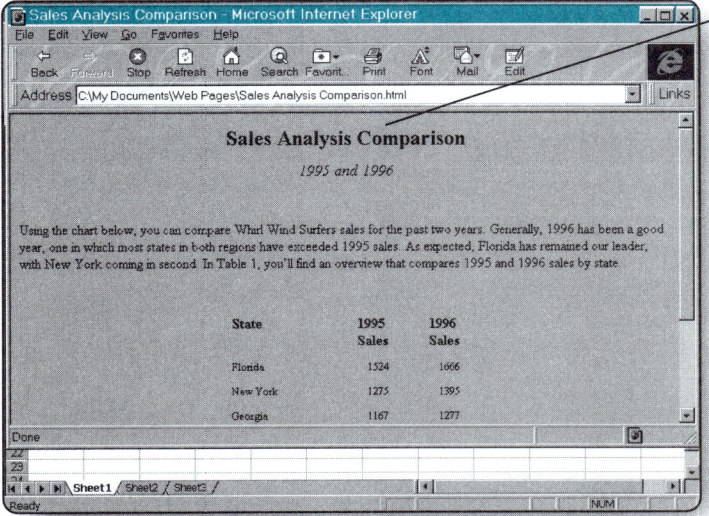

To view the document as others will see it on the Web, click on the Web Page Preview button. Your Web browser will open and display the document.

SAVING AN EXCEL WORKBOOK AS A WEB DOCUMENT

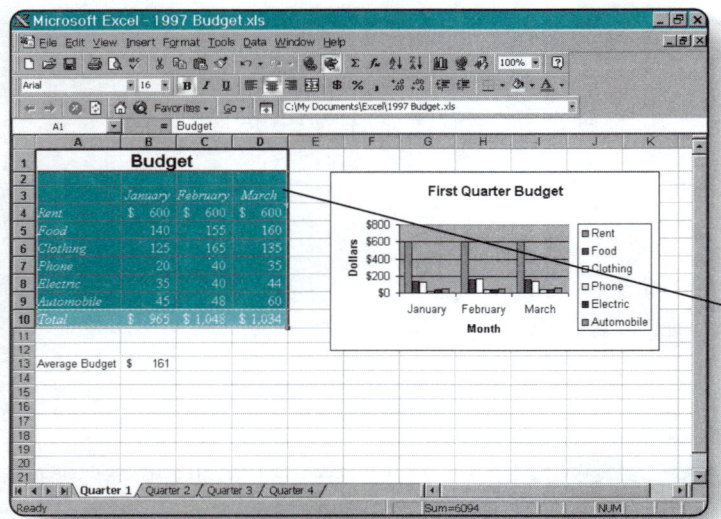

Excel provides a wizard to help you through the process of saving a workbook to HTML format.

1. **Open** or **create** the **Excel workbook** you want to save as a Web page.

2. **Select** the **range of cells** you want to convert.

TIP

Don't worry about selecting charts. Chart ranges appear automatically in the wizard, even if you select cells.

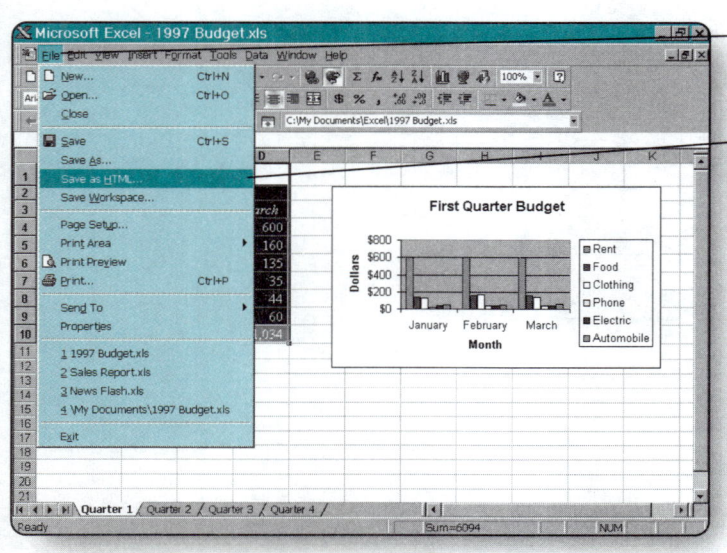

3. **Click** on **File**. The File menu will appear.

4. **Click** on **Save as HTML**. The Internet Assistant Wizard – Step 1 of 4 dialog box will open.

NOTE

The Office Assistant might appear, offering you help with the wizard. You can close the Office Assistant.

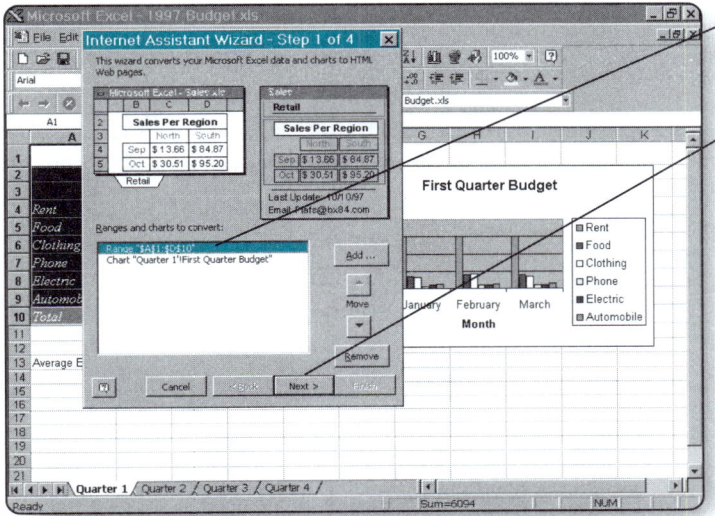

5. **Click** on the **range** you want to convert.

6. **Click** on **Next**. The Internet Assistant Wizard – Step 2 of 4 dialog box will open.

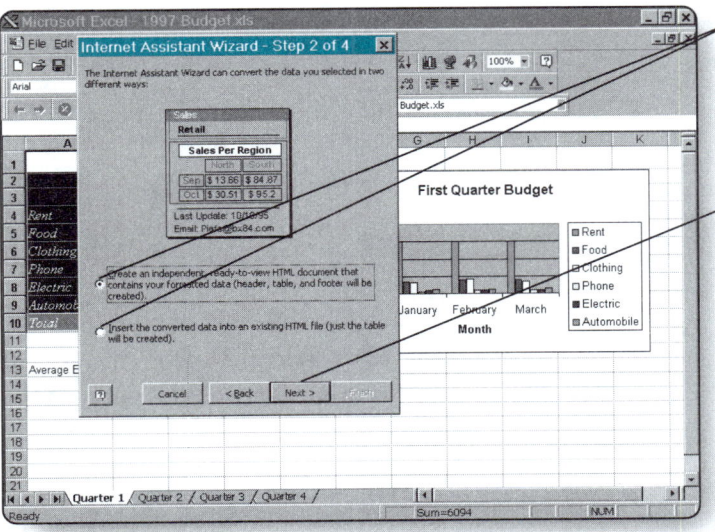

7. **Click** on an **option button** to choose how you want to save the HTML file (separately or in an existing file).

8. **Click** on **Next**. The Internet Assistant Wizard – Step 3 of 4 dialog box will open.

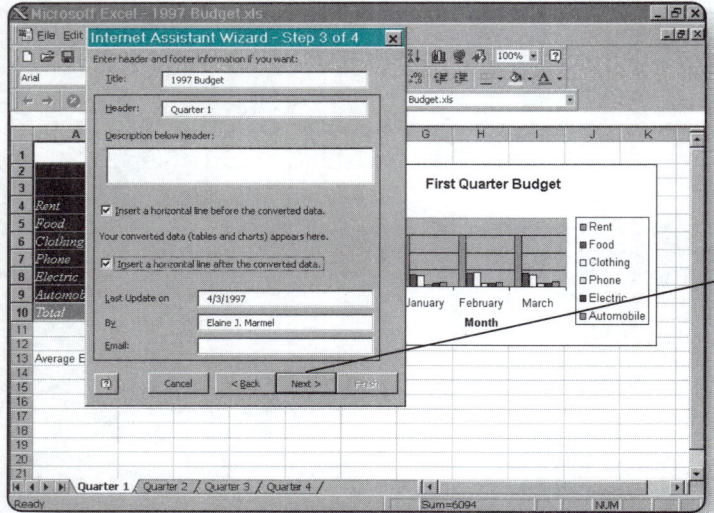

9. Set options for the data you convert, such as the title, the header, whether you want horizontal lines to appear above and below your data, and how to update information.

10. Click on Next. The Internet Assistant Wizard – Step 4 of 4 dialog box will open.

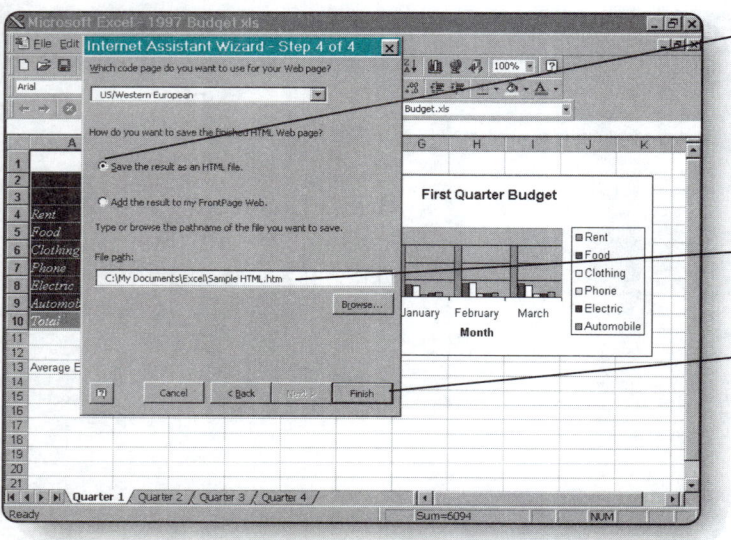

11. Click on an option button to describe how you want to save the finished Web document (as a separate file or as part of a FrontPage Web).

12. Type a filename for the Web document.

13. Click on Finish. The Internet Assistant Wizard – Step 4 of 4 dialog box will close and your workbook will reappear.

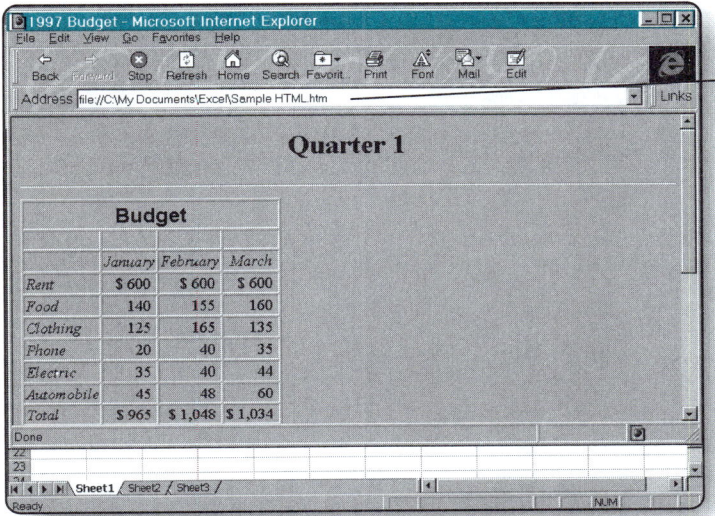

TIP

To view the workbook as others will see it on the Web, open your browser (do not log on to the Internet) and type the path to the folder in which you stored the Web document in the Address box.

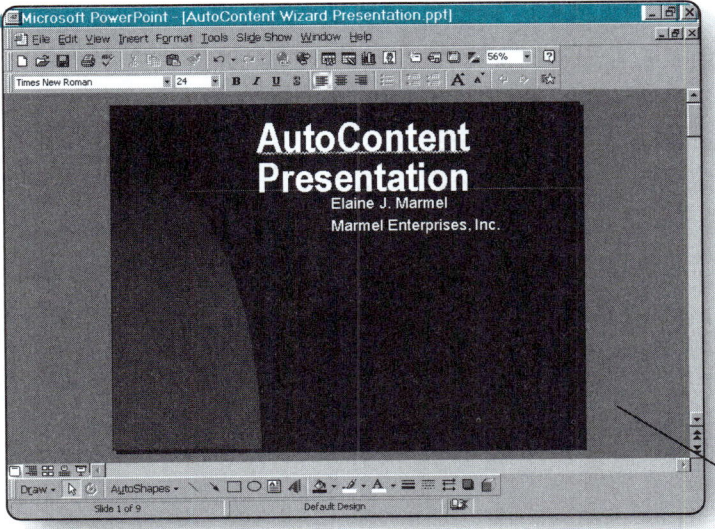

SAVING A POWERPOINT PRESENTATION AS A WEB DOCUMENT

PowerPoint also contains a wizard that will walk you through the process of saving a slide show as a Web document.

1. **Open** or **create** the **PowerPoint presentation** you want to save as a Web page. The presentation will appear onscreen.

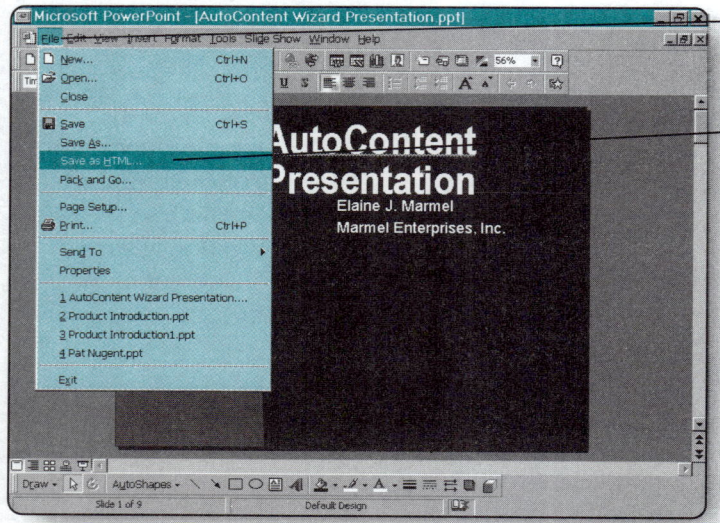

2. **Click** on **File**. The File menu will appear.

3. **Click** on **Save as HTML**. The Save as HTML wizard will open.

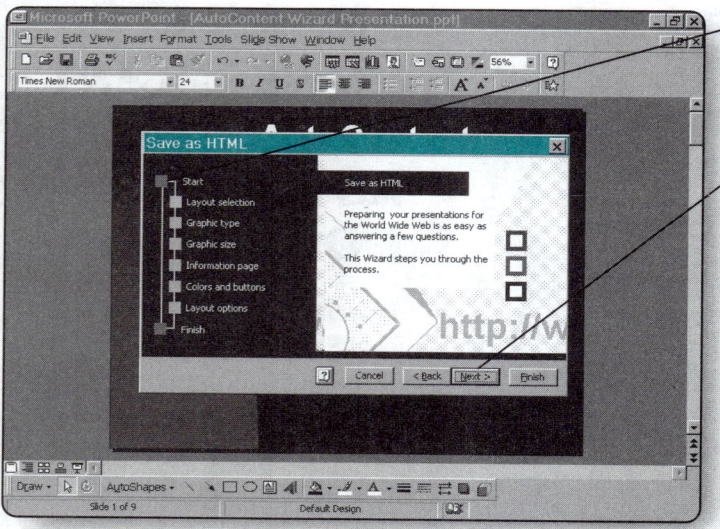

As you go through the wizard, you'll make choices about all these things.

4. **Click** on **Next**. The next screen of the Save as HTML wizard will open.

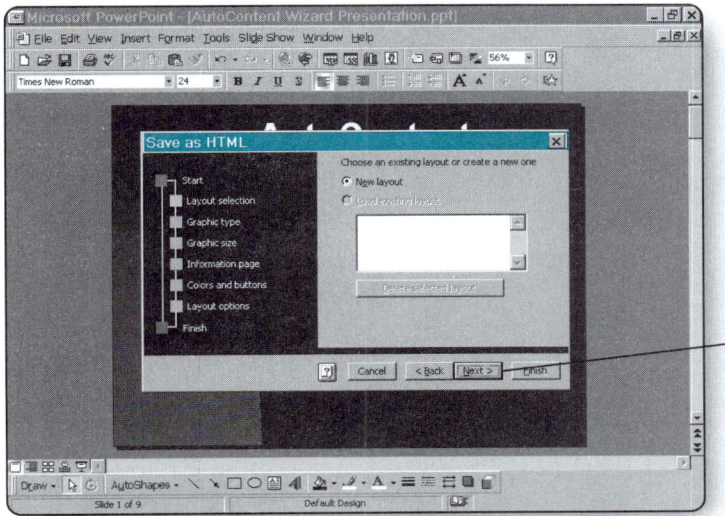

NOTE

Layouts refer to selections you've made previously in the Save as HTML wizard. If this is the first time you're using the wizard, you can click on New Layout only.

5. Click on **Next**. The next screen of the Save as HTML wizard will open.

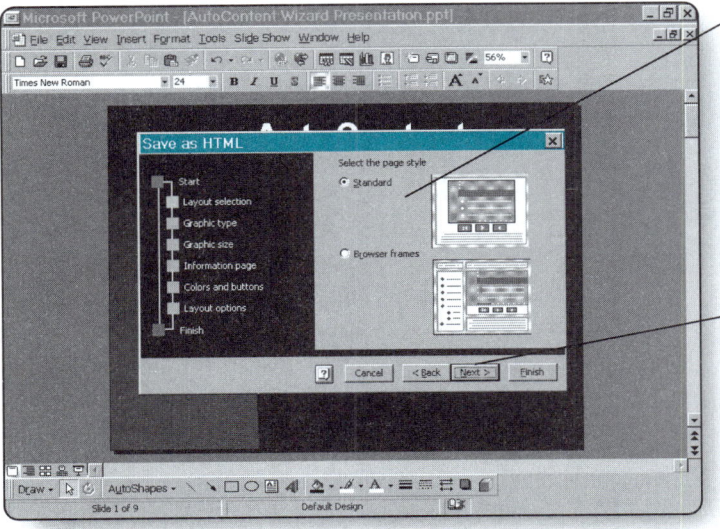

6. Click on a **page style**.

NOTE

Browser frames cannot be viewed by early versions of browsers.

7. Click on **Next**. The next screen of the Save as HTML wizard will open.

8. Click on an **option button** to choose a graphic type.

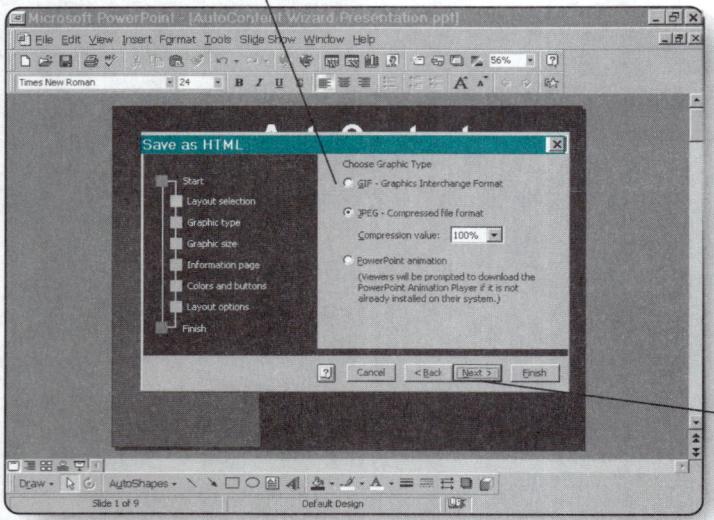

NOTE

GIF may provide slightly greater resolution, but with JPEG, you can adjust the image quality, which will allow you to reduce the size of graphic files. The smaller the size of a graphic file, the faster it will load.

9. Click on **Next**. The next screen of the Save as HTML wizard will open.

10. Click on an **option button** to choose a resolution.

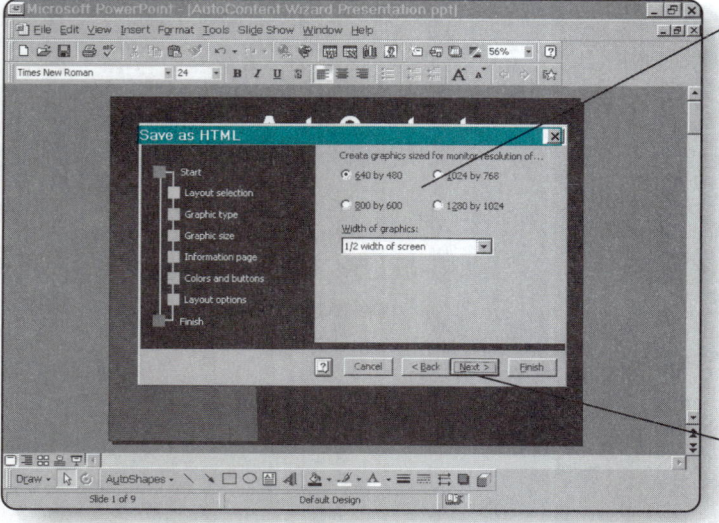

NOTE

The resolution you specify refers to the monitors that will be viewing your presentation. When in doubt, choose 640 × 480, the lowest resolution.

11. Click on **Next**. The next screen of the Save as HTML wizard will open.

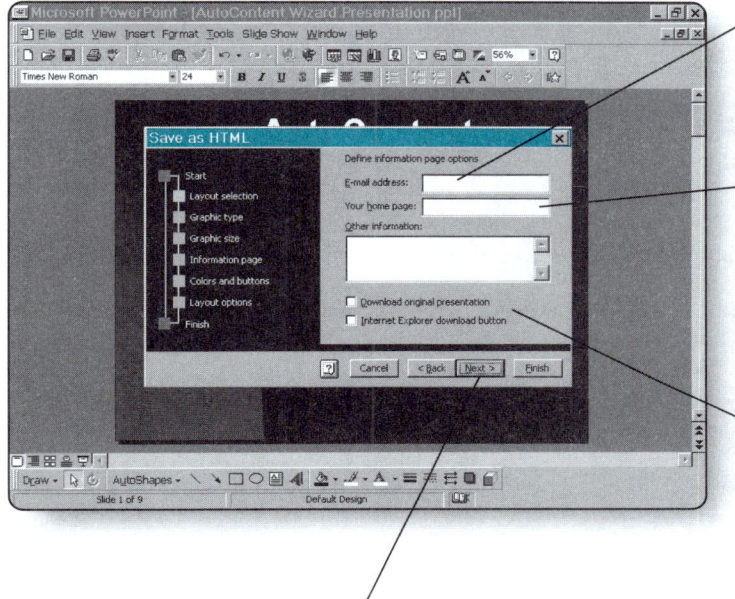

12. Type an **e-mail address**. This address will be used by others to contact you. Supplying an e-mail address is optional.

13. Type the **address** of your home page. This will appear on your Web page so people can visit your home page. Supplying the address of your home page is optional.

14. Click on **both check boxes**. Checking these boxes will add buttons to the presentation that will allow the user to download your presentation or the Internet Explorer browser.

15. Click on **Next**. The next screen of the Save as HTML wizard will open.

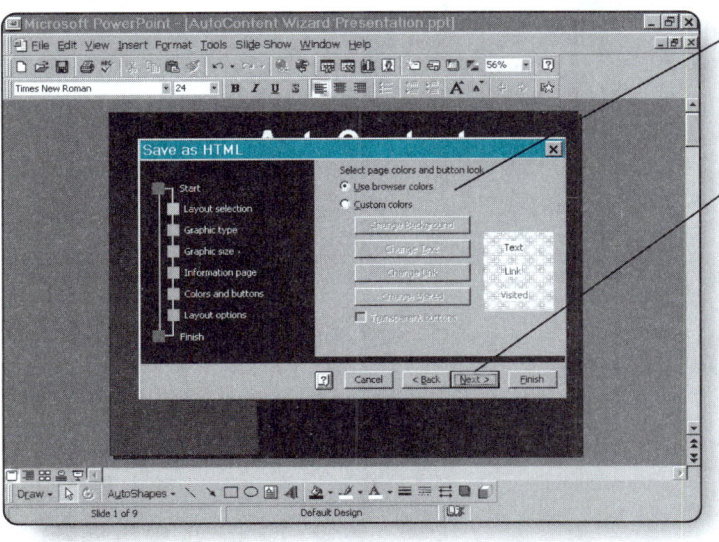

16. Click on an **option button** to decide the colors that will appear on your presentation.

17. Click on **Next**. The next screen of the Save as HTML wizard will open.

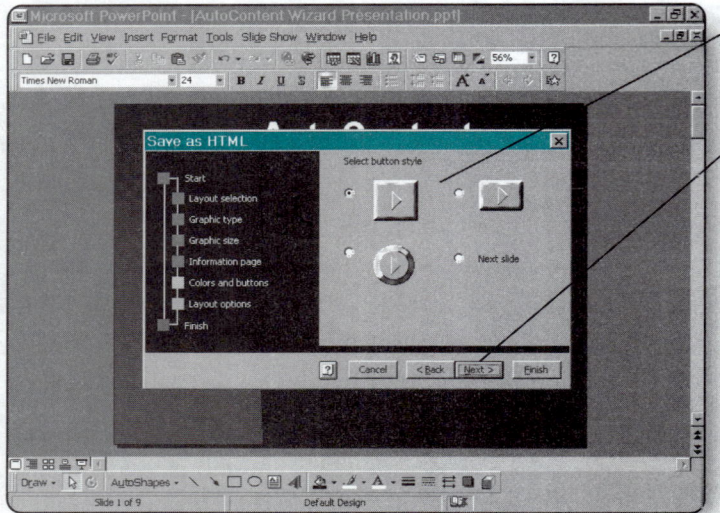

18. **Click** on an **option button** to choose a button style.

19. **Click** on **Next**. The next screen of the Save as HTML wizard will open.

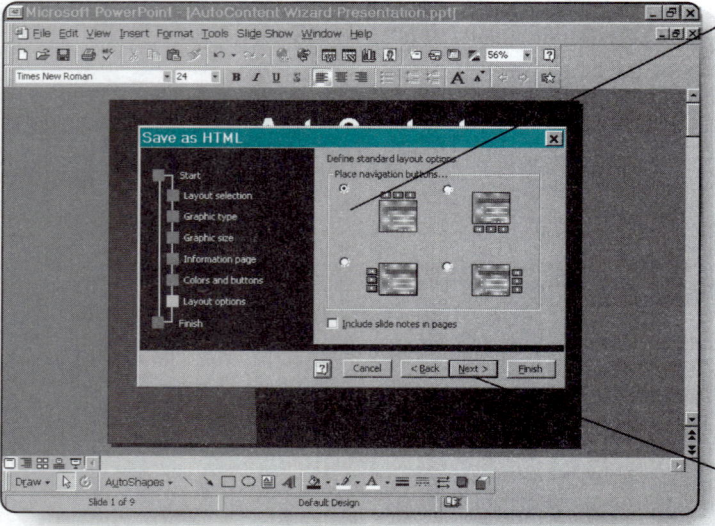

20. **Click** on an **option button** to choose where to place navigation buttons.

NOTE
If you chose Browser frames in step 6, the dialog box you see at this point contains a check box you can use to include or exclude slide notes in pages.

21. **Click** on **Next**. The next screen of the Save as HTML wizard will open.

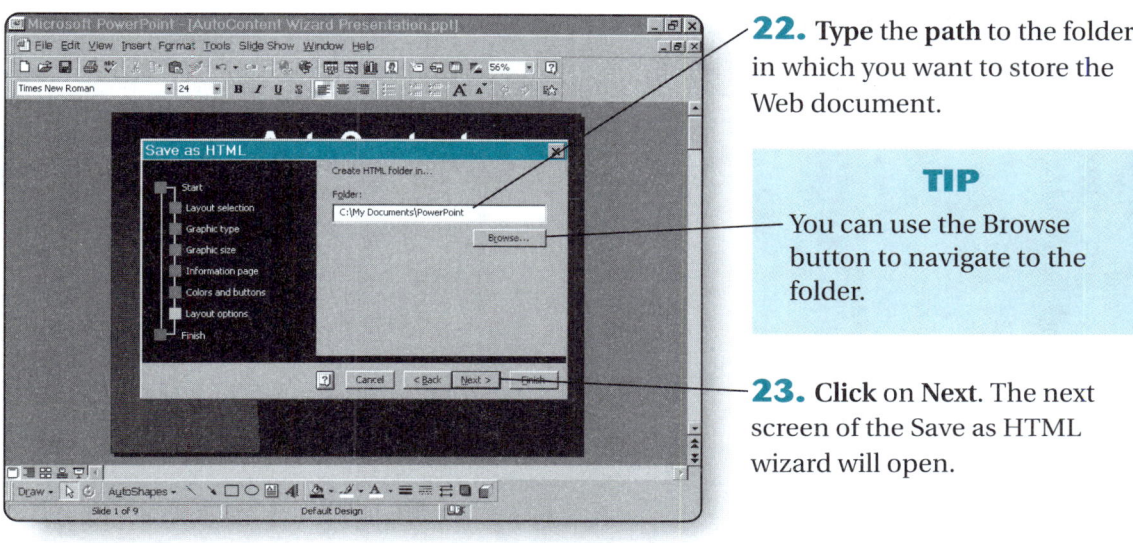

22. **Type** the **path** to the folder in which you want to store the Web document.

23. **Click** on **Next**. The next screen of the Save as HTML wizard will open.

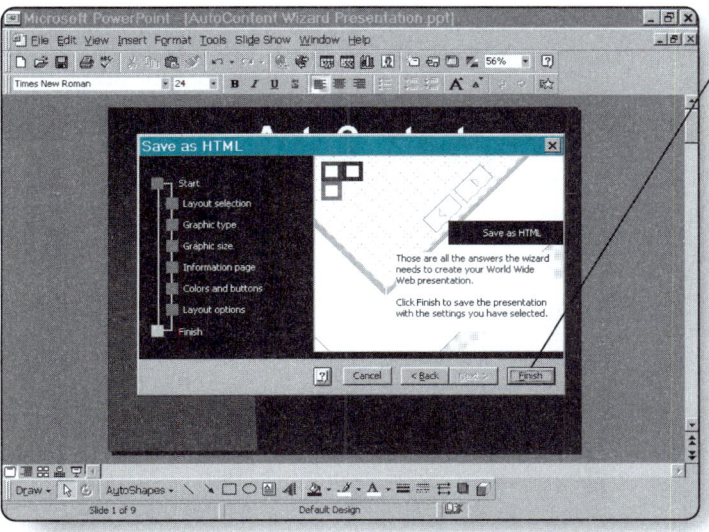

24. **Click** on **Finish**. You will see a dialog box acknowledging that your presentation was successfully saved as HTML.

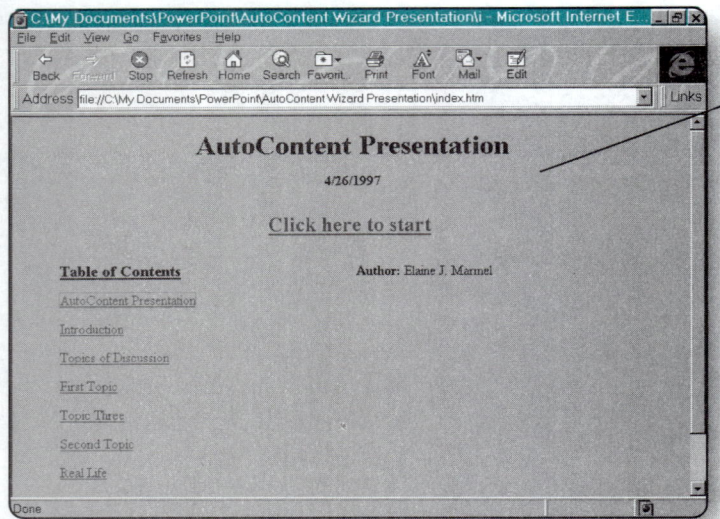

To view the presentation as others will see it on the Web, open your browser (do not log onto the Internet) and type the path of the folder in which you stored the presentation in the Address box. The first slide will be called index.htm.

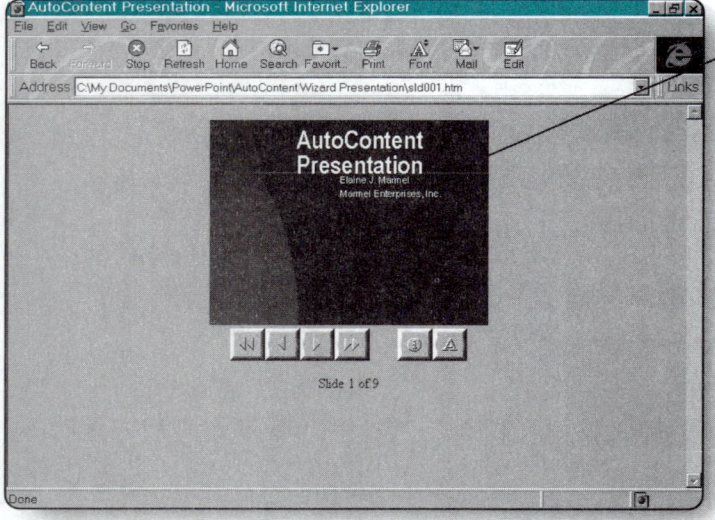

Click on any hyperlink to view the corresponding slide.

PART VII REVIEW QUESTIONS

1. Which Office programs contain a Web toolbar? *See Chapter 22*

2. Describe how to search the Web from inside an Office program. *See Chapter 22*

3. From which Office programs can you directly access the Web for help? *See Chapter 22*

4. How do you display your Start Page from inside an Office program? *See Chapter 22*

5. How do you display a specific Web address from inside an Office program? *See Chapter 22*

6. Describe how to save a Word document as a Web document. *See Chapter 23*

7. Describe how to save an Excel workbook as a Web document. *See Chapter 23*

8. Describe how to save a PowerPoint presentation as a Web document. *See Chapter 23*

9. Can you save a Binder as a Web document? *See Chapter 23*

10. Describe how to view a Web document you have created in an Office program using your Internet browser. *See Chapter 23*

PART VIII

Appendixes

na|

jumps

ice D

📁 Excel

Excel 8
s Data
ed.xls
ead-1.xls
leadblnk.xls
LEADS.xls
leadtst.xls
Mcn95v94.xls
News Flash.xls
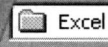Sales Report.xls

A Using the Newsletter Wizard

This appendix takes you through the Newsletter Wizard. This wizard is perhaps the most fun, because it uses graphic images as well as text and lines. It also provides the columns you need for a well-formatted newsletter, and styles for headings that make them stand out. In this appendix, you'll learn how to:

✦ Choose a newsletter style from the wizard

✦ Decide what information to include

✦ Insert text and add pictures

✦ Customize your newsletter

OPENING THE WIZARD

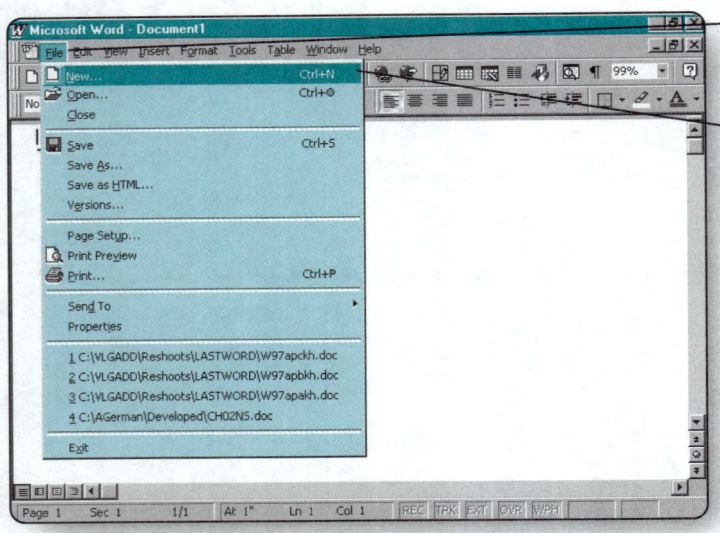

1. **Click** on **File**. The File menu will appear.

2. **Click** on **New**. The New dialog box will open.

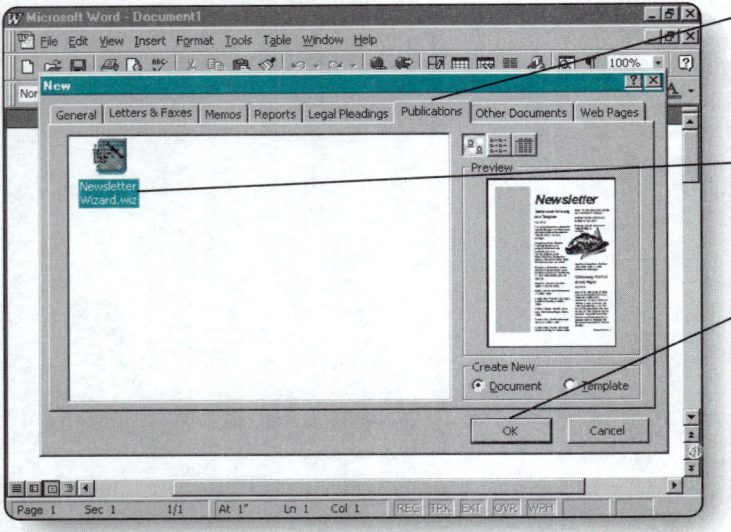

3. **Click** on the **Publications tab**. The tab will come to the front.

4. **Click** on the **Newsletter Wizard**. Notice that a preview of the newsletter will appear.

5. **Click** on **OK**. The Start dialog box will open.

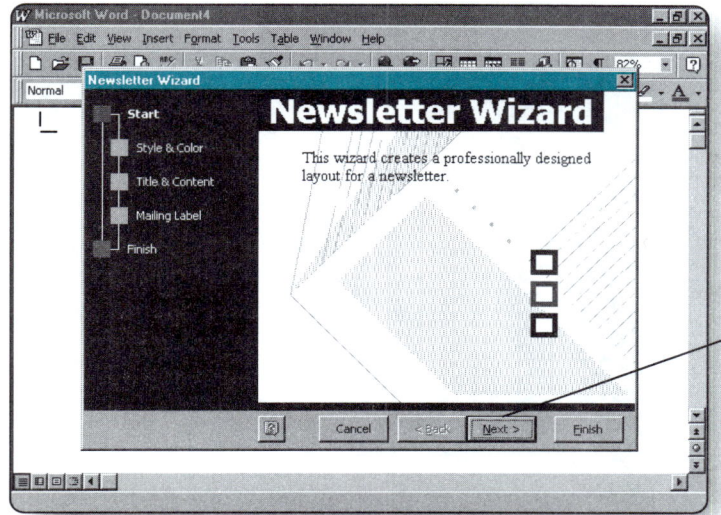

THE WIZARD BEGINS

Just as with other wizards, the steps are listed on the left, and you can move among them using this list.

1. Click on **Next**. The Style & Color dialog box will open.

WHAT'S YOUR STYLE?

Your next choice has to do with three styles. This dialog box also offers you the option of a color or black and white document.

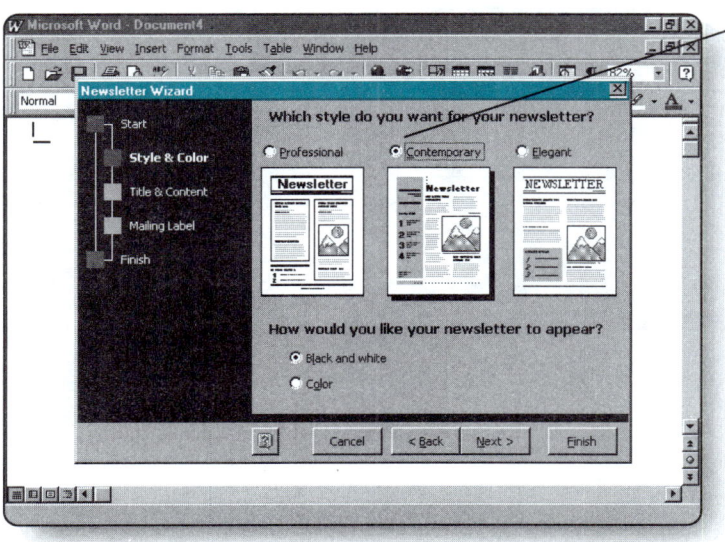

1. Click on **one** of the **option buttons** to the left of one of the three styles. The choice of your newsletter style may depend on what the newsletter will be used for:

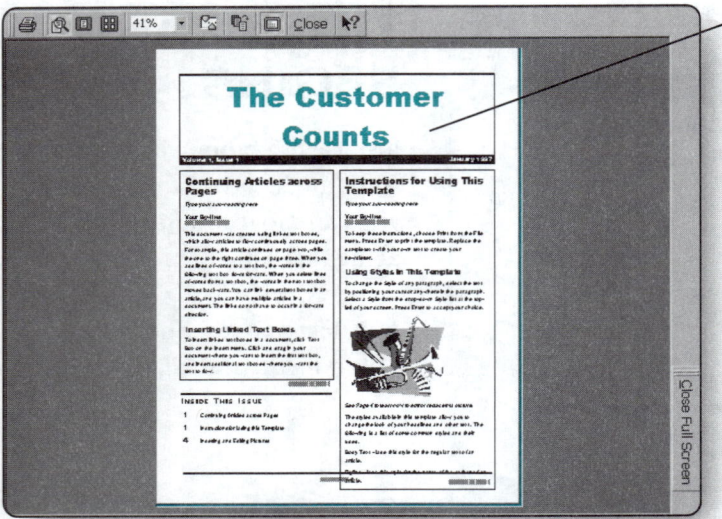

◆ **Professional.** A corporate newsletter, like the one a company sends to customers every month, would look nice with this style.

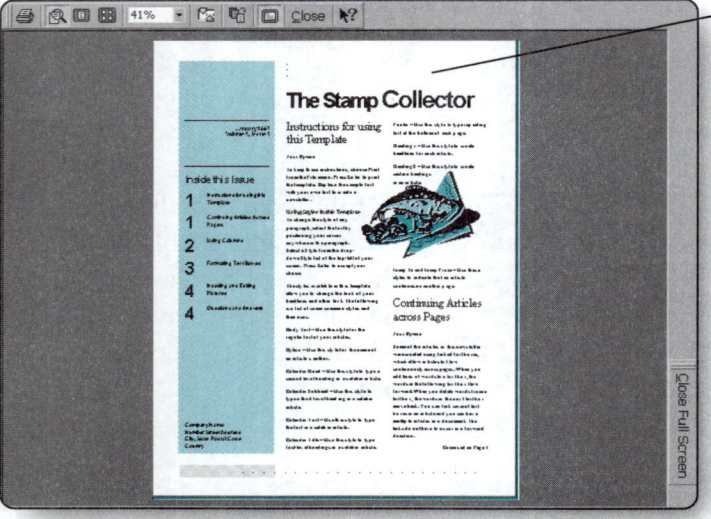

◆ **Contemporary.** A hobby, such as a stamp collecting club newsletter, might look best with this style.

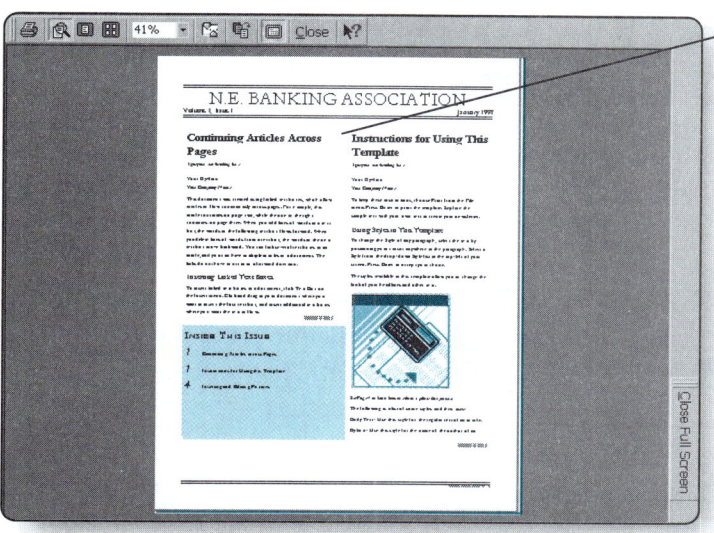

◆ **Elegant.** A professional association or more conservative organization might work best using this style of newsletter.

2. Click on the **option button** to the left of the Black and White setting. The option will be selected.

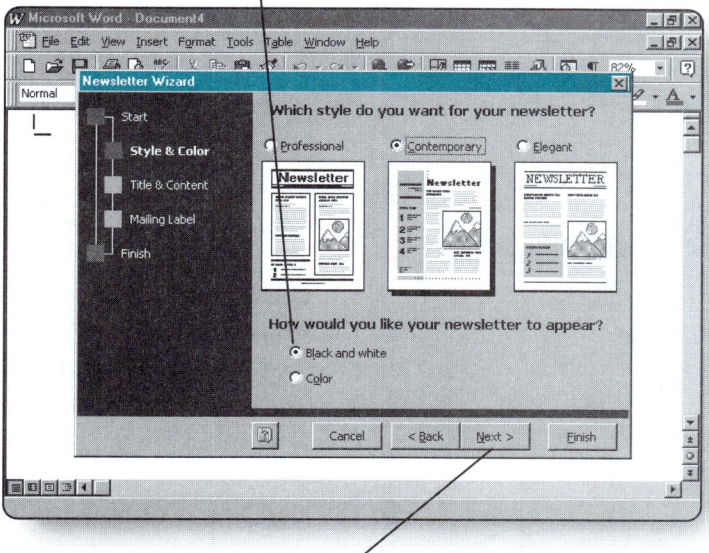

NOTE

Remember, unless you have a color printer, the color setting won't be of any use to you. Of course, with something like a newsletter, you might be planning to take it to a printer. The printer will probably want your newsletter file formatted for black and white, because that will provide the cleanest, sharpest images to work with. You can simply mark a copy with elements you'd like printed in a color, such as red for the headings.

3. Click on **Next**. The Title & Content dialog box will open.

WHAT INFORMATION TO INCLUDE

The Title & Content dialog box asks for three simple things: the title, whether you want a date for the newsletter, and whether you'd like to use a Volume or Issue notation.

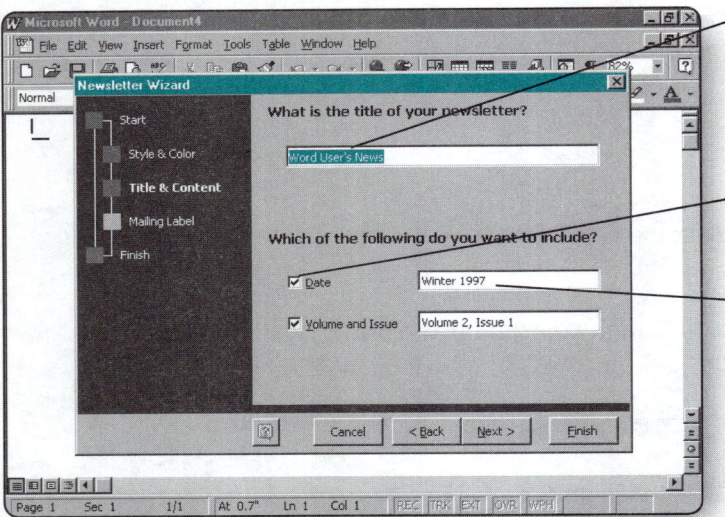

1. **Type** a **title** for your newsletter in the text box under, What is the title of your newsletter?

2. **Click** on the **check box** to the left of Date. A ✔ will be inserted.

3. **Click** on the **date** that's entered by default in the text box to the right and **type** the **edition name**.

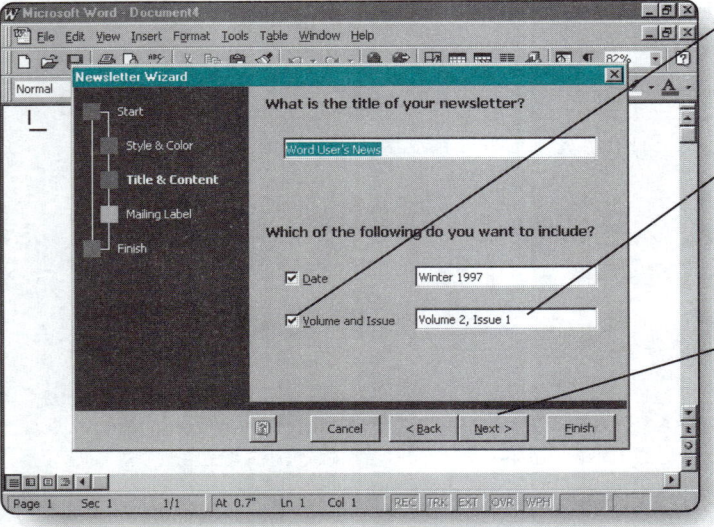

4. **Click** on the **check box** to the left of Volume and Issue. A ✔ will be inserted.

5. **Click** on the **number** that's entered by default in the text box to the right and type a **volume** and **issue number**.

6. **Click** on Next. The Mailing Label dialog box will open.

HOW WILL YOU MAIL THE NEWSLETTER?

The Mailing Label dialog box asks one simple question: Do you want to leave room for a mailing label on the back?

If your newsletter will be a self-mailer (folded and mailed or delivered to a specific individual on its own), you will need space on the newsletter to stick a mailing label. If, on the other hand, you throw one newsletter in every employee mailbox or leave a stack of them in your office reception area for people to pick up, there's no need for a personal address label. If you mail the newsletter in an envelope, there's also no need for this extra space.

1. **Click** on the **option button** to the left of Yes. The option will be selected.

2. **Click** on **Next**. The Finish dialog box will open.

FINISHING IT OFF

This is the last dialog box of the wizard. Once again, you can use this screen to go back and modify choices.

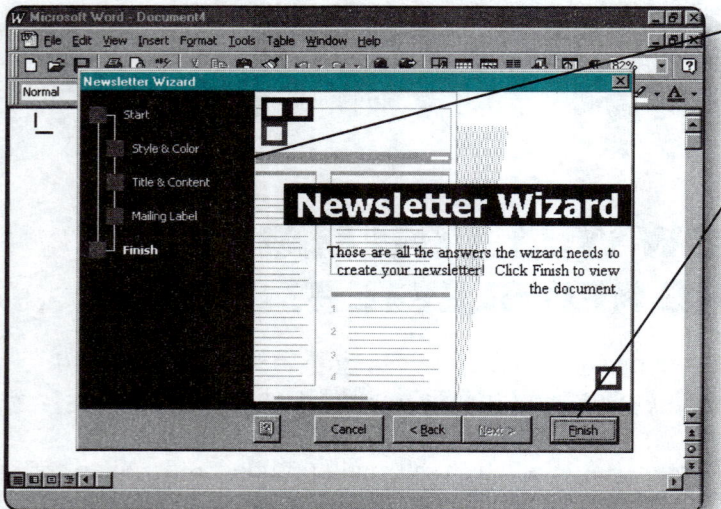

1. **Click** on **any step** in the list to the left to go back and make a change in that step.

2. **Click** on **Finish**. You will get a look at your newsletter. You may get a message telling you that Word is truncating text—that's because the title you entered for your newsletter may not fit in the space allowed. Truncating will cut off some of your text, but you'll fix that in a moment. Click on OK if you get that message.

MAKING YOUR NEWSLETTER YOUR OWN

You can do several things to complete your newsletter and adjust its contents to your particular organization.

Adjusting Your Newsletter's Heading

As mentioned in the last section, some of you will have to fix the heading in your newsletter before adding text and graphics.

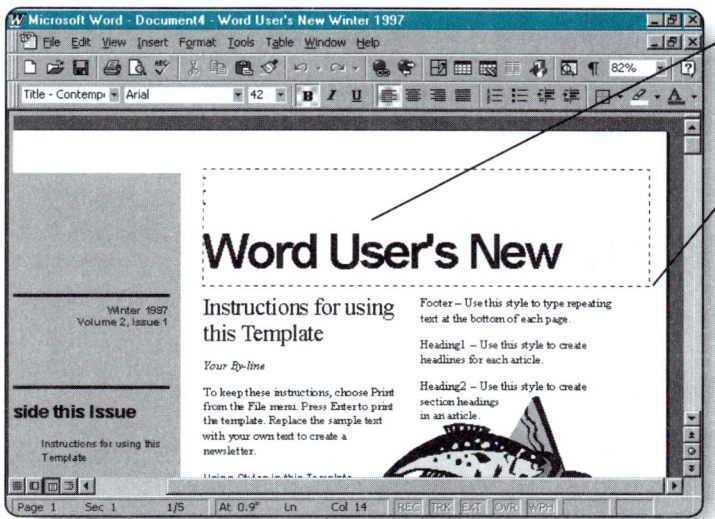

1. **Click** on the **heading**. A border with handles will appear around the heading.

2. **Press** and **hold** the **mouse button** on the handles and **drag** to widen the heading text object to accommodate more text.

3. **Release** the **mouse button**.

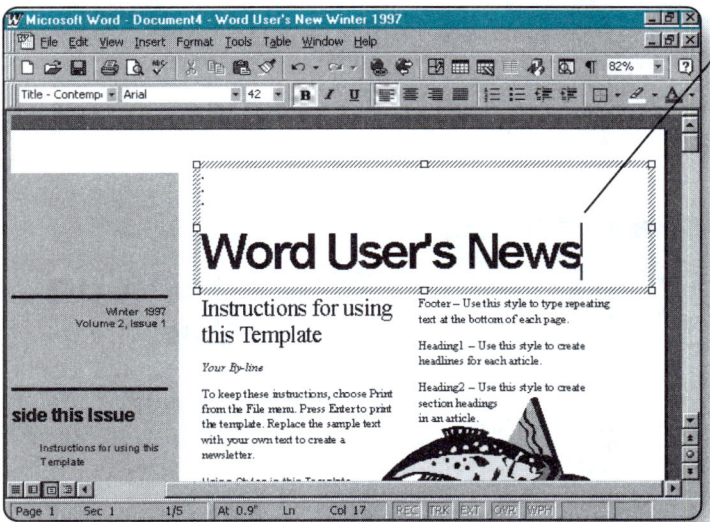

4. **Type** in the **additional letters**. This works best if you are missing only one or two letters. Otherwise, your text may run past the margin and make your document look out of balance.

TIP

Another way to adjust the heading text is to select it, and then adjust the font size to something smaller. You can also try changing it to a different font. Some fonts have smaller letter sizes than others, even within the same point size.

Inserting Text in Your Newsletter

The actual text of the newsletter provides instructions for personalizing it. You can print out a copy now and read through those.

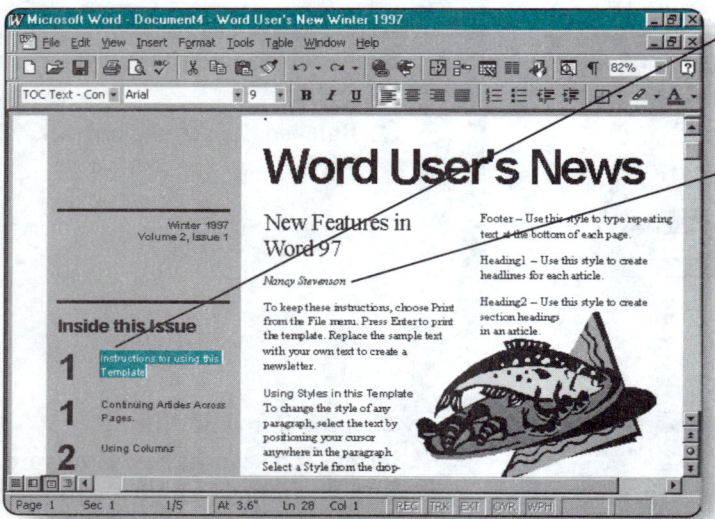

1. Select headings of articles, **bylines**, and the **text of the articles** themselves.

2. Type in your own **information**. Text will wrap from column to column and page to page automatically.

3. Modify the **items** in the Inside This Issue listing to match the articles you enter and their page number.

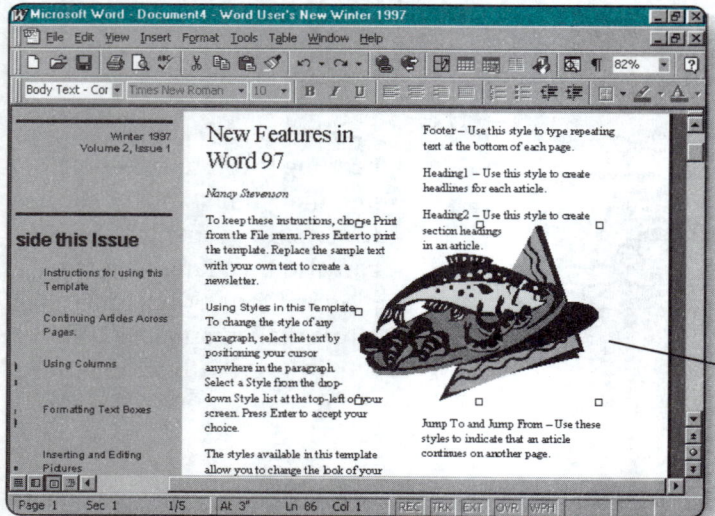

Adding a Picture to Your Newsletter

You can cut the graphic that's been placed by Word and insert a picture that works for your topic.

1. Click on the **graphic**. It will be selected.

2. Press the **Delete key**. The graphic will be deleted.

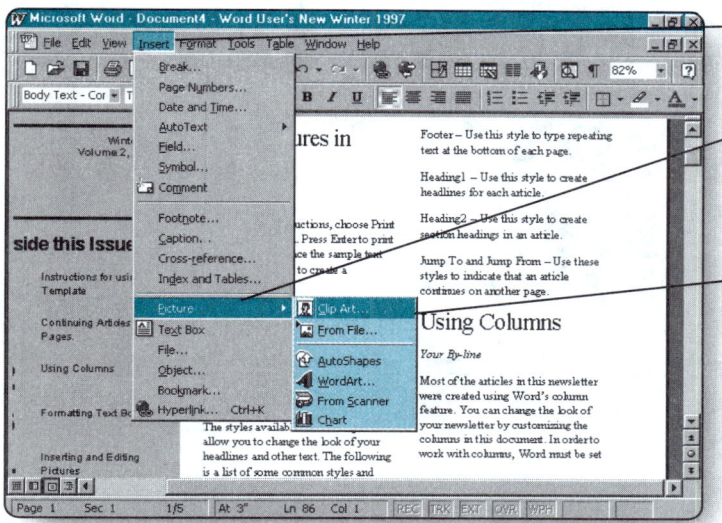

3. **Click** on **Insert**. The Insert menu will appear.

4. **Move** the **mouse pointer** down to Picture. A cascading menu will appear.

5. **Click** on **Clip Art**. The Clip Gallery dialog box will open.

6. **Select** a new piece of **art** from the Clip Gallery dialog box.

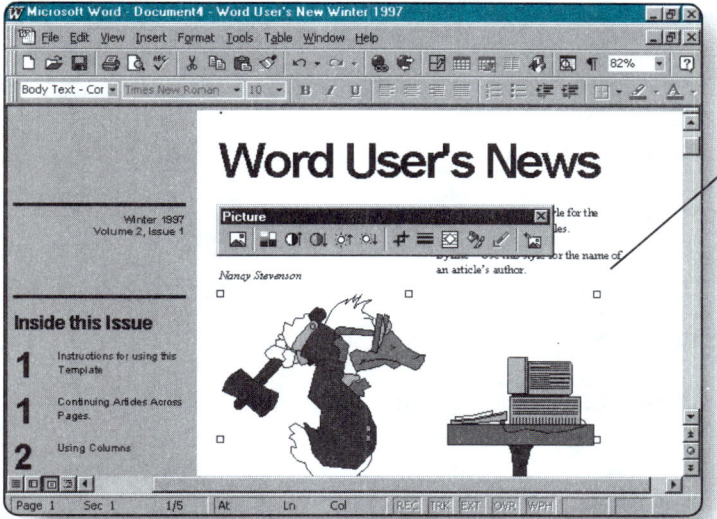

7. **Click** on **OK**. The Picture toolbar will appear, as well as resizing handles on the picture.

8. **Modify** or **resize** your picture, if needed.

NOTE

Note that with any wizard, if you run through it again, your previous settings and information stay in place. Word figures that you usually use the same styles and return address information in your documents.

B Setting Up Amortization Tables

If you have a loan of $2,000 and you have to pay it off in 10 months, an amortization table can give you some important information. You can use Excel to calculate the interest, principal, and total payment involved in the repayment of the loan. In this chapter, you'll learn how to:

✦ Set up labels for an amortization table

✦ Compute the interest amount of a payment

✦ Determine the principal amount of a payment

✦ Figure out the amount of a payment

✦ Calculate the decreasing balance

CREATING AN AMORTIZATION TABLE

Your table needs four columns for making calculations. You need to calculate how much each payment is, how much of the payment is interest, how much of the payment is principal (and actually reduces the balance), and what the balance is after you make each payment. You also need a fifth column for assigning a number to each payment.

Typing the Labels for a Table

You can begin your amortization table by preparing labels for the columns.

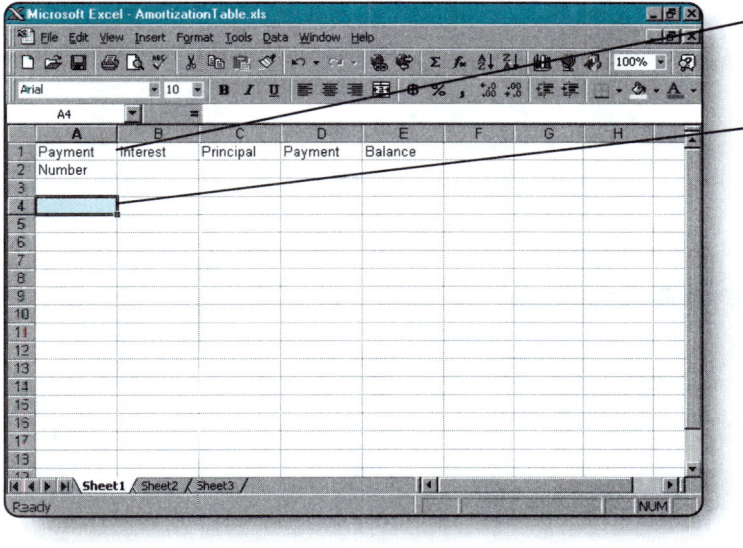

1. Type the **labels** you want to use.

2. Click on **A4**. The cell will be selected.

Setting Up the Column for the Payment Numbers

The first column, Payment Number, assigns a number to each payment.

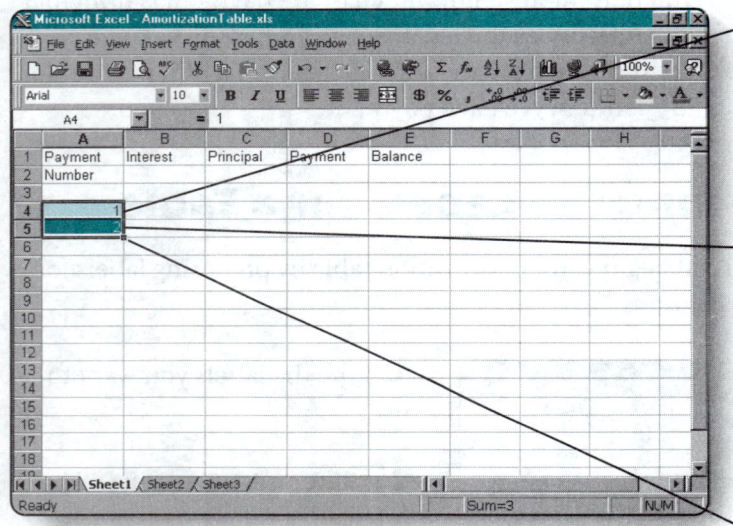

1. Type 1 in the first cell. The number will be entered.

2. Press the Enter key. The next cell in the column will be selected.

3. Type 2 in the second cell.

4. Press the Enter key.

5. Click on the **first cell** and **drag** the **mouse arrow** across the second. Both cells will be selected.

6. Move the **mouse arrow** over the fill handle. The mouse arrow will become a plus sign.

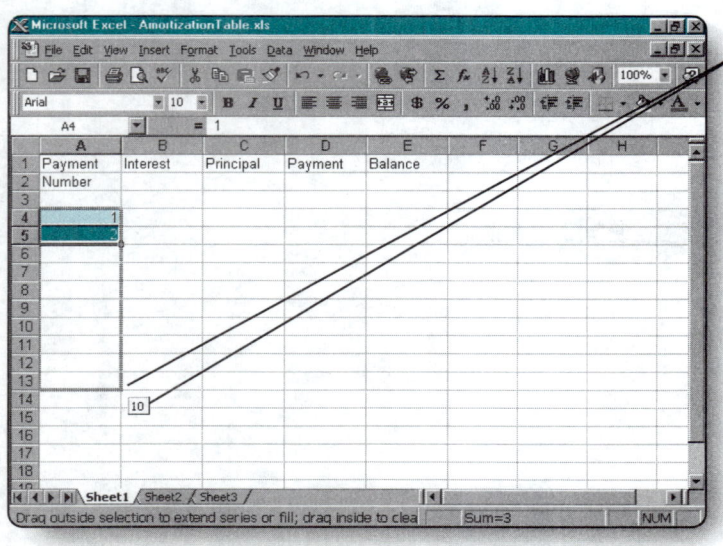

7. Click on the **fill handle** and **drag** it down until you see a small box containing the number of payments you will be making.

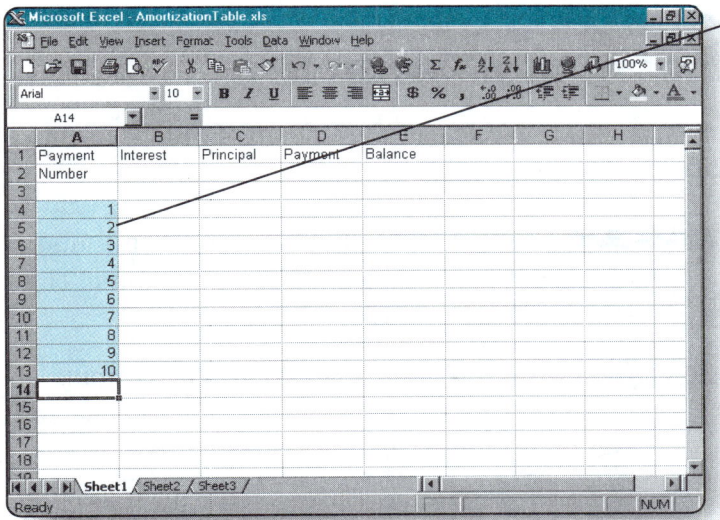

8. **Release** the **mouse button.** The payment numbers will appear in the cells.

Entering the Balance

Before you can calculate the interest per payment, you must place the beginning balance in the Balance column.

1. **Click** on the **cell** in the third row of the Balance column. The cell will be selected.

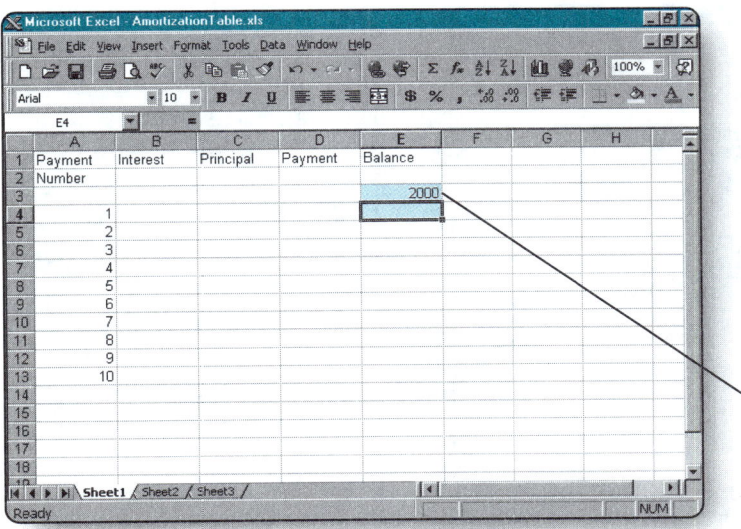

2. **Type** the **loan amount**.

> **TIP**
>
> If you want to avoid having negative numbers in your table, you can use -2000 as the loan amount.

3. **Press** the **Enter key**.

Calculating the Interest Amount of a Payment

Now you are ready to calculate the amount of your payment eaten up by interest.

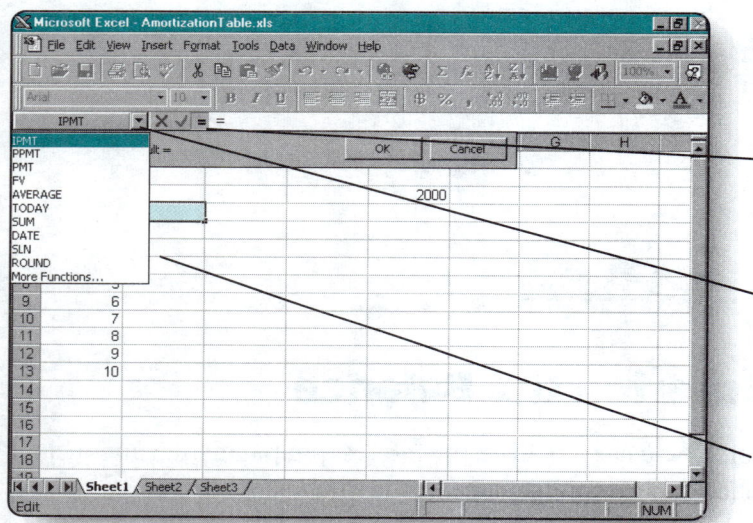

1. Click on the **cell** in the fourth row of the Interest column. The cell will be selected.

2. Click on the **Edit Formula button.** The Formula palette will open.

3. Click on the **arrow (▼)** to the right of the Function list box. A drop-down list of functions will appear.

4. Click on **IPMT**. The IPMT function dialog box will open.

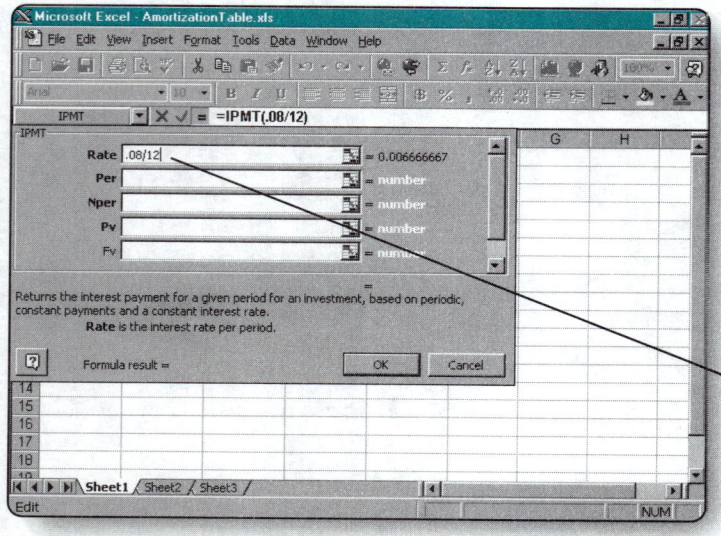

NOTE

If you don't see the function you want to use, click on the arrow (▼) to the right of Function list box. Click on More Functions… and select a function from the Paste Function dialog box.

5. Type the **interest rate divided by 12** in the Rate text box.

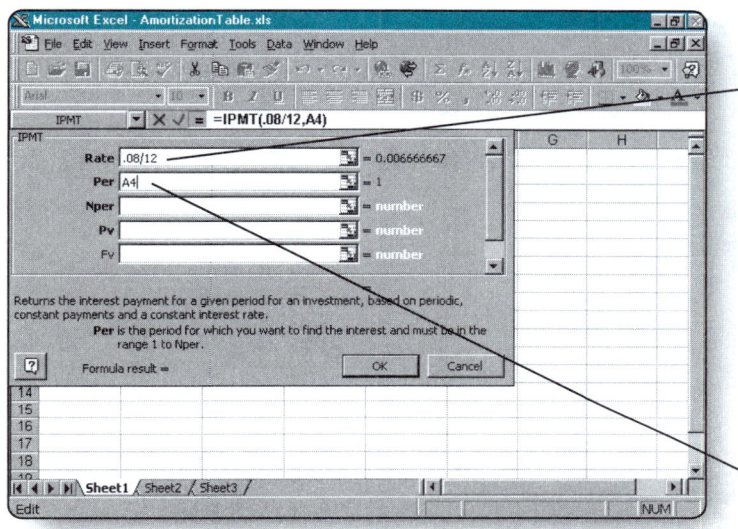

NOTE

Eight percent is the annual rate, but an amortization table uses the monthly interest rate. To determine that rate, you must divide the annual rate by 12.

6. **Press** the **Tab key**. The insertion point will move to the Per text box.

7. **Type** the **cell reference** of the first payment number.

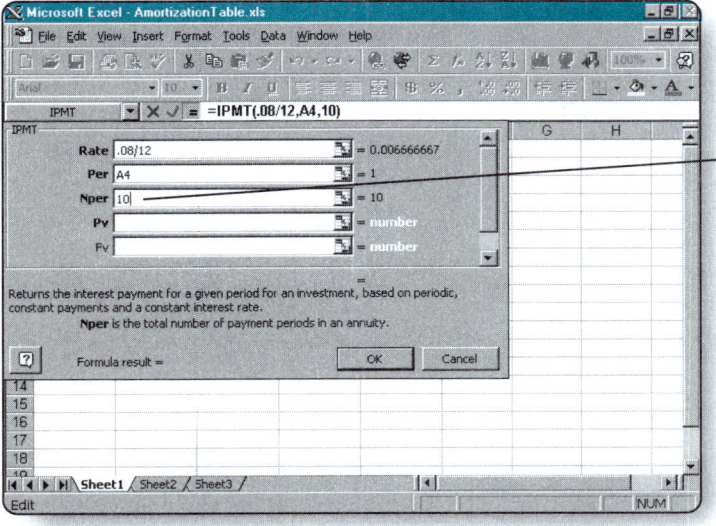

8. **Press** the **Tab key**. The insertion point will move to the Nper text box.

9. **Type** the **number of periods**.

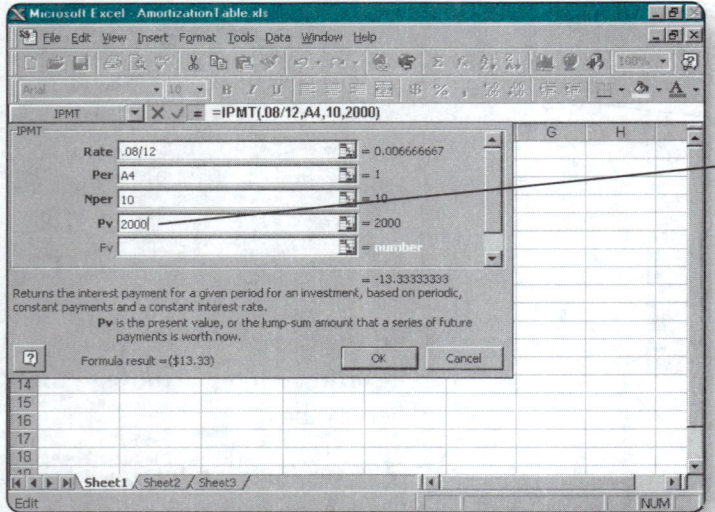

10. **Press** the **Tab key**. The insertion point will move to the Pv text box.

11. **Type** the **beginning balance**.

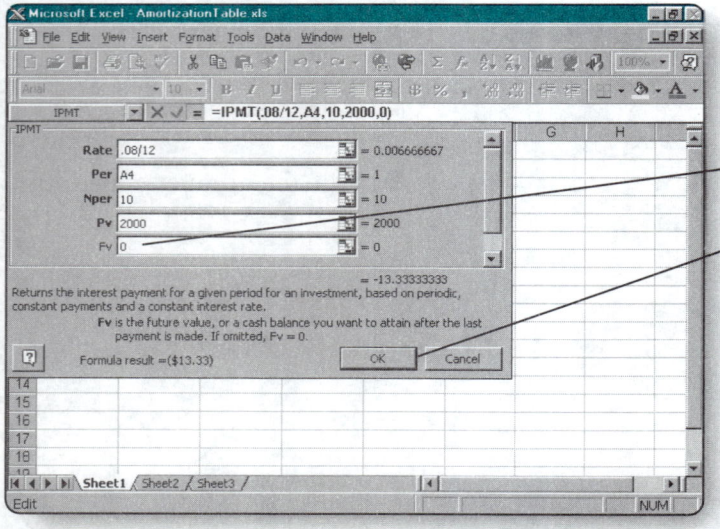

12. **Press** the **Tab key**. The insertion point will move to the Fv text box.

13. **Type** the **ending balance**.

14. **Click** on **OK**. The IPMT dialog box will close.

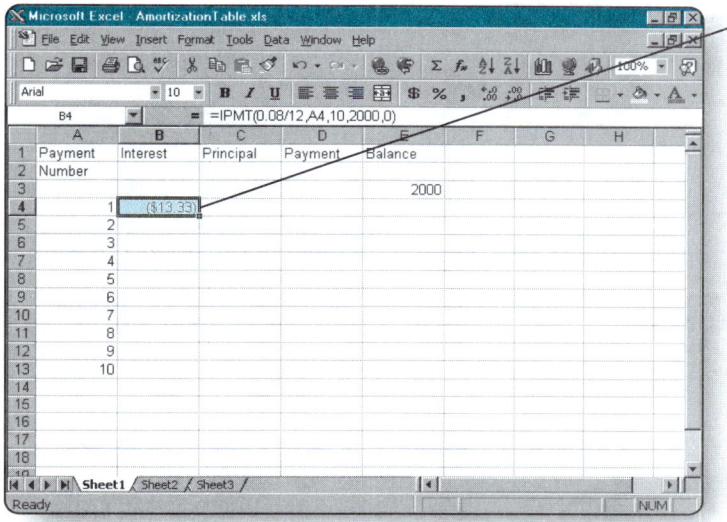

The interest amount will appear in the cell.

Calculating the Principal Amount of a Payment

The next calculation is the principal amount of the payment—the amount that the payment makes your balance drop.

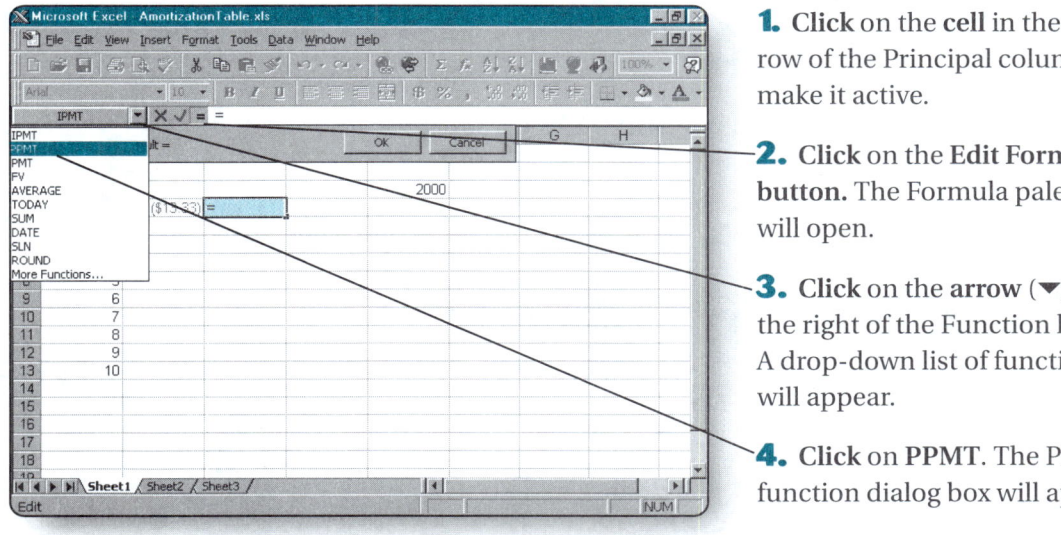

1. **Click** on the **cell** in the fourth row of the Principal column to make it active.

2. **Click** on the **Edit Formula button.** The Formula palette will open.

3. **Click** on the **arrow** (▼) to the right of the Function list box. A drop-down list of functions will appear.

4. **Click** on **PPMT.** The PPMT function dialog box will appear.

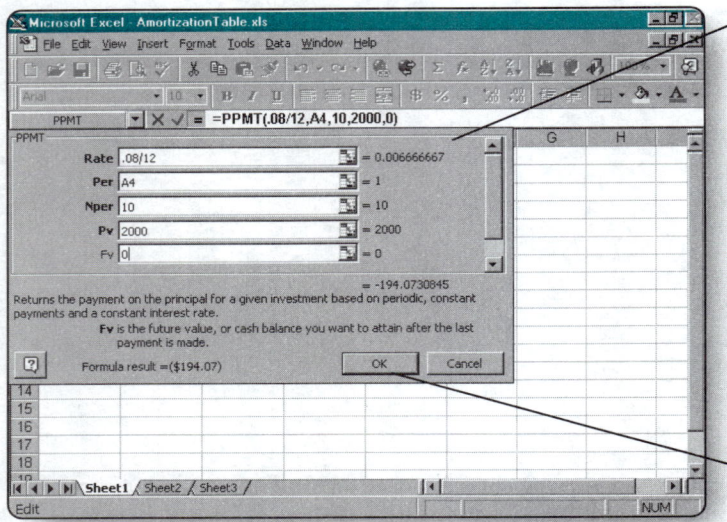

5. **Type data** in the PPMT function dialog box.

NOTE

The data for this dialog box is the same as the information entered in the IPMT function dialog box in "Calculating the Interest Amount of a Payment."

6. **Click** on **OK**. The PPMT function dialog box will close.

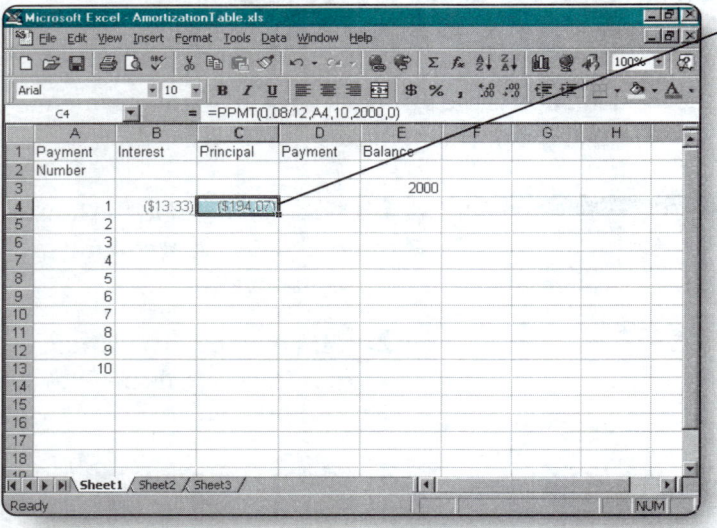

The principal amount of the payment will appear.

Entering the Payment Amount

Next, you enter the payment amount in the Payment column.

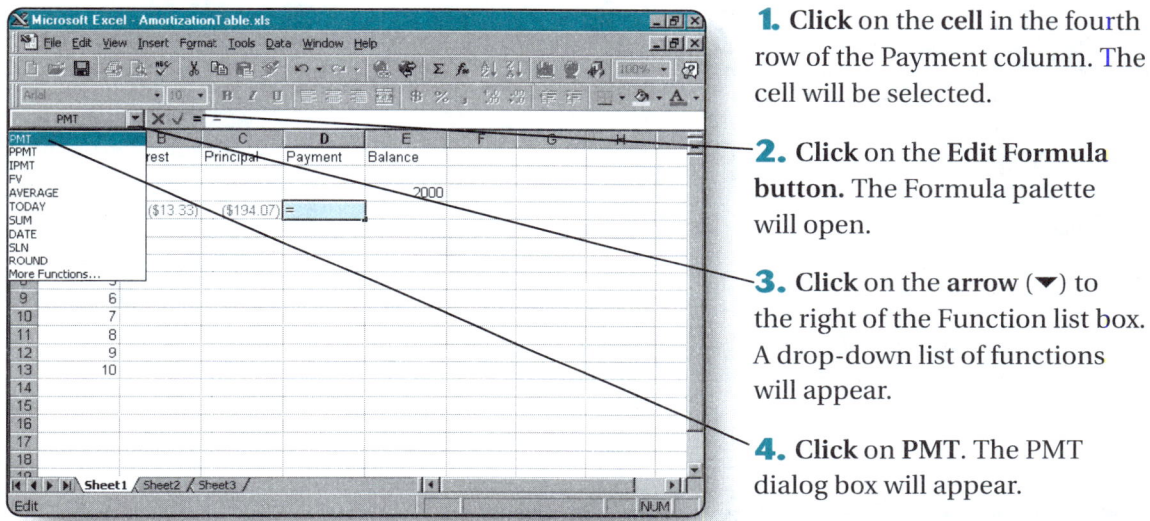

1. Click on the **cell** in the fourth row of the Payment column. The cell will be selected.

2. Click on the **Edit Formula button.** The Formula palette will open.

3. Click on the **arrow** (▼) to the right of the Function list box. A drop-down list of functions will appear.

4. Click on **PMT**. The PMT dialog box will appear.

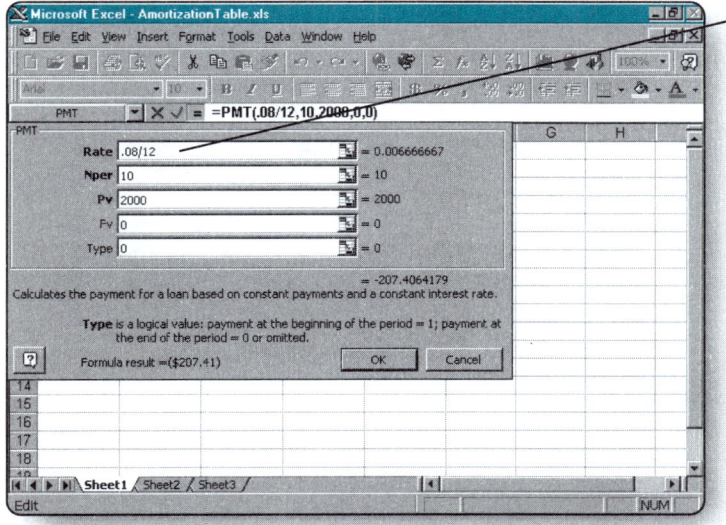

5. Type data in the first four lines of the PMT dialog box.

NOTE

This data is the same as the information entered in the preceding two function dialog boxes in "Calculating the Interest Amount of a Payment" and "Calculating the Principal Amount of a Payment." However, the Per text box is missing.

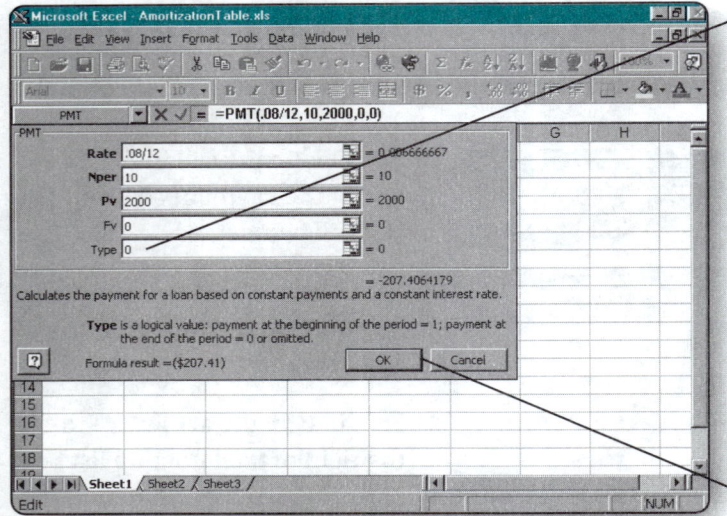

6. Type a **number** in the Type text box.

7. **Click** on **OK**. The PMT dialog box will close.

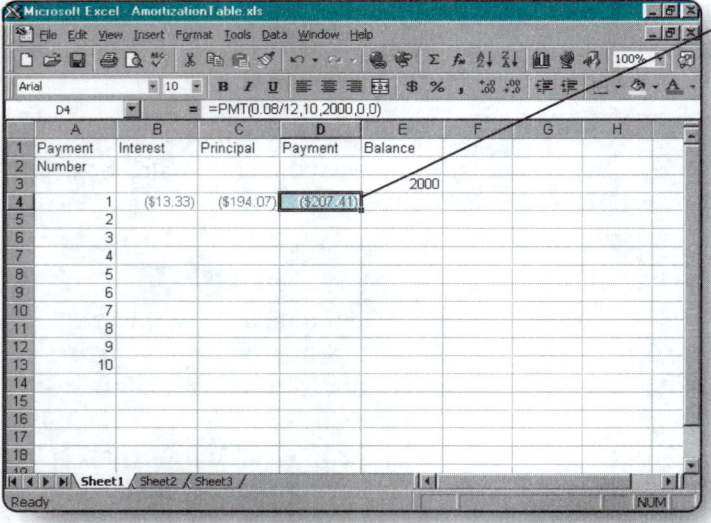

The payment amount will appear.

Calculating the Decreasing Balance

In this column, you begin to see the results of all that outgoing money.

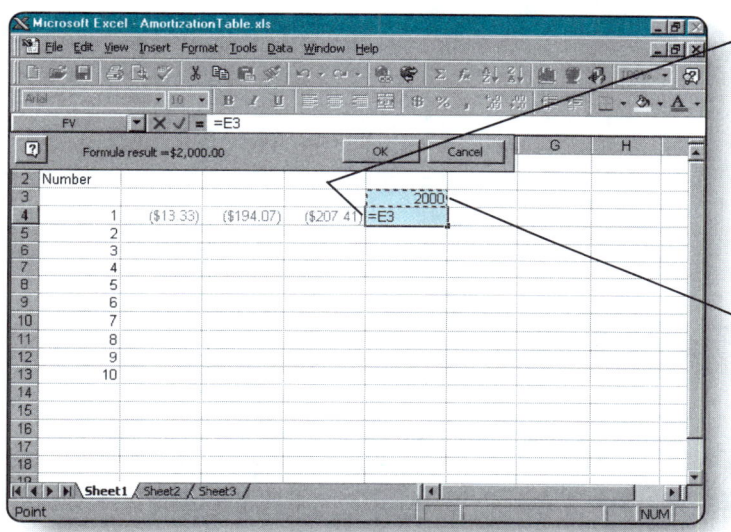

1. **Click** on the **cell** in the fourth row in the Balance column. The cell will be selected.

2. **Click** on the **Edit Formula button**. The Formula palette will open.

3. **Click** on the **cell containing the beginning balance**. An animated border will appear around the cell.

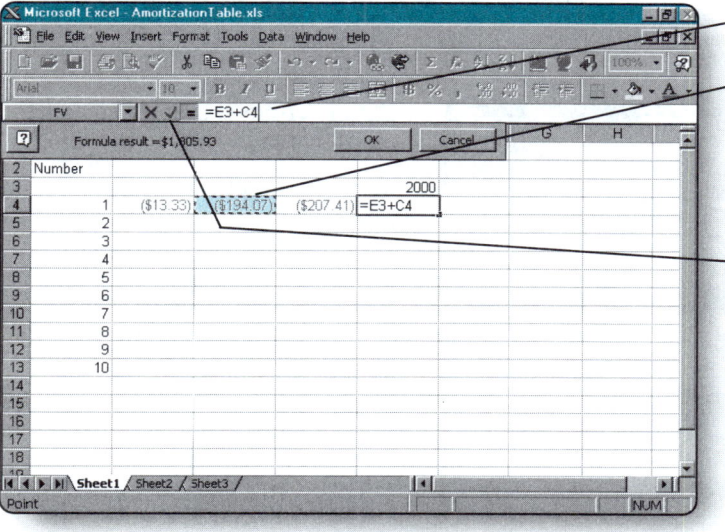

4. **Type +.**

5. **Click** on the **cell containing the principal**. An animated border will appear around the cell.

6. **Click** on the **Check Mark (✔) button**. The formula will be entered.

TIP

If you open a menu but don't want to make a selection, simply click anywhere on the screen outside of the menu box and the menu will close.

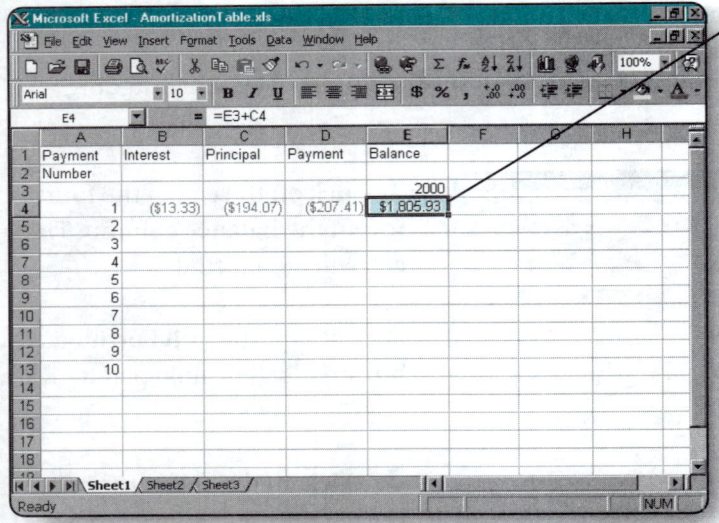

The new balance will appear.

COPYING THE FORMULAS DOWN THE WORKSHEET

Now that you've taken the time to enter the formulas in the first calculated row of the worksheet, you can just copy the formulas down the rest of the worksheet.

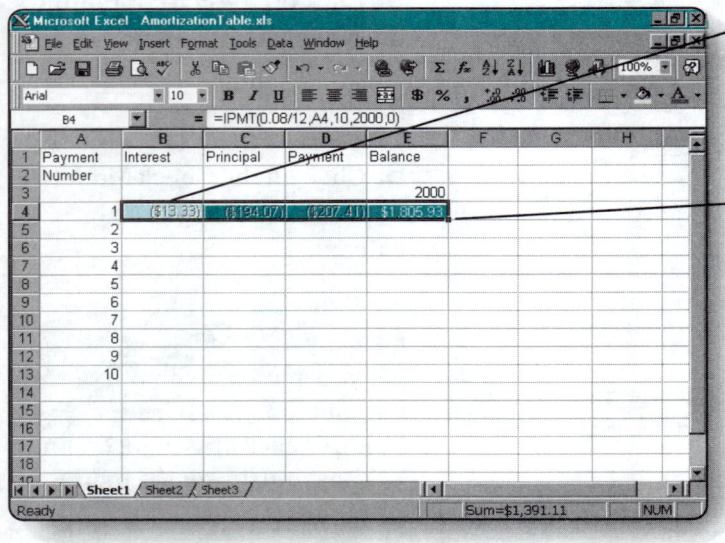

1. **Click** on a **cell** and **drag** with the **mouse arrow** across the range of data to be copied. The range will be selected.

2. **Click** on the **fill handle.** Excel will copy the contents of the range to the Windows Clipboard.

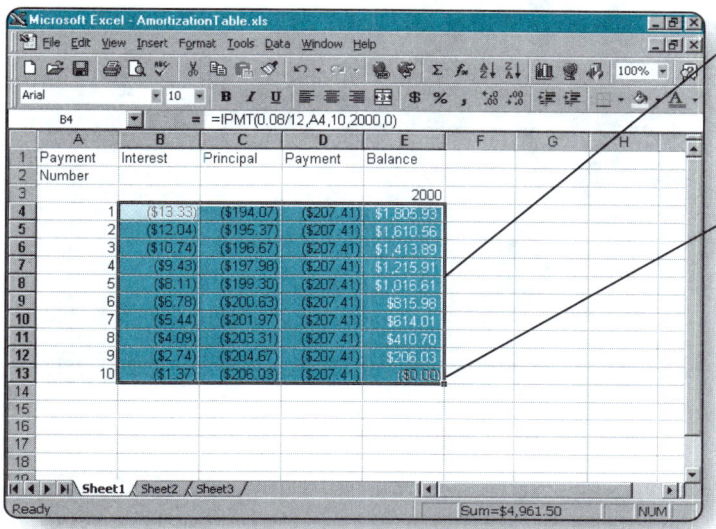

3. Press and **hold** the **mouse button** and **drag** down until you reach the last payment number. The cells will be selected.

4. **Release** the **mouse button**. Excel will fill the cells with the data resulting from the copied formulas.

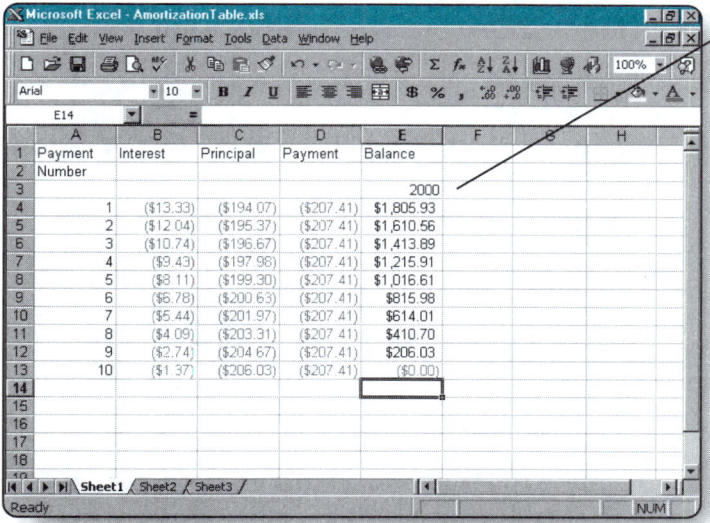

5. **Click outside** of the selected range. Excel will cancel the selection so that you can see the completed amortization table.

C Creating a Presentation with the AutoContent Wizard

The AutoContent Wizard walks you through creating a presentation. It's a wonderful tool for first-time users of PowerPoint who want to create professional-quality presentations quickly. When you create a presentation using the AutoContent Wizard, you define the following presentation elements:

- The *presentation type* is a category of presentation, such as corporate or sales and marketing.

- *Output options* refer to ways you intend to display your presentation. You may intend to create a presentation that you display on an overhead projector using transparencies or 35 mm slides, or on the Internet or in a kiosk situation, where the presentation runs continuously, replaying itself when it finishes.

- The *presentation style* helps determine the shades of colors PowerPoint will use when creating your presentation. When you choose a presentation style, you tell PowerPoint the type of output you will produce (paper, transparencies, slides, and so on) and whether you will print handouts.

- *Presentation options* include the presentation title, your name (or the name of the presenter, if you're only preparing the presentation), and any additional information.

TIP

If you are already working in PowerPoint, you can start the AutoContent Wizard by clicking on File, New, and then clicking on the Presentations tab. Finally, click on the AutoContent Wizard icon and then click on OK.

1. **Start PowerPoint**. The PowerPoint opening dialog box will open, and you will choose a method to start working in PowerPoint.

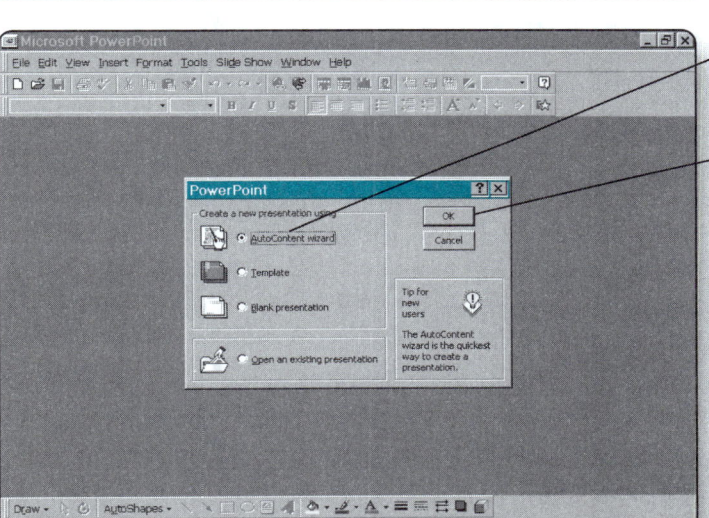

2. **Click** on **AutoContent wizard**.

3. **Click** on **OK**. PowerPoint will display the first of the AutoContent Wizard's dialog boxes, which will show you the elements of a presentation that you will set.

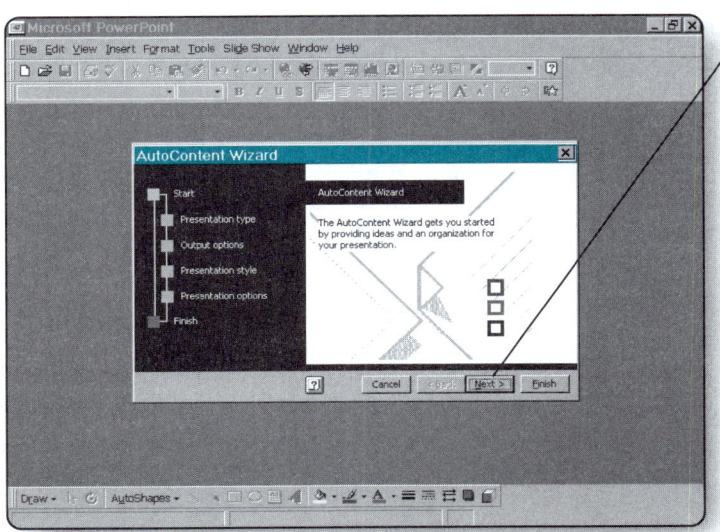

4. **Click** on **Next**.

SELECTING A PRESENTATION TYPE

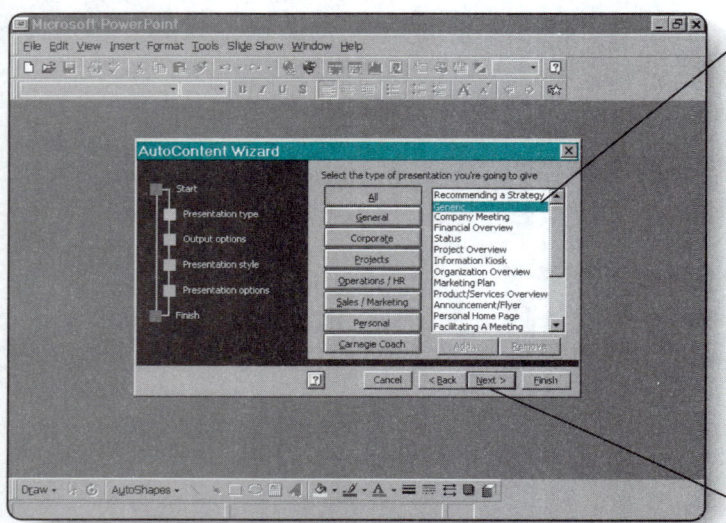

1. Click on the **type of presentation** you want to create.

TIP

If you prefer to see the presentation types organized in categories, click on one of the buttons to the left of the list. PowerPoint will display only the presentation types associated with that category.

2. Click on Next.

SELECTING OUTPUT OPTIONS

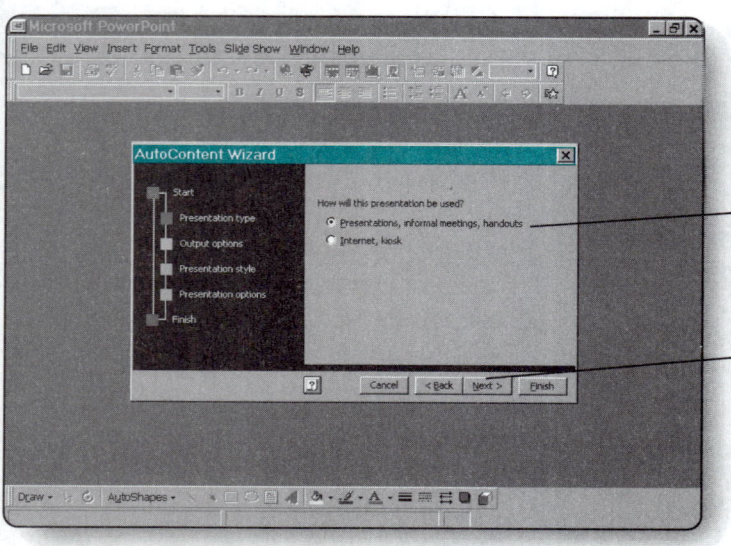

1. Click on the **option** you want to use. The option will be selected.

2. Click on Next.

> **TIP**
>
> A *kiosk* presentation is self-running and restarts when the presentation finishes.

SELECTING A PRESENTATION STYLE

When you select a presentation style, you identify the way you intend to display the presentation.

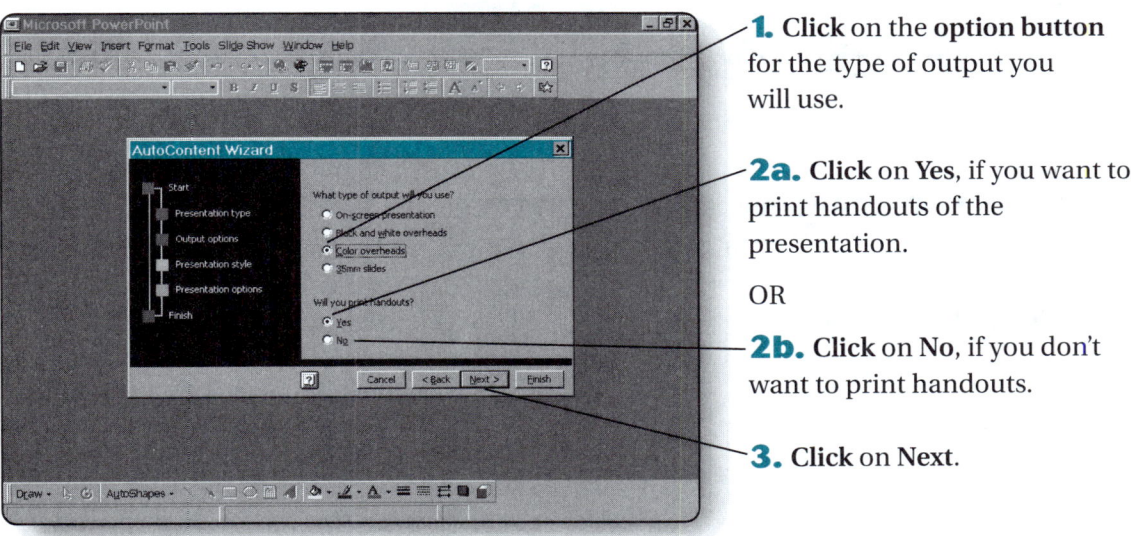

1. **Click** on the **option button** for the type of output you will use.

2a. **Click** on **Yes**, if you want to print handouts of the presentation.

OR

2b. **Click** on **No**, if you don't want to print handouts.

3. **Click** on **Next**.

IDENTIFYING PRESENTATION OPTIONS

You can identify the title of the presentation, the name of the person who will present or the person who prepared the presentation, and any other information you want to appear on the title slide of the presentation.

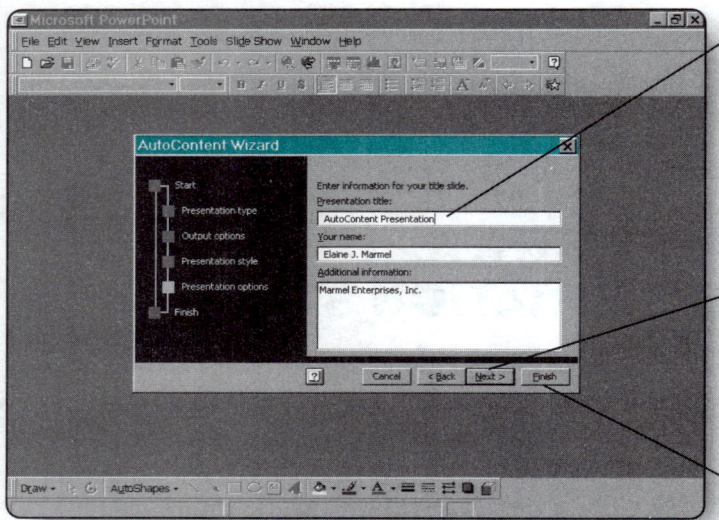

1. Select the text **Title goes here**, that appears in the Presentation title: text box.

2. Type the **title** of the presentation. The text you type will replace the existing text.

3. Click on **Next**. The last Auto-Content Wizard box will appear, explaining that the AutoContent Wizard doesn't need any more information from you.

4. Click on **Finish**.

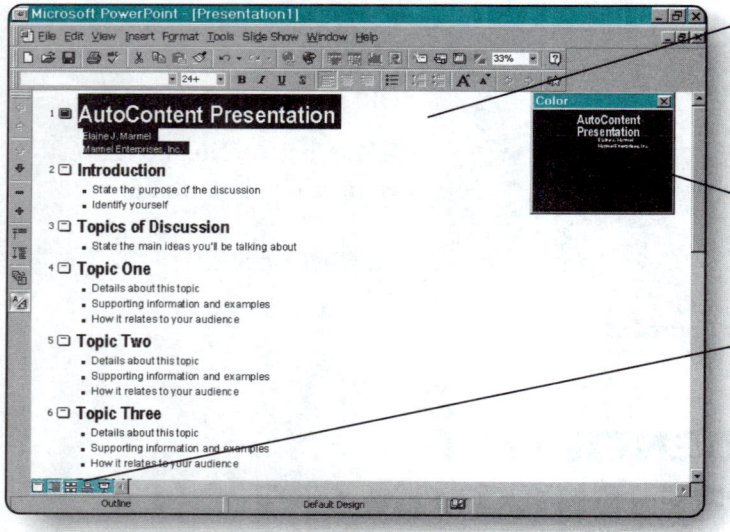

Your presentation will appear in Outline view, with the contents of the first slide selected. Notice that each slide is numbered.

In addition, you'll see a small window showing the appearance of the slides.

5. Click on any of the **view buttons**. You will change views and see your presentation.

Glossary

+. Addition operator.

-. Subtraction operator.

=. Initiates all formulas.

*. Multiplication operator.

/. Division operator.

>. Greater than operator.

<. Less than operator.

<>. Not equal to operator.

:. Range operator.

A

Absolute reference. References to cell addresses that don't change based on where a formula is located in a worksheet.

Active cell. The selected cell in a worksheet.

Address. A named reference to a cell based on its location at the intersection of a column and row; for example, the cell in the fourth row of the second column has an address of B4.

Alignment. The arrangement of text or an object in relation to the document's margins in Word, a slide's dimensions in PowerPoint, or a cell's edges in Excel.

Alignment can be left, right, centered, or justified.

Applet. A small software program provided with Word that enables you to perform additional operations, such as WordArt, for enhanced text effects.

Appointment. An entry in the Outlook calendar that spans less than one day to which no other individuals are invited.

Array. A contiguous set of cells in a worksheet.

AutoCorrect. A feature of Word that automatically corrects common spelling mistakes (such as "teh" for "the").

AutoFormat. AutoFormat enables you to apply pre-defined sets of formatting to a table's (or worksheet's) text, rows, and columns.

AutoSum. A built-in addition function that allows you to add a row or column of figures using the AutoSum button on the Excel toolbar.

AutoText. A feature of Word that enables you to save a set of text and insert it in your document by typing a word or phrase.

Axis (pl. axes). In a graph, one of two value sets (*see also* x-axis and y-axis).

B

Bar chart. A type of chart that uses bars of varying lengths to represent values.

Binder. The file you create when you save in Office Binder.

Binder pane. The panel that appears down the left side of the Microsoft Office Binder window, displaying sections in the binder.

Bold. A style applied to text to make the font lines thicker.

Border. A formatting option that places a line around any of the four sides of an object, such as a cell.

Break. An instruction embedded into a Word document that indicates a change, such as a Page Break, to start a new page.

Bullet. A symbol that precedes an item in a list. Bullets can be any shape found in a typeface, but most commonly, are solid black circles.

C

Cell. The area defined by a rectangle at which a row and column intersect in an Excel worksheet or a Word table.

Cell Reference. A method of referring to a cell in a formula by listing the location of its row and column intersection.

Chart. Also called *graph*. A chart is a visual representation of numerical data.

Circular Reference. In a formula, a circular reference indicates that a calculation should return to its starting point and repeat endlessly. A circular reference in a formula will result in an error message.

Clip art. Ready-made line drawings that are included with Office in the Clip Art Gallery. These drawings can be inserted into Office documents.

Clip Gallery. A collection of clip art, pictures, and sound files that comes with Word.

Column. A set of cells running vertically down a worksheet.

Combination chart. A chart that uses more than one style of representing data; for example, bars for one set of data and a line for another set of data. A chart that shows rainfall in a country by month with bars and the average rainfall in the world with a line is an example of a combination chart.

Contact. An entry that appears in an address book.

D

Data. Information, which can be either numerical or textual.

Data form. A place where data, such as data used in a mail merge operation, is stored in individual records.

Data series. In charts, elements that represent a set of data, such as pie segment, line, or bar.

Data source. In a Word mail merge, the information that is used to replace field codes with personalized information, such as names and addresses.

Data type. The category of numerical data, such as currency, scientific, or percentage.

Desktop. The main area of Windows where you can open and manage files and programs.

Dialog box. A window that appears during some procedures in Word that enables you to make settings by entering text, selecting things from lists, or checking boxes or buttons.

Drag-and-drop. A method of moving text or objects by clicking on an object with a mouse, dragging it to a new location, and releasing the mouse button to drop it into its new location.

E

e-mail. Messages sent electronically.

Equation. *See* formula.

Event. An entry in the Outlook calendar that spans an entire day.

F

Field. In a form letter, a field is a placeholder for corresponding data.

Fill. An action in Excel that automatically completes a series of numbers based on an established pattern.

Fill (color). A formatting feature used to apply color or a pattern to the interior of an object, such as a cell.

Fill Handle. A block at the bottom right corner of the active cell in a worksheet that is used to fill cells as it is dragged across them with a pattern of data.

Filter. To make settings so that only cells that meet certain criteria are displayed in your worksheet.

Financial functions. Functions (stored formulas) that are used with money, such as payments and interest rates.

Flip. To turn an object on a page 180 degrees.

Font. A design set of letters, symbols, and numbers, also called a *typeface*.

Footer. Text repeated at the bottom of each page of a document.

Format. To add settings for font, font style, color, and line style to text or an object.

Format painter. A feature of Word that enables you to easily copy all formatting that's applied to one set of text to any other.

Formula. An equation that instructs Excel to perform certain calculations based on numerical data in designated cells.

Formula bar. The location where all data and formulas are entered for a selected cell.

Freezing. In large worksheets it is sometimes desirable to freeze a portion of the sheet, such as column headings, so that it doesn't scroll off screen when you move down the page.

Function. A pre-defined, named formula.

G

General format. A numerical type applied to numbers in cells.

Go To. A feature that allows you to move quickly to a page or cell of your document based on criteria you provide.

Goal Seek. A feature that allows you to enter the result you want. Excel then determines changes in the formula or data required to obtain the result.

Gradient. A shading effect that moves from lighter to darker in such a way that it suggests a light source shining on the object containing the gradient.

Graph. Also called *chart*. A graph is a visual representation of numerical data.

Greater than. A function that restricts a number result to be higher than a named number.

Gridlines. Lines between the cells of a worksheet or the rows and columns of a table. You can choose to display or hide gridlines both onscreen and when you print.

H

Handle. Small squares that appear when you select an object that enable you to resize it.

Header. Text repeated at the top of each page of a document.

Hide. A feature of Excel that allows you to temporarily stop displaying designated cells in a worksheet.

Highlight. A feature that places colored highlighting onscreen for selected text.

Hyperlink. An element you create that consists of an address to a location, such as a folder on your computer or Web page. When you click on a hyperlink, you jump to the location defined in the hyperlink.

I

Icon. A graphic representation used on toolbars to represent the various functions performed when those buttons are clicked with a mouse.

IF function. A pre-defined formula indicating that a result is to occur only if some criteria is met. For example, you could use this function to indicate that "if the result of a sum is greater than 10, the result should appear in this cell."

Indent. To set text away from a margin by a specific distance, as at the beginning of a paragraph.

Italic. A font style that applies a slanted effect to text.

J

Justify. One type of alignment that spreads letters on a line or in a cell evenly between the left and right margin or across selected cells.

L

Label. A descriptive text element added to a chart to help the reader understand a visual element. Also refers to row or column headings.

Landscape. A page orientation that prints a document with the long edge of the paper across the top.

Legend. In a chart, a feature that defines the relationship of the graphic symbols to the data elements for the reader.

Less than. A pre-defined function that indicates a result should occur only if a number is less than the specified number.

Line style. Effects using width, arrows, and dashes that can be applied to a line.

Logical functions. Functions that are based on the logical consequence of a named set of circumstances, such as the IF . . . THEN function.

M

Macro. A saved series of keystrokes that can be played back to perform an action.

Mail merge. A procedure in which you use a form document, insert placeholders for types of data (called fields) and merge that document with specific data to produce personalized mailings.

Maps. Representing data in charts with geographical maps rather than traditional chart elements such as bars and lines.

Margin. A border that runs around the outside of a document page, in which nothing will print.

Mathematical functions. Functions that produce mathematical results, such as SUM and AVG.

Meeting. An entry in the Outlook calendar that spans less than one day to which others are invited.

N

Named ranges. Providing a name for a set of cells so you can use that name in formulas.

O

Object. A picture, map, or other graphic element that you can place in an Excel worksheet, a Word document, or a PowerPoint presentation.

Office Assistant. A help feature for Microsoft Office products that allows you to ask questions in standard English sentence format.

Office Shortcut Bar. A utility that ships with Microsoft Office. The Microsoft Office Shortcut Bar contains a series of toolbars that help speed up your work by providing quick access to the resources you use most often on your computer.

Operator. The parts of a formula that indicate an action to be performed, such as addition (+) or division (/).

Optional arguments. A portion of a formula which is not necessary to achieve the result, but that designates an action other than the default. An optional argument to include decimals in a result would include the decimal point and two zeros even if the number doesn't contain cents.

Orientation. The way a document prints on a piece of paper; landscape prints with the longer side of a page on top, while portrait prints with the shorter edge at the top.

Outline. A hierarchy of lines of text that suggests major and minor ideas.

Outlook bar. The panel that appears down the left side of the Outlook window. It contains shortcuts to the various sections in Outlook.

P

Page Break. An instruction that can be embedded into a Word document to instruct Word to move to a new page at that point.

Page Layout. A view in Word that is commonly used for arranging objects on a page and drawing.

Page Setup. The collection of settings that relate to how the pages of your document are set up, including margins, orientation, and the size of paper on which each page will print.

Passwords. A word selected by an Excel user to protect a worksheet; once a sheet is protected, the correct password must be entered to modify that sheet.

Paste. To place text or an object previously placed on the Windows Clipboard (through cutting or copying) in an Office document.

Pattern. Shading and line arrangements that can be used to fill the center of an object.

Pie chart. A round chart type in which each pie wedge represents a value.

Plot. The area of a chart where data is drawn using elements such as line, bars, or pie wedges.

Portrait. A page orientation where a document prints with the shorter edge of the paper along the top.

Precedent. Some formulas call on data that is the result of another formula; the precedent is the formula that originally created the data being named in the second formula.

Print area. The portion of a worksheet you designate to print.

Print Preview. A feature that allows you to view a document on your screen, appearing as it will when printed.

Protect. To make settings so that only someone with the correct password can modify a document.

R

Range. A collection of cells, ranging from the first named cell to the last.

Recalculation. Used with manual calculation, recalculation is applied to a formula when data has changed to receive the new result.

Redo. A feature that allows you to restore an action you have reversed using the Undo feature.

Reference. In a formula, a name or range that refers the formula to a cell or set of cells.

Relative. In a formula, making reference to a cell relative to the location of the cell where the formula is placed; if the formula cell is moved, the cell being referenced changes in relation to the new location.

Revisions. Highlighting effects applied to indicate any changes in text from one version of a document to another.

Right-aligned. Text that is lined up with the right side of a tab setting or document margin, as with a row of numbers in a column.

Rotate. To manipulate an object so that it moves around a 360 degree axis.

Row. A set of cells running from left to right across a worksheet.

Ruler. An on-screen feature provided to help you place text and objects accurately on a page.

S

Save as. To save a previously saved worksheet with a new name or properties.

Scroll bar. A device used with a mouse to move up and down or left to right in a document to display various portions of it onscreen.

Section. A "page" in a binder, represented by an icon that appears in the Binder pane. In actuality, a section might consist of several printed pages.

Selection bar. An invisible bar along the left side of a document. When you place your mouse cursor in the bar, it can be used to select a single line or multiple lines of text.

Shading. A color that fills cells or an object.

Shadow. A drawing effect that appears to place a shadow alongside an object.

Sheet. *See* Worksheet.

Slide. An element in a PowerPoint presentation, equivalent to a page.

Slide Layout. The term used to refer to the general appearance of a slide and the elements it contains; for example, you might have a bulleted list layout, or a chart layout, or a title only layout.

Solver. A feature that helps you locate the appropriate formula to achieve a specific result.

Sort. To arrange data alphanumerically in either ascending (A-Z) or descending (Z-A) order.

Spelling checker. A feature that checks the spelling in your document against a dictionary and flags possible errors for correction.

Spreadsheet. A software program used to perform calculations on data.

Start Page. The first Web page you see when you log onto the World Wide Web.

Status bar. An area at the bottom of a window that provides information about the document, such as what page, line, and column your cursor is currently resting in.

Style. A saved, named set of formatting such as color, size, and font that can be applied to text in a document.

SUM function. A saved, named function of addition that can be applied to cells by typing the term "SUM" in a formula.

Symbol. A typeface that uses graphics such as circles, percentage signs, or smiling faces in place of letters and numbers.

Syntax. The structure and order of the functions and references used in a formula.

T

Tab. A setting that can be placed along the width of a line of text that enables you to quickly jump your cursor to that setting.

Table. A collection of columns and rows, forming cells at their intersection, to organize sets of data.

Target cell. The cell where the results of a formula should be placed.

Task. An entry you make in Outlook's To Do section.

Template. A pre-defined collection of formatting and style settings on which you can base a new document.

Text box. A floating object containing text that you can create with the drawing feature of Office programs to place text anywhere in a document.

Text wrap. This feature forces newly entered text to wrap to the next line when the insertion point reaches the right margin.

Titles. Names of the elements of a chart.

Tool tip. A Help feature that displays the name of a tool in a small box when you move your cursor over the tool.

Transitions. In PowerPoint, elements you add to slide that determine what will appear during a slide show as you switch from slide to slide.

Trendline. A line that can be overlaid on a chart to indicate a trend from the data in the chart.

u

Undo. A feature that allows you to reverse the last action performed. You can undo actions by repeatedly using this feature.

Unhide. To reveal rows or columns previously hidden in a worksheet.

Unprotect. To remove password safeguards from a worksheet so that anyone can modify the worksheet.

Uppercase. A capital letter.

v

Value. Value is another term for a number.

Variable. Cells that are changed to see what results from that change.

View. In software, various displays of documents or information that enable you to perform different tasks or see different perspectives on information; for example, the Outline view in Word.

w

Web page. A document you see when you log onto the World Wide Web. Also called a Web document.

What if. A scenario that supposes certain criteria.

What's This?. A part of the Help system; once you select What's This? your cursor changes to a question mark and you can click on any on-screen element to receive an explanation of that element.

Wizard. A feature that walks you through a procedure step by step, producing something, such as a table, letter, or chart, based on answers you give to questions and selections made in Wizard dialog boxes.

Word count. A tally of the number of words in a document.

WordArt. An applet included with Word used for adding special effects to text, such as curving the text.

Workbook. A single Excel file containing a collection of Excel worksheets.

Worksheet. One of several pages in an Excel workbook.

Wrap. *See* Text Wrap.

x

X-axis. In a chart, the vertical-value axis.

y

Y-axis. In a chart, the horizontal-value axis.

Index

Send Us
YOUR COMMENTS

Dear Reader:

Thank you for buying this book. In order to offer you more quality books on the topics *you* would like to see, we need your input. At Prima Publishing, we pride ourselves on timely responsiveness to our readers needs. If you'll complete and return this brief questionnaire, *we will listen!*

Name: (first) _____ (M.I.) _____ (last) _____

Company: _____ Type of business: _____

Address: _____ City: _____ State: _____ Zip: _____

Phone: _____ Fax: _____ E-mail address: _____

May we contact you for research purposes? ❏ Yes ❏ No

(If you participate in a research project, we will supply you with your choice of a book from Prima CPD)

---

1 How would you rate this book, overall?

❏ Excellent ❏ Fair
❏ Very Good ❏ Below Average
❏ Good ❏ Poor

2 Why did you buy this book?

❏ Price of book ❏ Content
❏ Author's reputation ❏ Prima's reputation
❏ CD-ROM/disk included with book
❏ Information highlighted on cover
❏ Other (Please specify): _____

3 How did you discover this book?

❏ Found it on bookstore shelf
❏ Saw it in Prima Publishing catalog
❏ Recommended by store personnel
❏ Recommended by friend or colleague
❏ Saw an advertisement in: _____
❏ Read book review in: _____
❏ Saw it on Web site: _____
❏ Other (Please specify): _____

4 Where did you buy this book?

❏ Bookstore (name)_____
❏ Computer Store (name) _____
❏ Electronics Store (name) _____
❏ Wholesale Club (name) _____
❏ Mail Order (name) _____
❏ Direct from Prima Publishing
❏ Other (please specify): _____

5 Which computer periodicals do you read regularly? _____

_____
_____
_____

6 Would you like to see your name in print?

May we use your name and quote you in future Prima Publishing books or promotional materials?

❏ Yes ❏ No

---

7 Comments & Suggestions: _____

_____
_____

SAVE A STAMP

11 **I would be interested in computer books on these topics**

- ☐ Word Processing
- ☐ Networking
- ☐ Desktop Publishing
- ☐ Database:
- ☐ Spreadsheets
- ☐ Web site design

Other _____

9 **How do you rate your level of computer skills?**

- ☐ Beginner
- ☐ Advanced
- ☐ Intermediate

10 **What is your age?**

- ☐ Under 18
- ☐ 18-24
- ☐ 25-29
- ☐ 30-39
- ☐ 40-49
- ☐ 50-59
- ☐ 60-over

8 **Where do you use your computer?**

	100%	75%	50%	25%
Work	☐	☐	☐	☐
Home	☐	☐	☐	☐
School	☐	☐	☐	☐

Other _____

PLEASE
PLACE
STAMP
HERE

PRIMA PUBLISHING

Computer Products Division
701 Congressional Blvd., Suite 350
Carmel, IN 46032

Prima's Visual Learning Guides
fast & easy

Relax, learning new software is now a breeze. You are looking at a series of books dedicated to one idea: To help you learn to use software as quickly and easily as possible. No need to wade through boring pages of endless text. With Prima's Visual Learning Guides, you simply look and learn.

ACT! 3
Dick Cravens
0-7615-1175-X
352 pgs.
$16.99 (Can. $23.95)

Word 97
Nancy Stevenson
0-7615-1007-9
384 pgs.
$16.99 (Can. $23.95)

Excel 97
Nancy Stevenson
0-7615-1008-7
352 pgs.
$16.99 (Can. $23.95)

WordPerfect® 8
Diane Koers
0-7615-1083-4
352 pgs.
$16.99 (Can. $23.95)

Windows® 95
Grace Joely Beatty, Ph.D.
David C. Gardner, Ph.D.
1-55958-738-5
288 pgs.
$19.95 (Can. $29.95)

**WordPerfect® 6.1
for Windows**
Grace Joely Beatty, Ph.D.
David C. Gardner, Ph.D.
0-7615-0091-X
288 pgs.
$19.95 (Can. $29.95)

Excel 5 for Windows®
Grace Joely Beatty, Ph.D.
David C. Gardner, Ph.D.
1-55958-736-9
288 pgs.
$19.95 (Can. $29.95)

PRIMA

http://www.primapublishing.com

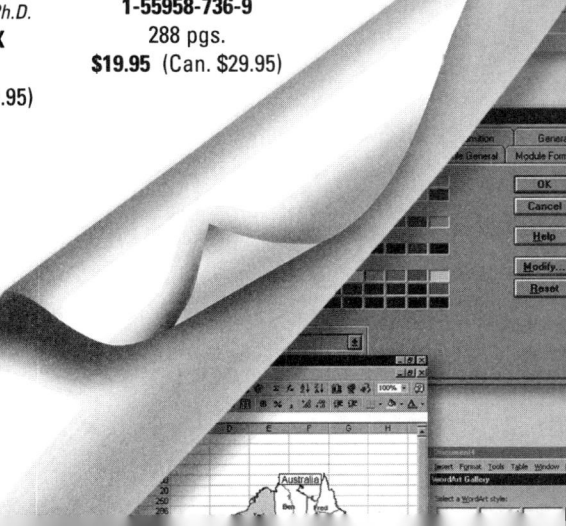

OTHER BOOKS FROM PRIMA PUBLISHING
Computer Products Division

ISBN	Title	Price	Release Date
0-7615-0801-5	ActiveX	$40.00	Available Now
0-7615-0680-2	America Online Complete Handbook and Membership Kit	$24.99	Available Now
0-7615-0915-1	Building Intranets with Internet Information Server and FrontPage	$40.00	Available Now
0-7615-0417-6	CompuServe Complete Handbook and Membership Kit	$24.95	Available Now
0-7615-1083-4	Corel WordPerfect 8 Visual Learning Guide	$16.99	Spring '97
0-7615-0849-X	Corporate Intranet Development	$45.00	Available Now
0-7615-0692-6	Create Your First Web Page in a Weekend	$29.99	Available Now
0-7615-0743-4	Create FrontPage Web Pages in a Weekend	$29.99	Available Now
0-7615-0428-1	The Essential Excel 97 Book	$27.99	Available Now
0-7615-0969-0	The Essential Office 97 Book	$27.99	Available Now
0-7615-0695-0	The Essential Photoshop Book	$35.00	Available Now
0-7615-0752-3	The Essential Windows NT 4 Book	$27.99	Available Now
0-7615-0427-3	The Essential Word 97 Book	$27.99	Available Now
0-7615-1008-7	Excel 97 Visual Learning Guide	$16.99	Available Now
0-7615-1013-3	Hands On Java	$40.00	Spring '97
0-7615-1046-X	Hands On Visual Basic 5	$40.00	Spring '97

ISBN	Title	Price	Release Date
0-7615-1005-2	Internet Information Server 3 Administrator's Guide	$40.00	Available Now
0-7615-0815-5	Introduction to ABAP/4 Programming for SAP	$45.00	Available Now
0-7615-0901-1	Leveraging Visual Basic with ActiveX Controls	$45.00	Available Now
0-7615-0690-X	Netscape Enterprise Server	$40.00	Available Now
0-7615-0691-8	Netscape FastTrack Server	$40.00	Available Now
0-7615-0852-X	Netscape Navigator 3 Complete Handbook	$24.99	Available Now
0-7615-0759-0	Professional Web Design	$40.00	Available Now
0-7615-0773-6	Programming Internet Controls	$45.00	Available Now
0-7615-0914-3	Programming ISAPI with Visual Basic 5	$40.00	Available Now
0-7615-0780-9	Programming Web Server Applications	$40.00	Available Now
0-7615-0063-4	Researching on the Internet	$29.95	Available Now
0-7615-0686-1	Researching on the World Wide Web	$24.99	Available Now
0-7615-0769-8	VBScript Master's Handbook	$45.00	Available Now
0-7615-0684-5	VBScript Web Page Interactivity	$40.00	Available Now
0-7615-0903-8	Visual FoxPro 5 Enterprise Development	$45.00	Available Now
0-7615-0814-7	Visual J++	$35.00	Available Now
0-7615-0726-4	Webmaster's Handbook	$40.00	Available Now
0-7615-0751-5	Windows NT Server 4 Administrator's Guide	$50.00	Available Now
0-7615-1007-9	Word 97 Visual Learning Guide	$16.99	Available Now

TO ORDER BOOKS

Please send me the following items:

Quantity	Title	Unit Price	Total
_____	_____	$_____	$_____
_____	_____	$_____	$_____
_____	_____	$_____	$_____
_____	_____	$_____	$_____
_____	_____	$_____	$_____

	Subtotal	$_____
	Deduct 10% when ordering 3–5 books	$_____
	7.25% Sales Tax (CA only)	$_____
	8.25% Sales Tax (TN only)	$_____
	5.0% Sales Tax (MD and IN only)	$_____
	Shipping and Handling*	$_____
	TOTAL ORDER	$_____

Shipping and Handling depend on Subtotal.

Subtotal	Shipping/Handling
$0.00–$14.99	$3.00
$15.00–29.99	$4.00
$30.00–49.99	$6.00
$50.00–99.99	$10.00
$100.00–199.99	$13.00
$200.00+	call for quote

Foreign and all Priority Request orders:
Call Order Entry department for price quote
at 1-916-632-4400

This chart represents the total retail price of books
only (before applicable discounts are taken).

By telephone: With Visa or MC, call 1-800-632-8676. Mon.–Fri. 8:30–4:00 PST.

By Internet e-mail: sales@primapub.com

By mail: Just fill out the information below and send with your remittance to:

PRIMA PUBLISHING

P.O. Box 1260BK

Rocklin, CA 95677-1260

http://www.primapublishing.com

Name_____ Daytime Telephone_____

Address _____

City _____ State _____ Zip_____

Visa /MC# _____Exp. _____

Check/Money Order enclosed for $_____ Payable to Prima Publishing

Signature_____